World Social Forum

WORLD SOCIAL FORUM
CHALLENGING EMPIRES

Jai Sen, Peter Waterman, editors

Montreal/New York/London

Black Rose Books No. MM360

National Library of Canada Cataloguing in Publication Data
World Social Forum : challenging empires /
edited by Jai Sen and Peter Waterman. -- Revised ed.
Associate Editor: Madhuresh Kumar

Includes bibliographical references.
ISBN 978-1-55164-309-0 (bound) ISBN 978-1-55164-308-3 (pbk.)

1. World Social Forum. 2. Anti-globalization movement.
I. Sen, Jai, 1946- II. Waterman, Peter, 1936-

HN18.3W67 2007 303.48'4 C2007-901919-6

First edition published by The Viveka Foundation, New Delhi, India (2004)

BLACK ROSE BOOKS

C.P. 1258	2250 Military Road	99 Wallis Road
Succ. Place du Parc	Tonawanda, NY	London, E9 5LN
Montréal, H2X 4A7	14150	England
Canada	USA	UK

To order books:
In Canada: (phone) 1-800-565-9523 (fax) 1-800-221-9985
email: utpbooks@utpress.utoronto.ca
In the United States: (phone) 1-800-283-3572 (fax) 1-800-351-5073
In the UK & Europe: (phone) 44 (0)20 8986-4854 (fax) 44 (0)20 8533-5821
email: order@centralbooks.com
Our Web Site address: http://www.blackrosebooks.net

Printed in Canada

Table Of Contents

Acknowledgements . . . . *viii*
Notes on the Editors . . . . *xi*
Notes on the Contributors . . . . *xii*
Introduction: Critically Engaging with the World Social Forum . . . . *xv*

PART 1 Antecedents: Critical Perspectives

For Struggles, Global and National
Samir Amin, interviewed by V. Sridhar *3*

Coming: A Rerun of the 1930s?
Walden Bello *11*

The Road From Genoa
Jeremy Brecher, Tim Costello, Brendan Smith *15*

Towards a New International?
Michael Löwy *19*

Transnational Feminism and the Struggle for Global Justice
Johanna Brenner *26*

Towards Another Anarchism
Andrej Grubacic *38*

Empire, Global Power Centres, and People's Alliances
Muto Ichiyo *48*

The Global Justice and Solidarity Movement and the World Social Forum
Peter Waterman *55*

World Social Forum Documents

World Social Forum Charter of Principles
WSF International Council, Porto Alegre, Brazil, 2001 . . . . *69*

WSF IC—Nature, Responsibilities, Composition, and Functioning
WSF Brazilian Organising Committee, Sao Paulo, Brazil, 2001 . . . . *72*

Note of Information, Fourth Day Activities at WSF Nairobi
WSF Organising Committee, WSF Nairobi, Kenya, 2007 . . . . *75*

Call for Day of Action/Mobilisation January 26th 2008
WSF International Council, Berlin, Germany, 2007 . . . . *77*

PART 2 Critical Engagement: The World Social Forum

The World Social Forum As Open Space
Chico Whitaker 81

The World Social Forum: Arena or Actor?
Teivo Teivainen 94

Another World Is Necessary
Nawal El Saadawi 104

The Secret of Fire
Peter Waterman 109

Is It Possible to Put a Human Face on Globalisation and War?
ILC 126

World Forum Movement: Abandon or Contaminate
Linden Farrer 134

De-Centering the Forum: Is Another Critique of the Forum Possible?
Michal Osterweil 145

Another (Also Feminist) World Is Possible
Sonia E. Alvarez, with Nalu Faria and Miriam Nobre 154

How Open? the Forum As Logo, the Forum As Religion
Jai Sen 162

The World Social Forum 3 and Tensions In the Construction of Global Alternative Thinking
Gina Vargas 185

The World Social Forum: Toward a Counter-Hegemonic Globalisation
Boaventura de Sousa Santos 191

World Social Forum's 'Many Alternatives' to Globalisation
P.J. James 205

The World Social Forum, Beyond Critique and Deconstruction
Emma Dowling, interviewed by Rebecca Shah 211

Movement And Other Independent Documents

Call of Social Movements
Social Movements Assembly, WSF Porto Alegre, Brazil, January 2002 228

Mumbai Declaration 2004
Mumbai Resistance, Mumbai, India, January 2004 233

Porto Alegre Manifesto
Group of Nineteen, WSF Porto Alegre, Brazil, January 2005 238

PART 3 Globalising The Forum: The Forum In The World

Globalising the WSF: Ironies, Contrasts, Challenges
Achin Vanaik 245

Citizen Mobilization In the Americas and the Birth of the WSF
Dorval Brunelle 258

The World Social Forum In Africa
Jean Nanga 276

The World Social Forum:Current Challenges and Future Perspectives
Irene León and Sally Burch 292

Another U.S. Is Happening!
Judy Rebick 305

The Road to Atlanta
Michael Leon Guerrero, Tammy Bang Luu, Cindy Wiesner 315

Asterix On the St. Lawrence
Pierre Beaudet 332

Movement And Other Independent Documents

The Bamako Appeal
World Forum for Alternatives, Third World Forum, Forum for Another Mali, ENDA, and others, WSF Bamako, Mali, January 2006 343

Call of Social Movements
Social Movements Assembly, WSF Caracas, Venezuela, January 2006 349

Declaration of Social Movements
Social Movements Assembly, WSF Nairobi, Kenya, January 2007 359

PART 4 Looking Beyond: Possible Futures, Possible Worlds

WSF: Where to Now?
Michael Albert 363

The Twilight of Vanguardism
David Graeber 370

The World Social Forum and the Future
Boaventura de Sousa Santos 378

Women's Global Charter for Humanity
World March of Women 387

Other Worlds Are (Already) Possible
Arturo Escobar 393

Glossary 405

References 409

Acknowledgements

This is the second edition of this book. So many individuals and institutions have been a part of this project, over these years, and who have therefore made this edition possible—and we would like to thank them all:

Anita Anand and Arturo Escobar, our co-editors for the first edition of this book, for their generous collaboration and contributions in the preparation of the first edition—and without whom it would not have been the book it was—and subsequently, their encouragement and support to the *Challenging Empires* Book Development Project (for which we raised funds and through which we have managed several things, including the translation into Hindi of much of the first edition); and for their support and encouragement to us to go ahead with this edition;

All contributors to the two editions of the book, respectively, for giving us permission to use their work, original or previously published, and to the editors and publishers of the media in which they appeared, for their cordial collaboration;

The Viveka Foundation, New Delhi, and especially Rukmini Shekhar and Rekha Natrajan, for preparing and publishing the first edition in record time and in time for the World Social Forum at Mumbai, India, in January 2004;

Pramod Bharti, in New Delhi, for the extraordinary design that he came up with for the first edition—for the cover and for the rest of the book—and which came to symbolise the book for so many; and for the permission he has now given us to use this for this edition;

Choike (in Montevideo, Uruguay), and especially Elsa Duhagon and Magela Sigillito, for so excellently posting the content of the first edition on their amazing site (http://www.choike.org/nuevo_eng/informes/1557.html)—and through this, for helping us to reach it out to so many more people;

All those whose amazing welcome to the first edition, over these years, has so strongly encouraged us as editors to continue in this work; and specifically:

Asbjørn Wahl (of the Campaign for the Welfare State, Norway, and Vice Chair of the Road Transport Workers Section of the International Transport Workers' Federation (ITF)); Immanuel Wallerstein (of the Fernand Braudel Center, USA); Milan Rai (anti-war activist and journalist, UK), and Massimo De Angelis (of The Commoner, UK), for their generous reviews of the first edition when it first came out.

Prof Rainer Rilling and Dr Wolfram Adolphi of the Rosa Luxemburg Stiftung, Berlin, for suggesting a German edition and for successfully bringing it out in 2004;

Muto Ichiyo (of the People's Plan Study Group (PPSG), Japan), for suggesting a Japanese edition; Ogura Toshimaru (also of the PPSG), for coordinating the translation; and Uchida Masato of Sakuhin-Sha, Tokyo, for publishing the book in 2004;

Gemma Galdon, then at El Viejo Topo/Ediciones de Intervención Cultural, in Mataró (Barcelona), and now at TNI, Amsterdam, for suggesting and then producing an edition in Spanish, in 2005;

Kishan Kaljayee (dramatist and editor, New Delhi), who has contributed to coordinating the translation of the first edition into Hindi during 2005–6;

And all the many people, all over the world, who have told us that they use or refer to the book in teaching, training, and/or in organising social forums and movements;

Novib (now Oxfam-Novib), Oxfam International, Heinrich Böll Foundation (India office), and KePa (Finland) for their grants for the first edition of the book, and Maral Kaprielian, Peter Wade, Richard Hyman, and the Studies in Political Economy group at Carleton University, Ottawa, for their solidarity donations towards the production of the first edition of this book;

Karl Dietz Verlag/the Rosa Luxemburg Stiftung and Sakuhin-Sha, respectively, for their donations to the *Challenging Empires* Book Development Project in exchange for the rights to publish their respective translations;

Oxfam-Novib, for its sustained support to CACIM (the India Institute for Critical Action: Centre in Movement), New Delhi, for its attempt over these years to constantly and critically engage with the WSF process—and substantially, on the basis of the credibility that we gained from the first edition of this book (and where all three of us who are in the editorial team, are now associated, in one way or another, with CACIM);

Sah Bittu, New Delhi, for helping us locate the new literature on the Forum that is being generated all over the world, especially for this edition;

Vipul Rikhi, New Delhi, for his excellent editorial skills and insightful comments on the new essays for this edition;

Priyani Roychoudhury, also of Delhi, for meticulously proofing the manuscripts of the first edition and also the new material added for this one, and therefore for her contribution towards the quality of this one;

Black Rose Books, and especially Dimitri Roussopoulos, for proposing to us that they would like to do this edition and for ideas for it, and for being extremely —though always critically!—cooperative, throughout the process of production of this book;

And finally, but most importantly, all the women and men, individually and collectively, all over the world, who make the World Social Forums happen and who, with others, through this and otherwise, are changing the world. Without them there would be no inspiration for this book, no writing, no book, and no Forum!

The Editors, May 2008

Notes On The Editors

JAI SEN, an activist, researcher, and installation architect based in New Delhi, India, has been involved in local community activism and international advocacy networking, and in research on popular movements in India and the history of the globalisation of social movement. He has also been involved in several World Social Forums, and is the author and editor/co-editor of several books and articles on the Forum and the globalisation of civil movement, including World Social Forum: Challenging Empires (2004), Are other worlds possible? Talking New Politics (2005), and most recently, A Political Programme for the World Social Forum? Democracy, Substance, and Debate in the Bamako Appeal and the Global Justice Movements—A Reader (2007). He is now a Director of CACIM (the India Institute for Critical Action: Centre in Movement), based in New Delhi (www.cacim.net), and was visiting scholar at the Institute of Political Economy at Carleton University, Ottawa, Canada, in the autumn of 2006 (www.critical-courses.cacim.net). jai.sen@cacim.net

PETER WATERMAN (London, 1936) retired from 27 years at the Institute of Social Studies, The Hague, in The Netherlands, in 1998. Since the mid-1980s he has specialised on labour and other social movement internationalisms, on communications/cultural internationalisms, and on the WSF itself. As a scholar-activist, he has initiated or contributed to movement dialogues on such themes as: Social movement unionism, the new labour internationalism, alternative international communication and culture, and a global labour charter movement. Most recently he has co-edited, with Jai Sen and others, *World Social Forum: Challenging Empires* (New Delhi 2004) and authored *Los nuevos tejidos del internacionalismo y la solidaridad* (*The New Nervous System of Internationalism and Solidarity*) (Lima 2006). He is currently writing his autobiography.

Notes On The Contributors

MICHAEL ALBERT lives in the United States and works for *Z Magazine* and ZNet.

SONIA E. ALVAREZ is the Leonard J. Horwitz Professor of Latin American Politics and Studies and Director of the Center for Latin American, Caribbean, and Latino Studies at the University of Massachusetts, Amherst, USA.

SAMIR AMIN is Director of the Third World Forum, Dakar, Senegal; Chair of World Forum for Alternatives located in Dakar, Cairo, Paris, and Belgium; and member of the WSF International Council.

PIERRE BEAUDET, currently teaching sociology at the University of Ottawa, Canada, is a founder of *Alternatives* in Montreal and has been involved in various social movements in Quebec since the 1970s.

WALDEN BELLO, recipient of the Right Livelihood Award, is a Senior Analyst with Focus on the Global South, Thailand, and Professor of Public Administration and Sociology at the University of the Philippines.

JEREMY BRECHER is a U.S.-based historian and author of books on labour and social movements.

JOHANNA BRENNER is Professor of Sociology and Women's Studies at Portland State University in Portland, Oregon, USA.

DORVAL BRUNELLE is Director of the Observatory of the Americas at the Université du Québec à Montréal, Canada.

SALLY BURCH is Executive Director of the Latin American Information Agency (ALAI- Agencia Latinoamericana de Informacion/América Latina en Movimiento), based in Ecuador, and a member of the WSF International Council.

TIM COSTELLO, a U.S. national, has been a truck driver, workplace activist, and union representative.

BOAVENTURA DE SOUSA SANTOS is Professor of Sociology at the University of Coímbra, Portugal, and Distinguished Scholar at the Institute for Legal Studies at the University of Wisconsin, Madison, USA.

EMMA DOWLING is a PhD candidate at Birkbeck College, University of London, UK, and has been an active participant in the organisation of official and autonomous spaces in both the European Social Forum (London, 2004) and the WSF in Porto Alegre.

NAWAL EL SAADAWI, a leading Egyptian feminist, is a novelist, psychiatrist, and author of many books on the liberation of women in Egypt and in the Arab region.

ARTURO ESCOBAR is Professor at the Department of Anthropology, University of North Carolina, Chapel Hill, USA, and the Colombian Institute of Anthropology and History, Bogotá, Colombia.

NALU FARIA is a psychologist and the Co-ordinator of Sempreviva Organização Feminista (SOF), in Brazil.

LINDEN FARRER, a historian and anthropologist, lives in southeast England and writes on social issues.

DAVID GRAEBER is an anthropologist at Goldsmiths, University of London, and has worked with the Direct Action Network, People's Global Action, and the Planetary Alternatives Network.

ANDREJ GRUBACIC is a historian and social critic, presently working as a researcher at the Fernand Braudel Center at the State University of New York at Binghamton, USA.

MICHAEL LEON GUERRERO, a long-time community organiser, is the Resources and Organizational Development Coordinator of the U.S.-based Grassroots Global Justice Alliance.

MUTO ICHIYO is a writer on political and social affairs, and has been active in the anti-war and other social movements in Japan since the 1950s.

ILC, the International Liaison Committee for a Workers International, is a multi-tendency regrouping of unionists and political activists.

P.J. JAMES is Lecturer at St Thomas College at Pala, Kerala, in India.

IRENE LEÓN is a sociologist and communicator specialised in international issues, a member of the board of ALAI (Agencia Latinoamericana de Informacion /América Latina en Movimiento), based in Ecuador, and member of the International Council of the World Social Forum.

MICHAEL LÖWY is a Franco-Brazilian Marxist intellectual and Director of Research in Sociology at the National Centre for Scientific Research, Paris.

TAMMY BANG LUU is a Senior Organiser at the Labor/Community Strategy Center in Los Angeles, California, USA.

JEAN NANGA is an African-internationalist socialist from Congo.

MIRIAM NOBRE is an agronomist and currently Programme Co-ordinator of Sempreviva Organização Feminista (SOF), Brazil.

MICHAL OSTERWEIL is a PhD candidate at the University of North Carolina, Chapel Hill, USA, and active in local anti-war movements and international global justice movements.

JUDY REBICK is a long-time socialist feminist from Toronto and holds the Canadian AutoWorkers Sam Gindin Chair in Social Justice and Democracy at Ryerson University, Toronto, Canada.

REBECCA SHAH is Associate Editor (Articles) at *In-Spire*, e-Journal of Politics, International Relations, and the Environment at Keele University, UK.

BRENDAN SMITH is a legal analyst and co-director of Global Labor Strategies and the UCLA Law School's Globalization and Labor Standards Project, USA.

TEIVO TEIVAINEN is Chair of World Politics at the University of Helsinki, Finland; Visiting Professor of Postgraduate Studies at the San Marcos University, Lima, Peru; co-ordinates activities of the Network Institute for Global Democratization in the Americas; and is a founding member of the WSF International Council.

ACHIN VANAIK is Professor of International Relations and Global Politics at the University of Delhi, India and a Fellow of the Transnational Institute, Amsterdam, The Netherlands.

GINA VARGAS is a veteran Peruvian feminist sociologist, founder of the Centro Flora Tristan, Peru, and a member of the WSF International Council.

CHICO WHITAKER, recipient of the Right Livelihood Award in 2006, is a founding figure of the World Social Forum and a member of the WSF Brazilian Organising Committee and of the WSF International Council.

CINDY WIESNER, now the Political Coordinator with Grassroots Global Justice in the U.S., was earlier working with the Miami Workers Center during the organising for the U.S. Social Forum.

THE WORLD MARCH OF WOMEN is an international feminist movement headquartered in Montreal, Quebec, connecting grassroots groups and organisations working to eliminate the causes at the root of poverty and violence against women.

Introduction: Critically Engaging With The World Social Forum

Jai Sen

Introducing this second, revised and updated edition of this book, when so much has happened since the time of the first edition (January 2004), while yet retaining the flavour of the original, is both a pleasure and a challenge.[1] Let me try.

In a well-known article back in 2002, Michael Hardt—co-author with Antonio Negri of *Empire* and of *Multitude*—compared the World Social Forum to the great NAM (Non-Aligned Movement) that shook the middle of the 20th century.[2] Noam Chomsky also suggested, in his address to the Forum in 2002, that it could well be the beginnings of a Fifth International.[3] Since those early days, the Forum has come to be widely and deeply discussed in terms of its contributions to world politics.[4] And many people, including this writer, have argued that the WSF is one of the most significant civil and political initiatives of the past several decades, and perhaps even of these past hundred years.

Whether it is playing—and can play—such a role remains to be seen, and this is something that is today under intense debate, with some key participants in the life of the Forum so far asking whether it deserves to continue.[5] But at any rate, it is not every day that an initiative like the World Social Forum takes shape, which simultaneously challenges the hegemony of so many empires, both 'external' and 'internal'; and there are even fewer instances of an idea with such sweep actually taking off and staying in flight. At the same time, and as some of the essays in this book discuss, the initiative is also today at a crucial stage. This is both in and of itself—as it struggles to consciously and strategically continue to globalise itself, among other things by holding its world meetings in different parts of the world, outside its birthplace and on other sides of the planet—and also, very much, on account of the enormous challenges of the historical moment at which it is doing this: of the rise and, it now seems, the disintegration of empire, but also of the rise of fundamentalisms of so many kinds—in the world at large but also within the body of the Forum.[6]

In essence, this book is an attempt to engage critically with this novel but complex world institution, and through this to contribute to a better understanding of this initiative. Specifically, we as editors hope that this better understanding will enable us all to view, relate to, and take part in this important idea in deeper ways than the more obvious, and especially at this significant time in world history. This introduction therefore lays out the nature of the book project, gives a brief description of the World Social Forum and some comments on it (there is much more on this, within the book), and presents and discusses the structure and content of the book.

The Book as Project

As such, this volume is a careful selection of diverse essays and documents, either on the Forum itself or engaging with it, or else engaging with related issues in ways that we believe shed light on the Forum and its potentials and limitations. Although a lot has now been written and published on the Forum, when we embarked on putting together the first edition of *Challenging Empires* our sense was that no single piece or volume had till then been able to fully portray the richness and depth of the initiative, let alone of the ideas behind it. But precisely because of the scale of the initiative, and of the fact that the Forum seemed to have so widely engaged—and in many cases, ignited—people's imaginations, and also because the Forum is at a crucial juncture of transition, we thought that it was essential to try to critically and comprehensively engage with the phenomenon. We tried to do so by bringing together essays and other writings from many parts of the world, written by people of different ages, experiences, ideological persuasions, and points of view; and by both women and men. We saw—and see—this book as a 'committed but critical' anthology on the Forum, and as something of the 'open space' that the Forum itself was, and still is, struggling to be.

All this is as true of this revised and updated edition, as of the first edition.

Perhaps not surprisingly, coming to this formulation and attempting to achieve this balance was itself a struggle. One of our many decisions towards this was to try to include in this collection both the critical but not committed, as well as the committed but not necessarily critical. Another was to focus on the Forum itself even while recognising the emergence of what some then began to call a 'world social movement' from within the Forum process, and that the Forum itself was only a part of much wider and still-emerging global movements—and even while the Forum itself was, as one of its architects phrased it, an 'incubator' of this emergence—giving birth to new movements.[7] We saw this struggle of ideas as reflecting the Forum at its best.

Yet another decision was to include thinking and writings both from established (or 'old') politics as well as new politics, and hard critique and rejection as well as analysis and celebration, and thereby to encourage dialogue across boundaries. And finally, in the same vein, was our decision to not edit out parts of pieces that seem to overlap—that gave different understandings of the 'same' histories (of the Forum, and of the movement) and of the future. We tried not to privilege any one view. To arrive at this collection as it stands, we therefore sought out, exchanged between ourselves, and went through a much larger number of texts—indeed, right up to the week before we went to press.

Again, all this is as true of this second edition as it was of the first. As editors, we have of course been delighted by the warm reception that the first edition received, so widely. This ranges from the reviews and reactions to it,[8] to the number of languages in which it has been published (German, Japanese, and Spanish, to our knowledge, and where we at CACIM in India are also bringing it out in four successive volumes in Hindi, complemented with additional material in Hindi from within the country)[9]—and including the important fact that it was individuals or publishers who approached us for the rights to do this, rather than our approaching them—to the comments of appreciation from so many people in so many parts of the world; to the fact that we are constantly learning of new people—activists, including Forum organisers, teachers, and others—all over the world who use the book as a basic reference in their work.

And this is not speak of the pleasure of hearing Dimitri Roussopoulos of Black Rose Books tell us in the autumn of 2006 that he felt that it was *essential* that the book be brought out in a new edition for the North American market (where, sadly, the book has been less available, because of distribution problems). Coming from someone like him, this was a wonderful affirmation of the value of the book. We were only too happy to agree, especially given that it was a publisher like Black Rose, with its extraordinary list, that was proposing this, and we have subsequently had the even greater pleasure of working with Dimitri in conceptualising this new edition.

But this decision has had its demands. On the one hand, we have had to face the somewhat harsh reality of bringing out a new edition that would include a substantial amount of cutting edge, new material that would appropriately bring it up to date and yet make the book of reasonable size (the first edition was itself a big book, of 390 pages); and on the other, it also placed on us the responsibility of meeting the standards that we ourselves had set for the book, in terms of diversity and balance. Inevitably, this has meant taking difficult decisions of eliminating some material of the first edition. (For those who are interested in seeing the full original collection, hard copies of the book are still available in bookshops and off the web, but in addition the collection remains permanently available in soft copy @ http://www.choike.org/nuevo_eng/informes/1557.html, and now also @ a new home, http://www.openspaceforum.net/twiki/tiki-index.php?page=WSFChallengingEmpires2004.)

This book—in its first edition, and now also this one—also has its limitations. One reason is because it is largely a collection of existing writings (with only a few commissioned papers and a small number of unpublished papers). We are aware that the collection remains uneven. Many parts of the world are not represented, and the proportion of contributions by women authors is also lower than we wanted.

This book has several objectives. By bringing together such a rich collection we hope to inform a wide reading public about this significant social and political phenomenon. Through this, we want to encourage and enable a process of engagement with the Forum, and with the phenomenon of global civil action—referred to by some as the 'anti-globalisation movement,' by others as the 'global social justice movement,' and by others yet as the 'alternative globalisation (or alter-globalisation) movement'—that we increasingly see taking shape around us: of which the battles of Seattle, Prague, Gothenburg, Québec City, Genoa, and Cancun—to mention only some of the sites of this struggle—the worldwide protest in February 2003 against the launching of the war on Iraq, and the more recent sustained actions against the G8 have been just the most visible manifestations.

In particular, we believe that the Forum brings together three novel and inter-related dimensions: The *form* of the political and of political discussion (the Forum's concept of 'open space'); the *question* of the renewal of imaginaries and utopias (how to give content to "Another world is possible"); and *questions of strategy* (including proposals, types of political organising, etc). We hope, through this book, to stimulate a more critical engagement with these three dimensions.

We believe that the World Social Forum is today at a critical juncture[10] and we hope that this book—both its former and its new content—can play a role in the debate that is so necessary at a time like this when the extraordinary vigour and success with which the Forum has manifested itself in North America (at the U.S. Social Forum in Atlanta, Georgia, in June 2007, and at the Québec Social Forum in Montréal in August 2007 described in this volume) suggests that this very current experience in North America might have a great deal to contribute.

Let me be concrete. On the one hand, now is a time when the future of the Forum is being very seriously questioned—and not only by some of the most seasoned strategists of the global movement but also, it seems, by some of its funders, who are, by all reports, stepping away, one by one—and presumably placing their bets elsewhere. Anyone who has taken part in the Forum, or who has even watched it from a distance, needs to pay close attention to these developments. But on the other hand, the vigour and success with which the Forum has manifested itself in North America, described in this book by organisers of the respective meetings, and the success in independent financeing and autonomous practice,[11] what does this efflorescence and reinvention mean? And what does it have to say to those who feel that the time of the Forum is over, or that it is time to move on?

The World Social Forum

The Forum was initiated in Brazil in January 2001 as a challenge to the World Economic Forum (held each January in Davos, Switzerland) in order to put forward another view of the world and its possibilities, encapsulated in its name, the World *Social* Forum, and in the motto it adopted, "Another World Is Possible!" Since 2001 the WSF has moved from being a singular major event each January in Porto Alegre, to being an efflorescence and celebration across the world. During 2002–3, a wave of continental meetings took place in Africa, Asia, Europe, and Latin America, and city, state, and national-level meetings have continued to take place in countries across much of the world.

In January 2006, the WSF tried a major new experiment: the idea of a *polycentric* world meeting, happening sequentially in the three continents of the

South (and reminding us that the Forum is, after all, an initiative of the South)—in Caracas (Venezuela, in South America), Bamako (Mali, in Africa), and in Karachi (Pakistan, in Asia). And in January 2007, it reverted to manifesting itself as a 'full' world meeting, and—having been held in South America four times (2001–3 and then 2005) and then Asia (2004)—it was organised in Africa for the first time.

For many people, especially perhaps for professional observers and commentators, it is the size of the WSF meetings that speaks the loudest and that therefore tends to be cited as the real measure of the relevance of the Forum. But it is not numbers alone that count.

First, even as numbers have grown, the *thrust* of the annual world event has also changed a lot, over the years. The first meeting in 2001 was predominantly a challenge to the World Economic Forum at Davos as a symbol of economic globalisation, and through that to neoliberalism itself. In 2002 it moved to being a meeting that also made a call for alternatives—it was the year when its slogan, "Another World Is Possible!" was coined. And the third meeting in January 2003, while centred on illuminating steps towards concrete alternatives, was one also marked by *critical self-reflection* on the WSF itself—both as structure and as process.

In 2004, when the Forum took place outside Brazil for the first time, in Mumbai, it tended to move back to being all about resistance—to neoliberalism and a host of other things—rather than being focussed on alternatives. (This fighting-from-the-bunkers view largely took shape because of the particular ideological make-up and imagination of those who had seized the leadership of the WSF in India.[12])

But from 2005, and freed somewhat from this leadership, the Forum has by and large moved back to a concern with alternatives as being the main mode of challenging empires.

This process has not been free of deep inversions, however. Major contradictions that have been hiding in the wings of the Forum emerged in full force at the Nairobi WSF—the commercialisation of the Forum, its 'militarisation' in the sense of its being overrun by 'security' measures, and its being overrun by big NGOs and religious interests. (See the essays in this book by Irene León and Sally Burch and, in particular, the interview with Emma Dowling.) In a different fashion, this also took place at the Caracas Forum, as a consequence of heavy state sponsorship and of the resultant loss of the WSF's soul as an autonomous, non-state initiative—despite all the other achievements of that Forum and of Hugo Chavez's role in hemispheric and world politics.[13]

Basically, however, the ideas of the WSF are firm.Over these years, and through the voice that it has articulated, it has made abundantly clear to the world at large that there *is* an alternative to neoliberal globalisation; indeed, that there are *several* alternatives. And equally, there is much reason to think that people all over the world are now mobilising to define and to live those alternatives. In this way, the WSF—along with all the other forms of transnational and global action that are also taking place—is playing a profound role in freeing peoples all over the world of the shackles of the colonisation of the mind. The essay in this book by Dorval Brunelle, on how this has taken place in the Americas, is a powerful exploration of how ideas, and mobilisation around ideas, can and do change the world.

The challenge that the Forum poses to empire has also been greatly widened. Starting from an initial position of opposing neoliberal globalisation alone, the Forum has also played an important role in the building of worldwide opinion against the war on Iraq. It did this not by taking a position itself but by being an arena, or a space, where anti-war forces from many parts of the world could meet at a critical point in the mobilisation. In particular however, it at that point became a space where those who had till then been opposing either neoliberal globalisation or war, alone, could meet and together develop a more comprehensive understanding of war and militarisation as instruments of economic globalisation and neoliberalism. The rest—the massive anti-war demonstration that took place on 15 February 2003—is history.

Beyond this, and more or less as a function of the 2004 world-wide meeting held in India and of the WSF having to relate to this part of the world and to its particular concerns, the Forum has also radically widened its perspective. Through the preparatory consultations in India as the WSF was being set up, and then carried through to the International Council, it came, in formal terms at least—by including these as axes for the world meeting—to also adopt a stance opposing *communalism* (religious sectarianism and fundamentalism), *casteism* (oppression, exclusion, and discrimination based on descent and work), *racism*, and—not because this is particular to India or South Asia but because this was a strong part of the social concerns of those who set up the WSF in India—*patriarchy*, and by extension, *sexuality*. With the first two being seen by some members of the IC as being peculiarly 'Asian' concerns, and therefore not 'universal,' these new axes never came to have the Forum's full support, but they entered its lexicon.

Equally, the fact that local, national, and regional/continental 'chapters' of the initiative have taken shape in many parts of the world since its formation, can also be seen as a deepening of the relevance of the idea globally. Another way of looking at this phenomenon however, is that the onslaught of neoliberalism and other fundamentalisms over the past period has brought together communities of people across the world with similar concerns and interests, and in this sense the World Social Forum is merely a vehicle for this common manifestation.

With this also comes the contradiction that the more 'local' the Forum is, the less open and the more controlled (and, sometimes, sectarian) it tends to be; as a function of the reality that the more local it gets, the more that participants tend to know each other and the less free and open they therefore tend to be: anonymity allows participants to be more open.

The challenge that the Forum poses is also deeply 'internal' as well as external, insofar as the *culture of politics* that the Forum professes to practice, of 'open space,' is—in principle, if not always in practice—a radical challenge to most existing modes of organisational practice and politics, in adopting this wide programme, the WSF has challenged those who take part in it to also adopt and practice these positions. (Even if the participating organisations do not relent, the chances are high that their cadres who drink of the Forum will be contaminated by the experience so that they will, in their own ways, gradually bring about changes in these directions.[14]) While the idea of the WSF as an open space, and of open space itself, has been deeply critiqued and challenged,[15] it would perhaps be agreed by most, including its critics, that it has nevertheless succeeded in introducing this idea into the political lexicon, and of challenging us all to think critically about the very idea of a conscious culture of open politics at a world scale.[16]

As such, the *very existence and practice* of the WSF includes a deep challenge to all discriminatory organisational practices, whether of class, communalism, caste discrimination, racism, patriarchy, and sexism (including the denial of freedom of sexual preference), as well as the play of power, that remain prevalent in subtle forms within most organisations, even the most professedly liberal. Indeed, there is now rigorous exploration available of how some of these discriminatory currents are playing themselves out *within* the World Social Forum.[17]

On the other hand, this dynamic growth and broadening has brought its own share of organisational problems, both at the events themselves and within the evolution of policy and strategy for the Forum as an idea, sometimes tending to overwhelm it. The Third World Forum (held in Porto Alegre, Brazil, in January 2003) is widely considered to be the point at which organisers, participants and observers began to seriously talk about alternatives to economic globalisation, and to reflect on the extent to which the Forum is practising the principles it preaches—but it is also the point at which the Forum came closest to collapsing, inwards.[18] Many key participants and theorists have commented, recently, that the Forum has become a place where it is impossible to hold an actual debate or to have real dialogue in the formal sessions.[19] Others—especially after the disastrous experience in this area at the Nairobi Forum, 2007—have also trenchantly commented that the Forum is far from being the open space it says it is, and that in reality it is only one more preserve of the already privileged, who jealously guard it as their territory.[20] These are serious criticisms, and surely demand our attention.

The continuing deliberations of the WSF International Council over the years show clearly however that the organisers of the Forum have become intensely aware of some of these issues, if not all, and of some of the contradictions of its globalisation. They have taken several initiatives in this period that have opened it up quite radically, and that suggest that 'the Forum' is learning from its experience and reinventing itself.[21] These include the introduction during 2004, for the 2005 edition of the Forum, of a participatory, online process of formulating (but not deciding) the themes for the world meetings, which by 2007 matured into the idea of having a day within the world meeting at Nairobi devoted to *live* convergence and transversal exchange among participants towards planning the 2008 Forum;[22] to the decision in 2005 to try out the experiment of a so-called 'polycentric' Forum in 2006; and most recently, to what is perhaps the boldest decision yet, to not have a single or polycentric Forum in 2008 but rather to replace it with a call for self-organised actions at all levels—local, national, and transnational—within a single week.[23] As I see it, this is the clearest indication yet of the Forum being willing to see itself, and the emerging global movement, as a cloud and not a clock, and where this, I suggest, is an essential prerequisite of its struggle to be an open space.[24]

But notwithstanding this, some key questions remain: Are the Forum's ruling bodies, structures, and processes—in short, its organisational culture—

appropriate to a network that is growing exponentially and globally? Are the decisions that the WSF International Office and the International Council are taking, including in terms of the proliferation of its structure, consistent with their objectives and values, or are they mired in the grammars and vocabularies of the past?

Most fundamentally, the WSF needs to be perceived and understood as a *process* that is still very much under construction and experiencing constant change; indeed, I believe there is reason to argue that the Forum has today already become something of an organism in the process of organic emergence.[25] Its future will depend on how it learns to evolve and respond to changing conditions, and on how 'we' all—movements, activists, intellectuals, and others—respond to its initiatives; and on how it responds to ours.

What is our place, within this?

The Structure of This Book

We see this book as our contribution to this process. In order to do so, we conceived of the first edition in terms of five main sections, and this edition, of four.[26] It opens with an exploration of *antecedents*—of the conceptual, ideological, and historical landscapes within which the Forum has taken shape and within which it continues to unfold and as a useful collection for locating the Forum within this wider world—and where each one of us work in our own ways. This section—though not a history of ideas as such—also provides a useful framework for an understanding of the next sectiong.

The second Section, *Critical Engagement*, is—together with the following one, *Globalising the Forum: The Forum in the World*—is the heart of this book: significant and sustained critical engagement with the Forum and its ideas and propositions. We have attempted here to include essays from as many viewpoints, and parts of the world, as we could find. They include pieces ranging from some based on very local experience, both within specific countries and within the Forum. The explorations range from the experiential to the philosophical, and include structural and post-structural analyses. The moods of the pieces range from high celebration to deep anguish—and rejection. Read individually, and read collectively, we believe that this section reveals the range of different struggles that are taking place, and is in itself simultaneously a manifestation and celebration of the struggle that the Forum itself is, and is so much a part of.

In this section, we have retained most of the essays in the original edition and added only one, a recent reflection (by Emma Dowling) which, though it refers to the most recent world meeting of the WSF (the Nairobi Forum in January 2007) contains thoughts that go much beyond this, transcending time and particular contexts. We have chosen to add this piece in particular because it creates a bridge between the other reflections—all written some years ago, but still very valid—and not only the present but also the next Section in this book.

The third section, *Globalising the Forum*, contains the major changes from the first edition.[27] The section from the first edition focussed on the Forum in India—which was relevant at the time. Instead this third section will deal with one of the major projects of the WSF developed since 2004 and will give readers a powerful insight into some of the most recent and most important developments in the Forum.

We start with three major essays that locate the Forum in India, the Americas, and Africa. The Forum in Mumbai was the first major step taken by the WSF in this historic journey. We therefore open with a contemporary essay by Achin Vanaik that discusses the Mumbai Forum but within the context of the politics and political economy of India at that time—and highlighting both the ironies and contrasts of the WSF coming to India from Brazil as well as the challenges facing it. The essay also asks, and addresses, two very direct questions that carry enormous meaning for the World Social Forum as a political project: what hopes and lessons did the 2004 WSF in Mumbai carry, for India and the world? And: What was, or was likely to be, the political impact of the Mumbai WSF on the Indian political scene at that time?

Two major essays follow, respectively by Dorval Brunelle and Jean Nanga, that locate the WSF not within particular countries but within two major continents, the Americas and Africa—and that set the scene for the subsequent discussion. It may be useful to mention that essays of this scope and sweep have perhaps been rarely attempted so far in the available literature on the Forum, at least in English. They thus constitute significant contributions to our understanding of the Forum.

With these broad essays before us, we then move to looking critically at all the three major Forums that have taken place during 2007: the WSF at Nairobi in January 2007, the U.S. Social Forum in Atlanta in June 2007—which some have argued may possibly change the course of U.S. politics[28]—and the Québec

Social Forum in Montréal in August 2007; which brings us, at the time of writing, to as close to the present as a hard copy book can be!

As editors, while we are profoundly grateful to all the contributors for writing for us or for allowing us to publish their work, we would like here to specially thank Pierre Beaudet, Judy Rebick, and Michael Leon Guerrero, Tammy Bang Luu, and Cindy Wiesner, for preparing their material for us—on the U.S. Social Forum and the Québec Social Forum—at extremely short notice. It goes without saying that being able to include this material provides to this book with a freshness of perspective that is very special—quite aside from the many insights the authors give us.

One further comment: collecting and juxtaposing essays is never a predictable process. But the essays that we have brought together in this edition clearly synergise, and demand to be read in relation to each other—for one then begins to see patterns that are otherwise less possible to discern. In his essay on the WSF in Africa, for instance, Jean Nanga makes the following observation, that speaks so clearly to what other contributors to this book are saying:

> This [the reductionist opposition between civil society, considered positive, and political society, considered essentially negative] is an idea promoted by International Financial Institutions, and it explains the hostility within the WSF to the participation of political organisations. In practice however, this also translates into an opposition to radically anti-neoliberal political organisations. Given this, the WSF in Nairobi could well be the theatre for an offensive by NGOs who support the addition of a social dimension to globalisation and by a charity-based movement for global justice, through the participation of local associations that they support financially.

The fourth and final section in this edition, *Looking Beyond: Possible Futures, Possible Worlds*, moves decisively past the Forum as Forum and looks ahead to what possible futures there are—for the Forum, for 'social movement' more generally, and for such initiatives at a world level. We have included five very different pieces, which open up different spaces and start from different points of entry, to try and portray something of the landscape that lies ahead of us, and its questions. Even though most of the pieces included here were in the first edition (only one is new, by the World March of Women), the view they open up for us remains extraordinary.

Some Special Features

Finally, there are four features of this book that we need to mention. One, interspersed between the sections are significant documents generated by the organisers of the World Social Forum process or that have been generated by social movements or other actors at one of the editions of the Forum. Rather than 'storing' all these in one reference section, we have preferred to make them part of the life of the book, enabling readers to dip into and then come out of the 'actually existing Forum' as they move through it.

The 'social movement documents' also require a special introduction. By choice, the World Social Forum refrains from taking positions on issues—even though it was specifically set up to provide a forum for opposing neoliberal globalisation—or from 'representing' the views of those who meet at Forum events. It thereby leaves the space open to all those meeting during the Forum to take whatever positions they wish, in their own names, and undertaking only to publish and circulate any statements made.

One of the important outcomes of the meetings of the World Social Forum have so far been the statements made by meetings that have taken place among social movements and/or other social and political actors during the world meetings. By definition, such statements do not represent the views of the Forum as a whole. But insofar as there is a strong school of thought that argues that the Forum is itself a 'movement of movements' and/or that it should be transformed into a 'world social movement' (or a movement network), these documents thereby assume a considerable added significance.

Presenting these documents gives a glimpse into a major new development in the life of the Forum: the increasingly insistent attempt, by intellectuals, to give programme (and bring 'order') to the Forum's apparently chaotic nature—and thereby, in the opinion of some, to overcome its apparent ineffectiveness. In our opinion, this debate—and this struggle, over order and the nature of order—is at the heart of the future of the Forum. We have therefore included the important even if somewhat ill fated statement from the 2005 Forum in Porto Alegre by a so-called Group of Nineteen as well as the introduction to a far more ambitious statement issued the following year, just before the 2006 polycentric Forum in Bamako, Mali, the Bamako Appeal.[29]

The Bamako Appeal is a large document, too long to publish here, but it is available as a whole either on the web (see the References section for details) or as one of the documents publishe elsewhered, *A Political Programme for the World Social Forum? Democracy, Substance, and Debate in the Bamako Appeal and the Global Justice Movements—A Reader* (available on our website, www.cacim.net).

All the references made by our contributors are collected into one Bibliography located near the end of the book, together with a Glossary, a rich resource list of key material in these fields.

In the interests of transparancy and readability all the names and titles in languages other than English, are translated into English. This, effort also used at CACIM, attempts to make bibliographies more multicultural and user-friendly, and has led to a somewhat unconventional presentation style in the bibliography (and which is also unconventional in other terms). But we are optimistic that the changes we have introduced at this level will also help readers to 'read' and understand this major world process better. The method behind our madness is explained in that section.

Finally, a fourth feature and a small request, in relation to this North American edition and perhaps especially to our readers in North America: in common usage, and because of the dominance till date of the trans-Atlantic Anglo-Saxon axis in the English-speaking world, the term *American* is used in English to refer exclusively to the U.S. (either as an adjective or to denote its citizens). But since the appropriation of this generic term by this one single country is widely resented by other peoples of the Americas (in North, Central, and South America), and perhaps also by some within the U.S., in this book we use the term only when it appears in a particular phrase or a title (for instance, in *American Revolution*) and otherwise use *U.S.* wherever possible. And in particular, for referring to citizenship we use *U.S. American* and not 'American' alone. We request readers to consider adopting this usage.

Although one tradition in edited volumes is to engage with the issues, positions, and propositions presented by the issues, authors, and texts, I—in concurrence with my co-editors—have chosen to not do so here; in large part, because our approach in this book is to merely present the various positions, and to thereby enable readers to navigate through them as they wish and to arrive at their own assessments. In all honesty, it would be extremely difficult to do justice in a brief survey to all the views expressed in this volume, which are in many places mutually contradictory; but more centrally, this is also beyond the scope of our role, as we see it.

In ending, I need only to mention that this second edition has been put together by only two of the four editors for the original edition, Peter Waterman and myself, and to warmly thank our colleagues in that venture, Arturo Escobar and Anita Anand, for their collaboration at that time and for their willing agreement now—as agreed upon, in fact, back in 2004—to Peter and my going ahead with producing this second edition (and also with a new series that we have now started work on, collectively titled *Challenging Empires*).

I know I speak for my co-editors, past and present, in saying that it has been a great privilege to find the pieces that we present in this book, to read all the essays, and to learn from them; and to have seen the first edition of this book get the warm reception that it did. It has been a powerful reminder of the scope and richness of the movement, and the struggle, that we are today engaged in. I thank Peter, my co-editor, for giving me the privilege of writing this introduction, and warmly invite readers to now enter this book.

Jai Sen, New Delhi, October 2007

Notes

1. I thank my co-editor, Peter Waterman, and our associate editor, Madhuresh Kumar, for their comments on a first draft of this introduction; and my co-editors on the first edition, Anita Anand, Arturo Escobar, and Peter Waterman, for their comments on early drafts for the introduction there, on which I have built this one. In some senses, this therefore now represents something of a collective formulation!
2. Hardt, July 2002.
3. Löwy, March 2003.
4. For instance: Sehm Patomäki and Ulvila, eds, August 2006; Samir 2006b; Smith et al, 2008.
5. Bello May 2007; Whitaker May 2007; also Sen and Kumar, compilers, January 2007.
6. For a discussion of the latter, see Daulatzai, November 2006 and Caruso, April 2007. For comments in terms of how religious fundamentalism played itself out at the Nairobi Forum in January 2007, see the chapters in this book by Irene León and Sally Burch and by Emma Dowling and Rebecca Shah, and Vargas, April 2007.
7. Whitaker 2004, p 113.
8. Sen, May 2004.
9. Anand, Escobar, Sen, und Waterman (Hrsg), 2004; Sen, Anand, Escobar, and Waterman, eds, 2005; Sen, Anand, Escobar, y Waterman (Editors), nd, c.2005; and Sen, Anand, Escobar, and Waterman, eds, 2006.
10. For those who would like to plug into this debate, subscribe to WSFDiscuss, an open and unmoderated forum on the World Social Forum and on related social and political movements and issues. To subscribe, simply send an empty email to worldsocialforum-discuss-subscribe@openspaceforum.net. You can also check out OpenSpaceForum, @www.openspaceforum.net, for an extensive collection of documents on the Forum and related movement.
11. See the essays in this volume by Michael Leon Guerrero, Tammy Bang Luu, and Cindy Wiesner on the U.S. Social Forum and by Pierre Beaudet on the Québec Social Forum; both in Section 3. And for a broader discussion of this issue in the North American context, see also: INCITE! Women of Color Against Violence, eds, April 2007.
12. For a discussion of the situation in India, see Sen, 2004c. This essay, titled "The Long March to Another World: Reflections of a member of the WSF India Committee in 2002 on the first year of the World Social Forum process in India," appeared in the first edition of this book but has been omitted here. See the original edition or the web link given in the reference. And for a contemporary discussion of the equivalent situation in Europe and in relation to the European Social Forum, see Treanor, November 2002.
13. Sen, Teivainen, and Wallerstein in debate, March 2006.
14. For one discussion of the potentially contaminating effects of open space, see Sen, May 2007.

15. For instance, Biccum 2005; Wright 2005; and see also the comments on this issue in the interview in this volume with Emma Dowling.

16. Keraghel and Sen, December 2004.

17. Especially: Caruso, December 2004; Caruso, October 2006; Caruso, April 2007; and Daulatzai, December 2004; Daulatzai, November 2006.

18. Albert, in this volume, Sec 4; Waterman, this volume, Sec 2.

19. Kagarlitsky, November 2002, and Wainwright, December 2002; and Judy Rebick in this volume.

20. See, for instance, Walsh, February 2007; and for an overview of the Nairobi Forum, the essay by Irene León and Sally Burch in this volume.

21. As discussed in Sen, January 2007.

22. See, in this volume, the planning Note issued by the WSF that summarises this decision. (WSF 2007 Nairobi: Note of Information, The 4th Day Activities and Proposals for Actions.)

23. See the Call as published in this volume. (Call for Day of Action/Mobilisation, January 26th 2008.)

24. Sen, May 2007.

25. Sen, January 2007.

26. De Angelis, May 2004. This powerful review in the first edition of this book is worth reading in itself, as an essay on alternatives and on the WSF.

27. Aside from the fact of our dropping the whole of the small Section 2 in the original edition, titled *Diaries*.

28. See Judy Rebick's essay in this volume, and also Sherman, July 2007, Uhlenbeck, July 2007.

29. Forum for Another Mali, World Forum for Alternatives (France), Third World Forum (Senegal), ENDA (Senegal), and others, January 2006.

PART 1

ANTECEDENTS: CRITICAL PERSPECTIVES

For Struggles, Global And National

Samir Amin interviewed by V. Sridhar

The antecedents of the World Social Forum (WSF) can be traced to January 2000 when a small group of about fifty activists, representing trade unions, intellectuals, peasant organisations, and other social groups, gathered in Davos. Samir Amin, who is Director of the Third World Forum, located in Dakar, Senegal, Egypt and Belgium, was among those assembled at this 'Anti-Davos in Davos.'

An economist and intellectual, Amin is regarded as one of the foremost thinkers on the changing dynamics of capitalism. Since 2001, he has been actively associated with the World Social Forum, as well as regional fora, which have evolved as a challenge to imperialist globalisation. Amin has authored many articles and books.

Amin spoke to V. Sridhar of India's *Frontline* magazine in Hyderabad, India, in January 2003, where he was participating in the Asian Social Forum (ASF). Excerpts[1] from the interview:

What is the significance of the WSF–ASF and the regional fora that have emerged in the last few years as a challenge to imperialist globalisation?

I consider these events important, although there may be problems with them. There are many, and growing, social movements around the world, different in nature, struggling either on social fronts—for the defence of labour and of the rights of the popular classes—or on political fronts for basic political rights. There are the feminist movements, ecological movements and many more. These movements are fragmented, in the sense that they are mostly national-based, or, in many cases, local-based. Most deal with a single issue or with a single dimension of the problem, without articulating it into an overall alternative political project.

This is the result of recent history. Social organisations that emerged after World War II gradually reached their historical limits. I am not only referring to the Soviet pattern of the alternative, but also to events in China, the erosion of the social democratic pattern in the developed capitalistic West, and the erosion of the 'national populist' alternatives in the South.

As a result of these developments we have moved into a period characterised by fragmentation. There will be no alternative to the present powerful system, neoliberal globalisation or imperialist globalisation, which is a new phase of imperialism, unless these movements come together to articulate an overall alternative. You cannot fight on a single front. Even if you are successful on that front, success will be limited, fragile and vulnerable because things are inter-related and because, in the final analysis, we need an overall alternative in all its dimensions. This alternative vision will have an economic dimension. But the political, social, and cultural dimensions will also have to be addressed. The WSF is not an organisation with a common political platform for devising strategies. It is not a forum open to everybody. Participating organisations must adhere to a charter saying they are opposed to neoliberalism, not necessarily to capitalism; opposed to militarisation of globalisation, not necessarily imperialism, which means much more.

You have said that a unified movement of the peoples of the South is a prerequisite for change in the present situation. What is the role of the peoples of the North in this?

I am an internationalist, a Marxist, socialist, and universalist. I am not a chauvinist, certainly not a Third Worldist. The world is one but a very unequal one. Capitalist development, which has shaped the modern world, has done it on the basis of growing inequality among nations and within them as well. For the last five centuries there have been countries at the centre and at the periphery. A major element of the global system is its imperialist dimension. Imperialism is synonymous with the growing polarisation among nations. It is based on the rationality of capitalist profitability. The awareness of popular forces in the South, which is at the periphery of the global system, is a fundamental prerequisite for any change.

After World War II, there was a gigantic movement of the peoples of Asia and Africa for national liberation. They had one target—independence. But the forces that united around this demand represented different classes. In countries such as China, Vietnam, and Cuba, the leadership was with the radical Left. In India it was with the middle classes during the fight against British imperialism. In Africa and in the Arab countries, a variety of forces led the movement. The leadership in these countries understood that they not only needed to support one another but also build a common front after independence, based on their common demands. That is how Bandung (the birthplace of the Non-Aligned Movement) happened in 1955.

The common front yielded results, creating a space for these countries to achieve several decades of relatively high rates of economic growth. There was industrialisation as well as great efforts in education and in other fields. In political terms, it enabled these countries to transgress ethnic, local and national chauvinisms. The alliance among nations was based on politics, depending heavily on the countries' position against imperialism. In Egypt, Nasser was an ally of India, and not Pakistan, because India had an anti-imperialist position unlike Pakistan. The fact that Pakistan was predominantly Muslim, like in Egypt, was not of any importance. During the last 20 to 30 years, the visions that came out of socialism, whether of the Russian or the Chinese kind, and out of the more radical of the national liberation movements, reached their historical limits.

Were these countries also not bargaining between two camps—imperialism, on the one hand, and socialism on the other?

Sure, that is true. The Soviet Union provided ideas—good in some cases, but bad in many cases—and, in some cases, good armaments (laughs) to these countries, which acted as a check against imperialism. It was not possible for the U.S. to act like a gangster as it does today, when it can unilaterally decide to bomb any country in the world.

But due to the erosion of the leaderships' support bases, these countries entered a vacuum, resulting in regression on all fronts. Afro-Asian solidarity eroded. This opened the way for other patterns of pseudo-solidarities, which are very reactionary, based on ethnic or pseudo-ethnic chauvinisms or on religious fundamentalism. Let me put it polemically: if the majority of the Indian people accept Hindutva, if the majority of people in the 'Muslim' countries accept the nonsense of political Islam, there will be no change on a world scale if these are not transgressed by another vision of human solidarity.

How were the limits in these countries reached?

There was some room for development because colonialism resulted in low levels of industrialisation in a few countries, and none at all in many others. So there was room for industrialisation after national liberation. But as they moved along, investment and technology became costlier. These countries inherited social systems with low levels of education, offering enormous room for upward mobility for people through education. As long as the children of the popular classes (the lower middle class and the peasantry) could move up through education—like in India, Egypt and many other countries— the system benefited from legitimacy. Even if they were not democratic, they were seen as delivering *something*. Countries that had high rates of economic growth, accompanied by not-increasing levels of inequality (I do not mean socially just), and those that offered upward mobility for large sections of society, enjoyed credibility and legitimacy. Some of these countries were semi-democratic, like India. Others, like Nasserite Egypt, were not democratic at all. But they were equally legitimate and credible because they delivered. Once the system could not progress within the same logic and same basis, the political system became more corrupt and lost legitimacy. This created a vacuum, which reactionary forces started to occupy.

How do you characterise the current phase of globalisation, in contrast to previous ones?

Globalisation and imperialism are not new. The history of capitalism is the history of imperialist expansion and was always global. What was the colonisation of India, if not globalisation? The building of the Americas since the 16th century was globalisation, as was the slave trade, which played a crucial role in the building of the Americas. Later, colonialism was globalisation. And globalisation has always been imperialist globalisation, never been achieved by peaceful and equal negotiations between peoples. That is history. But we would be wrong if we think that it is the same old story. An efficient counter-strategy can be developed if we focus on what is new.

The dominant discourse today, the Rightist one, says: "Well, change is always for the better and happens spontaneously. Change is always painful, but is only transitional. The market, that is, capitalism will by itself solve the problem in the long run (when everybody is dead)." That is not even ideology. It is propaganda. But this is what is repeated daily by politicians, written everyday in newspapers, shown daily on television and even presented as There Is No Alternative (TINA).

We have to look at what is new in a different way. How can popular forces re-organise to reduce the damage associated with global capitalist expansion? What can they do to impose their own agenda in the short run, to create the conditions for an alternative? The alternative, in my opinion, is socialism. It had the same name in the past and will remain the same in the future too. But the way we imagine socialism will not be the same as our fathers.

You said that the nature of imperialism today is different from that of the past. Has it anything to do with the way globalisation is different today?

Imperialism had always been characterised by rivalry among major powers. The Spanish and the Portuguese against the Dutch in the 17th century;

then the British against the French; and the German–Japanese against the others, still later. It was on this basis of rivalry among the imperialist nations that Lenin—correctly at the time before the First World War—thought the system must lead to a revolution because it will lead to war, which the proletariat, being the victims of the war, will revolt against. History proved Lenin right. There *was* a revolution. Whatever happened afterwards is another story, but there was a revolution.

After World War II, the U.S. and Japan became allies, Japan in a subaltern position. The U.S. and western capitalist Europe came together after the Marshall Plan and the formation of the North Atlantic Treaty Organisation (NATO). In geographical terms, the world capitalist system includes the U.S. and its outer province, Canada, capitalist Europe, at that time limited by the Iron Curtain, now also going a little further east, and Japan. After World War II, the imperialist powers put an end to their rivalry because they had a common enemy, the Soviet Union. They paid more attention to their common interests rather than the rivalry among themselves.

The Soviet Union has now disappeared, but these countries have not become rivals again. This is reflected in the economic management of the global system—the functioning of the G7, a group of the most powerful nations, the World Bank, the International Monetary Fund (IMF) and the World Trade Organisation (WTO). These are not global organisations; these are organisations of the *Global North*—of the capitalist centre. There are no major differences among these countries within these organisations. We ought to ask ourselves a number of questions. First, why are we in this situation? Second, does this mean there are no contradictions among these countries? Third, if there are contradictions, in what ways are they different from contradictions of the earlier period, in which imperialist countries were in rivalry? Fourth, how do the contradictions relate to North–South relations?

I suggest, as I have done at other meetings of the WSF, that capitalism has entered a new phase, of a higher level of centralisation of capital. This has laid the basis for the solidarity of capitalist interests at the global level. During Lenin's time, before World War I, and continuing till about thirty to forty years ago, monopoly capital needed a large market that could be accessed as an empire. A capitalist centre or metropolis with a number of colonies or areas of interests was the norm. That was the basis on which rivalries among the imperialist powers existed—on the sharing or re-shaping of colonies and the control of the global system. Today, the bosses of big business also say that in order to be efficient, transnational corporations (TNCs) need to access markets on a global scale. The globe is therefore the terrain on which competition among them is fought out.

But these monopolies also need a global system to operate. The change in the nature of imperialism does not negate the importance of changes in the processes of labour and other dimensions, which need to be taken into account so that the popular classes can reinvent efficient forms of organisations. But to be efficient at the global political level, and in North–South relations, it is a basic fact that imperialism now operates collectively as a triad, represented by the U.S., the EU and Japan.

There are contradictions among these powers but the nature of the contradictions is different. There is no common state, and capitalism cannot operate without a state. The claim that markets without a state rule capitalism is complete nonsense. There is no single state, even confederal, of the North. Even Europe with its Union is built on national states, which in many cases have deep historical roots. Therefore, how is the political dimension of collective imperialism to be run? That is an unsolved question.

You have said that there is a tendency for the "centres of gravity" of countries to fall outside the domain of nation states. What does this mean for the peoples of these nations, in terms of a search for an alternative? And, how does such a system operate and what are the contradictions in such a system?

The centre of gravity has moved from inside nations to elsewhere, and this has happened to all nations. This change is related to the size of dominant capital, which is global in scale. Since these are major decision-makers, they cannot be submitted to a national logic. At the European Social Forum (ESF) in Florence, many people felt that a new Europe should be built. They said that a political Europe was needed, not necessarily with a unified state because, for historical reasons, there are nations with a long history of a common language and culture. Some suggested a kind of confederation. But such a Europe also has to have a common political reality. Another Europe, like another Asia, is possible.

This new Europe ought to be based on a social compromise between capital (because we cannot imagine the end of capital immediately) and labour and other popular classes. But this other Europe cannot happen without changing its relationship to the South and if it continues to be a partner in the collective imperialist system.

Regionalisation will strengthen the capacities of the countries of the South. This can be based on, for instance, history and culture, as in the countries of Latin America, which have two closely related languages, Spanish and Portuguese, to link them. The other common factor is a common enemy for over two centuries—the U.S. I do not think Islam can provide the basis for such regionalisation. But the Arab countries, with a common language, could be the basis for unity among nations. There has never been a history of these countries being unified by a single state, except in the imagination of the nationalists. But this alliance must be based on politics, not merely a common market.

Even the larger countries face the menace of imperialism. The Americans do not like large countries. China and India are too big. There are differences within countries. Let me address frankly the case of India. There are different nationalities, languages and groups, and of course Hindus and Muslims. The way the power system deals with this diversity is creating problems such as the rise of communalism.

What is the position of the nation-state in this search for the alternative?

The need for a common front does not negate the crucial importance of the nation-state. For a long time in the future, we will need the nation-state. Markets have to be regulated at the regional and global level, but first at the national level. This change has to start from inside countries. That is why the nation-state is so important.

To summarize what are the principles that could govern another kind of global system? The first is the logic of the transition to socialism. This will combine the criterion of capitalism, that is, efficiency as measured by profitability; and the criterion of social justice. Although the term 'social justice' is very elastic, certain elements can be defined in concrete terms. It would mean jobs, reasonable and decent wages, schools for children and decent healthcare. That is social justice, not socialism. These are not going to be produced by the market, but will be imposed on the market by a social policy of the state. This however associates capitalistic criteria with social criteria, which will be in conflict. But the system recognises this and therefore manages them without allowing the market to dominate society unilaterally. It also recognises the fact that the free play of markets creates problems for society. Therefore, society will solve the problem through the exercise of political power. If such a system is obtained in several countries, then we can create the conditions for regional arrangements among them and for changes in the global system.

The second condition needed for substantial change is genuine democracy. Social change in the past—whether of the Soviet or Maoist type or of the national populist types in the Third World—had very little or no democracy at all. They were controlled and directed in many ways, with varying degrees of the negation of democracy. Very little was left to the initiative of the popular classes. But while people want progress, they also want liberty. We cannot remake the Soviet Union or Nehru's India. There are no remakes in history. Democracy in the dominant discourse is based on delinking it from the issue of social justice. This does not work if democracy does not result in social progress, because people no longer find it credible. The main reason for the move backward towards religious fundamentalism, ethnic solidarities and so on is the failure of democracy.

Imperialism and cultural fundamentalism go together. Market fundamentalism needs religious fundamentalism. Market fundamentalism says: subvert the state and leave it to the market at the global level to run the system. This is done when states are disempowered completely; and, within states, if the popular classes (the victims) are disempowered by the negation of their class identity. Moreover, the system can be run politically if the South is completely divided, with nations and nationalities hating one another. Religious and ethnic fundamentalisms are perfect instruments for ruling the political system. This is the reason why they are supported—ideologically, politically, even financially—by imperialism. The U.S. has always supported Islamic fundamentalism, for instance, the Saudi Arabian regime, Pakistan and the Taliban. It continues to support such regimes even today, though now in a covert manner. In Europe it uses ethnic movements to achieve its goals as in Yugoslavia.

Note

1. Reprinted with permission from *Frontline*. The original version appeared in Vol. 20, Issue 2. <http://www.flonnet.com/ fl2002/stories/20030131008201200.htm>

Coming: A Rerun Of The 1930s?[1]

Walden Bello

This meeting of the WSF International Council in Bangkok, in August 2002, is taking place against a background of what is shaping up as the worst crisis of global capitalism since the Great Depression seventy years ago. Charting our direction for the future is greatly dependent on understanding the nature and dynamics of this crisis.

Two methodological principles guide this discussion. First, never underestimate the resilience of capitalism. Second, never underestimate its vulnerability to crisis. Having said this, let me venture to say that we are entering a crisis that is an intersection of four crises—crisis of legitimacy, crisis of overproduction, crisis of liberal democracy and crisis of overextension.

Crisis of Legitimacy

The crisis of legitimacy refers to the increasing inability of the neoliberal ideology that underpins today's global capitalism to persuade people of its necessity and viability as a system of production, exchange and distribution. The disaster brought about by structural adjustment in Africa and Latin America; the chain reaction of financial crises in Mexico, Asia, Brazil, and Russia; the descent into chaos of free-market Argentina; and the combination of massive fraud and spectacular wiping out of $7 trillion of investors' wealth—a sum that nearly equals the U.S.'s annual GDP—have all eaten away at the credibility of capitalism.

The institutions that serve as global capitalism's system of global economic governance—the IMF, World Bank and the WTO—have been the most negatively affected by this crisis of legitimacy and thus stand exposed as the weak link in the system.

A sure sign of this crisis of legitimacy is the loss of some of the system's best ideologues in recent years—Jeffrey Sachs, creator of the 'shock treatment' of Eastern Europe in the early nineties, who now calls for developing countries not to pay their debts; Joseph Stiglitz, former World Bank Chief Economist, now the severest critic of the IMF; and Jagdish Bhagwati, who coined the term "Wall Street-Treasury Complex" to describe the interests that brought on the unending stream of global financial crises since the 1990s; and George Soros, capitalist par excellence who doubles as the enemy of "market fundamentalism."

Crisis of Overproduction

The crisis of overproduction and overcapacity could predict more than an ordinary recession. Profits stopped growing in the U.S. industrial sector after 1997, a condition caused by the massive overcapacity built up throughout the international economic system during the years of the U.S. boom in the 1990s. The depth of the problem is revealed by the fact that only 2.5 per cent of the global infrastructure in telecommunications is currently utilised.

Overcapacity has resulted in investment moving from the real economy to the speculative economy, to the financial sector; a development that was one of the factors behind the stock market bubble, especially in the technology sector. Enormous surplus capacity continues as a global condition and thus the continuing absence of profitability.

The global recession is, as a result, deepening. But precisely because severe imbalances had built up for so long in the global economy, this recession is likely to be prolonged; it is likely to be synchronised among the major centers of capitalism, and there is a great chance that it could turn into something worse, like a global depression.

Crisis of Liberal Democracy

Liberal democracy is the typical mode of governance of capitalist economic regimes. In countries such as the Philippines and Pakistan, popular disillusionment with elite democracies fuelled by money politics is rife among the lower classes and even the middle class. In Pakistan, this was one of the factors that allowed General Musharraf to seize political power.

Clearly, from Africa to Latin America, the phenomenon of the spread of the Washington or the Westminster-type of formal democracies that U.S. American political scientist Samuel P. Huntington called the "third wave of democratisation" is over. But the crisis of legitimacy is not limited to the South.

In the United States, there is widespread popular perception that, owing to massive corporate influence over the two political parties, plutocracy is now the U.S. system of governance, not democracy. Mass disaffection and cynicism have been compounded by the feeling of a vast sector of the electorate, that President George W. Bush stole the 2002 elections and, thanks to current revelations about his questionable ethics as a businessman, that he serves mainly as the president of Wall Street rather than of the country.

Despite Washington's current posturing about punishing corporate fraud, the spectacular developments in Wall Street are perceived as a moral collapse in which both economic and political elites are implicated. In Europe, there is also much concern over corporate control of political party finances, but even more threatening is the widespread sense that power has been hijacked from elected national parliaments by unelected, unaccountable Eurobodies such as the European Commission. Electoral revolts like the Le Pen and Pim Fortuyn phenomena in France and the Netherlands respectively are manifestations of a deep alienation with technocratic democracy.

Crisis of Overextension

The fourth crisis might not be immediately discernible, but it is operative as well. The recent expansion of U.S. military influence into Afghanistan, the Philippines, Central Asia and South Asia may communicate strength. Yet despite all this movement, the United States has not been able to consolidate victory anywhere, certainly not in Afghanistan, where anarchy, and not a stable pro-U.S. regime, reigns.

It is arguable that because of the massive disaffection they have created throughout the Muslim world, the U.S.'s politico-military moves, including its pro-Israel policies, have worsened rather than improved the U.S. strategic situation in the Middle East, South Asia and South East Asia. Meanwhile, even as Washington is obsessed with terrorism in the Middle East, political rebellions against neoliberalism are shaking its Latin American backyard.

Rise of the Anti-corporate Globalisation Movement

Intersecting crises are unfolding even as the movement against anti-corporate globalisation is gaining strength. During the 1990s, resistance to neoliberalism was widespread throughout the South and the North. In few places, however, they were able to become a sufficiently critical mass at a national level to decisively reverse neoliberal policies. But although they were not a critical mass nationally, they could become a critical mass globally when they came together at certain crucial events.

This was what happened in Seattle in December 1999, when massive mobilisations contributed to bringing down the Third Ministerial of the WTO. The other global confrontations of 2000, from Washington to Chiang Mai to Prague, also shook the confidence of the establishment. When the WSF was launched in Porto Alegre in January 2001 with 12,000 people in attendance, the ideological challenge became a very real threat to global capitalism.

Today, we may be witnessing a second moment in the trajectory of the resistance as many anti-neoliberal movements become a critical mass impacting on politics at the national level. This appears to be the case in Latin America, where espousal of neoliberal economic policies is now a surefire path to electoral disaster and progressive movements have either won electoral power or are on the cusp of power in Venezuela, Brazil and Bolivia.

Competing with the Right

Nevertheless, the crisis does not guarantee ultimate ascendancy for the forces against neoliberalism on the Left. For the Right is also on the move, taking advantage of the crisis of the neoliberal establishment to concoct ideological mixtures of reaction and populism that stoke the deepest fears of the masses. Note, for instance, the mass resonance of the fascist Le Pen's slogan "Socially I am Left, economically I am Right and politically I am for France."

With neoliberal ideology in retreat, the competition for the disenchanted masses is shaping up as an apocalyptic contest between the Left and the Right, though at this point one cannot definitely discount an ideological comeback by the global establishment.

Coming: The Battle of Cancun

In short, the immediate future promises a very fluid situation. In this regard, the Fifth Ministerial of the WTO in Cancun, Mexico, in September 2003, is shaping up as a confrontation between the old order and its challengers on the Left. Because of its decision-making structure, which is based on 'consensus' among all member-countries, the WTO is the weak link of the global capitalist system, much as Stalingrad was the weak link in German lines during World War II.

For the establishment, the aim is to launch another ambitious round of trade liberalisation in Cancun that would rival the Uruguay Round. For the opponents, the aim is to reverse globalisation by turning Cancun into the Stalingrad of the globalist project. In the space of just a decade, global capitalism has passed from triumphant celebration of the passing of the socialist states of Eastern Europe to a fundamental loss of confidence. It is entering a 'time of troubles' much like the second and third decades of the 20th century. Its successful emergence from the developing crisis is by no means assured.

Note

1. This talk was delivered at the meeting of the International Council of the World Social Forum, Bangkok, 13–15 August 2002.

The Road From Genoa

Jeremy Brecher, Tim Costello, Brendan Smith

In the year and a half from the Battle of Seattle to the Battle of Genoa, the WTO, World Bank, IMF and G8 have provided spectacular 'targets of opportunity' for the transnational movement challenging top-down globalisation. The movement has re-framed the debate on globalisation, put its advocates on the defensive and forced change in the rhetoric if not on the actions of world leaders and global institutions. But these actions are only the shining tip of the iceberg that is the movement for 'globalisation from below.' This movement is made up of grassroots groups around the world fighting to protect the environment, cancel Third World debt, prevent potential technological nightmares like genetically modified organisms, and recover democratic institutions from corporate domination. Also to mount effective global action against AIDS, halt capital punishment and other human rights abuses, and address a host of other problems that require global co-operation to solve.

Neither the repression conducted on behalf of the authorities nor the provocation of the violent fringe—nor the apparent de facto co-operation of the two—has anything to offer to the great majority of the world's people who want solutions to problems like global warming and global poverty. The key to addressing such problems lies precisely in grassroots, internationally linked action that goes beyond periodic meeting stalking.

Some have called the Genoa protests a failure because of the chaotic violence that accompanied them. But that is not so clear. There was also massive violence by police in Seattle, as well as by a fringe there also operating synergistically with the police. But the overall effect was still to establish that a huge international movement rejected actually existing globalisation and proposed an alternative based on global justice and common global interests. And that this movement for 'globalisation from below,' far from being a one-protest wonder, is continuing to grow.

The fact that nearly all the world's countries other than the U.S. decided to go ahead with a version of the Kyoto protocol is in part a tribute to the power of that movement. So is the decision to end G8 meetings, as we have known them and to hold only diminutive ones in remote hideaways far from the public eye. And so is the firestorm of criticism in Italy, Europe, and worldwide (though almost unreported in the U.S.) that has met Italy's brutalisation of the G8 protestors. There is little doubt that the lion's share of the violence in Genoa and other recent globalisation protests was the responsibility of the police and those who instruct them. But that doesn't mean that throwing rocks (or perhaps next time shooting) at the police is a good or wise response.

Indeed, there is a danger in the rise of violent and sectarian action within or alongside of what is an overwhelmingly non-violent movement. Movements that start with good intentions can indeed become deformed. A leader of the violent and sectarian Students for a Democratic Society (SDS) 'Weatherman' faction (in the sixties in the U.S.) recollected a quarter century later that, at a certain point, she lost touch with the very values that had led her to become involved in social action in the first place. The key to countering sectarianism and violence is not, however, to be "violently against violence" or to form "anti-sectarian sects," but to keep our focus on the movement's basic goal: empowering ordinary people to address the problems of our species and our environment.

There is a reason to eschew violence that should be considered even by those who do not reject it in principle. Violence and provocation have the effect of excluding ordinary people from participation in movement actions. (One might cite the example of the Palestinian Intifada, which initially was a mass non-violent movement involving whole communities including families and children. But as it moved to stone throwing and other forms of violence, it not only provided a pretext for disproportionate Israeli retaliation, but also made the movement the exclusive province of young men). Militant but non-violent action maximises the primary power of social movements: the threat they imply that the masses will withdraw their consent from the ruling authorities.

Notwithstanding some division over tactics, Genoa retained the two crucial dimensions of unity that made Seattle a global turning point. Far from pursuing a selfish or backward 'national interest,' people from different countries and regions around the world stood together for common objectives in a common internationalism. And the alliance of environmentalists and workers, those involved in First World issues and those pursuing Third World concerns, human rights and consumer movements, and the many other elements that compose globalisation from below continued the co-operation that so astonished the world at the Battle of Seattle.

We have now entered a new, and as-yet, little analysed phase in the development of globalisation. Its initial phase of manic expansion seems to be subsiding into economic stagnation. At the same time, the U.S. Government seems to be withdrawing from a role of 'first among equals' in establishing a global system on behalf of corporations and the rich. Instead, it is utilising its muscle as the world's only superpower to impose an old-fashioned version of 'national interest' (aka imperialism).

Whether this is an aberration or a long-term trend remains to be seen. The U.S. government's rejection of international co-operation on such matters as global warming, star wars, small arms trade, control of biological warfare, and economic coordination is creating a problem—and opening an opportunity for the movement for globalisation from below.

The interest of ordinary people in the U.S. and in the rest of the world is clearly in alignment—and in opposition to the destructive policies of the Bush administration. It provides one more opportunity (for example, the international campaigns against AIDS and the death penalty) for a global grassroots movement to outflank national policies.

Let's take the question of global warming. Immediately after the other 178 countries accepted and the U.S. rejected the modified version of the Kyoto climate accord, the city of Seattle announced that it would unilaterally abide by the accord and cut its carbon emissions by more than the required percentage. No doubt other U.S. cities will follow suit. This is a powerful example of the local dimension of globalisation from below. At a national level, environmentalists in Congress are proposing legislation to abide by the Kyoto accord.

In this situation, grassroots transnational people-to-people co-operation could transform global (as well as local and national) politics. Indeed, even very moderate action could have a big impact. If every person in the 178 countries that supported the Kyoto Protocol who is concerned about global warming would contact any Americans they know, express their concern, and ask them to act; if every trade union, religious group, sister city organisation, and similar citizen groups would do the same, it could have a significant impact in isolating Bush's already unpopular position. (Appeals to U.S. trade unionists could be particularly important here, since the American Federation of Labour-Congress of Industrial Organisations (AFL-CIO) has opposed the Kyoto Protocol and supported greenhouse-gas-promoting Bush administration initiatives.)

We've recently seen how the expression of concern about the death penalty expressed by Europeans and others has a big impact on capital punishment in the United States. The many people in the U.S. involved in Central American solidarity movements in the 1980s put significant limits on the Reagan administration's escalation of its interventions there. Global warming provides a brilliant opportunity for people inside and outside the U.S. to outflank national leaders who defy common human norms and interests.

The road from Seattle to Genoa has shown—and the road beyond Genoa will show even more clearly—that international cooperation at a grassroots level holds the key to effectively challenging 'globalisation from above.'

Towards A New International?[1]

Michael Löwy

The First International, founded in 1864 in London, had Karl Marx as the author of its inaugural Manifesto, which concludes with the famous formula: "The emancipation of the workers will be the work of the workers themselves."

The partisans of Marx and Proudhon participated in the International Working Men's Association (IWMA)—even though the former had much more influence, writing some of the main documents of the International, and relations between the two men were always poor. At the Brussels Congress (1868) the alliance between Marxist and Left Proudhonians like Eugène Varlin, future hero of the Commune of Paris, allowed the adoption of a collectivist programme that proposed collective ownership of the means of production. Relations with Bakunin and his supporters were more complex, which led to splits and to the dissolution of the IWMA after its ill-fated transfer to the United States in 1872 (one of Marx's less brilliant ideas).

The IWMA survives only in the form of those anarchist dissidents who consider themselves the heirs of what was founded in London in 1864. Its existence today is rather symbolic, but in 2001, the more dynamic and open currents of libertarian socialism established a network called Libertarian International Solidarity (LIS). It includes important organisations like the Confederación General de Trabajadores (Spain), l'Alternative Libertaire (France), the Uruguayan Anarchist Federation and so on. In addition, in recent years, there has been a significant development of anarchist currents inside the anti-neoliberal movement, some affiliated with the IWMA, others to the LIS, but many without international affiliation.

The Second International, founded by Friedrich Engels in 1889, was torn apart in 1914 with the support of its sections favouring the imperialist war. It was reconstituted in the twenties with a definitively reformist orientation, and reorganised itself once again, under a new name, that of the Socialist International (SI) after World War II.

The SI is currently a heterogeneous collection of parties and movements, mainly of European and Latin American origin, going from liberation fronts—

like the Sandinistas or the Farabundo Marti Front—to pro-imperialist parties, like Tony Blair's New Labour. A social democracy of moderate tendency—that is, social-liberal—predominates, like the German SDP, the French Socialist Party, Spain's PSOE. Its objective is no longer, as at the time of Friedrich Engels, Wilhelm Liebknecht, and Jean Jaurés, the suppression of capitalism and the socialist transformation of society, but rather the 'social' *management* of neoliberal capitalism. The Socialist International does not effectively function as a political organisation, rather as a discussion club, an area of political-diplomatic negotiation.

The Third International was the most significant attempt to create an international association of proletarian parties with an anti-imperialist and revolutionary character. In spite of many authoritarian characteristics and discipline of the military type, it was, during its first years (1919–24) a genuinely internationalist body, in which figures like Antonio Gramsci, Clara Zetkin, Andrés Nin, and Jose Carlos Mariátegui participated. After the death of Lenin, it became progressively transformed, under the leadership of the Stalinist bureaucracy, into an instrument of the Soviet policy of 'building socialism in one country.' Even so, authentic internationalist aspects survived among Communist militants, as shown by the significant participation in the International Brigades in Spain (1936–38).

In 1943, at the request of his allies, Churchill and Roosevelt, Stalin dissolved the Communist International without reducing the total political, ideological and organisational dependency of the Communist Parties of the world towards the Communist Party of the Soviet Union (CPSU). With the disintegration of the misnamed 'actually existing socialism' from 1989 onwards, the heirs of the Third International entered a crisis that has taken them, with few exceptions, towards political marginalisation or conversion to social democracy. Some parties, like the Communist Refoundation in Italy, succeeded in genuinely re-orienting themselves, breaking with their Stalinist past and taking a new direction, radical and open to the contributions of the social movements.

The Fourth International, founded by Leon Trotsky in 1938, emerged out of the International Left Opposition, an anti-bureaucratic tendency inside the Communist International. Weakened by the assassination of Trotsky and numerous other leaders—either at the hands of fascism or of Stalinism and by innumerable splits—it was never able to transform itself into a mass movement. However, its militants played an important role in the events of May 1968 in

France, the movement against the war in the U.S., and the resistance to the dictatorships in several Latin American countries. The Fourth International sought to salvage the heritage of the October revolution from the Stalinist disaster and to renew, with the help of its militants and leaders (Ernest Mandel, Livio Maitan, Hugo Blanco, Raul Pont, Alain Krivine, and Daniel Bensaïd) the theory and practice of revolutionary Marxism.

The Fourth International—to which the current author belongs—has grown stronger in recent years but remains a weak organisation both in numbers and resources. With the exception of the Philippines and Sri Lanka, its forces are essentially concentrated in Europe and Latin America. Its militants have participated, as an organised current, in the foundation of broader re-groupings, like the PRC in Italy, the Socialist Alliance in England and Wales, the Left Bloc in Portugal, the Frente Amplio in Uruguay, and the Workers' Party in Brazil. Unlike other groups or sects who identify with Trotskyism, the Fourth International does not consider itself as the sole revolutionary vanguard and its objective is to contribute to the formation of a new international, of a mass character, of which it would only be one component.

The question of internationalist resistance to capital has acquired a burning actuality today. Capital has never managed to exert such absolute and limitless power across the planet. Never before could it impose, as it does today, its rules, policies, dogmas and interests on all the nations of the world. Never before has there been such a dense network of international institutions—like the IMF, the World Bank, the WTO—destined to control, govern and administer the life of humanity according to the strict rules of the capitalist free market and free profit. Never before could the multinational companies and the financial markets exert in such a brutal way their global dictatorship. Finally, never before has the power of a sole imperialist state, the United States of America, been so extensive and so arrogant. Today we are witnessing, as sub-commander Marcos wrote in his message to the 'European Zapatistas' (August 28, 1995), "a true war of money and the forces of international financial capital against peoples, humanity, culture and history."

The offensive of capital and the neoliberal governments at its service —which began in 1980 with Ronald Reagan and Margaret Thatcher—reached its height after the fall of the Berlin Wall and the capitalist restoration in the countries of Eastern Europe. The "death of utopia" (or of the revolution, or of Marxism) and the "end of history" were proclaimed triumphantly in all the capitals of the West.

It was in a context of defeat and disorientation of the Left that there came, like a spark of light in the dark, the Zapatista uprising of 1994. And in 1996, the First Intercontinental Encounter for Humanity and Against Neoliberalism took place in the mountains of Chiapas. This event had a worldwide impact and brought together, for the first time in very many years, militants, activists and intellectuals of several tendencies, from the North and the South, from Latin America, the United States and Europe. From this meeting came the historic call to build the international of hope against "the international of terror represented by neoliberalism," as the Second Declaration of La Realidad puts it, and to take up the immense task of creating a collective network of all our struggles and specific resistances.

This was a call for an intercontinental network of resistance against neoliberalism, an intercontinental network for humanity. This intercontinental network will, recognising differences and similarities, seek to link up with other resistances worldwide and be the means through which different resistances learn from one another.

The meeting at Chiapas in 1996 can be considered as the first act of the great movement of anti-neoliberal struggle that manifests itself now in every corner of the planet. Although this initiative did not have any direct follow-up —the attempts to organise other encounters of this type, inspired by the Zapatista example, in Europe or Latin America were not successful—it was the point of departure, the moment of birth of a new internationalism, anti-neoliberal and anti-imperialist.

In 1999, when the great protest at Seattle took place, it became the main vector of this new internationalism, the Movement of Global Resistance —falsely characterised by the rightist press, as the 'anti-globalisation' movement. This 'movement of movements' would trigger protests in Prague, Stockholm, Brussels, Bangkok, Washington, Barcelona, Genoa and, more recently, Florence. There would be participation in tens, hundreds, and a million—and also in the WSF held in Porto Alegre (2001, 2002 and 2003), the ESF (2002), and other local or continental meetings.

This movement for another world is broad and heterogeneous, emerging with a worldwide international and internationalist character. In spite of its diversity, there is agreement on some fundamental principles: 'the world is not for sale'; 'another world is possible'; 'no to war.' These are general principles, but if they are defended seriously, they have a deep subversive potential. There is unity on concrete demand: abolition of the debt of the countries of the South; the suppression of tax havens and the imposition of a tax on financial transactions; a moratorium on transgenic products, etc. There is a broad consensus on the identification of the enemy: neoliberalism, the IMF, the World Bank, the WTO, the U.S. Empire. On the alternative to the dominant order, we see a broad range of answers, from the 'regulation' of the system to its revolutionary (socialist) transformation.

This diversity can be an obstacle, but it is also a source of strength. The Movement of Global Resistance involves trade unions, feminists, Marxists, anarchists, ecologists, Christians for liberation, socialists of several colours and shades, peasant and indigenous movements, non-government organisations (NGOs), intellectuals, and many young people, women and workers without other affiliations, who wish to protest, march, fight and discuss with others. It is a unique occasion for encounters, debate, mutual learning—a process of cultural interchange in which each actor, without abandoning their own ideas and convictions discovers those of others, and tries to integrate them in thought or practice.

The mixture and fusion of all these ingredients is creating an explosive cocktail, the new internationalist culture of the Movement of Global Resistance. This process is still in its beginnings, still far from having a common direction, but there is a sense of the formation of a common spirit of the movement, radical, combative, and hostile to institutional attempts to co-opt the movement.

The Movement of Global Resistance, or at least its most organised expression, the WSF, has a certain degree of international organisation. There is an International Committee, and a Parliamentary Forum was set up in 2002 in Porto Alegre. But these bodies, like the Forum itself, are very heterogeneous, and they do not function as an international political force. Their objective is more limited—the organisation of the WSF and the continental Forums. More important is the network of social movements—Via Campesina, the Brazilian MST and CUT, ATTAC and so on—who constitute the main force in the WSF and who have published a document containing some elements of political analyses, anti-imperialist and anti-neoliberal, and a call for common protest initiatives.

Does this amount to a 'Fifth International?' No. One, we are talking about social movements and not political organisations or a project of global social transformation. Two, the Movement of Global Resistance and its bodies are very heterogeneous—as they should be—including sectors who still believe in the possibility of a regulated, humanised, national and democratic capitalism. The same heterogeneity is found also inside the International Parliamentary Forum.

What is lacking is a network of political organisations—parties, fronts, movements—that can propose an alternative project inside the Movement, going beyond capitalism, and the perspective of a new society, with neither oppressor nor oppressed. Something similar exists in Europe—the Conference of the European Anti-Capitalist Left, which involves the PRC (Italy), the LCR (France), the Left Bloc (Portugal), the Socialist Alliance (England and Wales), the Red Green Alliance (Denmark), and several others. Despite differences, these currents share a similar rejection of capitalist globalisation, neoliberal policies and imperialist war. They also share the aspiration to have a 'positive' alternative: anti-capitalist, anti-patriarchal, ecological and internationalist "socialist and democratic society, without exploitation of labour and oppression of women, based on a sustainable development—a socialism from below, self-managed."[2]

If this experience were extended to other continents to constitute a network that included, in a broad manner, the most radical political positions in the great Movement of Global Resistance, we would have a 'New International.' This would not necessarily be the 'Fifth' because not all involved would necessarily identify with the history of the workers' and socialist Internationals of the past. It could be called the 'International Conference of the Anti-capitalist Left,' or the 'Tendency for the New International' or any other name invented by the creative imagination of its participants.

This new international could selectively integrate the positive contribution of the four proletarian internationals. It would be the heir of Babeuf and Fourier, Marx and Bakunin, Blanqui and Engels, Rosa Luxembourg and Lenin, Emma Goldman and Buenaventura Durruti, Gramsci and Trotsky, Emiliano Zapata and Jose Carlos Mariátegui, Augusto Caesar Sandino and Farabundo Martí, of Ernesto Ché Guevara and Camilo Torres, of Ho Chi Minh and Nazim Hikmet, Mehdi Ben Barka and Malcolm X and of many others. However, its main reference point would be the existing social movements and, in the first place, the Movement of Global Resistance to neoliberalism.

Of the internationals of the past, it would perhaps be the First that could serve as inspiration—although obviously in the political conditions of today which are totally different—as a multiple, diverse, democratic movement in which different political opinions could converge in thought and practice. This does not mean that the form in which the IWMA was constituted and functioned can be repeated today. It is impossible to anticipate what organisational forms this new internationalist force could have—decentralised federation, organised network, or simply a conference with periodic meetings—but it would necessarily have to be flexible, open and without formal bureaucratic structures. Ideally, it would include parties and fronts, but also Left magazines, research groups, organisations of social movements and intellectuals.

How could we delimit the political-social field of this new international? It seems evident to me that anti-imperialism and anti-capitalism—that is, the conviction that the suppression of capitalism as a worldwide system is a necessary condition, even if not a sufficient one, for the abolition of social injustice, exploitation and oppression—are essential criteria. The perspective of a new society—free, democratic, egalitarian, in solidarity, ecological, feminist (for me and my comrades, a socialist society, but that can be an open question) —is another essential element). But it is in the process of formation of this network, or federation, that we would define the common bases and the political platform of the New International.

Where must we begin? As our comrade Daniel Bensaïd puts it, the departure point is the irreducible force of indignation, the unconditional rejection of injustice, an attitude of non-resignation: "Indignation is a beginning. A way to get up and to begin to walk. Once you are indignant and have rebelled you can find out later what happens." If we can rally the forces which, across the planet, are motivated by indignation against the existing system, rebellion against the powerful and the hope that another world is possible, we will have the ingredients of a New International—with or without a number.

Notes

1. March 2003. First published as "Debate: Towards a New International?" in *International Viewpoints*, No. 348. Originally written for the Mexican magazine, *Revista Rebeldia*.
2. Conference of the European Anti-Capitalist Left, June 2002.

Transnational Feminism And The Struggle For Global Justice[1]

Johanna Brenner

Capitalist globalisation has had a profound yet contradictory impact on women's lives, and on the possibilities for contesting male domination in both the core and periphery of the world capitalist system. On the one hand, older forms of male dominance are being undermined; on the other, women's life conditions are getting worse. Capitalist penetration into the rural periphery has disrupted the settled economies that supported 'classic patriarchy'—a system in which men's power rests economically and politically on male property ownership and household headship.[2]

In the cities of the periphery, the 'Fordist gender regime'—the male breadwinner/female housewife household—which emerged in the sixties and seventies, the 'golden age' of economic development in some parts of the South, is crumbling as male wage and salary earners no longer earn a family wage. At the same time, based in part on women's incorporation into wage labour and their access to literacy and education, feminism has emerged as an organised political force. Women from the global South are mounting challenges in their countries and participating in a global feminist movement that is capable of affecting the policies of transnational organisations such as the UN and the European Union (EU).[3]

Yet, women and children, more than men, are victimised by global capitalist restructuring. Economic insecurity and impoverishment, exposure to toxics, degradation of water, high infant and maternal mortality rates, forced migration, increased hours spent in paid and unpaid work are only some indicators of women's burdens worldwide.[4] Women's organisations defending working class women and the rural and urban poor find themselves in a contradictory field of power relations defined by three contesting forces: national states, religious fundamentalist movements, and the global centres managing the neoliberal agenda.

Third World governments are male-dominated, often inefficient, plagued by cronyism and sometimes corrupt; the pressures of structural adjustment programmes imposed on them by the IMF and the World Bank have only aggravated these tendencies. Their failure to deliver on the promised benefits of 'free-market' policies has spurred the growth of religious fundamentalist political movements that target feminism and challenge governmental power. National governments respond to these movements with both political repression and accommodation, primarily at women's expense—for example, ceding local civil authority to religious courts and leaders. Such policies shore up traditional patriarchy in its social control functions while the capitalist transformation of local economies deprive women of whatever protection and security patriarchal systems did provide.[5]

In contrast to the weakened and male-dominated national state and the fundamentalist movements, key institutions of the neoliberal order, pre-eminently the World Bank but also government agencies of Northern countries such as the United States Agency for International Development (USAID), proclaim their support for modernisation and democratisation. Offering resources for women's economic development efforts, social services, and healthcare, the managers of the New World economic order present themselves as allies of liberal feminism.

Central feminist aspirations—full political citizenship, equal access to education and occupational opportunity, and an end to the culturally and legally authorised right of men to control women's bodies, sexuality, and reproductive potential—are fully compatible with neoliberalism. The forces that have the most to lose from the institutionalisation of liberal feminism's political goals are organisations representing groups threatened by the loss of older forms of patriarchal political and economic power. For example Islamic governments, conservative Muslim NGOs, the Vatican and Catholic organisations, the Protestant evangelicals, and the International Right to Life Committee.[6]

Of course, a neoliberal economic order will never usher in gender equality. But just as capitalism offers more room for self-determination and self-organisation for people than does feudalism, so too does the neoliberal gender order allow women more room to engage in public life and to contest with men for power and place. Yet in the South, as in the North, women's responsibilities in care-giving disadvantage them in relation to men within the increasingly competitive and individualised economic and political worlds associated with the demands of global capitalism. This continuing differential relationship of men and women to the important and necessary labour of care-giving—work that is increasingly privatised because of the demise of the welfare state—is preserving male dominance albeit in a new form.[7]

In this situation, feminists who want to create a movement that reflects the needs and interests of working class and poor rural and urban women, face intense and difficult political dilemmas. These can be analysed in three terms.

One, relations of class and racial domination reproduced or diminished among feminist organisations both transnationally and within national polities. Two, the particular pressures facing women's NGOs and the possibilities for resistance as well as co-optation. And three, the lines of tension and alliances between the global feminist and Global Justice Movements (GJMs).

Feminist Politics in the Space between Patriarchal Nationalism and Neo-Colonialism

Organised feminism has been most effective locally and globally in promoting liberal political rights for women and in raising issues that previously were invisible—such as sexual assault and domestic violence—and that got them into national politics as well as formal politics.[8] Locally and internationally, feminists continue to face the difficult and pressing issue of how to argue for and define women's rights in a way that does not align feminism with neo-colonial relations of domination. Women in the Third World are forced to contest two powerful and opposing forces. On the one side is a masculinist nationalism that selectively defines tradition and nation in ways that force women to be the bearers of cultural difference, while men are free to participate in the world of modern political and economic power. On the other side is transnational capital that in its current phase threatens to overpower the national state and subject women along with men to new forms of economic exploitation or even to exclude them from the economy altogether—at the same time that it offers opportunities for escaping from traditional male control.

In the U.S., women of colour challenged white feminists to recognise that their categories of analysis assumed the universality of white, middle-class experience and defined equality and opportunity in ways that marginalise the political interests of working class women and women of colour. Similarly, women from the neo-colonised South have challenged the dominant voice of women from the North.

Since the World Conference of the International Women's Year in Mexico City convened by the UN in 1975, international feminism has debated how to define women's interests. An important development is the adoption of a 'human rights' platform as an organising agenda that women can co-operate on transnationally and use locally. At the 1993 UN World Conference on Human Rights, women's groups—arguing that "Human Rights are Women's Rights and Women's Rights Are Human Rights"—called on the Conference to recognise "gender based violence as a violation of human rights requiring immediate action."

This effort included promoting the Convention on the Elimination of All Forms of Discrimination Against Women (CEDAW), adopted by the UN in 1979. Nationally, women's organisations have used the Universal Declaration of Human Rights, expanded by the UN in 1966 to include economic, social, and cultural rights, to demand accountability from their governments. However, as might be expected, given the current dominance of capitalist class forces, in practice, only political and civil rights have real support, while women's social rights, along with those of men, are increasingly violated and marginalised by the destruction of public services at the core and periphery.

Raising concerns about human rights as a political discourse is in no way an endorsement of cultural relativism—women from the global South are only too well aware of how assertions of cultural difference could be used to legitimate patriarchal practices. They are also very well aware of the need to defend their nations and cultures against Northern hegemony—that treats western practices as the measure of progress for women and for society and thus legitimises neo-colonial domination. Northern feminists have participated in this kind of 'universalising' political discourse, and denied that modernisation shaped by non-western cultures might offer women more dignity, power, and respect. In this, they have made it easier for anti-feminist forces in the Third World to define feminism as a part of the Northern imperial project.

A good example of the co-optation of 'women's rights' for imperialist purposes is George Bush's claim that the U.S. war on Afghanistan was carried out to promote human rights for Afghan women. The ground for this claim was laid in part by the international women's rights campaign begun in 1997 by a coalition of Northern women's rights organisations.[9] The campaign called on the international community to deny investment and recognition to the Taliban, completely ignored the complicity of the North in the installation of the Taliban in the first place, and the ways in which Washington's tolerance of Taliban rule was bound up in its overall neoliberal, geo-political agenda.

Under the leadership of Third World feminists, some organisations have tried to chart a course between patriarchal nationalism and colonising feminism. For example, the network, Women Living Under Muslim Law (WLUML) challenges religious/political fundamentalism from within an Islamic framework of discourse, re-defining, just as men have done historically, what constitutes an 'Islamic' practice. Radhika Coomaraswamy asks how human rights can be protected at the local level while avoiding being pawns of imperial strategy. She proposes two criteria. One, any practice that causes severe pain and suffering to the women concerned should be criminalised. And other practices should be evaluated through debate, dialogue and coalition-building by the women of the particular society who have "in different ways fought racism and communalism but who also struggle against patriarchy and for women's rights. Even within this group there are big differences."[10]

The proper role of feminist organisations in the imperialist core countries is to support this local dialogue respectfully, and with resources. Who defines women's interests and rights? The feminist insistence that freedom from sexual violence is a woman's human right offers an obvious basis for cross-class alliance. Yet, working class and poor women in the global South often shape their understandings of male violence in class terms. They locate it as an issue within a particular social context—for example in relation to government promotion of liquor sales to impoverished districts or rising unemployment and the disappearance of traditional male work. In contrast, middle class advocates translating international human rights politics into the local arena, are more likely to focus on the need for changing laws and police practices in isolation from the broader causes of violence against women.[11]

For its organisational growth, global feminism has depended on funds not from grassroots membership, but from institutions such as the UN, social democratic governments in the North, and private foundations in the capitalist core countries. In the early nineties, the United Nations, certainly as a consequence of feminist pressure from within, committed to funding the involvement of local women's groups in the national conferences projected to address development issues.[12]

External funding has several consequences. Within the Third World, women's NGOs rely on external funding sources. When grassroots groups become social movement organisations, and then primarily *advocates for* rather than be *mobilisers of* their constituency, an inevitable process of professionalisation and bureaucraticisation takes place. External funding has only aggravated this process. Some organisations have done better than others in maintaining connection with and accountability to their social base.[13]

However, stratification among women's groups has grown as those with elite ties, access to international funders, and the organisational characteristics that funders want to support are able to command more resources and political influence. In their structural position vis-à-vis their national states and international funders, these NGOs became advisors and gender 'experts' who play a brokering role between the state and its clientele.[14]

NGOs, Popular Feminism and the Problems of Cross-Class Alliances

In the sixties and seventies, even though political rights were relatively circumscribed, some development surplus was directed toward expansion of basic services particularly education and health care, which lowered maternal and infant mortality rates in many countries. The struggle for collective or social rights has been fundamental to the political mobilisation of women in the working class, urban and rural poor and indigenous communities. The declining standards in urban living, destruction of rural livelihoods and the shrinking of the state under Structural Adjustment Programmes imposed by the IMF created a virtual explosion of women's activism over the last two decades.

This activism has three characteristics. It is an activism motivated by survival needs; it is based in cross-household networks of mutual help and supported by communitarian values; it is legitimated by women's traditional gender roles, and at the same time expanded to include women's engagement in public life, separate from men. A politics based on maternal care does not challenge traditional gender roles, and may even reinforce women's identification with motherhood. But it can lead grassroots activists to challenge male power and re-shape gender identities—if it takes place in a context which includes feminist ideas about women's rights in relation not only to the state but to the men in their own communities, households, and movement organisations.[15]

In the seventies and early eighties, struggles among women activists in the Third World and internationally, tended to counterpose a politics of women's needs to a politics of liberal (civil and political) rights, with working class/peasant women. They argued that collective and social rights are 'more important' to Third World women than individual civil rights.

This conflict was in part determined by the encapsulation of women activists in the politics of the traditional organs of working class/popular political mobilisation —labour unions, organisations of the unemployed, Left political parties, and peasant organisations. Over time, grassroots women's groups emerged from the struggles of poor rural and urban women, and women in the new proletariat of the free trade zones developed their own versions of a working class/popular feminism. Moving out from under the masculinist politics of local social and political movements, they began to address issues of sexual politics and to develop distinctive feminist modes of organising: consciousness raising, participatory decision-making, and attention to personal empowerment as a basis for collective empowerment.[16]

This political evolution would have been truncated without the existence of transnational feminist organising. Regional and international gatherings gave locally marginal women's grassroots organisations moral and practical support. Middle class/elite women were the first to articulate a programme for women's equality and participation, and to identify new targets of feminist contestation broadly understood as 'sexual politics.' Although originating outside the working class, these feminist organisations create an environment in which a different kind of feminist politics among women of the working class, peasantry, and urban poor is possible.

However, these organisations can also play a very negative role—by reproducing relations of class privilege and domination within movements, framing feminist ideology and strategy within the limits of a liberal political project, and entering into conservative alliances with political and economic elites. An example of the latter is the proliferation of NGOs in the global South managing programmes of small-scale loans—microcredit—for women. Although the 1995 Beijing Platform of Action proposed a broad range of reforms and interventions to improve women's position in Third World economies, women's NGOs have been most successful in promoting microcredit programmes. Initiated by USAID and the World Bank, these programmes have garnered the vast majority of development funds targeted toward women. Microcredit has increased women's integration into the informal sectors of the economy, but women often exploit their own children, especially their daughters, in order to get their work done. This increases competitive relationships among women, and does little to lift women or their families out of poverty.[17]

Ideologically, microcredit reinforces the neo-colonial view that ascribes to Third World women both moral characteristics and personal powers that alleviate the need for state-controlled and regulated development. In valorising 'grassroots' women's maternal virtues and survival strengths, NGOs argue for targeting women as the 'best investment' for development funds. Since men are less likely than women to pay back loans, more likely to spend their income on themselves rather than their households, and to participate in the petty corruption that is a route to local political influence, these claims have real force.

On the other hand, like all powerful ideologies, microcredit also rests on a very partial picture and has the unintended consequence of further solidifying the neoliberal agenda. Third World women are set up as a reproach, not to the forces of capitalist domination, but to those who supposedly lack their courage and determination to negotiate the market, that is, the 'dependent' men of poor countries who have relied on the State to protect them from the competitive challenges of the market.

The emergence of the 'microcredit industry' indicates how NGOs staffed by women from privileged strata in the Third World find avenues for employment, international travel, and political influence through work in which they project themselves as representatives of women who are marginalised and excluded from the new economic order. Women advocates for women are forced to inhabit a niche that is simultaneously empowering and disempowering—incorporating women's representatives into state resource allocation processes at the cost of distancing them from their social base and shoring up, rather than contesting, neoliberal ideologies and policies. Similar kinds of pressures face NGOs working in the arena of women's reproductive rights.

Reproductive Rights

Since the fifties under pressure from the World Bank, USAID, and other development agencies, developing countries began implementing population control programmes, designed to lower women's fertility 'by any means necessary,' and their myriad abuses have been well documented.[18] Since the seventies, international networks of feminists, working through NGOs and the United Nations, sought to shift the focus from fertility to the promotion of health and well being of women and children. Establishing links between economic development, women's personal autonomy (education, maternal and child healthcare, changes in family law, etc.), they suggested such programmes would be an improvement in women's lives and also result in a decline in their fertility.

This transnational feminist effort achieved a significant victory at the 1994 UN International Conference on Population and Development in Cairo, which adopted a 'Platform of Action' affirming women's reproductive rights and specifically condemning government policies driven by numerical population targets. The Platform also endorsed the neoliberal assault on the State, calling for greater reliance on the private sector and NGOs for service delivery.

While achieving considerable success at the level of theoretical vision and UN (and even World Bank) rhetoric, NGOs have been entirely unsuccessful in promoting women's reproductive rights in practice at the national level. Across the Third World, fertility rates have plunged, in many cases achieving, just in twenty years, a demographic transition that took close to a century in the West. Economic transition and structural adjustment in the South have produced a 'crisis-led fertility decline.' The causes of this decline are complex and reflect, at least in part, women's own desires to control their reproductive lives, increasing demand for women's labour, and aggressive family planning promotion that has made sterilisation operations, IUD insertions, and hormone-based contraceptives easily available. However, the rapidity and depth of this change is also the result of more negative factors such as women's impoverishment and rise in female-headed households: increasing demands on women's working days, reducing their exposure to unprotected heterosexual contact; women's appropriate fears of the health risks of pregnancy, including maternal mortality (the result of illegal abortions); compromised health status from poverty; and lack of access to pre- and post-natal healthcare.[19]

Although numerical targets may no longer drive government programmes, abuses of women's basic bodily rights continue to pervade the system. The overall institutional context so severely restricts women's choices as to be inherently, if not purposively, coercive. Rates of sterilisation among poor women, and especially poor women in racially oppressed communities, are far higher than among women who are racially and economically privileged.[20]

Feminism in the Global Justice Movement

At the end of the 20th century, the managers of global capitalism, meeting at the Davos World Economic Forum (WEF), were forced to acknowledge a deep crisis of legitimacy in the neoliberal order.[21] Halfway around the globe, in Porto Alegre, activists gathered at the WSF, sought to create a political agenda for the GJM, that had put global elites on the defensive. The participation of women as leaders and as representatives of grassroots movements at the WSF holds real promise, as does the involvement of feminist organisations in the organisational networks that constitute local anti-globalisation forces.

Thirty years ago, it was unthinkable, even within radical social movements, to have women in leadership over men or to have issues of gender oppression anything other than a matter for a woman's auxiliary. Organisations that command most widespread respect for their militancy, revolutionary vision, and courage are deeply influenced by feminism—in their political agendas and their leadership cadres. For example, in 1993, following a process of convening local women's committees and holding hundreds of community assemblies, the Zapatista Clandestine Revolutionary Indigenous Committee in Mexico passed the Revolutionary Laws of Women. This programme of women's rights includes their right to decide the number of children they will have and care for, their right to work and receive a just salary, the right to choose their partners, and so forth.[22]

Yet, there are areas of tension between transnational feminism and other parts of the GJM. Reflecting a complex set of forces, these 'fault lines' cannot be fully analysed here. But, I give two examples of problems that the GJM will have to resolve. One, tensions between women's NGOs and labour unions, and two, strategic silences on the issue of abortion and sexual orientation.

Women's NGOs and the Labour Movement

Due to gender specific reasons, traditional modes of union organising have not been effective in organising women workers. Successful strategies are those that cross over the public/private and work/family divides, acknowledging women's care-giving responsibilities and strong ties to their communities. Women workers are joining trade unions across the globe, but NGOs, sometimes formed by women workers leaving male-dominated unions, and sometimes created when no unions were interested have also stepped in and these represent an important constituency of the working-class movement. Given the limited opportunities for women in the formal labour market, NGOs are striving to preserve women's jobs in the labour-intensive industries that will hire them, while they organise to improve wages and working conditions.

NGOs have tended to rely more on community organising, moral persuasion, international funding, and political support than on union dues and traditional weapons of struggle, especially the strike. Labour unions, unsympathetic to the reasons for the NGOs' strategic choices, have failed to enter into supportive alliances with grassroots organisations of women workers, driving the NGOs further away from the trade union movement. And NGOs have become more vulnerable to co-optation by management-dominated international 'watchdog' committees, which have become a major tool for transnational corporations responding to the anti-sweatshop movement.[23]

Silences in Community-Based Movements

Women's activism in community-based movements over the last two decades reflects historic continuity. For centuries, women have entered political struggle to secure the livelihoods of their families and communities. In addition to demanding resources from local government, many communities began to engage in alternative modes of production and provision of services—co-operative work schemes to produce food and clothing, building crèches and houses, organising trash collection.[24]

Women's leadership has emerged in these struggles and incorporation of feminist demands into their political programmes, especially where community-based organisations are part of broader movements that carry radical political worldviews (the Zapatistas in Mexico or the Workers Party in Brazil). These developments reflect tremendous gains and offer great hope. Within the GJM, some feminist political ideas and demands are more easily expressed than others, for example, the progress made on domestic violence and the silence on the issues of abortion and sexual orientation.

This could be because some feminist demands are more compatible with maternalist politics—the right to be free from domestic violence or to birth control and child spacing and can be framed in ways that preserve the essential relationships of the traditional heterosexual family. Fertility control can and has often been allied to claims about preserving the health of mothers and children. The notion that men have an obligation to care for women in their families—and should not expect to retain familial authority if they violate that obligation—is not fundamentally antagonistic to paternalistic gender norms.

Make no mistake: both these shifts in understanding substantially expand women's power and authority within marital relationships and represent a victory for feminism. But as difficult as these changes have been to make, abortion has generated far more opposition to feminism. Abortion could be regarded as simply a form of contraception (and is in some societies framed as 'menstrual regulation'). But it has come to be defined as an act of maternal rejection and a powerful symbol of women's ability to separate (hetero) sexuality from procreation and to claim sexual pleasure for its own sake. The validation of lesbian sexuality goes even further in the direction of denying the inevitable, natural, and moral status of families organised around a heterosexual bond.

A second possible reason for silences around issues central to sexual liberation could be the role of religious organisations, particularly the Catholic Church, in providing institutional and monetary support to popular movements. It might appear that their constituents' religiosity inhibits the political issues that organisers can raise. But illegal abortion is a fact of life for many Catholic women who find ways to make abortion compatible with their religious beliefs.[25] I would argue that it is the dependence of organisations on the Catholic hierarchy for funding and political legitimacy, rather than their women constituents' religious beliefs that enforces this code of silence.

Conclusion

Conflicts and tensions around gender relations and feminist politics within the GJM offer hope as well as words of caution. Conflicts exist because women activists and their organisations are serious players on the political stage, contesting male dominance not as outsiders but from within the networks of the GJM. Whether feminism will come to inform the radical vision and the everyday politics of global justice activists depends on how well the movements are able to sustain political coalitions that are participatory and willing to engage in dialogue. Movements that make a space for the political and strategic interventions of working class and popular feminist activists and their organisations will constitute a powerful pole of attraction, an alternative for those who now believe they have no choice but to compromise with the neoliberal order.

Notes

1. Edited excerpt of paper in *New Politics*, Vol. 9, No. 2 (new series), whole no. 34.
2. Gordon and Hunter 1998; Kandioyti September 1988.
3. Where 114 women's organisations attended the first UN sponsored women's NGO forum in Mexico City in 1975, 3,000 came to Beijing in 1995. Today, tens of thousands of NGOs participate in international conferences and gatherings. See Basu Autumn 2000, p. 73.
4. Bandarage 1998.
5. Feldman Summer 2001, p. 1108; Raj *et al.* 1998.
6. Basu, *Ibid.*, p. 72.
7. For more on this argument, see Brenner 2000.
8. Basu, *Ibid.*, p. 81.
9. *Ibid.*, p. 73.
10. Coomaraswamy 2002.
11. Basu p. 76. For the U.S., see Beth E. Richie 2000.
12. Basu p. 74. Major U.S. foundation grants to women's organisations working for women's rights and against violence against women increased thirteen-fold between 1988 and 1993. In the two years prior to the Beijing summit in 1995, the Latin American and Caribbean Regional NGO Coordination received $1,007,403 from the UN. See Alvarez, Autumn 2000, p. 16.
13. Thayer 2000.
14. Alvarez pp. 55–58.
15. Petchesky and Judd p. 310.
16. Townsend, *et al.*, 1999; Corcoran-Nantes 2000; Alvarez pp. 36–37.
17. Mindry Summer 2001, pp. 1187–1212; Poster and Salime 2002, pp. 189–219.
18. Hartmann 2002, pp. 259–284.

29. Bandarage pp. 170 and 183.

20. In Brazil's Northeast, an impoverished region with a large Black population, the proportion of women using sterilisation for contraception increased by 16.49 per cent between 1986 and 1992, by which time 64.39 per cent of contracepting women were 'choosing' sterilisation. In the same period, mortality showed a dramatic increase. See Thayer p. 228.
21. Bello 2001, p. Xv.
22. Bayes and Kelly 2001, pp. 160–161.
23. Mendez 2002, pp. 121–141.
24. Ortega, Amuchastegui and Rivas 1998. pp. 145–147.
25. Diniz, *et al.*, 1998, pp. 61–62.

Towards Another Anarchism[1]

Andrej Grubacic

A friend wrote recently:

> No one needs another 'ism' from the 19th century, another word which imprisons and fixes meaning; another word that seduces a number of people into the clarity and comfort of a sectarian box and leads others in front of the firing squad or a show trial. Labels lead so easily to fundamentalism, brands inevitably breed intolerance, delineating doctrines, defining dogma, and limiting the possibility of change.

It is difficult not to agree. However, I want to present and discuss here an 'ism' that is the dominant perspective of today's post-Marxist global social movement: Anarchism. I start with a short history of anarchism, in order to be able to subsequently suggest a model of modern anarchism and strategic implications which follow from accepting such a model.

I suggest that this idea of anarchism has coloured the sensibility of the 'movement of movements' of which we are the participants. Today, the ethical paradigm of anarchism represents the basic inspiration of our movement, which is less about seizing state power than about exposing, de-legitimising and dismantling mechanisms of rule whilst winning ever-wider spaces of autonomy from it.

I am inclined to agree with those who see anarchism as a tendency in the history of human thought and practice, which cannot be encompassed by a general theory of ideology, a tendency that—by posing a question of their legitimacy—identifies compulsory and authoritarian hierarchical social structures. If they cannot answer this challenge, which is usually the case, then anarchism becomes the effort to limit their power and to widen the scope of liberty.

Anarchism is a social phenomenon and its contents, as well as manifestations in political activity, change with time. Unlike all major ideologies, anarchism can never have a stable and continuous existence on the ground through being in government or a part of a party system. Its history and contemporary characteristics are determined by another factor—cycles of political struggle. As a result, anarchism has a 'generational' tendency, in fairly discreet historical phases, according to the period of struggle in which they were shaped and can be identified. Like any attempt at conceptualisation, this can be a simplification. But I hope that it will be useful for understanding this social phenomenon.

Historically, the first phase of anarchism was shaped by the late 19th century class struggles in Europe, exemplified both theoretically and practically by the Bakunin faction in the First International. It began in the run up to 1848, peaked with the Paris Commune (1871) and dwindled through the 1880s. This was an embryonic form of anarchism, mixing together anti-state tendencies, anti-capitalism and atheism whilst retaining an essential dependence on the skilled urban proletariat as a revolutionary agent. Bakunin, the magnificent dreamer, the "dynamite, not a man," in 1848, shouted, "Beethoven's Ninth Symphony should be saved from the coming fires of the world revolution at the price of giving up one's life." He bequeathed to us one of the most beautiful and perhaps the most precise descriptions of a single leading idea within the anarchist tradition:

> I am a fanatic lover of liberty, considering it as the unique condition under which intelligence, dignity and human happiness can develop and grow; not the purely formal liberty conceded, measured out and regulated by the State, an eternal lie which in reality represents nothing more than the privilege of some founded on the slavery of the rest; not the individualistic, egoistic, shabby, and fictitious liberty extolled by the School of J.J. Rousseau and other schools of bourgeois liberalism, which considers the would-be rights of all men, represented by the State which limits the rights of each—an idea that leads inevitably to the reduction of the rights of each to zero. No, I mean the only kind of liberty that is worthy of the name, liberty that consists in the full development of all the material, intellectual and moral powers that are latent in each person; liberty that recognises no restrictions other than those determined by the laws of our own individual nature, which cannot properly be regarded as restrictions since these laws are not imposed by any outside legislator beside or above us, but are immanent and inherent, forming the very basis of our material, intellectual and moral being—they do not limit us but are the real and immediate conditions of our freedom.[2]

The second phase, from the 1890s to the Russian civil war, saw a considerable shift to Eastern Europe, and thus had more of an agrarian orientation. Kropotkin's anarcho-communism was the most dominant feature in theoretical terms. It peaks with Makhno's army during the Russian Revolution and carries over after the Bolshevik victory in a Central European undercurrent.

The third stage, from the twenties until the late forties, focused on industrially oriented Central and Western Europe. This was the peak of anarcho-syndicalism in terms of theorisation, with much of the work being done by exiles from Russia. In this moment, the differentiation between two basic traditions in the history of anarchism has become clearly visible: anarcho-communist with, one might say, Kropotkin as representative; and on the other hand, anarcho-syndicalism which simply regarded anarchist ideas as the proper mode of organisation for highly complex, advanced industrial societies. And this tendency in anarchism merges, or interrelates, with a variety of left-wing Marxism—the kind one finds in, say, the Council Communists who grew from the tradition of Rosa Luxemburg, and that was later represented, in a very exciting fashion, by Marxist theorists like Anton Pannekoek.

After World War II, anarchism had a major downturn due to economic reconstruction and surfaced only marginally in anti-imperialist struggles in the South that were, however, largely dominated by pro-Soviet influences.

The struggles of the sixties and seventies did not signify a serious upsurge of anarchism, which was still carrying the dead weight of its history and could not yet adopt a new political language that was not class-oriented. Thus, anarchist leanings were found in very diverse groups, ranging through the anti-war movement, feminism, situationism, Black power etc., but not anything that is positively identifiable as anarchism. Explicitly 'anarchist' groups in this period were more or less a recycling of the previous two stages (communist and revolutionary syndicalist), and quite sectarian. Instead of engaging with these new forms of political expression they closed themselves off to them and usually adopted very rigid charters like the anarchists of so called 'platformist' Makhno tradition. This was a 'ghost' fourth generation.

Currently, there are two co-existing generations within anarchism: people whose political formation took place in the sixties and seventies (actually a reincarnation of the second and third generations), and younger people who are much more informed, among other elements, by indigenous, feminist, ecological and culture-critical thinking. The former exists in various Anarchist Federations, the Industrial Workers of the World, the International Workers Association, the Northeastern Federation of Anarcho-Communists and the like. The latter's incarnation is most prominent in the networks of the new social movement. From my point of view, Peoples Global Action is the main expression of the current fifth generation of anarchism.

What is sometimes confusing as a characteristic of current anarchism is that its constituent individuals and groups do not usually refer to themselves as 'anarchists.' There are some who take anarchist principles of anti-sectarianism and open-endedness so seriously that they are sometimes reluctant to call themselves anarchists for that very reason. But the three essentials running through all manifestations of anarchist ideology are definitely there. These are anti-statism, anti-capitalism and pre-figurative politics (in other words, modes of organisation that deliberately demonstrate the world you want to create; or, as an anarchist historian of the revolution in Spain has formulated it, "an effort to think of not only the ideas but the facts of the future itself"). This is present in anything from jamming collectives to IndyMedia—all of which can be called anarchist in the sense that we are referring to a new form. There is only a limited connection between the two co-existing generations, mostly implying the following of what each other is doing, but not much more.

The basic dilemma that permeates contemporary anarchism is between traditionalist and modern conceptions of anarchism. In both cases we are witnesses to the 'escape from tradition.' I would suggest that 'traditionalist anarchists' have not fully understood the tradition.

The term 'tradition' can, in the history of ideas, be comprehended in two different ways. One way (probably the more common one) is that a certain past is accepted as a complete structure that cannot or should not be changed, but should be preserved in its solid state and passed on into the future, unchanged. Such an understanding of tradition is connected to that part of human nature referred to as conservative, prone to stereotypical behaviour—Freud would even say "the compulsion of repetition." The other meaning of tradition, which I advocate here, relates to the new and creative way of reviving a historical experience. This positive manner of conveying the past, relates to the other side of human nature—provisionally considered revolutionary—along the lines of a paradoxically expressed truth: a wish for a change and, at the same time, a healthy need to remain the same.

Another 'escape from tradition' takes refuge in various 'post-modern' interpretations of anarchism. I think it is high time, to quote Max Weber, for a certain "disenchantment" of anarchism, an awakening from the dream of post-modernist nihilism, anti-rationalism, neo-primitivism, cultural terrorism, "simulacra." It is time to restore anarchism to the intellectual and political context of the Enlightenment project that is nothing else but understanding that "objective knowledge is a tool to be used so that individuals can take informed decisions on their own." Reason, says the famous Goya painting, does not produce monsters when it dreams, but when it sleeps.

Today, a dialogue between different generations within modern anarchism is necessary, as it is imbued with countless contradictions. It does not suffice to surrender to the habit of the majority of contemporary anarchist thinkers who insist on dichotomies. It would be good to abandon the exclusiveness of the either/or way of thinking, and engage in discussion, in search of synthesis. Is such a synthetic model possible? I think it is.

A new model of modern anarchism, which can be discerned today within the new social movement, is the one that insists on widening the anti-authoritarian focus, as well as on abandoning class reductionism. As Michael Albert puts it, such a model endeavours to recognise the 'totality of domination,' that is,

> To highlight not only the state but also gender relations, and not only the economy but also cultural relations and ecology, sexuality and freedom in every form it can be sought, and each not only through the sole prism of authority relations, but also informed by richer and more diverse concepts. This model not only doesn't decry technology per se, but it becomes familiar with and employs diverse types of technology as appropriate. It not only doesn't decry institutions *per se*, or political forms *per se*, it tries to conceive new institutions and new political forms for activism and for a new society, including new ways of meeting, new ways of decision making, new ways of coordinating, and so on, most recently including revitalised affinity groups and original spokes structures. And it not only doesn't decry reforms *per se*, but it struggles to define and win non-reformist reforms, attentive to people's immediate needs and bettering peoples' lives now as well as moving toward further gains, and eventually transformational gains, in the future.[3]

Anarchism can become effective only if it contains three essential components: worker's organisations, activists and researchers. How can one create a basis for a modern anarchism on the intellectual, union, and popular level? There are various ideas about another kind of anarchism, which would be capable of promoting the values I mentioned above.

First of all, anarchism must become reflexive, in that intellectual struggle must reaffirm its place in modern anarchism. One of the basic weaknesses of the anarchist movement today is, in comparison with the time of, say, Kropotkin or Recluse, or Herbert Read, exactly the neglect of the symbolic, and a sidelining of the effectiveness of theory.

Instead of the anarchists criticising the famous postmodern Marxist fairytale 'Empire,' they should write an anarchist 'Empire.' Religious Marxism has, for a long time, referred to theory and, by this token, has given itself a scientific appearance and the possibility of acting as a theory. Today, anarchism requires the overcoming of extremes of both anti-intellectualism and intellectualism. Like Noam Chomsky, I also have neither sympathy nor patience for these and believe that an opposition between science and anarchism should not exist:

> Within the anarchist tradition there has been a certain feeling that there is something regimented or oppressive about science itself. There is no argument that I know for irrationality, I don't think that the methods of science amount to anything more than being reasonable, and I don't see why anarchists shouldn't be reasonable.[4]

And like Chomsky, I have even less patience for a strange tendency that has spread, in various forms, within anarchism itself:

> It strikes me as remarkable that Left intellectuals today should seek to deprive oppressed people not only of the joys of understanding and insight, but also of the tools of emancipation, informing us that the project of Enlightenment is dead, that we must abandon the illusions of science and rationality—a message that will gladden the hearts of the powerful.[5]

Before us, further, lies the task of envisioning the anarchist researcher. What would be the role of an anarchist researcher? She would certainly not lecture, like the old Left intellectuals do. She should not be a teacher, but someone who envisages a new and very difficult role: she must listen, explore and discover. Her role is to expose the interest of the dominant elite carefully hidden behind supposedly objective discourses.

She has to help activists and supply them with facts. It is necessary to invent a new form of communication between activists and activist scholars. It is necessary to create a collective instrument that would connect libertarian scientists, workers and activists. It is necessary to found anarchist institutes, reviews, scientific communities and internationals, such as the PAN network (Planetary Anarchist Network). I believe that sectarianism, unfortunately a very widespread phenomenon in modern anarchism, would in this way lose its power. One of the organised attempts to resist sectarianism in modern anarchism is this outline by PAN of a new anarchist international:

> The Anarchist International is an initiative meant to provide a venue for anarchists in all parts of the world who wish to express their solidarity with each other, facilitate communication and co-ordination,

learn from one another's efforts and experiences, and encourage a more powerful anarchist voice and perspective in radical politics everywhere. But who wish to do so in a form which rejects all traces of sectarianism, vanguardism and revolutionary elitism.

We do not see anarchism as a philosophy invented in 19th century Europe, but rather, as the very theory and practice of freedom—that genuine freedom which is not constructed on the backs of others—an ideal that has been endlessly rediscovered, dreamed and fought for on every continent and in every period of human history. Anarchism will always have a thousand strands, because diversity will always be part of the essence of freedom, but creating webs of solidarity can make all of them more powerful.

Hallmarks

• We are anarchists because we believe that human freedom and happiness would be best guaranteed by a society based on principles of self-organisation, voluntary association, and mutual aid, and because we reject all forms of social relations based on systemic violence, such as the State or capitalism.

• We are, however, profoundly anti-sectarian, by which we mean two things: a) We do not attempt to enforce any particular form of anarchism on one another: Platformist, Syndicalist, Primitivist, Insurrectionist or any other. Neither do we wish to exclude anyone on this basis—we value diversity as a principle in itself, limited only by our common rejection of structures of domination such as racism, sexism, fundamentalism, etc. b) Since we see anarchism not as a doctrine so much as a process of movement towards a free, just, and sustainable society, we believe anarchists should not limit themselves to co-operating with those who self-identify as anarchists, but should actively seek to co-operate with anyone who is working to create a world based on those same broad liberatory principles, and, in fact, learn from them. One of the purposes of the International is to facilitate this: both to make it easier for us to bring some of those millions around the world who are, effectively, anarchists without knowing it, into touch with the thoughts of others who have worked in that same tradition, and, at the same time, to enrich the anarchist tradition itself through contact with their experiences.

- We reject all forms of vanguardism and believe that the proper role of the anarchist intellectual (a role that should be open to everyone) is to take part in an ongoing dialogue: to learn from the experience of popular community-building and struggle and offer back the fruits of reflection on that experience not in the spirit of the dictate, but of the gift.
- Anyone who accepts these principles is a member of the Anarchist International and everyone who is a member of the Anarchist International is empowered to act as a spokesperson if they so desire. Because we value diversity, we do not expect uniformity of views other than acceptance of the principles themselves (and, of course, acknowledgement that such diversity exists).
- Organisation is neither a value in itself nor an evil in itself; the level of organisational structure appropriate to any given project or task can never be dictated in advance but can only be determined by those actually engaged in it. So with any project initiated within the International, it should be up to those undertaking it to determine the form and level of organisation appropriate for that project. At this point, there is no need for a decision-making structure for the International itself but if in the future members feel there should be, it shall be up to the group itself to determine how that process should work, provided only that it be within the broad spirit of decentralisation and direct democracy.[6]

Furthermore, anarchism must turn to the experiences of other social movements. It must be included in the courses of progressive social science. It must be in collusion with ideas that come from the circles close to anarchism.

Let's take for example the idea of participatory economy, which represents an anarchist economist vision, par excellence, and which supplements and rectifies anarchist economic tradition. It would also be wise to listen to those voices that warn of the existence of three major classes in advanced capitalism, not just two. There is also another class of people, branded co-ordinator class by these theoreticians. Their role is that of controlling the labour of the working class. This is the class that includes the management hierarchy and the professional consultants and advisors central to their system of control—as lawyers, key engineers and accountants, and so on. They have their class position because of their relative monopolisation over knowledge, skills, and connections. This is what enables them to gain access to the positions they occupy in corporate and government hierarchies.

Another thing to note about the co-ordinator class is that it is capable of being a ruling class. This is, in fact, the true historical meaning of the Soviet Union and the other so called Communist countries. They are, in fact, systems that *empower* the co-ordinator class.

Finally, I believe that modern anarchism has to turn to envisioning the political. This is not to say that various schools of anarchism failed to advocate very specific forms of social organisation, albeit often markedly at variance with one another. Essentially, however, anarchism as a whole advanced what liberals call 'negative freedom,' that is to say, a formal 'freedom from' rather than a substantive 'freedom for.'

Indeed, anarchism often celebrated its commitment to negative freedom as evidence of its own pluralism, ideological tolerance, or creativity. The point, however, is that the failure of anarchism to enunciate the historical circumstances that would make possible a stateless anarchic society produced problems in anarchist thought that remain unresolved to this day. One friend told me, not so long ago that "you anarchists always strive to keep your hands clean, with the result that you are finally left with no hands at all." I believe that this remark relates exactly to the lack of more serious thinking about political vision.

Proudhon attempted to formulate a concrete image of a libertarian society. His attempt failed, and was utterly unsatisfactory. However, this failure should not discourage us, but rather point to the path followed by, for example, social ecologists in North America—a path leading to the formulation of a serious anarchist political vision. An anarchist model should also encompass the attempt to answer the question: "What is the anarchists' full set of positive institutional alternatives to contemporary legislatures, courts, police, and diverse executive agencies?" Quoting Michael Albert again, we need to:

> Offer a political vision that encompasses legislation, implementation, adjudication, and enforcement and that shows how each would be effectively accomplished in a non-authoritarian way, promoting positive outcomes would not only provide our contemporary activism much-needed long-term hope, it would also inform our immediate responses to today's electoral, law-making, law enforcement and court system, and thus many of our strategic choices.[7]

Finally, what would be the strategic implications of promoting such a model? I have often heard from anarchist activists a strategic proposition for which I have neither sympathy nor explanation. We should, they say, make an effort and live worse in order for things to be better. As opposed to this extraordinary logic, which reads "the worse, the better," I think it would be wiser, and far more sensible, to listen to the advice of Argentinean anarchists who advocate a strategy of "expanding the floor of the cage." Such a strategy will understand, instead, that it is possible to fight for and win reforms short of revolution in a way that both improve people's conditions and options now and create opportunities for further victories in the future.

This strategy implies that being in favour of a new society does not warrant ignoring people's current pain and suffering. What it does mean is that when we work to address current ills and work to make things immediately better, we do so in ways that raise our consciousness, empower our constituencies, and develop our organisations. And that, therefore, leads to a trajectory of on-going changes, culminating in new basic economic and social structures. Expanding the floor of the cage does not ignore people's short-term struggles for higher wages, an end to a war, affirmative action, better working conditions, a participatory budget, a progressive or radical tax, a shorter working week with full pay, abolishing the IMF—or whatever else—because it will recognise how people's consciousness and organisations develop through struggle. And it will actively avoid the kind of activist contempt for people's courageous efforts to improve the quality of their lives.

To conclude, I think that such a model of modern anarchism could have a significant role in building, amidst the current horrors of capitalism, a post-Marxist movement that would reclaim the values of the Enlightenment and make them finally realise their full potential.

Notes

1. Talk given at the 'Life After Capitalism' programme at the World Social Forum, Porto Alegre, Brazil, January 2003. I would like to thank my friends David Graeber, Uri Gordon and Michael Albert. Any idea you read here might very well actually have been invented by one of them.
2. Bakunin 1970.
3. Albert 2002.
4. Chomsky 1992.
5. *Ibid.*
6. According to the author, PAN, or AI, was in existence in January 2003 when he gave the talk on which this essay is based, but it has died since, leaving no documented trace; and where he too no longer has the reference details. The real name of the initiative was Planetary Anarchist Network. Personal correspondence, May 19 2008.
7. Albert 2002.

Empire, Global Power Centres, And People's Alliances: The Need for A Global People's Movement[1]

Muto Ichiyo

Did we step into a new distinct historical era with the attacks of September 11 2001 and the subsequent launch of the U.S.' war on terrorism? Yes and no. Yes, because this seems to represent the emergence of a persevering 'war-is-peace, peace-is-war' period under the single global U.S. Empire. No, because this is also the culmination of U.S. hegemony since 1945 (which stayed flawed and partial because of the Cold War), and because this is the logical consequence of the neoliberal globalisation processes of the 1990s.

Simple 'yes' views could imply, as do the dominant U.S. discourses, justification for the Bush action, while simple 'no' views could miss the signs of the times, thus justifying passive and reactive approaches (business-as-usual, responding to particular crises and injustices only individually and on the basis of the established framings, typically national, for instance: Japan—peace constitution; Philippines—national democracy; Korea—national unification; and Taiwan/China—Strait).

These national framings are certainly the necessary starting points but not sufficient because the Empire is global, with its particular strategies being merely instrumental to its global concerns (for instance, U.S. policy toward the Palestinian issue is geared to the creation of conditions allowing the U.S. to launch war against Iraq, and so has little to do with the resolution of this historic conflict). It is therefore necessary to establish a shared global framing vis-à-vis the whole logic, structure, discourses, and practice of the Empire, encompassing its socio-economic and military aspects. Such a global popular movement basis is yet to be established. In other words, we (social movements working in different national settings and on different issues) must seek a common understanding of the overarching Empire, take a common stand against this monstrous rule, resist and overturn it, while envisioning and promoting another world that is democratically organised and ecologically sustainable. The acquisition of this common context would certainly facilitate our struggle on individual issues, and for national solutions as well, since we then would be working for new, globally shared standards of justice.

Bush's Unilateralism

Is the imperial rule to be attributed only to the Bush administration's particular and peculiar behaviour? Will—say, Al Gore—if successful in the next presidential election, get things back to 'normal'?

As in the Cold War period, tense and lax phases may alternate in the new era too. But the general imperial frame set by Bush will stay, just as anti-communism and the East-West confrontation remained the tone of the Cold War period throughout its tense and lax phases. We need to differentiate what is particular to Bush from the persevering characteristics deriving from the evolution of the U.S. global hegemony. We need to address the over-determined structure as the single reality confronting us in the foreseeable future of this century.

Using 'terrorism' as Aladdin's lamp, Bush has claimed—and in fact succeeded in practicing—the right to militarily destroy and dispose of any states in U.S. disfavour ("You go with us or you go with the terrorists"). The second stage of the 'war on terrorism' declared by Bush in his 2002 State of the Union address—the axis of evil labelling, followed by the Nuclear Posture Review, among others—discarded the original 'self-defence' and 'retaliation' logic, to justify the U.S. right to carry out 'holy war' on a general basis. Bush has washed away the UN principles that made war illegal except for immediate self-defence, by bringing in the notion of pre-emptive defence. The notion of a 'just war' against evil has been reintroduced, with the U.S. as the supreme privileged body to judge who are the evil to be destroyed. U.S. national decisions are to be simultaneously and automatically global decisions. All constraints on U.S. sovereignty should go or be simply ignored. (Bush: "Some governments will be timid in the face of terror. And make no mistake about it. If they do not act, America will.")

One of the defining features of the imperial era is the overwhelming military power of the U.S.—rivalled by none. In the Cold War period, the U.S. was countervailed by the Soviet military power. The two Empires were symmetric in military terms, the Soviet Union serving as a humbling element relativising the U.S. as one of the contending parties. The Soviet military power, so to speak, was a measure to gauge the U.S. military stature. Now this external measure is gone, and the U.S. has to gauge its stature only with its own stature. This means that there is no external factor to delimit the U.S.'s military build-up. The U.S. gears its military directly to its cravings for an absolute and single-handed control of the whole world where no rivals are allowed to emerge. The U.S. strategic documents produced since 1995 have made this posture clear. Now Bush is enforcing these strategies in his permanent war on terrorism.

Anti-Terrorist Alliance: Why Is this Alliance Built Paradoxically Around U.S. Unilateralism?

The globalisation regime has already enmeshed almost all states which came to have heavy stakes in it, each finding it more advantageous and less risky for its self-interest to act within the U.S. Empire, imbibing its logic, for fear that turning its back on it would cause terrible problems, or in the hope of maximising its immediate interests by striking favourable deals accepting the Empire (for example, the U.S.-Russia deal on Caspian oil development).

The U.S. effectively blackmailed and silenced Southern countries' complaints about the Washington Consensus with the 'with-us-or-with-terrorists' threats. Northern core countries, already promoting globalisation as their recolonisation project, find the Bush scheme a new framework that facilitates their collective global domination and that protects Northern citadels from migrants and other intruders from the South. The U.S. logic of civilisation versus evil strengthens their deep-rooted conviction that western values and standards of living are supreme.

The Imperial logic of military prerogative and the claimed 'emergency' that is needed to boost the military and to curtail freedom and democracy, in many cases enable ruling political groups to put into practice reactionary schemes long-hatched but which could not be implemented (eg in Japan, the abolition of the war-renouncing constitution).

The U.S. logic of anti-terrorism is also useful for some states to justify their oppression of minorities by violent means without the fear of being accused of human rights violations—Russia, China, the Philippines, and most blatantly, Israel are examples.

These heterogeneous motivations make this alliance ad hoc and fragile. And in any event, this is a peculiar and even paradoxical alliance built around U.S. unilateralism. But the overwhelming U.S. military capability and readiness, coupled with the horror of ostracism, should not be minimised. The U.S. needs an alliance, but only tactically; the alliance is important but can be dispensed with. Forestalling its failure, Bush already declared his go-it-alone posture. This in itself works as a deterrence to dissent. Only pressure from below, by popular movements coalescing into a global people's movement, can free states from this alliance.

U.S. Hegemony: Continuity and Discontinuity

When its design emerged toward the end of WWII, U.S. hegemony, unlike the preceding British hegemony, was originally meant to integrate the whole world as a single U.S. market and domain of direct and indirect political control. The Bretton Woods system was so designed, and the Marshall Plan was proposed to cover Eastern Europe too. But the Kremlin disrupted this wholeness, and the Chinese revolution compromised it in Asia. The Cold War set in. The world was divided territorially, politically, and ideologically by the two ideologically antagonistic Empires. U.S. hegemony was functional in the 'free world' only, though the economic empire deeply penetrated the other imperial domain and increasingly undermined its social and economic basis. That was the Cold War, a long period of crippled U.S. hegemony. There, real issues in each of the two Empires were blamed on instigated subversion by the other Empire (Vietnam and Nicaragua as products of Moscow, and Gdansk and Warsaw as products of Washington).

The Cold War ended and the Soviet Union collapsed in the early 1990s, sending the U.S. back to its long-dreamt-of full hegemonic position. From then on, the U.S. has had to face the real problems of global capitalism. With Communism gone, it has had no alien body except the elusive terrorist networks on which to blame the world's hot, knotty, and very serious problems. The choices were either to tackle them seriously to resolve them, or to complete the U.S. Empire on a bulldozed ground under whose surface the real problems were to be buried and stay buried. The U.S. has definitely refused to take the first choice. The bulldozer being used is neoliberal globalisation, lubricated by plausible-sounding slogans of free market, free competition, free trade, deregulation, and privatisation (which have been carried out) as putative guarantees of democracy and human rights (which have never materialised).

Neoliberal globalisation had been promoted by, and served in turn to reinforce, a composite global power centre, whose core was the Northern states, multi-national corporations, and private and inter-governmental financial interests. The utterly undemocratic nature of the world structure was already exposed and resisted in the 1980s, with challenges around issues such as the debt crisis and structural adjustment, environment degradation, etc. The full U.S. Empire came back as the crudest machinery imaginable to keep this structure imposed on the majority of the world population who suffer from the destructive consequences of neoliberal globalisation.

The United States certainly has been, and is, the core of this whole process. But that it has come back as the full-fledged Empire also indicates a shift in the internal relationships of this global power centre. The U.S., without ceasing to be a nation-state, has appointed itself, even within the global centre, an entity beyond nation-states, and it claims its right as such. Of course in practice this is not new. Unilateralism wedded to isolationism has been one of the politico-ideological traditions of the United States, as U.S. history shows us. In recent decades, U.S. military forces have unilaterally intervened in many countries and ignored international criticisms (for instance, the International Court's ruling on its Nicaraguan intervention). But these were, so to speak, the U.S.'s private affairs.

A Changed World

But the rules of the game have now been changed. The U.S. has forced the world to accept that its decisions are automatically public policy that is globally applicable: that they are world decisions. International laws, the UN Charter, The Hague and Geneva treaties and conventions no longer apply, as the U.S. alone is the law. And the U.S. enforces the law with its nightmarishly colossal military machinery, by far out of proportion to the capacity of any possible adversary. There has been a major power shift in the composition of the global power centre.

George Bush (papa) dreamed of a similar post-Cold War setup and fought the Gulf War. But in retrospect, even he looks a dove. At that time, the war had a definite proclaimed purpose of driving away invading Iraqi forces from Kuwait, and Bush organised a multinational force somewhat on the basis of the UN resolution, and fought the war as a regular state-to-state war. Now George Bush (son) has launched a war against an unidentified enemy no one has clearly defined, whose whereabouts is not clear. Bush said, "Our war on terror is well begun, but it is only begun. This campaign may not be finished on our watch, yet it must be and it will be waged on our watch." If so, the events of September 11 triggered an Orwellian situation into which we are slipping, where war is synonymous with peace and peace synonymous with war and the line of demarcation between military and police operations is obliterated under ubiquitous systems of surveillance.

Challenges and Our Alliances

We need to face this whole situation squarely.

We, as a progressive movement, face the full U.S. Empire for the first time and therefore we have still to work out our shared position and strategies to cope with this new historical situation. The postures and strategies we established vis-à-vis the Cold War structure fall short of the needs we face now. On the other hand, the U.S. Empire has no capacity, nor any intention, to address the real problems of the world today. The world inevitably becomes increasingly violent because the Empire has taken on itself the impossible task of suppressing the expressions of the fundamental problems of the world today.

But we have the basis on which we can work out our strategies. Popular resistance to the varied aspects of neoliberal globalisation, especially since Seattle in 1999, certainly is a major base. But the popular resistance has been focused mostly on socio-economic and environmental aspects of the imperial design, staying indifferent to the military aspects. Now that the U.S. Empire has fully emerged through the current 'war on terrorism,' the nexus between the neoliberal globalisation and this war should be brought into our full view. This will enable broad alliances to emerge to confront the multi-faceted expressions of the imperial realities. In other words, the current war is not one of many issues, but it should be seen as the defining element of a whole period we have stepped into.

There is a crude revival and spread of the 'civilisation versus evil' discourses, including racism, jingoism, and various fundamentalisms. The people's alliances we envisage entail very serious efforts to overcome these discourses and practices. In intellectual fields, we have for decades accumulated knowledge and analyses in terms of multi-culturalism and post-colonial identities, in fact to a very sophisticated degree, and we almost believed that these had become established norms of our societies. But now we see in many parts of the world that these are washed away by crude racist arguments.

We need to recognise the fact that we are now being tested. And we must reflectively examine how we can intellectually cope with this.

Note

1. This paper was originally presented to a roundtable discussion on the war issue held by ARENA (Asian Exchange for New Alternatives) on May 8–9 2002 in Hong Kong; http://www.peaceworkmagazine.org/pwork/0209/020917.htm, accessed 070907. It is a replacement for the essay that appeared in the first edition of this book (The Viveka Foundation, New Delhi, 2004), titled 'Asian Peace Movements and Empire.' We have done this only on account of copyright issues. We have selected this particular, somewhat earlier (2002) piece from among Muto san's extensive body of writing in this area because it is similar in spirit to what it is replacing painting a horizon that those in the movement need to look at with this essay written soon after 9/11 and its aftermaths. It is instructive, today, in 2008, look at what has happened in these intervening years in terms of the questions that the author asks and the challenges he puts forward. Content editor for this essay was Vipul Rikhi.

The Global Justice And Solidarity Movement And The World Social Forum: A Backgrounder

Peter Waterman

The WSF is probably best identified with the recent international wave of protest known as the 'anti-globalisation movement.' While intimately interrelated with the latter, the WSF is just one emanation of this much more general phenomenon and process. How can these phenomena and their inter-relationships be best understood?

It is possible to make a 19th/20th century comparison, with the relationship between trade unions or labour parties on the one hand and 'the labour movement' on the other. But the labour movement, whilst obviously broader and looser than any particular institution, and having international expression, consisted largely of other, primarily national, institutions (co-operatives, women's organisations, publications). The WSF is an essentially international event (or an expanding series of such). And on the other hand, we have an essentially international movement that might not even (yet?) recognise itself as such. So we are confronted with two new social phenomena—of the period of globalisation, that are both international and global, and that have a novel relationship with each other.

The WSF—promoted by an identifiable group of Brazilian, French and other non-governmental organisations, trade unions and individuals—is itself linked organically to the more general movement. This is through an informal Forum event, known as the 'Call of Social Movements,' which has been attended, and its regular declarations signed, by many WSF participant bodies (see this volume). The Call formalised itself between WSF 2–3 with a Social Movements International Secretariat. But this body, or tendency, is a matter of discomfort for those within the WSF who want to see the Forum as a 'space' rather than a 'movement.'[1]

The 'Global Justice and Solidarity Movement' (GJ&SM) is actually a name *proposed by* the Call, for the general wave of protest against corporate-dominated globalisation, against U.S.-sponsored neoliberalism/neo-conservatism and war: one name for the new wave of radical-democratic protest and counter-proposition.

This 'movement of movements' is marked by its network form and communication activity; a matter recognised by friends and enemies alike.[2] Moreover, 'it' seems to change size, shape, reach, scale, target and aims according to events. So, at one moment it might be focused against neoliberal economic globalisation, at another against the U.S.-led war on Iraq. This makes it even more challenging to analyse than to name.

Like any novel phenomenon, the GJ&SM is easier to characterise by what it is *not* than by what it is:

- It is *not* an international labour or socialist movement, though unions and socialists are prominently involved;
- It is *not* a 'transnational advocacy network,'[3] though it is much marked by the presence of international and national NGOs;
- It is *not* a reincarnation of the international protest wave following 1968, though Che Guevara icons are still popular, and it includes other clear echoes of the sixties and seventies;
- It is *not* an anarchist movement, though anarchists, autonomists and libertarians are highly active within it;
- It is *not* a nationalist or thirdworldist movement, though nationalist, thirdworldist and anti-imperialist forces and notes can be clearly identified within it.

It is, on the other hand, not too difficult to identify a rising number of processes that have *provoked* this movement. These include:

- The increasing predominance, in the international sphere, of multinational corporations and international financial institutions, along with the neoliberal policies that have been imposed on both North and the South (Table);
- The shrinking of the public sphere and reduction of State social programmes and subsidies;
- The feminisation of poverty, the commodification of women (the sex trade), the simultaneous formal endorsement and political denial of women's and sexual rights;
- De-industrialisation, unemployment and the informalisation of employment;
- The ideology of competitiveness as the court of first and last appeal;
- The undermining of market protection (primarily of weaker national economies);
- The simultaneous preaching and practical undermining of traditional structures and notions of national sovereignty;

- The simultaneous creation of new international institutions and regulations, alongside the marginalisation of the United Nations and such agencies as the International Labour Organisation (ILO);
- Increasing talk of and the continuing undermining of ecological sustainability; corporate attempts to copyright genetic resources, to genetically modify foodstuffs, to commercialise them and then coerce people into buying them; the continuation and even increase of militarism, militarisation and warfare despite hopes raised by the end of the Cold War;
- The increase in globalised epidemics and threats to the climate;
- The demonisation of immigrants, asylum-seekers, and of Islam and other 'others.'

All these have dramatically raised social tensions, particularly in the South, but also in the East (the ex-Communist world) and even in such model core capitalist welfare states as Canada and Sweden. The pressures have also provoked major conservative, reactionary, religious and ethnic backlashes, of a violent and repressive nature, sometimes internationally co-ordinated.

Many identify the new protest movements of the emerging century with the North: Seattle 1999, Prague 2000, Genoa 2001, Gothenburg 2001, Barcelona 2002, Evian 2003. They also associate it with the middle classes, students and youth, who have indeed been prominent within it. But so have women, forming around 50 per cent at the World Social Forums, though this is little commented on.

But the movement cannot be limited to major protest events, nor to what has occurred since 1999. It must be traced both back and down, at least to the 'food riots' provoked by the IMF in the South of the eighties, when there were urban uprisings against the externally-imposed end of food subsidies. Widespread protests against gigantic and ecologically damaging dam projects, promoted by the World Bank and developmentalist local elites, go back to the eighties and earlier. There were major demonstrations and riots against the poll tax in Britain in 1990. Through the 1990s, there were myriad protests across the South against the euphemistically-named Structural Adjustment Policies (SAPs) in particular, and neoliberal policies more generally. And the appearance of the often corporatist, sometimes chauvinist and commonly quiescent U.S. AFL-CIO on the anti-WTO demonstration in Seattle, was welcomed—(somewhat prematurely?)—by the slogan 'Teamsters and Turtles: Together at Last!'[4]

One major manifestation of U.S.-initiated neoliberalism has been the North American Free Trade Agreement (NAFTA), which provoked widespread protest in both Canada and Mexico. In the case of Canada, it turned an initial national-protectionist campaign into one of international solidarity, first with Mexico, then with Latin America more generally, leading to the Hemispheric Social Alliance, which included the USA. In the case of Mexico, the launching date of the NAFTA, 1 January 1994, was also used for the launching of the Zapatista movement in the severely globalised, marginalised and exploited state of Chiapas, in the south of Mexico.[5]

Initially appearing as a classical armed guerrilla movement based on the discriminated upon and land-hungry Mayan ethnic communities of Chiapas, the Zapatistas rapidly revealed entirely novel characteristics: an address to Mexican civil society, high-profile internationalism, a sophisticated understanding and use of both the mass media and alternative electronic communications. All can be found in the speeches and writings of its primary spokesperson, Sub-Commander Marcos (Rafael Guillén) a university-educated non-indigene, trained in guerrilla warfare in Cuba. Activities of the Zapatistas, particularly two international *encuentros*, one in Chiapas, 1996, one in Spain, 1997, gave rise, or shape, to a new wave of internationalism. The powerful, poetic and playful words of Marcos, who switches between, or combines, popular Mayan and Mexican idiom with the language of cosmopolitan intellectuals, enchanted a dulled world. It had a dramatic appeal on several front, including an international Left, battered, bruised and disoriented by: the downscaling of the welfare state; the downsizing of the working class; the halting of the forward march of labour; the collapse of Eastern Communist and Southern Populist states; and the crisis of the international movements identified with such. Zapatista encounters also inspired at least two significant emanations of the movement, People's Global Action (PGA) and the WSF itself.[6]

Other major sources of, or contributors to the new movement must be mentioned, particularly the rising wave of protest against unemployment, privatisation and cuts in social services gathering steam throughout the nineties, markedly in Europe and the increasing development of 'counter-expertise,' concentrated in international and national NGOs which had been honed at a series of UN conferences and summits through the 1990s: notably the 1992 World Conference on Environment and Development and the 1995 UN Fourth World Conference on Women. Also, the rise of irreverent, often anarchist-tinted, direct action movements of customarily internationalist appeal, such as Reclaim the Streets in the UK. This supported the courageous, but eventually defeated Liverpool Dockers' protest against corporate attack, state legislation and union passivity in the face of such. A significant international libertarian initiative, related to this kind of national activity was that of PGA, which held meetings in Geneva, Bangalore and Cochabamba.[7]

Finally, the seventies and eighties movements served as forerunners to the rise of the so-called New Social Movements. Considered as expressing 'identity' more than 'interest,' these movements—of women, indigenous peoples, and sexual minorities, for media democratisation, on ecology and consumption—were noted in the South as well as the North. They brought to public attention hidden forms of alienation, suggested new forms of 'self-articulation' (both joining and expression). As much addressed to the transformation of civil society as of the economy or state, these movements raised issues that the major old international 'interest' movement—that of unionised labour—had long subordinated, ignored or marginalised.[8]

The rise of the 'anti-globalisation movement' did not so much re-assert 'interest' over 'identity' as surpass the alleged opposition or even the distinction. Highlighting the increasing power of corporations over states, and of their negative impact on people and peoples—North, South, East—the movement was as much a challenge to institutionalised labour and the Left worldwide as to an international women's movement suffering severe 'ngo-isation.'[9]

It is clear, from yet another name—the 'anti-capitalist movement'—that this 'movement of movements' is as much an *aspiration* as an *actuality*, as much a *becoming* as a *being*. It has, however, passed one major test. When the terrorist attack on New York and Washington occurred on 11 September 2001, there was a stalemate in the growing movement in North America (Seattle 1999; Washington DC 2000; Quebec 2001). Yet, with the U.S.-led wars against Afghanistan, 2002 and Iraq, 2003, a movement often considered to be primarily 'anti-corporate' morphed into the biggest international anti-war protest in history. A *New York Times* columnist stated, 18 February 2003, 'there may still be in our planet, two super-powers: the United States and world public opinion.' A 300-strong anti-war demonstration took place even in Lima, Peru. This is a country profoundly traumatised and isolated by decades of neoliberalism, counter-insurgency and authoritarian rule, and which had—unlike neighbouring Brazil, Ecuador and Bolivia—previously revealed only marginal awareness of the new internationalist wave.[10]

The language of the new radical-democratic protest movements is increasingly infecting some of the fifty- to onehundred-year-old international trade union organisations, such as the recently renamed Global Union Federations (GUFs). And trade unions, which have150–200 million members worldwide, are increasingly attracted by the WSF.[11] The WSF has been held in Porto Alegre, Brazil, 2001–3, and is scheduled for Mumbai, India, in 2004. If the earlier mentioned protest events were frequently marked more by *opposition* than *proposition,* the Forums have not only been devoted to *counter* proposition over a remarkably wide range of social issues (with a wide range of significant collective actors). They have also demonstrated that what is shaping up is much more than a northern, or even a western hemispheric internationalism. The Forum process, moreover, has now reached take off, with national, regional and thematic forums taking place all over the world. Some of these may be independent of the WSF itself. The WSF has also become both the subject and the site of intense reflection concerning its own significance, nature and future.[12]

Names and Definitions

This movement, as suggested, has many names, these reflecting sometimes conflicting, sometimes overlapping approaches, theories, strategies and aspirations. These understandings vary from the traditional leftist, the non-traditional leftist to the innovatory, and even the insistence that this is not a movement but a 'field.' Attempts have been made to capture, or at least conceptualise the phenomenon under the rubric of 'global civil society.' The ways even sympathetic theorists and strategists try to identify groups or tendencies within the movement is revealing both of their orientation and of the novel nature of the phenomenon.[13]

Thus, Alex Callinicos from the UK, while admitting that the majority of its activists are *not* anti-capitalist, refers to its 'developing consciousness' as justification for calling it so. He then draws up a typology of anti-capitalism that includes the 'reactionary,' 'bourgeois,' 'localist,' 'reformist,' 'autonomist' and 'socialist,' himself identifying with a sub-category of this last type, the 'revolutionary.'[14]

Christophe Aguiton from France, a Trotskyite of another feather, and a leading figure within the WSF, tentatively identifies three 'poles' within the global justice movement: 'Radical internationalist,' 'nationalist,' and 'neo-reformist.' The first looks beyond both capitalism and the nation-state, the second is a mostly-Southern response, and the third is the kind of 'global governance' tendency also strongly present within the WSF.[15]

Starr and Adams from the USA, who would be 'localists' in the Callinicos typology, characterise the movement as 'anti-globalisation,' and identify as significant, 'modes' or 'archetypes' within it: 'radical reform,' which is state-friendly; 'people's globalisation,' associated with the WSF; and 'autonomy,' identified with the ecological friendliness and democratic qualities of freely co-operating communities (their own).

The Portuguese researcher, Boaventura de Sousa Santos, who concentrates on the WSF, suggests its radical implications for the surpassing of traditional sociologies, Left strategies and even Western epistemology. He argues that any significant new emancipatory movement cannot be understood in pre-existing terms, and proposes the necessity, in our epoch, of developing a 'sociology of absence' and a 'sociology of emergence.' This is to surpass the sociologies of the existent and apparent, and allow voice to what has been ignored or suppressed. These new sociologies are also necessary to surpass 'conservative utopias,' whether of the Right or Left.

Italian Mario Pianta, considering the movement in 'global civil society' terms, divides responses to neoliberal globalisation into 'supporters of current arrangements,' 'reformists,' 'radical critics favouring another globalisation,' 'alternatives outside the mainstream,' and 'nationalist rejectionists.'

What is suggestive is that, with the exception of Callinicos, none of the above uses the terminology of Left (Right or Centre) and that, in practice, each of these understandings cuts across the Left-as-we-know-it, the Left of a national-industrial(anti-)colonial-capitalism. While many activists and some internationally influential Left movements do refer *solely* to this tradition, the question of whether the GS&JM is not potentially *surpassing* traditional Left internationalism is also being raised. 'Emancipation' might seem a more appropriate term than 'Left' when discussing today the transformation of society, nature, culture, work and psychology—as well as, of course, that increasingly important but placeless place, cyberspace.[16]

Formation of the Movement—The Local, National, Regional and Global

While some writers set up, in oppositional terms, the national and the global, the local and the global, it would seem more fruitful to see these as existing in creative tension, with each of these levels, instances or spaces informed by the other. Or at least needing to be so informed.[17]

If we compare the last major wave of world-wide protest symbolised by 1968, we have to recognise that the movements of that period were *parallel* rather than *linked.* Despite all the similarities, there appears to have been little direct contact or movement communication between Paris and Prague, between the European protests and uprisings and those of Dakar, Tokyo or Mexico City. Neither participant accounts nor contemporary ones seem to claim such.[18]

'1968' was certainly *inspired* by the Cuban Revolution (1959), the Chinese Cultural Revolution (1965), the Vietnamese resistance to the U.S. (1960s), by the dramatic rise of the U.S. Civil Rights Movement (1960s), by the creation of the Cuban-sponsored Tri-continental solidarity movement and the Organisation of Latin American Solidarity (1966–7). It was certainly also informed, in the literal sense, by mass media reports. But 1968 was neither organised nor co-ordinated by these. And the commercial media proved to be a predictably problematic means of movement communication.[19]

In so far as the movement was informed by the 'Situationist International' of that period, connected with the names of Vaneighem and Debord, this would have been in Paris rather than Prague and mostly because of such provocative new notions as 'the revolution in everyday life.' A hoped-for 'Coming of the New International' was confined to the Third World, marked by a state-oriented 'thirdworldism' and truncated even here.[20]

The period following 1968 can now be seen rather as revealing the crisis of the old, institutionalised, ideological, party, nationalist or bloc inter-nationalisms than as proposing an alternative kind of internationalism. What the vacuum was often filled with was a unidirectional 'First-World/ Third-World' solidarity, itself sometimes conflated with state-funded 'development co-operation' projects, carried out by NGOs with an often-ambiguous autonomy from states, North or South.[21]

For a meaningful alternative internationalism to take shape, a revolution within capitalism caused by the combination of globalisation and informatisation was needed. The nature of this alternative may be at least suggested by the world's biggest and most widespread (if unsuccessful) protest demonstration, the anti-war protest of 15–16 February 2003. This had been called for at the ESF 2002 and echoed at WSF 3. The provocation here was clearly the new kind of global war launched by the most conservative powers in the North. But the co-ordination of the protest was now largely dependent on dozens of 'alternative' websites and lists. It may have been further supported by traditional anti-war and anti-imperialist elements within the movement, but it would surely have been impossible without the web.[22]

The new localisms and internationalisms of the present day are inspired by the explicit or implicit recognition that "the nation-state...is at once too large and too small for the range of real social purposes."[23] What holds these levels, spaces, foci together, in a possibly conflictive but unavoidable tension, is the more-recent recognition, by the Zapatistas, of the necessity for "a world where many worlds fit."[24]

Let us reflect on the spatial relations of two national cases. There has been a dramatic wave of varied social protests across South Africa in the last few years: largely popular, non-white, poor, cross-class and multi-ethnic. As in the rather effective AIDS campaign, these movements can be seen, or presented, as local, and/or national, and/or regional (Southern African), and/or global. In much of the commentary, this kind of cross-scale referencing is quite spontaneous. To what extent such awareness exists amongst participants (or what significance a more-than-nationalist consciousness might have amongst them) remains to be investigated. But the very existence of such awareness amongst both *organisers* and *commentators* suggests a 'world of difference' from that of 1968, or of course, 1917. Its importance is indeed also witnessed in the South African case by those 'Left' politicians in power, and/or profoundly compromised with neoliberal policies, which appeal to old internationalisms against the new global movements![25]

India has seen similar or even greater waves of such protests over the last decade, traceable back to half a century or more. They include worker, rural, urban, regional, *adivasi* (indigenous) and *Dalit* ('untouchable'; oppressed) movements, religious and ethnic protests (often sectarian or communalist), ecology and women's movements. Over the past two decades there has been an increase in dramatic, often massive, protest demonstrations and marches, explicitly aimed against neoliberalisation, globalisation and imperialism. With the possible exception of the ecology and women's movements, and projects for regional civil society linkages; however, these have shown little consciousness of, or significant linkage with, movements elsewhere. That this has continued till recently may not be due simply to the relative size, poverty or isolation of India but to the framing of such protests within the protest discourses of the 19th/20th century, such as socialism (of a decreasingly internationalist nature), nationalism and populism. The recently rising consciousness of, and connection with, the GJ&SM, is symbolised by the holding of the first ASF (Hyderabad 2002), and the hosting of the first WSF outside Brazil, in Mumbai, in 2004. Exceptionally, in India, the old Left has taken this initiative. Whether, at Mumbai, the clearest note will be struck by the old traditions of national subaltern protest, or the new ones of global counter-assertion—or how these will be mutually articulated—may be significant for the future of not only the WSF but for the GJ&SM in general.[26]

Forming the Movement—Culture, Communication and Cyberspace

Distancing ourselves somewhat from current analyses, claims or prognostications concerning culture, communication or cyberspace, or aspects, of the new movement,[27] it is worthwhile tracing the line back to, or forward from, the old internationalisms.

Marx and Engels were excited by the communication impact of national railways and the telegraph as it became trans-European. When Lenin declared that "Cinema for us is the most important of arts," he meant that silent film could communicate across literacy and language barriers. Twentieth century communist internationalism was sensitive to the area of communications and culture, one of its most creative spirits declaring, notably, that "communications are the nervous system of...internationalism and human solidarity."[28] In the 1920s, the Moscow-based Third International sponsored a multitude of often-innovatory cultural and communication forms, both popular and avant-garde, from Germany to India and Japan.

Leaping forward to '1968,' we can note the brilliant poster art, often internationalist in spirit, following the Cuban Revolution, and that generated by Paris in 1968 itself. At the same time, however, the widespread hostility of the new Left to 'capitalist technology' and the 'commercial mass media' was criticised by Enzensberger.[29] He argued that engagement with the electronic media would allow people to mobilise *themselves*—to become "as free as dancers, as aware as football players, as surprising as guerrillas." From this period on we note the development of community-specific local-to-international radio, 'guerrilla' video groups and computer-communication experiments.[30]

A part of the new social movements of the eighties and nineties retained, and still retains, its suspicion of computer-based 'communications internationalism' and of the internet and cyberspace more generally. More pragmatic spirits simply adopted and adapted each new development. And the more visionary began to see the internet not simply as a tool but as a *space* to be disputed and even as *community creating*. Amongst the most pragmatic have been the union organisations and many independent labour and socialist internationalists. Amongst the more visionary and experimental have been the Zapatistas and their supporters, some feminists and those coming out of the 'community,' 'alternative' and other media movements—themselves descendents of 1968. The best-known expression is the de-centred, multi-media, Indymedia Center which sprang to life during Seattle 1999, and which now has nodes in such unlikely places as India, Palestine, and Russia.[31]

Alongside such new internationalist media practices we see democratic international media-campaigning, itself traceable back to the thirdworldist (i.e. statist) New World Information and Communication Order (NWICO) of the seventies and eighties Today this has a more radical-democratic or social-movement orientation. Media and cyberspace activity finds multi-faceted expression within the WSF, partly in official panels, partly in more marginal ones. It may also, however, find expression within alternative or oppositional spaces during the World Summit on the Information Society (WSIS), 2003–5. Such activities within the UN system may now be seen as secondary to activity within the framework of the WSF.[32]

Given their low-level of institutionalisation and of the conventional quest for political power, both the WSF and the GJ&SM have to be considered in cultural and communication terms. But whereas the Movement's protest events have been dramatically networked, and concerned with mass-media and alternative- media address, those of proposition, such as the WSF, have been rather less so, relying on such traditional (new) Left forms as the panel and the demonstration. A path-breaking exception here has been, however, the anti-fundamentalist and anti-war masks, videos, posters and hoardings of the feminist Marcosur group at WSF 2 and 3.[33]

Conclusion: A Fifth International?

A new internationalism is taking shape and place, though it might be more realistic to put this in the plural, or to distinguish it as 'the new global solidarity.' There will be argument about whether it surpasses the First-to-Fourth Internationals or provides a basis for some kind of Fifth one. However, it is also quite possible that it will reproduce the errors and failures of previous Internationals. The GJ&SM has not, so far, proven to be a movement much aware of *that* history, which is also part of its *own* history—or at least of its inheritance. Those involved in such debates are, however, likely to agree that a movement that is *not* aware of its history is in danger of repeating it.[34]

Patrick Bond's table (overleaf) may clarify positions and processes identified in the paper or provoke alternative conceptualisations of the Global Justice and Solidarity Movement.[35]

Political Current	Global Justice Movements	Third World Nationalism	Post-Washington Consensus	Washington Consensus	Resurgent Right Wing
Main Agenda	'De-globalisation' of capital (not people), 'globalisation-from-below,' anti-war, anti-racism, women's liberation, ecology, indigenous rights, 'de-commodification' of state services and mass-participatory democracy.	Increased (but fairer) global integration, i.e., reform (not transformation) of the interstate system through debt relief, democratisation of global governance, more market access, regional Cupertino and anti-imperialism.	Fix 'imperfect markets' and add 'sustainable development' to existing neoliberal framework through global state- building, while opposing U.S. unilateralism and militarism.	Neoliberalism revamped and renamed (PRSPs, HIPC and PPPs), slight provision for 'transparency' and (self)regulation, more effective bail-out mechanisms; and general support for Empire.	For petro-military imperialism, against multilateralism; protectionism, tariffs, subsidies, bail-outs and cronyism; racism; and reversing globalisation of people via xenophobia.
Internal Disputes	Role of the nation-state; party politics, fix-it vs. nix-it strategies for international agencies, and tactics (merits of symbolic property destruction).	Political alignments, degree of militancy vis-à-vis the North, divergent regional interests, religious differences, egos, internecine rivalries.	Some look leftward (for broader alliances) and others look to the Wash. Con. (for resources and legitimacy).	Differing reactions to U.S. imperialism, based in part upon divergent national-capitalist interests and domestic political dynamics.	Disagreements over extent of imperial reach, and over how to protect national cultures and patriarchy.

Political Current	Global Justice Movements	Third World Nationalism	Post-Washington Consensus	Washington Consensus	Resurgent Right Wing
Leading Institutions	Social movements; environmental justice advocates; radical activist networks; indigenous people's and autonomist groups; some militant labour movements; a few left wing think-tanks (eg. Focus on the Global South, Food First, Global Exchange, IBASE, IPS,IFG, Nader centres, TNI);leftist media/websites (eg. Indymedia, Pacifica, www.zmag.org); and sectoral or localised coalitions allied to the World Social Forum.	Self-selecting regimes(often authoritarian): Argentina, Chile, China, Egypt, India, Iraq, Libya, Malaysia, Nigeria, Pakistan, Palestine, Russia, S.Africa, Turkey, Zimbabwe with a few—like Brazil, Cuba and Venezuela—that lean Left (but others soft on imperialism, e.g. E Timor, Ecuador and Eritrea);Islamic nationalism; and supportive NGOs (eg. Third World Network, Seatini).	WSSD, some UN agencies (eg. UNCTAD, UNICEF, UNREAD); some int'l NGOs' (eg. Care, Civicus, IUCN, Oxfam, TI); large enviro. Groups (eg., Sierra and WWF);big labour (eg. ICFTU and AFLCIO); liberal foundations (eg. Carnegie, Ford, MacArthur, Mott, Open Society, Rockefeller); Columbia University Economics department; and German, Canadian and Scandinavian governments.	U.S. State (Federal Reserve, Treasury, USAID); corporate media and big business; World Bank, IMF, WTO; elite clubs(Bilderburgers, Tri-lateral Commission, World Economic Forum); some UN agencies (UNDP, Global Compact); universities and think-tanks (University of Chicago Economics department, Council on Foreign Relations, Institute of International Finance, Brookings); and most Japanese and EU governments.	U.S. Republican Party populist and libertarian wings; Project for New American Century; rightwing think-tanks (AEI, Cato, CSIS, Heritage, Manhattan); The Christian Right; petro-military complex; CIA, FBI, Pentagon; right-wing media (eg. Fox, National Interest, Washington Times); and proto-fascist European parties, but also Israel's Likud.

Notes

1. Social Movements World Network website; Vargas 2003; Whitaker 2003; World Social Forum website.
2. Arquilla and Ronfeldt 2001; Cleaver 1998; Escobar 2003; Klein 2001.
3. Keck and Sikkink 1998.
4. Aguiton 2003; Walton and Seddon 1994.
5. Alianza Social Continental website; Zapatista Index website.
6. de la Grange and Rico 1998; Holloway and Peláez 1998; Olesen [forthcoming]; Wahl 2002.
7. Abramsky 2001; PGA website; Reclaim the Streets website; Sweeney 1997.
8. Alvarez, Dagnino and Escobar 1998; Cohen 1985; Melucci 1989; Omvedt 1993a.
9. Alvarez *et al.* 2002.
10. Ashman 2003; Boyd 2003; Callinicos 2003; Starr 2000.
11. Aguiton 2003; Buckley 2003; International Transportworkers Federation 2002.
12. Fisher and Ponniah 2003; Transnational Alternatives 2002; Sen 2003; Santos 2003; Whitaker 2002.
13. Aguiton 2001; Callinicos 2003; Crossley 2002; Glasius, Kaldor and Anheier 2002; Pianta 2001; Starr 2000; Santos 2003.
14. Callinicos 2003, pp. 14–16.
15. Global Civil Society Yearbook website; Rikkilä and Patomäki 2001.
16. Boyd 2003; Cardon and Granjon 2003; Escobar 2003; Löwy 2003; Ngwane 2003; Waterman 2001a, b.
17. Massey 1991; Featherstone [forthcoming].
18. Ali and Watkins 1998; Carr 1998; Erickson 2002; Koning 1988, p. 192.
19. Ali and Watkins 1998; Gitlin 1980; Koning 1988, p. 192.
20. Gerassi 1971; Vague 2000.
21. Omvedt 1993.
22. Ashman 2003; Boyd 2003.
23. Williams 1983, p. 197.
24. EZLN 1997.
25. Bond 2003; Cock 2003; Desai 2002; Kingsnorth 2003; Ngwane 2003; Nzimande 2003; Weekes 2002.
26. *Desh Bachao* 2003; Dietrich and Nayak 2001; Featherstone 2002; Muricken 1999; Omvedt 1993; Sen 2003; Waterman 1982.
27. Cyberspace after Capitalism 2003.
28. Mariátegui 1973/1923.
29. Enzensberger 1976.
30. Ali and Watkins 1998; Art-For-A-Change website; Suarez 2003; Waterman 1992.
31. Harcourt 1999; Hellman 2000; Indy Media website; Olesen Forthcoming [ditto]; Suarez 2003; Waterman 1992, 2001b.
32. Cyberspace after Capitalism 2003; ISIS 2003; Leon, Burch and Tamayo 2001; Putting People First 2003; WSF Thematic Area 3 2003.
33. Articulación Feminista Marcosur website.
34. Löwy 2003; Waterman 1992, 2001a.
35. Buckley 2003.
36. Starr 2003.

WORLD SOCIAL FORUM CHARTER OF PRINCIPLES[1]

The committee of Brazilian organisations that conceived of, and organised, the first World Social Forum, held in Porto Alegre [Brazil] from January 25th to 30th 2001, after evaluating the results of that Forum and the expectations it raised, consider it necessary and legitimate to draw up a Charter of Principles to guide the continued pursuit of that initiative. While the principles contained in this Charter—to be respected by all those who wish to take part in the process and to organise new editions of the World Social Forum—are a consolidation of the decisions that presided over the holding of the Porto Alegre Forum and ensured its success, they extend the reach of those decisions and define orientations that flow from their logic.

1. The World Social Forum is an open meeting place for reflective thinking, democratic debate of ideas, formulation of proposals, free exchange of experiences and interlinking for effective action, by groups and movements of civil society that are opposed to neoliberalism and to domination of the world by capital and any form of imperialism, and are committed to building a planetary society directed towards fruitful relationships among humankind and between it and the Earth.

2. The World Social Forum at Porto Alegre was an event localised in time and place. From now on, in the certainty proclaimed at Porto Alegre that "another world is possible," it becomes a permanent process of seeking and building alternatives, which cannot be reduced to the events supporting it.

3. The World Social Forum is a world process. All the meetings that are held as part of this process have an international dimension.

4. The alternatives proposed at the World Social Forum stand in opposition to a process of globalisation commanded by the large multinational corporations and by the governments and international institutions at the service of those corporations' interests, with the complicity of national governments. They are designed to ensure that globalisation in solidarity will prevail as a new stage in world history. This will respect universal human rights, and those of all citizens—men and women—of all nations and the environment and will rest on democratic international systems and institutions at the service of social justice, equality and the sovereignty of peoples.

5. The World Social Forum brings together and interlinks only organisations and movements of civil society from all the countries in the world, but intends neither to be a body representing world civil society.

6. The meetings of the World Social Forum do not deliberate on behalf of the World Social Forum as a body. No one, therefore, will be authorised, on behalf of any of the editions of the Forum, to express positions claiming to be those of all its participants. The participants in the Forum shall not be called on to take decisions as a body, whether by vote or acclamation, on declarations or proposals for action that would commit all, or the majority, of them and that propose to be taken as establishing positions of the Forum as a body. It thus does not constitute a locus of power to be disputed by the participants in its meetings, nor does it intend to constitute the only option for interrelation and action by the organisations and movements that participate in it.

7. Nonetheless, organisations or groups of organisations that participate in the Forums meetings must be assured the right, during such meetings, to deliberate on declarations or actions they may decide on, whether singly or in coordination with other participants. The World Social Forum undertakes to circulate such decisions widely by the means at its disposal, without directing, creating hierarchies, censuring or restricting them, but as deliberations of the organisations or groups of organisations that made the decisions.

8. The World Social Forum is a plural, diversified, non-confessional, non-governmental and non-party context that, in a decentralised fashion, interrelates organisations and movements engaged in concrete action at levels from the local to the international to build another world.

9. The World Social Forum will always be a forum open to pluralism and to the diversity of activities and ways of engaging of the organisations and movements that decide to participate in it, as well as the diversity of genders, ethnicities, cultures, generations and physical capacities, providing they abide by this Charter of Principles. Neither party representations nor military organisations shall participate in the Forum. Government leaders and members of legislatures who accept the commitments of this Charter may be invited to participate in a personal capacity.

10. The World Social Forum is opposed to all totalitarian and reductionist views of economy, development and history and to the use of violence as a means of social control by the State. It upholds respect for Human Rights, the practices of real democracy, participatory democracy, peaceful relations, in equality and solidarity, among people, ethnicities, genders and peoples, and condemns all forms of domination and all subjection of one person by another.

11. As a forum for debate, the World Social Forum is a movement of ideas that prompts reflection, and the transparent circulation of the results of that reflec-

tion, on the mechanisms and instruments of domination by capital, on means and actions to resist and overcome that domination, and on the alternatives proposed to solve the problems of exclusion and social inequality that the process of capitalist globalisation with its racist, sexist and environmentally destructive dimensions is creating internationally and within countries.

12. As a framework for the exchange of experiences, the World Social Forum encourages understanding and mutual recognition among its participant organisations and movements, and places special value on the exchange among them, particularly on all that society is building to centre economic activity and political action on meeting the needs of people and respecting nature, in the present and for future generations.

13. As a context for interrelations, the World Social Forum seeks to strengthen and create new national and international links among organisations and movements of society, that—in both public and private life—will increase the capacity for non-violent social resistance to the process of dehumanisation the world is undergoing and to the violence used by the State, and reinforce the humanising measures being taken by the action of these movements and organisations.

14. The World Social Forum is a process that encourages its participant organisations and movements to situate their actions, from the local level to the national level and seeking active participation in international contexts, as issues of planetary citizenship, and to introduce onto the global agenda the change-inducing practices that they are experimenting in building a new world in solidarity.

First edition approved and adopted in São Paulo, Brazil, on 9 April 2001, by the organisations that make up the World Social Forum Organising Committee.

Approved with modifications by the World Social Forum International Council on 10 June 2001.

Note

1. Revised and finalised June 2001 version, World Social Forum International Council, on 08.10.07, available at: http://www.forumsocialmundial.org.br/main.php?id_menu=4&cd_language=2

WSF IC: NATURE, RESPONSIBILITIES, COMPOSITION AND FUNCTIONING[1]

The first meeting of the International Council (IC) of the WSF was held from June 9 to 11 2001. At that time, the following items regarding the nature, responsibilities, composition, and functioning of the IC were discussed and approved:

1) Nature:

The creation of the IC reflects the concept of the WSF as a permanent, long-term process, designed to build an international movement to bring together alternatives to neo-liberal thinking in favour of a new social order, one that will foster contact among a multiplicity and diversity of proposals.

Accordingly, the IC will be set up as a permanent body that will give continuity to the WSF beyond 2002, to consolidate the process of taking the WSF to the world level. The Council will play a leading role in defining policy guidelines and the WSF's strategic directions. National Organising Committees will serve as organisers and facilitators in tandem with the IC.

The IC must be a place of ongoing open dialogue and interlinking with other social movements and struggles. It will not be an authority in a power structure, and will not have mechanisms for disputing representation, nor for voting. Although the IC must have a balanced make-up in terms of regional and sectoral diversity, it will not be a bureaucratic structure with any claim to representing world civil society. The representativity of the IC will result from its ability to take the WSF to the world level, and to give it roots, organicity, and continuity.

2) Responsibilities:

With their main objective being to expand and consolidate the WSF, IC members must assume political and operational responsibilities such as the following:

Formulating WSF strategies

- Maintaining ongoing contact with international movements, campaigns, initiatives, struggles and other events;
- Making the WSF a familiar presence in their countries and regions, fostering widespread participation and debate on matters and proposals identified by the WSF;
- Promoting and supporting WSF meetings, identifying potential sites and encouraging participation;
- Ensuring reciprocal political, thematic, and operational action among WSFs;

- Promoting and supporting the formation of Committees in their countries;
- Together with WSF Organising Committees, providing a structure for topics, methodologies, formats, identification and invitations to speakers and exhibitors;
- Fund-raising.

3) Composition:

The IC consists of a basic core wherein regional imbalances still exist (sparse participation by Africa, Asia, and the Arab world), as well as sectoral ones (young people, blacks, among others), which must be eliminated.[2] The Council believes that confronting these imbalances and gaps must be seen as a goal to be attained by means of consultation, for which regions and groups require time. The IC must evaluate suggestions to take in new members resulting from these consultations, and subsequently extend the appropriate invitations. The IC must strive to raise funds so that networks will not be denied participation due to a lack of resources. Groups and organisations invited to the first meeting, but that were unable to attend, will of course be considered members of the IC.

The composition of the IC will obey the following criteria

- Adherence to the Charter of Principles;
- Geographical and regional balance aimed at diversity;
- Sectoral participation: trade unions, social movements, NGOs and others;
- Participation by heads of international and regional networks;
- Commitment to the continuity of the WSF, and with responsibilities referred to above;
- There is no pre-set number of members;
- Participants will include representatives from international and regional entities and organisations, and international networks and coordinators.

There will be two ways to participate in the IC, with the right to be heard guaranteed in each instance:

a) Permanent members;

b) Occasional guests and observers: Non-members whose participation is considered important at a given moment in the international situation or with regard to the WSFs organisational dynamics.

4) Functioning:

The IC is conceived as a dynamic arrangement reflecting society's initiatives. As such, each member will contribute to the IC according to the member's activities, and should make its commitments clear as regards the Councils functioning. Accordingly, during the meeting there was a proposal to create work groups to coordinate member's agendas.

Fund-raising efforts must get underway as soon as possible. Creating mechanisms for mobilisation and communication is also a pressing need, and must be quickly put in practice to foster coordination among members, and among members and WSF 2002 Organising Committees.

In order to ensure the IC functions dynamically, members should appoint a representative and a deputy. Each member will have a seat at IC meetings.

The next Council meeting will be held in Dakar, Senegal, in late October 2001 (where, among other matters, the site of WSF 2003 will be designated). Immediately afterward, the IC will meet again in Porto Alegre, just before WSF 2002 begins.

Notes

1. WSF Brazilian Organising Committee, not dated, approx mid-late 2001; posted August 2002. This document was first made available at the WSF website on 8 August 2002 @ http://www.forumsocialmundial.org.br/main.php?id_menu=4_2_2_1&cd_language=2. More details on the functioning of IC, its members, meeting minutes, and other details are available @ http://www.forumsocialmundial.org.br/main.php?id_menu=3_2&cd_language=2 and @ http://www.openspaceforum.net/twiki/tiki-index.php?page=WSFInternationalCouncil.
2. Note that this document was written in 2001 (*eds*).

NOTE OF INFORMATION, FOURTH DAY ACTIVITIES AT WSF NAIROBI[1]

In essence, the WSF process has moved from 'Thematic Terrains' to 'Objectives for Actions' around which all our struggles, actions, and alternatives are made visible and strengthened. The 4th day is the designated time for movements that have been participating in the first three days of the Nairobi Forum to present and share with everyone their *Proposals for Action*.

The *Proposal for Actions* should be the result of our reflections during the self-organised activities and these proposals must connect the different organisations, campaigns, struggles and alternatives.

The 4th day will be divided in three working sessions: the morning, with two periods of self-organised meetings and assemblies; an afternoon period that will consist of five big *Forums of Struggles, Alternatives and Actions*; a convergence rally ending up with a tree-planting event.

The morning periods are a continuation of the three previous days of self-organised activities. During all the days of self-organised activities, organisations are invited to draft their 'Proposal for Actions'. Each proposal must be signed by at least three organisations or networks, containing a brief description (no more than half a page) that conform with one of the following themes for actions. Since the objectives for actions guiding the self-organised activities were broad-based themes, the Content & Methodology Commission decided to expand them into actionable themes:

- Water;
- National/International Institutions and Democracy;
- Peace/War;
- Housing;
- Women's Struggles;
- Dignity/Human Being Diversity/Discriminations;
- Human Rights;
- Youth;
- Food Sovereignty/Land Reform;
- Labour;
- Education;

- Environment and Energy;
- Health;
- Knowledge/Information/Communication;
- Debt;
- Migrations;
- Free Trade;
- Culture;
- Transnational Corporations;
- Children;
- Alternative Economies.

A basic form will be available at each activity venue where the respective organisations/groups could fill it in at the end of the activity and submit it to a small office designated for that purpose. All proposals for actions will be posted at the same office currently identified as the *Hall of Proposals*. In that space, everyone can see the proposal for actions that will be presented in the 4th day.

During the afternoon of the 4th day, five *Forums of Struggles, Alternatives, and Actions* will be organised to present all the Proposals for Actions according to the proposed themes. The presentation of each proposal should not be more than three minutes long. The presentations will alternate with cultural performances related to the themes for action.

At 5 pm, all people present at the Forums will converge in a rally followed by a tree-planting event as a symbol of the planting of the seeds for alternatives.

Note

1. The 4th Day Activities and Proposals for Actions, January 2007, Note of Information. This note presents the methodological decisions debated in the Content and Methodology Commission meeting held in Nairobi from the 16th to 18th December 2006. This document is included here because the introduction of this "4th day of activities" at the Nairobi Forum in January 2007, inviting Proposal for Actions from all Forum participants and providing a whole day for deliberations on them, organised into actionable themes, constituted a major new item in the WSF's way of doing things at the world meetings and therefore a major new organisational and movement-building experiment. Its success remains to be seen. Sourced from WSF 2007 website @ http://wsf2007.org/program/note-of- information-fourth-day-activities.

WSF CALL FOR DAY OF ACTION/MOBILISATION, JANUARY 26TH 2008[1]

We are millions of women and men, organisations, networks, movements, trade unions from all parts of the world; we come from villages, regions, rural zones, urban centres; we are of all ages, peoples, cultures, beliefs, but we are united by the strong conviction that

ANOTHER WORLD IS POSSIBLE!

With all the richness of our plurality and diversity and our alternatives and proposals, we struggle against neo-liberalism, war, colonialism, racism, and patriarchy which produce violence, exploitation, exclusion, poverty, hunger, and ecological disaster and deprive people of human rights.

For many years we have been resisting and constructing innovative processes, new cultures of organisation and action from the local to the global, in particular within the processes and Charter of Principles of the World Social Forum from which this call emerges.

Aware of the need to set our own agenda and to increase the impact of these thousands of expressions and manifestations, we are committed to strengthening the solidarity and convergence amongst our struggles, campaigns, and constructions of alternatives and alliances.

We commit ourselves to a week of action which will culminate in a Global Day of Mobilisation and Action on January 26, 2008.

With our diversity which is our strength, we invite all men and women to undertake throughout this week creative actions, activities, events and convergences focusing on the issues and expressed in the ways they choose.

ACT TOGETHER FOR ANOTHER WORLD!

Note

1. Issued from the WSF International Council meeting, Berlin, Germany, 31 May 2007. For more information, including signatories, see www.wsf2008.net. Sourced from www.wsf 2008.net, 02.10.07

PART 2

CRITICAL ENGAGEMENT: THE WORLD SOCIAL FORUM

The World Social Forum As Open Space[1]

Chico Whitaker

The success of the World Social Forum 2003 in Porto Alegre and its process of globalisation during 2002 have raised many questions about its continuity. Many points of view have been expressed and new proposals put forward for the organisation of the 2003, 2004 and 2005 events.

The Forum faces a positive crisis three-fourths of growth, three-fourths that demands a deeper look at some of the issues in its Charter of Principles.[2] To avoid destroying its potential, some of these ambiguities have to be overcome before the process moves towards irretrievably crystallised, concrete orientations. To contribute to this debate, I explore here three themes that have become fundamental for the continuity of the Forum process:

- The choice between a Forum-as-space and a Forum-as-movement;
- The relative importance, in the Forum meetings, of the activities organised by the participants and the activities scheduled by the Organising Committees, and the respective nature of these two activities;
- The role of the Committees that organise the Forum events.

A fourth issue is, or could be, how the Forum should relate to political parties. I, however, will address only the first three themes in this note.

Forum: Space or Movement?

At this stage of the evolution of the Forum, the question of whether the Forum is a 'space' or a 'movement' has become a fundamental question and choice. To avoid answering this question, by not phrasing it clearly, would be the best way to create difficulties for ourselves. The Charter of Principles of the WSF emphatically defines it as a 'space.' Not everyone, however, thinks and acts as if it were really a space, or that it should always remain a space.

Many consider the Forum a 'space' that is something of a 'movement.' To others, it is 'still, only a space.' This means it can and should become an enormous movement, or a 'movement of movements' as some journalists call it. The great success of the 15 February 2002 demonstrations against the war on Iraq leads most enthusiasts to see this as a result of the Forum, even tending to say that it is the *product* of the Forum. It encourages others to want the Forum to take up a mobilising function, like all movements.

To begin with, movements and spaces are completely different things. Without over simplifying things in a Manichean way, either they are one or the other. Nevertheless, they can co-exist. Nor are they opposites, which means that they do not *neutralise* each other, but rather, they may even be *counterparts.* But you can't be both things at the same time, not even be a bit of each—which would end up by impairing one or the other. Movements and spaces may be seeking, each one performing its roles, the same general objectives. But each one works in a way of its own, aiming at different specific objectives.

The main question then becomes: would transforming the WSF into a movement, now or later, as the process advances—be a good strategy to achieve the objective of the overcoming of neoliberalism and the construction of 'another possible world?' Or conversely, would it be helpful for us to be able to count on spaces like those that are opened by the WSF now and in the future?

For me, there is no doubt that it is fundamental to ensure at all costs the continuity of the Forum as a *space* and to not yield to the temptation of transforming it now or even later, into a *movement*. If we maintain it as a space, it will not prevent nor hinder the formation and the development of movements—to the contrary it will ensure and enable this process. But if we opt for transforming it into a movement, it will inescapably fail to be a space, and all the potentialities inherent to spaces will then be lost.

Furthermore, if we do transform the Forum into a movement, we will be —without any help at all from those we are fighting against—throwing away a powerful instrument of struggle that we have been able to create by drawing on the most important recent political discovery, of the power of open, free, horizontal structures. It is this idea that explains the success in Porto Alegre as well as Seattle, and of the February 15 demonstrations against the war. And keeping in mind that this idea of 'horizontal social articulation' still has so much to contribute to our struggle today, it will also be necessary in the very process of the construction of the world we want.

This conviction is based on the analysis of the advantages of the current character of the Forum as a space as compared to a possible manifestation of the Forum as a movement.

What is the Difference between a Movement and a Space?

A movement *congregates* people—its activists, as the activists of a party who decide to organise themselves to collectively accomplish certain objectives. Its formation and existence entails the *definition* of strategies to reach these objectives, the *formulation* of action programmes, and the *distribution* of responsibilities among its members—including those concerning the direction of the movement. Those who assume this function will lead the activists of the movement, getting them—through authoritarian or democratic methods, according to the choice made by the founders of the movement—to take responsibility for their commitments in the collective action. Its organisational structure will necessarily be pyramidal however democratic the internal process of decision and the way used to choose those who will occupy different levels of management might be. On the other hand, its effectiveness will depend on the explicitness and precision of its *specific objectives*, and therefore, of its own boundaries in time and space.

A space has *no leaders*. It is only a place, basically a *horizontal space*, just like the earth's surface, even if it has some ups and downs. It is like a public *square without an owner*. If the square has an owner other than the collectivity, it fails to be a square, and becomes private territory. Squares are generally open spaces that can be visited by all those who find any kind of interest in using it. Their purpose is solely being a square, whatever service they render to its users. The longer they last as squares the better it is for those who use them for what they offer for the realisation of their respective objectives.

Even when a square contains trees and small hills, it is always a socially horizontal space. Those who climb the trees or the hills cannot control from above the actions of those inside the square. Being considered ridiculous by the others in the square is the least any such climbers would expect. Should they become insistent or inconvenient, they will end up talking to themselves, for those who are in the square will leave it. Or they may even come back with 'public authorities' who will make them leave or stop preaching from above to restore the peace and tranquillity typical of public squares.

The Forum: Space to Incubate Movements?

The Forum's Charter of Principles strongly opposes the assignment of any kind of direction or leadership inside it: nobody can speak on *behalf* of the Forum—there is no sense speaking on behalf of a space or its participants. Everyone, individuals and organisations, retains the right to self-expression and to act during and after the Forum according to convictions, embracing or not, positions or proposals that are introduced by other participants but never on behalf of the Forum or all of its participants.

Like the public square, the Forum is an open but not neutral space. The Forum opens from time to time in different parts of the world—in the events where it takes place—with one specific objective: to allow as many individuals, organisations, and movements as possible that oppose neoliberalism to get together freely, listen to each other, learn from the experiences and struggles of others, and discuss proposals of action; to become linked in new nets and organisations aiming at overcoming the present process of globalisation dominated by large international corporations and their financial interests.

Thus, it is a space created to serve a common objective of all those who converge to the Forum, functioning horizontally as a public square, without leaders or pyramids of power. The Forum works as a 'factory of ideas' or an *incubator*, from which initiatives, aiming at the construction of another world we consider feasible, necessary and urgent, can emerge. We can expect the birth of many movements, bigger or smaller, more or less combative, each with its specific objectives, to perform their own roles in the same struggle—and their development is the primary aim of the square.

The greatest potential of the Forum-as-space is to create movements that amplify this struggle. Conversely, when a movement generates new movements, this happens unwillingly as a result of internal divisions. And that is what would occur if the Forum became a movement.

The objectives of these initiatives do not have to be all clear and precise, quite different from what occurs in movements. Some are still being formed, waiting in the incubator to be hatched and need time to mature.

The Advantages of Not having a 'Final Document'

The Forum's Charter of Principles underlines this role by insisting that there be no 'final documents.' A public square does not make 'declarations,' but those inside it can do so. The participants of the WSF can make whatever final declarations they wish—and these are most welcome. But they will never be declarations of the Forum as a Forum. As a space common to all, it does not 'speak,' or rather, it 'speaks' a lot through its very existence. As more and more people and organisations get together in order to find ways to overcome neoliberalism, this in itself is an expressive political fact. Nobody therefore, needs to speak on behalf of the Forum.

This idea, as adopted by the Forum, was easily grasped by a great number of participants in its last edition in Porto Alegre, who contributed to the 'Notice Board' that was placed there for this purpose with 'Proposals for Action' adopted during the 2003 Forum. In addition to the fact that this notice board enabled participants to express themselves, the final proposals and declarations brought, or sent later, make clear the richness and the diversity of the engagement of the participants. The proposals can be found in the Forum's web page, but this year it was not possible to show everything that its participants decided to do, because the notice board was poorly publicised.

The diffusion of this information through the internet—indicating how to contact the authors of the proposals—opens other perspectives through new contacts and relationships now made possible, allowing new expressions around the proposals during the Forum. It is as if the Forum's square had become permanently open, outliving time and space, lasting longer than the limited five-day event of Porto Alegre. The contacts may be multiplied and lead to more concrete actions, fostered by the unlimited new possibilities opened by the internet. The same can happen with the 'notice board of proposals' set up in other events.

Diversity, a Prized Goal

But the Forum-as-space still has further advantages. As an open space, the Forum has the possibility of ensuring respect for diversity, unlike as if it were a movement. The principle of respecting diversity, adopted by the WSF Charter, is grounded on the conviction that one of the fundamental characteristics of the other world we intend to build must be respect for diversity.

Without becoming 'totally neutral,' the Forum allows each participant to maintain his/her own freedom to choose the sector or the level in which to act. This action can either be very wide and comprehensive or rather restricted; it might intend to address either the deeper causes of the problems the world faces or the superficial effects of these problems. The vast range of themes discussed during the Forum and the objectives sought in it can be thus very wide, such is the range of changes required for the construction of a new world. Nobody in the Forum has the power or the right to say that one action or proposal is more important than another. Nor should anyone have the power or the right to give or demand a bigger visibility to his or her proposals, 'usurping' for their own particular objectives a space that belongs to everybody.

This is an issue however, that requires more careful reflection, in view of what is being witnessed in the marches and street protests that tend to characterise the conclusion of the Forums. The banners should be the banners of all, as a final visible expression of the Forum's diversity and of the variety of proposals sheltered by it or born from it. To privilege this or that struggle, or to be in the first ranks in the marches or in the appointment of the public speakers at the end of the marches, contradicts the principle of respect for diversity and conveys a vision of a Forum-as-movement instead of a Forum-as-space. This question remains to be discussed in greater depth.

All these features of the Forum certainly account for its great acceptance and appeal and the success of its events. Its participants feel respected for the choices they make, for the rhythms they adopt and for their own level of engagement. Some may come to the Forum as activists of a specific movement. But the majority come driven by their individual beliefs that it is important to do so, to exchange experiences, to learn and to join others, keeping the freedom that they had before and will continue to have during and after their participation in the events.

They know that they will not be given orders nor will they have to follow commands, nor have to report back on what they have done or not done. Nor will they have to give proof of loyalty and discipline, nor will they be expelled if they don't do this—much the contrary of what would occur to them had they come to participate in any meeting of an organised movement.

Joy and Mutual Responsibility

This character of the Forum explains the great joy that reigns in this square. It is like an enormous fair, a real party with spaces for demonstrations and 'performances' of many different kinds. Nobody is anguished in the Forum, because no one has to fight to see one's own proposals and ideas prevail over others. Nor is anyone worried about having to defend oneself from others trying to control the Forum, or to impose orientations or rules of behaviour on the Forum that must get together to evaluate, decide, and undertake tasks. And, still less, political behaviour, as occurs in groups and 'delegations' as in good and disciplined parties or movements. Such meetings are possible but never obligatory for those who are activists of this or that movement.

It would be a pity if this joy of the square was lost, which may well happen if it is not a square any more. It is precisely this joy—the same joy we would all like to always see in the 'other possible world'—that takes ahold of and invigorates everybody, and that also destroys the divisions that segregate the struggles of different movements: the fact that we are *many* in the *same* fight.

In this way, activists of different movements meet up with and recognise each other in the open space provided to all by the Forum: those fighting for the rights of women, of rural and urban workers and of children; those fighting for the environment; those seeking new economic relations within countries or at the international level; and those seeking democratic participation in governments or for the enhancement of the spiritual dimension in the human being, in short, the great diversity of existing movements.

If the Forum becomes a 'movement of movements,' none of these movements would individually be able to create such a space and succeed in getting all the other movements to accept its invitation without conditions. The reunion would be curbed by the need to start building another structure that has the intention to unify, with all the rules—agreed upon by all—which would be required to make it possible. And then, competition would again emerge along with divisions as a result of the struggle for space and its control, and also for the definition of the objectives of the new movement.

Finally, a feature of the Forum-as-space is the feeling of mutual responsibility. The fact that it is a square without an owner makes this possible. Even the errors of the organisers—which are often many, given the scale that the events have taken—are accepted and corrected by the initiatives and by the creativity of the participants. In the 2003 edition of the WSF in Porto Alegre, there was a serious and involuntary mistake that forced the organisers to make a great effort to try to minimise its effects: the workshops' programmes were only published on the second day. This could easily have destroyed the entire event. Nevertheless, the participants found ways to compensate the failure on their own, and there were even initiatives from 'outside' in the form of a pirated publication of the programme prepared by people trawling the internet the evening before.

Risks We Face

To maintain the WSF as a space is then, perhaps, the best way to guarantee its biggest asset. This must be preserved at any cost. In this sense, those who want to transform it into a movement are working against our common cause. They are effectively acting against their own interests and against all our interests. As articulations and initiatives born in the Forum, they are hindering and suffocating their own source of life—or at least destroying a powerful instrument that is available to them, for expanding and enlarging their presence in the struggle we are all engaged in.

Initiatives that have been taken by certain self-nominated 'social movements' point in this direction. Justifiably concerned with the need of a popular mobilisation to fight against neoliberalism, they are however seeking to absorb the Forum inside their own mobilising dynamics, to serve their own objectives.

Such movements know that they do not and cannot ever congregate all the participants that come to each Forum, even if they manage to bring together a few important organisations. But even so, they think that their own final document can and should be presented and understood as a 'final document' of the Forum. One initiative of this kind—born in the incubator square of the 2001 Forum—has already given rise to several tensions and misunderstandings after the Forum. The pressure in this direction has also taken shape in other events, even after the 2003 Forum, though less easily. This last attempt jeopardised the mobilising effects and articulations that became possible with the 'Proposals for Action' Notice Board.

Recently the 'co-ordination' of these movements has gone farther: as members of the Organisation Committees for the WSF events, they have proposed that their own final meeting that is normally held towards the end of the Forum, be included in the last day of the Forum schedule. This meeting, which necessarily only gets limited participation, would then appear—at least to the media—as the concluding meeting of the Forum as a whole.

If they adopt this orientation, this will create a new tension. Everyone will then feel it necessary to bring the results of his or her own activity to this meeting, in order to ensure that these results are implemented by those who are going to 'coordinate' its effective realisation as in a well-organised movement. By focusing attention on the meeting they organise at the end of the Forum, and even if all Forum participants do not take part, this meeting will inevitably ignore or disrespect some proposals for action that are advanced. Or it will create the need of 'representations' that will transform the Forum into the usual pyramid, without the joy of the horizontal square.

The great challenge for the continuity of the Forum process therefore, and for it to fulfil its vocation of being an incubator for more and more movements and initiatives, is to *multiply* such spaces across the world that are genuinely open and free, without focussing attention only on specific proposals. We must hope that nobody, however inadvertently, contributes to 'closing down' the Forum to such a point that it disappears as an open space.

All this is a matter of choice. Individuals and organisations who are planning events this year or in the subsequent ones within the process of the WSF, and members of its present International Council or of the enlarged Council meeting in June 2003, may consider adopting an orientation of the type proposed by the so-called 'social movements.' Nobody can prevent such a decision. It is an option, but each participant in the Forum process will then have to decide about the continuity of their own participation. The Forum will not yet be a movement and therefore there will be no rules of membership nor will there be the need to respect majority decisions even if taken democratically. What we must not do is avoid clear recognition and consideration of this question, nor forget to analyse the consequences of such positions and decisions.

Organised versus Self-organised Activities

This discussion is essential because, quite aside from the pressure of participants to transform the WSF into a movement, the organisers of events themselves will tend to adopt this option if the present method of organising them is maintained. The choice between WSF-as-space and WSF-as-movement will necessarily return to face us in such an organisation.

In the Forum-as-space, self-organised activities would have priority in the minds of the event organisers once it is clear to them that the WSF works better as a space. Experience has shown us that events programmed by the organisers are overvalued and take place at the expense of meetings and seminars programmed by the participants themselves. These self-organised activities, which are at the *core* of Forum-as-space, are treated almost with negligence. Since the time that this way of organising the events was invented in the 2001 Porto Alegre Forum, these activities are almost looked down upon as secondary, less important activities that hold low prestige, almost as if they were a burden that the organisers are forced to carry.

It is, in fact, the case, that in all the Forums held so far, the process of choosing the themes and speakers at the conferences and panels has taken most of the organisers' time. This has also occurred at the International Council: the Bangkok and Florence meetings of the Council (in August and November 2002) devoted a great part of their working programme to this type of decision to prepare for the Porto Alegre Forum. Long meetings beyond the Council's schedule have become necessary, and even a special meeting in Brazil between Bangkok and Florence, of the new working group created for this—bringing together the 'co-ordinators of the main themes'—and with all the costs that such meetings entail. The themes and the lecturers have turned out to be the 'showcase' of the Forum, the most public and visible demonstration of what its concerns are and what is discussed in it; and this of course must be carefully planned in order to keep the positions and proposals clear. This is just the case with the Davos Forum which does not have self-organised activities and therefore has to choose the main theme of its events very carefully, each time.

On the other hand, the preparation of the other parts of the WSF—the events programmed by its participants which are, aside from its themes, a hallmark of the WSF—follows a purely administrative dynamic, which is nearly bureaucratic. A deadline is set for the submission of proposals for seminars and workshops; the ones that cannot be accepted according to the WSF Charter are identified through a process that is rather inadequate given the short time that the organisers have to do it in. In reality, it is only proposals made by persons and organisations that explicitly declare their relations with political parties and armed organisations that are set aside. Dates and places are then administratively allocated for these activities; a 'catalogue' is printed listing every activity, its proponent, its date, and place where it is going to be held. These are almost always issued at the last minute after making all the traditional corrections and last minute changes, and not all participants even receive them.

As the number of these self-organised activities tends to be big, only some can take place in the central areas of the event. The rest are distributed in the best possible way in all available spaces—sometimes in different parts of the cities, and even in areas that are difficult to reach. The final catalogue is usually only available on the first day of the event. The result is that the participants in the self-organised workshops and seminars tend to mostly be only their own organisers and those they themselves had invited, or those who were able to rapidly identify the activities that interested them.

The situation is worse when the organisers of the big events manage to bring renowned persons to their events and when these events overlap with the workshops and seminars, as occurred in Porto Alegre 2003. The big conferences end up attracting most of the participants, leaving the self-organised activities to those who really insist on participating in them. Given this situation, we clearly need to re-examine the function of the events, seminars, and panels.

There are several precautions that can be taken to avoid some of these problems. One, deadlines for submission of proposals for workshops and seminars could be fixed long before the event and at least two months in advance for the big events. This would make it possible to disseminate the proposals by internet ahead of time, in turn allow interlinks to be established well ahead of the workshops, better distribution of places and spaces that can facilitate such interlinking, and a better preparation by the participants themselves, allowing them to come to the Forum already knowing which activities they would like to join.

Secondly, space for self-organised activities should be located in the main spaces of the events, in the 'main square,' which has better infrastructure, easy access, and proper announcement. They should not have to suffer what happened in the Porto Alegre 2003 Forum, which led people to saying that the big 'stars' have usurped the Forum.

Self-organised activities are consistent with the idea of the Forum-as-space and not the Forum-as-movement. There can be no doubt that giving priority to self-organised activities would be much more conducive to achieving the objectives of the WSF as formulated in the WSF Charter and as indicated at the beginning of this article: to allow as many people, organisations, and movements opposed to neoliberalism to get freely together, listen to each other, learn from the experiences and the struggles of the others, discuss proposals of action, and become linked in new networks and organisations aimed at overcoming the present process of globalisation dominated by large international corporations and financial interests.

Organisation Committees: Facilitators or Directing a Movement?

As declared by the WSF Charter, the Forum is not meant to be a space for disputing power. Till now, it has had the character of a horizontal and open space, and this has effectively prevented the occurrence of such disputes in its events. But the Forum and its events are not immune to this happening.

When the Forum is looked at as a movement—which demands a 'political' orientation—it becomes strategically necessary, for the political forces that participate in it, to enter its OCs with the objective of influencing decisions. Tensions then arise between those who are already inside it and who virtually take 'possession' of it, and those who feel themselves excluded or simply want to get in and participate in setting that 'orientation.'

There are also those who feel it necessary to bring this struggle even to the Brazilian Organising Committee (BOC)—which is presently the Secretariat to the Forum process—and to its International Council (IC). They even say that the present composition of the Brazilian Committee is not representative, because it does not take into account the proportional participation of all the forces or political tendencies that should be in the leadership of the Forum process. They also say that the International Council should be 'conducted' by some persons, or reduced to a group that represents others.

These proposals would only be justified if the Forum were a movement, but they are not adequate to a Forum-as-space, to a 'square,' that—as we have already seen before—does not admit having or representing a 'political direction.' More than anything, the Forum needs people and institutions willing to perform the task of organising the use of the square without interfering with what is discussed in it, and even less in the freedom that should be guaranteed to all its participants.

On the face of it, it seems desirable that the composition of the OCs of the Forum-as-space have a diversity that respects and reflects the diversity in the events. But this does not mean that there has to be proportional diversity according to the importance of the organisations and movements that will participate in these events, because these organisations and movements are not coming to the Forum to receive orders. Far more important than having diversity in the committees is the credibility of people and organisations that make up the committees. They need to be able to invite people to the Forum without leaving them in any doubt about the real interest of the invitation they receive. Those invited must not be wary of the possibility of their being used by those who have invited them, to carry out their own real objectives—as happens when political parties decide to 'generously' support the process.

In this perspective, the concept that is more appropriate for the OCs and also for the IC, within the option of Forum-as-space, is that of a 'facilitator.' Facilitators do not command. What they do is make it possible for existing or future movements to progress in their struggles, to help avoid confrontations among them on alternatives about how to change the world. Still less do they have to try to impose their ideas and proposals on each other.

What they need is to be concerned, within a common perspective that they adopt, with ensuring that each event organised by them accomplishes the objectives of the Forum itself. They need to choose and put into effect, carefully taking into account the political reality at each moment, the best alternatives for organising the time and the space that will be made available.

It is, of course, the case that besides the OCs of the events, other levels of organisation for assessment and proposals for the Forum process—such as enlarged committees, councils, and assemblies—can amplify the effect of the process. This will be especially so if they can manage to incorporate an even larger variety and representation of movements engaged in the construction of the 'other world.' But in the option of Forum-as-space, this kind of organisation ought not to direct those movements and organisations, but only endorse and support the creation of more and more Forum spaces.

This kind of perspective is far more difficult to adopt because it is not as 'heroic' as the exercise of the political leadership that the option of Forum-as-movement requires. Adopting it will perhaps lead to less interest in participating in the organisation of the big events. It will then become even more crucial to conserve efforts and resources to amplify adhesions, links and articulations during the event.

But right now, it is useful and necessary that the barriers between different types and areas of engagement are brought down, and, that the articulation in the struggle against neoliberalism is spread all over the world. That it gets amplified, stronger, and denser; that more movements, networks, and initiatives of struggle are nurtured; and that the debate on proposals and ways to overcome the domination of capital are deepened.

If this is the moment we are living in, we can be sure that the task of multiplying Forum spaces is inestimably important, irreplaceable, and highly commendable in our common engagement to build other worlds.

Notes

1. This essay is an edited version of a larger piece circulated on email, 17 March 2003.
2. The Forum's Charter of Principles was first formulated by the eight members of the WSF Brazil Organising Committee in April 2001 (ABONG, ATTAC, CBJP, CIVES, CUT, IBASE, CJG, and MST, April 2001). It was then modified and approved by the first meeting of the 'WSF International Advisory Committee,' later renamed 'International Council,' in June 2001 (World Social Forum Organising Committee, June 2001). Whitaker is here referring to the June 2001 version; but since the April 2001 version, authored by the eight Brazilian organisations, has also been widely circulated and translated, across the world, different authors in this book in fact variously refer to these different 'versions' of 'the Charter.' So please carefully note the version that is being referred to, is distinguished by the date. Both versions were reproduced in this book, for reference, and are today still available on the web at the links given. For a discussion of the significance of there being two charters available, see: Sen, December 2003d.

The World Social Forum: Arena or Actor?[1]

Teivo Teivainen

The concentration of power in transnational and global institutions was one of the most significant social processes of the 20th century. Nevertheless, democratic theory and practice have remained very nation-state-centred. Although there were some examples of cosmopolitan democratic thinking and transnational democratic practice throughout the century (such as the seventies project of the New International Economic Order, NIEO), most analysts and politicians simply ignored them.

The solidarity movements related to earlier attempts to democratise global power, such as the NIEO project, saw the problem in terms of inter-state relations. Many of the early 2000's movements perceive the world in a less state-centric manner. Instead of asking that a particular Third World State be given more decision-making power in global affairs, today's activists may ask for more power to the civil society groups that confront both government and corporate power. This trend holds promises. However, in order to imagine and construct institutional features of alternative futures, we may need political structures that 'civil society,' as it is generally conceived, is unlikely to deliver.

In recent years, and in the wake of Seattle, we have observed the emergence of an increasing number of arenas that attract civil society organisations and citizens to express concern about capitalist globalisation. The arenas are varied, in terms of both political orientation and organisational design. The spectacular demonstrations from Okinawa to Gothenburg and Genoa have received ample media coverage and become prominent models of critical civil society organising. In most of them the main focus has been on defensive measures, being *against* something. Many of the most visible civil society gatherings have been explicitly, and often antagonistically, related to summits and well-known events of the global elite. But, more significantly, and even if with much less media attention, organised protests around these issues have been taking place in the more peripheral parts of our world.

From Anti-Davos to Porto Alegre: The Local Roots of a Global Event

In Brazil, a concrete initiative for a worldwide civil society event emerged in early 2000 with some connection to the first anti-Davos initiatives. The first formulation of the idea is generally attributed to Oded Grajew, co-ordinator of the Brazilian Business Association for Citizenship (CIVES).[2] In February 2000, Bernard Cassen, Chair of ATTAC and Director of Le Monde Diplomatique, met with Grajew and Francisco Whitaker of the Brazilian Justice and Peace Commission (CBJP) in Paris to discuss the possibility of organising such a forum. Their discussion produced three central ideas for the Forum. First, it should be held in the South, and more concretely, in the Brazilian city of Porto Alegre. Second, the name should be World Social Forum, changing only one key word from the name of a common adversary, the World Economic Forum (WEF). Third, it should be organised during the same dates as the WEF, partially because this symbolism was considered attractive for the media.[3]

Soon after, eight Brazilian organisations decided to form an Organising Committee (OC) for the event. In March 2000, they secured the support of the municipal government of Porto Alegre and the state government of Rio Grande do Sul, both controlled at the time by the Workers Party (PT—Partido dos Trabalhadores).[4] Initially it was the Mayor of Porto Alegre, Raul Pont, who received the idea with great enthusiasm. Soon, the state government led by Governor Olivio Dutra decided to dedicate plenty of time and effort into the WSF process.[5] Thus the WSF, unlike many transnational events in other localities, has strong local roots. During Brazil's military rule, the city was a centre of resistance with energetic neighbourhood associations.[6] Founded in 1980, the PT —with one of its main strongholds in Porto Alegre—has deep roots in these associations, trade unions, catholic organisations, women's movements and many other parts of vibrant Brazilian civil society.[7]

Porto Alegre was a smart choice for hosting the WSF, as both municipal and state governments were willing to allocate significant material and human resources to the event. In commercial terms most locals consider the WSF a good deal, but in ideological terms not everyone agrees.

Who Governs?

Naomi Klein characterised the organisational structure of the first WSF as "so opaque that it was nearly impossible to figure out how decisions were made."[8] Others have raised similar critical remarks in all the annual editions of the WSF's main event.

The formal decision-making power of the WSF process has been mainly in the hands of the Organising Committee consisting of the Central Trade Union Confederation (CUT—Central Única dos Trabalhadores), the Movement of

Landless Rural Workers (MST—Movimento dos Trabalhadores Rurais Sem Terra) and six smaller Brazilian civil society organisations.[9] In terms of affiliates, there is a huge difference between the two big ones and the others. The disparity in resources should not be exaggerated, however. Even if much smaller, some of the participating NGOs may have better access to financial resources than the MST. The role of IBASE, a Rio-based socially oriented research institute, has been particularly important in fund-raising for the WSF.

The other main organ of the WSF, the International Council (IC), was founded in São Paulo in June 2001. According to Cândido Grzybowski, director of IBASE, the idea to create an international council emerged in Porto Alegre on the last day of the first WSF. During the following months, the OC made a list of organisations that were then invited to the founding meeting in São Paulo. As of February 2003, the Council consisted of 113 organisations, though in practice many of them have not actively participated in the process. This number includes the eight members of the OC. Most IC members come from the Americas and Western Europe though many also have activities in other parts of the world. Organisations based in Asia and Africa include the Asian Regional Exchange for New Alternatives (ARENA), Environment et Développement du Tiers-Monde (ENDA), and the Palestinian NGO Network. Apart from the formal members, there are 15 observer organisations, mostly the representatives of regional and thematic social forums in various parts of the world.

The division of labour between the IC and the Brazilian Organising Committee has been ambiguous from the outset. The IC has gained increasing importance on paper and, to a lesser extent, in practice. It is fair to emphasise its role in giving international legitimacy to the Brazilian organisers,[10] though this has not been its only role. Until now, the system has worked relatively well, making decisions through what some of the Brazilian organisers call *construção*, constructing them in a critical debate and sometimes, laborious consensus building. The IC is not supposed to have mechanisms for disputing representation, nor for voting.[11] The only time there has been a vote was when in its first meeting it had to be decided whether the following meeting of the IC would take place somewhere in Europe or in Dakar. The overwhelming majority voted for Dakar. When it was decided that the WSF process in 2004 would take place in India, the linkage between the IC and the organisers both in Brazil and India became more complex.

The selection of the founding members of the IC, mostly through invitations by the Organising Committee, was reasonably easy when the overall process was still known to only relatively few networks. In the future, when there will be more groups interested in joining the IC, more explicit selection procedures will have to be established. There are indications that the question of fair representation will become more controversial in the WSF process. For the moment, initial procedures for selecting new members have been drafted at the meeting of the WSF International Council in June 2003 in Miami. They were not as detailed as some proposals, but some of the points were nevertheless contentious. For example, it was proposed that only those organisations that are active in several countries can be members of the IC, but this proposal was finally not accepted.

During 2002–03, the Brazilian Organising Committee was renamed 'The Secretariat.' The ambiguity of the relationship with the IC has, however, not been totally overcome. In some documents the renamed body is (self-defined as) 'Secretariat of the International Council,' whereas others refer to as 'Secretariat of the World Social Forum.' In practice, the terms Organising Committee and Secretariat have often been used synonymously.

Before the January 2004 Forum in Mumbai, Indian organisations will constitute a new Organising Committee. It is less clear what the composition and the role of the Organising Committee and the Secretariat will be in the next two years. As the WSF is not an event but a process with many events, it may become an established practice that these different events have particular organising committees, and the WSF as a whole has some co-ordinating body that, apart from the International Council, could be the Secretariat. At the same time, there are criticisms of the role of both the IC and the Brazilian Secretariat.

The decision to hold WSF 4 in India was made simultaneously with the decision to organise the WSF 5 again in Porto Alegre. Various IC members repeatedly expressed fears that if the WSF leaves Porto Alegre indefinitely, and the next venues do not meet the expectations, the whole process might die out. Fixing the place of the 2005 Forum, therefore, was seen as protection against the unlikely eventuality that the process to move the Forum to India was to result in a catastrophe.

In the WSF, organisers have been reluctant to explore ways in which cyberspace could be used in organising more formal decision-making processes. Peter Waterman has argued insightfully and provocatively that the WSF "*uses* the media, culture and cyberspace but it does not *think* of itself in primarily cultural/communicational terms, nor does it *live* fully within this increasingly central and infinitely expanding universe."[12] There has been a slightly more conscious use of cyberspace in the various projects of the governing bodies of the WSF after the meeting of the IC in Miami in June 2003.

From the Porto Alegre Events: Towards a Transnational Process

For many, the increasing numbers of participants have been one of the most important assets of the WSF. The 2003 Forum had over 20,000 official delegates and roughly 100,000 participants. Some, however, feel that this has led to an atomisation of dialogue.[13] Michael Albert (this volume) proposes that the main annual WSF gathering should be attended by from five to ten thousand people—delegates from the major regional Forums of the world.

The main mechanism for the globalisation of the Forum has been the regional and thematic Forums that are being held in various parts of the world. The more visible among these have been the Thematic Forum on neoliberalism in Argentina in August 2002, the European Social Forum (ESF) in Florence, Italy, in November 2002, the Asian Social Forum (ASF) in Hyderabad, India, in January 2003, and the Thematic Forum on Drugs, Human Rights and Democracy in Cartagena, Colombia, in June 2003. These Forums have formed part of the semi-official calendar maintained by the Organising Committee/Secretariat and the IC.

Sometimes there have been tensions between the WSF governance bodies and the organisers of the other Forums. For example, at the August 2002 IC meeting in Bangkok, the Brazilians, invoking the Charter of Principles, strongly opposed the plans of Italian organisers to invite political parties to formally take part in the ESF. The Italian delegates responded by accusing the Brazilian Organising Committee of hypocrisy, given the visibility of the Workers Party in all Porto Alegre Forums. A similar controversy occurred during the organising of an October 2002 Social Forum event in Quito, focusing on the Free Trade Area of the Americas (FTAA) that IC members found thematically and organisationally too narrow.

These controversies are examples of the organisational problems that the WSF is bound to encounter in its process of geographical and thematic expansion. While there are reasons to maintain coherence and some underlying rules in the process so that the WSF brand does not simply evaporate, too much control by the IC and the Secretariat is bound to limit the creativity of those in charge of the de-centralised events.

Apart from the semi-official list of regional and thematic Forums, myriad local events have been organised under the WSF banner but without any official recognition. Their proliferation is one of the most vital signs that the WSF process is indeed expanding, although it complicates attempts to see the WSF as a movement of movements with a more or less clearly defined political strategy.

How to Be and Not Be Political

The WSF provides a space for actors to construct projects in local and global contexts. The organisers that emphasise this role feel the WSF should avoid issuing declarations of support for any particular political processes. As stated by Cândido Grzybowski, "political action is the responsibility of each individual and the coalitions they form, not an attribute of the Forum."[14] Arguing a more pronounced dichotomy between the Forum as a space and the Forum as a movement, Chico Whitaker (this volume) has criticised "self-nominated social movements" that "seek to put the Forum inside their own mobilising dynamics, to serve their own objectives."

For some, the WSF's different identities are by no means incompatible: it is possible to be an *arena* and an *actor* simultaneously. Based on discussions in the IC and in the Forum sites in January 2003, I personally sense that there are increasing pressures to overcome the current reluctance to issue political statements.

Many in the governing bodies of the WSF, however, tend to conclude that the WSF should not plan to become a political actor since it does not have internal procedures for democratic collective will-formation. More critical voices argue that the correct way forward is to create mechanisms for democratic participation within the political architecture of the Forum. Once reasonably transparent and democratic mechanisms have been established, the WSF could more legitimately start to express itself as a collective movement.

Indeed, the unwillingness to formulate political statements is occasionally questioned among organisers and related actors, who would like to see the WSF expressing opinions on certain issues such as the crises in Argentina, Palestine and Venezuela. At the Bangkok meeting in August 2002, Walden Bello and others argued that the Council should produce a public statement encouraging movements around the world to take part in the protests planned for the WTO meeting in Cancun, in Mexico, in September 2003. In the January 2003 meeting of the Council, various delegates argued strongly in favour of making a public statement against the imminent war in Iraq. In both cases, the apparently consensual decision of the Council was not to issue any such statements. It is, however, likely that there will be more intense debates on this in the near future.

One way to avoid political silence without violating the Charter of Principles is to facilitate processes whereby organisations that take part in the WSF produce political declarations. Ideally, most participating organisations would sign such declarations, which could have powerful political impact. Until now, the social movement declarations produced during the WSF events have not been circulated very widely and thus, their impact is relatively modest. Nevertheless, they have created controversies among the WSF organisers. Even if these declarations do not officially claim to represent the WSF as a whole, Chico Whitaker fears that the media may consider them as semi-official conclusions. This can then lead to political disputes about whose concerns get to be expressed in the declarations.

Inclusions and Exclusions

The internal politics of the WSF have also been played out in how different groups have been given spaces during the main annual events. Racial tensions created some internal controversies, particularly in the first Forum.[15] The "whiteness" of the Forums is related to enduring racism, although it should be remembered that Rio Grande do Sul is one of the rare parts of Latin America where many locals are light-skinned people of European origin. Gender tensions have also been present. Even though there are no major gender differences in participant numbers, the Brazilian Organising Committee consists predominantly of middle-aged men. In the IC, representatives of feminist organisations have played a more visible role and gender issues have been included in the programme, although somewhat marginally. There have been other controversies on hierarchies and exclusions within the WSF—for example on the celebrity status of some participants, or the status of armed groups.

Even if it is not clear whether the WSF will become a more active political entity with developed internal will-formation mechanisms, it is clear that until now, the most important impact of the Forum on democratic projects has consisted of the encounters between different groups and activists within its confines. Geographically, most participants have come from the Southern Cone of Latin America and from Southern Europe, but there has been a conscious effort to facilitate the participation of people from Asia, Africa and other parts of Latin America. The process has attracted increasing attention in India, where the WSF 2004 will take place. The participation by groups from the United States has been growing every year.

Limits of Civil Society Purity: Connecting with and Distancing from Other Kinds of Actors

According to its Charter of Principles, the WSF is "a plural, diversified, non-confessional, non-governmental and non-party context." Even if the Brazilian media often portrays the events as almost directly organised by the PT, the party does not formally belong to the Organising Committee. The participation of Lula da Silva in WSF 2001 and 2002 was technically as representative of an NGO he had founded rather than as a representative of his party. Having become the President of Brazil, his participation was of a different status in WSF 2003, and as such, the object of controversy.

The participation of several ministers of the government of France in WSF 2 was criticised by many delegates, and the Belgian Prime Minister who had announced a visit was told by the OC that he was not welcome. Decisions on how to deal with governments and their representatives, inter-governmental organisations and UN agencies are inconsistent. Certain UN agencies have been actively involved in organising activities related to women, while the official line has been that inter-governmental bodies cannot participate.

In order to overcome these dilemmas, the IC meetings of 2002 decided that the WSF would have a new category of events: roundtables of dialogue and controversy, where representatives of institutions not allowed to attend as official delegates, could be invited to debate and discuss. This innovation was an effort to combine two contradictory aims: to keep the WSF as a purely civil society arena or actor, and not to become an inward-looking space for like-minded civil society organisations. The policy on who would be invited to these roundtables has not been clearly defined, but some key organisers think that representatives of some UN agencies could be invited, but not the World Bank and IMF.

In sum, the enthusiasm the WSF has generated around the world will lead to various dilemmas. Some organisers may emphasise the importance of clinging to strictly defined civil society partners; others are likely to have more pragmatic positions to obtain material and political support. The planned organisation of WSF 4 in India will be a crucial moment. On the one hand, it will provide a concrete possibility to give the process a better geographical and thematic balance. On the other hand, it may be difficult to find hosting local governments willing to dedicate as much energy to the process as has been the case in Porto Alegre. The organisers of WSF 4 in India will also have to deal critically with the question of foreign funding. In the Brazilian case, the importance of the foreign funding conditionality was there, but should not be exaggerated.

From Anti to Alternative

In most post-Seattle events, protesters have often been labelled 'anti-globalisation,' and some of them have used the expression themselves. It would, however, be analytically faulty and politically unwise to simply define the movements as being *against* globalisation, if the term is understood as the increasing transgression of nation-state borders on a worldwide level. Many of them are, I would claim, looking for a *different kind of* globalisation. *Outra globalização* (another globalisation) is an expression that has been emphasised by some of the key organisers of the Porto Alegre meetings.[16] Despite this insistence, the Latin American mainstream media talk of 'anti-globalisation activists' when referring to both Porto Alegre and other events inspired by it. These would be the February 2001 protests against the WEF regional meeting in Mexico and the March 2001 marches around the Inter-American Development Bank meeting in Santiago de Chile.

For those who want to argue for the possibility of a different kind of globalisation, there is a risk of ending up with strange bedfellows. It is not always easy to see the differences between the 'alternative' globalisation proposals with the idea of many business leaders that some democratisation is necessary in order to make the global expansion of capitalism acceptable. Those who cling to the 'anti-globalisation discourse' are often right when they claim that the alternative globalisation strategies would only lead to very moderate changes. Often, but not always.

It is frequently assumed that in the anti/alternative divide of globalisation debates, 'anti' represents more radical and revolutionary options whereas 'alternatives' are more superficial reforms. This assumption is not very helpful. Within the alternative globalisation spectrum, it is possible to find political projects that strive for a globalisation that radically transforms the world. While anti-globalisation people can be pro-capitalist, pro-globalisation people may be anti-capitalist. In principle, the WSF offers many opportunities for people on all sides of this debate to work together.

Despite various references to the necessity of imagining and constructing a different world, the issue of a democratic global order has not had a very high priority in the agenda of the WSF. There have been claims by intellectuals and groups working on issues of global democracy that the WSF process has been too much dominated by nationalists espousing anti-globalisation themes, when it might be the case that this is not even the position of the majority of the participants. Yet, one of the intellectual problems the WSF faces has been the lack of open debates between different visions of how the world should concretely be re-organised if, as the main slogan of the WSF says, another world is to be possible.[17]

Notes

1. Revised version of a paper presented at the Latin American Studies Association (LASA) meeting, Dallas, Texas, USA, 28 March 2003.
2. CIVES has sometimes been characterised as an association of business representatives that support the Workers Party (PT).
3. Personal communication with Bernard Cassen, 16 April 2002; also Cassen 2002.
4. On the origins of the WSF, see Whitaker April 2002.
5. Personal communication with Jefferson Miola, 20 April 2002.
6. Wainwright 2003.
7. On the origins of the PT in Rio Grande do Sul, see eg. Prestes 1999.
8. Klein 2001.
9. Associação Brasileira de Organizações Não Governamentais (ABONG); Ação pela Tributação das Transações Financeiras em Apoio aos Cidadãos (ATTAC); Comissão Brasileira Justiça e Paz (CBJP);Associação Brasileira de Empresários pela Cidadania (CIVES); Instituto Brasileiro de Análises Sociais e Econômicas (IBASE); and Rede Social de Justiça e Direitos Humanos.
10. See eg. Waterman 2003b.
11. World Social Forum, Brazil Organising Committee, August 2002 [April 2002].
12. Waterman 2003.

13 Savio January 2003b.

14. Grzybowski January 2003.
15. *Correio do Povo* January 2001.
16. Grzybowski 1998. See also Santos April 2001.
17. See Teivainen 2003a.

Another World Is Necessary[1]

Nawal El Saadawi

The international media ignored the big event that took place in Porto Alegre in January 2003, when thousands of women and men walked through the streets shouting, "Another World is Possible!" More than a hundred thousand people came to Porto Alegre this year (2003) to say why another world is not only possible, but also necessary. I live in Egypt, and have travelled in Africa, Asia, Europe, to the two Americas, to Australia, and everywhere I have seen how people are dying of hunger, in wars, in the so-called 'free market,' and under so-called 'democracy.' The media were occupied with the few who dominate the wealth of the world, who were meeting at the same time in Davos, at the World Economic Forum. This is not a world Forum. It is a Forum for the few individuals who own multinationals and the 'free market.'

Under capitalist democracy, 'freedom' means freedom to kill, to declare war, to exploit the oil, the land and natural resources of others. It is the freedom to occupy other countries by military force. It is the Israeli occupation of Palestine, the U.S. and British occupation of Iraq and Kuwait. These are only a few examples of what is happening in our post-modern era. In Davos, the Swiss police protected a small minority of the world's wealthy rulers. They could not move without police and military protection. However, they have now been exposed by billions of people in the world. People became aware of their lies, which they try to conceal with beautiful words such as democracy, the free market, human rights, development.

Lula, Brazil's Nasser?

Meanwhile in Porto Alegre's biggest public square, the third WSF was being inaugurated by 'Lula' (as they call Brazil's elected President, Luis Inácio Lula da Silva). In his speech, addressed to over 60,000 women and men, he began: "I am going tonight to Davos to tell them about your goals, to carry your message to them." But the crowd was not convinced. One of them shouted, "Why go all this long distance, Lula? Send them an email!" and the crowd roared with laughter. Many people in Brazil consider Lula a liberal capitalist, despite the twenty years he spent leading the Workers Party. Power corrupts revolutionary men and women and Lula may be no exception. A Brazilian woman told me his economic policies would benefit the "nationalist bourgeoisie." This reminded me of Gamal Abdel Nasser's economic policies during the sixties. The Egyptian capitalists corrupted the public sector and this led to the downfall and defeat of Nasser and finally to his death on 28 September 1970.

Some women and men in Porto Alegre believe that Lula is Brazil's Nasser. But others disagree. They still consider him the hero of the left wing groups fighting against globalisation and imperialism. Brazil's new Left is more radical, younger. They describe the old Left who dominate the WSF as dogmatic, rigid, undemocratic, linked to the new liberals who are playing a role in isolating the Forum from ordinary women and men, from the daily struggle of people.

In January 2004, the fourth WSF will be held in Hyderabad, India; the following year in Africa[2] Neither Brazil nor any other country should be allowed to dominate the WSF. It belongs to the world and not to one country. Since it started in 2001, it has been held in Porto Alegre. Why this monopoly? The participants from the Arab countries may one day have a World Social Forum in Palestine, Cairo or even Baghdad. For the time being, this seems to be just a dream. But why should we not have big dreams? In Porto Alegre everybody is dreaming of another world based on justice and freedom, in which women and men will be equal, in which there will be no wars and no poverty and no pollution of the environment by capitalists.

Listening to the Music of Words

I walk along the Jacui River under the sun of Porto Alegre. The smell of the air reminds me of my village in the Nile Delta—the waters of the river look the same, and the sunrays are almost the same sunrays. The faces around me are brown, sunburned, like the faces at home in Cairo. I feel at home. I do not know the Portuguese language but I understand the music of words and the beat of drums.

My talk was in a hall which seats 5,000 people. As they were giving me a standing ovation, an old German man with narrow eyes and a big nose pushed through the crowd and shouted angrily, "There's no bridge between the First and Third World—you'd better get used to it!" I laughed. Many women and men laughed too. A young Pakistani woman with a veil hiding her face was also angry. "I *chose* to wear the veil—it is my personal freedom!" she said. An U.S. woman with a coating of make-up on her face shouted, "I *chose* to put on make-up. Why are you against makeup? How can you call it a postmodern veil? It is a free choice! I feel I am free to do whatever I want!" I smiled, "Yes, you are free like the free market, like George W Bush, like Ariel Sharon, like Adolf Hitler; you are free!"

Creating an Alternative

For me, this third WSF tore the veil off the face of neoliberal capitalism, which dominates the world. NAFTA and the European Union (EU) are not democratic. They are key players in corporate globalisation. The European Referendum campaign[3] has been launched in order to build real democracy and ensure the full participation of women and young people in the EU. For it is the old men who still dominate the politics of the world (whether Left or Right, whether in the West or East, in the North or South). Across the globe, capitalist globalisation is still riding triumphant. The shadows of imperialism and neo-colonialism are very evident, especially in our region, the so-called Middle East (middle to whom, by the way?). The leaders of the so-called 'free world' who met at Davos are moving steadily to the Right, hiding their economic interests behind a religious veil, whether Christian or Jewish, using Islamic fundamentalism or post-modern terrorism to reinforce and expand their domination. The so-called 'War against Terrorism' has devastated Afghanistan, Palestine, Iraq, and is relentlessly building up plans to devastate Iran, Libya, Yemen, Syria, Egypt, Sudan, Korea and others.

The WSF is not merely an annual event in Porto Alegre. It has become a global movement, a continuous process to create an open space for free and equal exchange of thoughts and action. In terms of numbers it grew from 25,000 people in the first meeting in 2001 to more than 100,000 this year. But it is not just the numbers that count. The Forum has created an alternative to capitalist globalisation. It has created a new hope, a new power which is playing a profound role in helping to free people all over the world from the shackles of despair and false consciousness propagated by the global media. But more thinking is needed to close the gap between what is called political activities and social activities, between women's groups and socialist groups.

Look to Women, Look to the Future

The Left, the socialist movement (including the Marxists) have learned a great deal from women's movements in our countries and all over the world. They now tend to combine social activities with political, economic, religious, historical, and other activities. Women's input to human thought and to philosophy has been and continues to be significant and should not be ignored.

In Egypt, as in countries all over the world, the traditional left wing (including the new anti-globalisation groups) tends to exclude women in spite of having learnt new ideas from them. Traditional left-wing groups should change their old habits. Most of the people at Porto Alegre were women and youth. But there were old professional political groups there too, and they tended to regress to old habits in order to monopolise and exclude women and young people.

Right now we need to struggle against the WSF being hijacked by certain left wing groups in France, Europe, the U.S. or elsewhere. Left-wing groups in Europe are stronger than they are in Africa and they try to dominate. A French man, a leader of a group called ATTAC in Paris tried to control some of the groups from Africa. A U.S. man in a group called Habitat tried to control some groups from the Arab countries.

Advice to the West's Left

Revolutionary groups in Europe and the U.S. should know that we the women (and men) of the so-called 'Third World' are not backward, not in need of their leadership. We can lead ourselves. We do not need leaders from abroad to show us the way. We appreciate the ability of these revolutionary groups to transcend their nationality, religion, gender, colour, class, creed, language and other divisions inherited from the slave period. We appreciate their socialist leanings in the struggle against capitalist globalisation. But they must overcome their remaining prejudices. We refuse to submit to their domination under the guise of freeing us from local or global oppressors. We can fight our own battles just as they fought theirs. We want to co-operate, but on equal grounds. We want an equal exchange of ideas and experiences.

They need to move on from the concept of 'giving help' to that of equal exchange. They must stop focussing so obsessively on economic capitalist globalisation and look at other types of globalisation and exploitation in the everyday life of women and men. These myriad other forms of globalisations have been playing havoc with the private and public life of women, refugees, immigrants and workers under the guise of so-called revivals of religion or spirituality, or even socialist ideologies. We need to unmask the post-modern game of new political groups, and de-mystify the new language of progressive groups which work *for* us and not *with* us.

'Glocal' Action

We need to stop seeing the Forum at Porto Alegre as the only World Social Forum, and regarding the local or thematic ones as marginal. Self-critical reflection is an essential part of the WSF. Without this it cannot grow, create new ideas and new actions locally or globally. I like the new word 'glocal' since the local is inseparable from the global.

In Porto Alegre, I met a few participants from Egypt and other Arab countries. Most came from Europe and the U.S. However the Palestinian flag dominated the demonstrations, and the protesters against the war in Iraq were visible, though all the other flags were drowned in the red of the flags carried by Brazilian peasants and workers. The Forum in its totality condemned U.S. unilateralism, militarism and lack of global responsibility in spite of its claims as a global superpower. Power without responsibility is a political disease inherited from the patriarchal class system that was born with slavery. This is one of the dichotomies forced on us by religion and philosophy. We must resist this idea of an irrevocable split between a good, divine power and the devil's responsibility for evil. We must un-mask and strip away the language of George W Bush the father, son and holy ghost, and his axis of evil.

Notes

1. First appeared in *openDemocracy*, 20 March 2003. <http:// www.opendemocracy.net/ debates/article-6-91-1076.jsp#>
2. Two corrections: WSF 4 will be held in Mumbai, India, and not in Hyderabad; in 2005, the world meeting is being held again in Porto Alegre. There was a lot of confusion about locations of future events after the intense discussion that took place at the meeting of the WSF International Council in January 2003 where all this was decided, including as reported in the world media, and the views expressed here—written immediately after the 2003 meeting—only reflect this general situation.
3. See:<http://www.european-referendum.org/>

The Secret Of Fire

Peter Waterman

The WSF 1 in Porto Alegre, 2001, was mostly marked by protest against the WEF taking place at the same time. The WSF 2 in 2002 attempted to specify the meaning of "Another World is Possible!" The WSF 3 in 2003, was marked by a questioning of the extent to which the Forum—now an increasingly globalised phenomenon—itself embodies what it is preaching to others. I look at WSF 3 in terms of the:

- danger of going forward to the past of social movements and internationalism;
- problematic relationship with the 'old' trade unions;
- uneven age, gender, ethnic, composition of the Forum;
- uncertain future of a proposed global social movement network;
- necessity of a communications, media, and cultural internationalism;
- possibility of an academy of global empowerment.

My conclusion is that the 'secret of fire' of radical-democratic and internationalist social movements is now a public one, thus offering some guarantee of a continuation and deepening of the Forum process.[1]

The Future of the Movements and Internationalism: Forward to the Past?

At the centre of initiative and decision-making within the WSF have been the Brazilian national Organising Committee (OC) and the International Council (IC) it created. These are not subject to the principles of participatory or even representative democracy or of accountability to their respective communities (mass organisations, NGOs, funding agencies), the role of which seems to have been to give international legitimacy to the OC, whilst having a quite ambiguous relationship to it. The historical justification for the existence of both has been the quite remarkable vessel they have launched—an international and internationalist encounter, outside the immediate spheres of capital and State, targeted against neoliberalism and capitalist globalisation, increasingly concerned with proposing radical-democratic alternatives to such. And all this on the understanding that the place, space and form is the guarantee for the necessary democratic dialogue of countries and cultures, of ideologies, of political levels, collective subjects and movements and organisations. In so far as re-presentation is today as important, or even more important, than representation (a problematic quality within both liberal democracies and, for example, labour movements), the forms and contents of a new counter-hegemony have been at least sketched out by the committees of the Forum and on a global scale.[2]

This space however, has never been a neutral or innocent one, (like death and taxes, money and power are always with us, and the failure to confront these openly suggests either occupational blindness or bad faith). This space has not been as far beyond the old politics and parties and parliaments as it might like to claim.

The OC consists of a number of representatives of social movements and NGOs, the latter of which might address social movements and civil society but be answerable only to them. (It consists of two Brazilian movement organisations and six NGOs, and with seven men and only one woman.) These bodies have been oriented toward, or circulate around, the Partido dos Trabalhadores (PT), and/or its recently successful presidential candidate, Lula da Silva. Just as the Porto Alegre Forums have been places where this (and other Brazilian parties) could influence events and publicise themselves, so was the ESF in Florence in November 2002, one in which the Rifondazione Communista (and other Italian political parties) did. Such parties, and far-less-sophisticated and interesting others, have often hidden their political lights behind NGO bushels. The WSF has also been a site to which various inter-state agencies such as the UN have access or upon which they exercise influence. State-dependent funding agencies, national and international, and massive private-capitalist U.S. foundations have supported the Forum itself, or various, selected, inter/national NGOs influential within it.

The IC was created top-down by invitation of the OC (of ninety to a hundred members, mostly NGOs and inter/national unions of which only eight–ten are women's networks). This gargantuan assembly has no clear mandate or power, therefore acting for the OC largely as a sounding board and international legitimator. The nature and representation of the members, and the extent to which they are answerable to any but themselves, remain obscure. Many of them do little other work in the IC than turning up and then fighting for their corner—such as the maximum number of representatives within the Central part of Forum programmes in the hands of the OC/IC. The IC does not operate behind closed doors, but its proceedings are barely reported by its members to even the interested public. There has, recently, been formal discussion about the role and rules of the IC, consequent on an intended shift of weight from the Brazilian national to the international committee. But whilst part of this discussion—actually more like an interesting experiment in online consultation (see <http://www.delibera.info/fsm2003ci/GB/>)—is posted on a publicly accessible website, the existence of this is known to few. Moreover, only a tiny fraction of IC members have taken part in this consultation, again suggesting that their motivation for membership has more to do with a search for recognition and influence than with the advance of this—admittedly novel and complex—project as a whole. The Centre, however, is not a monolith. On the contrary, it is itself in movement, under its own momentum, as indicated by post-Forum web updates (http://www.forumsocialmundial.org.br/home.asp). At the very least, however, it has signally failed to *communicate itself* to even an interested public. This is a matter to be returned to below.

The Porto Alegre Forum is an agora in which there are a few large, well-publicised and well-placed circus tents, surrounded by a myriad of differently-sized others (now around 1,700 in all—which means 300–400 events per *day*), proposed by social movements, international agencies, political organisations, academic institutions and even individuals. The Suburban/Peripheral events compete for visibility, for sites, for translators/equipment and often overlap with or even *reproduce* each other, and—whilst certainly adding to the pluralism of the Forum—have an inevitably minor impact. Whilst, again, the decision that the Forum is not a policy-forming body allows for pluralism and creativity, the result is, inevitably, domination by the official programme—one which has been conceived without notable discussion beyond the governing committees.

The concentration of power at the Centre is reinforced by the presence of our very own celebrities—who may have to choose between appearance in a hall seating thousands, or in a classroom seating twenty-five. Indeed, even the major Central Themes (sets of panels on specific problem areas) were somewhat marginalised this year, either by being placed away from the central university site, or simply by the attention focused on celebrity events, rallies and demonstrations. This formula is out of control in different ways.

WSF 3, with maybe 70,000 Brazilian and 30,000 foreign participants, was too big for the hosts to handle. A number of experienced local organisers had apparently been lured away to Brasilia by the new government, and the original PT local-government sponsors had lost influence in both the city and the state. Unlike last year, the programme was never published completely in either English or Portuguese. A well-organised North American Left, internationalist, and pro-feminist group, invited to run a five-day programme on 'Life after Capitalism,' found itself without publicity, and then geographically marginalised in a country club unmarked on the Forum maps, unknown to information booths, and a taxi-ride away from the main site. The Brazilian feminist tent, a major focus of attention at WSF 2, had been moved to some anonymous site elsewhere in the city. Other radical groups, which consider themselves initiators of the GJ&SM more generally, likewise complained of marginalisation.

The Forum is also out of control in the sense that it is moving beyond the reach of the Centre, with regional, national, local and problem-specific Forums mushrooming worldwide. Here the OC–IC can give guidance and blessings (and even hypothetically withhold such) but little more. The Forum may slip out of the hands of the original international NGO elite (I use this term loosely) as it is challenged by those who are demanding that its decision-making bodies consist of regional and national representatives (or elites?).

The Forum is in danger of losing its social profile, as major politicians and governments recognise the importance of this agora, and turn up invited (President Lula da Silva) or uninvited (President Hugo Chavez). There was no way that the Forum could fail to invite Lula, or even to wish him well on his way to Davos. But well-wishers might have been alarmed by such newspaper headlines as 'Lula is Applauded in Davos and Starts the Dialogue between Porto Alegre and Davos,' and 'IMF Approves Financial Discipline of Lula Government.' This is not speaking of Lula's conciliatory Davos speech itself.

Those who seek to give it not only a national but also a nationalist character are putting into question the Forum's place as what I call the 'new global solidarity.'This is evidenced in the Indian case. Here a declaration of the Asian Social Forum (ASF), dominated by a major Indian Communist Party, attacked *imperialist* wars in Asia but forgot about the *nationalist* Indo-Pakistani conflict —in which nuclear threats are issued by two opposed chauvinist regimes—both enjoying U.S. imperial military cooperation! An informative report on the ASF proposed that strong nation-states, and alliances of such, were the necessary answer to globalisation.[3] This traditional—not to say archaic—notion was reinforced by an editorial sub-head that turned the writer's proposal into an ASF-WSF conclusion! An impressively open WSF 3 event on WSF 4 in India suggested that certain party-aligned leaders of recent Forums in India have learned to 'talk the talk,' but scepticism is in order about whether they can also 'walk the walk.'

Given all this, there is a danger that the Forum will be overwhelmed by the *past* of social movements and internationalism. This was one in which such movements were dominated by the institutions they spawned, by the political parties that instrumentalised them, in which the movements were state-oriented and or state-identified, and in which internationalism was literally that: a relationship between nations, nationals, nationalisms, nationalists. Proletarian solidarity turned into military aid to approved regimes. West-Rest solidarity came to be dominated by one-way state-funded 'development cooperation,' and in which Rest-Rest solidarity could be reduced, for example, to slogans of solidarity with the revolution in El Salvador, or in a tribal village of India, where any sign of solidarity with other tribals, or tribals in the neighbouring Indian state, were absent.

The Union-Forum Relationship: Moveable Objects and Resistible Forces

WSF 3 saw a growth and deepening of the relationship between the traditional international union institutions (TIUIs) and the Forum. There are already about a dozen international unions on the IC, most of which are anti-neoliberal but not anti-capitalist, and many of which are, due to globalisation, in considerable crisis. There is no evidence that they have tried to act as a bloc. With one or two exceptions, they may have been primarily concerned with finding out what kind of exotic animal this is.

The increasing interest of this major traditional movement in the Forum was demonstrated by the presence, for the first time, of the General Secretary of the International Confederation of Free Trade Unions (ICFTU). But top officers of Global Union Federations (GUFs, formerly International Trade Union Secretariats) were also present, either prominently on platforms or quietly testing the water. Present, further, were international union organisations and networks from beyond the ICFTU 'family' (now formalised as Global Unions). This year there were, in addition to the radical union networks from France or Italy, an independent left union confederation from the Philippines, two left mineworker activists from India, and, no doubt, hundreds of movement-oriented unionists from other countries. I noted also an increasing openness amongst even the most traditional of TIUIs. Whilst the first big union event was a formal panel with only gestures in the direction of discussion (here, admittedly, only reproducing a problematic Forum formula), another major panel saw the platform shared between the Global Unions, independent Left unions and articulate leaders of social movements or NGOs identified with the Forum process. The unions seem increasingly prepared to recognise that they are institutions, and they need to come to terms with a place and process that, whilst lacking in formal representation and often inchoate, nevertheless have the appeal, dynamism, public reach and mobilising capacity that they themselves lack but need.

But, what *kind* of relationship is developing here? From the first big union event, patronised by the charismatic Director of the ILO, veteran Chilean socialist, Juan Somavia, I got the strong impression that what was shaping up was some kind of understanding or alliance among the unions, the Social Forum and progressive states/men. The unconditionally praised PT Government and President Lula here evidently represented the latter. Somavia, who had just met Lula officially in Brasilia, made explicit comparison between the ILO's new programme/slogan of 'Decent Work' and Lula's election slogan 'For a Decent Brazil.' The fact that the TIUIs adopted 'Decent Work' as their slogan suggests the emergence of a global neo-Keynesianism, in which the unions and their ILO and WSF friends would recreate the post-1945 Social Partnership model (or ideology), but now on a global scale—and with the aid of friendly governments.

The model seems problematic in many ways. The main one is whether the role of the WSF, or the more general GJ&SM, is going to be limited to supporting a project aimed at making capitalist globalisation 'decent.' Or, should the movement not have a project for labour that might be simultaneously more *utopian* (post-capitalist) and, under present conditions, more *realistic* (making work-for-capital an ethical issue, treating 'non-workers' as equals of wage-earners, addressing the closely inter-related civil-social issues such as useful production, sustainable consumption)? There needs to be a discussion about the political, theoretical and ethical bases of the two labour utopianisms, one within and the other beyond the parameters of capitalism.[4]

When an old institution meets a new movement, something has got to give. The trade-union movement has been periodically transformed since 1800. Although decision-makers both of the TIUIs and the WSF could have quite instrumental reasons for relating to each other, one cannot be certain that the openness within the Forums will guarantee that the principles at stake will be continually and publicly raised. Which of the two international leaderships, for example, is going to even mention the extent to which the other is dependent on inter-state subsidies, direct or indirect?

Combined and Uneven Development: Gender, Ethnicity, Class and Age

I was somewhat alarmed, in the hotels, at the panels, at the receptions and in the news coverage, by the number of people who looked like me: White, Male, Middle-Aged (I was then not yet 70) and evidently, Middle-Class. I suspect the bias applies also to the decision-making committees. This does not mean that women, Africans, Indians, indigenous peoples, workers or the under-thirties are actually excluded from these—but the youth were under canvas in the Youth Camp or in private 'solidarity accommodation'; the Argentinean *piqueteros* were in the streets (sleeping who knows where?); and women were less visible than they had been at WSF 2, though this may have been an effect of the de-centralisation and dispersal at WSF 3 (including that of myself!).

Amilcar Cabral, assassinated leader of the anti-Portuguese struggle in colonial Africa, once suggested that after independence, there would (or should) occur the 'suicide of the petty-bourgeoisie.' As the more sceptical Frantz Fanon argued at the same time, however, the post-colonial elites were going to do everything they could to retain and increase their privileges. There are striking power and wealth differences between Forum participants, particularly visible, predictably, in the case of the South. In two or three Latin American cases known to me, the poorer participants travelled by bus—this sometimes meaning a 4–5 day journey, with entry obstacles at various border-crossings. I am not suggesting that the existent Forum elites are suicidal without irresistible pressure from outside or below (nor even that I was going to abandon a hotel with hot and cold running internet). Insofar, on the other hand, as the WSF has declared, certain principles relating to liberty, equality, solidarity, horizontality and pluralism, it might be possible to confront them (us) with the necessity of re-balancing the power equation. The elites could then put their efforts, in their home states/constituencies, into *facilitating* rather than dominating or *controlling* the Forum process.

The experience of women and feminists within the Forum might point to different directions. I have no figures for WSF 3, but at both previous events, women were almost fifty percent of the participants. There are powerful feminists and feminist networks on the panels and in the IC, quite capable of making the Forum a Feminist Issue, as also, of making a feminist contribution to, and impact within and beyond, the Core programme. There were regional and cross-regional meetings of feminists at Porto Alegre, an important one connected with planning for WSF 4. There were numerous panels on gender and sexuality in both the central and more marginal programmes. Feminists and feminisms at the Forum are, however, confronted with devising a strategy that combines working within decision-making bodies, making their presence felt within the Forum itself, and addressing a feminist and general public beyond the Forums. To me, the problem is one of publicly confronting the decision-making bodies (the shortcomings of which, with respect to women's representation, have been indicated above). Whereas leading figures might declare good intentions with respect to women and feminism within the Forum, the step from talking to walking has still to be taken here also.

The power and presence imbalances within the Forum might be corrected by two measures. One, quotas for under-represented categories and two, a Forum programme structured according to collective subjects as well as major problems. Thus, one could have major panels and programmes on Labour, Women, Youth, Indigenous Peoples—even the Aged (I hope to become such myself one day). At present, for example, Labour may be represented in a series of union-sponsored or union-approved events, some within and some beyond the Core programme. But this implies a dispersal of attention and impact where there should, surely, be concentration. (Fisher and Ponniah 2002 have but two contributions on the union movement as such, and the single one on feminism does not address the international/global at all!) Alternatively, or additionally, imbalances can, could and should be corrected by autonomous Forums. Or what about a re-invention, in the light of the WSF, of the World Youth Festivals of Communist origin?

A Social Movement Network: De/Centralised?

At two previous Forums there has been issued a 'Call of Social Movements.' The initiative for this has come from members of the OC and IC, some of these being recognisable social movement organisations, others being recognisable NGOs. Both Calls have been publicly presented and then signed by fifty–hundred other organisations and networks. This year, the notion of a 'Social Movements World Network' (SAWN) was widely circulated on the web and subject to a two-session public discussion within the Forum. This eventually produced a declaration, proposing a continuation of discussion about the nature of such a network, with further meetings to take place during major movement events this year.[5]

The Call—like other Forum bodies and initiatives—is surrounded by a certain amount of mystery. Given overlapping memberships, are we to understand the Call as a device for going beyond the Forum's self-limitation on making specific political declarations, taking specific political action? If so, how is it that the *Secretariat* of the Call, in Sao Paulo, only came to the attention of this interested observer eleven months after its creation? How come it took seven or eight months for the signatories of Call 2 to be identified (and then only in an obscure corner of a website), when those of Call 1 were published instantaneously? Doesn't discussion at specific events in specific continents automatically exclude from discussion those who can't afford to fly there? What, for the purposes of this new initiative, is a social movement? (Can it be a state-funded NGO? Can it be a group of academics and, if so, how many? And which trade unions qualify as social movements?) There is, here again, a serious lack of communication, which implies a concentration of crucial information amongst a limited circle.

I am actually favourable to, even enthusiastic about, the creation of such a network. In part because it doesn't exist internationally; and in part, because it is going to provide information and ideas on a continuing basis—and to those people/places otherwise excluded from the periodic Forums. In so far as this will have an existence in "real virtuality" (Manuel Castells), it may go beyond a WSF that remains largely earth-bound and institutional. The very experiment is going to be important for progress in this area.

Apart from the questions above, certain crucial others remain (about which I may only have yet other questions). Is the network going to be primarily political/institutional or primarily communicational? In the first case, communication is likely to be made functional to the political and institutional. And, there is likely to operate a 'banking' model of communication, in which information is collected, sorted and classified, to be then dealt out to customers/clients in terms of power, influence or profit, as determined by the information-bank managers. In the second case, we may be into a different ballpark. Here, the principle of the potlatch, or gift economy, can operate, in which individual generosity is taken to benefit the community. The underlying ontological principle here is the common African saying: "I am who I am because of other people."

Even in the best of all possible cyberworlds, however, there remain questions of appropriate modes (information, ideas, dialogue), of form (printed word at one end, multimedia at the other) and control (handling cybernuts and our own home-grown fundamentalists). There do exist various relevant models of international social-movement, civil society, anti-globalisation networks—earth-bound or cyberspatial. Indymedia Centre (IMC) has got to be the most important here, and needs to be publicly reflected upon both for what it does well and what it doesn't (dialogue?). Finally, any Social Movements World Network (SMWN) is going to have to go beyond network-babble and recognise that even networks do not exist on one, emancipatory, model. In discussing the issue, Arturo Escobar has suggested:

> It is possible to distinguish between two general types (of networks): more or less rigid hierarchies, and flexible, non-hierarchical, de-centralised and self-organising meshworks. Hierarchies entail a degree of centralised control, ranks, overt planning, homogenisation, and particular goals and rules of behaviour conducive to these goals. Meshworks...are based on decentralised decision-making... self-organisation, and heterogeneity and diversity. Since they are non-hierarchical, they have no overt goals. It can be said they follow the dynamics of life, developing through their encounter with their environments.[6]

In the end, however, it does not too much matter in which place/space, and on which model the SMWN takes shape. The existence of the web, combining low cost of entry, wide reach and high speed, provides the assurance that such a network will be supplemented or challenged by others.

From Organisation to Communication in the Global Justice and Solidarity Movement

The movement-in-general has shown, at its best, an almost instinctive feel for the logic of the computer,[7] and expressed itself in the most creative and provocative ways. For example, at the demonstrations in Quebec City in April 2001, a man was arrested for threatening to catapult a—possibly largish—teddy bear over the globalised razor wire. However, this is not the case for the WSF in particular. The WSF *uses* the media, culture and cyberspace. But it does not *think* of itself in cultural/communicational terms, nor does it live fully within this increasingly central and infinitely expanding universe.[8]

The WSF website remains problematic—promoting year-old ideas (chosen by whom?) in its meagre library. Trying to reach a human being on this site, to whom one could pose a question, reminds one strongly of Gertrude Stein (or whoever) on Oakland, California, "There is no *there,* there." The site's own claim, that it was visited during WSF 3 by X million, cannot deal with visitors such as myself, repeatedly seeking for information that wasn't there. The website perked up in the post-WSF 3 period, providing more useful information than it had during the previous year (http:// www.forumsocialmundial.org.br/dinamic/eng_portoalegrefinal.asp), but it is difficult to have confidence that this improvement will continue.[9]

The only WSF daily is *Terra Viva*, an admirable effort by the customarily unaccountable NGO, but which this year seemed to me to add to its space-limitations, delays and superficialities a heavier bias toward the Forum establishment. The commercial, professional, and substantial regional paper in Rio Grande do Sul, *Zero Hora*, gave wide coverage but, unsurprisingly, in Portuguese. For background information and orientation one was, this year, dependent on free handouts of *La Vie/Le Monde* (inspired by French social Catholicism), and *Ode*, a glossy, multi-lingual, New Age magazine from Rotterdam, with impressively relevant coverage (which I have used in this paper). Other alternatives, and non-Forum sites, provide better information and/or discussion than the Forum itself.[10]

The WSF seems to me something of a shrine to the written and spoken word. (Insofar as I worship both deities, I am throwing this stone from my own glasshouse.) At the core of the Forum is The Panel, in which 5–10 selected Panellists do their thing in front of an audience of anything from 5 to 5,000, the latter being thrown the bone of three to five minutes at a microphone. And these are the lucky ones! At the other end of the Forum's narrow spectrum of modes there is The Demonstration. Here euphoria is order of the day—how can it not be when surrounded by so many beautiful people, of all ages, genders and sexual options, of nationality and ethnicity, convinced that Another World is Possible? But here we must note the distinction made thirty years ago, between *mobilisation* and *mobility*, as related to the old organisation and the new media:

> The open secret of the electronic media, the decisive political factor, which has been waiting, suppressed or crippled, for its moment to come, is their mobilising power. When I say mobilise I mean *mobilise* ...namely to make [people] more mobile than they are. As free as dancers, as aware as football players, as surprising as guerrillas. Anyone who thinks of the masses only as the *object* of politics, cannot mobilise them. He wants to push them around. A parcel is not mobile; it can only be pushed to and fro. Marches, columns, parades,

> immobilise people. The new media are egalitarian in structure. Anyone can take part in them by a simple switching process. The new media are orientated towards action, not contemplation, towards the present, not tradition. It is wrong to regard media equipment as mere means of consumption. It is always, in principle, also means of production. In the socialist movements, the dialectic of discipline and spontaneity, centralism and decentralisation, authoritarian leadership and anti-authoritarian disintegration has long ago reached deadlock. Network like communication models built on the principle of reversibility of circuits might give indications of how to overcome this situation.[11]

And then there is also The Rally—a panel built on the scale of the Titanic. The paucity of cultural expression at WSF 3 is surprising, bearing in mind we are speaking of Brazil, the country that brought down the corrupt President Collor by cultural-political protest. The WSF 3 song, which has an attractive but complex lilt, is sung only in Portuguese, and was, in fact, the WSF 2 song. As in 2002, the tee shirts were still not going to win any design prizes. And the most popular icon (no fault of the organisers) remains Che. Something of an exception to the general Forum rule was, in 2002, the campaign against fundamentalisms of the Articulación Feminista Marcosur. I had and have doubts about the interpretation offered by this campaign, but it was one which intimately combined the customary Forum modes with dramatic cultural expression of undeniable originality and impact: last year there were masks, an enormous hot-air balloon, hoarding-sized posters and more. This year, activity was possibly less dramatic, but peaked with a packed-out book launch, at which was also projected a 10-minute CD production of considerable invention and power.[12] Lucy Garrido, the Uruguayan designer, opted for visuals, music and minimal words, in successive English and Spanish. We could have had, we should have had, a discussion around this. Or maybe even a panel...?

An Academy of Global Empowerment

A review of the recent literature on globalisation reminds us of what happened in the U.S. academy during the Vietnam War.[13] It was a moment at which the academy, not only in the USA, divided between those either committed to or complicit with the existing power relations and those who challenged these. There were, no doubt, excesses on the Left here (not yet free of the excesses of the Right), but opposition to the war in Vietnam, to racism, to class-discrimination, to sexism, to corporatism in the university, gave rise to a wave of high-quality radicalism, some of it still alive—despite neo-liberalism—today. Consider only the U.S.-based NACLA Report on the Americas (http://www.nacla.org/). What has happened in the intervening years is well summarised by Arturo Escobar:

> Social scientists have been in retreat. If the social sciences in the 1980s were infusing the natural sciences with new idioms and ideas, today it seems to be the other way around. Metaphors of complexity, webs, networks, self-organisation, etc. are now being more actively developed in the natural sciences, although of course there are attempts to bring it all back to the social sciences again. The re-conversion of the Humanities towards the production of critical inter-subjective knowledge for social transformation—while important in some fields such as cultural and so-called post-colonial studies, and feminist and critical race theories—has floundered in the persistent Achilles' heel of their engagement with extra-academic worlds. In this context, non-academic knowledge producers seem to have taken the lead.[14]

The last point here is significant. According to Raúl Zibechi, the capacity of popular movements to train their own leaders, to develop their own educational principles, and to develop their own intellectuals is amongst the seven or eight major characteristics of the newest wave of social movements in Latin America.[15] He mentions the Intercultural University of Indigenous Peoples and Nationalities, coming out of Ecuadorian struggles, the 1,500 schools of the MST (Landless Workers Movement) in Brazil, and others.

But there is also a growing alternative to this from within the academy. This lies, as one might expect, in individual academic staff and students turning their attention to either the GJ&SM in general or to the Forum process in particular. I mention here only a few new academic centres and recent initiatives, to give an impression of what must be taking place on a much wider and more varied scale and, hopefully, spilling out from the social sciences to the academy more generally.

First, the Centre for Civil Society, at the Centre for Global Governance at the London School of Economics in the UK, and second, the Observatorio Social de América Latina (Latin American Social Observatory) in Buenos Aires. The first is oriented towards a liberal-social-democratic notion of global civil society, and is inspired by the LSE's tradition of social reformism and social engineering. The second, concentrates on social movements, protest, and the global movement processes themselves. Though different, these two projects should not (for political reasons) and cannot (for epistemological ones) be set up in binary-oppositional terms. They represent two cases of academic response to the development of global civil society and global social movements. They are both worthy of closer attention than I can give them here.

Global Civil Society 2002 is the second of two weighty annuals produced by the Centre for Civil Society.[16] The first annual gave considerable attention to not only the title area but also to various global social movements and their dynamics.[17] The GCS project sets a standard for data collection and analysis that others are going to be challenged to surpass. And the accessibility of this work sets new standards, both in the sense of its excellent printed and graphical layout, but also because it is available, free, for chapter by chapter download, from the GCS website (see <http://www.lse.ac.uk/Depts/global/Yearbook/>).

The Observatorio Social de América Latina (OSAL) is sited within one of Latin America's premier research institutes, Latin American Council of Social Sciences, in Buenos Aires (CLACSO). This bland-sounding project represents what may be the most ambitious monitoring of social movements (under globalisation) anywhere. Although its basic publication form is that of a serial journal of the same name (nine since 2001), and although a large part of it is devoted to country-by-country reports, the current issue also extends beyond Latin America, and it includes analysis and theoretical debates.[18] OSAL/CLACSO has also published a number of books about the current wave of protest. This orientation is clearly toward the new global social movements. After years or decades in which social-movement studies, and commitment to social movements, were somewhat marginalised in Latin America, this is a dramatic declaration of commitment to movement-oriented research. Whilst the audio-visual offerings are from CLACSO rather than OSAL, these include numerous complete books and other resources (all, I think, in Spanish/Portuguese), the subjects and authors of which are often related to the OSAL project. Furthermore, CLACSO runs a computerised distance-education project, making its courses potentially available throughout the continent.

At WSF 3, CLACSO had a well-equipped stall with several staff at a major site, and is also an influential member of the International Council of the Forum. And OSAL was well represented in the Core programme of WSF 3. I have warned against setting up OSAL/CLACSO as a polar opposite to GCS/LSE, as some kind of model for a university of global emancipation. But it is a challenging experiment. Of particular interest might here be the extent to which the commitment of OSAL to the movement is reciprocated by the movements themselves—particularly those closest to it in its home base.

The mention of a university of global emancipation brings us to the pre-Forum proposal of Boaventura de Sousa Santos for a Popular University of Social Movements.[19] Launched with the blessing of IBASE, possibly the key Brazilian NGO behind the Forum, the proposal is for the mutual self-education of both scholars and activists, with a particular focus on the South, and with a specific rooting in the proposed locale. This was one of many individual, even personal, initiatives arising around the WSF and was proposed for discussion at WSF 3 and on the internet. The last initiative in my list is the most marginal in terms of recognition and power. This is less a specific project than the general orientation of a new feminist network, NextGENDERation. NG is a Netherlands-based network of young feminists in academia, which appears to combine the enthusiasm of seventies feminism with orientations and concerns of both postmodernism and, well, post-capitalism. What is of particular interest is its concentration on the transformation of the university itself:

> The NextGENDERation network wants to stand for a type of feminist knowledge politics, deeply concerned with the democratisation of higher education. This concern relates to different, although interconnected, dimensions. The access to higher education, and the way in which power mechanisms such as gender, ethnicity and class structure access this on different levels (with horizontal segregation according to disciplines, and vertical segregation according to academic hierarchies), are of primary concern to us. The production of knowledge is a second dimension on which our attention is focused: the brands of critical and situated knowledges produced from feminist, anti-racist, post-colonial and antiheterosexist points of view have already began to transform the old curricula and canons. We are committed to continuing this transformation. Both of these dimensions are related to a vision of what the university, and higher education in general, stands for. From our feminist perspectives, we start from a critical distance towards the classic conception of the university as an ivory tower. At the same time, we don't buy into the current neo-liberal ideals of higher education as a training-place in function of the needs of the labour mar-

> ket. We are invested [sic] in a vision of the university as a place for the production of critical and socially relevant knowledge, and want to work towards that ideal in our specific historical time and space. Another university is possible![20]

These rapid sketches may give some impression of an academic fermentation either caused or stimulated by the Forum. But after serious reflection on the rise and fall of post-1968 academic radicalism, the conclusion here must be that we need to think of sites and forms of research and education that can survive the next equivalent of the neoliberal backlash.

Conclusion—The Secret of Fire

I am concerned about the future of the Forum process, but not worried. Pandora has opened her box, the genie is out of the lamp, and the secret of fire for emancipatory movements is now an open one. This secret is to *keep moving*. In other words: a moment of stasis within a movement (institutionalisation, incorporation, bureaucratisation, collapse, regression) requires that activists be prepared to move to its periphery, or to move beyond it, or to create a new movement to advance, again, the potential represented by the old movement during its emancipatory moment. In Florence, young libertarians were grumbling and mumbling 'Another Forum is Possible.' This possibility is not only a matter of information and communication technology. It may be the combination, precisely, of this with youth—given that at least urban kids are growing up with cellular phones, playing arcade computer games, and therefore with an affinity for other computer technology (and a healthy disregard for attempts to coral such).

For the rest, I am inspired. By the energetic and innovative social protest, and original analyses of the local-national-global dialectic in Argentina. By the belated appearance of a network, Raiz (Root), in Peru that clearly has some feeling that the WSF is more than an NGO jamboree. By the Kidz in the Kamp who were discussing, under a tree, and with informal translation, how to ensure that the emancipatory and critical forces have more impact on the Forum process. By the struggle, against all odds, of the U.S. ZNet people to mount 'Life after Capitalism,' an event of post-capitalist *propuesta* within the Forum. By the massive global anti-war demonstrations of 15–16 February 2003—something that puzzled even radical specialists on the new social movements. By the increasing number of companer@s of various ages, identities, movements and sexual orientations, who believe that, in the construction of a meaningfully civil global society, transparency is not only the best policy but also the *only* one.

Notes

1. This is an edited and revised version of "Second Thoughts on The Third World Social Forum," Porto Alegre, 23–28 January 2003, Working Papers, Institute of Social Studies, The Hague, which reveals intellectual debts and includes an extensive bibliography. Edward Fullbrook, who cannot, regrettably, be held responsible for any of its continuing short- (or long) comings, provided stimulus for the production of this tauter version.
2. Since this piece was first drafted, Boaventura de Sousa Santos (March 2003) has produced the most original analysis and theorisation of the Forum that has yet appeared. He gives considerable importance to the 'self-democratisation' of the Forum—the aspect on which this paper concentrates.
3. Jain January 2003.
4. Waterman 2003e.
5. Social Movements World Network 2003.
6. Escobar 2003.
7. Klein 2001.
8. For more on this new and challenging area, see Cardon and Granjon 2003 and the Cyberspace panel within 'Life after Capitalism' <http://www.zmag.org/lacsite.htm.>
9. Later visits to the WSF website update revealed that my first and second reflections on WSF 3 had been posted. Gratified that, after five–ten previous efforts over two years, I had finally been given such recognition, I remain in ignorance about the selection principles or procedures involved. [NB : All this was true of 2003, when this note, and this essay, were written; and the link has also changed. *Eds*]
10. See <www.choike.org/links/about/index.html>, <www.nadir.org/nadir/initiativ/agp /free/wsf/>
11. Enzensberger 1976, pp. 21–53.
12. Cotidiano Mujer/CFMEA 2002.
13. Munck 2002.
14. Escobar 2003.
15. Zibechi 2003.
16. Glasius, Kaldor, and Anheier 2002.
17. Anheier, Glasius and Kaldor 2001, reviewed Waterman, 2003d.
18. OSAL 2003.
19. Santos 2003b.
20. NextGENDERation 2003.

Is It Possible To Put A Human Face On Globalisation And War?

International Liaison Committee for a Workers International[1]

An Open Letter to the Trade Unionists and Activists Participating in the WSF 2002 in Porto Alegre, Brazil, from the International Liaison Committee for a Workers International (ILC).

Dear Brothers and Sisters,

We, the undersigned Brazilian trade unionists, want to open a dialogue with you. We are living through a terrible situation the world over. The U.S. government, under the cover of the United Nations, is using the heinous terrorist attacks of 11 September to intensify a political agenda of "full-scale, protracted war"—as Bush himself has stated. It is a war that started with the bombing of Afghanistan and is far from over.

In neighboring Argentina, the people—after years of governments that had submitted to the dictates of the IMF and applied the politics of privatisation, destruction of workers' rights, and bleeding the nation to pay back foreign debt—took to the streets and threw out the 'centre-left' government of Fernando De la Rua. They made it clear they wanted an end to policies that had plunged millions of Argentineans into misery and hunger—all in the name of 'modernisation,' 'exigencies of globalisation,' the 'criteria' of the Mercosul regional 'free trade' pact, and the preparation of the country for the FTAA!

In this new situation, the 'powers that dominate the world,' that is, the multinationals, the financial speculators, the international financial institutions such as the WTO, World Bank and IMF and all the governments in their service, have declared an economic and political war against the workers, against their organisations, and against the peoples. Their aim is to use the tragic events of 11September to roll back all the rights and conquests wrested through bitter struggle by working and oppressed peoples. Their aim is to destroy any and all barriers to their plunder of natural resources and their unbridled quest for profit and exploitation. The struggles of resistance against these scorched-earth policies cry out for the unity of working people the world over—from North to South and from East to West. It requires the united struggle of oppressed and exploited peoples to stop this offensive of war and destruction, which is leading the world to the brink of barbarism. Only through such united struggle in defense of the rights and gains of working people will it be possible to chart a way forward for the future of humanity.

For our part, we are certain that this quest for unity in action to defend and advance the rights of working people is what has prompted thousands of unionists and activists from across the globe to participate in the second WSF in Porto Alegre.

But does the reality of the WSF correspond to this expectation? Does the WSF offer a way forward for this struggle? We want to raise some questions here about the WSF and invite you, our brothers and sisters, to draw your own conclusions.

The Trap of Civil Society

The WSF has presented itself, since its inception, as a Forum for 'civil society.' The very concept of 'civil society,' which is so popular of late, erases the borders between social classes that exist in society. How, for example, is it possible to include in the same category of 'civil society' both the exploited and the exploiters, the bosses and workers, the oppressors and oppressed—not to mention the churches, NGOs, government and UN representatives? The organising committee of the WSF in Brazil includes organisations such as the Brazilian Association of Employers for Citizens (CIVES) and the Brazilian Association of NGOs (ABONG). They are joined in the committee by other entities, which, to be sure, are connected to the struggles of the exploited and oppressed—such as the CUT (Unified Workers Federation) and the MST (Movement of Landless Peasants). Is this organising committee itself not an expression of the politics of 'civil society'—that is, of the attempt to group together in the same camp, interests that are in fact *contradictory* and diametrically opposed?

Let's take the example of the campaign in defense of workers' rights contained in the Brazilian Labour Code which we in the Brazilian trade union movement are now carrying out. The CUT has issued a call to prepare a General Strike in March 2002 to prevent the approval of PL 4583 by Minister Dornelles. It is clear that the CUT is determined to carry forth with this strike call should the situation require it. What do the so-called 'progressive bosses' think of these workers' rights? What do the NGOs—which practice as well as promote 'volunteerism' and other forms of precarious and unregulated labour—think about these workers' rights? Don't all the jobs 'created' by the NGOs, in fact, *re-*

place jobs in the public enterprises and services, in line with the policies implemented by (Brazilian President) Fernando Henrique Cardoso at the behest of the IMF? The politics of 'civil society' are today officially the politics of the World Bank. What is the content of these politics? Judge for yourself. The World Bank's World Development Report 2000/2001 puts it this way:

> It is appropriate for financial institutions to use their means...to develop an open and regular dialogue with the organisations of civil society, in particular those that represent the poor. Social fragmentation can be mitigated by bringing groups together in formal and informal forums and channelling their energies into political processes instead of open conflict.

Could it be a coincidence that among the funding sources of the WSF one can find the Ford Foundation or that the World Bank's Website promotes the Porto Alegre Forum?

What is the Role of NGOs?

Hundreds, if not thousands of NGOs will be participating in the World Economic Forum of Davos to be held this year in New York as well as in the WSF in Porto Alegre. What is the role that those who control the commanding heights of the global economy attribute to NGOs?

In the official World Bank document titled *The World Bank and Civil Society* (September 2000), one reads: "More than 70 per cent of the projects supported by the World Bank that were approved in 1999 involved non-governmental organisations (NGOs) and civil society in some manner."

There is a popular proverb that states, "He who pays the piper calls the tune." The World Bank, as we know, is part of the holy trinity of capitalist globalisation, alongside the IMF and the WTO. Could it be that these institutions are 'neutral' and that they do not express the interests of global capitalism? Let us look at this one concrete example: the International Council of the WSF met in Dakar, the capital of Senegal on October 31 and November 1, 2001. ENDA-Third World, which is an NGO that has been actively building the WSF across Africa, hosted and organised this WSF planning meeting. What are the politics of ENDA?

According to its own documents, ENDA believes that "to prohibit child labour is to deprive children, as well as their families, of an important means of subsistence." ENDA affirms that "it is necessary to take into account the socio-economic reality and, therefore, to fight for the rights of child labourers."

This stance by ENDA is in open contradiction to the positions of the CUT and the international labour movement—all of which call for the abolition of child labour and mandatory education till age fifteen of all children. The place for children is in school! But not only does ENDA advocate child labour, it is participating directly in the privatisation of the public water system, constructing wells and cisterns and charging users a fee for providing the water.[2]

And what about the Tobin Tax and ATTAC? In the name of James Tobin, winner of the Nobel Prize in economics and fervent advocate of corporate 'free trade,' an Association for the Taxation of Financial Transactions and for Assistance to Citizens (ATTAC) was created first in France (1998) and then on an international scale. Among its goals is the establishment of a Tobin Tax, which would create a tax of between 0.05 per cent and 0.1 per cent on international financial transactions. The money collected would serve to create an 'international fund' to help 'development and the struggle against poverty.'

As is widely known, ATTAC is today one of the main founders and organisers of the WSF of Porto Alegre. The Tobin Tax, for its part, has won the support of people as 'prominent' as the multi-billionaire speculator George Soros, Brazilian President Fernando Henrique Cardoso and others. Now, if a tax existed to finance an international 'fund' to aid the poor, one would think that the greater the financial speculation, the better it is because such a 'fund' would have more resources. This rationale is not far-fetched.

Be that as it may, along with the Tobin Tax, ATTAC today is dedicated to other ventures as well. It proposes to "change the world" under the slogan 'Another World is Possible!' through "better control over globalisation." But is it possible to change the world without questioning the fundamental relations of production, without challenging the private ownership of the major means of production? Is another world possible with a minimal Tobin Tax helping to "*control* globalisation?"

Bernard Cassen, President of ATTAC-France and Director of *Le Monde Diplomatique*, a newspaper controlled by the enterprise group of the daily *Le Monde*, declared at the founding congress of ATTAC-Germany (19–21 October 2001) that, "President Bush has taken steps in the direction of ATTAC's proposals since 11 September 2001. It is clear that we still have a long way to go. But it is necessary to note that...Mr. Bush is now against tax shelters. We register this fact. Bush has come closer to our positions concerning the role of the State, investing U.S. $120 billion in the economy...He has embraced our position on the cancellation of the debt, though he is doing this for his own reasons. The U.S., for example, has just cancelled Pakistan's debt, which proves that it is *possible* to cancel the debt." Bush has just launched one of the largest-scale offensives against working people ever, including the massive bombing of Afghanistan, and yet, according to the President of ATTAC-France, Bush is moving closer to the positions of ATTAC. This is very interesting.

"A World without War is Possible"

Under this title, a special session of the WSF will be devoted to a 'world without war.' According to the proposal from the organisers, this session "seeks to bring social and/or institutional representatives of the regions where wars are taking place together with Nobel Peace Prize recipients in a joint effort to reflect on the nature of wars and to identify the possibilities of elaborating peace plans." The following 'regions' will be discussed: Palestine, Kashmir, the Basque Country, Colombia and Chiapas. Curiously, the bombing of Afghanistan will not be part of the agenda. How is it possible for the "all-out and protracted" war launched by Bush—today in Afghanistan and tomorrow possibly in Iraq or Somalia—not to be part of the discussion under this point.

Palestine—which currently faces a dramatic situation, with the State of Israel attacking on all fronts in open war—will be discussed, with the objective of "elaborating a peace plan." But what is the origin of the current situation in Palestine? It is the Oslo Accords, *sponsored* by the United States (under Clinton) and then *legitimised* by the UN as a "peace plan." These accords created a pseudo-Palestinian 'State' (the Palestinian Authority, whose headquarters are now being bombed), which was but a conglomeration of miniscule so-called Palestinian territories surrounded by the State of Israel.

Speaking of Nobel Peace Prizes, it was the Oslo Accords that garnered that prize for Yasir Arafat and for the Israeli Chief of State at that time, Shimon Peres. As a matter of fact, the Secretary General of the UN, Kofi Annan, has also been graced with the Nobel Peace Prize, perhaps in recognition for the role that the UN played in perpetrating the genocide in Rwanda—or was it for the embargo that the UN has imposed on Iraq, or better yet for the cover provided by the UN to the NATO bombers in ex-Yugoslavia?

'Participatory Democracy' and the 'Participatory Budget'

The World Bank has just created an international department charged with overseeing the implementation of 'participatory democracy' in 26 countries. It has also translated, published and distributed the book *The Participatory Bud-*

get: The Experience of Porto Alegre, written by Tarso Genro (former Mayor of Porto Alegre) and Ubirata de Souza. Is this simply disinterested propaganda of the World Bank? Or, on the contrary, do the 'participatory democracy' and 'participatory budget' processes not, in fact, embody the above-cited strategy of 'channeling energies' to avoid 'open conflict?' All the documents which came out of the first WSF of Porto Alegre discuss the 'model' experiences of participatory democracy that have existed in the capital of Rio Grande do Sul. The Second WSF continues on the same line. Among the list of WSF workshops there is one titled 'World Participatory Budget' (neither more nor less!), organised by the Governor of Rio Grande do Sul, "in participation with citizens' movements."

But how does the 'participatory budget' function in reality? In the unsuspecting voice of its co-ordinator in the city of Sao Paulo, it is meant to be a "filter for popular demands!"

Only one small portion of the municipal budgets—in the case of Porto Alegre the sum amounts to 17 per cent—is earmarked for discussion and allocation by the assemblies of representatives of popular organisations (the council of the 'participatory budget'). These assemblies define how the priorities should be set for the disbursement of these limited funds. (The bulk of municipal budget monies are untouchable, as they have been earmarked to pay back the foreign debt and other expenses). As resources are limited, there is constant in-fighting among activist groups over how the priorities should be set. The 'participatory budget' councillors are forced to choose what they would prefer—the creation of a school or health clinic, paving of roads or childcare centres, etc. This is how the responsibility for NOT meeting the demands of the population is shifted...onto the backs of the participants in the 'participatory budget' themselves!

Now, who participates in the participatory budgets? The answer is 'civil society.' In the case of a participatory budget assembly in the municipality of Camacua, a businessperson sent 'his' representatives as delegates and won close to 70 per cent of the votes to prioritise the pavement of a road—to the detriment of all the other demands!

Is this, as its supporter's claim, 'an innovative form of democracy?' Or, on the contrary, isn't it a trap that seeks to co-opt popular movements and associations into the implementation of the city government's austerity plans, thereby making them responsible for the 'choices' that inevitably do untold harm to other popular movements and associations?

And what conception of society lies behind this 'participatory budget?' It is that of a society without conflicts, without contradictions, based on 'consensus among equals.' But is this not the inverse of democracy which demands the recognition that contradictory interests exist in society, as well as the recognition of the right of the exploited and oppressed to independent organisation in the face of the State and the exploiters? What would be, for example, the participation of a union of public service workers in the 'participatory budget?' There is no lack of voices that say that unions "should learn to function in labour-management co-operation committees" and therefore should enter such "participatory" Forums. It is reasonable to expect that the union delegate would seek improvements in wages and conditions as a priority. But the association of homeowners may want light in their neighbourhood. Instead of directing their demands for public power and mobilising to achieve them through collective action, they will be played against each other in the assemblies of the participatory budget. Many of you have participated in such assemblies. Is what we are saying not the complete truth?

Brothers and Sisters, we, the undersigned unionists, will participate in the Trade Union and Popular Assembly which the CUT has called in Porto Alegre on 1 February to discuss and prepare the General Strike next March. But we will not participate in the panels, workshops and official sessions of the World Social Forum.

We will not be there because we are convinced that the defence of the organisations that workers have created to fight against capitalist exploitation is contradictory with the politics of civil society, which dissolve the borders of social class. It is contradictory, moreover, with the politics of 'giving a human face to globalisation,' which, as we know, is not a phenomenon of nature, but rather the product of global capitalism. 'Globalisation' by definition necessitates the destruction of our workplaces, our jobs and our rights. Capitalist globalisation has destroyed nations, democracy, and the sovereignty of the poor. It cannot be 'humanised.' We, who affirm the need to defend the trade unions as instruments of working class struggle, deny any legitimacy or authority to the NGOs to speak in the name of the exploited and oppressed. We do not claim to be the sole possessors of the truth. We simply want to put forward our point of view —which is part of the democratic process. We respectfully submit these views for the consideration of all our brothers and sisters in struggle.

You can count on us as fighters in the struggle against war and exploitation; in defence of social and labour rights, against de-regulation; in defense of trade union independence and democracy! You can count on us in the struggle against the FTAA, and for the withdrawal of Brazil from the negotiations to implement it! You can count on us in the struggle against privatisation and in defence of public services! You can count on us for the preparation of the General Strike to stop the destruction of our labour rights and to impose a defeat on the governments of FHC-IMF!

Militant Greetings, 2 January 2002

Signatories, Unions and Titles:

Julio Turra, National Executive Committee, CUT trade union federation
Hélcia de Oliveira, Vice President, CUT-DF
Josenildo Vieira, Executive Committee, CUT-PE
Maurício Rosa, Executive Committee, CUT-SC
Mônica Giovanetti, Executive Committee, CUT-PR
Gardênia Baima, Executive Committee, CUT-CE
Walter Matos, Executive Committee, CUT-AM
Marília Penna, Executive Committee, CUT-SP
Luiz Gomes, Executive Committee, CUT-AL
Gilmar Gonçalves, Executive Committee, CUT-MS
Cláudio Santana, Executive Committee, CONDSEF
Jesualdo Campos, Executive Committee, CONTEE
Cely Taffarel, Executive Committee, ANDES-SN
Roque Ferreira, Executive Committee, FNITST (ferroviários)
Jaqueline Albuquerque, Executive Committee, FENAJUFE
João Batista Gomes, Executive Committee, SINDSEP (municipais SP)
Luis Bicalho, Executive Committee, SINDSEP-DF (federais)
Verivaldo Mota, Executive Committee, Sindicato dos Vidreiros-SP
Nilton de Martins, Executive Committee, Sindicato dos Radialistas-SP
Roberto Luque, Executive Committee, SINTSEF-CE (federais)
International Liaison Committee for a Workers International (ILC)

Notes

1. International Liaison Committee for a Workers International (ILC) was constituted in Barcelona, Spain, in January 1991 at a conference of working class and socialist delegates from fifty-three countries. Its objective was to unite the working class, the youth and all the oppressed peoples of the world to fight back. The ILC has grown into a multi-tendency re-groupment of unionists and political activists in ninety-two countries. It takes as its historical precedent the International Workingmen's Association, the 'First International,' founded in 1864 in London.
2. ENDA: Water and Urban Poverty.

World Forum Movement: Abandon Or Contaminate

Linden Farrer

In November 2002, 60,000 activists from all over Europe converged in Florence, Italy, for the ESF at the same time as the neoliberal elite met at the TABD in Chicago.[1] The ESF promised to be a meeting space for "in-depth reflection, democratic debate, free exchange of experience and planning of effective action among movements of civil society engaged in building a planetary society centred on the human being."[2]

Preparatory meetings in Brussels, Vienna, and Thessaloniki led to the involvement of more than 600 organisations and 40,000 more participants attending than expected. The final day saw an anti-war march attracting a million Italians from all over Italy to Florence (which has a population of just 400,000). The ESF was clearly one in the eye for the Berlusconi regime, particularly since none of the promised violence and damage to monuments publicised in the right-wing media actually occurred. The eventual crackdown on dissent took place fairly quickly, with up to forty 'No-Global' activists arrested or held under house arrest.[3]

The ESF's parent organisation, the WSF, first anticipated the creation of a European Forum and other regional Forums in 2002. The WSF sees itself not only as a meeting-place for discussion of alternatives to neoliberalism, but also as a counterpoint to the WEF.[4] Whilst the WEF met in Davos (Switzerland) in 2001, in 2002 it was forced to meet in New York. This was not a powerful statement by the neoliberal elite standing firm against its opponents but due to the costs of protecting the 2001 WEF conference from protestors. The security operation for the 2001 conference was the Swiss government's most expensive since the Second World War, provoking cries of protest from within Switzerland. While the WSF has risen in status the WEF has steadily fallen, having lost its prime-magnet for corporate and financial heads—the serene mountain top location it has met at since 1971. It now describes itself as a gathering to "discuss how to maintain hegemony over the rest of us."[5]

The power of the anti-capitalist movement has been felt not only by the WEF, but also by other organs of world neoliberal government. The WTO in

Seattle (1999) was disrupted by workers and 'fair trade' protestors and trade unionists. The World Bank and IMF in Prague (2000) abandoned meetings a day early as protestors scaled and surrounded delegates at their conference centre. And world leaders had trouble declaring benevolent intentions over the thick tear gas, savage beating of protestors and the murder of activist Carlo Guiliani by the police at the G8 meeting in Genoa (2001).[6] The legitimacy of world leaders and their organisations has been put into question and the "violence of some of the actions, as well as the violence of the State, has led the mainstream media to focus on what the 'anti-capitalists' have been saying and doing, rather than on the communiqués issued by the summits themselves."[7]

But disrupting the conferences is not nearly enough, particularly when they can be moved to inaccessible locations and violent means used to suppress protest. This is where the WSF and its continental (and local) offshoots offer the liberal anti-globalisation and radical anti-capitalist movement a summit of its own, able to devise alternative strategies of globalisation, or in the WSF's own words, to make 'another world possible.'

However, the contradictions inherent in (what has loosely been termed) the anti-globalisation movement are all too apparent at protestor summits, and has led to conflict and uncertainty for some sections of the movement. The actions of activists engaged in direct action and militants on the street have captured the headlines and brought about concrete, but arguably short-lived results. Others, such as liberal-reformists (who want to reform capitalism), NGOs (who want money to carry out their activities and are often happy to enter into negotiations with big-business and government), and authoritarian leftists (who want to enter government to affect reform or build a mass party for revolution), enter into a dynamic push-and-shove to hash out a way forward in the form of the Social Forums. Unfortunately, this vocal leadership, which has the money and experience to organise, are moving the Forums away from the direction initiated by radicals, and into the self-destructive orbit of conventional politics.

The anti-capitalist movement, the WSF and the ESF, are all direct responses to declining involvement in party politics. This is due to a neoliberal consensus that stifles opportunity for change, resulting in growing radicalism. Nick Dearden succinctly says, "it is acute political and economic disempowerment, the violent death dance of a tiny global elite hell bent on turning a majority of the world's population to the margins in a push towards war, blood, starvation, and unending inequality and impoverishment that has brought these diverse groups and individuals together into what is surely the largest movement in history."[8]

According to Hilary Wainwright, the concerns of participants at the ESF included the democratic autonomy of nations, regions, cities and communities; the social right to health, housing, asylum and a "high-quality" environment, "and the desire to live in something other than a shopping mall for big corporations." At the top of the list is a de-militarised Europe at peace with itself and the world, taking a high moral stance against U.S. imperialism. High on the list too was a radical rethink or complete rejection of predatory capitalism, conceiving of a Europe that rejected crude market ideology and with fully accountable institutions.

There were specifics too—Europe should have open borders, and people within it have the right to work and to have a home; there should be a Tobin tax on financial markets and regulation of corporations; there should be no GM foods, no privatisation of public services; the media should be in the hands of the many, not the few, and racism should be driven out. Wainwright stated that the ESF's task is to create a "much more vigorous, more democratic control over the quasi-state institutions of the EU than the ones the European Parliament currently provides."[9]

But while these demands sound progressive, even radical, they beg question as to whose agenda Wainwright is describing—that of the grassroots or that of the organisers and their selected speakers? This question harks back to the foundation of the WSF as an idea conceived by the Workers Party (PT) of Brazil. Noam Chomsky stated in a keynote address to the 2002 WSF that it offered the beginnings of a sketch of what a 21st century international might look like, but warned that in order to avoid the destructive fractures of previous internationals (that caused a split between Karl Marx who headed the statist faction, and Bakunin who headed the anti-state anarchists), the WSF had to organise on an anti-hegemonic basis.

This lesson has gone unheeded, and as Jason Adams writes, the PT "jealously controlled the organising committee of the WSF" with the result that one anarchist spokesperson remarked, "with all of the rhetoric that has gone around, we thought the WSF was going to be an open event, but then when we attempted to get involved and take part, it was made clear to us that we would be given no decision making power at all...we were given menial tasks and were excluded from the actual planning and execution of the event." At WSF

2001, anarchists and ecologists loosely affiliated with People's Global Action protested against this exclusion and in 2002 their protests led to the Workers Party calling in riot police; as Indymedia posters pointed out, "Porto Alegre isn't the social democratic paradise that the PT makes it out to be."[10]

Likewise at the ESF, certain sections of a widely defined anti-globalisation movement were more active—or more able—to undertake organisation of the Forum.[11] The first decisions of the ESF in Italy were taken by a group of six people meeting at the Rimini congress of the Rifondazione Comunista. This group included Tom Benetollo (the national President of the ARCI), a cultural association closely linked to the old Italian Communist Party and now seen as a front for the Left Democrats—the equivalent of New Labour—who control the Tuscan regional government and Florence city. Although the Left Democrats helped set up and arrange the ESF, their policies in regional government have included privatisation of local services and entailed environmental destruction. Also from a parliamentary Left background is Peppe De Cristofaro (of Giovani Comunisti—the youth organisation of the Rifondazione Comunista, which got 5 per cent of the vote in the 2001 elections and now has an opinion poll rating of 8 or 9 per cent).

Their leader Fausto Bertinotti urged all Italians to come to Genoa the day after Carlo Giuliani was murdered at the anti-G8 demonstrations in 2001 to "defend democracy." Also present were Pierluigi Sullo (Carta), Alfio Nicotra (a representative for the Italian Social Forums), Bruno Paladini of Cobas (an anarcho-syndicalist union that had a prominent presence at the anti-G8 demonstrations), and Marco Bersani of ATTAC Italia that helped set up the WSF and calls for a tax on financial speculation amongst other demands, and is linked closely to the French Parti Socialiste, especially when Lionel Jospin was Prime Minister.

These six individuals took important decisions about the ESF's structure, ultimately deciding who spoke in Florence, at what time, and on what subject. All the main speakers were chosen in advance by the organisers—anyone else got a maximum of three minutes speaking time and international NGOs, such as Amnesty International had priority. The inevitable result was meetings with the celebrity names you would expect—such as José Bové, Johan Galtung, Cees Hamelink, Jacek Kuron, Tony Bunyan, Alex Callinicos, Susan George, Wolfgang Sachs, Riccardo Petrella, Tariq Ali—and the organisations you would expect—SOS Racisme, ATTAC, Amnesty International, European trade union federations, Oxfam, Friends of the Earth, Le Monde Diplomatique, Statewatch, Pax Christi, and Rosa Luxemburg Stiftung.[12]

In addition to the leadership's ability to define the ESF's agenda, their choice of speakers led to much of the initiative and organisation coming from NGOs who rely on lobbying politicians and parliament to achieve change —quite the opposite of putting grassroots resistance into action. The liberal anti-globalisation movement's call for a tax on financial speculation might explain the presence of NGOs, since the revenues raised by this tax are to be distributed to the NGOs themselves. Some of the funding for the WSF and ESF even comes from government organisations, such as the Norwegian Foreign Ministry and Netherlands Ministry of Foreign Affairs. In addition, the involvement of the 'old guard' of political parties such as the PT, the RC and even Blair's equivalent—the Left Democrats—should be seen as a key test of the integrity of the ESF.

In Britain, the main organising group was Globalise Resistance, who are considered a front-group for the Socialist Workers Party (SWP). Chris Nineham of Globalise Resistance doesn't shy away from his position in regard to political parties, stating that "left wing parties are already central to the movement," mirroring a recent spate of SWP propaganda proclaiming the party to be "at the heart of the anti-capitalist movement."[13] So while the Socialist Workers Party was officially not there the much more 'movement' sounding Globalise Resistance was present, though not surprisingly GR's 'star' speaker was SWP Central Committee member, Alex Callinicos. The Alliance for Workers Liberty came as the anti-sweatshop group, No Sweat, Workers Power came in their pseudo-anarcho (but ultimately Trotskyist) 'Revo' outfit and the Socialist Party adopted the unimaginative title 'International Socialist Resistance' Façade. Although these organisations are involved either as a source of funding or in an attempt to grasp hegemonic control over the disparate anti-capitalist movement, the fact that these hierarchical and authoritarian organisations are involved at all should ring alarm bells for activists.

Not surprisingly, the involvement of establishment, hierarchical, organisations and parties led to bureaucratic control over the proceedings, disliked by many participants—mirroring the experiences of some activists at the WSF. Boris Kagarlitsky claims that organisational difficulties—quite impossible to avoid considering the numbers that turned up—would have been minor annoyances if the organisational muddle had been redeemed by interesting or substantial discussion. In fact, he claims that discussion at the Forum never happened and that people who gathered in Florence to talk about the prospects for the movement found that they had come to a three-day rally instead. General statements were delivered from the podiums; successive speakers voiced delight at how many of us there were, and how young and good-looking everyone was, and that "initiating serious debate in the halls full of thousands of people, warmed up by mass-meeting rhetoric, was impossible."[14] Wainwright echoes this when she writes that the "Florence Forum certainly achieved diversity, but often failed to establish real dialogue in the formal sessions."[15]

So whilst the WEF meets in what it terms a "unique club atmosphere," it could be expected that the ESF and WSF would organise in a form quite distinct from these organisations—after all, the kind of world we want to create can only arise out of organisational structures that mimic and set a blueprint for future society. Instead, we see that hierarchical and authoritarian means of organisation have been employed, preventing direct grassroots democracy within the Forums. More positively, the sheer scale of a Forum with simultaneous translation in five languages for 1,000 speakers at thirty conference sessions, and over 200 workshops, 150 seminars and twenty-five campaign meetings in addition to a range of cultural and fringe events, show that authoritarian control from above was nigh impossible for the majority of sessions.

More worryingly however, the liberal-establishment that controlled the ESF, managed the agenda with radical questions such as the legitimacy of the 'war on terror' and 'anti-terrorist legislation' excluded, as this was seen as too provocative to the government. Other discussions, such as the legitimacy of the nation state and parliamentary democracy that allows post-fascists (or even fascists on occasion) to enter government—like in Italy today under Berlusconi—were also left off the agenda.[16]

Instead, the main theme of the Forum was the war on Iraq. One of the main proposals to come out of the ESF was a call for national demonstrations against a war on Iraq (or whatever the next target happens to be) in every European capital city on 15 February 2002, which will pose a symbolic show of strength and unity by the anti-war/globalisation movement that will be hard to ignore completely.[17] Unfortunately, a war with Iraq must be seen within the wider context of capitalism and imperialism, and the effort and time concentrated on discussing the war is explained by the accommodation afforded to it through the support of the liberals opposing it.

In addition, the limelight ensured to 'establishment' speakers by the leadership of the ESF led to dangerous assertions being made in regard to the EU and the world economic system. One theme that emerged for example, was the need for 'widespread and conscious participation by citizens in the European political process,' a call that ignores the very reasons for the growth of the movement. The fact that 60,000 people turned up at the Forum rather than join a political party or meet their parliamentary representative shows that the movement has grown out of a recognition of the fallacy of parliamentary democracy and liberal reform. A demand that the EU's constitution include 'provisions to safeguard labour, environmental, health and education rights' is in effect, demanding (without threat) that the master of capitalism in the EU should reform itself—of course, it can't. Wainwright's desire that the ESF hold the EU to 'account' masks the truth that the EU is the friend of the capitalist system that demands the destruction of the earth, our rights, our liberties and freedoms. There is no way for the EU to be reformed, its undemocratic, anti-grassroots, authoritarian and centralised nature is directly opposed to all the demands of the anti-capitalist movement, even if some EU departments work towards progressive ends.

Even more naively, Sousa Santos said that the only way to achieve a "true and independent European identity was for the EU to clearly differentiate its socio-economic system from the U.S. neoliberal model," urging the rehabilitation of the state in economic affairs. As if pre-World War I colonialism and the laissez-faire capitalism of nineteenth century European nation states were ultimately different from those of the U.S. today, and that non-neoliberal *capitalism* was a solution to the problems of neoliberalism! The danger inherent in this approach is that it is self-destructive, ignoring the reasons that made the Forum possible in the first place.

Potentially more troublesome tendencies within the liberal leadership of the ESF are indicated by the symbolic dates for the meetings of the Forums —the same dates as the self-appointed global elite meet; this points to an even more impotent and self-destructive direction. When Pascal Lamy (EU Trade Commissioner) stated at a TABD dinner speech that the TABD "continues to put forward recommendations to which governments on both sides of the Atlantic (will) do well to listen carefully."[18] U.S. Vice President Al Gore stated that of over a hundred recommendations put forward by the TABD, over half had been implemented into law, wishing that the Senate was as effective as this in drawing up legislation.[19] The most dangerous route that the leadership of the ESF can take is to see the Forums as potentially stronger negotiating partners for government than the TABD or WEF.[20]

Instead, the ESF and WSF should see themselves as an embryonic form of direct, grassroots democracy, capable of forging ahead in gaining power through undermining the legitimacy of existing structures of power, distributing this power as widely and diffusely as possible.

Attendance at the ESF—three times than expected—and the anti-war march that shocked Italy in its size, show that discontent is strong for a different order. The ESF is a chance for the Trade Union movement and anti-capitalist movement to create permanent links without the go-between of a political party, and to help people from all over the world with experiences of different struggles to come together and share ideas, tactics and strategy for change. The stale bureaucracy displayed in some sections of the leadership, and those who would divert the anti-capitalist movement to further their own aims looked out of touch with the grassroots composition of the ESF. Jonathan Neale of Globalise Resistance (also a member of the SWP) told me that the leadership had been wholly reluctant to call an anti-war demonstration from the start—because it would upset Berlusconi—and was far too timid in its demands and rigid in organisational framework. He said that it was the grassroots that were forcing the leadership into more radical positions as it saw itself superseded by a groundswell of radicalism. Perhaps the next ESF could see a complete removal of those who want to create a hierarchical, old-fashioned party-type Forum, replacing it with representatives of grassroots struggle from below instead.

For the anti-capitalist movement to achieve real change, it will have to do so through a confrontational approach to liberal democracy. This could involve the setting up of Social Forums throughout Europe, at local levels, creating direct links with local communities in struggle. These, organised in a federal structure—but respecting local autonomy—would undermine and ultimately make obsolete the earth-destroying, authoritarian and oppressive governmental structures that currently control the planet. Activists have the opportunity to wrest the ESF from its current 'leadership' and steer it in a truly progressive direction, rather than seeing it become a negotiating partner on par with the TABD, or able to lobby the EU more effectively.

The vision that minds can have without the experience of years of political deadlock, sectarianism and cynicism, arising from the failure of party and parliamentary politics is definitely a bonus for the movement despite Kagarlitsky's lament about the lack of middle-aged "leaders" who have a better historical perspective. He writes that real power lies in military headquarters, ministries and, in the best case, elected assemblies that have developed an immunity to pressure from the streets, unless, as happened in Buenos Aires in December 2001, the events unfolding on the streets directly threaten the stability of the institutions themselves.[21] Confrontation with the State or world government cannot, ultimately, be won by force. And this is where the ESF and regional Forums have the potential strength to bypass existing structures that are part of the old order and create grassroots associations of free individuals, linked locally and worldwide, making existing structures obsolete.

Instead of a grassroots approach, which takes some time to build up, the organisers of the Social Forums appear at present to be rushing the process, attempting to establish themselves as the leadership of a movement that has developed without their participation in the first place. In a series of letters made public on Indymedia UK, between Professor Nanjundaswamy of the Karnataka Indian Farmers' Union (KRRS) and Bernard Cassen of ATTAC, Nanjundaswamy makes it clear that the KRRS cannot participate in the Asian Social Forum (ASF). This is because it expresses its "dissatisfaction about the way in which the ASF is being launched by NGOs little known to the people of India, approaching mass based grassroots movements in December 2002 to have the ASF in January 2003." Additionally he asks why "ATTAC never apologised for the death of Carlo Giovani, where instead of looking at the violence of the fascist police that tortures in police stations, declarations focused on the violence of the black block?"[22] This was surely a gross example of liberal leadership out of touch with the radical anti-capitalism that has helped build the movement to the position it occupies today.

The second meeting of the ESF takes place in Paris in November 2003. For it to be considered a step forward, it will have to consist of a more representative cross-section of activists (up to 90 per cent of the delegates at the first ESF meeting were Italian), and as stated in an article on Indymedia UK, needs to be "more diverse and less bureaucratic."[23] People's Global Action (PGA), a network of grassroots organisations that have organised 'Global Days of Action' against capitalism(and are overtly anti-capitalist rather than anti-neoliberal) feel particularly strongly about the WSF process, seeing it (in 2000) as, "an attempt by sectors of the traditional Left, the old established and bureaucratic Left, to take over the struggle against capitalist globalisation" within the perspective of national development—a Left which desires a "humanised" capitalism; which wants to "socialise" the market; which wants to govern the State. They also observe that the "Forum is hierarchical, verticalised, like the events of the bureaucratic Left...speakers/conferences on the one hand, and, at another, public spectators."[24]

At last year's ESF meeting they organised an autonomous space, "not in competition" and "not anti-ESF," to facilitate networking between groups and individuals and to "contaminate by association, the ESF with non-hierarchical practices." They noted that the ESF had many young activists and held potential to develop existing anti-capitalist networks.[25] This is the best way of working with the ESF; being constructive in criticism, attempting to change the organisation from inside and outside, preventing liberals from tending towards their self-destructive habits of strengthening existing structures of government through voting and lobbying. Rather than abolishing the ESF because it had a shaky, but ultimately successful start, we should work to make the ESF a truly revolutionary force to change society from below, not of lobbying those above.[26] Florence was a beginning, the "site where the foundations for an alternative Europe were laid"[27]; as Noam Chomsky has noted, the WSF and its continental offspring "potentially offer the best hopes of the Left for a true international."[28]

Notes

1. The TABD's purpose is to offer "an effective framework for enhanced co-operation between the transatlantic business community and the governments of the EU and U.S." (http://www.tabd.org). Its agenda is pro-business and anti-environment; one priority has been to block efforts made to phase out hydro fluorocarbons (HFCs), one of the most potent greenhouse gases used in refrigerators. The Danish Government had decided to implement a ban on these that was to take effect in 2006, but the TABD described it as a potential trade barrier that would restrict free flow of trade and hence established a special working group to obstruct or at least postpone the decision. Another priority has been to demonstrate to EU and U.S. officials its concerns over plans to limit corporate tax evasion. See <http://www.corporateeurope.org/observer10/tabd.html>
2. See ESF website at <http://www.fse-esf.org/rubrique.php3?id_rubrique=1>
3. This led to an immediate response from civil society throughout Italy, with demonstrations of 30,000 in Rome, 20,000 in Naples and demonstrations in twenty-eight other cities throughout Italy. See <http://www.ainfos.ca/en/ainfos10442.html> and <http://uk.indymedia.orgfront.php3?article_id=47220&group=webcast>
4. The WEF is an annual gathering of 1,000 business leaders, 250 political leaders, 250 academic leaders, 250 media leaders along with token labour, social justice, and entertainment leaders. They aren't leaders "because an electorate or the public says so but by virtue of their wealth, influence, and power, and their farsightedness in being able to maintain all three" (Milstein C at <http://struggle.ws/global/issues/wsf.html>). This is reflected in the composition of the membership of the WEF (which numbers around a thousand corporations), 68 per cent being based in North America and Europe, and less than 1 per cent in Africa (<http://www.geocities.com/pwdyson/ wef_orgs.htm> lists WEF member organisations).
5. Walden Bello at <http://www.zmag.org/Sustainers/content/2002-01/31bello.cfm>
6. Numerous other 'days of action' have taken place, all over the world; the ones listed here are the movement's best-known successes. Reports from these days of action can be found at <http://www.pcworks.demon.co.uk/magazine/campaign/zzgda.htm>

7. *Aufheben* #10 (2002), p. 2.
8. N Dearden at <http://www.resist.org.uk/reports/archive/esf/esfdearden.html>.
9. Wainwright December 2002, p. 5.
10. J Adams at <http://www.zmag.org/content/VisionStrategy/AdamsWSF.cfm>
11. Questions have even been asked as to who compromises the International Council of the WSF that decided that the ESF should be set up.
12. *Socialist Review* (November 2002), p. 17 and Treanor P <http://web.inter.nl.net/users/Paul.Treanor/esf.html>
13. *Socialist Review* (November 2002), p. 19.
14. Kagarlitsky B at <http://www.zmag.org/sustainers/content/200211/21kagarlitsky.cfm>
15. Wainwright *Ibid*.
16. Treanor *Ibid*.
17. See <http://www.resist.org.uk/reports/archive/esf/esfantiwarcall.html>
18. Quote from <http://www.tabd.org/media/2001/lamy060502.html>
19. See <http://www.xs4all.nl/~ceo/tabd/troubled.html>
20. It is also possible that these symbolic dates have been chosen because corporations are seen as the enemy rather than elected national or world governments, or that the capitalist system itself is perceived to be a more powerful force than nation states and government apparatus; either way, these dangers remain.
21. Kagarlitsky *Ibid*.
22. Letters at <http://uk.indymedia.org/front.php3?article_id=48336&group=webcast>
23. From an article advertising preparatory meetings for the 2003 ESF at <http://uk.indymedia.org/front.php3?article_id=47814&group=webcast>
24. From <http://www.nadir.org/nadir/initiativ/agp/free/wsf/nowsf.htm >
25. See the text of the 'final plenary' of the autonomous space at <http://www.nadir.org/nadir/initiativ/agp/space/finalplenary.htm>
26. Treanor *Ibid*, argues that the ESF should be abolished. Peter Waterman notes in regard to the Treanor piece that,

    "abolishing something that has hardly begun—and that is capable of assembling massive numbers of young people, old people, workers, and women from all over Europe—seems both hasty and extreme...whilst much of his alternative agenda is eccentric (in the sense of representing a personalised wish-list, hallmarked by impossibilism, and unarticulated with any familiar group, worldview or utopia), his challenges, concerning what I have elsewhere called the political-economy of the Forum (Waterman 2002b), are surely reasonable. In the case of the Amin-Houtart book, for example, the financial sponsors of the World Forum of Alternatives are actually identified as including not only European NGO funding agencies (themselves mostly state dependent) but the General Commission of International Relations of the French Community in Belgium—presumably a sub- or quasi-state body. Treanor is also, admittedly, a 'fundingmentalist—someone who believes that ideas and behaviour are totally determined by funders. Insofar as most critiques of capitalism have come from universities funded by Capital and The State, and insofar as even Marx's *Kapital* was funded out of the surplus value of Engels' textile mill, this assumption does not meet the evidence of either actually-existing or historical radicalism." (See <http://hubproject.org/news/2002/11/44.php>.)
27. Longhi V, *Red Pepper* (December 2002), p. 15.
28. Adams J, *Ibid*.

De-Centering The Forum: Is Another Critique Of The Forum Possible?

Michal Osterweil

In the weeks following my return from WSF 3, whenever someone would ask me, "How was it?" I would reply, "Amazing! I had an amazing time. The official event itself was somewhat of a disaster, but the people it brought together, the spaces and encounters it made possible—even unintentionally—exceeded most of the limitations the Forum itself had." And I meant it. I had learned so much and gained so much political inspiration, even as my pessimism about certain forms of traditional politics increased. As I repeat this to myself now —however, in spite of, or perhaps in lieu of the myriad critiques and discussions in the months following the Forum—I wonder why the more mixed and exhilarated sentiment I had by the Forum's end did not appear to be more widely shared.

Why does it seem that even many critical and progressive people are discussing giving up on the Forum, when even in its current form, it is an incomplete, plural, and contradictory space that far exceeds both the event itself and its official manifestations? We cannot forget that both the Forum and the 'movement of movements' of which the Forum is just one part, are messy, dynamic and radically plural entities whose parameters and objectives are by their very natures neither stable nor easily explicable. It is certainly important to recognise that there was an 'official' Forum, one that emerged from a concrete set of actors, ideas and events, and that was, in fact, what the majority of people did have the opportunity to experience, but there was also much more. While disappointment, disillusionment and even anger with the 'official' Forum are valid and important subjects to discuss, they may be obscuring the alternative and diverse practices that, though less visible, were still very much a part of Porto Alegre.

How we think about this Forum is important for how we imagine our critiques. Even more, how we write about and discuss the Forum does, in fact, contribute to producing it. It also produces it for the thousands who could not attend or for those who look to such discussions to process their own assessment. The fact is that the Forum is not just an event, but also a process; not simply something that happened but a political concept and a potentiality. Thus all our analyses play an important role in developing and shaping it and by extension the 'movement of movements' of which it is a part.

I believe that all too often, even our most critical writings have perpetuated a shallow understanding of the Forum and its critiques. Rather than focus only on the Forum and its shortcomings, I believe we need to *de-centre* our own vision and critiques. We need to make visible the various alternative spaces, the rich political diversity that were part of the WSF, even if the faults of the larger Forum rendered them largely invisible.

Situating Critiques of the Forum: From Structure to Politics

Since the conclusion of WSF 3 in Porto Alegre, there have been a number of critiques and discussions about its problems and weaknesses. In addition to concern about the effectiveness of a Forum that now has 100,000 participants—a number that in itself makes functioning difficult at many obvious and practical levels—there have been a number of rather serious critiques about the internal contradictions and the lack of democracy in its functioning.

Many people from various geographical and political backgrounds have criticised the Forum for a series of formal or organisational problems that they believe make it an undemocratic space. These problems include a lack of transparency in decision making, hierarchical organisation, as well as special treatment of celebrities and the creation of elitist tiers that privilege the more well known and consolidated components of the movement over many of the smaller and more grassroots and perhaps more radical organisations. A number of people have also criticised what they consider to be the privileging and co-optation of the Forum by institutionalised political structures like political parties, trade unions, and mainstream NGOs that, in addition to being hierarchical organisations themselves, tend to be reformist or social democratic in their outlook. This is seen as integrally related to the lack of transparency and democracy within the Forum structure. Many also highlight the need for being more critical of the State in the struggle against neoliberal globalisation, a position that is seen as precluded by the presence of more conventional (state-related) actors within and around the Forum.

These critiques have come from a variety of sources—from those who identify with the 'official' Forum, but are weary of its declining effectiveness as its size and popularity grow; to those who identify themselves as somewhat 'outside' it and consider the Forum in its current form to be actually opposed to the spirit of the new alternative globalisation movement. It is significant that these criticisms have come from such a wide array of political actors. But criticisms of organisational structure, vision and political approach existed long before (as well as during) this particular forum. Such criticisms did not emerge only as reactions to the technical and functional difficulties evidenced at the Forum, but from larger ethico-political disagreements and debates about what resistance to this phase of neoliberal globalisation and the political crises that accompany it ought to look like.[1] In fact for some, notions of 'true' democracy, hierarchical and non-hierarchical organisation, self-organisation and anti-authoritarianism, are at the heart of the political projects they seek to develop—at the Forum, and within the 'movement of movements' more generally.

For example, even before the Forum began, many groups and networks —including Indymedia, Intergalactika Laboratory of Global Resistance, Life After Capitalism, and many others—had planned and organised alternative and autonomous spaces and meetings outside of (and within) the official Forum.[2] They liked the original idea of a truly free space and they too wanted to participate in an international encounter of this sort. But they saw the official Forum with its planned panels, plenaries, and celebrity focus, as structurally, and therefore politically, problematic. They did not want to replicate political forms and approaches that they believe perpetuate the systems and relations of power they hope to oppose and overcome. So they set up alternative spaces.

The Intergalaktica Laboratory of Global Resistance, where I spent a great deal of time, was such an autonomous space. It was housed in a humble white tent at the edge of the Youth Camp; it had no blackboards or air-conditioning, and was in all senses rather far removed from the well-equipped PUC classrooms.[3] Although many participants at the Forum might not have realised it, the Youth Camp—located about fifteen minutes from the Port and almost directly behind the arena where Lula spoke on the first day—was truly a world within the Forum. Filled with food stands and various vendors, its own media centre, several concert venues, and countless spaces set up for various meetings—including Intergalaktica—the large expanse of green that had been planned and organised by a committee of youth, housed nearly 30,000 people. They slept in tents, showered outdoors, and practically ate, drank and breathed the Forum experience! Long after many of us retreated to our hotels, the Youth Camp was still very much active—filled with live music, intense meetings, film viewings, and myriad other events and activities!

Despite its distance, Intergalactika attracted a variety of people, including some who identified as anarchists, autonomist Marxists, and others who refused any political labels but saw their politics as inspired and co-authored by the Zapatistas. The events held there consisted of a variety of workshops committed to sharing experiences, debating ideas, and developing a political praxis based on the principles of horizontality, self-organisation, anti-authoritarianism, participatory democracy and direct action. In Laboratorio Intergalaktica—as well as for a significant part of the alternative globalisation movement—organisational form, process and the more micro-political and quotidian elements usually excluded from conventional politics are key sites for political intervention and elaboration. This was also the case in Porto Alegre.

For example, at a Saturday morning workshop in the Laboratorio, Masco, a member of the Argentinean Movimiento de Trabajadores Desocupados (MTD) emphasised the importance of such micro-politics. He recounted how becoming unemployed, and thereby experiencing a total rejection by the capitalist system, radically shifted the political outlook and praxis of his group. It forced them to realise that in order to be truly and "radically opposed to capitalism" they needed to think beyond traditional organisational forms like unions and political parties, they needed to, promote "another way of living." This meant producing "new practices, and new social relations" that worked against the pursuit of power and against inclusion into the capitalist system. He acknowledged that this was an incredibly difficult task, but that being unemployed (en masse) produces a "rupture so strong that it allows one to dream again." For him, and many others, radically democratising micro-political spaces and processes —and thereby pointing to the inherently political nature of such spaces—is necessary if people really hope to work towards effective social change.

For these groups, this movement was certainly about opposing institutions like the WTO, IMF, World Bank, but it was also about *reinventing* politics. It was about making visible the political nature of practices and spaces that were not traditionally considered political, while at the same time mobilising new forms of political practice that embody anti-authoritarianism as well as a critique of all forms of sovereign power. Looking to the Zapatistas, Situationists, Anarchists and Autonomist thinkers/activists, these activists emphasise what some have referred to as 'pre-figurative politics'—"modes of organisation that consciously resemble the world you want to create."[4]

> Now it will be necessary to create new spaces of encounter, exchange and articulation; plural spaces, that are open and truly autonomous. Spaces that are free, not only of vertical organisations, but also of vertical, 'unidimensional' words/discourses—free of old and new prestiges, of new and old authorities. We are going to think in situation, name in situation and in action.[5]

For those who participated in Intergalactika, institutional structures, meeting process and daily elements of living are inherently political and constitute critical points for elaborating effective opposition practices. Moreover, it is the historic Left's failure to recognise these new spaces of politics that has contributed to its complicity in producing the current crisis in political institutions and democracy. Previous leftist movements and organisations—including the older versions of Marxism and communism, political parties, as well as some of the 'new social movements' of the seventies and beyond—failed to achieve lasting social change because they had a narrow understanding of what constitutes 'the political.' Today, many actors working to change the world have still not realised that if they truly hope to combat neoliberalism and oppression they cannot work only in the traditional political terrain. They have to recognise that how panels are formatted, decisions made, and inclusion/exclusion enacted, are themselves powerful political acts. They cannot ignore the political logic, institutions and social relations that are a part of how capitalist and other forms of oppression manifest themselves—often within leftist struggles and spaces like the WSF itself.

Attention to democratic form and structure is not simply a procedural or technical topic of critique; it is central to an ethico-political and strategic vision.[6] Critiques of institutional and organisational democracy are as much an attempt to actively work to create and spread a new form of political engagement, as they are critiques of the Forum as it exists.

Too often, however, our critiques do not point to the political sources or the highly political nature of these critiques. We make it look as if such criticisms were 'just' structural. This stems from a larger problem: for the most part critiques and assessments of the Forum tend to reinforce the privileging of the 'official' Forum, and the marginalisation of the alternative spaces. While we have taken the critiques and analyses seriously, especially those of its organisation and undemocratic functioning, we have done so from a vantage point that takes the official Forum—with its panels at the well equipped PUC, the Stadium and the Port—as the necessary object of critique. We have said what the Forum lacks, but have not pointed to the participants of the Forum who were very deliberately already democratising spaces within and around the movement. Rather than engaging the multiple peripheries, alternative, coincidental and contradictory spaces that comprise the Forum in its totality, we write as if it is the 'official' Forum that must be fixed (or dismissed).

Even writing and arguing for 'abandonment' of the Forum has obscured the fact that the Forum is *already* a plural and contested space, and have perpetuated the invisibility of those who actively contest it. Instead of explaining the political trajectories and projects of these alternative actors, writing positively about them, their histories, and their ideas—in other words, rather than making them visible in their own terms—we have tended to write as if the Forum, and the movement of which it is a part, has a more important central part, and it is a single, unified, entity. In writing and speaking this way, we contribute to producing it as a reality: we simultaneously bolster the importance of the mainstream and perpetuate the marginalisation and invisibility of multiple alternatives.

Although spaces like Intergalactika might have been marginal compared to the 'official' Forum, they were very much part of the Porto Alegre process, and for some people (like myself) they even constituted a central part of the entire Social Forum experience. It is not enough to point out that such places were marginalised and largely invisible;[7] we need to show and explain why it is so important that they not be. Unless we write concretely about spaces like Intergalactika and the histories and movements from which such projects emerge, we maintain their invisibility, and contribute to an impoverished understanding of the criticisms of the 'official' Forum—and of the Forum itself. We prevent people from comprehending the ways in which criticisms of organisational democracy are as political as they are functional, and on the other, what an internally democratic Forum might look and feel like.

My being able to witness and participate in alternative and critical spaces has had a profound effect on the way I read and engage in the debates and discussions that have proliferated since the close of the Forum. Augmenting my intellectual and analytical engagements, my actual experiences have made the various critiques of the Forum resonant and palpable in a different way. Rather than thinking (abstractly) about participatory democracy, horizontality and self-organisation as things the (official) Forum lacked, I have a positive sense of what they are and why they are critical to a politics that is desperate not to replicate failures of the past. This is not to deny that Intergalactika and other 'alternative' spaces themselves had myriad problems and were rife with tensions and divisions of their own. But it is precisely the sense of these as spaces as real, lived places, and not only as conceptual counterpoints to the mainstream Forum that has given me a different understanding, an odd combination of intellectual and visceral comprehension, of what 'another Forum' (or forums) might look and feel like.

De-centering the Forum: De-centering Theory

Why have our critiques fallen into this trap? I believe it is because of our tendency to perpetuate the marginalisation of the peripheries and the privileging of the centre. It has to do with both our dominant modes of critique—particularly a certain style of de-construction—as well as with the nature of the diversity with which these new movements compel us to deal. While we are constantly stating how diverse and plural this 'movement of movements' is,[8] our analytical tools and vocabularies have themselves not caught up with this intellectual recognition.

The problem with most forms of de-construction or criticism is that, even as they critique or deconstruct something they see as problematic, they almost always maintain the centrality of that 'dominant' or 'hegemonic' term and phenomenon. In addition, they are highly intellectual and rationalistic. For example, critiques of capitalism can make capitalism seem to be such a coherent and total system that it renders existing alternatives and struggles within the system irrelevant.[9]

A different strategy is to destabilise or destroy the dominance or totality of a hegemonic concept or entity by showing that it is not so total or coherent as one might think; and, by making visible the plethora of actors, experiences, and differences, that its seeming unity or dominance has obscured. For example, it is one thing to say the Forum was problematic. It is quite another thing to recognise that while the 'official' Forum was problematic according to certain criteria, there were myriad effects, occurrences, meetings events, contingencies that the occasion of the Forum made possible. These might have been less obvious, but they were present. Similarly, it is one thing to say that having panels that featuring experts and stars is problematic because it produces hierarchy. It is quite another to actually *show* a workshop that attempts to challenge such hierarchies by locating everyone in a circle, and combining 'experts' with grassroots activists. One approach relies on the intellectual and abstract agreement that hierarchy is bad, the other gives a more visceral and positive sense of why alternatives might be better. It is not that the first mode of critique is wrong; on the contrary I believe it is quite necessary. But it should not be our only mode of intervention.

I believe that there is an interesting parallel to be made between the fact that our modes of critique reinforce the 'mainstream' by always criticising it according to its own terms, and the ways in which these new movements hope to re-define politics. If many of the critiques are premised on mobilising areas not traditionally considered political, their critiques cannot be understood according to the regular (political) terms of the conversation. Said differently, to my mind it is no coincidence that the 'official' Forum—that aspect associated with a more 'traditional' understanding of politics—is more visible than the Forum of the actors seeking to expand politics to new spaces precisely because the 'official' actors are favoured by the current common sense of politics. The fact of the matter is that we just don't have the categories in our political and sociological vocabularies to treat critiques of organisation, forms and micro-politics in the same way as do more traditional political categories such as ideology, tactics.[10]

We know how to talk about the differences among the various *issues* and *actors* in the movement, and about the remarkable fact that this movement is comprised of so many different actors—environmental groups and labour unions, political parties and NGOs, environmental campaigns and economic ones. But it is much more difficult to speak of the *differences* that exist between groups that function according to principles of horizontality and radical democracy and those that don't. For even when we speak about diverse political approaches, such as anarchists and communists, political parties and NGOs, we tend to rely on categorical descriptions and generalised statements about ideologies, and rarely on concrete political practices.

As a consequence of the paucity of our own analytical tools and categories, we then relegate critiques of process—or the belief that process is an essential part of democratising daily life—to non-political space. Such critiques then appear to be *additional* to rather than *part of* substantive political debates. In this way discussions and critiques about democratising the Forum appear to be a way of making the Forum function better, rather than re-constituting the political potential of the Forum itself.

In addition to the significant work of analysing and assessing the problems of the 'official' Forum, it is important that those engaged in such work be attentive to the ways in which we do so, and to the effects that our modes of critique have. I truly believe that we should augment the current debates with more vivid descriptions and narratives of the 'other' parts of the movements and point to their histories, ideas and perspectives as relevant in their own right. And that we should emphasise the fact that in spite of the official Forum's flaws, the occasion of Porte Alegre included a wide variety of interesting and important alternatives, and unexpected encounters and outcomes. We will then be giving not only a more accurate picture of the Forum and this movement, but we will also begin to pluralise the political categories and visions that currently constrain both our analyses and the ability of movement actors to communicate with one another on more equal grounds.

Notes

1. The relationship between neoliberalism as an economic process and a political one is key.
2. It is hard to speak of inside/outside the Forum with much exactness. Not only are there multiple potential parameters, a space might be 'within' the Forum in one sense but against and outside it in another. For example, 'Life after Capitalism' is slightly different from other radical spaces. Although critical of the Forum and its narrow view of politics, it too had a traditional panel form and sought to be housed within the official facilities of the Forum.
3. Notably, Intergalactika was named after the first Intercontinental Meeting against Neoliberalism and For Humanity. The meeting called for by the Zapatistas in 1996 was attended by representatives from over forty-three countries. In a way, the concept was quite similar to the Social Forums, though I have rarely heard them spoken of in relation to one another. In my mind this is another manifestation of how the one part of a movement, and its history, is seen as *the* only history. For more information on the first and second Intergalaktics see Holloway 1998a, as well as 1998b.
4. Grubacic 2003. Also in this volume.
5. Translated from the Hub listserv: a discussion listserv in which many of the critiques of the Forum were posted and hotly debated.
6. I do not mean to suggest that this is the only dimension of these actors' political visions or analyses. I focus on it because it serves to emphasise how what is taken to be 'merely' procedural, and logistical. by some, is in fact of utmost political relevance to others.
7. Whether or not this marginalisation was intended or the fault of the official Forum, is not something that I would like to address at this moment. I am personally of the opinion, (like Grubacic), that it was the combined effect of the myopia of the bureaucracy of the official Forum, and mistakes made by the organisers of the space, as well as a general chaos and confusion.
8. Even the term 'movement of movements' is a product of this!
9. Gibson-Graham 1996.
10. Perhaps it is true, as Boaventura de Sousa Santos says, that we need a new epistemology to assess experiences such as the WSF since the assessment will always be found wanting when gauged with established criteria.

Another (Also Feminist) World Is Possible: Constructing Transnational Spaces And Global Alternatives From The Movements

Sonia E Alvarez, with Nalu Faria and Miriam Nobré

The nineties are considered the decade in which feminist movements in Brazil, as well as in Latin America and other world regions, 'went global' or became transnationalised. Academic analyses typically explain this globalisation of feminisms in terms of the growing participation of sectors representing feminist movements in the hegemonic spheres of international politics, particularly the conferences or world summits sponsored by the United Nations during the same period.[2]

Without a doubt, the incursion of scores of feminists into these official spaces of global politics had a marked, and contradictory, impact on Latin American feminisms.[3] A wide spectrum of feminist reflections gathered together in a recent dossier on 'Feminisms and the World Social Forum' affirm, however, that 'other transnationalisms'—other processes and modalities of feminist activism that transcend the borders of the nation-state—also emerged *from the movements themselves*.[4] The articles in the dossier attest to the existence of multiple feminisms that have been constructing alternative and counter-hegemonic public spaces at the regional and global levels, in which new meanings, identities, transgressive practices, and forms of resistance and rebelliousness have been forged and fed back into the process.

The bulk of the essays analyse the participation and intervention of feminists, particularly those from Latin America, in one of the most recent, innovative and promising of these counter-hegemonic transnational spaces, and one of the first concrete expressions of the so-called 'anti-globalisation movement,' namely, the WSF. In order to contextualise this most recent form of feminist action in the space of the global movements, the dossier starts with a reflection on another transnational process, well prior to the WSF, which has been of the utmost importance to the development of the feminist movements in Brazil and all over Latin America: the region-wide feminist meetings (*encuentros*, or encounters) that took place during the eighties and the nineties.

Since the beginning of the eighties, as this first essay documents, Latin American feminists have been building networks of advocacy and activism *(militancia)*, weaving personal-political linkages and constructing regional identities and forms of solidarity through the Latin American and Caribbean Feminist *Encuentros*. These events have taken place every two to three years since the First *Encuentro* was convened in Bogotá, Colombia, in 1981, with the tenth edition scheduled to take place in Brazil in 2005.

The Latin American *Encuentros*, as well as the national meetings periodically organised in a number of countries, are places of dialogue, negotiation, coalition-building, conflict, and contestation *among women* who are self-proclaimed feminists or who in one way or another identify themselves, or seek to become closer to, feminism. In other words, these *Encuentros* are critical spaces where Latin American feminist activists exchange ideas, discuss strategies, and imagine utopias *among themselves*, along with 'other' feminists who—although belonging to different countries, social classes, ethnic and racial groups, age groups, or sexual preference, with the most diverse personal-political trajectories and involved in the broadest array of political practices—share visions of the world and declare their political commitments to a wide gamut of feminist and social justice struggles.

More than mere 'events' in the life of the movement, the *Encuentros* foster processes of both solidarity and contention among the region's feminists. They constitute a sort of supranational platform where key issues confronting Latin American feminisms can be staged, debated and (re)formulated. Among the most contentious axes of discussion have been: the meaning and practices of the movements' autonomy and 'institutionalisation'; the diversity and inequality among women and among feminists; and the relationship of different feminisms to other movements, particularly to the larger women's movement, political parties, the State, and the sphere of international policy making. Already at the Sixth *Encuentro*, held in 1993 in Costa del Sol (El Salvador), the involvement of many feminist NGOs and regional networks with dominant national and international political institutions, especially the UN processes, had become one of the most heated topics of debate.

In the second half of the nineties, the various '+5' UN conferences, intended as follow-up to the Rio, Vienna, Cairo, Copenhagen, and Beijing summits, made clear—even to many of those who most actively participated in such processes—that the feminist project of influencing official international spheres had yielded meagre concrete results. If it is true that it was possible to incorporate some of the elements (the most palatable) of the feminist agenda in the international accords and platforms of the nineties, it is also true that any possibility for more significant changes in the rights and life conditions of most women were in effect blocked by the intensification of neoliberal globalisation, the ever more dramatic rolling back of the State, structural adjustment processes, and the concomitant erosion of citizenship and social policies.

The obvious deficiencies of neoliberalism unleashed an innovative and dynamic resistance to the 'single thought' doctrine in Latin America in the most recent times. This resistance, which first appeared in the public eye with the Zapatista uprising of 1994, branching out and becoming broader and more diverse in the entire region during the last decade of the 20th century and the opening years of the 2000s, has included from the massive mobilisations of the MST, the continental articulation of indigenous and Afro-descendent peoples movements, and the neighbourhood assemblies *(asambleas barriales)* and the pickets of the unemployed *(piquetero)* movement in Argentina to the most recent confrontations between coca growers *(cocaleros)* and repressive forces in Bolivia. At the same time that the cycle of UN conferences was coming to a close and that the 'disenchantment' among many of those who had participated in these official processes was growing, there emerged a new global social force that found its point of articulation precisely in its radical opposition to the reigning global neoliberal regime—that is, the anti-globalisation movement or, as others would have it, the 'global justice and solidarity movement.' Many feminist activists were, from the very beginning, part of these ample, yet diffuse, new regional and global movements that found their most enduring expression in the WSF. Among the 112 regional or global organisations making up the International Council, nine are feminist networks.[5]

The 2003 WSF was organised around five axes: 1) democratic sustainable development; 2) principles and values, human rights, diversity and equality; 3) media, culture and counter-hegemony; 4) political power, civil society, and democracy; and 5) democratic world order, fight against militarism, and promoting peace. The second and fourth of these axes were organised by two feminist networks, The World March of Women against Poverty and Violence and the Marcosur Feminist Articulation, respectively. These thematic axes functioned as parameters for the registration of participants and seminars by hundreds of entities participating in the WSF. There were 1,286 self-organised activities at the 2003 Forum. Public demonstrations and cultural activities have been growing with each successive Forum, introducing new languages to the Forum debates.

Along with a broad and heterogeneous gamut of movements, NGOs, and networks of all imaginable types, the Forum saw the confluence of the most diverse expressions of Latin American and global feminism. Feminists, like activists from other social movements, arrived at the Forum in large numbers and with enormous, albeit not always convergent, expectations about the WSF.[6] In such a wide and diverse space/process as the Forum, important political and strategic differences and divergences were evident among participants. Even if united in their opposition to the most egregious effects of neoliberal globalisation, participants at the WSF espouse the most diverse, and at times antagonistic, visions and strategies about how to combat those effects; these range from those who seek to 'democratise' the World Bank, the IMF, or WTO to those who want to 'nix them'; from NGOs and networks that 'negotiate' with national and international public policy arenas to groups and movements that reject and 'expose' these official spaces while advocating for radical structural transformations; from those who promote 'other globalisations'—more horizontal and based on solidarity—among the planet's peoples to those who prefer to strengthen national sovereignty or that of their peoples and ethnic groups; from those who defend mobilisation and direct action against global capitalism to those who persist in lobbying and advocacy strategies; from sectarian positions advocating *one* other world all the way to those who defend the notion that many other worlds are possible or that want to foster another world where, as the Zapatistas put it, many worlds can fit. All of these positions and many others—that oscillate between the more polarised ones above—meet each other at the Forum, dialogue, debate, diverge, and sometimes articulate tactics and strategies in common agreement.

Needless to say, these agreements and differences also characterise feminist engagements with the WSF process. The collaborators in the dossier, who include feminist activists from Argentina, Uruguay, Ecuador, Italy, Canada and Brazil, are unanimous in affirming that the WSF is an indispensable space of action for the feminisms. For Uruguayan Lilian Celiberti and Peruvian Virginia Vargas, from the Marcosur Feminist Articulation, the WSF "has become a space of confluence of the struggles and proposals of movements, organisations, networks, campaigns, and multiple actors who have assumed this space as their own, developing new perspectives for a utopian imagination, something which had been almost completely lost in the social horizon of the last decades." "To me it seems a cauldron where all the elements necessary for the construction of a better world find a place," proclaims Brazilian Maria Edinalva Bezerra Lima from the Brazilian Workers' Union Central, CUT. They all concur with the fact that, as Canadian Dianne Matte (Coordinator of the World March of Women) suggests, feminist participation in the WSF process is fundamental to tighten "the relations between the feminist movement and the movement for another globalisation, and to inscribe our priorities in it and strengthen the possibilities for a real social transformation." "Another world, without feminism," Matte insists, 'is impossible.' And Uruguayan Lucy Garrido, from the journal, *Cotidiano Mujer* and the Marcosur Feminist Articulation, states that, "we want the feminist agenda (symbolic-cultural subversion, sexual rights, equity) to become an integral component of the agenda for economic justice and the deepening of democracy."

For Ecuadorean Irene León from ALAI (Latin American Information Agency), the WSF represents an unparalleled opportunity to construct and consolidate alliances not only among feminists but, principally, between the feminisms and the forces of the world movement for another kind of globalisation. As she says, "the participation of the movement in the making of alliances and in the creation of critical discourses and new proposals is a necessary effort if we want the vision of a different world to be inclusive and have a gender perspective." At the same time, Nadia Du Mond, from the World March of Women in Italy, points out that, "the expansion of the WSF at the regional and continental level enabled the creation of international spaces of encounter and articulation which the women's movements would have had difficulty finding under other circumstances"; she also observes that the Forum process has fostered the growth of feminism, given that many young women and other women who "had become activists in all kinds of mixed movements along the road from Seattle or Porto Alegre looked for the first time with interest at the presence of a feminist component, becoming interested in a gender approach in relation to their own sphere of engagement." For Brazilian Júlia Ruiz de Giovanni, one of these young feminists, the young women who participated in the Forum "are the bearers of a renovated feminism since they have to respond continuously to the historical challenges that arise today not only for feminism but also for the ensemble of emancipatory projects for which the 'movement of movements' pretends to be the channel of convergence."

Beyond these points of convergence, of course, lie differences of approach, emphasis, and strategy among those feminists who come together at the WSF. First, similarly to other participants in the Forum process, feminists also encompass a broad spectrum of positions on the best way to face and combat neoliberal globalisation in general and its devastating impact on women's lives in particular. Second, feminists also differ in relation to the strategies that are best suited to promote alliances with other social forces who participate in the Forum process and to ensure that the questions that are central to the feminisms become an integral part of those 'other worlds' envisioned by the new global movements.

As the essay by Argentineans Silvia Chejter and Claudia Laudano suggests, for example, from the Second WSF, there have been significant differences between those feminists that insist on the need for an autonomous space *(espacio propio)* with its own programme within the WSF, on the one hand— "a space of encounter, debate, creativity, artistic expression, embodied activities, and circulation of information on themes such as health, development, sexuality, environment, theology, and violence, all of them approached from a women's perspective"; and, on the other, those feminists who place their bets on achieving a more effective political insertion in all of the Forum spaces. Arguing that, "a parallel women's Forum, following the format of the civil society events at the UN conferences," is not the best feminist strategy for the WSF, the Ecuadorian Magdalena León T, from the Latin American Network of Women Transforming the Economy, proposes that, "this does not mean that women do not need their own spaces, nor that the Forum is lived as in an ideal world of equality, but that here we are dealing with a qualitatively different process...it is a collective and solidarity effort where power—in its institutional and formal meaning—is not exerted or struggled over and where feminism can occupy a central role in the advancement of its utopias and proposals, which are of a radical and global character." Others, however, such as Brazilian Maria Betânia Avila from SOS-Corpo and the Brazilian Women's Articulation, state that unequal power relations "still shape this political space in movement," insisting that "as a form of thought and political practice, feminism forms part of such a construction (that is the Forum process), and part of that construction is the overcoming" of the inequalities that are manifested at the interior of the WSF and of those movements that make it up. For this author and for several others in this dossier, the WSF presents itself as "a space where feminisms find a productive *locus* to weave their alliances and ideas with other subjects, but also to act in the sense of demarcating feminism's contribution to a democratised form of politics." In this way, as Irene León suggests, feminist participation in the WSF faces "a double challenge: on one side, to break away from androcentric and ethnocentric visions and practices, in order to move towards all-inclusive kinds of ethics; on the other, to call on so-called issue-specific movements to widen the scope of their action and proposals so that they include the full set of social problematics in their approaches."

We hope that these thoughts and discussions will contribute to stimulating the debate on how to deal with this double challenge, and also will give greater visibility to feminist actions in alternative transnational spheres and to the contributions and interventions of the diverse expressions of feminism that participated in the first three Forums—in the events themselves as much as in the regional and global processes triggered and articulated through the WSF. Towards this, we asked our authors to address the following questions, on the basis of their specific perspectives and subject 'positionality': what does the WSF mean, as both event and process, for feminisms, especially for those in Latin America? What have been/should be the significance and contributions of the diverse feminisms to the Forum? Does the participation of feminisms in the Forum constitute a new or different form of action, insertion, intervention, or articulation in the international sphere? In particular, how could one compare this action with the regional feminist articulation in the *Encuentros* and with the feminist participation in the various preparatory processes for UN conferences and/or other official international processes?

We attempted to secure reflections that could account for the widest possible range of feminist networks that have participated in the WSF, both Latin American and global. The various voices are all militant feminists who developed their feminist practice in various countries and regional and global articulations and/or speak from different feminist places: from the feminisms of the new generations, of labour unions, NGOs, activist and advocacy networks, and so forth. Without pretending to be representative of the vast gamut of feminist positions at play in the WSF, these voices hope to contribute to a debate and a process that are still under construction. The debate on the feminisms and the Forum will continue in Mumbai with the realisation of the Fourth WSF, and also in all of those spaces where the most diverse forms of resistance to neoliberal globalisation are articulated on a daily basis.

Notes

1. Essay authored by Sonia E. Alvarez based on the introduction to a dossier on "Feminisms and the World Social Forum" edited by Sonia E Alvarez, Nalu Faria and Miriam Nobre, in a special issue of *Revista Estudos Feministas* (*Journal of Feminist Studies*), Brazil, Volume 11, No. 2, 2003. Translation by Arturo Escobar from Portuguese. The issue is available online at www.portalfeminista.org.br and <http://www.scielo.br scielo.php?script=sci_serial&pid=0104-026X&lng=en&nrm=iso>. Arturo Escobar translated this version from the Portuguese. Contributing authors to the Dossier include : Maria Betânia Ávila, SOS-Corpo and Articulação de Mulheres Brasileiras in Brazil; Ericka Beckman, Stanford University, USA; Maria Edinalva Bezerra Lima of CUT, Brazil; Maylei Blackwell, University of California-Los Angeles, USA; Lilián Celiberti, Cotidiano Mujer and Articulação Feminista Marcosur, Uruguay; Silvia Chejter, Revista Travessia, Argentina; Norma Chinchilla, California State University-Long Beach, USA; Nadia De Monde, World March of Women, Italy; Elisabeth Jay Friedman, Barnard College, USA; Julia di Giovanni, SOF—Sempreviva Organização Feminista and World March of Women, Brazil; Nalu Faria, SOF—Sempreviva Organização Feminista and World March of Women, Brazil; Lucy Garrido, Cotidiano Mujer and Articulação Feminista Marcosur, Uruguay; Nathalie Lebon, Randolph Macon College, USA; Irene León and Magdalena León T, ALAI, Ecuador; Diane Matte, World March of Women; Marysa Navarro, Dartmouth College, USA; Miriam Nobre, SOF—Sempreviva Organização Feminista and World March of Women, Brazil; Marcela Ríos-Tobar, University of Wisconsin, Madison, USA. For a full set of references and bibliography, please see the Dossier.
2. For a sample of this literature, see Chen 1996; West 1999; O'Brien *et al* 2000; Keck and Sikkink 1998; and Meyer and Prugl 1999. For analyses that examine the inter-relation between local social movements and transnational activism, see Naples and Desai 2002; Friedman 1999; Alvarez 2000b; and Basu 2000.
3. For analyses of the engagement of some feminist sectors from Latin America in the process of UN conferences, see Clark, Friedman and Hoechstetler 1998; Friedman 2003; Alvarez 2000a; Olea Mauleón 1998; and Vargas 1998.
4. Alvarez, Faria, and Nobre, eds, 2003.
5. These are: Articulación Feminista Marcosur (Marcosur Feminist Articulation; mujeresdelsur @mujersur.org.uy, *www.mujeresdelsur.org.uy*); International Gender and Trade Network. secretariat@coc.org, <www.genderandtrade.net>; Red Latinoamericana Mulheres Transformando a Economia (Latin American Network of Women Transforming the Economy) mujerdialogo @prodigy.net.mx], <http://movimientos.org/remte>; Rede Dawn de Mulheres (Dawn Women's Network dawn@is.com.fj, www.dawn.org.fj); Rede Latino Americana e Caribenha de Mulheres Negras (Latin American and Caribbean Black Women Network criola @alternex.com.br, *www.criola.ong.org*); Rede Mulher e Habitat (Women and Habitat Network gem@agora.com.ar, <http://www.redmujer.org.ar>); Rede Mundial de Mulheres pelos Direitos Reprodutivos (World Network of Women for Rerpoductive Rights office@wgnrr.nl, <www.wgnrr.org>); REPEM–Rede de Educação Popular entre Mulheres (Popular Education Women's Network repem@repem.org.uy, www.repem.org.uy); World March of Women, www.ffq.qc.ca/marche2000/en/index.html, dmatte@ffq.qc.ca>
6. Other analyses of the participation of feminists in the WSF include León 2002; Faria 2003; Celiberti 2001; Rosemberg 2003.

How Open?

The Forum As Logo, The Forum As Religion: Scepticism Of The Intellect, Optimism Of The Will

Jai Sen

During the third world meeting of the World Social Forum in Porto Alegre in January 2003, a new initiative named 'WSF Itself' organised a workshop on power relations within the WSF. An exercise during the workshop required participants to imagine the kinds of policies that could be adopted that would kill—or certainly, cripple—the Forum. In its words, the 'toxics.' The idea was to reveal, through this exercise in intense negativism, what needed to not be done. But as a participant, I gradually became aware that the exercise gave me an insight into some of what is, in fact, already taking place but is not being 'read' given the positivist lenses through which we normally tend to see the world around us, including the Forum.[1]

In some senses, this essay is a continuation of that exercise, of trying to *read* the Forum.[2] I have written this essay because even as I celebrate the fact of the Forum and what it is doing, I also believe that there are several tendencies taking shape within it that are deeply negative and contradictory to its very spirit. Most centrally, they include the Forum becoming a commodity and a brand name and its motto a logo and the beginning of a kind of worldwide franchising; and an increasing struggle for its control. In large part this is happening because the very success of the WSF as an enterprise has, as Roberto Bissio put it, "created a power (and a value) around the logo, whether we like it or not. And this has to be recognised and acknowledged, since denial of reality would become manipulative."[3]

But the list goes deeper. Even if, in principle, it should be possible to address (and arrest) these trends, they are accompanied by other more structural factors. These include the related fact that the actually existing Forum is not the 'open space' that it is said to be, but is instead highly structured and, in several dimensions, exclusive. Among other features, the Forum—though declaring itself 'open'—is in reality 'open' only to particular sections: to those who already agree with certain policy formulations, which largely limit it to those who can broadly be said to be on 'the Left,' and beyond this, increasingly, to those who are willing to declare in writing their adherence to certain given policy formulations. The Forum also discriminates against individuals, as I explain subsequently. All this adds up to a rising dogmatism and an organisational fundamentalism that is a hallmark of old politics.

In short, we are already witnessing the crystallisation and rise not only of corporatism but also of *orthodoxy* and *dogma*, which I suggest constitutes a fundamental challenge to the future of the WSF. The WSF is showing distinct signs of behaving like a tightly controlled corporation, a movement, or an institutionalised religion. This is reflected by, among other things, a growing discourse of 'we' and 'they' in the WSF International Council and its counterpart bodies at national levels, such as the WSF India Organising Committee. The Forum is therefore gradually becoming a place *only* for gatherings of the committed and converted.

Even though I am deeply worried about what I see taking place in the Forum today, I still hold to my earlier argument that the crystallisation of the WSF is one of the more significant developments of the past many decades, and perhaps of the past century.[4] I therefore believe that all of us who share some or all of this position, need to urgently look at what needs to be done.

In this article, I attempt to both analyse what I see happening and make some suggestions for a more creative future. In particular, I propose that the Forum must recognise the fact of grey areas and open itself to those who are concerned about the empires it has chosen to challenge but may not yet have clear positions on them. To the opposite of weakening it, this can be one of its most significant contributions in today's world of growing fundamentalisms.

The Forum needs also to explicitly recognise that individuals play myriad roles in social life and transformation, and that modes of civil and political association are changing; and it must abandon the discriminatory policies it has institutionalised against them. Its central historical role must remain to encourage and enable free and open debate and not to overtly or covertly build a world movement of organisations of The Left. Those who are today concerned about the possibilities of movements taking over the Forum are, in fact, only moving in what in generic terms is the *same* direction, but via a different path; and the growing and almost knee-jerk reactions of some among the leadership to criticism and opposition, are only leading the Forum to lose its soul.

Fundamentals

I believe the primary significance of the Forum lies in the *political culture* it represents, and that its main contribution is in *political-strategic* terms. The Forum, as argued by those who initiated it, is not an organisation or a movement, nor a world federation, but a *space*—and to boot, a relatively non-directed space, from and within which movements and other civil initiatives of many kinds can meet, exchange views, and find space to take forward their work and their visions, locally, nationally, regionally, and globally. Literally, a free space, for free thought, where people can dream of other worlds, individually and collectively, and struggle to forge ways of achieving their dreams, or to use Marx's term, a 'space for human self-development.'

The original organisers of the Forum saw their task as being not the building of movement, or the co-ordination of opinion and position, but simply as the building of space—literally and metaphorically—where free exchange is possible, and as widely as possible. This is most resonantly expressed in the Forum's Charter of Principles.[5] A principal architect of the Forum has recently issued an interesting note reflecting on 'the Forum as space, the Forum as movement,' and has come out strongly against seeing the Forum—the space—as being primarily occupied by movements.[6]

The real 'success' of the Forum is that it is making possible a scale of talking across boundaries that has rarely been dreamt of before, and contributing to building a culture of open debate across conventional walls. The real 'alternative' it offers is showing that it is possible to create, and to sustain, a non-directed space. In my understanding, helping to *bridge* old politics and the new is arguably one of the most crucial but most difficult challenges for the Forum, and quite possibly also one of its historically most important.

The Forum, as it takes place, is thus a challenge not only to mainstream, orthodox, and conservative thinking and practice, but also to all those organisations and initiatives that claim to be working in terms of 'alternatives.' It implies, and requires, new cultures of politics. But this is precisely one of the areas where it is already showing signs of imploding.

The External Challenge

The growth of the WSF has to be understood in the backdrop of the world context. September 11 took place in the same year as the first Forum and gave to an impatient imperial power the opportunity to unleash its so-called 'war against terrorism,' to link it with the war for so-called 'free trade,' and for its President to declare that "Those who are not with us are against us." The numbers attending the Forum, which has explicitly opposed this war and this 'free trade,' have continued to dramatically grow, in spite of—and in the face of—this threat.

Two years later, and even though now increasingly challenged in terms of moral authority, capitalist globalisation is still riding triumphant across the globe even as the economy of its heart unravels from within. Nation-states across the world are relentlessly tightening 'security' and surveillance measures, supposedly in defence against those labelled terrorists but also aimed at protestors of state politics and market operations. There are also periodic signs that Europe is moving to the Right, and Hindu, Islamic, Christian, and Jewish fundamentalisms are rampant in different parts of the world, intertwining with variants of economic fundamentalism. And in 2003 we have seen the 'coalition of the coerced' defiantly launch its war on Iraq in the face of world opinion, as an obvious widening of the reach of its empire.

Equally, other 'coalitions of the coerced' are also pushing hard—to bring in the FTAA (Free Trade Agreement of the Americas), to open all of the Americas to "free trade" and to bring in major changes at the WTO. If their efforts succeed, the results will represent major advances in the neoliberal project. In all this—all done in the name of freedom, the deep shadows of imperialism and authoritarianism are evident.[7]

Certain developments in India have been equally discouraging. In early 2002, India experienced a brutal anti-Muslim pogrom in the state of Gujarat. Later in the same year, voters of the state returned to power, with a landslide victory, the Bharatiya Janata Party (BJP), the party that is widely seen as having been responsible for the communal violence, and its neo-fascist Chief Minister. In late 2003, the same party won elections in three more states in north India, routing its opponents. These remain crucial developments even if elections in the bitterly contested and brutalised state of Kashmir in late 2002 yielded a new, moderate government, and during 2003, the Congress (I), a more centrist party, won state elections in another state and also in the small state of Delhi, within which the capital is located. Although public and international reaction to the Gujarat experiment forced the BJP to move to taking a more centrist stance after the pogrom, the shadows of fascism still threaten India since its allied 'popular' organisations see Gujarat as a model for what should happen in the rest of the country. If this were to take place, it would have worldwide repercussions.

Against this grim scene, the developments in Brazil and in global transnational space over this past year have been encouraging. In 2002, the Brazilian presidential elections brought Lula, the leader of the Workers' Party to the Presidency. Among many other initiatives, Lula has stressed that his government's foreign policy sees the building of relations across the South as a key element, and especially with three major countries—South Africa, India, and China.

The massive and sustained demonstrations across the North over the past few years, along with demonstrations in many countries of the South, and the growing sense of self-confidence of global civil movement, have also been important indications of another politics and of other possibilities. The recent toppling of the President in Bolivia by a popular movement is a dramatic suggestion that new barriers are being broken.

How does the Forum fit into all this? Most importantly perhaps, the WSF has struck at the level of *meaning:* along with the struggle that is still emerging across the globe against neoliberal globalisation, it has made resonantly clear that the TINA (There Is No Alternative) dictum does not hold good, and that there *is* world wide resistance to neoliberal globalisation and its attendant depredations; and that there *are* alternatives. The challenge for the Forum is now to envision how to relate to today's extraordinarily fluid and volatile context, and how it can most effectively realise the potential of a world transformative power that it seems to be gathering. It needs to consider what role(s) it can play in translating these possibilities into real social and political alternatives; how, to use Teivo Teivainen's terminology, to remain primarily an arena, and not become a leading actor.[8] This ambiguity of identity and role has been its strength, and a secret of its magic, as is the case with many social and political actors. But it is going to have to re-invent itself, as it constantly tends to become more an actor than an arena.

An important indication of how the WSF is working to both globalise itself and to relate to the wider world situation is its decision to hold its next world meeting in India—on the continent where imperial interests have now so decisively landed.[9]

The Internal Challenge

But aside from this major 'external' challenge, there are several *internal* challenges that also demand its attention. In the pages that follow, I discuss these challenges in terms of a series of descriptive metaphors intended to highlight particular problems.[10]

The Forum as Market, the Forum as Alienation

As many others have pointed out, despite all its other virtues, the Forum is becoming an *alienating* event suffering from giganticism.[11] It has become a place of a thousand events, but with too few transversal connections, and not a real meeting of minds. This problem also arises from the undeclared emphasis in the Forum on individualised, separate initiative, and from the lack of prioritisation given to the collective and to sharing, among participants, and among organisers and participants.

In the theorisation of the Forum as 'open space,' the basic but undeclared assumption is that if people come together in a large open space, they will necessarily interact. To a substantial extent, this does seem to be happening. This 'self-organisation,' individually and collectively, is increasingly seen to be the strength and the magic—of the Forum.[12] But individuals and organisations belonging to particular streams of thought and action, or coming from different cultures and language-groups, also tend to stick together, especially in large, overwhelming experiences such as the Forum, unless major efforts are made by the organisers to help participants to overcome the differences. One consequence is that large numbers of events are therefore in reality not 'open,' because of language problems, and that in reality most events happen autonomously with little or no exchange of content.

Although the Brazil Organising Committee has had volunteer translators and helpdesks available in many parts of the Forum and crucial information available in several languages, and from the January 2003 meeting is now also developing a post facto 'systematisation' (documentation) of events,[13] there have so far been no arrangements for real-time transverse sharing of ideas. The International Secretariat does not even respond to suggestions that it should consider creating a discussion space on the Forum's website. While there is reason to argue that this sharing best happens through spontaneous self-organised initiatives, this is no reason for not making any such provisions at all, and becomes a case in point of the emphasis in the Forum on *private enterprise* and the lack of prioritisation given to *the collective*.

Although there are some signs that this might be changing, these tendencies have been only accentuated by the tendency of the organisers, both in Brazil and India, to *control* things: by making closed-door decisions about key organisational issues, by reserving 'sensitive' roles to its own members (such as who takes part in roundtable discussions with political parties), and tending to act as a vanguard and politburo.[14] Equally, as Naomi Klein and others have pointed out, the Forum is also increasingly coming to be dominated by 'big events' and big names.[15] All these factors emphasise a certain culture that 'separates out' participants and produces alienation, tending to make events discrete and isolated rather than a meeting of minds that the Forum has the potential of being.

The Forum as an Event, not World Process

This problem of alienation, disintegration, and commodification is reproducing itself on a world scale. The WSF started off as an event in January 2001. Inspired by its success, the Brazil Organising Committee (BOC) had the foresight to say, in the Charter of Principles they drafted for the Forum just three months later in April 2001, that, "The World Social Forum at Porto Alegre was an event localised in time and place. From now on, in the certainty proclaimed at Porto Alegre that 'another world is possible,' *it becomes a permanent process of seeking and building alternatives*, which cannot be reduced to the *events* supporting it."[16] And when the BOC formed the International Council (IC) in June 2001, it had the vision to see that the main purpose of the Council was to, "take the Forum to the world level."[17] Consistent with this vision, the IC decided at its meeting in Porto Alegre in January 2002, to give a call for the organisation of 'regional' and 'thematic' forums from 2002 onwards.

A series of such meetings have now taken place—the Asian Social Forum, the first and second European Social Forums, the World Social Thematic Forum on Democracy, Human Rights, War, Drug Trafficking (held in Colombia), and others. But while it is good to see and understand this flowering as a manifestation of the globalisation of the WSF, each event is taking place in an isolated way. Although this again seems to be changing in small ways through the 'systematisation' process, as well as the working groups that the International Council is increasingly working through, between events—there seems as yet all too little or no exchange of experience, of strategy, of information, and no larger culture of being an international political process.

A small but encouraging sign in this area has been a shift in the Forum's language. As opposed to earlier, when the term 'the World Social Forum' was reserved exclusively for the event each January, the International Secretariat is now referring to *all* WSF-related meetings as 'World Social Forums' in the plural, which is what some of us have been calling them for the past two years. But this remains a long way from achieving a large composite vision of the whole, and of its politics. One of the most important roles that the Forum is playing is providing a space where old movement and new movement, as well as other actors, can meet and speak. The task of the WSF as actor—here, as manifested in the International Secretariat and the International Council—therefore needs to be one of moving past organising big events to one of joining the struggle for forging a new vocabulary and grammar of world politics and of looking beyond the Forum as a *world event* to seeing it as a *world process*.

The Forum as Temple

How open is the Forum? Or, is the Forum, in fact, already highly mediated and structured at a number of levels, and further demarcated and gradually closed down, as happens in religion as it gets institutionalised?

The Forum's Charter of Principles says, "The meetings of the WSF are *always open to all those who wish to take part in them*, except organisations that seek to take people's lives as a method of political action" (Clause 11, emphasis mine). In this section, I am concerned not with the second part of this clause but with the first, the assertion of openness.

For Fisher and Ponniah (editors of the first major English language book on the WSF), the WSF is "not a social movement in and of itself. It's an open forum, and in that there's a commitment to its openness, to the participatory nature of it, to *open democracy*. That's the key convergence."[18] This is the fundamental working assumption of participants at the Forum, the idea that it is best known for, and the idea that many researchers and observers most celebrate it for: a culture of openness. But it is precisely because this is such a fundamental aspect of what the Forum is about that we need to look at this question in some detail.

In his thought-provoking recent paper that I have already referred to, Chico Whitaker has compared the open space to a 'square' (*praça* in Portuguese) clarifying that this is "an open but not a neutral space," and is open (only) to those "that oppose neoliberalism...For this reason, in order to join the square, one must agree with its Charter of Principles."[19]

Samir Amin, one of the founders of the 'Anti-Davos meeting' in January 2000 and a member of the WSF International Council, emphatically underlines this when he says that the Forum is "*...not a forum that is open to everybody.* It has a charter to which participating organisations *must adhere*. They *must make it clear* that they are opposed to neoliberalism, not necessarily to capitalism. They *must also be opposed* to militarisation of globalisation—not necessarily imperialism, which means much more."[20]

It is clear from this that the architects of the Forum have themselves never intended that the Forum should be *fully* open. Notwithstanding the formal provision in Clause 11 of the Charter, in reality, it is *only* open to those who have clear positions on certain issues. Exploring Whitaker's metaphor a little further, we also need to recognise that no space that is created by someone ever exists by itself, uncontrolled. Just as all squares and *praças* have historically been and still are produced by someone—religious institutions, a feudal power, a landowner, and more recently, an institution of State or the market (and sometimes but rarely, of popular power)—so has the 'open space' that is the Forum. In this case, the 'square' that is the Forum has been created by the BOC, and is maintained by the IC.

Similarly, just as institutions have rules of their own, in the case of the WSF, the Charter of Principles are the rules. More local interpretations provide even more specific rules, such as the 'WSF *India* Policy Statement' that was generated in India during 2002, modifying the Charter of Principles somewhat to suit local conditions.[21] These rules specify who is and is not welcome in the space, and either openly or covertly suggest the use of force to ensure that the rules are observed. The debate presently going on within the WSF about the role and possible dominance of social movements is a case in point, and it is this that has led Chico Whitaker to produce his recent note, as above, which specifically cautions against the Forum being "turned into" a movement.

Aside from rules as to who is and is not welcome to use the space, are also the important questions of position, the drawing of boundaries, and the tolerance (or intolerance) of grey areas and of internal contradictions. For instance, even while declaring elsewhere that it is "open to all," Clause 1 of the Charter of Principles makes clear that the WSF is, in fact, restricted—that it is a space (only) for:

> ...groups and movements of civil society *that are opposed to neoliberalism and to domination of the world by capital and any form of imperialism*, and are committed to building a planetary society centred on the human person.[22]

If the Forum is indeed restricted to only those who already have a clear and defined position, how can it be considered to be 'open'?

This is not only a moral and ethical question, but also a deeply political and strategic one. Can the struggle against neoliberalism be won only by those—and we remain a minority—who have already taken committed positions against it? In this struggle, as in any other, is it not necessary, at the minimum, to engage with those who are less sure of their positions on the issue (likely to be the vast majority), and to try and win them over—as well as to listen to their arguments to deepen our own analysis and strategy?

A related argument applies to another important clause of the Charter of Principles regarding armed groups. As earlier noted, Clause 11 says, "The meetings of the WSF are always open to all those who wish to take part in them, *except organisations that seek to take people's lives as a method of political action*." I am here concerned with the second part of the Clause. There have been concrete cases where this provision has been applied—where groups who have been judged to be of this character, and even supporters of such movements, have been denied access to the 'open space' that the Forum is said to be.[23]

While a literal interpretation of this provision ("organisations that seek ...of political action") may be acceptable as a boundary for such an initiative, it is tending to be applied equally to those who allow that it might be sometimes necessary for movements to use violence. But there are clearly contexts in which this question of violence in political action is grey, such as in the context of national liberation, resistance against oppression, self-defence or defence of common property, such as forests for forest dwellers. What the Forum is therefore doing is the classic 'conflation' in human rights discourse: in its opposition to "the use of violence as a means of social control by the State" (Clause 10), it is equating this to the actions of movements and individuals, in *all* circumstances.

Again, and especially given the mission it has taken up, is it not necessary for the Forum to, at the minimum, provide space that allows exchange with such groups ? And on the other hand, what is the strategic purpose of closing the Forum to such exchange?

Over the past six months, the leadership of the WSF has taken some strong policy decisions in this area that have only reinforced the status quo. In India, it has already reached the stage where those wishing to become members of the newly formed 'India General Council' must first sign a form declaring their adherence to the Forum's Charter of Principles. This development might be viewed by some as being merely an aberration. I believe however, that it reflects a deep-seated culture that is coming to the surface as the menu of the now 'global' Forum is interpreted locally.

In June 2003, the IC of the WSF also took a decision to precisely this effect, requiring written declarations of adherence for all those who wish to become members of the IC. Consistent with this, the online form for registering events at the Mumbai Forum requires those applying to declare 'Yes/No' as to whether they are willing to adhere to the Forum's Charter. This extraordinary requirement is clearly coercive in nature. The consequence for those who have dared to say 'No' remains to be seen—and should be closely analysed by those undertaking the systemisation of the Forum.

In sum, the World (Social Forum) is being rendered in black and white, with no spaces for shades of grey. If this is so, what is the difference between the Forum and any other ideologically driven organisation, such as a political party or an organised religion? There are many signs that the WSF is fast becoming a *closed* space, reserved for the committed and converted alone. And that 'the Forum' is becoming a party or institutionalised religion with its own leaders, priests and congregation.

In a major paper earlier this year, analysing the dynamics of the Forum, Boaventura de Sousa Santos put forward the important proposition that conventional social and political processes create 'absences,' through marginalisation and exclusion, and that a 'sociology of absences' is required if one wishes to understand them in terms of their full meaning and in order to "explain that what does not exist is in fact actively produced as non-existent." He went on to argue that the WSF itself "is a broad exercise of the sociology of absences."[24] I venture however to suggest that the Forum too is creating absences by virtue of the political culture it is increasingly tending to practice.

Indeed, notwithstanding Santos' radical analysis of the Forum, it is noticeable that the Forum is not, as yet, the arena of spontaneous choice of victims of violence, of oppression, of history. Both in India and Brazil, many of the mainstream organisations of the excluded—such as of indigenous peoples —are as yet keeping away, and many of those who come to the Forum to give testimony to their oppression come because they are brought there by issue-based civil organisations. As I see it, this is happening because the Forum is an initiative that still belongs mostly to the middle class, middle and upper caste, and male leadership of the 'civil,' 'present' world. Insofar as it has taken a position against oppression and imperialism of all kinds, the possibility that it may well be causing 'absences' is something that the Forum needs to consider.

This question has now moved into a new dimension. WSF India took a resolution at its last National Consultation in April 2003, expressing its opposition to what we in India and South Asia term 'fundamentalism' (extremism), caste discrimination, communalism, patriarchy, war and militarism, as well as to neoliberal globalisation.[25] As a direct consequence of this Resolution, the WSF India Organising Committee adopted and proposed all these five as 'axes' for the world meeting at Mumbai in January 2004.[26]

Apparently after considerable debate at its June 2003 meeting in Miami about the arguable cultural particularity of some formulations, the IC gave the go-ahead to WSF India to use these themes for the world meeting. In principle therefore, and even if all these new formulations have not yet been formally incorporated into the WSF Charter of Principles, the IC has taken the first step of accepting this much-widened vocabulary as the *Forum's* vocabulary: for the world meeting in Mumbai will, after all, be seen as 'The *World* Social Forum' speaking, not just WSF India. This widened vocabulary will enter world language in an important way.

There are different ways of looking at this development, however. On the one hand, from the point of view of progressive movements in many parts of Asia, possibly also more widely, this widening of the vocabulary of the WSF constitutes a major advance. Sections of the Dalit movement in India for example, have struggled hard to bring caste onto the international agenda, and succeeded in doing so through the Durban conference on Racism, Xenophobia, and Other Forums of Discrimination.

For the issue to be accepted at another world initiative such as the WSF is another major step forward, similarly, for those fighting religious and national fundamentalism and for those fighting patriarchy—even if women's groups have succeeded in bringing patriarchy to the world stage much earlier.

The big question is whether the leadership of the WSF will be willing to formally include these new issues in its Charter of Principles. Aside from the question of ruling out debate with those who hold different opinions, the Charter of Principles at present takes a position only on neoliberalism and imperialism. In world politics, the WSF Charter of Principles focusses on these because the initiative was conceived, born, and given shape during the rise of global civil action against the WTO and the Bretton Woods institutions.

But since that time, new questions have emerged on the world scene, such as war. So far, the Brazil Organising Committee/International Secretariat and the IC have shown themselves to be remarkably quick in terms of embracing the issues of war and militarisation, by centre-staging these in the agenda of the Forum, although they have not yet formally modified the Charter of Principles accordingly.

The issues of religious nationalism, communalism, caste, and patriarchy have not yet entered the Forum's vocabulary despite their having been specifically articulated in IC meetings and elsewhere.[27] This non-acceptance could be seen as being nothing more than a reflection of dominance in the Council by regions where these issues are not strong (the first three, in any case). The Council's willingness to handle these essentially cultural issues will be an important indicator of the degree to which the Forum is an open space.

On the other hand, lies the question of strategy—and of the ironic possibility that accepting this wider agenda might work to make the Forum an even more exclusive space. As above, if the WSF is truly to be a world initiative, then it is only appropriate that it embraces this more comprehensive agenda. But if this wider agenda is accepted into the Charter, then the WSF will become a space for:

> ...groups and movements of civil society that are opposed to ... imperialist globalisation, militarism, patriarchy, communalism (religious sectarianism and fundamentalism), and casteism and racism (oppression, exclusion and discrimination based on descent and work), and are committed to building a planetary society centred on the human person.

This in turn, will mean that all those who wish to take part in the Forum, and more specifically, to play any role in the decision-making bodies of the Forum, will need to declare their opposition to all of the above—and in writing. This is no longer a hypothetical possibility. WSF India already requires those wishing to join its 'India General Council' to declare adherence to this full spectrum.[28]

The Forum as Real Estate

There is one further dimension of 'openness'—or closure—that demands discussion by itself: the question of the openness of the Forum to *individuals*. Notwithstanding the Forum's assertion and reputation of being 'open,' participants in the WSF meetings held in Porto Alegre have so far been divided into two broad categories: organisational representatives, who have been classified when registering as 'delegates,' and individuals, who have been classified as 'Observers' (or 'Hearers'). This is also more or less the proposal for the WSF world meeting in 2004, in Mumbai.[29]

This division is also reflected in the organisational structure of the Forum. I do not know the rules for the organising committee for the European Social Forum, but the WSF India Committees and the WSF International Council are made up exclusively of the first 'class.' But in insisting upon this formula, are the organisers of the Forum only creating divisive social relations, and thereby again, in effect, acting towards closing down the 'open' space? And insofar as we today live in an age where classical 'organisations' are increasingly being replaced by virtual organisations and networks, where people are increasingly *not* belonging to organisations but preferring to work as individuals perhaps loosely affiliated, is this approach not also following obsolete organisational theory and strategy?

It is a fact that the Forum's Charter of Principles as it stands, provides space only for organisations and not individuals ("The World Social Forum brings together and interlinks only organisations and movements of civil society from all the countries in the world..."). While the Forum is declared to be an 'open space,' in reality, the organisers have therefore created two 'classes' for access to and use of the space. There are some who have the legitimacy to participate, and there are others who are only meant to 'observe' and to 'hear.' In actual practice and as implied even in the term, the rule about 'Observers' is not completely exclusive. It 'only' means that they do not have full privileges, such as (in Porto Alegre) being eligible to have translation headsets, or the right of access to all meetings. And they are given identity plaques—to be hung around their necks—of a different colour, so that they can be easily identified. By contrast, this division was absent at the Youth Camp at Porto Alegre, where the difference between 'organisational representatives' and 'individuals' was apparently ignored.[30]

According to one of the architects of the Forum, the thinking behind this discrimination is 'to push organised people to come (forward) and to avoid transforming the Forum into a traditional congress.'[31] Beyond this, the thinking behind not having individuals on committees is that the committees should be made up only of organisations fighting neoliberalism—since 'who do individuals represent?' In short, it is organisations that 'represent' society, and therefore are and should be the vanguard of change in society. The formation of the IC as it stands essentially reflects this wider thinking, which has now come to dominate thinking in India as well, after a brief one year when we thought more freely.

I suggest that this marginalisation of individuals is a reflection and manifestation of two closely related forces: a deep belief in the primacy of organisations (and especially of movements) in social change, and a subliminal reassertion of property relations—here, in terms of the ownership of the open space that the Forum is meant to be. In terms of the latter, the unstated and undeclared structure of the Forum is that organisations *are* the owners of the space that is the Forum. This is never openly said, but is the underlying theory and reality. But I suggest that it is precisely this attitude and unstated ideology that underlies the struggle and debate that continues and is sharpening in the Forum, regarding understanding the Forum as space or seeing it as movement.[32] Because the Forum is now real estate.

In terms of the former, the primacy of organisations, even while recognising the importance of organisations in social processes, we need to be willing to recognise and acknowledge the significance of the many roles that individuals play, perhaps especially in civil organisations. To start with, many such organisations, are in fact, built around particular individuals, and even if those individuals claim to be representing 'their' organisations, they often actually act largely as proprietors, representing their own interests as much as those of their organisations and its members. So the distinction between organisational representatives and individuals is often thin.

Civil organisations also generally practice some degree of voluntarism on the part of those working in them. Beyond this, in this day and age, we know that the vast majority of people in most societies across the world do not belong to formal organisations, and are, to the contrary, increasingly associating informally and often only temporarily, such as through myriad networks. This has historically been the case because the majority of sections has been forced to remain 'unorganised,' but is increasingly now the case for those who could, in principle, be within organisations but who prefer a higher form of being organised, of living and acting autarchically. In such a situation, and at such a time in history, can we still argue that formally organised, permanent organisations are and should be the vanguard of society? In short, do we believe that organisations represent the *only* vehicle for the self-development of human potential and of the social individual?[33]

In some ways, it can be said that the history of organisational development—in general, and also those with emancipatory and transformative goals—has been one of simultaneously developing and articulating both individual and collective social identities (class, caste, ethnicity, language, race, and gender, and more recently, sexual preference), and through this, of cultures and structures of authentic representation. In today's conditions, this is intersecting with another trajectory, of more highly *individualised* emancipation and empowerment, and of the building of virtual identities and cultures, of 'imagined communities' (to use and extend Benedict Anderson's phrase).[34] As Naomi Klein, among others, has pointed out, the global civil movement emerging today in many ways mirrors and models itself on the net.[35] Whether it does so consciously or not is not the question.

As I see it, these two trajectories—of formal, permanent, and putatively representative *organisation*, and informal and transient *association*—are to some extent working with different purposes, and the Forum is an arena where the two paths cross. Even while, as I have argued above and elsewhere, the Forum has a vital role to play in providing a space for different modes of movement to meet and carry out a dialogue, what is crucial for our analysis is that the WSF itself is a part of this new phenomenon—of transient association. So we need to reconcile these two different 'memberships,' constituencies and realities that make up the actually existing Forum—and most crucially, we need not insist that the rules of one trajectory must be the rules of the whole.

In formal terms, although the Forum's Charter of Principles declares that it does not intend to be "a body representing world civil society" (Clause 5), the reality today is that in many ways, this is *precisely* how the International Council is structured, with old rules of formation, and where movement organisations, which overtly 'represent' large masses of people, are increasingly privileged. 'The Forum' today is trapped within a vision of seeing itself as an 'organisation,' and there are now strong calls for it to create a more federal structure for itself.[36]

Finally, by excluding or marginalising individuals, the Forum is also marginalising a huge and vital section of societies in the world and weakening the larger movement against neoliberalism, imperialism, and fundamentalisms of all kinds. This is especially so in those countries of the world which do not enjoy electoral democracy or the freedom to associate and organise, and where it is individuals who often play the most vital roles in building and protecting democracy.

The Forum as Logo

My final point: as the Forum spreads across the world, there is a distinct possibility that it is fast becoming a commodity, a brand name, a monoculture, and its motto, 'Another World Is Possible!' a logo, and that the 'regional' and thematic events are becoming *franchised* events.[37] If this is at all the case, then the

WSF is itself becoming corporatised—and is thereby contributing to the globalisation of a certain, very specific civilisation—a monoculture. This is surely deeply problematic ground for an initiative such as the WSF that overtly celebrates plurality.[38]

The organisers of the Porto Alegre Forum, the BOC (now called the International Secretariat), have come up with a very particular vocabulary for the organisation of the WSF.[39] Despite initial discussions within WSF India towards coming up with a more indigenous formula, this menu is being more or less duplicated at the Mumbai Forum. The International Secretariat continues to struggle with this formula however, sometimes creatively. It has, for instance, come up with the proposal that the conferences, which earlier used to be at the centre of the Forum and dominated the event (and where this design was replicated at, say, the Asian Social Forum), should now be at the margins, and the self-organised events should be brought organisationally to the centre.[40] The WSF India Committee has taken this idea to heart and further reduced the proportion of events at the Forum that will be organised by the WSF itself, thereby further emphasising the self-organised events.[41]

There is now already something of a standard formula that has also developed for peripheral events, even within three years. In Porto Alegre, there was a World Youth Forum, a World Parliamentary Forum, a World Forum of Mayors and Local Authorities, and a World Education Forum that are held along with the WSF. There were rallies and marches, and the obligatory formal parts of the menu are the colourful inauguration and closing ceremonies. The problem is that since the Porto Alegre Forum is widely seen as having been 'successful,' this menu is now being widely copied, and there is much reason to think that this *menu* is tending to become standard, as a kind of recipe for success—for replicating the richness, vigour, and flavour of Porto Alegre. There is also the difficult reality that precisely because the Forum has so far been 'successful,' this has created a power and value to it, and so there is now struggle for control over it as it spreads. This is as true of the European Social Forum as of the Asian Social Forum.[42] The fact that the Forum has declared through its Charter that it "intends neither to be a body representing world civil society" (Clause 5), and that it "does not constitute a locus of power to be disputed by the participants in its meetings" (Clause 8), cannot prevent it, if it is successful, from accumulating power.

But this is what creating a brand is all about, and why and how franchising comes about; and even if this may be somewhat exaggerating the situation, there now seems to be a distinct possibility of the Forum becoming a world chain, with a *standard* recipe, and The Forum—the event—something that comes out of a cookie-cutter; and where particular interests start developing local control over the product. Can the day be far off when someone suggests that patenting the Forum's motto 'Another World Is Possible!' just in case someone else tries using it?

The Forum is also catching. Besides the regional and thematic fora mentioned earlier, there are now city-level forums all over Brazil, in several parts of Europe and the U.S., and state-level forums in parts of India and surely elsewhere as well. On the one hand, it is exciting to see all this as a part of the globalisation of the WSF. At another level we have to ask ourselves: is what is taking place a spreading of the *culture* of the Forum, along with creative local re-interpretation, or is it more a reproduction of the *outer* form, the menu?

The Forum and the Challenge of History

Two points remain to be made. One, as I said earlier: I believe that helping to bridge old politics and the new, in different countries and historical contexts and also in transnational space but at the same time in history is one of the most crucial but most difficult challenges for the Forum, and possibly also one of its historically most important.[43] If we agree that the larger struggle is the war of ideas, then one can reasonably argue that the Forum must move from focussing on exchange among the converted to progressively opening up to the non-converted. It must also open itself up to those who live outside established political channels, such as migrants and refugees, and also to the huge 'uncivil societies' of the world who are today in the historical process of finding voices of their own by which they are challenging both states and traditional civil societies where power resides.[44] It must learn to respond meaningfully to those who keep away from it, to those who criticise it, and even to those who oppose it.

I believe it is of great concern that the Forum is not doing this, and to the contrary seems to be becoming increasingly exclusive and arrogant about those 'it' disagrees with. These are trappings of power that 'it'—here, the IC, the International Secretariat, and the various Organising Committees—need urgently to shed.

Two: I believe that the 'conservatives' in the Forum are in any case missing the forest for the trees. Try as they might, they are not going to be able to control and discipline the Forum as a whole—not in the way they are approaching the subject, at least. As Chico Whitaker of the Brazil Organising Committee so often says, the Forum (as planned, by the organisers) is always overwhelmed by the self-organised events. This, indeed, is the magic of the Forum. But the approach that those wanting to retain a certain pristine quality are taking, ignores this, even violates this.

As already mentioned, although the Forum tends to be seen as a six-day wonder that takes place each year, the reality is that 'the Forum' is not limited to the real-time connections and exchanges that take place during those days. The real reality today is that 'the Forum' is today more virtual than real: That its reality is the myriad selforganised connections and exchanges that take place in cyberspace throughout the rest of the 359 days of the year (and also during those six days), seamlessly related to and a part of a much larger universe of exchange that cyberspace allows; and also the myriad other real-world meetings that all this generates. This in many ways is surely what the Forum is all about, and the spirit it generates. But the crucial issue is that all this is outside the control of those who seek to guide the Forum.

This is the real Forum; and just as states are, till date, not capable of controlling this, though they are trying, there is also no way that anyone within the Forum is going to be able to create rules for this larger universe, put up fences for who comes in, and demand adherence. This, the real Forum, is a free space. The space that has been imagined and defined in the WSF Charter of Principles, and then manifested in the real world in Porto Alegre, Mumbai, and elsewhere, is only a small part of this wider and much larger Forum. The Forum of life.

In one sense, this is a manifestation of Peter Waterman's point, that the Forum tends to *use* cyberspace, but not to *live* it. What we so far term and see as the 'virtual' has in many ways become the real (and in some senses, 'the real' virtual). We need to take stock of this and fundamentally re-think the Forum, our relationships, and the event and process that is so far called 'The Forum,' in these terms and in terms of the times we live in and that are emerging. In short, we—and especially the leadership of the Forum—need to re-think the culture of politics that we bring to the Forum.

In Conclusion: From Symbol to Logo

For many, the WSF has become something of a symbol of a larger global struggle. But there are deep trends taking shape within it that suggest that it is currently going through a process of sharp involution and succumbing to forces of conventionalism and orthodoxy. On the one hand, it is showing all signs of becoming corporate, with the symbol morphing into the logo that 'the WSF' has already become. On the other, it is beginning to increasingly behave like institutionalised religion. The two, of course, are not mutually exclusive, but together they sharply articulate the question of whether another world is really possible.

Both trends seem in part to be a function of the success that the Forum has already become, and of the power and influence that is not only being ascribed to it but was, surely, sought by it. But they are also a result of 'simpler' forces—of conventional organisational dynamics and of its leadership often drawing from a known, familiar (and 'old') vocabulary of structure and management. This seems sometimes to have been a subconscious choice, and sometimes a conscious, ideological choice.

But the WSF now has to face the challenge of how to realise and creatively deploy the potential of the power that it is gathering. Given the trends in this essay, this is of concern to all, even the small individual participant in the Forum. This is particularly important given the juncture in history at which the Forum has taken shape and is acting. It has a responsibility to a much larger history than its own. It can only do this by forging new vocabularies and grammars of thought and action, and not by relying on old categories, as its leaders are tending to do. As with all initiatives, the Forum is too important to be left to its leaders.

In particular, participants in the Forum—individuals and organisational delegates alike—must struggle to regain the spirit of the 'open space' that it started out saying that it wanted to be. It can only do so by abandoning the hard-line, discriminatory policies it has adopted against individuals and against including those who are 'concerned' but not necessarily yet 'committed.' To repeat, its central historical role must remain to *encourage* and *enable* free and open exchange and debate, not to overtly or covertly build a world movement of organisations of The Left.

We need, in short, to struggle to regain the dream. We can only do so if we persist in attempts to read and interrogate the actually existing Forum—and if we insist on dreaming the dream.

Notes

1. The workshop was titled 'Getting over issues of rivalry and power: a challenge for the FSM?' More information from Celina Whitaker at wsfitself@no-log.org. One of the key participants was Chico Whitaker, member of the Brazil Organising Committee and one of the architects of the WSF, and the author of an important essay (also in this volume) that I discuss in this article.
2. This is a revised excerpt from an earlier essay, Jai Sen, May 2003. The first version was a revised and expanded version of a Note I was invited to prepare by Carola Reintjes on the WSF for the 'VI Encuentro de Economía Solidaria' held in Córdoba, Spain, May 1–3, 2003. I thank Carola for giving me the opportunity to spell out these thoughts; Roberto Bissio, Jeremy Brecher, Sundar Chaterji, Taran Khan, Dave Ranney, Carola Reintjes, David Szanton, Teivo Teivainen, and Peter Waterman for their comments on earlier drafts; and Arturo Escobar and Rukmini Shekhar for editing the text.
3. Roberto Bissio, personal communication, 29 May 2003.
4. Sen 2002.
5. ABONG, ATTAC, CBJP, CIVES, CUT, IBASE, CJG, and MST, April 2001, and WSF Organising Committee, June 2001.
6. Whitaker, March 2003. See this volume. See Whitaker February 2002 for an earlier statement of this position. Whitaker represents the CBJP on the WSF Brazil Organising Committee, but is only one out of eight members, representing different organisations and tendencies.
7. Bhushan, March 2003, and Hussain and Tiwari, April 2003.
8. Teivainen, March 2003. For some of the same ground, see also Teivainen, 2002.
9. For more discussion of this point, see Samir Amin's interview in this volume and also: Sen 2004c, which was a companion essay to this essay in the first edition of this book (2004).
10. See Sen 2003 for a fuller treatment.
11. Albert, see this volume; Savio, January 2003; and Waterman, 'The Secret of Fire,' in this volume.
12. See Whitaker, February 2002; Escobar, and Vargas, in this volume; and Anand 2004, for a discussion of some of its internal dynamics.
13. See the WSF website for details of the systematisation project: <www.forumsocialmundial.org.br>
14. Albert, this volume.
15. Klein, January 2003.
16. From: ABONG, ATTAC, CBJP, CIVES, CUT, IBASE, CJG, and MST, April 2001. Emphasis supplied.
17. WSF, Brazil Organising Committee, August 2002.
18. Fisher and Ponniah, eds, 2003. See also Ponniah and Fisher 2004.
19. Whitaker, March 2003; emphasis given. See this volume.

20. See Amin, January 2003; also in this volume. Emphasis mine.

21. WSF India, July 2002.

22. ABONG, ATTAC, CBJP, and others, April 2001, as above. See this volume. Emphasis given.

23. At the world meetings, the Zapatistas have been among those denied access, and the clause has also been use to exclude some Basque organisations. In India and at the Asian Social Forum in January 2003, organisations affiliated or sympathetic to the PWG (People's War Group, a militant Maoist organisation operating in the region around Hyderabad, the city where the meeting was held) were kept out of the meeting. This and other dynamics led to a group named FAIG (Forum Against Imperialist Globalisation), which had initially been actively involved with the organization of the Forum, to withdraw and to organise a major rally in opposition to the Forum, during the Asian Social Forum.

24. Santos, March 2003. Edited version in this volume, Section 2.

25. Resolution taken at the WSF India National Conference in Nagpur, India, March 21–22, 2003.

26. WSF India 2004. The specific wording WSF India has used for the axes is:"Imperialist globalisation; Patriarchy; Militarism and peace; Communalism (religious sectarianism and fundamentalism); and—Casteism & racism (oppression, exclusion and discrimination based on descent and work)."

27. Several speakers at the meeting of the International Council in Bangkok in August 2002, the first time that it met in Asia, raised the questions of religious nationalism, communalism, and caste,and the need for the Council to embrace them. The proposals found wide support among participants and observers, especially among those from Asia.

28. WSF India, nd(b).

29. The online literature for the Mumbai meeting, while distinguishing clearly between individuals and organisational representatives—by offering a clear choice going to different registration forms, uses the terms 'participant' and 'individual' somewhat interchangeably, sometimes along with the term 'delegate,' but does not say anywhere what the respective rights and privileges of individual participants and organisational participants are. The registration form for 'Individuals' (at <http://www.wsfindia.org/participantForm.php>) curiously provides for three categories : 'Event Organiser,' 'Delegate,' or 'Observer,' and also gives no explanation for what the terms respectively mean or imply, or what the consequences are, of choosing one or the other of the latter two categories.

30. I thank Taran Khan for pointing this out to me.

31. Personal correspondence with Chico Whitaker during March 2003.

32. Whitaker March 2003.

33. My thanks to Dave Ranney for summing up this issue so succinctly.

34. Anderson, 1983.

35. Klein, July 2000b.

36. Albert, this volume.
37. While I cannot think of any specific documents I have seen making this analysis, I do not claim originality over these thoughts, such as 'logo,' 'franchise.' I think that there are many of us involved with the Forum who share these concerns, and I see myself voicing them here only an expression of a wide and deep concern. Roberto Bissio, of the Third World Institute in Uruguay, has for instance informed me that he apparently used these same terms during the meeting of the International Council in Porto Alegre in January 2003.
38. For a discussion of the issue of the globalisation of civilisation, see Sen, November 2002d.
39. For an exploration of the menu—and experience—of the Forum, see Wolfwood 2004.
40. Whitaker, March 2003. See this volume.
41. It is interesting and significant however, how strongly this shift—which was approved by the IC at its meeting in Miami in June 2003—was resisted by some members of the WSF's Content Commission, even at the last minute before the Mumbai Forum, at its meeting in Peruggia, Italy, in October 2003.
42. For a discussion of the politics of the Asian Social Forum, see Sen 2004c this volume. Rivalry over control of the European Social Forum is now legendary 'within the WSF,' and one can only hope that someone will perhaps write on it soon.
43. Sen 2002.
44. I see 'civil society'—as the term is used today—as referring to the attempted hegemony by the middle and upper classes, and by the middle and upper castes in those parts of the world where this stratification applies, and to its celebration—essentially, by members of these sections—as embracing 'all of society' outside the State. I see it as being merely a way of these sections disguising their historical project of struggling for hegemony, including by 'civilising' the 'uncivil (ised).' For earlier and more detailed discussion of this idea, see Gera, Howell, and Sen, June 2002, and Sen, November 2002d. And for an early discussion of the concept of unintendedness, see Sen, April 2001 (April 1975).

World Social Forum 3 And Tensions In The Construction Of Alternative Global Thinking[1]

Gina Vargas

The WSF, which began in Porto Alegre, Brazil in 2001 is established on the horizon and within the strategies of globally oriented networks and social movements. The two powerful and mobilising slogans of the Forum—"Against Monolithic Thinking!"(of neoliberalism) and "Another World is Possible!"—express the orientation of this other globalisation whose force is the ethical and utopian conviction that alternatives can be constructed by democratic, global and emancipatory forces. For this, there is no existing recipe or a specific agent, only multiple social actors contributing their forms of resistance and constructing democracy with social justice and equity.

The WSF Charter of Principles approved at the end of 2001 (see this volume) provides the principle of cohesion for numerous attitudes and strategies accompanying the development of the Forum. Specifying this as a space for social movements that act within civil society, the Charter positions the Forum as a space of plurality and autonomy, non-confessional, non-governmental and non-partisan. It explicitly highlights the necessity for respect and positive affirmation of differences among movements and forces of change. It clarifies that the Forum is more a space and a process that is being progressively constructed and expanded, with contributions and strategies from this plurality, and not so much an event. It does not reach conclusions or produce formal public declarations, as this would undermine the variety of different networks, organisations and movements taking part, and who would feel bound, in some way, to accept a single position. The Charter of Principles establishes the rules of the game in this global space.

The WSF is a space for the affirmation, amplification and construction of rights in the global arena. It is a space for widening democratic, subjective and symbolic horizons—for the recovery of a utopian perspective and for thinking about a different possible world. Everyone experiencing this interactive process is affected by it—by new questions, new presences, and the possibility provided for generating new democratic political cultures, which in turn feed our democratic imagination. This is the most important legacy of the WSF.

The process of globalisation of the Forum initiated in 2002—seeking to extend the global space of interaction—has had consequences. It is incorporating new subjects, actors, movements and topics (the Pan-Amazonian, the Argentinean, Palestinian and Colombian Forums).[2] It is now also manifesting itself in different contexts (the European, Asian, African and the Hemispherical Forum of the Americas). And, it has moved geographically—WSF 4 will be held in India in 2004. From 2005 it will move back, every two years to Porto Alegre, its symbolical and original base.

With the Forum's success and expansion, have come difficulties and misunderstandings. This is inevitable: the construction of a space-process of such scale and importance is unimaginable—except by idealising it—without tensions, struggles for understanding, confusions, and power dynamics. There are issues of growth and evolution, with ambivalence between old and new subjectivities; difficulties of generating new forms of political debate and of proposing new contents and forms for democratic political cultures. There is a challenge to create spaces for thinking globally, in pluralistic and radical-democratic terms, about current dilemmas. As Julieta Kirkwood says, in her case for the feminist movement, in order to confront new challenges it is necessary to be open to a certain ambiguity.[3]

In this context, dynamics, initiatives, connections or disconnections multiply, expressing the enormous diversity of the movements for an alternative globalisation as opposed to just a 'Forum.' The WSF is also setting new trends —by publicly accounting its income and expenses, reporting its decisions, and opening the meetings of its International Committee (IC) to observers. These steps are also messages, warnings, to the wider world within which it is taking shape.

The Forum means different things to different people. For some, it is an 'agora' where ideas, experiences, movements, networks come together, for exchange and dialogue, and self-reflection.[4] For others it is a 'market' for the exchange of goods and knowledge; a 'movement of movements'; an official, reformist space (the Organising Committee and the International Committee); and an alternative or revolutionary space (the networks and movements).

Without doubt, the idea of space, an agora, a public square, is the one that best expresses the intention and dynamics of the Forum. One of the most heated debates, well expressed by Chico Whitaker, highlights the dilemma between Forum-as-space and Forum-as-movement.[5]

To be a Forum-as-space implies that the Forum must be, as its Charter reveals, an open meeting place for reflective thinking, democratic debate of ideas, formulation of proposals, free exchange of experiences and interlinking for effective action, by groups and movements of civil society that are opposed to neoliberalism and to domination of the world by capital and any form of imperialism, and are committed to building a planetary society centred on the human being. The WSF asserts democracy as the avenue to resolving society's problems politically. As a meeting place, it is open to pluralism and to the diversity of activities and ways of engaging the organisations and movements that decide to participate in it, as well as the diversity of genders, races, ethnicities and cultures.[6]

This said, it is clear that the WSF is not a neutral space. To enter this space implies acceptance of its Charter. For the WSF to be Forum-as- movement—in other words, if the WSF were to be understood, as some suggest, as a movement—this would mean giving it the roles of mobilising and of defining strategies and leadership responsibilities. On the other hand, Forum-as-space implies a 'movement of ideas,' facilitating the development of many movements, the possibility of interaction, each contributing from its own space of transformation, without excluding themselves from a global vision. The Forum-as-movement denies this horizontal space, prevents it from being 'a place without an owner,' the collective property of all those interested to so use it.[7] It converts it into an organic social movement (singular), or a new international coalition (some people call it a new internationalism), [8] acting in the name of a wide and generic global movement, in which inclusion is not guaranteed. [9] For the WSF to be Forum-as-movement, the present Charter of Principles is not valid—and also no longer necessary, any more than the diversity.

This is a complicated issue. As Celiberti suggests, neither organisational centralisation nor an agenda of mobilisation can shorten the distance that must be walked to further the dialogue between the diverse priorities that movements have (anti-capitalist, anti-patriarchal, anti-racist, anti-homophobic, including the various oppositions to neoliberalism). The Forum is a space-dialogue for advancing this process.

And it is a space par excellence. Social movements, networks and coalitions and party activism (represented by individuals and/or as parts of different movements), infect the Forum with their hopes and visions—and also their limitations. All the logics of change, and all the different actors —the transgressors and the radicals, the more or less conciliatory, the more or less democratic, the more or less authoritarian—that are found within different democratic social movements, equally find place and expression within the WSF.

Here, notions of primary and secondary struggles, fed by monolithic understandings of neoliberal globalisation, are unhelpful. Each has to confront their own contradictions, and to commit themselves to the multiple democratisations, forms of justice, ways of constructing freedom—with different faces, ethnicities, sexes, sexual options, capacities, ages. And, without male hegemony. These dynamics, once assumed, also result in the transformation of subjectivities, and lead also to the recognition of the vital roles of diversity.

To have a space to struggle for recognition, it is necessary to politicise difference, "to celebrate...the advancement of the idea of solidarity and the protection of differences as the political capital of democracy."[10] The WSF is such a space, created by the politicisation of differences in a world shaped by the neoliberal capitalist globalisation process. The idea of solidarity and the protection of differences as the political capital of democracy are to be celebrated. But the effects of economic policies on the most vulnerable sectors of society, including women, are to be lamented.

There are other concerns of space and meaning of the Forum, as understood in the Charter, which have yet to be discussed fully. For example, are there limits to the autonomy of organisers of thematic and regional Forums (or of the WSF itself)? Can autonomy mean freedom to modify the Charter? And would such a measure mean the exclusion of certain visions or presences? [11] Does the Forum risk becoming a mega event instead of a mega process (13,000 participants at WSF 1 and 100,000 at WSF 3)?

Proposals to reduce participation in the WSF to delegates of Regional and Thematic Forums, as well as of certain movements, networks or countries, mean confronting the meaning of 'representation.' This is problematic enough at the national level. But what is representation at the global level, which is a space where movements expand and diversify and where there is more interaction between movements? In this space, there are no struggles or homogeneous identities to be 'represented' (such as women or homosexuals), but rather multiple visions, experiences and strategies.[12] National level crises cannot be resolved in a global space.

Other tensions include the desire of Forum-as-movement position holders to convert the WSF into spokesperson for the movements gathered, through declarations and proposals—necessarily monolithic—in the name of the Forum itself. Experience however, shows that other ways are possible. In practice, the Forum did not require a formal public declaration for the global movements to co-ordinate and stimulate the successful world mobilisation against the U.S. war on Iraq on 15 February 2003.

For many at the Forum, the formal presence of political parties would only be possible and fruitful if and when they democratise themselves. However, to open up participation even to democratic parties—which have a clear alliance with social movements (such as Rifondazione Communista in Italy)—would mean opening up to parties that want to be in the Forum, and whose democratic credentials are weak or non-existent. This is a major risk. Even for this reason alone, the space for civil society, separate and free from state-political forces, needs to be preserved, in the interests of democracy.

Finally, what is 'official' and what is 'alternative' at the Forum? Are differences in strategy—towards neoliberalism and the current imperial dynamics of the U.S.—sufficient to de-legitimise one part of the Forum? Any process, born alternative, takes on a particular dynamic of change, fundamental for its own renewal. Do alternatives have limits? What are the limits of alternatives? Can alternatives be plural? In such processes, a degree of both cohesion and flexibility is necessary, to avoid the 'tyranny of structurelessness,' and to be dynamic and open.

The most striking characteristic of WSF 3, in relation to previous ones, has been its self-reflection. The well-known imbalances in the Forum are also raw material for the boldest of proposals that can extend our vision—and in so doing, that reverse the fragmentation that neoliberalism brings and encourage deep exploration of the dynamics of change. The problem is not the existence of trends or conflicts—these are natural in a laboratory of democracy—but their existence in parallel and opposite form, without consideration of the 'translation' that Sousa Santos calls for.[13]

We are today constructing civil, democratic society on a global scale. The progress and changes between the three Forums, including its globalisation, proves that this construction is underway. The tensions that the process is experiencing are a part of constructing these global spaces in a democratic way. Far from being a problem, they can infinitely enrich the possibilities of experience and inclusion. Answers on how to avoid the implosion of the Forum require democratic intelligence and collective search.[14]

This is the moment of the Forum. The tensions that today face the Forum are part of the difficulty in attempting to capture the democratic imagination of the new millennium.

Notes

1. Edited from an unpublished original, '*El Foro Social Mundial III y las tensiones en la construcción del pensamiento global alternativo*,' Lima, March 2003. <http:// www.forumsocialmundial.org.br/dinamic.asp?pagina=bal_vvargas_esp> Translation: Maria Eugenia Miranda, Peter Waterman; further work Anita Anand, Jai Sen. This is a personal and political view, from an activist commitment to this global space under construction. I have participated in the three Forums as a feminist activist. I have also been a member of the WSF International Council, along with Lilian Celiberti, as a representative of the Montevideo-based Articulación Feminista Marcosur.
2. These are not country-specific Forums, but of particular situations that reveal global tensions. In Argentina the Forum addressed structural adjustment policies and neoliberal economic orthodoxy; in Palestine, the Middle East conflict; and in Colombia, the problem of violence and war.
3. Kirkwood 1996.
4. Waterman 2003. See this volume.
5. Chico Whitaker 2003. See this volume.
6. ABONG, ATTAC, CBJP, CIVES, CUT, IBASE, CJG, and MST, April 2001, Clauses 1 and 9. See this volume.
7. Whitaker 2003, in this volume.
8. Internationalism is one of the historical values of global solidarity that globalisation is re-creating and expanding. Nevertheless, no Fifth International can be conceived without recognition of the multiplicity of new-old social actors affecting the global.
9. Celiberti 2002.
10. Rosemberg 2002.
11. Modifying the Charter is a right of the movements. But it is also the right of the movements to prevent this global instrument from being defined by or for regional or thematic particularities, or worse, for possibly authoritarian and exclusionary ends.
12. In the emerging global movement, there is consensus around the fight against neo-liberalism and neo-liberal globalisation, for reasons of justice and equity. There is no consensus, however, on whether the fight is against capitalism. There are anti-globalisation positions and also alternative globalisation ones. There are preferences for a democratic capitalism and others that doubt its very possibility. There are socialists of all varieties, trade unionists of all the global tendencies (including those that participate in the World Economic Forum at Davos).
13. Santos 2002.
14. Whitaker 2003, *ibid*. This volume.

The World Social Forum: Toward A Counter-Hegemonic Globalisation[1]

Boaventura de Sousa Santos

The Newness of the World Social Forum

The World Social Forum is a new social and political phenomenon. The fact that it does have antecedents does not diminish its newness. Rather, it is quite the opposite. It is not an event, nor a mere succession of events. It is not a scholarly conference, although the contributions of many scholars converge in it. It is not a party or an international of parties, although militants and activists of many parties all over the world take part in it. It is not an NGO or a confederation of NGOs, even though its conception and organisation owes a great deal to them. It is not a social movement, even though it often designates itself as a movement of movements. Although it presents itself as an agent of social change, the WSF rejects the concept of a historical subject and confers no priority on any specific social actor in this process of social change. It holds no clearly defined ideology, either in defining what it rejects or what it asserts.

Given that the WSF conceives of itself as a struggle against neoliberal globalisation, is it a struggle against a *form* of capitalism or against capitalism in general? Given that it sees itself as a struggle against discrimination, exclusion and oppression, does the success of its struggle presuppose a postcapitalist, socialist, anarchist horizon, or does it presuppose that no context be clearly defined at all?

Since the vast majority of people taking part in the WSF identify themselves as favouring a politics of the Left, how many definitions of 'the Left' fit the WSF? And what about those who refuse to be defined because they believe that the Left-Right dichotomy is a North-centric or West-centric particularism, and look for alternative political definitions?

The social struggles that find expression in the WSF do not adequately fit either of the ways of social change sanctioned by western modernity: reform and revolution. Aside from the consensus on non-violence, its modes of struggle are extremely diverse and appear spread out in a continuum between the poles of institutionality and insurgency. Even the concept of non-violence is open to widely disparate interpretations.

Finally, the WSF is not structured according to any of the models of modern political organisation, be they democratic centralism, representative democracy, or participatory democracy. In other words, the 'movement of movements' is not one more movement. It is a *different* movement.

The challenge posed by the WSF has one more dimension still. Beyond the theoretical, analytical and epistemological questions, it raises a new political issue: it aims to fulfil a utopia in a world devoid of utopias. This utopian will is expressed in the slogan 'Another World is Possible!" At stake is less a utopian world than a world that *allows* for utopia.

In this paper, I therefore deal with the WSF as critical utopia, epistemology of the South, and emergent politics.

The WSF as Critical Utopia

"Utopias have their timetable," says Ernst Bloch.[2] The conceptions of and aspirations to a better life and society, ever present in human history, vary as to form and content according to time and space. They express the tendencies and latencies of a given epoch and a given society. They constitute an anticipatory consciousness that manifests itself by enlarging the signs or traces of emerging realities. Does the WSF have a utopian dimension? And, if so, what is its timetable?

The WSF is a set of initiatives—of transnational exchange among social movements, NGOs and their practices and knowledge of local, national or global social struggles against the forms of exclusion and inclusion, discrimination and equality, universalism and particularism, cultural imposition and relativism, that have been brought about or made possible by the current phase of capitalism known as neoliberal globalisation. The utopian dimension of the WSF consists in claiming the existence of alternatives to neoliberal globalisation.

As Franz Hinkelammert says, "we live in a time of conservative utopias whose utopian character resides in its radical denial of alternatives to present-day reality."[3] The possibility of alternatives is discredited precisely for being utopian, idealistic, and unrealistic. Under neoliberalism, the criterion is the market. The total *market* becomes a perfect institution. Its utopian character resides in the promise that its total application cancels out all utopias. What distinguishes conservative utopias such as the market from critical utopias is the fact that they identify themselves with present-day reality and discover their utopian dimension in the radicalisation or complete fulfilment of the present. Moreover, if there is unemployment and social exclusion, if there is starvation and death in the periphery of the world system, that is not the consequence of the deficiencies or limits of the laws of the market; it results rather from the fact that such laws have not yet been fully applied. The horizon of conservative utopias is thus a closed horizon, an end to history.

This is the context in which the utopian dimension of the WSF must be understood. The WSF signifies the re-emergence of critical utopia, that is, of a radical critique of present-day reality and the aspiration to a better society. This occurs, however, when the antiutopian utopia of neoliberalism is dominant. The utopian dimension of the WSF consists in affirming the possibility of a counter-hegemonic globalisation; it is a radically democratic utopia. In this sense, the utopia of the WSF asserts itself more as negativity (the definition of what it critiques) than as positivity (the definition of that to which it aspires).

The specificity of the WSF as critical utopia has one more explanation. For the WSF, the claim of alternatives is plural, both as to the form of the claim and the content of the alternatives. The other possible world is a utopian aspiration that comprises several possible worlds. It may be many things, but never a world with no alternative.

Yet the question remains: once the counter-hegemonic globalisation is consolidated, and hence the idea that another world is possible is made credible, will it be possible to fulfil this idea with the same level of radical democracy that helped formulate it?

The World Social Forum as Epistemology of the South

Neoliberal globalisation is presided over by technico-scientific knowledge, and owes its hegemony to the credible way in which it discredits all rival knowledge, by suggesting that they are not comparable, as to efficiency and coherence, to the scientific nature of market laws. This is why the practices circulating in the WSF have their origin in very distinct epistemological assumptions (what counts as knowledge) and ontological universes (what it means to be human). Such diversity exists not only among the different movements but also *inside* each one of them. The differences within the feminist movement, for instance, are not merely political. They are differences regarding what counts as relevant knowledge, on the one hand, and on the other, differences about identifying, validating or hierarchising the relations between western-based scientific knowledge and other knowledges derived from other practices, rationalities or cultural universes. They are differences, ultimately, about what it means to be a human being, whether male or female. The practice of the WSF also reveals, in this context, that the knowledge we have of globalisation is much less global than globalisation itself.

To be sure, many counter-hegemonic practices resort to the hegemonic scientific and technological knowledge paradigm, and many of them would not even be thinkable without it. This is true of the WSF itself, which would not exist without the technologies of information and communication. The question is: to what extent is such knowledge useful and valid, and what other knowledges are available and usable beyond the limits of utility and validity of scientific knowledge? To approach these problems raises an additional epistemological problem: on the basis of which knowledge or epistemology are these problems to be formulated?

Science is doubly at the service of hegemonic globalisation, whether by the way in which it promotes and legitimates it, or by which it discredits, conceals or trivialises counter-hegemonic globalisation. Hegemony presupposes a constant policing and repressing of counter-hegemonic practices and agents. This goes largely hand in hand with discrediting, concealing and trivialising bodies of knowledge that inform counter-hegemonic practices and agents. Faced with rival bodies of knowledge, hegemonic scientific knowledge either turns them into raw material (as is the case of indigenous or peasant knowledge about biodiversity) or rejects them on the basis of their falsity or inefficiency in the light of the hegemonic criteria of truth and efficiency. Confronted with this situation, the epistemological alternative proposed by the WSF is that there is no global *social* justice without global *cognitive* justice.

This alternative is grounded on two basic ideas. First, if the objectivity of science does not imply neutrality, science and technology may as well be put at the service of counter-hegemonic practices. The extent to which science is used is arguable inside the movements, and it may vary according to circumstances and practices. Second, whatever the extent to which science is resorted to, counter-hegemonic practices are mainly practices of nonscientific knowledge, practical, often tacit bodies of knowledge that must be made credible to render such practices credible in turn.

The second point is more polemical because it confronts the hegemonic concepts of truth and efficiency directly. The epistemological denunciation that the WSF engages in consists of showing that the concepts of rationality and efficiency presiding over hegemonic technico-scientific knowledge are too restrictive. They cannot capture the richness and diversity of the social experience of the world, and specially that they discriminate against practices of resistance and production of counter-hegemonic alternatives. The concealment and discrediting of these practices constitute a waste of social experience, both social experience that is available but not yet visible, and social experience not yet available but realistically possible.

The epistemological operation carried out by the WSF consists of two processes that I designate as *sociology of absences and sociology of emergences*. I speak of sociologies because my aim is to critically identify the conditions that destroy non-hegemonic and potentially counter-hegemonic social experience. Through these sociologies, social experience that resists destruction is unconcealed, and the space-time capable of identifying and rendering credible new counter-hegemonic social experiences is opened up. The following description of the sociology of absences and the sociology of emergences represents the ideal-type of the epistemological operation featured by the WSF.

The WSF and the Sociology of Absences

The sociology of absences consists of an inquiry that aims to explain that what does not exist is, in fact, actively produced as non-existent, that is, as a non-credible alternative to what exists. The objective of the sociology of absences is to transform impossible into possible objects, absent into present objects. The logics and processes through which hegemonic criteria of rationality and efficiency produce non-existence are various. Non-existence is produced whenever a certain entity is disqualified and rendered invisible, unintelligible, or irreversibly discardable. What unites the different logics of production of non-existence is that they are all manifestations of the same rational monoculture.

I distinguish five logics or modes of production of non-existence. The first derives from the *monoculture of knowledge*. It turns modern science and high culture into the sole criterion of truth and aesthetic quality, respectively. All that is not recognised or legitimated by the canon is declared non-existent. Non-existence appears in this case in the form of ignorance or lack of culture.

The second logic resides in the *monoculture of linear time*, the idea that time is linear and that ahead of time precedes the core countries of the world system. This logic produces non-existence by describing as 'backward' (pre-modern or under-developed) whatever is asymmetrical vis-à-vis whatever is declared 'forward.' The third logic is the *monoculture of classification*, based on the naturalisation of differences. It consists of distributing populations according to categories that naturalise hierarchies. Racial and sexual classifications are the most salient manifestations of this logic, with racial classification as one of the one most deeply reconstructed by capitalism.[4]

The fourth logic of production of non-existence is the logic of the dominant scale: the *monoculture of the universal and the global*. Globalisation privileges entities or realities that widen their scope to the whole globe, thus earning the prerogative to designate rival entities as local. Non-existence is produced under the form of the particular and the local. The entities or realities defined as particular or local are captured in scales that render them incapable of being credible alternatives to what exists globally and universally.

Finally, the fifth logic is that of productivity. It resides in the *monoculture of criteria of capitalist productivity and efficiency*, which privileges growth through market forces. This criterion applies both to nature and to human labour. Non-existence is produced in the form of non-productiveness. Applied to nature, non-productiveness is sterility; applied to labour, "discardable populations," laziness, professional disqualification, lack of skills.

There are thus five principal social forms of non-existence produced by hegemonic epistemology and rationality: the ignorant, the residual, the inferior, the local and the non-productive. The realities to which they give shape are present only as obstacle vis-à-vis the realities deemed relevant, be they scientific, advanced, superior, global, or productive realities. They are what exist under irretrievably disqualified forms of existing. To be made present, these absences need to be constructed as alternatives to hegemonic experience, to have their credibility discussed and argued for and their relations taken as object of political dispute. The sociology of absences therefore creates the conditions to enlarge the field of credible experiences. The enlargement of the world occurs not only because the field of credible experiences is widened but also because the possibilities of social experimentation in the future are increased.

The sociology of absence proceeds by confronting each one of the modes of production of absence mentioned above and by replacing monocultures by ecologies. I therefore identify and propose five ecologies: *the ecology of knowledge*, which confronts the logic of the monoculture of scientific knowledge with the identification of other knowledge and criteria of rigour that operate credibly in social practices. The central idea is that there is no ignorance or knowledge in general. All ignorance is ignorant of certain knowledge, and all knowledge is the overcoming of a particular ignorance. In this domain, the sociology of absences aims to substitute an ecology of knowledge for the monoculture of scientific knowledge.

Second, the *ecology of temporalities*, which questions the monoculture of linear time with the idea that linear time is only one among many conceptions of time and that, if we take the world as our unit of analysis, it is not even the most commonly adopted. Linear time was adopted by western modernity, but it never erased, not even in the West, other conceptions of time such as circular time, cyclical time, the doctrine of the eternal return, and still others that are not adequately grasped by the images of the arrow of time. In this domain, the sociology of absences aims to free social practices from their status as residuum, devolving to them their own temporality and thus the possibility of autonomous development. In this way, the activity of the African or Asian peasant becomes contemporaneous of the activity of the hi-tech farmer in the USA or the activity of the World Bank executive; it becomes another form of contemporaneity.

The *ecology of recognition*, thirdly, opposes the monoculture of classification. It confronts the colonial mentality of race and unequal sexuality;[6] it looks for a new articulation between the principles of equality and difference, thus allowing for the possibility of equal differences—an ecology of differences comprised of mutual recognition. The differences that remain when hierarchy vanishes become a powerful denunciation of the differences that hierarchy reclaims in order not to vanish.

The *ecology of trans-scale* confronts the logic of global scale by recuperating what in the local is not the result of hegemonic globalisation. The local that has been integrated in hegemonic globalisation is what I designate as localised globalism, that is, the specific impact of hegemonic globalisation on the local.[7] The de-globalisation of the local and its eventual counter-hegemonic re-globalisation broadens the diversity of social practices by offering alternatives to localised globalisms. The sociology of absences requires in this domain, the use of cartographic imagination, to deal with cognitive maps that operate simultaneously with different scales, namely to identify local/global articulations.[8]

The *ecology of productivity*, finally, consists in recuperating and valorising alternative systems of production, popular economic organisations, workers' co-operatives, self-managed enterprises, solidarity economy, which have been hidden or discredited by the capitalist orthodoxy of productivity. This is perhaps the most controversial domain of the sociology of absences, for it confronts directly both the paradigm of development and infinite economic growth and the logic of the primacy of the objectives of accumulation over the objectives of distribution that sustain global capitalism.

In each of the five domains, the objective of the sociology of absences is to disclose, and give credit to, the diversity and multiplicity of social practices in opposition to the exclusive credibility of hegemonic practices. The idea of multiplicity and non-destructive relations is suggested by the concept of ecology. The WSF is a broad exercise of the sociology of absences. But there are variations. If it is, in general, unequivocally a refusal of monocultures and an adoption of ecologies, this process is not present with the same intensity in all movements, organisations and articulations. If for some, opting for ecologies are unconditional, for others hybridity between monocultures and ecologies is permissible. Some movements or organisations act, in some domains, according to a monocultural logic and, in others, according to an ecological logic. It is also possible that the adoption of an ecological logic is de-characterised by the factionalism and power struggle inside one movement or organisation, and turn into a new monocultural logic. Finally, I offer as an hypothesis that even the movements that claim different ecologies are vulnerable to the temptation of evaluating themselves according to an ecological logic, while evaluating the other movements according to a hegemonic monocultural logic.

The World Social Forum and the Sociology of Emergences

The sociology of emergence is the second epistemological operation conducted by the WSF. Whereas the goal of the sociology of absences is to identify and valorise social experiences available in the world—although declared non-existent by hegemonic rationality—the sociology of emergences aims to identify and enlarge the signs of possible future experiences, under the guise of tendencies and latencies, that are actively ignored by hegemonic rationality and knowledge.

For some thinkers, the possible is the most uncertain and the most ignored concept in western philosophy.[9] Yet, only the possible allows us to reveal the inexhaustible wealth of the world. Besides All and Nothing, Bloch, for instance, introduces two new concepts: Not (Nicht) and Not Yet (Noch Nicht). The Not is the lack of something, but also the expression of the will to *surmount that lack*. The Not is thus distinguished from the Nothing.[10] To say No is to say yes to something different.

The Not Yet is the more complex category because it expresses what exists as mere tendency, a movement that is latent in the very process of manifesting itself. The Not Yet is the way in which the future is inscribed in the present. It is not an indeterminate or infinite future, rather a concrete possibility and a capacity that neither exists in a vacuum nor is completely predetermined. Subjectively, the Not Yet is anticipatory consciousness, a form of consciousness that is extremely important in people's lives. Objectively, the Not Yet is, on the one hand, capacity (potency) and, on the other, possibility (potentiality). Possibility has a dimension of darkness as it originates in the lived moment, which is never fully visible to it; it is also, as a crucial component of uncertainty that derives from a double want: one, the fact that conditions that render possibility concrete are only partially known; and two, the fact that such conditions only exist partially.

At every moment, there is a limited horizon of possibilities, and so it is important not to waste the unique opportunity of a specific change offered by the present: *carpe diem* (seize the day). Considering the three modal categories of existence—reality, necessity, and possibility— hegemonic rationality and knowledge focus on the first two and neglect the third one entirely. The sociology of emergences focuses on possibility. Possibility is the world's engine. Its moments are want (the manifestation of something lacking), tendency (process and meaning), and latency (what goes ahead in the process). Want is the realm of the Not, tendency the realm of the Not Yet, and latency the realm of the Nothing and the All, for latency can end up either in frustration or hope.

The sociology of emergences is the inquiry into the alternatives that are contained in the horizon of concrete possibilities. It consists in undertaking a symbolic enlargement of knowledge, practices and agents in order to identify therein the tendencies of the future (the Not Yet) upon which it is possible to intervene so as to maximise the probability of hope vis-à-vis the probability of frustration. Such symbolic enlargement is actually a form of sociological imagination with a double aim: on the one hand, to know better the conditions of the possibility of hope; on the other, to define principles of action to promote the fulfilment of those conditions. The Not Yet has meaning (as possibility), but no direction, for it can end either in hope or disaster.

The sociology of emergences therefore replaces the idea of determination by the idea of *care*. The axiology of progress and development, which have justified untold destruction, is thus replaced by the axiology of care. Whereas in the sociology of absences the axiology of care is exerted vis-à-vis alternatives available in the present, in the sociology of emergences the axiology of care is exerted vis-à-vis possible future alternatives. Because of this ethical dimension, neither the sociology of absences nor the sociology of emergences are conventional sociologies. But they are not conventional for another reason: their objectivity depends upon the quality of their subjective dimension. The subjective element of the sociology of absences is cosmopolitan consciousness and non- conformism before the waste of experience. The subjective element of the sociology of emergences is anticipatory consciousness and non-conformism before a want whose fulfilment is within the horizon of possibilities.

The symbolic enlargement brought about by a sociology of emergences consists in identifying signals, clues, or traces of future possibilities in whatever exists. Hegemonic rationality and science has totally dismissed this kind of inquiry, either because it assumes that the future is predetermined, or can only be identified by precise indicators. For them, clues are too vague, subjective, and chaotic to be credible predictors. By focussing intensely on the clue side of reality, the sociology of emergences aims to enlarge symbolically the possibilities of the future that lie, in latent form, in concrete social experiences. The sociology of emergences valorises clues as pathways toward discussing and arguing for concrete alternative futures. The care of the future exerts itself in such argumentation and negotiation.

As in the case of the sociology of absences, the practices of the WSF also come more or less close to the ideal type of the sociology of emergences. I submit as a working hypothesis that the stronger and more consolidated movements and organisations tend to engage less in the sociology of emergences than the less strong or consolidated. As regards the relations between movements or organisations, the signs and clues given by the less consolidated movements may be devalued as subjective or inconsistent by the more consolidated movements. In this as well, the practice of the sociology of emergences is unequal, and inequalities must be the object of analysis and evaluation.

The World Social Forum as Political Emergence[11]

The newness of the WSF is more unequivocal at the utopian and epistemological level than at the political level. Its political newness does exist, but it exists as a field of tensions and dilemmas, where the new and the old confront each another. The political newness of the WSF resides in the way in which these confrontations have been handled, avoided, and negotiated.

Generally speaking, the political novelties of the WSF can be seen, first, in terms of the very *broad conception of power and oppression* that it seems to have adopted, and which responds to the fact that neoliberal globalisation is linked with many other forms of oppression that affect women, ethnic minorities, peasants, the unemployed, workers of the informal sector, immigrants, ghetto sub- classes, gays and lesbians, children and youth. This requires that movements and organisations give priority to the articulation among them, and ultimately explains the organisational novelty of a WSF with no leaders, its rejection of hierarchies, and its emphasis on networks made possible by the internet.

Second, the WSF strives for *equivalence between the principles of equality and of recognition of difference*, grounding the option for participatory democracy, which addresses equality without the exclusion of difference.

Third, the WSF *privileges rebellion and non-conformity at the expense of revolution*. There is no unique theory to guide the movements, because the aim is not so much to seize power but rather to change the many faces of power as they present themselves in the institutions and sociabilities. At this level, the novelty consists in the celebration of diversity and pluralism, experimentalism, and radical democracy.

It has become common to examine the WSF's political experience in terms of problems and tensions at three levels: representation, organisation, political strategy and political action. According to its Charter of Principles, the WSF does not claim to be representative of counter-hegemonic globalisation, and no one represents the WSF nor can speak in its name. But then: whom does the WSF represent? Who represents the WSF? The WSF's restricted geographical scope so far has led some critics to affirm that the WSF is far from having a world dimension. Some proposals have been made in this regard, including the decision to hold the fourth WSF in India. While this problem is real, I believe that the WSF must not be de-legitimised for not being worldwide enough.

A second, hotly debated question is the WSF's organisation, particularly the relation between the Organising Committee (OC) and the International Council (IC), the organisation of each of the three Porto Alegre Forums, and each event's structure. These aspects have raised many issues, which I cannot discuss at length here. (See other essays in this section, and other sections in this volume—Eds). Among the most discussed are: internal democracy, including issues of transparency of decisions and the articulation between the IC and the OC; the hierarchical structure of the events, chiefly the distinction among different kinds of sessions and the importance accorded to each, a feature of which feminist movements have been particularly critical (following the two mottos—'Another World is Possible!' and 'No One Single Way of Thinking'); and the top-down organisation of the events.

A third site of tension and critique is the relation with political parties, social movements, and NGOs. The Charter of Principles is clear on the subordinate role of parties in the WSF. The WSF is an emanation of civil society as organised in social movements and non-governmental organisations. In practice, however, things are ambiguous.[12] In my mind, the issue is not whether relations with parties should exist or not, but rather to define the exact terms of these. If the relations are transparent, horizontal, and mutually respectful, they may well be, in some contexts, an important lever for the consolidation of the WSF.

A fourth area of contestation is size and continuity. To the steady increase in the size of the annual event, the IC has responded with a proposal to stimulate theme and regional, national and local events, that intercommunicate horizontally and that will not be articulated as preparatory for one another but as meetings with their own political value.

Finally, there are issues of strategy and political action. As a radical utopia, the WSF celebrates diversity, plurality, and horizontality. The newness of this utopia in Left thinking cannot but be problematical as it translates itself into strategic planning and political action.

The organisers themselves acknowledge many of these tensions and criticisms, which suggest that these tensions are part of the Forum's learning process. Some measures have been suggested, including the current restructuring of the IC and a deepening of horizontal organisational practices and systems of co-responsibility. Although it is clear that much remains to be done, it is fair to say that the WSF's organisational structure was the most adequate to launch the Forum and render it credible internationally. The current consolidation of the WSF will lead it to another phase of development, in which case its organisational structure will have to be reconsidered so as to adjust it to its new demands and tasks ahead. For now, it should be acknowledged that the desire to highlight what the movements and organisations have in common has prevailed over the desire to underscore what separates them. The manifestation of tensions or cleavages has been relatively tenuous and, above all, has not resulted in mutual exclusions. It remains to be seen for how long this will to convergence and this chaotic sharing of differences will last.

The last point concerns precisely this, the notion of cleavages. Here again we find a site of political novelty. There is a meta-cleavage between western and non-western political cultures. Up to a point, this meta-cleavage also exists between the North and the South. Given the strong presence of movements and organisations of the North Atlantic and white Latin America, it is no wonder that the most salient cleavages reflect the political culture and historical trajectory of the Left in these parts of the world. What is most instructive however, is that despite the reality of the cleavages that could be at play —reform or revolution; socialism or social emancipation; the State as enemy or potential ally; national and global struggles; direct action or institutional action; and that between the principles of equality and difference—it is clear that what is new about the WSF is that the majority of the movements and organisations that participate in it do not recognise themselves in these cleavages. They have political experiences in which there are moments of confrontation alternating or combining with moments of dialogue and engagement. In these long range visions of social change cohabit the tactical possibilities of the moment, in which radical denunciations of capitalism do not paralyse the energy for small changes when the big changes are not possible. Indeed, many movements of the South think that no general labels—even Left and Right—need be attached to the goals of the struggles.

According to the large majority of the movements, these conventionally conceived cleavages do not do justice to the concrete needs of concrete struggles. The decision on which scale to privilege, for instance, is a political decision that must be taken in accordance with concrete political conditions. Similarly, for many movements it is no longer a question of choosing between the struggle for equality and difference, but of articulating one with the other, for the fulfilment of either is condition of the fulfilment of the other.

Nonetheless, there is a cleavage among the movements and even, sometimes, inside the same movement on whether priority should be given to one of these principles. Concrete political conditions will dictate which of the principles is to be privileged in a given struggle. Any struggle conceived under the aegis of one of these two principles must be organised so as to open space for the other principle. Many of the tensions and cleavages mentioned above are not specific to the WSF, but belong to the legacy of struggles over the past 200 years. The specificity of the WSF resides in the fact that all these cleavages co-exist in its bosom without upsetting its aggregating power. The different cleavages are important in different ways for the different movements and organisations, providing room for action and discourse. Second, there has so far been no tactical or strategic demand that would intensify the cleavages by radicalising positions. On the contrary, cleavages have been fairly low intensity. For the movements and organisations in general, what unites has been more important than what divides. Third, if a given movement opposes another in a given cleavage, it may well be on the same side in another. In this way are precluded the accumulation and strengthening of divergences that could result from the alignment of the movements in multiple cleavages. On the contrary, the cleavages end up neutralising or disempowering one another. Herein lies the WSF's aggregating power.

Notes

1. Edited version of part of a paper presented at the XXIV International Congress of the Latin American Studies Association, Dallas, USA, March 27–29, 2003. The second part appears later in this volume.
2. Bloch 1995, p 479.
3. Hinkelammert 2002.
4. Wallerstein and Balibar 1991; Quijano 2000.
5. Santos 1995, p 25.
6. Quijano 2000.
7. Santos 1998, 2000.
8. Santos 1995, pp 456-473; Santos 2001.
9. For instance, Bloch 1995, p 241.
10. Bloch 1995, p 306.
11. This is a drastically abridged version of the corresponding section in the original text (Santos 2003). Please refer to this text for the lengthy and enlightening discussion of political novelty, tensions, problems and possibilities surrounding the Forum's experience. —Eds.
12. Sen 2003.

The World Social Forum's 'Many Alternatives' To Globalisation[1]

P.J. James

Until recently, the discourse of TINA (There Is No Alternative) has been dominant in mainstream discussions pertaining to neoliberal globalisation. But now, the enchanting catchword is TAMA (There Are Many Alternatives). The immediate context for the ascendancy of this populist slogan is the launching of the WSF and the propaganda blitz unleashed through its websites. Quite reminiscent of the utopian and Christian socialists of yesteryears, WSF is now envisioning 'many alternatives' and even 'many worlds' to globalisation. With this perspective, the WSF is reincarnating itself in continent-wise and country-wise 'editions' such as the European Social Forum, African Social Forum, Asian Social Forum, and WSF-Brazil, WSF-Argentina, WSF-Palestine, WSF-India. Within countries there are even attempts for regional editions of WSF such as Kerala Social Forum (KSF) where the slogan is "Another Kerala is Possible!" Meanwhile, the catchword of the Hyderabad 'event' scheduled during January, the Asian Social Forum (ASF) with an "Asian vision and content" is "Another Asia is Possible!"

Conceived by eight Brazilian civil society and left libertarian groups, the idea of the WSF drew its inspiration from a Participatory Budgeting Programme, an experiment in 'civic governance' first proposed by the Union of Neighbourhood Associations of Porto Alegre (UAMPA) during the 1990s. Exactly a year before the formal launch of WSF in January 2001, an international conference, 'Real Utopias Project: Experiments in Empowered Democracy' was held at the University of Wisconsin in Madison, USA, to theorise on the empowerment dimension of the Porto Alegre participatory experiment and related experiments elsewhere. Along with the participatory municipal budgeting of Porto Alegre, the conference examined the Neighbourhood Governance Councils and Community Policing of Chicago, the Habitat Conservation Plan in the U.S., and the Participatory People's Plan in Kerala as 'real world utopias' or instances of 'empowered participatory governance.' The intellectual resources including the evolution of the conceptualisation culminating in the launching of WSF with its slogans of 'many alternatives' and 'many worlds' can be traced back to this 'utopian' conference held in the USA.

The WSF and the global NGOs associated with it have produced a flood of literature on various aspects and adverse effects of neoliberal globalisation in Afro-Asian-Latin American countries. The structural analysis of poverty, hunger, oppression, state repression, and environmental degradation, made by specialised intellectuals belonging to the WSF have certainly enhanced the global peoples' understanding of imperialist plunder. However, despite its eloquent critique of neoliberalism and rhetoric on 'many alternatives' to globalisation, the WSF approach to the problem is an impediment to a scientific understanding of neoliberal globalisation that is firmly rooted in the logic or laws of motion of imperialist capital. It does not extend a comprehensive understanding on globalisation. In its critique on globalisation, though the WSF keeps a radical posture, its newer and newer 'editions' or re-incarnations do not appear to be focussing on the political economy behind the global operations of capital.

To be specific, the ultimate outcome of WSF's analytical or academic exercises is to deviate the anti-imperialist struggles of working class people away from the badly needed political alternative. Rather than specifying the underlying political economy of neoliberal globalisation, the innumerable WSF events —conferences, seminars, workshops—are attempting to fragment and divert the whole issue. For instance, a participant in the scheduled ASF at Hyderabad is going to get a disaggregated view of globalisation—akin to the blind man's experience of the elephant—thereby nullifying a badly needed political approach. There is no question that this fragmentation and multiplication of social reality to the extreme ultimately serves the neoliberal objective of making it difficult to comprehend the historical dynamics and global working of imperialist capital.

This is well exemplified in the WSF theme of 'many alternatives.' According to its websites, as already noted, each 'edition' or 'event' of the WSF results in a hybridisation or localisation of its own alternative to globalisation such as "another Asia," "another Africa," "another India," or even "another Kerala" and so on, *ad infinitum*. Though attractive, implicit in this populist approach is a de-ideologisation and de-politicisation that betrays the indispensable internationalist perspective on neoliberal globalisation. This perspective demands an anti-imperialist alternative based on the solidarity and unity of the global working classes, in which the validity of the national terrain as the launching pad of anti-globalisation struggles is fully accepted. It also brings to the fore the utmost relevance of a socialist alternative to the decaying capitalist-imperialist system.

The WSF's sole orientation on national and regional specificities as is manifested in its absolutism with country-wise alternatives in gross disregard of the anti-imperialist socialist alternatives is an ingenious move to de-ideologise and deviate working people away from a class-based political economy and proletarian internationalism. In this specific historical context —where alternatives as 'socialism with Chinese characteristics' have degenerated to national chauvinism and narrow economic nationalism—the WSF's clarion call for country-specific 'many alternatives' which conspicuously avoids an ideological and political confrontation with global capital will have the hidden agenda of de-ideologising anti-imperialist struggles worldwide.

This position of the WSF is inseparably linked with its sectarian approach towards political movements and political parties in general. On the one hand, it says that the "WSF will always be a Forum open to pluralism and to diversity of activities and ways of engaging of organisations and movements that decide to participate in it."[2] It also says, "Neither party representations nor military organisations shall participate in the Forum." Thus, the WSF not only prohibits the entry of political parties in its 'events' but also, very revealingly, places them in the category of military organisations.

This highly illiberal and hence truly neoliberal position is not new nor an isolated one. It is a time-tested escapist attitude systematically cultivated by conservatives, and recently by the New Right, to keep the working class and its party away from mainstream discussions. Anti-communist theoreticians such as Kothari who now share common platforms with the WSF's Hyderabad 'event' have long been ardent proponents of 'a non-party process' in their version of people's alternatives led by what they call "motivated middle-class professionals."

The so-called 'pluralism' advocated by the WSF, its close affinity to 'new social movements' (NSMs), and its hatred towards class movements, all have wider ideological ramifications. Their roots lie deep in the post-Marxist prognosis on the decline or disappearance of the working class as a revolutionary force and the ascendancy of NSMs and NGOs as the "new revolutionary subject of history."

In a similar vein, the WSF Charter also speaks of its opposition "to all totalitarian and reductionist views of economy, development and history."[3] To be specific, the terminology 'totalitarian' and 'reductionism' are part of the usual mudslinging carried out by imperialist think tanks and postmodernists against the class approach upheld by communists. The WSF is simply parroting this malicious slander. As is obvious now, its very orientation is at variance with the class interests of workers, peasants and other toiling masses who are bound to fight capital's onslaught with a political orientation.

Perhaps the most debatable issue pertains to the ideological basis of the WSF itself. Its published documents reveal that the WSF is a forum of global civil society with a focus on NSMs and NGOs. WSF "brings together and interlinks only organisations and movements of civil society from all the countries in the world"[4] and "seeks to strengthen and create new national and international links among organisations and movements of civil society."[5] Thus, the WSF Charter and related documents can be seen making a line of demarcation between the politically oriented 'old movements' and the civic oriented 'new movements.'[6] Obviously, the WSF's emphasis is on civil society led by 'new movements' composed of voluntary organisations/NGOs, civil and community-based organisations at local, national and global levels.

Its antipathy towards political parties and 'statist' politics and affinity towards so-called civil society movements emanate from the post-modern conceptualisation of civil society as a counter to the State. This new discourse on civil society is part of a general trend that assumed prominence in neoliberal-postmodern thinking in the context of the collapse of the welfare state in the seventies.

Today, the post-modern emphasis on the centrality of civil society is used to fill the gap created by the withdrawal of the State from the sphere of development. Both post-Marxists and postmodernists visualise civil society as emerging out of the deconstruction of the political sphere and the consequent neutralisation of both the Left and the Right. Thus, the WSF's fascination with civil society is, at present, shared by a broad ideological spectrum ranging from the neoliberalists to the degenerated Left.

The conceptualisation of civil society is useful to neoliberal globalisation —not only to replace the public sector with private sector—but also to shift the burden of social service provision to the shoulders of people themselves under the garb of participatory people's alternatives. It is no wonder that the biggest votaries of civil society today are none other than the World Bank, USAID, UNDP, Ford Foundation, and so on. Regarding the idealisation of civil society, neoliberal agencies and the WSF are on the same wavelength. The World Bank defines civil society as the whole of the private sector led by NGOs and has established an executive wing called the 'World Bank/NGO Committee.' For the World Bank, market and civil society are synonymous; it defines the growth of democracy and 'good governance' in Afro-Asian-Latin American countries in terms of the degree of replacement of the traditional political sphere by civic action.

In this context, the neoliberal agencies' new-found affinity to civil society arises directly from their reluctance to recognise the existence of class society and class struggle. In contrast to this, according to working class positions firmly rooted in historical materialism, the so-called 'civil society' is a class society. Even much before the advent of Marxism, Rousseau, prophet of the French revolution, noted that the objective of all civil societies was "to stabilise and give legal status to inequalities originally based on force." Gramsci is only reiterating this when he defines civil society as the realm where the "hegemony or political power on one social group over the entire nation is exercised through subtle, intangible and invisible forms." In other words, dominant groups in civil society are always legitimised and sheltered by the State which exercises effective power through the hegemonisation of civil society. Rather than understanding state and political power as extensions of so-called civil society, post-Marxists, postmodernists and neoliberalists are placing both state and civil society in watertight compartments.

In fact, post-Marxists, postmodernists and neoliberal agencies are now resorting to a neo-Gramscian interpretation (which views Gramsci through a post-Marxist angle) on civil society as the site of radical and plural struggle against coercion by the State. They do this by negating his central emphasis on class and discarding the essentially dialectic and continuous relation between state and civil society that he stressed. A glance at WSF documents reveals the same visualisation. As the whole of the private sector including MNCs are part of civil society, there is a significant danger that even global civic action itself may reproduce the dangers of neoliberal globalisation—an aspect that the WSF cannot comprehend due to its negation of classes and of class struggles.

Of course, a number of organisations that share the WSF platform are fighting along with the organised working class and progressive forces against globalisation and IMF-WB-WTO agencies. These united moves are to be nurtured and further developed, though without any let-up on the part of progressive forces to achieve maximum possible solidarity among various sections fighting globalisation from different standpoints. At the same time, there must be an uncompromising ideological struggle to impart a correct orientation to such struggles, based on an objective evaluation of the underlying logic of globalisation. Here, the political struggles waged by the organised working class, peasants, and other toiling masses must form the core of the move. However, since such struggles belong to the domain of 'old movements,' the WSF cannot uphold them.

In India, unprecedented anti-globalisation struggles including all-India *bandhs* (strikes) are developing in the country, led by the organised working class. At one stage, the number was a staggering figure of 45 million—the biggest ever in recorded history. Obviously, the need of the hour is to give an anti-imperialist ideological and political orientation to these ever-mounting struggles in the political sphere. At this crucial juncture, the entry of the WSF with its 'many alternatives' and utopias which, rooted in the ideology of civil society and NSMs, and which refrain from addressing the crucial political economy of neoliberalism, will not be helpful for extending this anti-imperialist orientation to them. Alternatives propounded by the WSF are bound to be utopian on account of the latter's basic incapacity to unravel the laws of motion of capital, which is the driving force behind globalisation. As such, the advent of the WSF and its reincarnations or 'editions' including its academic exercises or 'events' may also have the hidden agenda of diverting people's struggles from an anti-imperialist political orientation.

Notes

1. Edited version of article in *Red Star, Platform for Communist Revolutionaries,* January 2003.
2. WSF Charter of Principles, Clause 9. See World Social Forum Organizing Committee, June 2001.
3. *Ibid.*, Clause 10.
4. *Ibid.*, Clause 5.
5. WSF India Policy Guidelines, Clause 18. See WSF India, July 2002.
6. See Programme Note for the Asian Social Fprum, Hyderabad, India, January 2003, page 9.

The World Social Forum, Beyond Critique And Deconstruction[1]

Emma Dowling, interviewed by Rebecca Shah

In this interview Rebecca Shah asks Emma Dowling to subject this year's 2007 World Social Forum at Nairobi and wider alter-globalisation movements to critique and to explore how it might be possible to move beyond critique and deconstruction into envisaging and creating an alternative possible world.

Can you start by telling us how the WSF movement came about and how you became involved with it?

The WSF started with ATTAC (Association for the Taxation of Financial Transactions for the Aid of Citizens, an alter-globalisation organisation), NGOs in Brazil, and left wing political movements who were organising around the issue of globalisation and against global financial institutions. Perhaps similarly to the Zapatista *Encuentro* (encounter, open meeting) that had already taken place in Chiapas in Mexico; the idea was to have an event where members of different movements and organisations could come together and network in order to strengthen their projects. Important in this is not just the moment that is the WSF with workshops and seminars, plenary sessions, and other meetings, but also that people have a continued engagement with each other year after year and can build a more coherent movement through the process of exchange of information, strategy, or ideas. People become friends and comrades in the process.

I first became involved with the WSF because I was active with ATTAC around the time that the first European Social Forum (ESF) happened in Florence, November 2002. I knew about the first WSF taking place in Porto Alegre before that and wasn't able to go, but attended the ESF 2003 in Paris. So I've been around the social forum process since near the beginning and became involved directly in the organisational process when the ESF came to London, in November 2004. And after that I went to the WSF in Brazil in 2005 as part of a project called *Explorations in Open Space*, which explored what the Forum as an open space means in terms of political practice, whether the Forum should remain an open space or have a more clearly articulated political programme. I personally think the Forum has never been an open space; I think it's a logical contradiction![2]

How far do you think the movement can be seen as an attitude of critique and deconstruction on the history of the dominant world order?

Very much so. The Forum comprises a vast array of different actors that come together under the theme 'Another World is Possible,' or, as some people prefer to put it, 'Other Worlds Are Possible,' which doesn't reinforce a universalising discourse around one world being possible. The movement comes out of wanting to critique the Thatcherite slogan that 'there is no alternative' to the globalisation of capitalist social relations. It's very difficult to put labels on the Forum but if anything it is anti-neoliberal, not anti-capitalist. It calls into question neoliberalism, the Washington Consensus, the fact that people are less important than profit. It is part of the whole new wave of global politics around neoliberal restructuring.

There are different narratives about when this movement started to coalesce. Many people argue that it was 1994 with the Zapatista uprising, others talk about Seattle, and others see it as a new cycle of struggles that has its antecedents in the 1968 movements, but this particular phase is about critiquing capitalist, neoliberal globalisation. The first WSF tried to put this critique onto the agenda, which is why it organised its timing each year to coincide with the World Economic Forum.

Let's talk about the physical WSF space. This year, you went to the WSF in Nairobi. What were your impressions? How did it compare to previous Forums?

There have been social forums on the African continent before—last year there was a polycentric Forum in Bamako, Mali—but it's the first time that the WSF as one unified event has taken place in Africa. It was very different to my experiences of being in Porto Alegre. The Forum is so diverse that it is a difficult thing to label. There are multiple subjectivities, from left-wing anti-capitalists to liberal lobby groups, NGOs, anarchists and independent activists, citizen activists, environmental campaigners, and feminists, so once you start trying to label the WSF you run into problems. Bearing that in mind, I felt that there was one particular discourse which seemed to permeate this year's Forum: the big influence of large NGOs that have money.

There are a number of reasons for this. The first is that the Forum was taking place without political or financial support from the local council or the Kenyan government. They weren't opposed to the Forum taking place—it was viewed as a lucrative opportunity for local businesses—but it was not actively endorsed or funded, as far as I can tell. That meant funding had to come from elsewhere. WSF funding always comes from multiple sources, but in the past local councils have provided funding or infrastructure or something. When the Forum took place in London, the Mayor Ken Livingstone's office gave a lot of money to the Forum. I don't know enough about the events in the run up to the Forum, nor am I familiar with Kenyan politics in any detail, but a Kenyan friend of mine mused that even if there might at some point have been money allocated to the WSF, it probably would have never reached its destination because of the high levels of corruption within governmental structures.

The second reason why there was a presence of large NGOs is that Nairobi is the United Nations and aid-agency capital of east and central Africa; thus these organisations are there and obviously they're going to get involved in something that's happening on their doorstep. Given the evident shift in discourse that has taken place in recent years, from one in which neoliberal restructuring was imposed as an inevitable global development, to one which promotes 'globalisation with a human face,' maybe even as a result of the alter-globalisation movements, organisations that wouldn't have seen themselves as part of this space ten years ago do see themselves as part of it now.

The third reason is that in Africa, from what I can tell, the legacy of the Christian mission and the neo-colonial politics of charity helping developing countries to 'develop' still loom large, which is a really problematic issue. This is different to Latin America where there have been these organisations but in a very different historical context.

So the big NGOs represent not only the dominant, wealthy, capital-based societies, but also the ideas of neoliberalism and neo-colonialism which the WSF was set up in opposition to?

Many of them do. Although you could argue that a good deal of the people that are part of this movement don't necessarily see charitable causes or the format they take as problems, so they have a different politics from my politics. There are also religious organisations that see themselves as part of the alter-globalisation movement, so it is a space that encompasses all these forces. Church organisations and poverty and development NGOs exist in this space because they think they're also about making the world a better place and helping people. They are also there because of the self-organised nature of the Forum.

It is precisely because the space is articulated as some sort of non-partisan space (whether it can or should be non-partisan is another question) that it is an opportunity for people with power and money to monopolise that process. In that moment, self-organisation backfires because those with more money are able to put on bigger events. For example, the Human Rights and Human Dignity caucus, which was a UN-related group and that had about eighty sessions in the Nairobi WSF with a massive tent in a very prominent place, could do that because the Forum is a self-organised space. In the London ESF, larger organisations like trade unions and particularly the Mayor's office made concerted, very well-organised attempts to completely monopolise the Forum and succeeded in doing so because they had money and power. The challenge is how we can come together and have these networking moments without reproducing these relations.

What happened recently in Nairobi after the Forum took place is, I think, indicative of the contradictions that are embodied in the participation of some of the larger NGOs and UN agencies in the WSF events. In March this year (2007), fifty-six activists who had been using Nairobi's Jeevanjee Gardens as a meeting space for their open Forum for many years, and who organised an alternative forum during the Nairobi Forum, were beaten and arrested for 'unlawful assembly' in a dispute over the planned 'regeneration' of the gardens which the activists were opposed to because they claimed it was being turned into a public bus park without any consultation with the people who use the space, as well as being an attempt to take it away from the people that currently access this public space. According to reports I've read, the Nairobi city council is working on this in partnership with UN Habitat, which was also a major player within the Human Rights and Human Dignity Caucus at this year's WSF.

How do the big NGOs influence what happens within the Forum space?

There used to be a lot of large-scale plenary sessions within the WSF, which—because of the investment involved—were organised only by the WSF's own organising committee or the big NGOs, so they used to dominate the space in this way at that time. But the emphasis within the Forum has shifted and is now more on smaller workshops and seminars where different groups come together to organise sessions on different political themes. These range from neoliberalism or capitalism to human rights, environmental concerns, land and housing, financial markets... There's very focused networking that goes on, or showcasing of campaigns but also information and ideas sharing, as well as political exchange. All of these things take place. What I think was a problem is that this year, one of these again became more dominant —there was a lot of showcasing. It's a form of politics which feels a bit like a trade fair or business meeting.

I think it's also useful to remember the context in which the larger NGOs play a role in African countries. These organisations have been working in an African context for many years, and they have African partners, so it's not that the WSF itself puts poverty alleviation on the map when it comes to town. There are connections that already exist. But the way that they in some instances played themselves out within Forum meetings was quite problematic. For example, I was in a session about the G8, and the organisations from the global north who were there had their partners—who are from African countries—either on stage with them or sitting in the audience, and together they both proliferated the same discourse. But if you want to challenge that, but you are yourself from the global north, you can't—because it then looks as though you're imposing your white, western, middle class way of looking at the world, when the 'African' people say that they want the same things as these northern organisations. Do you see what I mean?

Yes, the WSF is supposed to be a place without power structures within it, but clearly there are power differences, not only in terms of money—between those that can afford to self-organise and those that can't—but also in terms of the interpersonal interactions.

Any social forum exists within existing neoliberal social relations and not outside of the system, and it would be foolish to think otherwise. I say 'open space' is a logical misnomer because to declare a space in which power doesn't exist or shouldn't play a role is impossible. If we understand power as being a relation and as something that permeates our relations, then power never goes away. Power is not a commodity that you can leave at the door; it comes with you in your spaces, through your interactions with other people. You can't just declare power to not matter anymore. Political practice has to be informed by that notion so that we can understand the power relations that exist in those spaces and deal with them, not so that then we can live in a world without power. We need to find better ways of dealing with it and also generate contestation and conflict in a productive way so that we can move forward.

Do you think that the WSF is a space that is able to engage with ideas about power?

I think it can if we have a different political practice. There are many problems that fed into why I felt frustrated at the Nairobi Forum—both the declarative politics and the opposite, when people start invoking 'the other' the whole time, like "Where are the African people? Where are the African social movements? We need an African to talk about this!"

This becomes a reification of 'the African' without understanding that Africa is a complex place. You can't really have 'the African' who comes and gives the 'subaltern' perspective on whatever problem you're discussing at that moment. I think the problem is two-fold: On the one hand, this invocation of the African voice stems from a desire not to reproduce white privilege, which is a good thing, but on the other, it appeals to an identity that does not exist in such a simplistic way, nor does it address the complexities of social and capitalist hierarchies that exist within Africa.

Furthermore, I feel there is a tendency to universalise the subjectivity of people involved with the WSF movement. We tend to say that we see ourselves as all being part of the same movement or having the same enemy, whether that's imperialism, capitalism, environmental degradation, human rights abuses or whatever, and within that there seems to be very little space to understand how we as individuals with our different locations, struggles, and subjectivities come together or conflict; and how to work through that if we're going to get anywhere beyond fictional solidarities, statements of intent or lowest common denominator politics, which is what it often ends up being. So on the one hand, we celebrate our diversity and multiplicity and we see that as our strength (and sometimes also our problem); but on the other, what permeates that is actually a denial of difference, because we do not understand our different localities in relation to one another within the struggle and within global capitalism.

Does the WSF, as it stands, have the space or the ability to consider these ideas of identity politics, or will focusing on these things subvert the purpose of a non-directive space?

I don't think we should talk about identity politics in the sense of something static. One of the problems of some 'new' social movements is too static an understanding of different identities—the homosexual, the woman, the environmental activist—which are different identities as opposed to subjectivities. Then organising happens around those different identities and it becomes much more about lobby-politics to have your identity represented in a space than trying to understand the different power relations, interconnections, and sites of contestation between these different moments.

This is also a problem when class is ignored. Class isn't talked about much any more because it's supposedly an antiquated way of understanding the world now we have these multiple social identities more important than class or capitalist social relations. But it should be the *interconnections* between capitalism and social identities, as well as reconfiguration of class composition, that we address within our movements, not one or the other. What I find lacking is bringing it back to ourselves and who we are in that space. It becomes about something that exists outside of that space, and not something we bring with us into the space. The WSF is then seen as standing outside of the relations that we're trying to deal with—as if neoliberalism, capitalism, and human rights violations only exist 'out there.' The WSF is, of course, a space where we bring all of that with us, so we have to be able to deal with it within the structures as well as in the outside world.

Returning to your experiences at this year's Forum—I have read reports that this Forum attracted only a fraction of the numbers that attended last year's Forum. Can you reflect on why this may be, for example, whether it is a practical matter to do with where and how it was organised or more to do with diminishing global interest in the WSF?

I thought a lot about this because at the Forum I had a sense of emptiness. There was a lot of hustle and bustle and there were obviously lots of people around, but I still had a sense of emptiness. Rooms were empty. There was also a sense of an absence. For me that absence was ordinary people and local movements. There seemed to be representatives of local organisations and there were lots of people from the slums but they had been brought there through organisations.

So you think attendance had a lot to do with the context of where it was held?

I think so. If it had been in South Africa for example, it might have been very different because South Africa has quite strong movements and the anti-apartheid struggle still figures quite largely in people's politicisation. By comparison, in Kenya the Mau Mau movement was defeated, and although it did pave the way for Kenyan independence, two quite autocratic regimes followed under presidents Kenyatta and Moi. There is also the idea that the WSF is a place where representatives of organisations come together, not the members of organisations. Not everybody agrees with this but the discourse does exist. We also have to remember that the ability to travel depends on one's financial and visa situation. But maybe it's also that people are now wondering whether the WSF is a politically useful process for them.

I haven't spoken to anybody about this in any detail, but I think some people who view themselves as anti-capitalist, and who maybe trace their history back more directly to the Zapatista movement, feel that going to the Forum doesn't make sense because it's dislocated from local contexts and local struggles because it is dominated by the old left, NGOs, or other forces they feel uncomfortable with. Maybe they felt that there wouldn't be anybody that they want to connect with because those people can't afford to go. But there is a sense that a lot of people are beginning to ask, 'Well, what purpose does the Forum serve in any sort of effective way?'

The Forum is different from more traditional political movements because it doesn't aim at a particular solution, it is purely a space. But are participants able to value it as a space and a process or do they need a purpose—goals and outcomes—in order to value it?

I think problems start when we try to impose an overarching purpose on our everyday struggles. The WSF tries to avoid that by saying that it's not trying to be a political programme. At the same time, if you've got an open space, all that can be is a space! You have to understand what the limitations of the WSF are. You can use it to meet people and strengthen your networks, but if the right people aren't there then you can't connect with them! It becomes a vicious circle.

I don't think that the movement needs an overarching programme, which is what some people within the Forum have tried to do. Or, rather, they have said not that the WSF needs to develop a programme itself but that the WSF space should be used to develop a programme for the movement. For example, the *Porto Alegre Manifesto* of the G19 at the 2005 Forum resulted from nineteen predominantly male intellectuals and activists who got together to develop a programme for what they thought should happen in the world.[3] But because many people at that Forum were very critical of their trying to impose a programme on the movement, they later retracted it saying it was only one proposal amongst many others. But after that, it happened again, in Bamako the next year, when some people—including some of the authors of the Porto Alegre Manifesto—developed and put forward a new document, the *Bamako Appeal*, which was pages and pages of what should happen to make the world a better place, tackling everything from gender politics to labour struggles, environmental struggles, new forms of democracy, global capitalism.[4] And that has started a debate about open space verses political programme. This is unresolved.

Immanuel Wallerstein, who has been quite supportive of the Bamako Appeal, said in the Herald Tribune that this year's Forum moved beyond the debate about whether the Forum is a space or a political programme, or whether it needs a political programme, because in Nairobi everybody got together and just got on with it. A similar argument was put forward in a German newspaper article I read, that because the Forum was taking place on the African continent where poverty and reality were staring us in the face, we couldn't have airy-fairy debates about left-wing politics any more.[5] It said that we actually had to get down to reality and start organising practically because hunger and starvation were screaming at us.

But do you think they were? According to the reports I've read, hunger and poverty were kept at some distance away from the Nairobi Forum, by the high entrance fees!

Yes, but hunger and poverty also came to the Forum and challenged it, which is really important because what I think the Forum needs to be is not an open space but a space of contestation where we can actually engage with one another. Contestations were happening at the Forum which was very positive but also very tragic because local Kenyan people had to storm the gates and demand free entry. Slum kids were swarming through the Forum and demanding free food from the Windsor Hotel and the Norfolk Hotel, which respectively belong to the Kenyan Interior Minister and was the first colonial hotel in Nairobi. These two, that would otherwise be considered the enemy in anybody's book, were providing five-star food for Forum participants at extortionate prices. It was a massive problem. The kids were demanding free food and there were actual food riots. I was there to show my support and solidarity with these young people because it was absolutely outrageous. Why were the small local traders providing food relegated to some place further away and in our faces were five star hotels that were selling us food?

Things that I had read were very critical of those aspects of this year's Forum—the commercialism and lack of access for local poor people—but you make it sound like an example of what the Forum is all about: A space where genuine challenges and contestations can happen. Would you say it wasn't altogether a negative experience, perhaps even a strength that problems can be challenged and dealt with in the space?

Yes, in this sense we can understand conflict as producing change. Though it remains to be seen how the Forum process responds to these issues. It was addressed formally by the Assembly of Social Movements, an assembly which exists within the Forum because the Forum is not supposed to make any decisions. The idea is that the different movements which participate in the Forum can come together and make some decisions on what may be the focus of campaigns. The February 15th anti-war march in 2003 was something that came out of the Forum process, for example, or the pledge to participate in the G8 summit protests. This year, at the Nairobi Forum, the Assembly of Social Movements' declaration condemned the commercialisation, the NGOisation, and the militarisation of the WSF.[6]

I haven't mentioned that we not only had five-star hotels providing food, but we also had to buy air time from a mobile phone company in order to register for the Forum. The Forum was sponsored by Celtel, which is a Kuwaiti-owned corporation providing cell-phone infrastructure in fifteen different African countries and in countries in the Middle East.[7]

Funding would appear to be an ongoing problem, especially if the Forum is to behave in a way that embodies the ideals it intends to promote and discuss.

I think one problem is that of scale. It's very easy to have a gathering of a hundred people and live up to your anti-profit ideals. But if you're trying to cater for hundreds of thousands of people, it shifts. I fully understand that. I think, however, that we have already come a very long way in trying to generate alternatives and that wasn't apparent at this year's Forum. For example, in Porto Alegre there was a massive solidarity economy space. Granted, there's a bigger solidarity economy movement in Latin America, but even in Africa there are many cooperatives that function very well, but they were not involved. In the same token, if you can use open source software, why use Microsoft? They might not solve all of the problems but alternatives do exist, and so we at least need to be engaging with them. It seemed to me that too many compromises were made this year.

I understand that some local organisers took alternative action outside the Forum to voice their discontent with some of these compromises.

That's right; as I said, there was an alternative forum that was organised in the Jeevanjee Gardens in the centre of town by the Citizen's Assembly, which is a coalition of local groups including the emerging Social Activism

Network and People's Parliament. These organisations—which have been meeting on a weekly basis throughout the year for some time now, in the Gardens—felt the need to have an event that was visible and accessible to the local Kenyan population and that was free. It was also a political statement that the Forum was deeply problematic in how it involved or did not involve local people. The people that I spoke to there weren't against the Forum, but they were against some of the things we've talked about here that happened around it.

If this was planned in advance, it must have been known before the WSF took place that it would encounter problems and fail to allow suitable access for local people?

Yes, I think the forum at the Jenvanjee Gardens was planned from back in December (2006). It wasn't advertised on the WSF website but I found out about it because of a protest at the WSF opening ceremony where people came with banners that said: 'Five hundred KSH (Kenyan shillings, or about U.S. $ 7) to go to the Forum, or feed my children for a week? Come to the alternative forum in the Jeevanjee Gardens.'

So I went to an event there that had over a hundred local Kenyan people and a few white people dotted around, including myself. Immediately I felt quite uncomfortable. I wasn't used to being in a space where I was in the minority, so that was already an experience for me. People were talking about the WTO and youth and their experiences as farmers or living in the slums, about rape, about not being able to feed themselves, send their children to school, or to get an adequate price for their produce. It was interesting to see how people there were saying 'Well, we've had NGOs for forty years and our problems remain' - indicating that there are problems with the way certain NGOs are doing politics. We can't throw every NGO into the same pot, but I mean the big poverty and development NGOs, the church organisations. There was critique. One guy gave a message to 'civil society' critiquing the whole problem of colonial liberalism, which I thought was very interesting.

Was this debate happening inside the WSF as well?

In some spaces it was, but I felt it wasn't problematised sufficiently because there were too many organisations there that were heralding their successes as opposed to critiquing and deconstructing problems. There was a lot of 'look at the fantastic sanitation project that we're doing in this slum' or 'this brilliant education project that we're doing here, isn't it great that we have brought all these slum dwellers to the Forum?' or 'come to the slum and see our project.' It was interesting that the message across the board was: 'The subject of social transformation is in the slum. Let's go and see it.' Whatever the politics of the people saying it, the message seemed to be the same. Everyone was looking for this subject of social transformation or the victim that needed to be helped. All of us were looking for 'them.'

Over 50% of the population of Nairobi lives in slums. I went to Korogocho slum because I had met a person from Kibera (another slum) at the opening ceremony. He took me to Korogocho with another friend. First we went to this Catholic mission where there were lots of white people with cameras taking pictures of the slum and all the slum children were performing for the visitors. I found this very problematic. Then we went looking for a radio and newspaper project which is being run by local youth from the slum, which I was interested in because it was more self-organised.

It was interesting for me to deal with who I was, why I was there, and whether I was also on my own little mission to find the people that I'm supposed to be in solidarity with or wanting to help. It was interesting to try to understand how that plays itself out for me personally and my politics but also how this problem was situated within and around the Forum. I found it problematic that slum dwellers became the 'what's hot' of the Forum. But I also felt I had found the self-organised project fantastic! That is the kind of politics that I support here—a politics of the first person where you engage with your own struggles, rather than the struggles of the other that you're in solidarity with or you're trying to help.

But I found some of the material produced in the newspaper produced by this project to be really problematic. There were pro-life, anti-abortion articles and an article that read almost as if women were blaming themselves for rape, saying 'If we weren't so corrupted by capitalism and the images of women half-naked on television then we wouldn't go around wearing mini-skirts and then we wouldn't be raped.' On the one hand, I think it is important that the needs and demands of people who have been marginalised, excluded, or exploited, are put at the centre of our movements' politics. But at the same time, I don't think this should lead to a reification or a deification of a supposedly unified 'subaltern.' So how do we engage with one another? I want to be able to critique others if I think that there is a problem with their politics, but at the same time we need to be able to do that in a space where it's an engagement, where we don't simply judge or accuse each other and then walk away. How does that play itself out? Am I acting out a moment of privilege if I criticise an African person? How do we forge real solidarities and common projects?

What is diversity, and what is solidarity? There was a demonstration of people from the Kibera slum at the WSF opening ceremony and it was unclear what the demonstration was about. There were organised slum-dweller groups, many of them connected to local churches. They had people dancing with headscarves and t-shirts about their organisation and all these people waving Palestinian flags. There were Christians and pro-Palestinians marching together. Was this a celebration of diversity? Or did people get confused about what it was about? We asked some young people who were waving Palestinian flags what flag they were waving. They were very indignant. One said, 'Don't you know? This is the Kenyan flag,' and then another said 'It's the Spanish flag.' That was a real moment where I thought 'Wow, who's been going round here distributing these flags not actually telling people what the hell they're waving?.'

This reminds me of people waving banners distributed by the Socialist Worker's Party (SWP) at the anti-war march in London in 2003 without understanding what the SWP stood for and how it related to the shared anti-war issue. My question is whether your experiences were really special because of the context or just indicative of a global problem?

I think it's a problem of political practice, not of location. It's a problem when we don't give enough space to forms of education or understanding that try to unpack things, critique, deconstruct, and move beyond the immediate context and simplicity. It's very easy to say that Africans are corrupt, women are oppressed, and so on, and if only people had the right moral values then the world would be a better place—or whatever it is that you choose to brand as the key to unlocking all the problems of the world. I think we need to start from people's experiences to try to make sense of it, rather than starting from explanation and trying to match the experience to the explanation.

But also, where does our own humility come in? I have a problem with the Catholic Church and all organised religion because that is the conclusion I have come to through my own experience of life and politics. How do I then acknowledge and have the humility to understand that religion is, for many of the Kenyan people I met, central to their lives and their politics? Also, how can I critique the problems I see with the way that the Catholic Church operates?

I was talking to a friend I made who was involved in organising the events in the Jeevanjee Gardens, and he was saying one of the biggest problems in trying to organise at a grass-roots level was that African people are still in this mind-set that 'White people know better.' In a binary construct, white people are seen as either the problem or the solution. Whether it's a positive or negative image of the white person, the construction is always in relation to the white person. He told me that when the white person left his group, it seemed as if other people didn't have faith in themselves to know what to do.

The WSF is supposed to be a place where we can critique some of these things and then move beyond them. But if our practices within and around the Forum space don't engage with these problems, then we're not going to be able to move on. Reading the résumé of the international council meeting after the WSF, there was some self-criticism about mistakes such as the huge military presence at the Forum—massive machine guns turning away four-year-old children from the slums, and so on—and also commercialisation. But there was no discussion of political practice. We need, on so many levels, to ask ourselves: How we can get back to—or get forward to—a sort of politics which engages us with one another?

Is this failure to engage related to the fact that the Forum promotes a particular form of social and political organisation (eg NGOs) under what is ostensibly a non-directive approach to social organisation?

Absolutely. I think that this happens when we lose our sense of critique and our understanding of the constellation of forces within which we are situated. In the same way, if you look at the G8 summit protest in the UK in 2005, the massive campaign of Make Poverty History and the Live 8 concerts to all intents and purposes hijacked the movement, and even though NGOs that were involved in the Make Poverty History campaign have always been part of the movement protesting against the G8 in a lobbying capacity.

What seemed to happen in Gleneagles—the G8 summit protest in the UK —was that the movement became a force to *legitimise* rather than *delegitimise* the G8. The G8 became elevated to a position where it could be, if only it was willing to listen to the movement, a force for good in the world—instead of understanding that structurally speaking, this institution can never change the rules of the game because it is an epiphenomenon of the system where the rules are being set. How can giving it more power and more legitimacy solve the problem?

The alter-globalisation movement has been successful in shifting discourse by challenging neoliberalism and the idea that there is no alternative to it, but shifts in discourse do not necessarily mean shifts in material realities. The G8 is talking about climate change and Africa using discourses that are coming out of the movement and translating them into policies which on the surface *look* like they're moving towards something different. It is not necessarily lying, even though a lot of it is rhetoric, but actually if we unpack the policies they are just doing the same old thing. It is a problem when discourses shift but practice doesn't. That is the problem with lobby politics. If you're asking the problem to sort out the problem, then the problem is unlikely to be solved!

Do you think that the WSF, as a place where process is said to matter above outcomes, unlike the G8 protests, might present a better opportunity for longer-term genuinely transformative change—if it isn't subverted along the way in power struggles?

Yes. And if our struggles also aren't about trying to find different ways of doing things simply in abstract terms, but also on a practical level, then we actually need to think not only how to confront global capitalism but also how to organise our every-day lives differently. And that doesn't mean having some sort of utopia at the end of it. It means engaging in our everyday struggles that then transform things on multiple levels.

Maybe having these massive events is counter-productive. Maybe we need to think of different ways of doing things like going back to more decentralised ways of organising. I don't know what the answer is. I've gained a lot from going to Forums. I think they have been useful—but you can't have only one moment of attack to the system. And so it's interesting in this respect, that there is going to be no single WSF event in the coming year (2008). I think that the Forum organisers were feeling over-stretched trying to organise annual Forums. It seems that people want to go back to what I call 'visibility exercises,' so later this year (2007) there will be a big focus on the G8 and next year, instead of a Forum, there will be a week of decentralised global days of action. These decentralised actions will be in direct confrontation with the system but will also say 'We're still here! We're still doing what we do and it's still important,' rather than having a one-off meeting that the media and others aren't really interested in.

It's like trying to change the form in order to gain some ground again, but in some ways it's also a return to an emphasis on direct confrontation with the system, like the much-heralded anti-WTO protests in Seattle in 1999.

It may seem retrogressive, but it's also engaging with the ideas that you mentioned of the Forum recognising itself, its internal power structures and its situation within the world. Maybe decentralised and contextualised action will strengthen the global meetings of the future?

Yes, I hope so. I still have faith! Then we have to ask: How do we use the connections that we've made? We've been meeting with each other for a long time now, so has that strengthened what we've been trying to do or not? I think it has. I think it's been an amazing resurgence of political activity, not just in the social forums but everyday communication over the internet coupled with people travelling, exchanging analyses, strategies, and visions, visiting different struggles all over the world. These exchanges have strengthened our networks and we've learned a lot in the process. It's been incredibly useful, and my critiques of the Forum and the different movements are in that spirit. I don't think it's all wrong, but we do need to think about how this is working, what direction it's going in, and how different events and process are necessary at different moments in time.

Do you think it's meaningful to start thinking about beyond critique and deconstruction? Is it possible to imagine another possible world before we deconstruct what we have now, who we are and how we relate to each other?

I don't think we can see it in those terms. I think it's a false dichotomy to talk about critique and deconstruction as things that are different from reconstruction. Part of changing the world or reconfiguring social and power relations is about critique and deconstruction. It has to be an ongoing process. I don't believe in utopias. We should see critique and deconstruction as something ongoing in our political practice, that never goes away. We're always re-instituting something that isn't perfect so we always have to be critiquing and deconstructing that and prefiguring these social relations as we go along.

I think we're always prefiguring in the here and now something that we want to exist, and whereas that opens up a whole new space to talk about politics, it doesn't mean that then all that matters is the every-day practices of human interaction and alternative modes of production and consumption. Of course there is still a political sphere and there are still nation states, and there are many different sites of politics and of struggle. Thus, simply pre-figuring the desired world is not sufficient for social and political change to occur; but it's an important element. So I think 'deconstruction' and 'reconfiguration' are two sides of the same coin. They go together and we can't see it in this linear way. So the Forum can't move through stages of first critique, then deconstruction, then reconstructing this other world.

So we should more see it as an ongoing and hopefully eternally incomplete project?

Yes, I would say so. And that relates to what we think the purpose of the Forum is. We need to be looking at the struggles that go on every day. That's where we can change things, have successes and gain ground. The Forum should be this space where we can engage with one another. Whether the Forum as an event is a good idea or not might change in the next five years, but that doesn't mean that it is wrong now, or that it was wrong five years ago. It means that there comes a point when we have to reconfigure and rethink and maybe have a different strategy for some time which might then change again depending on the needs of that moment.

I was really reassured to have a conversation with someone from the Nairobi citizen's assembly about these issues. He had a real bone to pick with civil society—if the WSF is civil society—because it's not involving ordinary people. My question to him was: 'What is it that we have to do to win? Is it involving local people, or something else? What is the key to changing things?' And he said, 'I think we're actually already winning, because we're sitting here having this conversation.'

That sounds trite, but at the same time if we don't start from who we are and build from there then I don't think we're going to get very far.

That sounds like a positive place to end our conversation too. Thank you for your insights into the complex praxis and politics that underlie the WSF. Given our conversation, it will clearly not be an easy journey, but I want to ask you in closing; Do you think another world is possible?

I think other worlds already exist!

Notes

1. This is an edited version of the interview first published in *In-spire—e-Journal of Politics, International Relations, and the Environment,* www.in-spire.org, Vol 2, No 1, June 2007, issue title 'Beyond Critiques and Deconstruction.' Available at http://www.in-spire.org/current.html. The editors thank the author Emma Dowling, and Rohee Dasgupta, Managing Editor of In-spire, for permission to include this interview in this book.
2. For a report and assessment of the *Explorations in Open Space* workshops in 2005, see Juris and Nunes, June 2005.
3. See the Group of Nineteen's statement, in this volume.
4. See the introduction to the Bamako Appeal, in this volume.
5. Brand, January 2007.
6. See this volume.
7. See http://www.celtel.com/en/our-company/our-investors/index.html.

RESISTANCE TO NEOLIBERALISM AND MILITARISM: FOR PEACE AND SOCIAL JUSTICE

Call of Social Movements, the 2nd World Social Forum Porto Alegre, January 2002[1]

1) In the face of continuing deterioration in the living conditions of people, we, social movements from all around the world, have come together in the tens of thousands at the second World Social Forum in the Porto Alegre. We are here in spite of the attempts to break our solidarity. We come together again to continue our struggles against neoliberalism and war, to confirm the agreements of the last Forum and to reaffirm that another world is possible.

2) We are diverse—women and men, adults and youth, indigenous peoples, rural and urban, workers and unemployed, homeless, the elderly, students, professionals, peoples of every creed, colour and sexual orientation. The expression of this diversity is our strength and the basis of our unity. We are a global solidarity movement, united in our determination to fight against the concentration of wealth, the proliferation of poverty and inequalities, and the destruction of our earth. We are constructing alternative systems, and using creative ways to promote them. We are building a large alliance from our struggles and resistance against a system based on patriarchy, racism and violence, which privileges the interests of capital over the need and aspirations of people.

3) This system produces a daily drama of women, children and the elderly dying because of hunger, lack of health care and preventable diseases. Families are forced to leave their homes because of wars, the impact of 'big development', landlessness and environmental disasters, unemployment, attack on public services and the destruction of social solidarity. Both in the South and in the North, vibrant struggles and resistance to uphold the dignity of life are flourishing.

4) September 11 marked a dramatic change. After the terrorist attacks, which we absolutely condemn, as we condemn all other attacks on civilians in other parts of the world, the government of the United States and its allies has launched a massive military operation. In the name of the 'war against terrorism', civil and political rights are being attacked all over the world. The terrorist war against Afghanistan is now being extended to other fronts. Thus there is the beginning of a permanent global war to cement the domination of US government and its allies. This war reveals another face of neoliberalism, a face which is brutal and unacceptable. Islam is being demonised, while racism and xenophobia are

deliberately propagated. The mass media is actively taking part in this belligerent campaign which divides the world into 'good' and 'evil'. The opposition to this war is at the heart of our movement.

5) The situation of war has further destabilised the Middle East region, providing a pretext for further repression of Palestinian people and their struggle for self-determination as they face brutal suppression by the Israeli State. This is vital to collective security of all peoples in the region.

6) Further events also confirm the urgency of our struggles. In Argentina the financial crisis caused by the failure of IMF structural adjustment, and mounting debt precipitated a social and political crisis. This crisis generated spontaneous protests of the middle and working classes, repression, which caused deaths, changes in the government, and new alliances between different social groups. With the force of *cacerolazos*, the people have ensured the satisfaction of their demands.

7) The collapse of the multinational Enron exemplifies the bankruptcy of the casino economy and the corruption of businessmen and politicians. Workers have been left without jobs and pensions. In developing countries this multinational engaged in fraudulent activities and its projects pushed people off their land and led to sharp increases in the price of water and electricity.

8) The United States government, in its efforts to protect the interests of big corporations, arrogantly walked away from negotiations on global warming, the antiballistic missile treaty, the Convention on Biodiversity, the UN conference on racism and intolerance, and the talks to reduce the supply of small arms, proving once again that U.S. unilateralism undermines attempts to find multilateral solutions to global problems.

9) In Genoa the G8 failed completely in its self-assumed task of global government. In the face of massive mobilisation and resistance, they responded with violence and repression, denouncing as criminals those who dared to protest. But they failed to intimidate our movement.

10) All this is happening in the context of a global recession. The neoliberal economic model is destroying the rights, living conditions and livelihoods of people. Using every means to protect their 'share value', multinational companies lay off workers, slash wages and close factories, squeezing the last dollar from the workers. Government faced with this economic crisis responds by privatising, cutting social sector expenditures and permanently reducing worker's rights. This recession exposes the fact that the neoliberal promise of growth and prosperity is a lie.

11) The global movement for social justice and solidarity faces enormous challenges: its fight for peace and collective security implies confronting poverty, discriminations, domination and the creation of an alternative sustainable society.

Social movements energetically condemn violence and militarism as a means of conflict resolution; the promotion of low intensity conflicts and military operations in the Colombia Plan as part of Andes regional initiative, the Puebla Panama plan, the arms trade and higher military budgets, economic blockades against people and nations especially against Cuba and Iraq, and the growing repression against trade unionists and activists.

We support the trade unions and informal sector worker struggles as an essential instrument to maintain work and life conditions, the genuine right to get organised, to go on strike, to negotiate collective agreements at different levels, and to achieve equality in wages and working conditions between women and men. We reject slavery and the exploitation of children. We support workers struggles and the trade union fights against casualisation, subcontracting of labour and lay off, and demand new international rights for the employees of multinational companies, and their affiliates, in particular the right to unionise and space for collective bargaining.

12) Neoliberal policies create further misery and insecurity. They have dramatically increased the trafficking and sexual exploitation of women and children that we condemn strongly. Poverty and insecurity also lead to migration and millions of human beings are denied their dignity, freedom and rights. We therefore demand the right of free movement; the right to physical integrity and legal status and legal status of all migrant workers. We support the rights of indigenous people and the fulfilment of ILO article169 in national legal frameworks.

13) The external debt of the countries of the South has been repaid several times over. Illegitimate, unjust and fraudulent, debt functions as an instrument of domination, depriving people of their fundamental human rights with the sole aim of increasing international usury. We demand unconditional cancellation of debt and the reparation of historical, social and ecological debts. The countries demanding repayment of debt have engaged in exploitation of the natural resources and knowledge of South.

14) Water, land, food, forests, seeds, culture and people's identities are common assets of humanity for present and future generations. It is essential to preserve biodiversity. People have the right to safe and permanent food free from genetically modified organisms. Food sovereignty at the national, regional and local

level is a basic human right; in this regard, democratic land reforms and peasant's access to land are fundamental requirements.

15) The meeting in Doha confirmed the illegitimacy of the WTO. The supposed adopted "development agenda" only defends corporate interests. By launching a new round, the WTO is moving closer to its goal of converting everything into a commodity. For us, food, public services, agriculture, health, education and genes are not for sale. In addition we reject the patenting of all biological life forms.

The WTO agenda is perpetuated at the continental level by regional free trade and investment agreements. By organising protests such as the huge demonstrations and plebiscites against FTAA, people have rejected such agreements as representing a recolonisation and the destruction of fundamental, social, economical, cultural and environmental rights and values.

16) We will strengthen our movement through common actions and mobilisation for social justice for the respect of rights and liberties; and for quality of life, equality, dignity and peace. We are fighting:

- For democracy: people have the right to know about and criticise the decisions of their own governments, especially with respect to dealings with international institutions. Governments are ultimately accountable to their people. While we support the establishment of electoral democracy across the world, we emphasise the need for democratisation of states and societies and the struggle against dictatorship.
- For abolition of external debt, and reparation.
- Against speculative activities: we demand the creation of specific taxes such as the Tobin tax, and the abolition of tax heavens.
- For the right to information.
- For women's rights, freedom from violence, poverty and exploitation.
- Against war and militarism, against foreign military bases and interventions, and the systematic interventions, and the systematic escalation of violence. We choose to privilege negotiation and non-violent conflict resolution.
- For a democratic, social European Union based on the needs of European workers and people, on the need of solidarity and cooperation of the eastern and southern people.
- For the rights of youth, their access to free public education and social autonomy, and the abolition of compulsory military service.

In the years to come, we will organise collective mobilisation such as:

In 2002

8th of March: International Women's Day

17th of April: International day of Peasant's Struggle.

1st of May: Labour Day

12th October: Cry of the Excluded

16th October: World Food Day

Other global mobilisations will take place

15th to 16th of March: Barcelona (Spain), summit of the EU.

18th to 22nd of March: Monterrey (Mexico), United Nations conference on financing for development.

17th to 18th of May: Madrid (Spain), summit of Latin America, Caribbean and European.

31st May: International Day of action against militarism and peace

June: Rome (Italy), world food summit; 22nd–23rd Seville EU summit

July: Toronto and Calgary (Canada), G8 summit.

22nd July: USA campaign against Coca-Cola

September: Johannesburg (South Africa), Rio + 10

October: Quito (Ecuador), Social continental forum 'A new integration is possible'

November: Cuba, 2nd Hemispheric meeting against FTAA

December: Copenhagen (Denmark), summit of EU

In 2003

April: Buenos Aires (Argentina), summit of the FTAA.

June: Thessaloniki EU Summit

WTO, IMF and World Bank will meet somewhere, sometimes. And we will be there!

And many more events that have not been listed.

Note

1. Sourced from http://www.movsoc.org/htm/call_2002_english.htm on 19.07.03.

MUMBAI DECLARATION 2004 AGAINST IMPERIALIST GLOBALISATION AND WAR[1]

We, 'Mumbai Resistance 2004 Against Imperialist Globalisation and War', an international event held in Mumbai, India, 17–20 January 2004, participated in by more than 300 organisations and thousands of individuals from all parts of India and from other countries all over the world, hereby adopt the following declaration:

We have successfully achieved the objectives of MR 2004 as conceived by the International League of People's Struggles (ILPS) at the Thessaloniki Resistance in June 2003, to hold an international event co-sponsored by the broadest range of anti-imperialist groups, to consolidate and strengthen the anti-imperialist movement.

Drawing inspiration and strength from the unity, commitment, energy and international co-ordination that MR 2004 has gathered, generated and heightened, we make the following pledges and calls to action:

WE PLEDGE to fight imperialist globalisation and war to the end. For this we will unite with all forces that stand in opposition to the horrors resulting from this new anti-people offensive.

WE PLEDGE to steadfastly stand by the poverty-stricken masses, who are the worst victims of imperialist globalisation. We will unite with them in their struggles against imperialist plunder and war throughout the world.

WE PLEDGE to vehemently oppose the disastrous impact on society in the form of the dehumanising poverty, destruction of the peoples' livelihood, the destruction of the environment, the crass consumerism, the heightened alienation, and the increasing degeneration of the cultural life of the people.

We PLEDGE to fight against the further infringement and even whole assault on the sovereignty of all oppressed countries, that has come under massive attack by the forces of imperialist globalisation and their institutions like the TNCs, World Bank, IMF, WTO, etc. and also their imperialist governments, specifically that of U.S. imperialism.

WE PLEDGE to fight back the growing fascist attacks of ruling classes around the world and their whipping up of parochial hysteria, pitting one community against another. Particularly, Racism, Zionism, etc, which act as the ideological content of fascism in various regions of the world, will be opposed tooth and nail.

WE PLEDGE to fight shoulder to shoulder together with the people of various countries that have come under the jackboots of imperialist aggression, particularly that of the U.S. imperialists.

WE PLEDGE to fight for the abrogation of all the loans to the third world by the imperialists and their agencies like IMF, World Bank, etc.

We resolve to put up a formidable fight alongside the Iraqi people until all U.S. and other occupation troops are withdrawn from Iraq.

We resolve to fight alongside the Palestinian and other Arab people shoulder to shoulder in getting back their land and sovereignty; and that the Jewish and Palestinian people live in peace, with equal rights.

We resolve to fight for the withdrawal of all foreign troops from Afghanistan and all other countries of the world, and the disbandment of all U.S. military bases around the globe.

We resolve to fight for the unconditional release of all political prisoners incarcerated by the reactionary regimes, particularly of those fighting U.S. imperialism and their lackeys.

We resolve to fight for the scrapping of all the multilateral institutions like the IMF, World Bank and WTO, etc, and the removal of TNC operations in the oppressed countries of the world.

We resolve to fight for the forthwith annulment of all unequal Treaties, Agreements and Military Pacts signed between the imperialists and the oppressed countries of the world.

We are determined to achieve our full and total sovereignty—economical, political and military—of all nation-states of the world, and their fundamental right to national self-determination of all nationalities, where these have been infringed in any way.

In India, where this Conference is being held, we resolved to fight for:

- The end of 'economic reforms', liberalisation, privatisation, and globalisation of the economy, and the unhindered entry of foreign capital into the country.
- The end of imperialist paradigm of governance and development model. We stand for the establishment of people-centred development and institutions of real democracy with full employment and equitable entitlements. We resolve to fight for right to work.
- The end of all forms of State terror, in the form of undemocratic legislations like POTA, banning strikes and TU activities, extra-judicial killings, torture, custodial rape, disappearances and the banning of various parties and organisations.
- The end of state-sponsored Hindutva Fascism and defence of all rights of the minorities, and punishment for all those responsible for the demolition of Babri Masjid and the Gujarat genocide.
- The end of army operations against the nationality movements and withdrawal of all Indian forces from Bhutan being used to crush the movements based there; grant all nationalities their right to self-determination.
- The end of State terror against all democratic movements, including the armed revolutionary struggles of the masses, and demand the right to organisation and free speech to all.
- The end of the further infringement of our Sovereignty by imperialism in general and the U.S./ Israel axis in particular.
- The end of attacks on the peasantry, badly hit by: the flood of cheap imports; cut in investments; end to concessional credit, electricity, water; cut in subsidies, de facto scrapping of PDS; and corporatisation of agriculture.
- The end of attacks on students and youth as manifested in the privatisation of education, the loss of jobs, opportunities, and the extensive promotion of degenerate cultural values.
- The end of the incessant marginalisation of tribal people and the scrapping of all big projects leading to their displacement and their right to the forest land, wealth and self rule.
- The end of attacks on the working class and the growing spectre of unemployment; the repeal of the anti-labour laws, and end to VRS, a stop to the contractualisation of labour, etc.
- The end of all forms of casteism and the despicable practice of untouchability, and an immediate stop to the growing attacks on Dalits with overt and covert state

support. We commit ourselves to the struggles of all the oppressed caste people against Brahmanism that has regained in strength under neo-liberal globalization. A large majority of Indian population constitutes artisan castes and classes they have been adversely affected by the policies of globalisation. Without showing any alternative their livelihood is destroyed. We resolve to fight against this situation.

- The end the cultural onslaughts of Hindutva forces on the Dalits, Adivasis and other oppressed castes and their intrigues to use them as their cannon fodder for achieving their vile goal of Hindu Rashtra.
- The end of all manifestations of patriarchy and the growing commodification of women in this period of globalisation; particularly the growing trafficking of women and the intensified debasement of women through advertising, tourism, pornography, etc.
- The end of Indian expansionism and the outright bullying and treaties to the neighbouring countries by the Indian ruling classes in close alliance with their U.S. bosses.

WE CALL on the people to boycott the products of TNCs/MNCs and thereby bringing massive losses on the imperialists and their empires markets, to leave the country particularly American imperialists' and build militant mass struggles to drive away them from our countries.

WE CALL on the people to build firm resistance to the U.S. military camps worldwide. We resolve to take up a consistent mass protest movement, till all U.S. and other imperialist military camps are completely withdrawn.

WE CALL on the people of all countries of the world, including India, to unite to fight back the imperialist offensive going on under the signboard of 'globalisation' and join to defend the rights of the working people throughout the world.

WE CALL on the people to smash the imperialist aggressors, particularly the U.S., and ally firmly with the resistance movements, particularly in Iraq, Afghanistan and Palestine until victory.

WE CALL on the people to oppose State terror, and anti-democratic laws like POTA whatever its form, and fight back their growing fascist onslaught across the world.

WE CALL on the people not to be taken in by imperialist schemes and tricks to diffuse discontent, particularly by NGOs and Social democrats, but to build a mighty militant movement to smash imperialism and its agents throughout the world, and work towards building a new order, based on equality and justice for all—a world moving towards socialism.

We express our deep sense of solidarity and oneness with all people worldwide in struggles against imperialism and all reaction and strongly seek coordination in building common battlegrounds against our common enemy, that is, imperialism and the classes, which constitute its composition.

On this, the 18th day of January 2004, let us all PLEDGE to unite and march forward in the path of struggle. Let us create a new bright future for all the toiling masses of the world. As a first step, let us OBSERVE March 20 as Anti-imperialist War-Day; the Day U.S./British forces aggressed on Iraq—a day to be observed by mass protests against the imperialists, and militant actions against imperialist forces and their agents in India and throughout the world.

18 January 2004
Signed by
311 organisations that comprise MR-2004

Note

1. Declaration adopted at the end of Mumbai Resistance 2004 against imperialist globalisation and war—an event held parallel to World Social Forum at Mumbai. Sourced from Indymedia Ireland @ http://ireland.indymedia.org/article/63143; accessed 05.10.06.

PORTO ALEGRE MANIFESTO

GROUP OF NINETEEN, 29 JANUARY 2005[1]

Twelve Proposals For Another Possible World

Since the first World Social Forum took place on January 2001, the social forum phenomenon has extended itself to all continents, at both national and local levels. It has resulted in the emergence of a worldwide public space for citizenship and strife, and permitted the elaboration of political proposals as alternatives to the tyranny of neoliberal globalisation by financial markets and transnational corporations, with the imperialistic, military power of the United States as its armed exponent.

Thanks to its diversity and solidarity between its actors, and the social movements of which it is composed, the alternative global movement has become a force to be taken into consideration globally. Many of the innumerable proposals which have been put forward on the forums have been supported by many social movements worldwide. We, the signers of the Porto Alegre Manifesto, by no means pretend to speak in the name of the entire World Social Forum, but speak on a strictly personal basis.

We have identified twelve such proposals, which we believe, together, give sense and direction to the construction of another, different world. If they would be implemented, it would allow citizens to take back their own future. We therefore want to submit these fundamentals points to the scrutiny of actors and social movements of all countries. It will be them that, at all levels—worldwide, continentally, nationally and locally—will move forward and fight for these proposals to become reality.

Indeed, we have no illusions about the real commitment of governments and international institutions to spontaneously implement any of these proposals, even though they might claim to do so, out of opportunism.

A. Another different world must respect the rights for all human beings to live, by the implementations of new economic measures. Therefore, it's necessary to:

1. Cancel the external debt of southern countries, which has been already paid many times over, and which constitutes the privileged means of creditor states, local and international financial institutions, to keep the largest part of humanity under their control and sustain their misery. This measure needs to be complemented by the restitution of the gigantic sums which have been stolen by their corrupt leaders.

2. Implement international taxes on financial transactions (most notably the Tobin tax on speculative capital), on direct foreign investments, on consolidated profit from multinationals, on weapon trade and on activities accompanied by large greenhouse effect gas emissions. Such financial means, complemented by public development help which should imperatively be 0.7% of the GNP of rich countries, should be directed towards fighting big epidemics (like AIDS), guarantee access to all humanity to clean water, housing, energy, health services and medication, education, and other social services.

3. Progressively dismantle all forms of fiscal, juridical and banking paradises, which do nothing more than facilitate organized crime, corruption, illegal trafficking of all kinds, fraud and fiscal evasion, and large illegal operations by large corporations and even governments. These fiscal paradises are not only limited to certain states, existing in areas of non-legality; they also exist within the legislation of developed countries. In a first instance, it would be advisable to strongly tax capital flux entering and leaving these 'paradises,' as well as all establishments and actors, financial or otherwise, taking part in these gigantic transactions.

4. All inhabitants of this planet must have the right to be employed, to social protection and retirement/pension, respecting equal rights between men and women. This should be an imperative of all public polity systems, both national and international.

5. Promote all forms of equitable trade, reject all free-trade agreements and laws proposed by the World Trade Organization, and putting in motion mechanisms allowing a progressive upward equalisation of social and environmental norms (as defined under the conventions by the International Labour Organization) on the production of goods and services. Education, health, social services and culture should be excluded from the scope of the General Agreement on Trades and Services (GATS) by the WTO.

The convention on cultural diversity, currently being negotiated at UNESCO, must result in cultural rights and politics of public cultural support to explicitly prevail over commercial rights.

6. Guarantee the right to for all countries to alimentary sovereignty and security by promoting peasant, rural agriculture. This means a total suppression of all sub-

ventions to the export of agricultural products, mainly by the USA and the European Union, and the ability to tax imports to avoid dumping practices. In the same way, every country or group of countries must be able to decide in a sovereign way to forbid the production and import of genetically modified organism, meant for consumption.

7. Forbid all type of patenting of knowledge on living beings (human, animal or vegetal) as well as any privatization of common goods for humanity, particularly water.

B. Another possible world must sustain community life in peace and justice, for all humanity. Therefore it is necessary to:

8. Fight by means of public policies against all kinds of discrimination, sexism, xenophobia, anti-Semitism and racism. Fully recognize the political, cultural and economic rights (including the access to natural resources) of indigenous populations.

9. Take urgent steps to end the destruction of the environment and the threat of severe climate changes due to the greenhouse effect, resulting from the proliferation of individual transportation and the excessive use of non-renewable energy sources. Start with the execution of an alternative development model, based on the sparing/efficient use of energy, and a democratic control of natural resources, most notably potable water, on a global scale.

10. Demand the dismantling of all foreign military bases and the removal of troops on all countries, except when operating under explicit mandate of the United Nations. Especially for Iraq and Palestine.

C. Another possible world must promote democracy from the neighbouring level to the global level. Therefore, it's necessary to:

11. Guarantee the right to access information and the right to inform, for/by all citizens, by legislation which should:

a) End the concentration of media under gigantic communication groups

b) Guarantee the autonomy of journalists relative to actionnaries [sic]

c) Favour the development of non-profit press, alternative media, and community networks.

Respecting these right implies setting up a system of [checks and balances?][2] for citizens, in particular [through] national and international media observation institutions.

12. Reform and deeply democratize international institutions by making sure human, economic, social and cultural rights prevail, as stipulated by the Universal Declaration of Human Rights. This implies incorporating the World Bank, the International Monetary Fund and the World Trade Organization into the decision-making mechanism and systems of the United Nations. In case of persisting violation by the USA of international law, transfer the United Nations headquarters outside New York, to another country, preferably southern.

Porto Alegre, 29 January 2005, Signed by:

Aminata Traoré
Adolfo Pérez Esquivel
Eduardo Galeano
José Saramago
François Houtart
Boaventura de Sousa Santos
Armand Mattelart
Roberto Savio
Riccardo Petrella
Ignacio Ramonet
Bernard Cassen
Samir Amin
Atilio Boron
Samuel Ruiz Garcia
Tariq Ali
Frei Betto
Emir Sader
Walden Bello
Immanuel Wallerstein

Notes

1. Sourced from *Z Mag* at http://www.zmag.org/sustainers/content/2005-02/20group_of_nineteen.cfm; posted on 20 February 2005.
2. Wording not clear at source.

Part 3

Globalising The Forum: The Forum in The World

Globalising The World Social Forum: Ironies, Contrasts, Challenges[1]

Achin Vanaik

There was an obvious irony in organising the 4th World Social Forum that was held in Mumbai, India, from January 16–21 2004, by shifting it from Porto Alegre, the city of the participatory budget that is fully geared to welcome the WSF, to an indifferent Mumbai. To the absolute opposite of Porto Alegre, Mumbai is the city in India that most starkly symbolised the impact of neoliberalism. It is a rapidly de-industrialising, financial-commercial-services centre with an expanding informal sector of self-employed and unorganised labour, where over 40 percent of its 17 million population are forced to live in slums. It has heavy vehicular and small factory pollution. The choice of venue for the Mumbai WSF—a dusty, environment-unfriendly, and long disused industrial site—only completed the ironic symbolism. But on the other hand, whereas the restricted and dusty venue in Mumbai contrasted sharply with the sprawling and verdant geography of the WSF site in Porto Alegre, it also forced an extraordinary physical mingling among the over a hundred thousand participants, with more than 15,000 from outside India.

Asia from the West, South, and East was well represented at Mumbai, as was Western Europe; the rest of the world much less so. When coupled with the unmatchable social and cultural diversity of India, which was fully represented at this WSF, this concentration created a general atmosphere of collective political solidarity and vitality that has clearly set a new standard for future WSFs.[2] By contrast, the social composition of participants at the 3rd WSF that was held in Porto Alegre in January 2003 was far more uniformly middle class. But again, on the other hand, if the youth camp in Porto Alegre is always a considerable success, in Mumbai it was organisationally and politically a big disappointment.

The ironies and contrasts do not end here. Lula, trade unionist, populist leader, and President of Brazil, who was so warmly welcomed at both WSF 2 and 3 in Brazil, was unwanted at, and uninvited to, the WSF in Mumbai. But he was in India right at that time, and instead of being invited by the WSF, was the honoured guest of the Indian state at this year's official Republic Day celebrations on 26 January 2004, just days after Mumbai and even before the dust had settled there!

There was a legitimate worry that shifting the WSF from South America, the continent of greatest resistance to neoliberalism, to the Indian subcontinent where the government's neoliberal trajectory is still only weakly challenged, could be a mistake. It is in South America that, indisputably, mass politicisation is deepest and widest. In contrast, the flip side of the Mumbai WSF's wonderful diversity, of the delightful displays of music, dance, and street theatre, and of the strong presence of Dalits, tribals, women's groups, and trade unions, was the fact that political awareness was more limited and sectoral in character. Neither the leaders nor the ordinary members of so many of the large movements and groups that gathered there showed much interest or involvement in the conferences, seminars, and workshops lying outside their specific areas of concern. Low literacy levels combined with constant breakdowns in the technical facilities provided for translation do not fully explain this weakness, whose basic roots are political.[3]

The Social Forum project that first emerged in South America reflected a new historical conjuncture—not just the two decades of assault by neoliberalism on that continent but also the effective disintegration of the old left and its replacement by a more inchoate, plural, and diverse set of progressive actors in civil society. Their growing radicalisation in the late 90s found its organisational expression in the WSF and its associated 'politics of open space.' India, however, is where the old left (still largely unrepentant about its Stalinist and Maoist legacies and traditions) survives as a substantial force replete with 'their' mass fronts of trade unions and of women, peasant, and student wings. But since out of a total labour force of some 340 million, only nine million—or less than three percent—are unionised, it is hardly surprising that there also exists, in the Indian landscape, a breathtaking array of social movements, single issue groups, and a spectrum of NGOs from the most progressive and radical to those whose principal function is to be the new 'privatised' service-providers offsetting the impact of the neoliberal state's abandonment of its multiple social responsibilities in health, education, social security, and basic needs.

All these contradictions were clearly present in Mumbai. And where else would you find, for the first time in the history of the WSF, an alternative forum called Mumbai Resistance (MR) being organised across the road from the official one, by a variety of Maoist groups and fronts whose principal ballasts were the People's War Group of India and the Communist Party of the Philippines?

Much smaller, with an overall attendance in the few thousands, MR's main purpose was to call attention to itself. Its inaugural function spent nearly as much time criticising the WSF as it did attacking neoliberalism or U.S. imperialism.[4]

But even at the entrances of the main WSF, in a manner that was clearly inconsistent certainly with the prevailing spirit of the Social Forum project, the CPI and the CPM had strategically placed (hitting visitor eyes well before the WSF signs themselves) huge billboards declaring that their idea of another world, at least, was a *Communist* future. Mimicking the WSF's slogan 'Another World is Possible!' their billboards instead shouted 'Another World will be a Socialist World!' A strongly instrumentalist attitude towards the Social Forum project still prevails amongst these left parties.

Nonetheless, after allowing for all reservations and qualifications, the end result justified the decision to hold the WSF 4 in India. Asian presence and involvement in the Social Forum project, hitherto marked by a strong Latin American and European 'face,' has taken a leap forward. Africa and North America remain laggards. Porto Alegre last year brought together for the first time the two great global streams—the movement against neoliberalism and that against U.S. imperialism. This confluence has been sustained and further consolidated in Mumbai. The introduction of newer themes and a stronger emphasis on some older ones also took place enhancing the awareness-raising aspect of the WSF. The Indian organisers gave some shape to the otherwise amorphous character of the 'WSF as open space' by holding a series of WSF-sponsored events focusing on five broad themes—imperialist globalisation; patriarchy, gender and sexuality; militarism and peace; casteism and racism, work and descent-based exclusions and discriminations; religious fanaticism, sectarian violence—themselves subdivided to include issues of ecologically sustainable development; matters of food, land and water sovereignty; media culture and knowledge; labour and the world of work; and health, education and social security.

In addition, the Mumbai WSF made a conscious effort (with uneven success) to promote more thorough reflection on the relationship between political parties and social movements, on discussing alternatives to neoliberal globalisation, and on the role of the nation-state and nationalism in an era when many are calling for new structures of global governance. The extent to which various activist groups were able to utilise Mumbai WSF to enhance international coordination, networking and planning for common actions clearly varied, and the results of their endeavours will only become evident in the future.

So the question arises: What hopes and lessons does WSF 2004 carry, for India and globally? But before addressing this crucial question, there is another shorter-term question that needs a direct answer. What has been, or is likely to be, the political impact of the Mumbai WSF on the current Indian political scene?

The National Scene

Frankly, the answer must be little or none. Mega-event though it might have been, the mainstream national (ie English language) media treated it as a one-off, self-indulgent jamboree of the politically marginalised. Reportage was limited and inadequate. Commentary, with few exceptions, ranged from the contemptuous to the patronising.

This was also true of political parties. Control of Mumbai municipality rests with the Shiv Sena, the most rightwing and Hindu chauvinist of the regional party allies of the Bharatiya Janata Party (BJP). Both the Shiv Sena and the BJP-led central government decided it was less fruitful politically to disrupt the WSF than to ignore it. So they stayed away. The Maharashtra state government, which is currently run by an alliance of the Congress and an earlier breakaway from it, similarly paid little heed. But this is hardly surprising, given that the Congress leadership is as committed to the post-1991 neoliberal reforms as in the BJP (indeed, it sees it as its own offspring)[5] and believes that there is no alternative for itself but to pursue a 'soft Hindutva' domestically and befriend the U.S. externally, albeit less effusively. The WSF was too radical for its liking, though the odd Congress political bigwig did register his presence, only to go largely unnoticed.

We need to face the fact that there remains a significant disjunction between the political realities on the ground and the kind of political context that would be required where the holding of a WSF could be expected to have any immediate and meaningful impact. To the contrary of this, since the beginning of 2002 the fulcrum of Indian politics has moved further to the right. We have to understand this political reality and the context within which the Mumbai WSF took place, if we are to be able to understand the possible relevance of the WSF to politics in India.

The Indian economy continues to move along the neoliberal path at a steady if controlled pace. Worries about a slowing down of average annual growth rates after 1997 have been temporarily assuaged by the spectacularly good monsoons in 2003 that have dramatically raised agricultural growth rates and now promise a GDP growth rate in 2003–04 of around 8 percent. Thus the average annual growth rate for the last five years will reach the 5.7 to 5.8 percent level that has sustained itself over the last two decades. True, the average annual growth in manufacturing over the last five years is an unimpressive 5.3 percent. Agriculture will undoubtedly revert to its normal pattern of low and slackening growth. Annual software exports have now reached the $16 billion mark and there are brighter prospects for export of auto parts, but the trade imbalance continues. Remittances by Indians abroad (mainly from the Gulf and the U.S.), at 3 percent of GDP, are still more than double the annual FDI flows which since 1997 have not crossed the peak that year of $4 billion. Though the $100 billion reserves position has a disturbingly large component of more volatile portfolio investments and Non-Resident Indian (NRI) short term bank deposits as well as a high proportion of commercial borrowings by the government, it is large enough to be cited as evidence of a now "Shining India" and of a "feel good factor" that are the new slogans being internalised by the Indian 'middle class,' courtesy of incessant media repetition.[6]

The central government in India is clearly determined to push through privatisation of valuable public properties. Since few would wish to buy up loss-making or sick industries unless they have high-value assets worth stripping, or can easily be made highly profitable, New Delhi has tried to follow a dual strategy. This is to sell off some of the big profit makers (oil companies like Hindustan Petroleum and Chemicals Limited and Bharat Petroleum and Chemicals Limited) and to starve potential profit-makers of necessary modernisation-investment funds. The latter tactic is being applied to Air India and Indian Airlines whose most profitable air routes are being opened up to competitors. Failing balance sheets and profit and loss accounts can then be used to justify equity divestment and privatisation. HPCL and BPCL were nationalised by Acts of Parliament, and a Court ruling that this status can only be changed by a similar political process has stalled matters; meanwhile resistance to efforts at privatisation of the Indian banking system is still strong.[7] In the beginning of the nineties, public sector assets were around 15 percent of GDP. Today, they are around 12 percent of GDP.

After the 1997 East Asian financial crisis, the Indian government congratulated itself on not prematurely moving towards full capital convertibility. It is still some way from this but the intent is clear. In the new millennium New Delhi eased restrictions to allow Indian companies to invest up to 25 percent of their net worth abroad, no questions asked. Today, free capital investment abroad is allowed up to 100 percent of a company's net worth. Apart from stubbornly high fiscal deficits, stagnant savings rates, persistent poverty, growing social and regional inequalities, the major area of unease for the government is the relatively jobless character of current growth patterns compared to even the eighties. The number of the registered unemployed reached a staggering 34.85 million in 2002, and is expected to reach 40.47 million in 2007. The employment elasticity of output has fallen from 0.52 between 1983–94 to 0.16 between 1993–2000. It is here that the political weak spot of Indian neoliberalism resides —in the not too distant prospect of a substantially greater proportion of youth mostly educated in provincial colleges and belonging to the middle and lower echelons of the 'middle class' becoming disillusioned with the heady promises of neoliberal project that currently still retains its appeal.[8]

Markers

But even if the economy has chugged along expected paths, the polity has also witnessed significant new turbulences. The two crucial markers here have been the terrible pogrom against Muslims organised by the state government of Gujarat (headed by its Chief Minister Narendra Modi) in March/April 2002 and the depressing outcome of the provincial assembly elections in December 2003 in the key Hindi heartland states of Rajasthan, Madhya Pradesh, Chattisgarh, and Delhi.

On 27 February 2002, a brutal communal assault by an angry Muslim mob in the town of Godhra, in the state of Gujarat in western India, served as the awaited trigger for a carefully pre-planned, state-organised 'retaliatory' pogrom in which even according to official figures (the actual figures were much higher), over 2,000 Muslims were butchered and around 150,000 driven out of their homes. There was looting, property destruction, sadistic beatings, injuries, and rape on a massive scale.

This was not only the worst case of sustained communal violence since Partition but the first time that a state government had been so deeply involved in preparing and carrying out such a massacre.[9] What marked it as a decisive turning point was not so much that the direct perpetrators got away with their criminal behaviour—this has happened in India often enough before—but that the Sangh Parivar-BJP combine that was responsible for it, got away politically. During the pogrom and its aftermath, strong recriminatory pressure was built up not only by the Opposition parties, but also among the BJP's allies in the ruling National Democratic Alliance (NDA). Massive extra-parliamentary mobilisation by the Opposition at the national and regional levels, inside and outside Gujarat, could have broken the ruling coalition government. But this never happened. The Congress, which should have led such a campaign, did not have the courage, the confidence, or the anti-communal commitment to take such action.

In its absence, Prime Minister Vajpayee at the BJP party conclave in Goa at the end of May 2002 made a speech that in retrospect can be seen as marking the point at which the Indian polity took another qualitative lurch rightwards. In his decisive, agenda-setting speech, Vajpayee openly rationalised the pogrom as an unavoidable reaction to the Godhra incident. He categorically rejected the demand from his NDA allies to remove Narendra Modi as chief minister of Gujarat, effectively challenging them to make their choice—either to pull down his government and precipitate early elections or to fall quietly into line. He also made a pitch internationally to the U.S. ideological right by declaring Islamic fundamentalism/terrorism as the world's principal danger.

The rest is history. The ruling NDA remained intact, with the BJP's authority within it greatly strengthened. Gujarat under Modi called early polls in December 2002, campaigning on an openly communal platform of not just justification but celebration of the pogrom, a tactic the Congress was scared to directly oppose, instead highlighting the Modi government's 'general performance' failure. For the first time ever, the right-wing BJP obtained a two-thirds majority in the Gujarat assembly because of a massive gain in votes and seats in central Gujarat where most of the communal violence had been concentrated. The result only further deadened the already enfeebled anti-communal reflexes of the Congress.

The December 2003 elections in the country were a further boost to the BJP. In this case, Hindutva was not the major factor behind the Congress debacle but it did contribute to the BJP success. In a single day, the BJP gained absolute majorities in the three states of Madhya Pradesh, Rajasthan, and Chattisgarh where the Congress had been in power and was expected to do reasonably well, retaining at least two if not all three states. It ended up retaining power only in Delhi.

Suddenly, the most sober and downbeat assessments of the coming general elections, which have now been advanced to sometime in April 2004, are that the BJP-led NDA coalition has easily the best chances of coming back to power. To be sure, the parties comprising the NDA, including the BJP would seem to have reached their electoral peak in terms of seats secured during the last 1999 general elections.[10] So how can they sustain their performance, let alone expand their reach? In the last two general elections, the BJP tally has plateaued at around 180 seats (out of a total of 552 members in the Lok Sabha, the 'House of the People'). It peaked everywhere in 1999 and can hope to considerably improve this time only in one state, Uttar Pradesh. But after the elections, if the NDA seems the most likely candidate for central rule, then its ranks could well expand through the wholesale defection of some of the pre-poll Congress allies.

The coming elections can prove to be a turning point not because the BJP will make a qualitative leap forward in its individual tally but because the Congress may collapse as a national party. Programmatically, it is in all key respects a softer version of the BJP but without its powerful cadre base (courtesy of the RSS), or its aggressive policy of transforming (through major personnel changes) all governing institutions and structures it can lay its hands on whether in civil society or in the state apparatuses at Central and provincial levels, or its determination to eventually bring about a *Hindu Rashtra* (a Hindu State). Socially, the Congress, as evidenced by the recent assembly elections, is losing its last, hitherto stable base—the tribals in central India—to the BJP. For a full five decades after independence, every single breakaway from the Congress, even when led by leaders whose national stature had been forged in the great freedom struggle before 1947, quickly faded into total oblivion. But this is changing. Since 1997, two such breakaways—the Trinamul Congress of West Bengal and then the National Congress Party of Maharashtra—have stabilised as major regional parties, because they have not been afraid to hobnob with the BJP.

What holds the Congress together today is not ideology nor organisational solidity but the promise of governance at the Centre. If this time around it fails to achieve such power as the hub of an alternative ruling coalition (supported from the outside by the CPI and CPM), it will very likely suffer defections from its ranks to the BJP/NDA as well as further splits into one or more regional parties in the northern states of Rajasthan, Madhya Pradesh, and Chattisgarh. The Congress is today prepared to make the kind of concessions to forge a coalition that it has never contemplated before—leaving a 150 to 200 seats for its allies to contest; assuring sought-for allies that in case of victory, the prime ministership will be decided collectively and will not automatically devolve on Sonia Gandhi as leader of the largest single party in the bloc. As a measure of Congress desperation, Rahul the son and Priyanka the daughter of Rajiv and Sonia Gandhi, who do not suffer from the 'foreign' tag, are likely to be thrown into the campaign fray as electable candidates. All this is to counter the BJP effort to promote the 'Vajpayee charisma' as its way of extending its tally well beyond the 180 mark.

But should the Congress collapse, the BJP will become the only national party and will have institutionalised its status as the 'normal' fulcrum of bourgeois political rule, a deeply disturbing development with momentous implications and ramifications.

The WSF: Hopes and Lessons

This unfolding scenario has direct implications for the WSF in India. One of the central aims of the Indian organisers of the Mumbai WSF, even if not declared and always kept in the background, was that it should stimulate the further development of an 'anti-fascist front' nationally against the Sangh/BJP. The intent here was not an electoral bloc but the formation of a long-term alliance of left parties and their mass fronts with the big social movements and a range of progressive NGOs to collectively mobilise in civil society. Has the Asian Social Forum that took place at Hyderabad in January 2003 and now the WSF 2004 organised in Mumbai, helped bring these forces together?

The answer, again, has to be No. Mutual suspicions and tensions remain within the social movements and parties, as well as between them. There has been the constant jockeying for public representation in the 'star system' that is a seemingly unavoidable aspect of the Social Forum process. There are the inevitable fears about manipulation and doubts about ulterior motives.

Indeed, one of the most important issues thrown up by the Mumbai WSF, and by the experience of the World Social Forum in Brazil and in India, is whether it might not be better for parties to participate openly as such instead of informally exercising their substantial influence behind-the-scenes as they now do—whether it is the PT (Workers' Party) in Brazil or the CPM and CPI in India.

This could result in a more honest dialogue between party spokespersons and others. The former could no longer dodge direct critiques of their record of behaviour in and out of office. Surely this would encourage a less manipulative relationship whereby genuine adjustments and greater mutual respect could be forged.

The fear in India is that if this were done, Social Forums would become arenas in which the pressures of electoral/political competition would then trump efforts at accommodation. Besides, it might lead to interminable arguments as to which parties to allow in or keep out. If the CPM—which has made major concessions to neoliberal pressures in West Bengal—is to allowed in, then why not also the Congress?

Overall, it would be fair to say that in part as a result of the experience of the WSF over the past two years, the mass fronts of the left parties, and substantial sections within the parties including many major leaders, have moved closer to social movements and progressive NGOs, and vice versa. This movement towards closer collaboration however, is still hesitant, wary, and uneasy. There remains a lack of that kind of general perspective that could help systematise forms of collaboration going beyond occasional common actions. But the movement forward is real.

Internationally, at this point in time the Indian left has nowhere to turn except towards a global radical milieu that is instinctively anti-Stalinist and much more developed in its attitudes on matters concerning sexual choice, female oppression, and ecological sustainability. Domestically, much greater co-ordination amongst radical forces is required to confront the neoliberal project, and even if public opposition to neoliberalism is likely to grow. In South America, what tipped the balance towards successful mass resistance was the antagonism of whole swathes of the middle class whose savings were destroyed by the combination of unstable currencies, recession and unemployment. This has not yet happened in India. The neoliberal reforms have a shorter history, and a more cautious approach to capital convertibility has provided a measure of protection. But the problem of educated unemployment is rising to serious proportions. Youth belonging to the lower echelons of the 'middle class' are finding neither secure nor well-paid jobs. A growing crisis of expectations is emerging. If seen in this light, Mumbai 2004 might well be identified as the first major collective warning of the shape of things to come.

There are parallel concerns at the international level. Greater collaboration between the main radical actors—parties, unions, movements, and the best NGOs—is urgently required. The crucial task remains what it has always been: How best to combine the politics of the universal and the politics of the particular. The first is most powerful and effective precisely when it encompasses and respects the latter. Historically, the classical—indeed, the only—organisational form that has shown itself capable of embodying this combination has been the party. One need not assume that this must remain the case. But the principal challenge facing the Social Forum project is whether it will be able to contribute to the creation of those new organisational forms that are equipped with the general vision and capacity to simultaneously and systematically pursue the politics of the universal and the particular. Insofar as the State remains a crucial nodal point of concentrated bourgeois power, no radical strategy can afford to merely ignore or sidestep it.

Rather than maintain the hectic pace of a WSF every year, which drains the time and energy of too many activists away from their basic areas of implantation and concern, it would be much better after the WSF 5 in Porto Alegre next year (2005) to schedule WSFs for every second or even third year. This would allow for holding more forums at intermediate (city, provincial, national and regional) levels. The time has surely also come to take a breather and synthesise the experiences and lessons of the major local, national, continental and global forums that have so far been held.[11]

Moreover, the one great lacuna in the Social Forum project is the failure to extend it to North America, particularly the U.S. Even at the WSFs, U.S. American participation has always been disproportionately much smaller than the size and importance of the progressive sectors of U.S. American society has warranted. This insularity must be broken.[12]

It can be claimed with some legitimacy that without the Social Forum project, neither the massive global anti-war mobilisation of 15 February 2003 nor the mobilisation at Cancun against the WTO in September 2003 would have been anywhere near as successful as they were. By this measure, the proposed anti-war demonstrations on 20 March 2004 will be a major test. They need not reach the level of the 2003 demonstrations. We must recognise that calling for an end to the U.S. occupation is unlikely to have the same appeal as the call not to start an avoidable war. But if even a few millions can be mobilised worldwide, it will give an undoubted boost to progressive forces everywhere. Far more is at stake than just the Social Forum project.

Notes

1. This essay is an edited version of "Ironies and Contrasts," 29 March 2004, accessed from the WSF's Library of Alternatives on 1 October 2007 <http://www.forumsocialmundial.org.br/dinamic.php?pagina=bal_achin_2004_ing>.
2. The remarkable diversity of participation from within India was ensured by the involvement of 190 organisations in the Indian General Council (IGC), the ultimate decision-making authority for the 4th WSF. In contrast, last year's Brazilian Organising Committee comprised just eight organisations. The IGC nominated the main executive body, the Indian Organising Committee, which in turn selected the Mumbai Organising Committee. In the IOC, the two mainstream left parties—the Communist Party of India

(CPI) and the Communist Party of India (Marxist), or CPM—certain NGOs, and a number of big Dalit organisations from southern India played the major roles.

3. But it is a fact that inadequate infrastructure also hampered proper discussion and mass participation, especially in the big conferences. This failing was linked to the otherwise laudable determination of the organisers to limit foreign funding sources and to keep overall costs low. An approximate total estimate for holding the event (excluding all other costs) would be around $2.4 million—or just a third of what it was at Porto Alegre.
4. See, in this volume, the Mumbai Declaration issued by the Mumbai Resistance meeting in 2004. Though many of their criticisms are valid—pointing out the political limitations of the WSF as currently constituted, the continuing legitimacy in at least certain situations of violent self-defence, the dangers of NGOisation, the ulterior motives and purposes of certain funding sources—none of this precluded their participation in the WSF even while retaining and expressing these criticisms. Respect for the role played by some of the major groups in MR in defending the poorest sections of society in their countries (this is certainly the case in India) should not prevent one from recognising their time-warped politics, nor their unfortunate sectarianism.
5. The phase of neoliberalism that India is going through was initiated in 1991 by a Congress government, starting with so-called 'structural adjustment policies.' At the time of publication of this book, the present prime minister of India, Manmohan Singh, who was still earlier an employee of the World Bank, was, as finance minister in 1991, the architect of the reforms. —Eds.
6. A fuller treatment of the Indian economy's basic character is to be found in my 'India's New Right,' in the May-June 2001 issue of the *New Left Review*. A booming stock market provides further reassurances to an Indian elite that includes the misnamed 'middle class,' which far from being a median category, comprises the top 10 to 15 percent of Indian society. Of the Rs 100,000 crores (U.S.$ 204 billion, @ 2004 rates) that went into the secondary market in 2003, only Rs 2,000 crores (U.S.$ 4.08 billion) was new investment in new ventures.
7. In 2000, the government introduced the Banking Companies and Financial Institution Laws (Amendment) Bill in Parliament, which seeks to reduce the minimum share holding by government to 33 percent. Resistance from bank unions forced the government to refer the Bill to the Standing Committee on Finance where it currently remains.
8. Just as one example, in 2003 there were 740,000 applicants for 20,000 posts in the lowest 'group D' category in Indian railways. Among the applicants for railway gangmen jobs were MBAs, both graduates and post-graduates, and engineers.
9. Godhra, a town of roughly equal proportions of Hindus and Muslims, has a long history of communal tension and violence that has usually been triggered by some 'provocation' or the other. Tensions had been building up over the week as a result of a 'March on Ayodhya' organised by the *Sangh Parivar*. (The *Sangh Parivar* is the Hindutva family of organisations of which the main components are the cadre-based *Rashtriya Swayamsevak Sangh*, the BJP, and the lumpen storm-troopers of the *Bajrang Dal*. Ayodhya is a town in middle India where there was a mosque that Hindu fundamentalists asserted was built over a particularly sacred Hindu temple, and which they therefore then, led by members of the *Sangh Parivar*, proceeded to demolish in 1991, leading to Hindu-Muslim riots across much of India.) Sangh activists and their families as well as ordinary passengers were returning by train to Gujarat when a molestation of a Muslim girl on the platform of Godhra station provided the spark igniting an already simmering situation, leading to the burning of one railway bogey suspected of harbouring the molesters. Fifty-eight people including women and children were burnt to death. The same afternoon the Gujarat government

deliberately decided to inflame the situation by calling for a statewide 'bandh' or closure of all public activities on 28 February 2002, when orchestrated violence on Muslim neighbourhoods began, spreading throughout Gujarat including into the villages and lasting for over a month.

Enormous documentation of the atrocities now exists and is easily available. For a detailed account of Godhra and its immediate aftermath including the extent to which the police and bureaucracy of Gujarat (up to its highest officer levels) was suborned, see *Gujarat Carnage 2002: A Report to the Nation* prepared by an Independent Fact Finding Mission comprising Prof. Kamal Chenoy (Jawaharlal Nehru University), S.P. Shukla (former Finance Secretary in the central government and former member of the Planning Commission of India), K.S. Subramanian (retired Director-General of Police in Tripura state), and Achin Vanaik. Major communal riots took place in India in 1984 after the assassination of Mrs Gandhi, in this case anti-Sikh. But while the officail tally of deaths was higher in these riots (around 3,000) and local political (here, Congress party) leaders were again behind this, it pales in comparison to what happened in Gujarat. The communal character, context and history surrounding the two cases were very different. Anti-Sikh sentiment was the result of a specific conjuncture marked by the rise of the Khalistan separatist movement. Anti-Muslim sentiment has a much longer history, wider roots and, above all, the existence of a powerful grassroots organisation whose raison d'etre is the cultivation for political purposes of an enduring hatred for Muslims. Anti-Sikh communalism has withered as the Khalistan movement withered. While the leaders most responsible for the 1984 violence have not been punished, the Congress has publicly apologised for what happened and for the role played by its local leaders. The levels of brutality and sadism reached, and the scale, geographic extent, and duration of communal violence, was much greater in the case of Gujarat. The degree and extent of complicity on the part of the apparatuses of the state was also far greater, and the negative political implications of Gujarat 2002 were much more profound.

10. In 1999, the NDA won all the 23 seats of Haryana, Delhi, Himachal and Goa put together; 20 out of 26 in Gujarat, 36 out of 42 in Andhra Pradesh, 16 out of 25 in Rajasthan, 26 out of 39 in Tamil Nadu, 28 out of 48 in Maharashtra, 41 out of 54 in Bihar, 19 out of 21 in Orissa, and 29 out of 40 in Madhya Pradesh-Chattisgarh.
11. A start has been made through the publication in 2004 of *World Social Forum: Challenging Empires*, an anthology of essays on the theory and practice of the WSF. Edited by Jai Sen, Anita Anand, Arturo Escobar and Peter Waterman, and carrying a thoughtful foreword by Hilary Wainwright, the book was released at the Mumbai WSF.
12. It has now been broken! See the essays in this book on the first U.S. Social Forum, by Michael Leon Guerrero, Tammy Bang Luu, and Cindy Wiesner and by Judy Rebick. —Eds.

Citizen Mobilisation In The Americas And The Birth Of The World Social Forum[1]

Dorval Brunelle

The World Social Forum (WSF) is undoubtedly the most important social phenomenon of the new millennium. Analysts have identified a number of factors that have played a significant role in its emergence as well as in the proliferation of social forums at the local, national, and continental levels all over the world.

These forums establish "novel forms of political organisation"[2] on the part of social movements that have set up the WSF process as "a form of polycentric governance, or a transborder political body with an organisational architecture that remains fluid, decentralised, and ever evolving."[3] In turn, "the WSF process offers a fresh start for struggles *for* social justice and *against* neoliberal capitalism."[4] In fact, the WSF *as process* would seem to answer to calls for more democracy and more social justice in a way that formal elections cannot hope to achieve. This is because the militants and activists involved in these movements direct their actions and strategies at global institutions and in transnational space as opposed to directing it against only their own national states.[5]

On the other hand, such a conclusion also does not seem to entirely fit with what is going on presently in Latin America where, in parallel to the social movements' involvement with the WSF process and in transnational campaigns, we have seen the dramatic emergence of a series of left-leaning governments on that continent over the past decade or so. Even if the mobilisation may not be alone responsible for these major changes at the state level, these changes also cannot be seen in isolation from the extensive and sustained mobilisation process that has been going on all over Latin America.

In this context, this essay argues that organisations and movements in Latin America framed their actions, strategies, and protests differently from what was done by others in other parts of the world, with the result that they did indeed achieve a measure of political impact that has not so far been seen elsewhere.

In the following section, I list four factors that according to some authors, have had an important influence on the setting up of the WSF process.[6] I then go on to introduce my own take on the fourth of these, which is the roles played by social mobilisation in the Americas as a whole—North, Central, and

South America. This factor deserves closer scrutiny for two reasons: first, because, as I will show, intense social organisation and mobilisation in the Americas acted as important forerunners of the WSF process itself; and second, because their continued involvement served to enhance their own organising and politicising capabilities, even as they induced a marked shift to the left in the political spectrum of South America.

Factors That Set The WSF Process In motion

The first factor that stands out is the mobilisation of the protests against the World Economic Forum (WEF), whose annual meeting takes place each January in Davos, Switzerland. This initiative, known as 'the Other Davos' (*l'Autre Davos*, in French), was launched in Zurich in 1999, and has been convened ever since at the same time as the WEF. This mobilisation called attention to two salient features of the new neoliberal global order coming out of the post-Cold War era: one, that this was an order founded on the alliance of governments with international organisations and big business; and two, that this alliance was deliberately being forged in a remote area, shielded from any open debate and public scrutiny—in short, in an undemocratic way that challenged all previous norms of governance.

Opposition to not only the political economic ideology of the order but also to its increasingly private and unaccountable culture, and the advocacy of the opposite, became the central characteristics of the WSF that took shape in time.

The second factor that is given a prominent role in the literature is the decisive emergence at the turn of the century of popular movements that challenged and successfully disrupted international institutions and processes that had seemed invincible. One of the strongest expressions of the new movement was in the protest that emerged in 1998 against the Multilateral Agreement on Investment (MAI), negotiations for which were being held at the time under the aegis of the Organisation for Economic Cooperation and Development (OECD) in Paris. This was soon followed by a series of mobilisations and actions, which included the celebrated action against the third Ministers' Meeting of the World Trade Organisation (WTO) in November 1999, in Seattle; the mobilisation against the joint annual meetings of the International Monetary Fund (IMF) and the World Bank in 2000 and 2001; protests against the annual meetings of heads of states of the European Union and the Asia-Pacific Economic Cooperation (APEC); as well as annual mobilisations against the G-7, later to become the G-8.

On the one hand, this series of actions led over time to a sense within the movements of a growing power and the emergence of a 'movement of movements'; and on the other, many authors have seen the creation of the WSF as an initiative to allow all these various different movements a space and opportunity to meet and exchange notes, and perhaps even to build alliances.

To these two seemingly more immediate factors, some authors add a third one which was the growing dissatisfaction on the part of non-governmental organisations (NGOs) with the United Nations system and its incapacity to overhaul the prevailing practices concerning NGO involvement in international affairs.[7] Dissatisfaction soon took the form of mounting disillusionment after the world conferences on the environment (the second Earth Summit in Rio de Janeiro, 1992), on women (the fourth World Conference on Women in Beijing, 1995), and on social development (the World Summit on Social Development in Copenhagen, in March 1995). This was further deepened by the many setbacks experienced during the five-year review processes of these Summits that were held in 1997 and in 2000, respectively. Even if these disillusionments cannot be tied to the setting up of the WSF as such, the disillusioned themselves—such as those involved in setting up the World March of Women, initiated from Canada —were quite ready to come on board a new and different process.[8]

Latin America and the Fourth Factor: The Importance of Multiple Framing

Finally, there is a fourth factor that I want to look at here, separately from the previous ones. This is the very nature of the mobilisation undertaken by the social movements of the Americas, where a clear consciousness emerged, particularly during the campaigns against inter-state negotiations around the Free Trade of the Americas Agreement (FTAA), that struggles at the national level against one's own government's involvement in these negotiations must go hand in hand with mobilisation on a transnational scale; and vice versa.

In Latin America, in particular, it is important to note that organisations and coalitions were already in place in the nineties to protest against a host of measures, economic plans, and other 'structural adjustments' imposed from above, under the so-called *Washington Consensus*. In addition, organisations from each and every country on the continent were already directly concerned by the actions of the World Bank, the IMF, and others, and involved in actions against them. So there was a kind of a 'piling up' effect at play here, of layers of experience in resistance, which was not the case for the organisations from the North and where organisations from the other continents of the South—Africa and Asia—were newer to the practice of transnationalising on a scale comparable to that in the Latin Americas.

So, somewhat contrary to what was going on elsewhere within the global social movement, here the movements did not neglect the national state or the national scene during the process of transnational coalition building at the regional and hemispherical levels; they worked simultaneously at both levels.[9]

This *multiple framing*, I would like to contend, was necessitated *by the nature of the agreements themselves* that were sought to be put into place. I aim to show how a particular model of economic integration based on a so-called *free trade* agreement exacted such major 'structural adjustments' from other countries in the hemisphere that it led to convergence between opponents to the deals both at the national *and* at the transnational level.[10]

The connection between the two levels is important here, and I will argue that it is precisely this frontal attack against state sovereignty and its ability to promote the common good that led to the emergence of a new practice of mobilisation. It also explains the *extent of the transnationalisation* that emerged among major social organisations in Latin America, which it did not to a comparable extent elsewhere. It also points to the scope and depth of the *impact of this new kind of social mobilisation* on the political sphere at the national level, most evidently in South America.

It is important also to underline that these mobilisations in the hemisphere eventually led to the demise of the FTAA. In this regard, the 'FTAA victory'—a bracketing which will be made clear in a moment—represents a momentous event that should be ascribed concurrently to the mobilisations in the Americas and to the WSF itself, which in turn had a determinant impact on the positions taken by some governments in the region on this issue.

The significance of these developments lies at several levels. Both in turn explain the large presence and visibility of organisations from Latin America at the first WSF while the better known world organisations—Amnesty International, Oxfam, Greenpeace—only came on board later and at a much slower pace. And even if geographical proximity facilitated Latin American organisations being there, the somewhat more sparse showing on the part of organisations from the USA is probably more attributable to the strategy that prevailed there of concentrating struggles either on the national or at the international and global levels, and where both were to the detriment of struggle at the hemispheric one. This is all the more striking since, as noted above, the mobilisation in Seattle in November 1999, is widely seen as having played the part of being a distant forerunner of the WSF process. But many organisations in the USA tended to concentrate their actions against their own government and within their own political institutions, such as concentrating their energies on lobbying Congress and, in some cases, throwing their support behind the Democratic Party, while others carried on their struggles against the IMF and the G-8 as before. One notable exception however, is the Alliance for Responsible Trade (ART), which played a significant role both in the mobilisation against NAFTA and against the FTAA.

I start with a discussion of the campaign in the Americas around NAFTA (the North American Free Trade Agreement) and move on to look at the mobilisations in the hemisphere against the FTAA, a project spearheaded by the USA from late 1994 onward. This is not a particularly original starting point since many authors before me have pointed to the emergence of the *Ejercito Zapatista de Liberacion Nacional* (EZLN, or Zapatista National Liberation Army), on 1 January 1994, the very day NAFTA—which was the forerunner of the FTAA—came into force, as *the* momentous event that ushered in a new type of mobilisation against neoliberal economic integration on a grand scale.[11]

But my own take on this argument, as indicated earlier, will be somewhat different. I will concentrate my attention on the features of the agreements themselves before moving on to the protest movements that were set up to oppose them.

NAFTA: New Modes of Hegemony and of Mobilisation

The main reason why I use NAFTA as a starting point is because this agreement was in itself a milestone in the establishment of a neoliberal agenda, which in turn triggered new modes of citizen mobilisation. From this point on, free trade agreements would be argued to be—and would prove to be—the most efficient way to implement structural adjustment programmes since they now, instead of being imposed on countries from the outside by the IMF and others, are agreed to by a consenting party.

Beyond this, it was the first so-called 'free trade' agreement that involved two totally asymmetrical partners: The U.S., which was the imperial power par excellence, and Mexico. (In actuality, although NAFTA is called a trilateral agreement between Canada, Mexico, and the USA, it is essentially bilateral, because by that time Canada had already signed its own bilateral trade deal with the USA in 1989, CANUSFTA, and thus had nothing to offer to the new treaty.)

In a sense, NAFTA is both a concentrate of the *Washington Consensus* and its requirements and also a plan of action incorporating what the WEF, the IMF, the World Bank, the WTO and the G-8 had been demanding for years. Furthermore, NAFTA is much more efficient than any measures by the likes of the IMF or the World Bank. As a *treaty* between supposedly consenting nation-states it pretends to be a consensual agreement between *equal* parties. NAFTA therefore achieved what no single agreement had ever achieved before this: it imposed 'structural adjustments' on a grand scale, it established complete transborder mobility for capital, goods, and services—the so-called *three freedoms*[12]—and it liberalised internal public and private markets, including the agricultural sector. The latter is an objective that, to this day, the WTO has been unable to accomplish. It also implemented what was termed an *evolutionary approach*—as opposed to the traditional one-time agreement—which implied that the negotiation process was and would remain open-ended and continuous, thanks to the setting up of thirty odd Working Groups which in turn answer directly to the NAFTA Commission set up under chapters 19 and 20 of the agreement.[13]

The implementation of a NAFTA-type strategy and approach goes far beyond the terms of any previous free trade agreement, and one of the most telling indicators of this is the fact that the two countries involved with the U.S. had to undergo major *constitutional* amendments in order to bring the basic institutions and the basic norms of the state in line with the requirements of the agreement. The fact that the enforcement of norms and institutions coming out of NAFTA required prior constitutional amendments is a telling indicator of its importance as an agreement. There was, however, another, deeper significance, since NAFTA would now be used as a template for each and every subsequent free trade negotiation and, in many instances, at the same constitutional cost.[14]

Furthermore, some provisions of NAFTA, notably chapter 11 on the liberalisation of investments and investor rights, in time proved so appealing to neoliberal-minded power brokers that the Organisation for Economic Cooperation and Development (OECD) took it upon itself in 1998 to set up negotiations for a *Multilateral Agreement on Investment* (MAI) among its member states. This was however an initiative that collapsed over the following year because of the major campaign that came to be launched against it and mounting social opposition to the deal in many of the countries involved.[15]

To sum up, there are several reasons why NAFTA provides a crucial starting point. First, because of its contractual nature, where any government that enters into such an agreement does so voluntarily, a situation arises that is markedly different from the one that prevails when the same requirements come out of the IMF, the World Bank, or the G-8. A central aspect of this is that national governments became directly and openly accountable and responsible themselves, and not just the institutions of which they were members.

Second, because the sheer extent of these requirements—which cut right across a host of issues from constitutional revision to collective versus individual rights, the survival of agriculture, the equality of women, the status of indigenous peoples, and the environment, among many others—it aroused public debates and provoked large scale mobilisation. And third, NAFTA therefore not only acted as a template for many other neoliberal international treaties (and attempts at treaties) but also precipitated the forging of a new mode of social response, one that came to maturity in the course of fighting NAFTA, MAI, and then the FTAA.

Looked at from the perspective of citizen action, the requirements and exigencies coming out of a so-called *free trade treaty* crystallised a new multidimensional and multifaceted onslaught against the common good. This challenge called for the critical examination of past practices on the part of social organisations operating on the national scene, and the reaching out towards other organisations in the other countries involved. Previously, coalition building against issues of importance had led to the creation of temporary coalitions that were soon dissolved once the issue in question dropped out of view, whereas this time around the coalitions set up to confront NAFTA were set up on a permanent basis, and are still very much active to this day. In this case, all four coalitions—including one from Quebec—were built around the same model of a confluence of seemingly diverse causes, with the union movement playing an important role in each case, in conjunction with other social organisations, such as the women's movement, First Nations (in some cases, not all), the environmental movement, social justice organisations, and research groups.[16]

Furthermore, national cooperation between organisations was intimately tied to transnational cooperation, essentially because the external outreach afforded an effective and credible leverage to the internal opposition itself, especially in contexts where free trade was immediately seized upon by the media as an essential and indispensable instrument for the promotion of economic growth in the country.[17] All these factors would play in and be important to the mobilisations against the FTAA as well.

Mobilisation on a large scale against a free trade deal between U.S. and Mexico started off in both countries in 1990, quite a while before the launching of the official negotiations, while Canadian organisations came on board only after their government was admitted to the negotiating table in March 1991. Ultimately however, these campaigns were unsuccessful. Apart from the addition of two side-accords to the agreement, NAFTA was duly signed by the three countries and came into force 1 January 1994, as planned.

Even if the struggles against NAFTA were unsuccessful, and therefore may at best have had only an indirect impact on the WSF, as we shall see below their subsequent branching out into a host of struggles against the FTAA came to have a very direct impact.

The Struggle against the FTAA and the Road to the WSF

No sooner was NAFTA signed than the White House came up with an even grander scheme. This project was first spelled out in a memorandum issued by the National Security Council (NSC), dated 29 November 1993, sent by National Security advisor, Anthony Lake, to President Clinton. The object of the memo was 'Proposed Hemispheric Summit,' and its purpose, the following: "To seek your approval for a summit meeting of Western Hemisphere heads of state in Washington in May 1994 *to build on the NAFTA victory* to generate a broad hemispheric consensus behind our key policy objectives (...)."[18]

The memo's 'background' unfolds the argument in the following manner:

> The moment is ripe for an historic initiative—of the weight of the Good Neighbour policy and the Alliance for Progress—to establish the themes for inter-American relations for the rest of the decade and beyond: The NAFTA is the foundation for the gradual expansion of hemispheric free trade (...)
>
> Hemispheric institutions, including the OAS and Inter-American Development Bank and now the NAFTA institutions, can be forged into the vital mechanisms of hemispheric governance.
>
> The organising concept could be a hemispheric 'Community of Democracies' increasingly integrated by economic exchange and shared political values. Whatever the slogan, your vision of an inte-

> grated Western Hemisphere could be a model for international relations in general and for North-South relations more specifically. (...)[19]

This eventually led to an event held in Miami in December 1994 where the project of a *Free Trade Area of the Americas* (FTAA) was unveiled by the U.S. to the thirty-four heads of state and government in attendance.[20] But for the national coalitions that had mobilised against NAFTA,[21] the opening of this new and expanded round of commercial negotiations was a challenge that called for even more intense transnational collaborations between the North and the South of the hemisphere, in order to defeat the FTAA.

Here, it is important to note that the economic and political situation in South America, and a long history behind it, led to a somewhat different approach and strategy than what was used in the campaigns against NAFTA. This was because the labour union movement in South America—and most notably, the *Coordenadora das Centrais Sindicais do Cono Sul* (CCSCS, or the Coordination of Trade Unions of the Southern Cone)[22]—were, like their counterparts in the European Union,[23] more supportive of the creation of a different, *regional* alliance named MERCOSUR.[24] This project of regional economic integration in the so-called 'southern cone' of South America had been launched in 1991 by Argentina, Brazil, Paraguay, and Uruguay,[25] and the unions' support to this can be understood both as a means to gain greater political leverage on their part at the national level and as a part of a much longer tradition of Latin American integration as a political and economic project that emerged soon after the wars of independence in the 19th century, at the first Pan-American Congress convened by Simón Bolívar, in Panama, in 1826.

In other words, in some countries of South America at least, and especially in those that were members of MERCOSUR in particular, the labour movement and its allies did not oppose economic integration *per se*. In fact, they were quite open to confronting their own governments on occasions when they took positions that could have a detrimental effect on the consolidation of MERCOSUR. But this approval and support by the union movement was limited to MERCOSUR and not extended to the FTAA project, and even though some of the concerned governments pretended to advance the MERCOSUR agenda through their negotiations around FTAA.

For their part, governments were also conscious of the importance of this support by the trade unions. This led them to extend the right of participation in the MERCOSUR process to the union movement and to other social organisations, under the Protocol of Ouro Preto, signed in 1995. This openness on the part of governments involved in the MERCOSUR process towards the participation of unions and other social organisations established a clear-cut difference with the NAFTA process, where such opportunity absolutely did not exist.

This distinction became all the more discriminatory in the light of the fact that many of the unions from the South involved in MERCOSUR, as well as the unions from the North all of whom were excluded from NAFTA, were members of the same regional organisation (ORIT) and were affiliated to the International Conference of Free Trade Unions (ICFTU). One of the basic tenets of ICFTU philosophy and practice since its creation back in 1949 was collaboration with business and governments under what was called *tripartism*—an approach and philosophy that was binding on all parties This had allowed ICFTU union members to participate actively in organisations that implemented *tripartism*, like the Economic and Social Forum of the UN (ECOSOC) or the OECD.[26] Consequently, in implementing *tripartism* in the MERCOSUR process in the same way as the European Community—now the European Union —had done before, governments of the MERCOSUR in effect aligned themselves with this philosophy, while governments from North America refused to do so. In fact, the latter went even further and practiced *bipartism*—by extending consultative status to the Americas Business Forum (ABF) in 1995 even while excluding all other citizen organisations, like the unions.[27]

Consequently, when civil society organisations from the South and from the North in the Americas came together at a parallel social summit convened during a meeting of the ministers of commerce of the Americas in Belo Horizonte (Brazil) in 1997, and founded the Hemispheric Social Alliance (HSA) as an instrument in their common struggle against the FTAA, MERCOSUR did not figure on their agenda.

From then on, and over the ensuing years, there emerged an ever-widening circle of mobilisation concentrating attention and efforts against the FTAA in the Americas, not only at the continental level but at the national and local levels as well—as the struggle against water privatisation in Cochabamba, Bolivia, showed so well. The HSA organised a string of People's Summits held in parallel to the Summits of the Americas, in Santiago (Chile) in 1998, in Québec City (Canada) in 2001, in Monterrey (Mexico) in 2003, and in Mar del Plata (Argentina) in 2005. Local chapters of the HSA also organised two Social Forums of the Americas, one in Quito (Ecuador) in 2004 and the other in Caracas (Venezuela) in 2006, the latter at the same time as the polycentric sixth world meeting of the WSF that was held there. Each time, the results of the debates were fed into the founding document of the HSA, *Alternatives for the Americas*, which went through a number of revisions over the years.[28]

The HSA also received an important political boost and a continent-wide recognition when *comandante* Fidel Castro convened the first *Campana continental de lucha contra el ALCA*, (Continental Campaign of Struggle against the FTAA)—which has been convened yearly ever since then—at La Havana (Cuba) in November 2001, in the wake of the second Peoples' Summit of the Americas held in Québec in April of the previous year, 2000.[29]

This strategy—of a sustained process of both mass mobilisation and of idea development—proved very successful. The heads of state and government finally abandoned their project of a hemispheric free trade area at their fifth Summit of the Americas, that took place in 2005 in Mar del Plata (Argentina). This happened because the mobilisation that took place around the FTAA along with other factors led to a shift leftwards in country after country, and by 2005, the opposition to the treaty at the governmental level had grown to such an extent that it was no longer a feasible proposition. I will discuss this in more detail below.

But this outcome would not have been possible if the HSA and its member organisations had concentrated and limited their involvement only at the continental level, and if they had not also invested heavily in organising, mobilising, and networking at the local and national levels as well. It is here that the bulk of the work was done, by countless grassroots organisations, with the result that barely three years after its launch in December 1994, the FTAA came to be condemned in almost every city and town in the Americas; and where several years later, in January 2002, opposition to the FTAA was the main theme on the banners stringing the opening march of the second WSF held in Porto Alegre.[30]

Other Contributing Factors

As indicated earlier however, it would be simplifying matters greatly to suggest that this extensive social mobilisation, networking, and alliance building that took place in the Americas came exclusively out of a response to the new strategies of free trade, liberalisation and imperialist dominance alone, to the exclusion of other historical issues. Two important reminders are in order in this respect. The first has to do with the proclamation by the UN General Assembly, on 21 December 1993, of the International Decade of the World's Indigenous People (1995–2004),[31] whose main objective was "strengthening international cooperation for the solution of problems faced by indigenous people in such areas as human rights, the environment, development, education and health."[32] The second has been the emergence during the same period of the women's movement throughout the Americas.

In the Americas, the pivotal moment in the re-emergence of indigenous peoples as historical and collective actors had occurred a few years earlier, from 1992 onwards, in the wake of the celebrations surrounding the quincentennial anniversary of Columbus's landing in 1492. This event spurred a host of mobilisations throughout the hemisphere, which took the form of Native American Protests against the official celebrations.[33] Over the ensuing years, countless gatherings, meetings, and assemblies were convened and numerous organisations set up. Among many initiatives, *Enlace*—a Continental Network of Indigenous Women set up in 1993—organised four continental meetings in Quito, Mexico City, Panama City, and Lima. Most notably, the indigenous peoples of the Americas organised important forums through the hemisphere during the 1990s that acted as forerunners of the WSF itself. And the indigenous peoples of the Americas have also preserved their organisational autonomy to this day, within and in relation to the WSF. Each year, their annual Social Forum of Indigenous People takes place immediately prior to the WSF itself, in which however they also claim their own space.[34]

Furthermore, in many contexts in Latin America, most notably in Mexico, Bolivia, Peru, Venezuela, Brazil, Chile, Ecuador, Paraguay, and Guatemala, indigenous organisations have played an important political role as well. The most important examples are the *Confederacion de Nacionalidades Indigenas del Ecuador* (CONAIE, or the Confederation of Indigenous Nationalities of Ecuador) and the *Asamblea por la Soberania de los Pueblos* (ASP, or Assembly for the Peoples' Sovereignty), which became the Bolivian *Movimiento al Socialismo* (MAS, or Movement Towards Socialism), as well as the *Movimiento indigeno Pachacuti* (MIP, or Indigenous Pachacuti Movement), also in Bolivia.

Finally, the women's movement in the Americas also re-emerged in full view at the turn of the millennium, in particular through the organisation of the World March of Women in 2000.[35] This initiative has a most impressive following throughout the continent. Today, there are as many chapters of the March as there are countries in the hemisphere, and each is involved in the setting up of Women's Forums both inside and outside the WSF venue itself.

Some authors have credited both the women's and the indigenous peoples' movements for the implementation of many of the innovative rules and codes of conduct that have subsequently been adopted by participating organisations during social forums at all levels, and which have also filtered into the WSF charter and *modus operandi*. Most notable in this regard are the respect for pluralism, tolerance of dissent, and the implementation of horizontality in discussions and decision-making, as well as gender balancing.[36]

The Shift to the Left In South American Politics and the WSF

Neoliberalism seeks to depoliticise issues, organisations, and people. Both its profound distrust of the State and its reverence for market forces serve this purpose. From the mid-eighties on, civil governments bent on state reform replaced military regimes in South America. In economic terms, these reforms reflected ideas contained in the so-called *Washington Consensus* that came to be defined in 1989, ideas that provided for the privatisation of public assets and the liberalisation of national markets (also articulated as *the four freedoms*—the free and unhindered mobility of goods, services, investments, and labour). This was at a time when the economic nationalism that had been advocated by the Economic Commission for Latin America and the Caribbean (ECLAC)[37] was under heavy criticism both from within and from outside the country, such as by the World Bank and the International Monetary Fund, and when the newly elected democratic governments of Latin America substituted a new, more neoliberal model of development based on export promotion (*hacia afuera*) in place of the more inwardly-oriented model of import substitution (*hacia adentro*) that had prevailed since the late forties.

But this fling with neoliberalism was to be short-lived. Following the Asiatic financial crisis of 1997 and the economic meltdown in Argentina in December 2001, and in the wake of increasing social inequality, mounting economic insecurity, and creeping political corruption, disillusionment quickly set in, with the result that, at the turn of the millennium, the extensive social mobilisation that had taken place in the region assisted in ushering in a host of political parties belonging to the Left at various levels of governments.

From soon after the return to civilian rule in Brazil in 1986, the socio-political context in this country provides an interesting example of the cross-fertilisation between social mobilisation and politicisation. The involvement of two of its major civil society organisations—the *Movimento dos Trabalhadores Rurais Sem Terra* (MST, or the Landless Workers' Movement) and the *Central Única dos Trabalhadores* (CUT, or the Workers' Union)—in conjunction with the *Partido do Trabalhadores* (PT, or the Workers' Party)—served as stepping stones in the conquest of power in cities (for example, São Paulo and Porto Alegre in 1988, 1992, 1996, and 2000) as well as in states (for instance, Rio Grande do Sul in 1998) before the accession of Luis Ignacio da Silva (Lula) to the presidency in 2002. During their battle against the neoliberal model of development, these organisations brought to the fore new initiatives and alternatives and, among them, a protocol for participatory democracy implemented by the PT in the city of Porto Alegre, which, among other things, explains why this city was chosen as the host of the first WSF.

In turn, the Workers' Party of Brazil—a key player in this process—played a central role in the founding of the WSF itself. This was well illustrated at the very first WSF in Porto Alegre, in January 2001, when the organisers welcomed the president of the PT, Lula who had lost his presidential bids in 1989, 1994 and 1998, and who would try again in 2002. Lula was extremely well received at the WSF, and this probably fired up his troops even more, so much so that he would win the next elections and return to the WSF, in January 2003, but now as head of state, in a bid to gather momentum before flying off to Davos to present his *Fome Zero* (Zero Hunger) programme to fight malnutrition in his own country and worldwide.

But this shift to the left of the political spectrum is not limited to Brazil.[38] To give an idea of its importance and swiftness, one has but to recall that at the third Summit of the Americas, in Québec City in April 2001, among the thirty-four in attendance President Hugo Chavez of Venezuela was the only head of state who opposed the FTAA project. But barely two years later, at the fourth 'special' Summit of the Americas,[39] at Monterrey (Mexico), in January 2003, the project was seriously questioned by a number of states, most notably Brazil and Argentina, and with the result that at the last Summit of the Americas, in Mar del Plata in November 2005, governments from Uruguay and Bolivia joined the opposition and the project was kept off the official agenda, which concentrated on job creation and democracy instead.

This demise is basically imputable to the numerous changes in governments that had occurred in the intervening years, starting off with Venezuela and Brazil, followed by Argentina, Bolivia, Chile, and Uruguay and, more recently, Ecuador and Nicaragua. Furthermore, in many other contexts, the electorate has been remarkably polarised on the issue of free trade, liberalisation, privatisation, and commercial integration with the North, as the recent electoral jousts in Mexico, Costa Rica and Peru have shown all too well. And these results are all the more striking when we compare them to what has been happening in the U.S. and in Canada that have both veered resolutely to the right of the political spectrum in recent years.

This juxtaposition in fact brings to the fore a historical opposition dating back to the first decades of the 19th century that played itself out in the rival plans for continental integration in the Americas: one put forward and defended by Simón Bolívar (of Venezuela but who is widely regarded in Latin America as one of the liberators of Spanish South America as a whole), who favoured a Latin American integration, and the other by President James Monroe of the U.S., who declared a U.S. guardianship over the Americas.

Conclusion

To sum up, the multiplication, extension, and plurality of citizen mobilisation in the Americas at the turn of the millennium not only played a seminal and determinant role in the convocation of the first WSF in Brazil in 2001 but more importantly, these mobilisations assured that this new initiative would be active not only at the transnational and world levels but would proliferate at all levels. This proliferation was all the more applicable and relevant given that the organisations that had led this mobilisation were already in place and had previously engaged in similar initiatives on their own. In other words, having acted as the immediate vectors if not the immediate inspiration for the WSF, they could henceforth act as the *natural* relays of its objectives and mandate, and proceed to implement its slogan, 'Another world is possible,' in their actions and activities on a day-to-day basis.

In the Americas, as we have seen, these changes also played themselves out at the political level and in the political sphere with the result that Latin America is presently, in many instances, ruled by progressive governments that owe their accession to power to the innumerable social mobilisations in the hemisphere. And this is precisely what the WSF is all about: to serve as a catalyst and as a facilitator of mobilisations the world over, but especially on the more practical and pressing social as well as political issues at the national, local, and community levels.

Notes

1. The author wishes to thank Georges LeBel and Jai Sen for their comments on an earlier version of this paper. Content editor for this essay is Vipul Rikhi.
2. J. Smith, *et al.* 2008, p 131.
3. *Idem*, p 133.
4. *Idem*.
5. Della Porta, *et al.* 2006.
6. Barlow and Clarke 2002; Foster, in Bandy and Smith 2005, p 223; J Smith, *et al.* 2008, p 14.
7. Smith, *et al.* 2008, p 14.
8. Matte and Guay, in Seoane and Taddei, 2001, pp 169-178.
9. This applies most notably to Via Campesina: an international movement created in Latin America—which coordinates peasant organisations throughout the world, to the World March of Women, as well as to the indigenous movement, the ecological movement and the Inter-American Regional Organisation of Workers (IAROW, better known as the *Organisation Regional Interamericana de Trabajadores*, ORIT) affiliated at the time to the International Confederation of Free Trade Unions (ICFTU). The ICFTU merged with the World Confederation of Labour (WCL) and formed the International Trade Union Conference (ITUC) in 2006.
10. In Canada, a *Memorandum to the Cabinet* spelled this out quite explicitly. The secret document in question, dated 7 August 2002, was entitled *Mandate for WTO Negotiations* and was tabled by the Minister of International Commerce and the Minister of Industry. It had this to say about NAFTA and other such agreements: "The challenges of NAFTA and bilateral free trade agreements provided the impetus for the *structural adjustments* (*emphasis added, DB*) needed not only to face competition at home but also to compete and win abroad, including in the world's largest market, the U.S." p 18.
11. Benasayag and Scavino 1997; Benasayag and Sztulwark 2002; Beck, 2003, p 516.
12. Out of four, the fourth being complete mobility ('freedom' [sic]) of *labour* which is provided for, with limitations, in the European Union.
13. For instance, negotiations on the issue of agriculture between the U.S. and Mexico under NAFTA have been going on since 1995, ie for the past thirteen years.
14. There is a simple explanation for this: since states had provided for the constitutional protection of land, natural resources, public utilities or social rights, among others, liberalisation required the *deconstitutionalisation* of these collective rights. This debate will in all probability re-emerge in Mexico when the issue of the privatisation of Pemex is brought to the fore.
15. See: Barlow and Clarke 2002, pp 103–4 and 155–6. Also: Deblock and Brunelle 2000.
16. The four are: The *Red Mexicana de Accion Frente al Libre Comercio* (RMALC: www.rmalc.org.mx), the Alliance for Responsible Trade (ART: www.art-us.org), Common Frontiers (www.commonfrontiers.ca), and the *Réseau québécois sur l'intégration continentale* (RQIC: www.rqic.alternatives.ca).
17. Cross-border liaising between coalitions started off as early as 1990, but took on an extended and more permanent turn after the Miami Summit and the launching of the FTAA negotiations in 1994, and the creation of the Hemispheric Social Alliance (HSA) in 1997, as we shall see below. These exchanges have been going on ever since.

18. The use of the expression 'NAFTA victory' in the present context explains why I chose to emphasise the expression 'FTAA victory' earlier on, when mentioning the successful outcome of social mobilisation in defeating the deal.
19. National Security Council, *Memorandum for the President*, 29 November 1993. Declassified 3/8/96. Emphasis added. This memo was readily available on the NSC web site for a while, but was subsequently removed. The memo, as well as its political and strategic implications are further analysed in Dorval Brunelle 2003.
20. The 35th, Cuba, long excluded from pan-American affairs, is obviously not involved in this process.
21. There are four *national* coalitions in North America against free trade. The Quebec coalition has kept its own autonomy through the process and played an important role in the organisation and as co-host of the second People's Summit in Quebec City in April 2001.
22. The founding members of the CCSCS were the *Central Obrera de Bolivia* (COB); the *Movimento Intersindical de Trabajadores* (MIT), from Paraguay—later renamed the *Central Unitaria de Trabajadores*, CUT; the *Comando Nacional de Trabajadores* (CNT) and the *Central Democratica de Trabajadores* (CDT) from Chile—which later merged into the *Central Unica de Trabajadores*, CUT; the *Confederacion General del Trabajo* (CGT) from Argentina; the *Plenario Sindical de Trabajadores / Convencion Nacional de Trabajadores* (PIT-CNT) from Uruguay; and finally, the *Central Unica de Trabajadores* (CUT) and *Central General de Trabajadores* (CGT), both from Brazil. See Vigevani and ors, 1998, p 109.
23. The European Trade Union Confederation (ETUC) plays a similar role in the EU. It gave full support to the integration process from the outset and has sought to strengthen its social dimension.
24. The unions of South America belonging to ORIT / ICFTU had set up the CCSCS as early as 1986. In a declaration issued in 1998, the CCSCS stated: "Representatives of the workers were always in favour of the creation of Mercosur, which should foster commercial exchanges among the four countries." On line: www.ccscs.org.
25. The negotiation process between Brazil and Argentina started off in 1985, under the governments of Sarney and Alfonsin. The main conceptual influence on the MERCOSUR project at the time was, and still is, the European model of social and economic integration.
26. This involvement in OECD affairs of the Trade Union Advisory Committee (TUAC) however, alongside the Business and Industry Advisory Committee (BIAC), was of little use during the MAI negotiations in 1998, either because the union representatives at the OECD failed to see the relation to Chapter 11 of NAFTA or because of sheer thoughtlessness on their part. Be that as it may, the net result was the same: it is not thanks to union presence that civil society was provided with a draft of the document, but through other channels, most notably, in North America, through the doings of the particularly *unradical* Western Governor's Association which posted the draft on its website to denounce what they saw as an assault on 'state sovereignty.'
27. *Tripartism* is one of the reasons why unions from Canada and the U.S.—since this does not apply to Mexico—were often at odds with other social organisations that did not, by

definition, have this kind of privileged access to governments and businesses. Consequently, the fact that they were deprived of this access under NAFTA played an important part in allowing them to open themselves up towards civil society organisations. To this we must now add another factor: that for their part within MERCOSUR, unions from the South benefited from *tripartism*, while the unions from the North did not. This is probably why the issue of civil society consultation and participation would play such a prominent role in the document *Alternatives for the Americas* prepared under the aegis of the HSA.

28. For details on the Hemispheric Social Alliance, see http://www.asc-hsa.org/ or http://www.web.ca/comfront/hems2.htm

29. Significantly enough, the final declaration of the first encounter was entitled: *Consenso de La Havana* (the 'Havana Consensus') as a direct attack on the 'Washington Consensus.'

30. The sheer number of such encounters against the FTAA, citywide, nation-wide or even continent-wide in a short span of time defies the imagination. To which one should add all the other social struggles (workers, peasants, women, First Nations) where the FTAA was not the central issue, but was appended to other claims or denunciations. Some of these are listed on numerous websites. See, for instance: www.asc-has.org; www.laneta.apc.org/asc/; www.socialmovements.org/; and www.elhabanero.cubaweb.cu/2001.

31. Followed, it must be added, by the proclamation of a Second International Decade of the World's Indigenous People commencing 1 January 2005.

32. See: http://www.ohchr.org/english/issues/indigenous/decade.htm.

33. In some instances, these activities led to the cancellation of the Columbus Day parade, an important yearly celebration in the U.S. For an overview of activities organised in 1992, see : http://faculty.smu.edu/twalker/protest4.htm.

34. See the WSF web site: www.forumsocialmundial.org.br/ noticias_01.php?cd_language=1&cd_news=1394.

35. See: http://www.marchemondiale.org/qui_nous_sommes/en/. This initiative came out of and was initiated by the *Federation des femmes du Québec* (FFQ) which had staged an important march in Québec, in 1995, 'La Marche du pain et des roses' (*The Bread and Roses March*).

36. For instance: Smith *et al, op cit.*

37. ECLAC is a geographical organisation set up in 1948 under Article 59 of the UN Charter. It answers to the ECOSOC.

38. A caveat is in order here since this 'shift to the Left' should neither imply that the governments involved are of the same ilk, nor that *left* is here synonymous with socialism. After all, Argentina's Kirchner is more a *peronist* than a socialist, and in Chile, the *Coalicion* headed by Michelle Bachelet comprises socialists as well as Christian democrats, while in Uruguay, the ruling *Encuentro Progresista-Frente Amplio-Nueva Mayoria* of Tabaré Vasquez is an even more complex mix.

39. 'Special' because the negotiation process relied on four summits of heads of state and government in all. But mounting difficulties and numerous changes of governments called for the convocation of an additional summit.

The World Social Forum In Africa[1]

Jean Nanga

The arrogance of neoliberalism, although challenged in some Latin American countries, seems to face a cooling of opposition everywhere else, as if the movement for global justice is exhausted. Starting with a sketch of Africa's place in the world system, this essay proceeds to ask: What should we expect from the World Social Forum to be held in Nairobi, Kenya, in January 2007, the second WSF to be held in Africa—the continent where all of globalisation's evils are concentrated? Will this WSF give a second breath to the movement, both in Africa and globally, and create a greater and firmer radicalism?

The Underhand Dealings of Africa's Leaders

Successive conflicts, AIDS, high infant mortality, malnutrition, meagre access to drinkable water and electricity, illiteracy, the immense and hazardous exodus to countries in the capitalist centre—all this presents an Africa victimised by its exteriority to globalisation.

Some experts have not hesitated to speak of Africa's suicidal drive vis-à-vis the opportunities offered to 'develop' itself like Asia. This happens so often that generous western donors have lost interest, weary of seeing what has supposedly succeeded elsewhere fail in Africa. They have chosen to ensure a minimum of aid and leave the African peoples to their leaders' incompetence and corruption.

The underhanded dealings of Africa's governing elites are a fact. The democratisation of the 1990s has not eradicated the oligarchic virus. To the contrary, being neo-liberal in character it has developed an obsession with enrichment, even if illicit. Fortunes are being made or increased, whether in the post-Mobutu or the post-Houphouët-Boigny eras, to cite these major figures of sub-Saharan oligarchism. Heads of State like Dos Santos (Angola), Sassou Nguesso (Congo), Biya (Cameroon), and Bongo (Gabon), although not listed in *Forbes*, have accumulated as much as some multinationals by embezzling funds and other public property, through commissions in attributing strategic markets, and so on.

But they have also invested their gains, as much in their countries as elsewhere, thus becoming veritable capitalists, unusual only in the public source of their primitive accumulation. Even Mobutu (of Zaire, now the Democratic Republic of Congo) did not just hoard money. His fortune existed in numbered bank accounts in so-called 'democratic' countries, but was also invested in real estate and shares in companies outside Zaire. Thus we see the constitution and consolidation of a class of local hucksters developing in Africa.

Recently, Idrissa Seck, former prime minister of the Senegalese president Abdoulaye Wade, stated that he had enriched himself from the coffers of the Senegalese State to invest in real estate, particularly in Paris. In South Africa, the ANC's establishment in power allowed some its leaders and those of its trade union ally, COSATU, to lead or own private companies in the name of 'black empowerment,' a so-called positive discrimination that amounts to putting a little more colour in the South African bourgeoisie.

These governing elites are thus attached to the global neo-liberal economy; hence their indifference to the consequences of globalisation. They tolerate the 'fight against poverty' only when it is compatible with their individual and class interests.

Corruption: A Relationship

Without denying the reality of corruption and its harmful impact on African societies, where adults and children die unable to oil the machine of corruption in public care centres, such criticisms of Africa smack more of moralism informed by racist considerations about the immaturity of Africans than of politics. In fact, the African continent is the victim of a culture of corruption linked to the system imposed on it. If we are to realise the structural nature of corruption in capitalist systems, we must reject the fraudulent image of capitalism and its democracy that is propagated by economists and political scientists supportive of the dominant order and then relayed by media of the same stripe.

Corruption in the political class is enclosed in silence, or benefits from a guarantee of being forgotten. This forgetfulness has consequences on human lives, as in the Elf affair in France, when thousands of deaths in the Congo reminded us that the most harmful corruption for African societies is that which links the continent's governing elites with the centre's economic and political powers.

This link has now been discovered even by the NGO Transparency International, which says, "The big exporters compromise development by dubious practices abroad...In the economically weakest African countries, for example, those questions have designated French and Italian companies as being most frequently at the origin of these practices."[2] No western country, however, receives a 10/10 mark from this NGO. In some countries, foreign corruption is even encouraged and fiscally covered by law, because it is necessary to compete with others. Thus the exceptional character of the inquiry was carried out by Britain's Africa All Parliamentary Group, denouncing British multinationals.[3]

From the viewpoint of the struggle against structural social injustice, the World Bank's crusade against corruption seems diversionary: its sole concern to establish rules of competition between imperial powers. In particular, U.S. expansion into African markets is sometimes blocked by certain historical complicities between African elites and their equivalents in European multinationals. The World Bank is only an instrument for correcting this 'imbalance.'

This crusade against corruption has a variable character; and it is not surprising that French and British ministers in charge of cooperation have criticised the Bank's recourse to sanctions for backsliders in the area of corruption. This rivalry is further exacerbated by China's arrival in the African market. As the French foreign minister Philippe Douste-Blazy recently put it: "[A]s this century begins, Africa has become a strategic stake of the first order."[4]

Africa Again a Strategic Focus

Officially sanctioned economists have figures to prove Africa's virtual exclusion from the world economy: Africa's GDP represents only 1% of the world total; its share in world trade is 2% (against 8% in the 1990s); and its share of foreign direct investment is around 1%. But these figures are used with the erroneous postulate of an equitable exchange between partners.

The recent copper deal in the Democratic Republic of Congo (DRC) is an example:

> The U.S. company Phelps Dodge[5] has shares in the biggest mining project in Katanga. In Tenke Fungurume, the most important reserves of copper of the world, still not exploited, are located...around 18 million tonnes of copper and 1.5 million tonnes of cobalt, which would yield around 100 billion dollars according to the prices of recent years. Tenke Mining is part of the Lundin group based in Geneva.
>
> Whereas Phelps Dodge has a shareholding of 57.75%, Gécamines has only 17.5%. Gécamines has received [only] 15 million dollars in all from Phelps Dodge. How is it that a mine whose reserves are worth 100 billion dollars is sold at such a derisory price?[6]

Just as was the case at the end of the 19th century, since the end of this last century Africa has become a strategic focus for capitalist imperial powers. In its 2006 report, the World Bank notes that "[T]he increase of income per inhabitant in Africa is currently equivalent to that of other developing countries" —which is unhappily only an average, excluding great inequalities of real income and very unequal divisions of wealth—and that "the productivity of the best African companies is comparable to that of their competitors in Asia (India and Vietnam), for example."[7] Foreign direct investment has increased, and neoliberal reforms are well under way. The International Finance Corporation has praised Africa's progress: "Globally, the most popular reform in 2005-2006 has consisted in facilitating the formalities of creation of enterprises. Forty-three countries have simplified them, and have thus reduced the costs and the time periods. The second most popular reform, implemented in thirty-one countries, has been to reduce the amount of taxes and steps necessary for the payment of taxes."[8] In 2005, foreign companies in Africa had a turnover of 200 billion dollars.

Great Britain has also profited from Africa. From July 2005, the date of the celebrated G8 summit at Gleneagles, to July 2006, financial flows from Great Britain to sub-Saharan Africa were 17 billion pounds sterling (1.35 billion as contributions; 6.8 billion direct investment; and 7 billion imported commodities); but financial flows from sub-Saharan Africa to Great Britain were *over 27 billion pounds sterling* (1 billion in repayment of the Nigerian debt; 4 billion in profits by British companies; 4.5 billion in imports of commodities; and 17 billion in capital flight).[9]

This is a picture that justifies the words of the French foreign minister:

> It is a continent whose average growth is henceforth durably superior to world growth and is triple the European growth rate. In 2006, according to the IMF, the growth of sub-Saharan Africa will exceed 5% for the ninth consecutive year. The investors are moreover not ignorant of this, when international and financial flows to the African continent have doubled in the past three years...France does not intend to disengage from a continent which is near to it, and with which it has for such a long time had privileged relations.

The bombardments of villages controlled by Central African and Chadian rebels in December 2006 by the Mirages of the French army only affirm this closeness.

U.S. Expansion

Contrary to widespread opinion, the U.S. has only rarely been absent from Africa, as evidenced in its support to Mobutu in Zaire or to apartheid in South Africa, and its significant investments in Nigeria and Liberia. Now, jealous of its hegemony in the capitalist camp, the U.S. has undertaken to also strengthen it in the world in general.

In Liberia, the permanence of the U.S. economic presence is symbolised by Firestone/Bridgestone, which benefited from a concession of half a million hectares for rubber production for 99 years in 1926, prolonged by 37 years in 2005. Working conditions (of men, women, children) remain practically unchanged since 1926, to such an extent that this enterprise is accused of "torture" and "forced labour" in a complaint filed by the U.S. Labour Rights Fund.[10]

The events of 11 September 2001, preceded by two bombings of U.S. embassies—in Dar es Salaam and Nairobi—also served as pretexts for U.S. expansion in Africa. In 2001, George W. Bush took over the bilateral policy created by Bill Clinton, the *African Growth and Opportunities Act* (AGOA), to compete in the area of the so-called preferential market with the European Union's *Agreement with the African, Caribbean, and Pacific Group of States* (ACP), initiated in the 1970s.

The U.S. absense of a colonial or neo-colonial past allied to an effective propaganda apparatus can make it seem that the AGOA and the *Millennium Challenge Corporation* (MCC) are different from the scams traditionally proposed by imperial powers. Under cover of the 'struggle against poverty,' and within the framework of the MCC, the U.S. finances projects relating to the deepened neoliberal restructuring of African economies, such as the agreements signed with Mali and Benin in October 2006 from which they hope to benefit.

Concerning the first, "the most important element of the agreement is the Alatona irrigation project [234.6 million dollars] which should increase agricultural yields and food production while improving the land regime" and even "strengthen the property rights of the poor." Moreover, "the Alatona project will introduce innovatory techniques in the area of credit and management of water, as well as reforms seeking to realise part of the potential of the Office of the Niger as [the] locomotive of growth in the rural areas of Mali."[11]

It is this agreement that the Malian government, guided by the World Bank, is selling to its poor peasants. But this peasantry realises how these 'reforms' will aggravate its situation, to the profit of local private capital often accumulated in the State apparatus.

Among the 'innovations' to improve cotton yields in West Africa are genetically modified seeds, which have already appeared in countries of the sub-region, co-financed by multinationals. The offensive for their use is led by university elites, Since education budgets were reduced, numerous researchers have entered this breach to escape the breadline. Their talents are sought by multinational firms (Monsanto, DuPont with the U.S. Rockefeller Foundation; Bayer of Germany; Syngenta of Switzerland, and so on) with salaries that are individually profitable but socially damaging.

Kenya is one of the laboratories for the U.S. offensive against the small African peasantry, the goal being to create food dependency even if through famine. The same neoliberal themes inform the February 2006 agreement with Benin to "... increase investment and private activity by improving the land regime, access to financial services and the legal apparatus, as well as by suppressing obstacles to trade in the port of Cotonou."[12] Such bilateral 'cooperation' strengthens the agricultural policy of international financial institutions within which the U.S. is hegemonic.

The "war against terrorism" also helps, and this expansion is accompanied by a military presence in Kenya, on the oil-producing coasts of the Gulf of Guinea, and in the Indian Ocean where, in addition to its base at Diego Garcia, the U.S. coexists with France in Djibouti. U.S. oil interests in Algeria also benefit from an apparatus of protection.

Similarly, the traditional French hegemony in this Sahelian zone is challenged by the *Trans-Saharan Initiative of Struggle Against Terrorism* and the *African Centre of Study and Research on Terrorism* that aligns ten Sahelian states with the U.S. With the establishment of the *Combined Joint Task Force-Horn of Africa* (CJTF-HOA), the USA's national security appears assured in Africa.

The latest manifestation of this hegemonic will is U.S. military involvement in the Somali conflict against the Union of Islamic Courts, accused of belonging to the nebulous Al Qaeda. Ineffective logistical support is accompanied by diplomatic action through Resolution 1725 of the UN Security Council deploying a force in Somalia.

The version of this Resolution adopted on 6 November 2005 excludes the provisions most expressive of U.S. imperial will, but there is no doubt about its wish to control the Somali subsoil. Silence on this motivation is well respected among analysts of the Somali crisis, who thus credit the false justification concerning the U.S. 'war on terror.' According to Eunice Reddick (director of East African affairs at the U.S. State Department),[13]

> [I]n this unstable context, the objectives of U.S. policy in Somalia remain clear: to fight the terrorist menace, [to] support the establishment of an effective governance and of political stability, [and] to respond to the humanitarian needs of the Somalis and promote regional security.

The same is true of the Sudan where the U.S.'s investment in sending an intervention force to Darfur is supposedly motivated by the humanitarian desire to end the "genocide" of the "black" population by "Arab" militias serving Khartoum.[14]

The U.S. would like the world to believe that its interest in Africa has nothing to do with African oil. But from 2005 on, U.S. imports of the latter have overtaken imports from the Near East, and the proven reserves of this region have been revised upwards. African-Americans in the U.S. establishment contribute to this patriotic mystification, and racial identity thus serves the Corporate Council on Africa, which is composed of imperialistic crusaders like Boeing, Cargill, Citigroup, Coca-Cola, Exxon, General Motors, Halliburton, Microsoft, and Mobil, who benefit the most from today's neoliberal version of gunboat diplomacy.

European Imperialism

Europe has long been more visible in Africa than the U.S. simply because of France and Britain's colonial pasts. Their national policies reproduce colonial domination and are accompanied by a 'European' partnership with the African, Caribbean, and Pacific states in the context of the EEC—the ACP agreements of Yaoundé (Cameroon), Lomé (Togo), and currently the EU-ACP Cotonou agreement—establishing a preferential market.[15] However, rather than establishing infrastructure for economic autonomy, this cooperation has restricted Africa to producing raw materials for Europe.

To conform to the rules of the World Trade Organisation (WTO), the EU has now proposed Economic Partnership Agreements (EPAs) for free trade. Their consequences will be catastrophic for the small peasantry, small local units of production and local finances, by positioning subsidised products imported from the EU against local products, and encouraging the suppression of customs duties. Indeed, "... despite its importance, agriculture has for some decades undergone a crisis whose main cause is the unjust measures of the Agriculture Agreement inside of the WTO. Taking account of the weakness of agricultural incomes, very few rural households manage to cover their food needs seven months out of twelve, and many do not even reach four months."[16] The consequences of these agreements will affect even non-members of the ACP group, both through the sub-regional integration of African economies, and via the project for continental integration represented by the *New Partnership for Africa's Development* (NEPAD).

African governing elites are, for now, dragging their feet over these EPAs, not only because they could cause social revolts but above all because they know their own interests as economic entrepreneurs, invested particularly in agriculture, could suffer.

Meanwhile the EU, without claiming to oppose the hegemonic project od the U.S. in Africa, is deepening its autonomous presence and defending the image of European power—including on military terrain—by ignoring NATO. The 2006 general elections in the DRC gave Europe the chance for a truly multinational military deployment: twenty of the twenty-five EU states provided the mission's 1,500 soldiers. The European Force (Eufor) is led by France and Germany—a French general commands in the DRC but the headquarters of the Force are in Potsdam, Germany. Each supplied one-third of the troops, the last one-third being shared among the eighteen other states.

This expedition was the first time the German army returned to Africa since the colonial period, which provoked widespread debate in Germany. German participation in Eufor was decided only after a parliamentary debate; and Prime Minister Angela Merkel represented the mission as motivated exclusively by support for democratic processes and concern to avoid the resumption of a war that would bring more migrants to Europe.[17]

This was reiterated by the German foreign minister, Frank-Walter Steinemeier: "[F]rom the viewpoint of security and strategy, we act because we know that failing states end up becoming exporters of troubles, terrorism and serious refugee problems. Our objective consists in preventing these dangers."[18]

But this opinion was not shared by the German foreign minister's colleague in defence, Franz Joseph Jung, who said frankly enough that "... stability in this region rich in minerals is a benefit for German industry"; nor by Eckart Von Klaeden, senior member of the German Parliament, who said: "There is significant subterranean wealth there for security, like uranium and beryllium. They can fall into the wrong hands." [19]

Thus, Europe and the U.S. articulate the relationship between the military and the economy as what Leopold II called "the sharing of the cake" and what contemporary specialists in 'post-conflict' situations call "economic return on military investment." It was for a bigger share of the cake that Europe forced the UN's hand to obtain the Congo mission, without first consulting the Congolese state or the African Union.

This also caused great chagrin in South Africa, where the post-apartheid state has not broken with the imperial ambition on the continent dreamt of by Cecil Rhodes. As for the U.S., given its involvement in the war in Congo from 1998-2003—through Rwanda, Uganda, and a part of the Congolese opposition transformed for the episode into an armed opposition—it was poorly placed to obtain such a mission. Nonetheless, being absent from the ground has not disqualified it from sharing the cake. The head of the Congolese state, Joseph Kabila, has not ceased to play his cards to maintain equilibrium between different imperialist appetites.[20] This has succeeded, at least with regard to the outcome of the last presidential elections.

Since the publicity received by the DRC's oil reserves, the U.S. has already displayed its interest by sending a signal to the regime in Kinshasa. By a presidential decree of 30 October 2006, Bush froze the shares of the heads of the last pocket of armed rebels and their accomplices, like the arms and precious stones trafficker Viktor Bout, long a U.S. protégé whose misdeeds were shown on screen in *Lord of War*. It also shows awareness of the increasing complexity of inter-imperialist competition in Africa with the arrival of China, which does not seem ready, unlike Europe, for a position subordinate to the U.S.

Chinese Imperialism?

A spectre haunts western imperialism in Africa. Unhappily, it is not the African movement for global justice, but China, this hybrid country led by a nominally Communist party deaf to calls for respecting of human rights, but with an impressive rate of capitalist economic growth, its GDP ranked fifth in the world. This involves a significant consumption of raw materials, and thus China has turned towards Africa—clearly an obligatory passage for those having imperial ambitions. Although Chinese traders are accused by small local traders of unfair competition and the Chinese practice of using its own workforce in its worksites is widely denounced, China has nevertheless succeeded in creating sympathy for its goods—simply because they are accessible to the poor as purchasing power from the Cape to Cairo gets drastically lowered.

Few African states are indifferent to the economic boom of a country that is still supposedly of the South but which seems willing to share its fruits with

African countries (though only to those that it needs to realise its ambitions as a world power). China needs wood, cobalt, cotton, copper, steel, manganese, oil, platinum, and uranium. All this is imported from Africa. This obviously affects those imperial powers that have controlled these resources for over a century. The Chinese appetite has, for example, already produced rising oil prices, which certainly doesn't displease western oil multinationals. Nonetheless, this Chinese bulimia could disturb the imperial order.

What does seem to annoy the western imperial order is the alternative Chinese model for exchange within the capitalist framework, which the Chinese call *common* or *shared development*. In aid, preferential loans, debt cancellation, market opening, support for agriculture, education, or health, China has already shown its resolve to do more than the west. Agreements with China have shown African rulers that in exchange for raw materials and at relatively lower costs, China is willing to give Africa infrastructure and to purchase African goods at prices that Africans consider equitable.

The success of the Africa-China Summit of November 3–5 2006 in Beijing is not unrelated to the low participation by African heads of state in the 'European Days on Development' in Brussels, just two weeks after Beijing—seventeen, as against forty-eight in Beijing. Something concrete emerged from the first, for example the Ivory Coast received 3 billion francs CFA; whereas the Afro-European summit ended as usual with promises that remain unfulfilled or are subject to conditions that trample the states' internal sovereignty.

At the European "Days," Ugandan president Yuweri Museveni told his European counterparts. "Do not force people to do what you want them to do." China has only one demand, the non-recognition of Taiwan by its African partners. Further, it also applies the principle of non-interference: "We respect the free choice of each of its own road of development; we attach a high importance to the concerns of each."[21] This allows states like Angola some relief from the grip of international financial institutions; and also makes it an ideal partner for African autocrats-oligarchs, who are often appalled by how the west uses 'respect for human rights' to strengthen its own domination and exploitation.

Yet let us be clear. The cynicism and indifference of Chinese pragmatism can only harm the real democratic movements in Africa, which do not adhere to the reproduction of the capitalist and neo-colonial order. Worse, Afro-Chinese cooperation could resemble Franco-African cooperation, not only supplying arms to autocratic regimes but also participating in army training. The French press has already questioned Chinese support to Chad rebels during their advance towards N'Djamena. China, it should be recalled, is part of the club of the major arms merchants, all permanent members of the UN Security Council.

This principle of non-interference is often accompanied with support to regimes confronted with the antipathy of western powers. For example, at the UN Security Council, resolutions proposed by the French state against Laurent Gbagbo in the Ivory Coast, or the U.S. against Omar El Béchir in Sudan invite the Chinese veto if they are not revised to a more moderate version.

China's interests in the Ivory Coast, where oil enterprises do not hide their ambitions, explain its support for Gbagbo. Moreover, to get around the embargo, the Gbagbo regime can purchase Chinese weapons, to the great chagrin of French companies who had exclusivity in these sectors.

Notwithstanding, French capital in the Ivory Coast remains dominant and the operating account of the Ivorian state at the French Treasury remains the most significant of the West African sub-zone of the franc CFA. But we should not exclude the possibility that in case of electoral victory, Laurent Gbagbo might rely on Chinese, not French, cooperation as the basis for his neoliberal nationalism. This resembles the oligarchic regime of El Béchir in Sudan, where Chinese support based on oil operations is creating growth and attracting investors, thus allowing him to stand up to the U.S.

Chinese global ambition is accompanied by an official conception of cooperation that follows "...the correct principles of sincere friendship, of equal-to-equal treatment, of mutual support, and of common development."[22] But despite this posture, it remains motivated by capitalist interest, which inevitably limits its 'generosity' and maintains inequality.

This is clearly shown by the internal situation of China at present, which cannot escape 'the historic law of combined and uneven development.' As Chinese capital reaches the summits of the world economy and produces a capitalist and middle class, there is pauperisation of the peasants, withdrawal of free access to public services, the abandonment of certain regions, repression of social demands, and so on.[23]

Moreover, Chinese adhesion to the religion of growth also risks exhausting natural resources in Africa and constituting a serious ecological threat. The Chinese state, with the U.S. and some others, bears chief responsibility for the threat facing the planet, and is the least disposed to commit itself to fighting it.

Its friendship for Africa cannot be effective without an awareness of the severe floods experienced in 2006 by Kenya, ironically the host of a conference on climate change—from which no real programme of struggle emerged.

An Africa that Struggles

Imperialism is not dead. It has merely become neoliberal. Africa is a primary location of the natural resources necessary to capitalist growth, at the price of human lives and the production and reproduction of poverty, as capital develops business from poverty and misery. This poverty has made Nairobi, for instance, an area where severe gang violence has developed, recruiting its cadres from the milieus of uneducated youth—youth without decent jobs or the hope of finding any. This is a phenomenon familiar to the South African or Brazilian economies, and indeed also to the U.S., though with an evident racial aspect.

Even charity is used—such as by Bill Gates, who plays the role of messiah but is also the biggest beneficiary of the neoliberal order. He chooses Africa for his generosity rather than the zones of poverty in which millions of his U.S. compatriots live. He does this not only in relation to AIDS but also in supporting the Rockefeller Foundation's campaign to impose genetically modified seeds on African agriculture. The continent seems condemned to this 'assistance' by international capital, and the responsibility lies in the corruption of African rulers.

Yet, there is also an Africa that struggles against neoliberalised neo-colonialism. Activists in the struggle against privatisation and for social justice in South Africa, participants in Niger's Social Forum, peasants of the Office of the Niger, employees of Gacilienne in Burkina Faso, radical activists of Swaziland, Woman of Zimbabwe Arise (WOZA), trades unionists of the Union of Kenya Civil Servants (UKCS), the Aviation and Allied Workers Union (AAWU)...the flame to defend social, cultural, and political rights, and emancipate workers and victims of capitalist exploitation, is not extinguished.

From the first World Social Forum (WSF) in 2001 to the Polycentric World Social Forum in Bamako, Mali, in 2006, this flame has become increasingly visible. At the Polycentric Forum, the peasants of Mali—victims of the Bretton Woods institutions, multinational seed companies, European anti-immigration policies, and the Malian government—united. The tension of African public debt and the social consequences of its repayment have ceased to concern only a handful of individuals.

Peasants have set up regional networks to resist neoliberal attacks against small agriculture. Women's networks show great dynamism at each meeting. Youth organisations, conscious of the murky future that neoliberal capitalism promises, try to recreate the revolutionary Pan-Africanism symbolised by Amilcar Cabral and Thomas Sankara. Trade unions are also active, but much less than is necessary to change the relationship between Capital and Labour. Victims of the policies of the capitalist centre and its periphery against the free circulation of persons are trying to coordinate. Ecological organisations are emerging in reaction to the plunder of forests, pollution of coastlines, and depredations in mining areas.

These struggles still suffer from a lack of continental networks between different organisations, although they often confront the same multinationals, such as Bi-Water, Suez, or Vivendi for water, Chevron-Texaco, Shell, Total for oil, Anglo-Gold for gold, as well as Chinese enterprises like Zhonging Telecommunications Ltd (ZTE), which are competing with western telecommunications to monopolise state telecommunications.

Greater participation by trade unions and national trade union federations in the Social Forums could help coordination. Above all, this requires a clear distancing between the campaign to promote so-called 'responsible trade unionism,' and the 'social partnership' between employers and governments.[24] In the case of the Congress of South African Trade Union (COSATU), this led to internal frictions between certain federations and the leadership, accused of privileging its tripartite alliance with the ANC and the South African Communist party. Moreover, it is under the influence of this education in 'responsibility'—which accentuates bureaucratic and egoist interests—that the Movement for Democratic Change (MDC, originating mainly from the Zimbabwean trade union movement) seems to be moving to the right, even while opposing attacks by the autocratic regime of Robert Mugabe and the Zimbabwe African National Union (ZANU) on workers and others. This tendency should also worry the Labour Party of Nigeria, modelled on the MDC by, among others, Adam Oshiomole, president of the powerful Nigeria Labour Congress union federation.[25]

The Contradictions of the WSF Sharpen In Nairobi

This emerging African movement for social justice also suffers from the financial heteronomy of numerous associations and social movements. Many such movements depend on western partners, including multinationals. This affects the definition of their projects, both locally and internationally. For example, in a great part of the movement the reductionist opposition between civil society, considered positive, and political society, considered essentially negative, still prevails.

This is an idea promoted by International Financial Institutions, and it explains the hostility within the WSF to the participation of political organisations. In practice however, this also translates into an opposition to radically anti-neoliberal political organisations. Given this, the WSF in Nairobi could well be the theatre for an offensive by NGOs who support the addition of a social dimension to globalisation and by a charity-based movement for global justice, through the participation of local associations that they support financially.

With increasing poverty, religion has again become "the opium of the people." The Islamophobic campaign orchestrated by U.S. neoconservatives and relayed so widely in Europe tends to cover the reactionary offensive waged by Christian churches around the world. Kenya is one of the African societies where, alongside traditional Christianities and traditional, indeed fundamentalist, Islam, Christian fundamentalisms proliferate, and surf on the poverty generated by the system they co-manage.

In this context, the apparent anti-capitalism of Caritas, a charity organisation that is statutorily established in the Vatican itself, is unsurprising[26]:

> Caritas Europa considers the World Social Forum (WSF) as being a permanent world process, which groups together in an open meeting place the social movements, networks, NGOs and other bodies of civil society opposed to neoliberalism and to a world dominated by capital or by any form of imperialism.[27]

Has Caritas passed bag and baggage into the camp of Christian liberation theology? Does this signal a radical progressive change in the Pontifical Justice and Peace Council at the very time when the Vatican is led by the former head of the Sacred Congregation of the Faith (an inquisitorial body, charged with the clerical repression of liberation theologians), Cardinal Ratzinger, alias Benedict XVI? And where one of its most influential members is Michel Camdessus, former director general of the IMF, former adviser of Nicolas Sarkozy at the French ministry of economy and finance, and allegedly a member of Opus Dei?

Such participation by reactionary Christianity threatens feminist and LGTB movements. In Africa, homophobic and anti-feminist prejudices remain fairly developed within the movement for global justice. Onyango Oloo, of the Kenya Social Forum, drew attention to the persistent male supremacy in the WSF during the preparation in Nairobi: "Of the seven commissions of the WSF Organising Committee, one alone is chaired by a woman despite the fact that women constitute nearly half the members of these commissions."[28]

This, in a context where the movement for global justice and the WSF should be one of the main spaces of real education against phallocracy and for gender equality.

The movement is also not immune to penetration by neoliberal values. This is exemplified by the operation led against Babel (a free translators' network) to the profit of commercial translators. Democratic access to the debates will thus be subordinated to the financial resources of workshop organisers, and exclude languages other than those used in the leading bodies of the "international community." This might mean that Swahili might be little used at the WSF 2007, despite being Kenya's language.

On the other hand, the 2007 WSF has the potential develop a permanent Pan-African solidarity in the fight against neoliberalism. From Cape Town to Tunis, the rich diversity of peoples could organise a coordinated struggle against the Pan-African declaration of neoliberalism represented by NEPAD, and support an alternative pan-Africanism that is emancipatory, egalitarian, socially just, and ecological. And, so far as humanity as a whole is concerned, the consolidation of the global justice movement would favour the development of a new internationalism whose effectiveness will depend on the capacity to democratically draw the lessons of internationalisms past and present.[29]

But this goal can only be attained through dialogue or debate between anti-neoliberal social movements and anti-capitalist political organisations. This implies rebuilding politics, no longer sacrificing the interest of the majorities or of the exploited and oppressed minorities on the altar of electoral interests, and not diluting the strategic in the tactical; in other words, a transformation of all radical social and political organisations.

Notes

1. This is an abridged and edited version of an essay titled 'The Nairobi Social Forum' that was published in *International Viewpoint—News and analysis from the Fourth International, IV Online magazine*, IV385, January 2007, http://www.internationalviewpoint.org/spip.php?article1191 (accessed js 13/02/07). Content Editor is Parvati Sharma. The editors thank the author for his permission. We have also tried our best to get in touch with the publisher of the original essay to get permission from them for republishing it, but despite repeated attempts have not got a reply from the journal.
2. Transparency International 2006.
3. Africa All Party Parliamentary Group, March 2006.

4. Session of 5 October 2006.
5. One of the world's biggest copper producers.
6. Pelda, August 2006.
7. Press release number 2007/115/AFR.
8. Press release, 'Doing Business 2007,' Washington DC, 6 September 2006.
9. Christian Aid, July 2006.
10. Pailey, February 2002.
11. Corey, nd.
12. U.S. Representative for Foreign Trade, October 2006.
13. Greenberg, October 2006.
14. Nanga, October 2004.
15. European Commission, nd. In the wake of decolonisation, ACP and EEC countries signed the Yaounde I (1963–1969) and Yaounde II (1969–1975) agreements. Following the accession of the United Kingdom to the EEC in 1973, this led to the incorporation of Commonwealth colonies to the ACP group, and in 1975, the Yaounde agreements were replaced by the Lome Convention, involving forty-six ACP countries and nine EEC member states.
16. Ndao, November 2006.
17. See the articles by Custers, April 2006 and May 2006.
18. Steinmeier, July 2006.
19. See Greenberg, *op cit*.
20. Joseph Kabila's father, Laurent-Désiré Kabila, came to power in 1997, after a war against Mobutu's army, with the support of the U.S., via the Rwanda of Paul Kagame and the Uganda of Yuweri Museveni. He was assassinated in 2001, when confronted with a war against his former allies who had produced internal armed oppositions.
21. Hu Jin Tao, November 2006.
22. Idem.
23. Alternatives Sud, April 2005; and McGregor, November 2006.
24. Mouhamadou Tidiane Kasse seems to credit the idea of "the construction of a partnership with the governments and the multinationals" as one of the stages of the dynamisation of the African trade union movement. See Tidiane Kasse, nd, c.2007.
25. Obono, March 2006.
26. Article 5 of the Additional Protocol to the Statutes of Caritas Internationalis, 16 May 2002.
27. Caritas Europa at the World Social Forum 2007.
28. Oloo 2007.
29. See Löwy, March 2003.

The World Social Forum: Current Challenges And Future Perspectives[1]

Irene León and Sally Burch

Due to its plural character and diverse participation, the World Social Forum continues to be the most significant space for the construction of anti-neoliberal thought, ideas, and alternatives. The 1,200 activities that made up the agenda for the seventh forum that took place in Nairobi, Kenya from January 20–25 2007, pay tribute to its vitality. This vitality has grown out of the innovative original proposal for the World Social Forum and whose backbone are the social processes present at each meeting of the Forum and in its process: the movements, networks, campaigns, and intellectuals that have provided the basic material for its substance and dynamics. On this particular occasion, they took the vantage point of Africa, a continent rich in social and political initiatives but which also suffers the most from the incongruence of the neoliberal model.

The incredible mosaic of experiences and cultures of which Africa is composed was reflected in the diversity of participants and wide variety of issues raised, from long-standing struggles, such as the fight for independence of the people of the Western Sahara to more contemporary issues such as HIV-AIDS and the right to water.

Without a doubt, this recent Forum provided the possibility of considering global struggles from the political perspective of a continent in resistance, bringing with it significant experiences gained from recent triumphs: independence from colonialism achieved over the last fifty years, the abolition of apartheid in 1990 in South Africa, as well as steps towards socialism in Angola and Mozambique, and more. New social movements on the continent have also set interesting and important precedents, such as the historic victory for free import and access to generic drugs for HIV-AIDS, achieved in 2001 by the Treatment Action Campaign (TAC) in South Africa against a group of transnational corporations that were leveraging WTO accords to gain exclusive control over drug patents.

The Forum in Nairobi also enabled a greater number of networks and organisations to establish new or stronger relationships, to define new areas of common interest, and to develop innovative solidarity initiatives, such as that of the Global Campaign for Agrarian Reform in Africa, a project of Vía Campesina and others. In addition, the Forum motivated participants to broaden their scope of intercontinental relationships. This was demonstrated, for instance, by the priority established by the Americas Social Forum to orient its activities toward giving visibility to Africa's presence in the Western hemisphere and highlighting their shared history and experiences, present and future. This significant policy decision was reflected in various joint activities organised in collaboration with the African Forum.

However, like every work in progress, this recent Forum also brought to the forefront several critical issues, some of which have existed from before and while others were new. In this regard, the commercialisation of the Forum and the contracting out of services must be mentioned, as well as the undeniable NGO-isation, the Forum's distancing from popular participation, the invasive police presence, the high profile presence of various Christian churches and other related matters, all of which were thoroughly reported by the media. The avalanche of critiques, whose most relentless proponents arose from African delegations, need to be gathered and seriously considered with regard to the Forum's future. Unfortunately, they reaffirmed the impression of an event marked by poor organisation and a distancing from the original intentions that have animated this process for the last seven years.

In this context, it is vital that we think about the future and open up debate and encourage discussion. That is, we need to compile and establish a dialogue between the different evaluations and ideas so that this initiative—that is widely considered to be the greatest social proposal of our time—can renew its meaning and vitality.

In order to accomplish this, it is essential to confront the economic and power relationships internal to the Forum since these are fundamental to any decision concerning its character, approach, participation, format and architecture. Furthermore, these are determining factors for making a choice between its two competing tendencies: that of the 'World Social Fair,' supported by some organisations, and that of the Forum as a collective process to uphold and strengthen changes, proposed and defended by a wide range of movements and organisations.

The African intellectual Samir Amín points out that between these two approaches there is another, that of

> ... an *altermondialisme* (another-world-ism) whose adherents are primarily drawn from the middle-class within rich countries and who

> are critical of the way of life proposed by capitalism, but who have little interest in the real concerns of the popular classes within their own countries, and less still of those in the South, where this 'moderate' *altermondialisme* is often misunderstood. Paradoxically however, as a result of their greater access to financial support, these groups often seem to be over-represented in the World and Regional Social Forums and are at times perceived to be holding back the strengthening of popular struggles.

Examples of this trend can however, of course also be identified in the South.

The most fundamental challenge before us is to determine a way forward for the Forum without abandoning its openness to diverse manifestations and broad participation. This means that we need to establish some guidelines that take into consideration what it hopes to achieve.

Forum as Fair, Forum as Process

Broadly speaking, there are two conceptualisations of the Forum: one, the 'Forum as Fair' and two, the 'Forum as Process.'

In the *Forum as Fair*, each person is supposedly meant to be able to freely find or do what they want and, just as in the market system, everyone achieves their own ends based upon their own possibilities, though in this case, apparently in a more humane atmosphere. Those with greater resources however become more visible within the 'mainstream' part of the Forum, as happened in Nairobi. The 'main avenue' was primarily occupied by Christian churches —though not the vast ecumenical diversity existing within Africa and globally—as well as by development organisations, international institutions, and some NGOs. Many of the events that got reasonable participation seemed to gain their attendance from among the faithful who were sponsored to be there—or the equivalent, those who were beneficiaries of projects. In addition, the criterion established in Nairobi that self-organised events should pay a fee based on the size of each event, without consideration of ability to pay, nor of social representation or ability to draw participation, generated a disconcerting skew in the programme. Within this, there were ultimately only a few organisations that were able to organise dozens of events, and others were forced to limit their activities.

In the *Forum as Process*, on the other hand, there are one or more critiques of the state of the world and an inventory of existing standpoints present in the proposals of the live movements that come together in this space. Up until now, one of the most important contributions of the Forum has been its potential to expand the arena for exchange and convergence among various social struggles and to allow for the visioning of a common agenda. Perhaps the key example is that which has come together in the Assembly of Social Movements. This initiative is fostering collaboration between many different issues, producing a declaration and calendar of joint actions, and interconnecting proposals and efforts to build movements and networks in their ongoing struggles against the various impacts of the neoliberal model and its institutions.

One of the greatest achievements of the World Social Forum to date has been the global day of action against the invasion and war against Iraq, on 15 February 2003. (The decision to organise this action originated at the European Social Forum in Florence in November 2002 and was finalised at the forum in Porto Alegre, Brazil, in January 2003.) This could only have happened through the open space that the WSF provides, for people to meet and to converge. To sacrifice this possibility of methodological experiment could put the future of the Forum at risk, since occurrences such as those in Kenya where the Assembly had to forge its own space on the go, and where open participation became an issue of internal protest, could lead to the demotivation of participants whose contributions are essential in the common struggle against neoliberalism.

Outstanding Themes during the Forum In Nairobi

Given the scope of the agenda at the Nairobi Forum, it is not feasible to take a look at the full scope of issues that were raised in Nairobi. Instead, we will indicate a few that stood out for their novelty or breadth.

The principal thematic achievement of the Forum in Nairobi was, without a doubt, its *thorough exploration of the issue of HIV-AIDS*. It highlighted the various socio-economic problems that are related to tackling this affliction, from which about 39.5 million people in the world are suffering and of which two thirds are in Sub-Saharan Africa. It is for this reason that the most important initiatives, proposals, and actions related to this pandemic are emerging from this continent—a part of the world that has made abundant contributions to making correlations between the expansion of this disease and poverty, and to analysing the impact of neoliberal policies in this regard.

Given the magnitude of the problem and considering its macroeconomic and human aspects, socially conservative campaigns that only promote sexual abstinence are clearly not relevant. For the first time though, this trend of thought was visible during the Nairobi Forum, including belligerent demonstrations against programmes that more explicitly address the issue. These demonstrations reduced a complex and multi-factoral issue down to a question of morality, far removed from a vision of rights and liberties such as is upheld by various social movements.

The issue of *External Debt* also drew broad attention and participation, including an innovative proposal to associate debt with a demand for reparations for damages inflicted upon the peoples of the South, given that, as expressed by Camille Chalmers from Jubilee South: "The basic idea is to recognise that the present debt is the result of a historical process of looting and of ecological destruction, both physical and social, such that the North owes an enormous debt towards the South." For this reason, future campaigns are being developed around three key words: *repudiation, restitution,* and *reparations*.

More than forty global and continental organisations and networks from Africa, Latin America, and Asia participated in an assembly to develop their positions and strengthen coordination among movements around these issues, renewing their rejection of the new formulas proposed by the International Financial Institutions that continue to advocate structural adjustment policies. There was agreement to encourage governments of the South to enter into processes of *repudiation* and to back them in this effort. In this regard, they welcomed the decision by the government of Norway to cancel part of the illegitimate 'debt' of certain Latin American countries, recognising that the joint campaign by social movements in Norway with those of affected countries has been an effective model.

They also set out to reinforce initiatives to raise awareness about the illegitimacy of the debt and to further pursue studies on the *reparations* process. Finally, they emphasised the importance of collaboration with other organisations and movements on related issues such as free trade, militarisation, and military bases, as a way to develop more effective strategies to confront all projects for domination.

The focus given by Vía Campesina and other organisations concerning the issue of *Agrarian Reform and Food Sovereignty* also had significant outcomes during the Forum. A *Global Campaign for Agrarian Reform in Africa* was launched as a significant contribution of the farmers' movement towards the resolution of one of the greatest problems on the continent and for humanity, that of hunger. Indeed, with continued concentration of land ownership and control over natural resources such as water, poverty continues to grow, particularly in the countryside where unprecedented levels are being registered: 75% of poor people worldwide live in rural areas.

Policies relating to land and rural development, such as those of the World Bank, which push for land liberalisation, expansion of commercial agriculture, and the advance of genetically modified crops, among others, were outlined as the greatest threats facing peasant livelihoods and their need of sustainability. This was reflected in the words of Adamantine Nhampossa from Mozambique, Coordinator of Vía Campesina in Africa: "Five hundred years ago, colonialism took our land. Since the 80s, the World Bank is taking our land. Currently, the only thing that we have left is to become mobilised and to organise campaigns such as this, encouraging people to struggle for their rights."

Many participants saw the proposal for *Food Sovereignty*, which concerns the right of peoples to decide on their own agricultural and nutritional policies, as being highly relevant—not only because of the high levels of hunger and malnutrition across the African continent but also because of their agricultural customs and knowledge of sustenance and sustainability. These customs and this knowledge are today being undermined by the imposition of policies and market practices, and are further threatened by the advance of free trade agreements such as the Economic Partnership Agreements (EPAs).

For this reasons and others such as this, the issue of *Free Trade* was another important subject of debate; an area in which various agreements were advanced, particularly with regard to strengthening ties between Africa and other continents. In this area, the consolidation of the international movement against the EPAs stood out (agreements of economic cooperation and partnership that are being negotiated between the European Union and various countries in Africa, the Caribbean, and the Pacific).[2]

The most immediate actions agreed upon include an international mobilisation on 19 April 2007, whose epicentre will be in Europe and Africa but which will also take place in Caribbean countries. Meanwhile, the Hemispheric Social Alliance will encourage actions of solidarity throughout the rest of Latin America. In Africa, EPAs are equivalent to the *Free Trade Area of the Americas* (FTAA) for Latin America.[3] Ever since the process of negotiations began about two years ago, significant growth has taken place in mobilisations against these agreements across the continent, primarily led by the African Trade Network bringing together unions, farmers' organisations, and NGOs from about forty African countries.

The theme of *Diversity* was expressed and explored in a variety of ways. *Sexual diversity*, in particular, and the demands for the rights of people discriminated against as a result of their sexual orientation, received wide attention. This happened despite a supposedly adverse context where repeated arguments concerning cultural incompatibility with this form of diversity even included attempts to exclude it from the agenda of the Forum. On this subject, the Assembly of Social Movements echoed proposals from the 4th Social Forum (that took place in Mumbai, India, in January 2004) in its final resolutions, reaffirming its commitment to struggles to eradicate such discrimination wherever it might arise. The resolution in question also endorsed the campaign "In a diverse world, equality is first" that was put forward by the LGBT South-South Dialogue together with other networks, as a mechanism to foster a culture of respect for diversity, a central element toward the construction of alternatives.

Women's concerns and their proposals for humanity were expressed in new ways on the African continent. Among the new issues raised by this movement, food sovereignty was put forward by the Women's Network of the Vía Campesina and the World March of Women (WMW), who presented the particular challenges for the affirmation of rights concerning agriculture and food production. The WMW also contributed debates around the commercialisation of the bodies and the lives of women, as expressed in different realms associated with the reproduction of life, and various discussions concerning globalisation, such as migration. In collaboration with the LGTB South-South Dialogue and other networks, they also considered questions of diversity as a substantial part of struggles against patriarchy and for universal equality.

Communication, which is constantly invoked as an indispensable resource for reinforcement of the Forum's goals, was also the object of several resolutions. In a meeting to pool conclusions called by the International Campaign for Communication Rights (CRIS), and with the participation of international and regional networks as well as African organisations, several proposals for action were exchanged. The meeting reached consensus on the necessity to mobilise a wide range of support around the *democratisation of communication*. These included proposals to raise awareness concerning the fact that communication rights are fundamental: as part of democratic process, for the organisation and struggles of social movements, and for the exercise of all human rights. It was also emphasised that information, communication, and knowledge, and in particular the radio spectrum and the internet, must be recognised as public goods and services rather than as commodities, and that they must therefore remain outside of free trade agreements; and moreover, that in the areas of information and communication public policies need to be only further extended.

There was a varied and plural presence in Nairobi from the Americas. The *Americas Social Forum Tent*, organised by the Hemispheric Council, became an important meeting space for participants from the continent while also providing a venue for meetings and exchanges with other realities such as that of Palestine and the Sahara, as well as for others who arranged their gatherings there. Among the range of activities that took place, two in particular stand out. Both were organised by the women's movement.

The first was the Preparatory Meeting for the World Forum on Food Sovereignty, named 'Nyeleni 2007,' that was to be organised in Mali in February 2007 by Vía Campesina and the World March of Women. This meeting gathered important contributions concerning the role of women as creators of knowledge with regard to the substance and provision of human nutrition.

The second was the launch of the book *Fidel y las Mujeres* ('Fidel and Women') during an event organised by the Cuban Women's Federation. In addition to emphasising the important role of women in the Cuban revolution, this event became a global space of expression for the warm appreciation of Cuba's contributions to people's struggles. Participants from five continents spontaneously took part emphasising the importance of Cuban solidarity in education, health, science, and culture, with special emphasis from Africa, a continent to which that country has offered its solidarity for so many causes.

Other Activities

Among the wide range of other issues that were presented during the Forum in Nairobi, we might briefly mention the *Anti-War Assembly*, which called for global days of action from the March 17-20 2007; the launching of the new *African Water Network*, with the participation of people from more than forty countries, which will struggle against the privatisation of water in cooperation with allied networks such as the *Red Vida* (Network for Life) in the Americas. The *Assembly on Work and Globalisation* also made an important proposal for the creation of a permanent international network among unions, social movements, and research centres, focusing on work, culture, and labour rights, so as to confront the attacks by neoliberal globalisation.

An *Alternative Social Forum* was also organised during the Nairobi Forum, on January 21–23 2007. It took place in one of the city's central parks, Jeevanjee Gardens, and was a response to the obstacles that Nairobi's poor faced in terms of participating in the main forum. The People's Parliament is an established institution in Nairobi that gathers in the park each afternoon throughout the year, in order to debate diverse subjects from local, national, and international levels. In this Forum, issues such as housing, unemployment, social security, land, water, health, and the provision of public services, were raised and discussed. Ideological debates also took place, such as with regard to capitalism and socialism. Some four thousand people took part in all, over the three days, including some participants of the World Social Forum who visited the park.

The Alternative Forum went forward and presented its resolutions to the Assembly of Social Movements that took place within the Forum. Among them were the public provision of housing by the State as a basic human right; the fair distribution of natural resources, giving priority to local communities; the elimination of disparities in wages and guaranteeing everyone with a fair minimum wage; and the reversal of historical injustices such as the expropriation of peasant farmers' land in Kenya and treaties that limit the use within Kenya of water from Lake Victoria.

Current Challenges

We turn now to reflecting on the Forum—on its character, and on participation, 'architecture,' and methodology. We want to do this by reflecting not only on the Nairobi Forum but also more generally, and by looking ahead to an important upcoming year.

With regard to its character, it is crucial to recognise that the options facing the Forum today relate back to its original Charter of Principles. The Forum-as-event, envisioned originally as the confluence of a broad-based proposal as well as being open to plural strands of thought and debate, needs now to give priority to new practices being developed by participants in their day-to-day work. This includes, among others, the alternative solidarity economy, ecological practice, gender diversity, and equality. One of the strongest critiques of the forum in Kenya was the scarce presence of participants from the alternative solidarity economy and to the contrary, the front-line presence of private and corporate actors.

In the same sense, the 'architecture' of the Forum must respond, and be far more sensitive, to the local reality and context in which it takes place. The idea of designing, in the here and now, an 'alternative city' that allows those in attendance to experience a different model during this timeframe, must be balanced with the importance of creating a participatory framework. The Forum needs to be in a location accessible to the local population—whether in an urban or rural context—and should take maximum advantage of existing public infrastructure. This is all the more so if creating special 'architecture' for the purpose of the Forum incurs higher costs, obliging the organisers to appeal to private companies, and which are ever more present in the Forums. One example is Petrobras, which was the sponsor of the 2005 Forum in Brazil but which was also very visible during the forum in Nairobi, as sponsor of the Brazilian delegation as well as the Brazilian Pavilion. Another example was the multinational cell phone company, Celtel, which was given the responsibility for registration during the Nairobi Forum.

The notion of holding gigantic events, which has gained hold gradually over time, motivates organisers to want to make each Forum larger. This leads to the inevitable drawbacks in terms of space and economic investment, which in the case of 2005 Forum in Brazil actually led to a substantial deficit. The Forum in Nairobi also fell victim to this rationale. Participation was calculated at more than 100,000 people, while all indications suggested that attendance would be less. The official tally of 66,000 registrants also seems greater than the actual number present. These miscalculations led to the selection of a remote location for the Forum on the outskirts of Nairobi, Moi Stadium, whose cost to access was prohibitive, not only for local popular sectors but also for the average participant from the South. Additionally, that the large tents being used were largely empty during the Forum indicates that the investment was far out of proportion with actual attendance.

However, beyond these seemingly logistical elements, one of the major challenges for the Forum is the search for *methodological procedures that contribute to reinforcing the underlying goals*. This means ensuring that all the distinct perspectives that are present in the process are taken into account in the definitions.

The International Council (IC) has come to consensus about the importance of providing opportunities for convergence as well as of ensuring balance with regard to various factors (geography, sectors, gender, ethnicity) in the major WSF events. Two important proposals in this regard, which came out of the first Americas Social Forum held in Quito, Ecuador, in July 2004, were partially implemented as part of the Forum in Nairobi. This however took place in a way that ended up actually diminishing their effectiveness, not enhancing them.

First, *co-organised events* must be envisioned as a mid-way alternative to the central conferences and panels of the early forums and to the opposite idea of having only 'self-organised events'—but which do not guarantee diversity within the major arenas. In this idea, co-organised events are set up by the co-ordinating bodies of the Forum taking into account all the organisations and networks that come together to register joint activities within the principal themes that have been established for the particular Forum. In Nairobi, thirteen events of this kind were programmed for the forum, and were assigned large venues. However, last-minute preparation and poor promotion and publicity for these events resulted in very poor turnout, absent speakers and, in some cases, cancellation.

The second proposal implemented in Nairobi was that of 'the fourth day,' that was *dedicated to convergence, evaluation, and the planning of coordinated actions*.[4] One of the key achievements of the WSF has been precisely in the bringing together of diverse actors, issues, sectors, and agendas. While this coming together in a sense takes place in general in the Forum as a whole, the role of actually *bringing it all together* has in practice been taken up by the Assembly of Social Movements, on behalf of all participating sectors.

Thus, in Nairobi, on the morning of January 24, the one-but-last day of the Forum, self-coordinated thematic assemblies—where attendance was, just as throughout the Forum, purely voluntary—dealt in turn with such issues as war, migration, AIDS, sexual diversity, the union movement, and globalisation, among others, and effectively allowed for the identification of common goals and actions.

The reality of the assemblies was however, very different from its promise. First, the agenda for the day did not provide broader spaces for convergence *between* different themes; all the themes were deliberated on separately. Instead, the agenda outlined twenty-one issue-based workshops for the afternoon session, "of struggles, alternatives, and actions." These were also defined by keywords that lacked political meaning, and many of them repeated topics from the morning's sessions. And beyond this, the agenda for the afternoon's session was limited to only presenting proposals for action that would be later displayed on the Forum's webpage. And so, once again, and under these circumstances, it was up to the Assembly of Social Movements, in a packed tent, to take on this role of making space for the convergences that—as we have mentioned above—are so necessary.

From the outset, the Forum has been a space for convergence in the broadest sense imaginable, as part of the struggle against neoliberalism. Its pluralism, diversity, and gender perspective are fundamental elements; its character as an agora for the exchange of ideas and proposals is essential to its make up; and its participatory character is its driving force for the construction of alternatives. But if it is to retain this essence, it cannot become reduced to the coordination of disconnected events, redesigned each time like a new experiment. It is time now to invest in the idea of the *forum as process*, such that the accumulated experiences may serve as a broad platform for new initiatives, and continue contributing to the construction of a plural social and political force that will bring about in-depth changes as alternatives to the neoliberal model.

Future Perspectives: Looking Ahead to the 2008 World Social Forum

The 2008 Forum will explore a new organisational model. Instead of one central event, organised somewhere in the world in January 2008 as has become the WSF's custom, this time the WSF has issued a worldwide call to its participants to organise high-profile gatherings and actions around the world on the same date in January 2008, January 26.[5] In principle, this concept will allow for the participation of a far greater number of people while also having a truly *global* manifestation and impact. In any case, on the one hand, since this is not something that can be orchestrated in a centralised way, its success will depend on the situation within each country and the decision of local participants to invest their selves in its organisation and therefore, in autonomous, self-organised activities. Clearly, the cohesion of the Forum and its international visibility in 2008 will depend to a great extent on a global communication initiative, as much during the lead up as at the time of the Forum.

Debate has already begun about whether or not the 2008 Forum/day of action should have one or several central themes, or whether it should be based on freely determined themes; and whether or not there will be a common slogan beyond "Another World is Possible." During the meeting of the International Council in Nairobi in January 2007, a significant group of international networks and regional Forums brought forward a new idea—the idea of a *global day of action against the crimes of the transnational companies and governments* who participate in the World Economic Forum, to take place concurrently in

Davos. Such an initiative would ensure that a clear and forceful message is sent about the commitment of the World Social Forum in the struggle against neoliberalism.

And in 2009, the World Social Forum is scheduled to again take place in a central location. Spacing out the World Forums has been an ongoing demand by several sectors, particularly social movements. Since the time that the WSF International Council was established in 2001, the movements have insisted on the need to have more space and time to invest in their own social struggles as well as to develop local and continental processes for the Forum. In any case, if the problems that arose in Nairobi are warning signs of fatigue with the mega-forum approach—and these are issues that have already been voiced on previous occasions—then 2008 presents both a major challenge and an opportunity for participants all around the world to look for and develop new ways for the Forum process to take root in the different corners of the world.

Notes

1. This essay is an edited version of an article by the authors posted on ALAI—América Latina en Movimiento, titled 'The 7th World Social Forum: Facing Current Challenges and Future Perspectives,' @ http://alainet.org/active/15665. The editors thank the authors for permission to publish their essay here, and the authors thank Magdalena León for her contributions to the first version of this article. Translation of original article by ALAI.
2. For a discussion of these and other inter-state Agreements and a broad historical and political economic background to the Nairobi Forum, see the essay by Jean Nanga in the volume.
3. See the essay in this volume by Dorval Brunelle.
4. See the WSF document on the 4th day, in this volume.
5. See the WSF's Call for a Day of Action, in this volume.

Another U.S. Is Happening![1]

Judy Rebick

After spending five weeks in Bolivia last summer, I was convinced that new paths out of this destructive, hateful morass we call neoliberalism could only come from those most marginalised by its greed and violence. Little did I imagine that one of the strongest signs of this direction would come from the belly of the beast itself. Fifteen thousand people, overwhelmingly poor and working class, majority people of colour, at least half women, and including a massive number of youth, gathered at the end of June 2007 in Atlanta, Georgia, for the U.S. Social Forum (USSF), signalling what could be the birth of the most powerful social movement the U.S. has ever seen.

"People are asking me when Atlanta has ever seen something like this," said Jerome Scott of Project South and a veteran Atlanta activist, speaking of the opening march of the USSF. "I've been reflecting on that and my answer is Atlanta has never seen anything like this. The Civil Rights movement was mostly African American and last year's May 1st (immigration rights) demo was mostly Latinos—but this march was the most multi-national action I have ever seen. It was beautiful."

Similarly, Carlos Torres, a Chilean refugee now living in Canada, told me halfway through the forum, "Never in my wildest imagination did I think I would ever see something like this in the United States!" This sentiment was repeated again and again by Latin American visitors who were there as emissaries from the World Social Forum (WSF). It was radical, it was militant, it was feminist, it was anti-capitalist and anti-imperialist, it was queer, it was loud and lively, and it was brimming with love, kindness, and a deep sense of solidarity. The slogan of the USSF was 'Another World is Possible, Another U.S. is necessary.' But this was widely understood as referring not only to another U.S. but also to another 'us'—meaning that the Left has to reinvent itself.

Marisa Franco from San Francisco's POWER (People Organized to Win Employment Rights) said at the opening plenary of the June 29 session[2]:

> We're not talking about a platform or demands here. We're talking about how we can make things work better. We must connect with each other, walk vision as well as talk vision. No one else will do it for us. If another U.S. is necessary, another 'us' is necessary, too.

And it was a major step forward for the World Social Forum movement as a whole. The idea of a U.S. Social Forum came from a couple of people who went to the 2001 WSF in Brazil and then brought a few more with them in 2002. They formed a group called Grassroots Global Justice and began the process of organising a U.S. Social Forum, firmly in the WSF spirit. One of them, Fred Azcarate, then with Jobs with Justice and now with the AFL-CIO (American Federation of Labor and Congress of Industrial Organizations), explained to the opening plenary that "It took this long because we wanted to do it right by building the necessary relationships among the grassroots organisations and ensuring the right outcomes." And the right outcomes were to create the conditions to unite the disparate grassroots people's movements around the U.S. across race, age, sector, and region. They got the idea from the WSF but they took it beyond where anyone else has managed to go, except perhaps in Mumbai. In Nairobi, poor people demanded a significant place in the WSF planning process—and in Atlanta, they had one.[3]

Hundreds of participants arrived via the 'Freedom Caravan,' commemorating the civil rights Freedom Rides of 1961. Buses began in Albuquerque, New Mexico, and linked with others from the Gulf Coast and then various places in the South that symbolise the civil rights struggle. In addition, a lot of fundraising was done to bring poor and low-income people to Atlanta.[4] Instead of a majority of privileged middle class people who are usually the majority of World Social Forums, working class, poor people, and students formed a large part of the participants there. It was also just about the most diverse and multi-racial gathering I've ever seen. According to veteran left activist Stephen Sherman writing in *Monthly Review* [5]:

> The remarkable accomplishment of the United States Social Forum was to bring together the largely white activists whose touchstone was the direct action at the WTO protests in Seattle with community and labor activists who mostly come from communities of color.

This was all the more remarkable given the de facto racial segregation endemic on the U.S. Left for the last thirty years.

I think it's fair to say that, by the end of the Forum, the confidence of both groups that they belong together and can work with each other had increased. The National Planning Committee represented what they call national and regional 'base-building' groups, whose base is mostly poor and working class people. It seemed to this observer that the Forum shifted the balance of power on the U.S. Left to the poor and oppressed from the middle class. The burst of brilliance in the anti-WTO protests in Seattle settled on the one hand into a marginalised, mostly white 'anti-globalisation movement,' and on the other, reinforced a fairly mainstream Left focused on improving the fortunes of the Democratic Party. Even the Seattle protests were highly problematic. As Latino activist Betita Martinez asked in a famous article of hers in the magazine *ColorLines*, "Where was the colour in Seattle?"[6]

These and other questions since that time made people realise that what was called at the time the *anti-globalisation movement*, and later the *global justice movement*, were both entirely white and also focused on one issue—protesting corporate globalisation. The visible Left in the U.S. was, and remains, mostly intellectuals, and many of them in Washington-based think tanks and foundation-funded NGOs. The grassroots organising that has been going on over the last number of years has been invisible to most of us outside of the country. The genius of the organisers of the USSF was to bring together all these local and grassroots groups in one place using the social forum open space process as a way to do it.

Every plenary focused on building alliances among the myriad of grassroots movement across the United States. Most emphasis was on a 'black-brown' alliance to combat the racism that divides African Americans from their Latino and immigrant brothers and sisters. But there was a lot of focus on student/labour alliances, and environmental issues were completely linked to social justice issues. One of the remarkable things about the resurgence of the student movement in the United States in the 21st century is that it has been very linked first to anti-globalisation and then to workers' rights. The resurgence of campus activism a few years ago was linked to an anti-sweatshop campaign protesting the use of campus branded clothing made in sweatshops. At the Forum I heard stories of student alliances with workers on campus and in the community helping organise poorly paid workers.

Another important feature of the Forum was to link corporate globalisation and war to a wide variety of local struggles. Speakers linked local struggles to international ones, something very rare in the United States. This seemed to have been a central factor in their ability to bring together such a diversity of forces. Most speakers linked the issues and everyone spoke of the need to unify all the struggles and to develop a deeper solidarity across movements. Support for gays, lesbians, and transgendered people—who have been major targets of the Bush administration—seemed universal.

The Forum ended in a People's Movements Assembly where various regional and issue caucuses presented their resolutions. Several new national networks were formed and the bonds of solidarity were deeply forged among those who are usually divided. People left with the commitment to organise social forums in their regions, cities, and neighbourhoods. Over the course of the week, the social forum became a metaphor for creating a movement of movements everywhere.

Almost all the 900 workshops over the four days were filled to the brim with activists who were sharing strategies in everything from food security to community/labour alliances to a new 'taking back our cities' movement against gentrification.[7] The majority of the plenary speakers were women, people of colour, and young people. There was not a single 'star' among them, left wing or other. In a culture obsessed with celebrity, the organising committee decided they didn't need any, even the good ones.

Also as a result, none of the big NGOs in the United States was on the planning committee. There is a big debate going on in the United States about what they call the NGO-industrial complex.[8] The idea was present throughout the Forum that foundation-funded, majority white, centrist, and Washington-dominated NGOs and think tanks have hijacked the Left. These groups were welcome to participate but not in a leadership capacity. Some participants went overboard and 'pied' (threw a pie in the face of) Medea Benjamin, the spokesperson of Code Pink.[9] The organisers apologised and dissociated themselves from the action, but it was clear that that action reflected and symbolised deep disaffection with the larger social justice and anti-war groups.

While the location of the Forum in Atlanta—in the southern part of the U.S.—and the participation of several veteran civil rights leaders planted the roots of the Forum firmly in the history of the civil rights movement, there was less reference to its relationship to the women's movement or the workers' movement. To this writer, the plenary on gender was the most disappointing. It is true that the women's movement in the United States has been race divided and the movement most publicly recognised is almost all white; nevertheless some of the most important feminist theorists in the United States are African Americans like bell hooks and Audre Lorde. The women who did speak about the history, like Betita Martinez, veteran Latina activist and author, were almost apologetic about it.

On the other hand, an extraordinary feature of the Forum was the role of indigenous people. They led the opening march and participated on several panels as well as holding their own plenary. Much of the vision came from them. After talking about the melting of the glaciers, Faith Gemmill from REDOIL (Resisting Environmental Destruction on Indigenous Land) in Alaska said,[10]

> Our people have a prophecy that there will come a time in the history of humanity when people are in danger of destroying ourselves. When that time comes, a voice will arise from the North to warn us. That time is now. I was sent here to give you part of our burden to speak up now against the greed.

And Tom Goldtooth, who represents the Indigenous Environmental Network on the National Planning Committee, said,[11]

> We must talk from the heart and shake hands with one another. A prayer has taken place that this spirit is going to grow. No matter who we are we must demand not reform of a broken system but transformation. We need to organise from the grassroots.

And many did speak from the heart.

The plenary on Katrina was stunning. Afterwards I felt that if the first American Revolution was started by a callous colonial power dumping tea into Boston Harbour, the second one might be caused by a callous, racist, arrogant government thinking it could wipe out the hard fought place of Afro-Americans in New Orleans after a storm provided them the opportunity. Monique Hardin from Advocates for Environmental Human Rights opened the plenary saying, "New Orleans is a man-made disaster. Bush is the man and Bush is the disaster. Reconstruction on the Gulf Coast is a massive privatisation scheme to destroy people of colour and poor white people." Dr Beverley Wright, speaking from the floor, said, "Our parents and our grandparents fought to buy a house to pass on to their family and they are trying to take that away from us when they talk about turning the place we lived in East New Orleans into a green space. They're not talking about turning the place [where] rich white folks live into green space." Another community leader said, "Katrina is both a reality and a symbol. If you work in justice, if you work in health care, if you work in housing, you are in Katrina."

One of the most powerful speeches was from Javier Gallardo from the New Orleans Workers' Centre, a guest worker from Peru.[12] He explained that while African Americans were displaced from the region in huge numbers, hundreds of workers like him had been brought in from Latin America for the reconstruction of the Gulf Coast, and their employers' names are on the passports. Their ability to stay in the U.S. is dependent on the employer. He said that there is now a practice that when the employer is finished with the workers, he sells them to another employer for $2,000 each. "What is that?" Javier Gallardo asked. "We call it modern day slavery. They want to divide us but the old slaves and the new slaves can join together and together we can defeat them," he continued to thunderous applause. This old slaves / new slaves metaphor wove its way through the rest of the Forum in the powerful idea of a black-brown alliance that veteran activists felt will transform left-wing politics in the United States and especially in the South where the vast majority of the working class is now black and brown.

Another impressive feature of the Forum was in the handling of conflict. When the Palestinian contingent objected that they were the only group not permitted to speak for themselves in the anti-war plenary, the organisers read their letter of protest to the next plenary. When the moderator of the People's Movement Assembly stopped the report of the indigenous caucus at the end of their allotted time by removing their mike, they took grave offence and felt silenced. Within ten minutes, most of the indigenous people in the room were on the stage with the consent of the organisers. What could have been an explosive divisive moment with a lot of anger and hurt was handled with incredible skill by both permitting the protest and by making sure it was interpreted in a way that created unity rather than division. I had the feeling that a new culture of solidarity was being born, one we tried for in the feminist movement but never quite accomplished.

Of course there were weaknesses in the Forum. While the issue of the war and U.S. imperialism had pride of place, the mainstream anti-war movement had little presence. The anti-war movement has lost a lot of its steam over the last few years. A debate on strategy for broadening the movement is desperately needed. Yet the anti-war plenary had little such discussion.

In fact, there was little space at the Forum for debate of any kind. Plenaries were informative and motivational and workshops were very practical and mostly based on sharing tactics and strategies. However, there were no sessions set up to debate critical issues. There was an assumption of agreement on many things that probably need further discussion. A break with the sectarian bickering of the past is no doubt desperately needed but there is also a need to learn how to constructively debate and discuss difference. For example, in the statement from the Palestinians about how they were not represented on the anti-war panel, they suggested that no one outside Palestine had a right to express an opinion about the Hamas. From a feminist point of view, it is difficult to understand how we can work in solidarity with the Palestinian cause without being able to express solidarity with the struggle of Palestinian feminists against the policies of the Hamas. But there was no place to discuss such contentious questions.

As is often the case, the strengths of the Forum were in some ways also its weaknesses. The planning committee bent the stick quite far towards people speaking for themselves rather than the usual parade of academics and leaders of major NGOs on display at such events. Yet, while strengthening the voices of the grassroots organisations is no doubt critically important, there also has to be a discussion on building alliances with the more mainstream and middle class groups. My experience in the women's movement tells me that building these kinds of alliances is critical to the ultimate success of a struggle—and this is probably triply true in the United States.

Nevertheless, and despite all these problems, there is no question that the U.S. Social Forum was probably the most significant event on the U.S. Left for a generation. The organisers of the USSF addressed the central weaknesses of the U.S. Left and showed to everyone who was there or who reads alternative press that another U.S., one which reflects the interests of poor and working class people, is indeed possible, particularly by modelling a level of unity across race and culture divides that few had ever seen before. But beyond the symbolic, the Forum also created links of solidarity that will no doubt continue to deepen and expand.

The last time there was a significant upsurge in the United States was in the 1960s when the civil rights movement combined with the anti-war movement and then the women's movement to produce a tremendous wave of protest against the imperialist adventures outside, and race and gender discrimination within the United States. The forces gathered in Atlanta were even broader. In particular, while the labour movement did not have a strong presence, workers' issues were front and centre and integrated with issues of racism, sexism, and heterosexism. There was a strong class-consciousness in the discussions that I have rarely seen in U.S. social movements. The need to organise workers was front and centre in the debates about strategies. The potential of an alliance among all those groups who are oppressed and exploited in the United States seemed within reach by the end of the Forum and such a development would surely challenge the ruling elites in the United States in a much more profound way than even in the 1960s.

Just as important were the links made between the local struggles in the U.S. with international struggles. Not since the days of the Viet Nam war have we seen an event more rooted in internationalism. While it was subtle, there was nevertheless a strong message that every struggle discussed at the USSF was of vital importance to the people of the world. Taking down the imperial power requires a battle both inside and outside the beast. Too often international issues in North America are segregated, with young middle class activists taking on the anti-war, anti-corporate globalisation issues and immigrants focussing on their home countries. The USSF brought together these forces for the first time in a generation.

Andrea Smith, a young feminist academic speaking at the gender plenary, said, "I don't really like the slogan of this Forum, 'another U.S. is necessary.' Surely our collective imaginations can come up with something better than a kinder, gentler country based on genocide, slavery, and imperialism," she proclaimed, to thunderous applause.

Turning the Mirror on Ourselves

In Atlanta, at some points I couldn't believe I was in the United States of America. As Canadians, we often feel a vague sense of superiority over our U.S. American friends and comrades. After all, we are said to be that 'kinder, gentler country' that Andrea Smith referred to. As one of the founders of the Toronto Social Forum that was held in Toronto in 2003, I worked long and hard with Alternatives, a Quebec NGO, to build a Canada / Quebec / First Nations Social Forum. Canada is very much a multi-national country, with Quebec and Indigenous Peoples each identifying as a nation, with little identification with the Canadian state. Our idea was to recognise the three founding nations of Canada in the preparation of a social forum here. But we failed for a number of reasons, not the least of which were the tensions between different movements and the manifest lack of interest in solidarity among these national groups.

Though there have been a number of local social forums across Canada, we have still not succeeded in creating the conditions for a cross-country social forum. Another attempt at a social forum in Canada can surely learn some lessons from the U.S. Social Forum.

At the end of the summer of 2007 however, just two months after the U.S. Forum, a highly successful Quebec Social Forum may also have set the stage for another try at a cross-Canada social forum. Vastly exceeding the predictions of even the organisers, more than 5,000 people participated in the first Quebec Forum (FSQ, or the *Forum Social Quebecois*) in Montreal. It was the largest gathering of the Left in the history of Quebec.[13]

(Cont'd)

Reflecting a bit on the FSQ, it could be seen that the Social Forum process permitted, like the U.S. Forum and like the Forum in other places around the world, a gathering of all the social movements in Quebec in one place. More than 300 workshops over two days discussed a vast range of issues. Unlike the USSF, however, the major NGOs and social movements dominated the Quebec Social Forum. For example, the NGO Alternatives merged their summer school into the social forum and as a result, brought in many activists and intellectuals from all over the world. But the consequence of this was that there was also a much stronger focus on international issues and on building transnational alliances than there was at the USSF.

On the other hand, while Quebec is not as diverse as the U.S. , the most visible absence at the Québec Forum was from what the Quebecois call the 'cultural communities.' The enormous diversity of communities in Montreal was not at all reflected, with the exception of a strong participation from the Latin American community. But then again, almost one third of participants came from outside the Montreal area, showing that the Left is strong around the province. The unions helped to finance the Forum but with the exception of a few unions, there was little evidence that they had mobilised their members to participate. Others like the women's, housing, anti-poverty, environmental, and student movements were highly present. The Forum concluded with a cross-Quebec, cross-sectoral call for action on 26 January 2008, as part of the World Social Forum Global Day of Action.

While the Quebec Social Forum was an important moment for the Left in Quebec, showing its strength and unity, it did not have the transformative character of the USSF. Quebec is probably the last country to be hit by a neoliberal shift. Powerful social movements and the labour movement have been able to resist the assault until very recently. The Quebec Left is still in a bit of a state of shock in response to the rise of the Right and the new experience of marginalisation by a neoliberal media and government. The Forum was an important event in encouraging the social movements to keep up the fight and in provoking discussions about strategies in the times to come.

As a Canadian, I have often returned from political gatherings in the United States with a sense of gratitude that I don't live there and don't have to deal with the morass of U.S. politics whether on the Left or the Right. Even as a young woman, I moved to New York in 1968 and was horrified by the level of sectarianism on the U.S. Left when SDS (Students for a Democratic Society) meetings broke out in fist fights and Black Panthers were hiding in white comrades' apartments because they were so infiltrated by the FBI. I think that Atlanta was really the first time that I felt more hope from a gathering in the U.S. than from my own experiences in Canada.

In her celebrated speech at the 2003 World Social Forum in Brazil, Arundhati Roy famously said,[14]

> Remember this: We be many and they be few. They need us more than we need them. Another world is not only possible, she is on her way. On a quiet day, I can hear her breathing.

It wasn't a quiet day that day, but on that day in Atlanta I could hear her not just breathing but shouting, loud and clear:

"What do we want? *Justice!* How will we get it? *People Power!*"

Notes

1. Content editor for this essay is Vipul Rikhi.
2. Rein, July 2007.
3. For a detailed discussion on the genesis and formation of the U.S. Social Forum, see the chapter in this book by Michael Leon Guerrero, Tammy Bang Luu, and Cindy Wiesner; and for a discussion of the World Social Forum in Nairobi, Kenya, that took place in January 2007, see the essay by Irene León and Sally Burch.
4. See the essay in this book by Michael Leon Guerrero, Tammy Bang Luu, and Cindy Wiesner for a discussion of the realities of fund-raising for the USSF. —Eds.
5. Sherman, July 2007.
6. Martinez, January 2000.
7. The taking over of often pleasant immigrant / ethnic or working class neighbourhoods in cities by property redevelopers to clean them up for wealthier classes—the gentry—to move in.
8. For details, see: INCITE! Women of Color against Violence, eds, April 2007.
9. Code Pink is a particularly effective and militant feminist anti-war group that among other things dogged Hilary Clinton for two years until she changed her position on the war in Iraq.
10. Author's notes.
11. Author's notes.
12. Workers' Centres have been created mostly in immigrant communities for workers to organise themselves. They have grown from a handful in the early 1990s to more than 120 today and they were very present at the Forum.
13. For a more detailed discussion of on the Québec Social Forum, see the essay by Pierre Beaudet in this volume.
14. Roy, January 2003.

The Road to Atlanta: Reflections on The Organising History of The U.S. Social Forum[1]

Michael Leon Guerrero, Tammy Bang Luu, Cindy Wiesner

Written by us as members of the National Planning Committee (NPC) for the United States Social Forum (USSF), this essay attempts to provide both documentation and some reflections on the process of organising the USSF from its inception in 2003 until the actual Forum in June 2007. Originally written to serve as a narrative for new members joining the USSF NPC, that report has been adapted to prepare this article. We feel it is useful and important to understand how the USSF evolved, socially, politically, and organisationally, and the challenges that we faced, particularly around issues of participation, accountability, and decision-making.

By all accounts published so far,[2] the U.S. Social Forum was a great success. But in our estimate, as organisers who participated in the planning process, even though we view the USSF as a significant step in movement-building in the United States we feel that it is still too early to assess every dimension of the success and meaning of this first USSF. Nevertheless, we can say that participants in the Forum were inspired and spoke of their hope in the possibility of significant political change in the United States; and that this experience tells us that a new, young leadership of the grassroots movements—darker, queerer, and more anti-imperialist, and clearer about the need for systemic social transformation—is emerging. In terms of numbers alone, we exceeded our goal of 10,000 participants, and estimate that more than 12,000 people participated over the course of the five days. But we want here to go beyond this. The NPC had established certain political objectives for the USSF: introducing the Social Forum process to U.S. social movements; creating an understanding, in cities, regions and sectors, of the USSF as a movement-building process; and focusing on grassroots people of colour groups at the base as our key constituency to organise, thus recognising their critical role in creating systemic change in this country. We were also clear that we wanted movements and sectors to intersect, and we tried to help this happen by creating a convergence of issues, dialogues, and debates—in the event but also in the process. Our hope was that the Social Forum would help different social movements develop strategic alliances and relationships, and so make more effective advances against neo-liberalism, imperialism, white supremacy, patriarchy, and homophobia. We also considered it important to challenge U.S. chauvinism, so the NPC made spaces in the Forum's plenaries and other activities to acknowledge our international obligations to movement-building in alignment with the Global South.

We will reflect on these objectives in the course of this essay.

A Seed Is Planted

As much as its success in terms of numbers, reports on the USSF featured its cultural and regional diversity.[3] It is a fact, however, that some key sectors of movements in the U.S. were not represented strongly, particularly faith-based networks and the environmental conservation movement, and also the larger national and international non-governmental organisations. To a large extent, this was an outcome of how we designed the USSF process, and of the NPC's intention to make the Forum both a process and an event. We wanted to build from the 'bottom up,' focusing on sections and communities traditionally marginalised from national political processes. In our view, the Global Justice Movement in the United States had so far been largely white-led[4]—we identify even the celebrated Battle of Seattle as young, white, and anarchist, albeit composed of many decentralised affinity groups—and we saw the USSF as an opportunity for change. Our aim was to shift the focus of the movement to those most impacted by the ravages of neo-liberal capitalism. Thus, the driving force organising the USSF were grassroots organisations that have so far been largely overlooked in national politics. For the past three decades, these organisations have been building dynamic community and worker institutions in indigenous nations, working-class neighbourhoods, and communities of colour. This grassroots Global Justice Movement represents the potential for a new political direction, and hope for fundamental political change within the U.S. The groups on the NPC that helped anchor this process included Project South, Jobs with Justice, SouthWest Organizing Project, Labor/Community Strategy Center, Indigenous Environmental Network, Southwest Workers Union, Miami Workers' Center, People Organizing to Win Employment Rights, CAAAV, Organizing Asian Communities, St Peter's Housing Committee, Southwest Network for Environmental and Economic Justice, and the Praxis Project.Though no unifying vision or ideology binds us, we share traits, histories, and objectives. Many of us have antecedents in the political struggles of the 1960s and 70s, and leaderships that view their work within a broader global context, seeking social justice and environmental sustainability. We promote human rights and social justice, and many of us share anti-racist and anti-imperialist perspectives. We emphasise creating a grassroots, democratic membership base as essential for fundamental social change, and we organise in poor, working-class communities, largely composed of people of colour and of Indigenous peoples; and we build coalitions, networks, and alliances—locally, nationally, and internationally. Though small, our non-profits have some of the most politically developed organisers; and even though under-resourced and overworked, in the end it was this sector that launched what is perhaps the most important contemporary political process in the U.S.

Genesis: Initiating the Process

During the early years of the World Social Forum (WSF), several members of the WSF International Council (WSFIC) had called for a United States Social Forum. Some early U.S. participants, including Jobs with Justice (JwJ) and later Grassroots Global Justice (GGJ), resisted the call. Our caution was based on the fact that there was no broad public awareness in the U.S. about the WSF process. With social movements neither strong nor broad-based enough, a U.S. Social Forum would have been premature. If convened in the early years of the WSF, it would have been dominated by national policy organisations without grassroots membership and not representative of working-class communities of colour.Meanwhile, however, some activists experienced, and many others read about, major Social Forum convergences in Brazil, and we witnessed the power of the coordinated actions organised against the Iraq War in 2003 and the social movement convergences throughout Latin America that had their genesis at the Forums in Brazil. GGJ was in fact founded in July 2002 after a number of U.S.-based organisations, including Jobs with Justice, South West Organizing Project, Strategic Concepts in Organizing and Policy Education, and the United Electrical, Radio, and Machine Workers' Union, attended the second WSF in Porto Alegre, Brazil. The event provided an inspiring backdrop for dialogue within the U.S. delegation. It also sparked a critical self-examination about why the movement in the U.S. was unable to build organisations on a scale as massive as from other countries at the WSF. Several organisations agreed to continue the dialogue in the U.S., and so the GGJ was eventually founded, as an alliance.

The alliance was created to allow the grassroots sector in the U.S. to both strengthen the national grassroots movement and to proactively participate in the international arena. Initially a loose affiliation of organisations, GGJ's first function was to organise delegations of grassroots leaders to the World Social Forums over the subsequent years—to Porto Alegre in 2003 and 2005, Mumbai (India) in 2004, Caracas (Venezuela) in 2006, and Nairobi (Kenya) in 2007. These delegations allowed grassroots organisers to meet and interact with their international global justice colleagues and to gain insights and inspiration from organising models and strategies developed and used by our international allies. GGJ finally agreed to initiate discussions about the concept of a USSF at a WSFIC meeting that was held in Miami, Florida, in June 2003, specifically to allow the full IC to engage in depth with movement organisations in the U.S.—looking ahead to such a Forum. Following this, we from GGJ convened two meetings of organisations within the U.S., in April 2004. The USSF process began out of those dialogues, and GGJ was asked by the consultations to shepherd the process until a National Planning Committee was formed.We realised, however, that the conditions that would allow the Forum to accommodate the broad diversity of social movements that we have in the U.S., still did not exist. It became clear to us that we would first have to create awareness and understanding among grassroots organisations. As we began to speak with organisations from around the country, several asked why the USSF would be different from any other national process. Others had heard about the chaotic nature of the Social Forums elsewhere and wondered how such an event could be productive to their purposes. This scepticism was compounded by the collapse of the Northwest Social Forum in October 2004. Just two weeks before the event was to take place, the Forum was cancelled when the Native American Programming Committee (and subsequently the Youth Programming Committee) withdrew from the event, on the argument that Native Americans were being marginalised from the organising process.

There was also the question of who was leading what was happening in the U.S., in relation to the WSF. Although the Boston Social Forum had, even earlier than this, succeeded in drawing some 5,000 participants in July 2004, some also questioned the limited participation by grassroots communities of colour in Boston. In fact, it is true that all the Forums that took place within the U.S. before the USSF in Atlanta, including Chicago in May 2006 and the Midwest Forum in July 2006, were white-led. This history had major implications for the USSF process we were to build. Undeterred by scepticism however, in the summer of 2004 GGJ put out a broad call to build a National Planning Committee (NPC) for the USSF, and twenty-two organisations agreed to serve on it. All founding members agreed that we would expand the body only over time, and though we were not all grassroots organisations we all agreed to be deliberate in our outreach to ensure that grassroots groups anchored the process. We did not want advocacy, academics, and other sectors to dominate the process from the beginning, and so we agreed to conduct broader recruitment to the NPC only later on. Such a founding principle was critical because, as already mentioned, grassroots sectors based in communities of people of colour, working-class communities, and poor communities are historically marginalised from national dialogues and political strategies. We also decided to focus our outreach on organisations rather than individuals, in order to ensure accountability to a community or collective—though anyone could participate in the process. Our first year of organising, 2004–5, was a difficult and formative period. Firstly, our initial goal to convene the USSF in the summer of 2006 may have been overly ambitious. Most crucially, the fact that we chose to build the foundation of the NPC with grassroots organisations meant that the organising process was under-resourced. Foundations tend to provide little support to grassroots organising in the U.S., and, in any case, by early 2005 a high level of scepticism had begun to emerge among foundations about the Social Forum process. The Ford Foundation, a major contributor to early Social Forums internationally, cut off support for the WSF after 2003. Other funders expressed concern that their huge investment in Social Forums did not result in tangible political outcomes. Still others were sceptical whether the core of organisations comprising the NPC could handle an event of the scale we were projecting. Besides, after the Republican Party stole two Presidential elections in 2000 and 2004, many liberal foundations shifted their focus to supporting electoral organising strategies. This meant that for the first three years, the U.S. Social Forum process was primarily carried on the backs of smaller organisations, which committed staff time, in-kind support, and money to the effort. This presented enormous challenges, and uncertainty about whether the USSF would ever even take place. Conversely, it also strengthened the resolve and unity of the NPC's active core. It also forced us to develop a dynamic and diverse fundraising strategy that relied on in-kind donors and on income from registration fees. Indeed, an important though side achievement of the USSF process is that despite these handicaps, we completed the event with a surplus.In early 2005, the Site and Outreach Committee selected Atlanta, in Georgia, a state in the southeast of the U.S., as the site for the USSF. Atlanta was chosen, by vote, because the legacy of slavery and of the genocide of Indigenous people is still palpable in the southern region of the country; and also because the city is an important symbolic location for the civil rights movement, being home to Dr Martin Luther King Jr and Coretta Scott King. But Atlanta is also located in a region that is politically conservative; the state of Georgia has blatantly anti-labour, anti-immigrant, and anti-gay laws, and the region has fewer movement organisations than others. All this only added to the challenge of raising funds and securing logistical and infrastructural support. In a larger sense, the choice of Atlanta thus broke with historical norms in the global WSF process—especially in Porto Alegre—in that the USSF was going to be held in a region that was politically conservative and therefore also financially unyielding. Notwithstanding, Project South took on the responsibility of acting as the host organisation in Atlanta.

Atlanta: The First Face-to-Face Meeting

The NPC decided to adopt the WSF organisational culture and structure and, during the first half of 2005, put it into practice. This included forming several working groups, for Communications, Culture, Fundraising, Outreach and Programme, as well as a Local Host Committee. We made the process as open as possible to allow more organisations to participate. Organisations that wanted to join the NPC still had to apply, but anyone could participate in the working groups. All NPC member organisations were required to also participate in the working groups because we wanted participation in the NPC to be based on work.The formative stage of the USSF organising process culminated with the first face-to-face meeting of the NPC in Atlanta in August 2005. The fact that it was a full year after the NPC was founded before we could convene a meeting is in itself testament to our lack of resources! At this first meeting, we created a Youth Working Group. Also, consistent with our movement-building objective, we established a *regional* structure to encourage greater participation from the grassroots. Ten regions were designated: Alaska, Northwest, Northeast, Rocky Mountains/Great Plains, Great Lakes/Midwest, Southeast, Pacific, West, Southwest, and the Caribbean. Each region was to have a regional committee and to develop its own process for mobilising towards the USSF. This idea evolved into an interesting, ongoing learning experience. Over time, debates emerged in each region about whether the regional designations made sense because functionally, various areas self-defined their regions differently, through their own lenses of history, politics, and culture.

We also created an Organising Committee (OC), made up of one representative from each working group and regional committee; and eventually the OC came to serve as a coordinating body. The NPC, however, still provided the overall political direction to the process. Just two weeks after this first NPC meeting however, on 29 August 2005, Hurricane Katrina struck New Orleans and the Gulf Coast. Hurricane Rita soon followed. Tens of thousands of displaced people—several of whom were organisers—moved to Atlanta. New Orleans is a majority Black city and the negligence by local, state, and federal agencies after the disaster brought renewed attention to institutionalised racism in the South.

Organisations who were on the Local Host Committee in Atlanta naturally now focused all their attention on relief efforts; and the reconstruction of the Gulf Coast region thus became a central focus of the USSF, while also reaffirming the importance of holding the USSF in the South. But on the other hand, this also meant that the Southeast Regional Committee and the Local Host Committee decided in the fall of 2005 that, given the circumstances, the date of the USSF be postponed from 2006 to the summer of 2007.

The Need for Convergence

Important political events between 2002–2006 had already highlighted the limitations of progressive movements in the U.S. In 2002–3, the Bush administration invaded Afghanistan and Iraq, sparking massive anti-war protest across the world. Although the issue provoked the largest-ever global mobilisation, on 15 February 2003, when it is estimated that some 30 million people participated, the protest was unable to prevent the military invasion and occupation of Afghanistan and Iraq. By 2005, it was clear to us in the U.S. that the anti-war movement lacked both the unified vision and political strength necessary either to force a withdrawal from the region or to redefine national policy towards the Middle East. Equally, Hurricane Katrina and the breech of the levees in New Orleans had created the worst natural and man-made disaster in U.S. history, only compounded by the government's criminal neglect—and yet movements were barely able to influence the situation. The neglect and abandonment of the population by local, state, and federal governments during the fatal crisis amounted to the veritable manslaughter of the majority Black population: at least 1,500 people died, and up to 1.2 million were displaced. Progressive movements responded with material support at the scene, but not with a coordinated national effort or protest.

Politically, the response was even weaker. In fact, the lack of a mass movement initiative in support of the Gulf Coast allowed the Bush Administration to leave the people displaced, the region in ruins and its reconstruction in the hands of corporate developers.[5] The lack of a national effort for reconstructing the Gulf Coast region again highlighted the fragmentation and isolation of progressive social movement in the U.S. The next year, another crisis hit the U.S., and once again progressive movements failed to unite. In early 2006, the House of Representatives passed House Bill 4437, introduced by Rep. James Sensenbrenner. The Sensenbrenner Bill, as it came to be known, called for massive increases in the militarisation of the U.S.-Mexico border, including a 700-mile expansion of the Border wall, the mandatory detention and deportation of undocumented immigrants, and an increase in the authority of police agencies to enforce immigration laws. The wall had already become a stark, oppressive symbol of the militarisation of the U.S., and thousands had died attempting to cross the border through the deserts and rivers of Mexico and the southwest United States. Now, under the jurisdiction of the Homeland Security Agency, tens of thousands of armed Border Patrol agents and National Guardsmen began to patrol the region to prevent entry by economic refugees from Latin America. The Bill propelled a massive wave of marches by immigrants and supporters in the smallest towns and largest cities of the country, while also precipitating other, also regressive, Congressional initiatives. In March 2006, millions of people, primarily Latino immigrants, mobilised in cities throughout the United States, walking out of schools, workplaces, and homes. The marches were followed by boycotts and strikes on International Workers' Day on May 1. These mobilisations halted the momentum of the extreme Right, and ultimately stopped the Sensenbrenner's initiative in the Senate, and also prevented any new immigration legislation. Yet, progressive movements failed to embrace a unified vision of a just immigration policy and were left merely with the role of responding to the extreme right measures proposed in Congress, or of bolstering a weak liberal response. In April 2006, the USSF OC met and discussed these major upheavals and setbacks: growing public opposition to the U.S. occupation of and war on Iraq; the aftermath of the Gulf Coast hurricanes and continued apathy of the U.S.

government; massive immigrant rights mobilisations against the Sensenbrenner Bill; and the weakness of social movement in the country, in all these crises. We also talked about the growing concern about climate change in the context of the exploitation of Native lands, particularly the Arctic National Wildlife Refuge.

The impact of these events and actions touched almost everyone in the United States. However, the political movements in response to these events developed not in relation to each other but in parallel. We recognised each of these issues as 'movement-building moments,' during which a national progressive response *could* have galvanised the country. The NPC decided to further explore these issues through the USSF process and to attempt to create a space that would enable convergence or coordination among the different movements working on these issues. We saw it as a space in which to develop an integrated analysis of a broader vision and programme for social transformation. These ideas later became the focus of plenaries at the USSF.

South by Southwest: Regional Social Forums

In January 2006, a number of significant events that were key to the organising process occurred. A Lead Staff Organiser was hired, the first staff person for the USSF. In mid-January, Project South helped convene the Southeast Regional Committee (SERC), attended by over 100 representatives of forty organisations. The organisations attending agreed to organise a broader meeting, with a goal of 500 participants, in the summer of 2006. This would become the *Southeast Social Forum* in Durham, North Carolina. Weeks later, at the 6th WSF in Caracas, Venezuela, a small set of organisations who organise on the U.S.-Mexico Border, including Southwest Workers' Union and the National Network for Immigrant and Refugee Rights, decided to convene a *Border Social Forum* in October 2006. These two Social Forums would set the tone for the USSF in 2007.The Southeast Social Forum (SESF), held during June 15–17 2006, marked a significant milestone on the road to Atlanta. Roughly 700 people participated. Groups throughout the region mobilised their memberships and constituencies—a majority of them people of colour. Latino and South Asian immigrants from Virginia, African-Americans fighting displacement in Miami, and homeless people from Atlanta—they all came in busloads. Rich and profound discussions were held on the tensions between African-American and Latino immigrant communities, and a dialogue took place on the development of Black-Brown alliances. The success of the event had a ripple effect throughout the country. Key regional organisations that anchored the SESF continued to help build the USSF, and groups and people that were sceptical of Social Forums before began to see the value of the process. It was a preview of what the USSF could be. This was followed by the Border Social Forum. Energised by the Polycentric WSF in Caracas, Venezuela, in January 2006, the immigrant rights mobilisations in March, and the SESF in June, one thousand people converged at the Border Social Forum in Ciudad Juarez, Mexico. The Forum helped consolidate participation not just in the Southwest United States but in northern Mexico as well. Braceros—workers who had come to the U.S. under the guest worker programme of the 1940s—as well as farmers and farm workers from northern Mexico attended. A march was organised to denounce the Wall of Death on the U.S.-Mexico Border. The discussions that had been initiated in Durham about building Black-Brown alliances, continued in Ciudad Juarez.These two Forums were the first to be organised by member organisations of the NPC, and they were based on the same intention of starting with working-class, poor, and people of colour communities. Some other Forums, organised independently of the USSF process, such as the Houston, Chicago, Midwest, and Maine Social Forums, all held in the summer of 2006, were perhaps successful in other terms, but failed to integrate leadership and participation by people of colour. The NPC however made efforts to reach out to each of these Forums, make connections, and encourage their participation in the USSF process.

Later however, in November 2006, a significant Forum took place in Puerto Rico. Although it too was organised independently of the USSF process, the USSF NPC sent a representative to attend the event and established a relationship between the USSF and the Caribbean. The next year, another sympathetic Forum was the *DC Metro Social Forum* in March 2007, which introduced grassroots organisations and national NGOs to each other.Meanwhile, several citywide processes were beginning to take shape in places like Los Angeles, the San Francisco Bay Area, and New York City—but other regions were developing only very slowly. The Pacific and Alaska regions, in particular, faced huge challenges in terms of marshalling resources to organise and effectively participate in the national process. The relationship of Indigenous nations and occupied territories in the Caribbean and Pacific became an important question. Since many political activists in these regions are still in the process of resisting occupation by the U.S., they were wary of participating in a U.S. Social Forum.

In the course of these discussions, we realised that the regional designations formulated in the first NPC meeting were arbitrary, and that cultural, political, and historical conditions made for more organic definitions of regional boundaries. Many of the designated regions didn't have a history of regional organising or a shared regional identity. Indeed, some of them did not even consider themselves part of the U.S., but sovereign nations. Hawaii and Puerto Rico, for instance, asked to participate as international delegates. Prior to the SESF, the OC held a second face-to-face meeting. At the meeting we discussed the growing importance of the regional processes, particularly in the Southeast and in the Border between Mexico and the U.S. As in the Southeast, the Border process was breaking down historical barriers between groups and generating buy-in from organisations throughout the region. We recognised that there was a growing disconnect between the national and regional processes—participation in the NPC as a body was declining while participation of groups in some regions was increasing, even though many of those groups were not involved in the national discussions.Further, Indigenous involvement and leadership in the Social Forum process did not have a good historical precedent. To ensure ongoing outreach and coordination, it was vital to invest resources in Indigenous participation. So, in February 2007, the USSF created its second staff position and a Native American Outreach Coordinator was hired; and alongside, a Native American Advisory Committee was created to help guide the outreach to Indigenous nations.

Involving More Sectors

Participation by some other sectors, particularly labour, also developed only slowly. This was partly because of the split in the American Federation of Labor-Congress of Industrial Organizations (AFL-CIO) in 2005, which made it difficult to discuss the USSF with any of the unions. Eventually, in December 2006 a Labour Working Group (including independent worker organisations, AFL-CIO, and the new Change to Win labour federation) was established, and the *impact of neo-liberalism on the working class* was included as one of our core issues. Simultaneously the Outreach Working Group began to focus on the peace movement, meeting with anti-war coalitions such as United for Peace and Justice and the Palestinian Solidarity Movement. A Women's Working Group was created to ensure women's participation and leadership, and we also approached Lesbian, Gay, Bisexual, Transgender, Two-Spirited, Intersex, Questioning (LGBTTIQ) leaders and organisations. Given that the Right often uses gender and sexuality as wedge issues in our communities, *liberating gender and sexuality* was integrated as the sixth area of struggle for focus in the plenaries. Taken together, the six areas we had defined by this stage—late 2006—as themes for the Atlanta Forum were as follows:

1) *War and Militarism,*
2) *Gulf Coast Reconstruction,*
3) *Immigrant Rights,*
4) *Indigenous Rights* (the emphasis at first was on energy exploitation on native lands, and later focused on indigenous rights as a whole);
5) the *Impact of Neoliberalism on the Working Class,* and;
6) *Liberating Gender and Sexuality.*

Structure

At the Durham meeting, we had clarified that the NPC would define the overall political direction of the USSF, and that the OC would be an organising body working more directly with the staff. During 2006 however, the division of labour between, and decision-making roles of, the two bodies became unclear. As the OC took on more ongoing coordinating and organising responsibilities, it grew in significance, eventually making decisions that shaped our overall political direction. This tension was not unique to the USSF. We observed similar struggles with the Americas Social Forum. Equally, the WSFIC is currently debating whether to form a Facilitation Group to organise its processes. The USSF OC felt it was critical to resolve this question at the next NPC meeting. In the NPC meeting following the Border Social Forum, some members argued for expanding the staff to coordinate the overall organising process and for creating a Secretariat to fulfil this function. Others proposed flattening the structure and eliminating the OC to broaden participation and decision-making. Finally, the latter proposal was adopted. We agreed that all NPC members would make a concerted, dedicated effort from October 2006 to June 2007, and adopted a theme for the eight-month stretch: *The Road to Atlanta.* This decision eventually set us back. For some, it created a false sense of democracy, because the change did not arouse the required surge in participation; and when several organisations did not step up, this left a structural gap. The sudden lack of a committee driving the organising effort cost us valuable time over the next eight weeks. As a result, the December 2006 NPC meeting created a new Accountability Team (A-Team), mandated to coordinate the overall NPC process. The A-Team worked with lead staff organisers, meeting weekly by conference call, to make short term coordinating decisions, define a process for decisions to be made by the NPC or other bodies, and so on. The A-team, like the OC before it, struggled with its identity as an administrative, facilitating body versus its role as a political leadership body.

Where Are the Funds?

In the U.S., very few foundations and donors support social justice work and, among those that do, grassroots organising is often considered less valid than electoral, media, or legislative strategies. Even those foundations that support grassroots organising were sceptical of the USSF process and doubted the grassroots sector's ability to organise the Forum. This meant that from the start it was difficult to raise funds for the USSF; its eventual success depended on the political will of NPC members who committed staff hours, office space, and other in-kind resources as well as hard cash. It also meant that just four months from the actual Forum, our bare-bones budget of $350,000 wasn't guaranteed! Feedback from our organising work and outreach staff made it clear that lack of funds was the main barrier preventing many organisations and individuals from participating in the USSF. Consequently, and despite its financial crunch, the NPC established a Solidarity Fund and developed criteria that prioritised assistance to the Gulf Coast region, Indigenous nations, particularly in Alaska and the Pacific, working-class communities of colour, and rural communities. Overall, we raised roughly $60,000 for travel stipends.

The 100-Day Countdown

We made important strides in the fifth meeting of the NPC in March 2007. For one, convening the meeting in Chicago helped consolidate the Midwest's participation. However, we were also experiencing new structural challenges. Working groups were operating somewhat independently and we needed to strengthen their integration. Being clear about the political and material commitment of the NPC's member organisations was also crucial. Some organisations were clearly shouldering the bulk of its work, and we needed to know who would be willing to share this burden during the final stretch. We created two documents: one described the political commitment of NPC members, and another documented specific fundraising goals determined by each organisation and the amount they could contribute if we faced a deficit. We also developed a minimum budget and prioritised expenditures if there were to be a shortfall. Translation and interpretation were another concern. Politically, we agreed on the fundamental importance of providing support for multiple languages, but we realised that we only had the capacity to provide interpretation in Spanish and American Sign. At that late date, we had no resources, nor anyone to coordinate this work. Not having money made it difficult to recruit qualified interpreters; but the Chicago meeting had prioritised translation as a top budget item. Eventually, we raised enough resources to cover the costs of a few interpreters.

The Final Stretch

This period was characterised by a great sense of urgency—in the need to address both unresolved logistics issues and political challenges. Although some resources began to come in, we were still well short of our bare-bones budget. Also, we needed to have as clear a picture as possible of the actual programme of the Forum before we convened in Atlanta. We began to map out the Forum's agenda and made final decisions on the overall themes and content for NPC-organised activities. The debate over the plenaries intensified. Following the model of co-generated activities at the 2006 WSF in Caracas, the NPC decided to organise plenaries on each of the *Areas of Struggle* identified in 2006, along with the two later additions. The six final areas were:

1) The Reconstruction of the Gulf Coast in the Post Katrina era: Challenges, visions, and strategies

2) Imperialism, War, Militarism, and Prisons: Towards a U.S. based on peace, economic, and environmental justice

3) Voices of the Indigenous Community: From the heart of Mother Earth

4) Immigrant Rights

5) Gender and Sexual Liberation: Integrating gender and sexuality throughout the Movement

6) Workers' Rights in the Global Economy.

We chose these issues in order to highlight political moments that we understood as opportunities to catalyse a national progressive movement. Each of these was an area in which organising and mobilisation tended to be isolated, and we wanted to encourage a dialogue and promote integration between them. The first debate was whether each plenary would address a single topic, or different topics would be integrated in one plenary, the speakers addressing each separate issue and its relationship with the others. The NPC decided to organise the plenaries by theme. A second debate centred on whether well-known intellectuals or movement celebrities should be invited to speak.

Although they might draw a broader audience, many were concerned that their presence would drown the voices of grassroots organisers. We also wanted to challenge the notion that people working on the ground cannot theorise their struggle. The NPC decided on an 80/20 split, the majority being leaders working on the ground. Thirdly, there was constant pressure to add more plenaries. Several organisations expressed concern that their issues would not get enough visibility if they were not represented in a plenary. But limited time during the Forum meant that the NPC could not make additions, and ultimately we finalised six plenaries. The NPC also struggled to ensure diversity in each of them. Each committee organising plenaries was given guidelines for representation, including ethnic and gender balance, representation by youth, and diversity in sexual orientation. We also realised somewhat late that the USSF was taking place at the same time as the 38th Anniversary of the Stonewall Rebellion. To address this, we established a Queer Visibility Committee to add *diversity in sexual orientation* throughout NPC-organised events and to develop guidelines to ensure that the USSF was a safe and supportive space for queer and transgender people.Of course, and just as in all national and international events, local and the national organising bodies faced challenges about roles, expectations, and responsibilities. We needed to improve the integration and communication between the Atlanta Organising Committee (AOC) and the NPC, and to better coordinate the work of local organisations with the national process. The AOC felt it was not getting a clear picture of the political objectives and nuances of the NPC, and vice-versa. Tensions had arisen between the NPC and AOC over division of labour and authority, and over political conversations that needed to happen and logistical decisions that had to be made. We increased participation by local Atlanta organisers in the NPC meetings; and although this did not resolve tensions, it created greater communication and joint work between the two bodies. Meanwhile, we also approved the proposal for a second USSF to take place in 2010. We were hearing from regional and local organising processes that groups had already begun to talk with each other in an unprecedented way. Possibilities for new collaborations were developing. We saw this as a major success for the USSF, even before the event took place. The NPC decided to call for these processes to continue past the USSF, and for local, regional, sectoral, and thematic dialogues to eventually build towards another USSF.

Trials and Tests

In mid-May 2007, just six weeks before the USSF, a subset of the NPC met in New York City to ensure that all working groups and committees were clear about their goals in the final weeks. The group reviewed plans submitted by working groups and conducted a 'walk-through' of each day of the USSF. This allowed us to envision what would take place, and also note any unaddressed organising gaps and potential problems. In June, the full NPC met in Washington DC to review final preparations. NPC members would now transition from the existing working groups to new teams that would coordinate the event itself. An Integrated Team (iTeam) with members from both the NPC and the AOC was established to address immediate logistical and political questions at the USSF. Each iTeam member was also to liaison with logistical teams such as registration, the tent area, and other major sites for venues, security, and translation. Meanwhile, by now the lack of volunteers had reached crisis level. We estimated that we needed 2,000 volunteer shifts of four hours, and in early June we were still well short of that goal. Fortunately, registrations began to pick up, bringing in a steady stream of revenue. Foundations, meanwhile, were hearing their grantees' excitement about the USSF and began to provide funding. This allowed us to hire adjunct staff in key areas for the final few weeks of the organising process. Security was another concern. The City of Atlanta and the Atlanta Civic Centre required us to hire a private firm for Civic Centre security and allow city police presence at the opening march. With the growth of the prison, police, and security state in the U.S., we couldn't invite extremely oppressed communities to the Forum and then bring in security that implemented policies they were fighting. Since we couldn't count on hired security to uphold our principles, we created our own system of volunteers for security. Members of the NPC experienced in movement security helped develop a security plan from a social movement perspective. The NPC decided to set aside time on the fourth day for regional and issue-based caucuses. Alongside, a working group of the NPC also organised a People's Movements Assembly (PMA), modelled on the Social Movements Assembly process that has evolved within the WSF. The process was advertised in advance of the Forum, encouraging organisations to bring resolutions and declarations to the USSF, and the last day was dedicated primarily to the PMA, with fifty declarations to be presented. At the time of writing, resolutions and declarations are still being accepted. They will be compiled and published on the USSF website for organisations, with a timeline of movement activities.[6]

Significance of the USSF Itself

One of the most enduring lessons that arose from the three-year process of organising the USSF is that we must keep evaluating, theorising, and putting back into practice what we learn. We—the NPC, as a whole—organised the USSF because we knew that we, in the United States, have a responsibility to challenge our own government and corporations; and our own prejudices. The USSF came to be the largest gathering of progressive organisations in the history of the U.S.—not to mention the largest convergence of anti-racist organisations rooted in oppressed communities of colour. The political imperative for radical social change helped us focus on the operational unity needed to ensure the success of the USSF. It was no accident that the NPC's composition differed so drastically from other U.S. movement spaces: our demographic spread was roughly 85% people of colour, 64% women, 51% under the age of 40, and 15% queer identified. This affected the composition of the USSF itself, who came, who spoke, what issues got highlighted, and how we did our work. We believe that one of the most important outcomes out of this process was the relationships built within the NPC. For those of us who served on the NPC, it was the first time that our organisations and networks worked together, and we were able in most cases to build trust, a sense of camaraderie, and to leave our comfort zones to work with people we might not know or like. We believe that within the ranks of this NPC is a core of leadership with functional unity that will impact the next crucial decade of movement-building in this country. While more time and much exchange are needed to sum up the gathering, we are proud to have played a role in bringing it into being.

Another World is Possible! Another U.S. is Necessary!

Notes

1. Content Editors for this essay are Vipul Rikhi and Parvati Sharma.
2. See essay by Judy Rebick this volume. Also Ponniah 2007, Rebick 2007, Sherman, July 2007, and Uhlenbeck, July 2007. For an archive of essays on the U.S. Social Forum, http://www.openspaceforum.net/twiki/tiki-index.php?page=SocialForums%3AUSSocialForum.
3. *Ibid.*, Rebick in this volume, Ponniah 2007.
4. See, for instance, Martinez, 2000.
5. Kromm and Sturgis, August/September 2007.
6. See <https://www.ussf2007.org/>

Asterix On The St Lawrence

Pierre Beaudet

From August 23 to 27 2007, over 5,000 people came to meet, talk, observe, strategise, explore, argue, and have fun during the Quebec Social Forum held in downtown Montreal. It was in many ways an extraordinary gathering, reflecting the richness, the scope, and the contradictions of a quite singular social movement in North America. Like the small Gaulois village where Asterix once lived, endlessly resisting Roman barbarism and aggression, the Quebec 'village' stands out from surroundings.[1] But we need to take a brief detour through history before getting into the dynamics of the Forum and the momentum that led to it.

The Not-So-Quiet Revolution of the 1960s

Quebec society has had a particular trajectory to it, linked to its conquest by the British Empire (1763) and the defeat of the national-democratic revolution (1837-38). As in many other parts of the world, British domination consolidated itself through various forms of 'indirect rule' that made the local elite (particularly the Catholic clergy) the managers of the Empire in Quebec. For over a hundred and thirty years, that deal kept the predominantly French speaking population under the yoke of a barbaric and archaic State.[2] But waves upon waves of popular and working class struggles slowly eroded that power, such that by the early 1960s the cracks were all too visible.

Quebec and Canada: The Prolonged Crisis

The land that is today called 'Canada' was first colonised by French settlers in the 1700s who pushed out Aboriginal communities.[3] By and large, they entered the land through the St Lawrence River valley, around which present-day Quebec is organised. In 1763, the region was conquered by the emerging British Empire. But by then, the Saint Lawrence Valley was already occupied by a large group of French-speaking inhabitants. In 1837, these communities led a republican and national uprising that was defeated. In 1867, the Empire gave the local Anglo-Canadian elite the power to create a Canadian State based on a certain devolution of power to 'provinces,' including Quebec where the majority of French-speaking people reside.[4]

Political crises of a nationalist nature erupted several times in the 20th century, but the movement really took off only from the 1960s onwards. A new radical nationalism took shape in Quebec based on the popular and middle classes expressing their will to disengage from English Canada while putting forward an agenda of social transformation. That movement was later captured by a rising Quebec bourgeoisie who created a nationalist political formation, the *Parti Québécois* (PQ), which won the provincial elections in 1976, thus triggering a new cycle of political fragility. Two referendums on independence were held (in 1980 and 1995), leaving the Nationalists defeated—but only just.

In this subsequent and more recent period, the Canadian State has been reorganised under the shadow of neoliberal policies with its elites looking south (to the USA) for business and ideology, and for integrating Canada in a sort of North-South axis, therefore weakening the more traditional east-west patterns. This is likely to create more turbulence in the near future.

Class and nation in Quebec actually merged to create a strong social and national movement expressing the aspirations of a young and urbanised proletariat, with its expression through the *Parti Québécois*. Canadian (mostly Anglo) elites started to waver in front of this movement. The dominant bloc within the PQ also split, leaving more and more space for popular protest.

This movement wich later came to be called the *quiet revolution* in Quebec was the combination of two contradictory processes: on the one hand, the emergence of a popular movement largely influenced by the Catholic Left, independent unionism, and student radicalism, and later evolving towards various forms of radical nationalism influenced by anti-colonial and anti-imperialist movements in the world[5]; and on the other, the irruption of a 'moderate' pro-capitalist nationalist elite, drifting slowly but surely towards the idea of creating an independent national State.

Masses and Movements Up and Down

By the early 1970s, Quebec was the site of major struggles and, in particular, of the most important strikes in the western world after Italy. From the general strike of 1972 down to continuous unrest involving proletarians, urban dwellers, communities, and students, the movement was radical, rebellious, and autonomous.[6] In 1976 however, the nationalist elite that had created the PQ won the provincial election which really shocked the Canadian establishment. But from immediately after that, and in reaction, the elite in Canada started to reorganise itself and soon positioned itself to launch a global counter offensive that successfully destabilised more local social struggles.

For the social and political movements in Quebec, the decline was steep and led to various attempts to create substitutist and illusory vanguard parties that slowly vanished in the 1980s. In the meantime, the nationalist elites consolidated their grip over the political space locking out the popular movement. They went so far as aligning themselves with the U.S. through the twisted logic of 'the enemy of my enemy (the Canadian establishment) is my friend' argument, and supported the North American Free Trade Agreement (NAFTA) signed in 1994.[7]

The Comeback

After years of stagnation in social struggles, the *Fédération des Femmes du Québec* (FFQ, or 'Quebec Women's Federation') in 1995 launched a spectacular march against poverty and violence against women. Registered only in 1996, the FFQ—as a federation of several hundred affiliated groups—already had major roots in most parts of Quebec, and was able to mobilise an extraordinary rainbow coalition of not only women's organisations but also popular and trade union groups. The initiative led to hundreds and later thousands of women and men marching through the villages and cities of Quebec. More than a march, the FFQ mobilisation was highly successful in involving masses of young and not so young people around a fairly open platform of social justice.[8]

During the same period however, the turmoil of neoliberal globalisation was starting to seriously affect popular classes in Quebec through massive cutbacks in health, education, and social security. Dormant trade unions that had capitulated to the nationalist elites were forced to take stock. A new social animal started to emerge against and beyond globalisation and focused on NAFTA. In April 2001, that movement finally came out in the open, with thousands of protesters grouping as part of the Summit of the People in Quebec City, actually blockading the Official Summit there of the thirty-four heads of states in the Americas (every head of state except Fidel Castro).[9]

A large delegation of South American popular movements also came to Quebec for this action, and they all later came together in a vast Social Alliance that played a big role in debunking the *Free Trade Agreement of the Americas* (FTAA) that was elaborated by U.S. and Canadian elites to extend NAFTA.[10]

The success of the People's Summit gave a huge boost to the emerging multi-class alliance rooted in the communities throughout Quebec. And so in

2003, when a new hard-line neoliberal government was elected (defeating the nationalist), social movements came to the forefront paralysing the 'reforms' that were put on the agenda. Once again, women's groups, community organisations, and youth collectives played the principal roles, with trade unions tailing more or less combatively.

Equally, in March 2003 immense anti-war demonstrations took place against the imminent attacks against Iraq, bringing into the streets of all major cities of Quebec something like one adult out of four, in a show of force that obliged the Canadian government to stay away from the U.S. aggression.[11]

And most recently, in 2005 the movement exploded again with a massively popular student general strike that technically speaking was a protest against a proposed hike of fees, but more fundamentally was against the commodification of education. With public opinion behind them, 250,000 students came out and won!

Internationalisation of the Movement

During the 1990s, the Quebec movement made new international connections, mostly in the context of the growing hemispheric resistance against FTAA. Common strategies were elaborated with Mexican, Brazilian, Argentinean, and Cuban organisations, also via linkages in the United States and English Canada.

In 2001, before the People's Summit in Quebec City, an important Quebec delegation of trade unionists and alterglobalists attended the first World Social Forum, in Porto Alegre, Brazil. By 2002, the numbers of people attending the WSF from Quebec were greatly multiplied. They now involved alterglobalist movements like the Montreal-based *Alternatives*, trade unions, and more and more young activists. Up to 500 activists went from Quebec.

Participation from Quebec has continued to grow at the subsequent Forums in Brazil, India, Mali, Venezuela, Pakistan, Kenya, and elsewhere. All in all, over 5,000 people from Quebec have now participated in the WSF process since its beginning in 2001. The match was instant and instinctive. The idea of social movements coming together, strategising together (without a pre-established blueprint), avoiding unnecessary sectarian strife, and above all, resisting subordination to narrow political platforms, was somehow 'natural.' In many ways, the major ingredients of the WSF 'soup,' captured in its famous Charter of Principles, were already in the 'genetic code' of the social movement in Quebec.[12]

Politicising the Social and Socialising the Political

In the most recent period, this evolution has continued in the social movement. Distinctly however, the labour movements that used to be at the forefront in the 1970s are tailing. For sure, the impact of the neoliberal restructuring also taking place in Quebec is leading to a fragmented proletariat, and this is taking its toll. At the ideological level, the social democratic and Keynesian 'instincts' of the trade unions have been paralysed by the gloomy atmosphere. Post- and ex-proletarians are constantly drifting in and out, reconstituting nomadic and flexible organisational identities, through all sorts of resistances. The historical strength of the movement, which is founded on its capacity to coalesce, enables it to resist—because in this form, it remains mobile and creative.

Although the dominant elites are organising large-scale offensives, the movement has shown itself capable of throwing big grains of sand into the gears. For example, it has successfully blocked huge pseudo 'development' projects in the cities, involving the gentrification of working class neighbourhoods. Faced with the prospect of a right-wing fallout of the nationalist movement, it has also made attempts to reinvent itself as a political coalition. This was finally created in 2006 under the soft name of *Québec Solidaire* (QS, or 'Solidary Quebec'). This new formation has a wide appeal, related perhaps to the fact that a former President of the FFQ, Françoise David, heads it.

More importantly, the QS is formed to insure it does not centralize the social movements that provide it with support.[13] It brings together not only the multiple variants of the Left (from ex- and post- communists to dissident anarcho-libertarians and critical social democrats) but also a substantial percentage of social activists involved in labour, women, student, and community struggles.[14]

Why Not a Quebec Social Forum?

The idea of organising a Forum in Quebec had been on the table for some time. It was first conceived between seminars and hard drinks in the heat of the WSF in Porto Alegre, 2003. Members of *Alternatives* and a few associates developed the grandiose idea of bringing together social movements from Quebec, English Canada, and the First Nations. That dream was later opposed by the leadership of the trade unions who considered this too closely related to the thinking of the radical alterglobalists. By and large, important sectors of the trade unions have remained fearful of confronting neoliberalism head on, preferring instead to negotiate the terms by which it can be softened or 'humanised.'

But as time went by and ideas developed, the concept was adopted and developed by the Urban Ecology Centre in cooperation with a large Montreal-based urban partnership that organised four 'Citizen's Summits' from 2001 to 2007, bringing together hundreds of community activists. Successful regional Social Forums were also organised in smaller towns and in some of the popular neighbourhoods of Montreal like Pointe Saint Charles or Villeray.

Early in 2007, the idea of a Quebec Forum was re-launched by an enlarged coalition involving at its core the *Confédération des Syndicats Nationaux* (CSN, or the 'Confederation of National Labour Unions,' one of the labour federations that have traditionally leaned towards the Left), *Alternatives*, the FFQ, Left Christian groups, and a range of regional coalitions. It also got the attention of the Aboriginal movements in Quebec through their own structures (the Assembly of First Nations). A series of accountable structures were very rapidly put in place along with considerable resources provided by the movements themselves.[15] The idea that the Forum needed to be an 'open space' and not some sort of defining moment of the Left, was never discussed, because from the start this intention was assumed to be at the core of the process. There was never any tension or controversy about the fact that the event was for and by social movements, and was meant as a creative, inclusive, and open-ended process.

Canadian Social Forum Or Quebec Social Forum?

In the early stages, Quebec and Canadian social movements tried to work together in the spirit of the WSF calling for a 'tripartite' Forum involving also the Aboriginal communities and organisations. But rapidly, that project proved to be too ambitious. It appears that social movements across the Ottawa river had already concluded that Quebec had become *de facto* if not *de jure* a separate country, at least at the level of civil society. For English Canadians, this is a sort of enigma. Although some parts of the radical Left recognise the national character of Quebec and support the right to self-determination, mainstream organisations like trade unions and the social democratic NDP have not been able to cope with this phenomenon. Is this a 'great power chauvinism' or simply ignorance? On the Quebec side, social movements have been influenced by different brands of radical nationalism focusing on the creation of an independent and progressive State, and not a 'reform' of Canada. Today the options are clearly demarcated and it is unlikely that the polarisation will be reversed.

Who Was There?

The Quebec Social Forum was structured around self-organised activities that took centre stage, with over 400 workshops and panels along eight axes:

Human rights and the struggle for equality of peoples;

Environment and ecology;

Public services and the common good;

Labour, trade unions, social economy;

Arts, culture, communication;

Citizen participation, democracy and people's power;

International solidarity, peace and anti-imperialism; and

Ethics, spirituality and religions.

This programme was conceived and elaborated by three large general assemblies prior to the Forum, in all comprising over 100 organisations. In the Forum itself, around 5,000 participants took part. The inspiration for the decentralized format was the WSF Charter of Principles.

In substance, participation was massive, across the spectrum of social movements from all the different regions of Quebec.[16] Women's organisations, student groups, and community-based groups working on health, day-care, education, and food security, were present en masse. The age of the participants was widely distributed with the predominance of the under 30s.

Immigrant groups and Aboriginal organisations were also visible throughout, both in their own panels and as invited by other labour and community organisations. For Aboriginals or First Nations, the principle of their struggle of self-determination was widely publicised and supported throughout the Forum. Because of the right-wing onslaught against immigrants and refugees, particularly Muslims and Arabs, many discussions targeted that particular challenge, emphasising the necessity of regrouping and fighting together.

Finally, most of the trade unions also came in force, except the *Fédération des Travailleurs du Québec* (FTQ, or the 'Quebec Workers' Federation'), the largest labour federation in Quebec, which boycotted the Forum primarily because it felt the Forum was critical of its pro-PQ policies. What was interesting however, was the participation despite this, of newly organised segments of labour from both the public and private sectors, by and large representing precarious labour conditions of workers in the service sector.[17]

Politically speaking, there was ample creative space for intellectuals and Left activists from different political formations, but with an obviously overwhelming presence of *Quebec Solidaire*.

At another level, over 150 foreign guests also took part, mostly from South America, the United States, Europe, and the Middle East. The historical linkages with South America, dating from the time of the Left Catholics in the 1960s until later battles in the 1990s against the FTAA, created a critical mass of solidarity at a practical level, among likeminded groups engaged in common struggles, strategies, and perspectives.

As often happens in productive Social Forums, the discussion was as much 'outside' the formal settings as 'inside' the workshops and panels. There was a huge outdoor location called the Ecofest, with exhibits, kiosks, performances (with over 150 artists), and free food (for 5,000 people, including many homeless). More importantly perhaps, the external activities were heavily green-focussed with a whole range of activities on roof gardening, compost production, and green agriculture.

As it has become the case with the WSF process, the last day of the Forum was taken over by a thousand social movement activists who agreed on a global platform related to the call by the WSF for a *global day of action* on 26 January 2008.

The one and only big deficit was the lack of participation of the English Canadian social movements. Two major reasons can explain this deficit: on the one hand, social movements in (English) Canada are currently weak, moreso than in the past. Canadian trade unions in particular are in full retreat faced with hard-line federal government. On the other hand, and as mentioned before, civil societies from both sides of the Ottawa River have perhaps internalised the idea that Quebec independence has become inevitable, even if not acceptable. In the mind of this writer, this might become one of the biggest challenges for social movements, both in Quebec and in Canada, in the near future.

Movements of Movements and Networks of Networks

Like many (but not all) Forums, the QSF was by and large a success. It brought the different components of the movement together. It forced (or encouraged) participants to think, reflect, and analyse. For example, the more or less four hundred workshops were resourced by a thousand participants who took the time to prepare and organise their thinking. Small working groups were set up to support that, widely using the internet of course.

At the end of the day, the ultra-decentralised nature of the Forum and its vast colouring socially and politically makes it difficult to draw conclusions that would not be premature. However, at least a few trends are visibly emerging. One was a general capacity on the part of the participants, rooted in communities and social activism, to focus on 'hard' issues like political power, imperialism, and the State. The tone was more explicit, as if people were massively willing to name the enemy more precisely, for instance, capitalism. Call it a re-politicisation of the movement: olitics understood as the struggle for power.

At another level, some of the inhibitions of the past, like a certain shyness about the idea of a progressive political platform, are fading, allowing the political process larger spaces to invest in, including (but not exclusively) through *Quebec Solidaire*. More and more, movements do not want yet another political party 'leaning toward the Left,' but something different. QS appears as one (out of many) 'tools' for widening the web, enlarging the alliances, and strengthening the visible and invisible threads between movements and the movements of movements.

Is it capable of responding to the call? It is too early to say. If QS does not come out of the box and invent new modes of political communication and mobilisation, it will probably become the left-wing of the nationalist movement. If it does, then there is a large space out there to occupy at the local, national, and international levels.

One of the difficulties in this endless dialogue between the 'social' and the 'political' is the questionable capacity to reconcile the two distinct 'moments' of the struggle: the short-term political moment and the long-term, more cultural and social, moment. What was interesting at the QSF was that we did not waste time on easy 'magic formulas' but focused on the will to constitute counter-hegemonies through 'wars of positions' involving patient and in-depth movement building, as indicated by the overriding nature and tone of the discussions.

At another level, the QSF and its participants expressed a very tough, realist stand in the face of the current (and upcoming) neoliberal onslaught. Dominant elites in Canada and certainly in the U.S., with whom the Quebec elites are associated, are coming hard on two fronts: first, to destroy the legacy of Keynesianism, and second, to criminalise dissent and jump on to the bandwagon of the U.S.-led 'endless war. Although in many ways the social movement has won the 'battle of ideas' and gained widespread legitimacy and support, it is still looking for ways to challenge the neoliberal elites at the highest levels. But these elites are also not wavering. On the contrary, they are becoming more violent, bolder, and more aggressive, transforming the State into a mere tool to repress and criminalise popular classes; the Guantanamoisation of society.

For sure in North America, hard times are ahead of us, including in our big Quebec village. And just as surely, Asterix will be tested again.

Notes

1. Asterix is a widely known character in a series of comic books published in France and distributed throughout the Francophone and Anglophone worlds since the 1960s. In these worlds, his resistance in what was then Gaul (now within present-day France) to the Roman Empire bulldozing everything in sight has become a sort of metaphor for the 'small guys' standing up to the big ones.
2. On the genesis of the Canadian State, see Stanley Brehaut Ryerson, 1973.
3. The land was named 'Canada,' and is still called this, by the immigrant, settler communities, and through them by the wider world. The Aboriginal communities refer to the land as Turtle Island.
4. There are seven million people living in Quebec (out of a total of thirty four million in Canada). Over 85% of the population is French speaking, with a still small but growing part of that majority coming from immigrant communities like the Haitians and the Lebanese. There are also over 200,000 Aboriginals (sometimes called 'First Nations') in Quebec. [Eds: A smaller but still significant number of French-speaking settlers also live in other parts of Canada, both east of Quebec and further west.]
5. The social movement in Quebec became distanced from popular and trade union movements taking place in the rest of Canada, partly because of its view of nationalism as a vehicle for social transformation, and partly because of the refusal of the Left in English Canada to recognise the importance of the national struggle in Quebec.
6. Most of the documentation about this period is in French. There are translations of key documents on the website of the Socialist History Project (http://www.socialisthistory.ca/).
7. See Brunelle April 1999, and also the chapter by Dorval Brunelle in this book.
8. The FFQ (www.ffq.qc.ca) also came to be known widely in the world because it took the lead in launching an international women's march that took off in 2002 in several countries with hundreds of women's groups participating across continents; now known as the World March of Women, www.marchemondiale.org. (See also its most recent declaration, in this book.)
9. See Drainville 2004.

10. See Dorval Brunelle's chapter in this book.

11. Over 250,000 people came out in Montreal, in February 2003, a city of less than 2 million. In English Canada, the anti-war demonstrations were also strong, but not to the same extent.

12. For the WSF Charter, see this book.

13. QS went into its first election in 2007 and got nearly 4% of the vote. David and her co-chair of the party got nearly 20% of the vote each in their respective ridings.

14. In many ways, QS acts as a 'non political' political party. For example, it refuses to focus on a leader; instead, there are two 'spokespersons.' Its programme is more a reference document than a rigid platform, and is constantly reshaped by permanent commissions. Commissions and working groups are open to non–members.

15. Most of the expenses were paid by contributions from trade unions and a few sympathetic NGOs, with a trickle from the City of Montreal. Registration @ $20 per person also brought in close to Can$100,000.

16. The population of more or less seven million is split between the large metropolitan area of Montreal (3m) and other regions spread out over a vast territory.

17. As in most western societies, the changes imposed by neoliberalism have fragmented and weakened (but not smashed) the 'traditional' working class in industry.

THE BAMAKO APPEAL

Forum for Another Mali, World Forum for Alternatives (France), Third World Forum (Senegal), ENDA (Senegal), and others, January 2006[1]

I. Introduction

More than five years of worldwide gatherings of people and organisations who oppose neo-liberalism have provided an experience leading to the creation of a new collective conscience. The social forums—world, thematic, continental, or national—and the Assembly of Social Movements have been the principal architects of this conscience. Meeting in Bamako on Jan. 18, 2006, on the eve of the opening of the Polycentric World Social Forum, the participants during this day dedicated to the 50th anniversary of the Bandung Conference have expressed the need to define alternate goals of development, creating a balance of societies, abolishing exploitation by class, gender, race and caste, and marking the route to a new relation of forces between North and South.

The Bamako Appeal aims at contributing to the emergence of a new popular and historical subject, and at consolidating the gains made at these meetings. It seeks to advance the principle of the right to an equitable existence for everyone; to affirm a collective life of peace, justice and diversity; and to promote the means to reach these goals at the local level and for all of humanity.

In order that an historical subject come into existence—one that is diverse, multipolar, and from the people—it is necessary to define and promote alternatives capable of mobilising social and political forces. The goal is a radical transformation of the capitalist system. The destruction of the planet and of millions of human beings, the individualist and consumerist culture that accompanies and nourishes this system, along with its imposition by imperialist powers are no longer tolerable, since what is at stake is the existence of humanity itself. Alternatives to the wastefulness and destructiveness of capitalism draw their strength from a long tradition of popular resistance that also embraces all of the short steps forward indispensable to the daily life of the system's victims.

The Bamako Appeal, built around the broad themes discussed in subcommittees, expresses the commitment to:

(i) Construct an internationalism joining the peoples of the South and the North who suffer the ravages engendered by the dictatorship of financial markets and by the uncontrolled global deployment of the transnational firms;

(ii) Construct the solidarity of the peoples of Asia, Africa, Europe, and the Americas confronted with challenges of development in the 21st century;

(iii) Construct a political, economic and cultural consensus that is an alternative to militarised and neo-liberal globalisation and to the hegemony of the United States and its allies.

II. The Principles

1. Construct a world founded on the solidarity of human beings and peoples: Our epoch is dominated by the imposition of competition among workers, nations and peoples. However, historically the principle of solidarity has played a role much more conducive to the efficient organisation of intellectual and material production. We want to give to this principle of solidarity the place it deserves and diminish the role of competition.

2. Construct a world founded on the full affirmation of citizenship and equality of the sexes: The politically active citizen must ultimately become responsible for the management of all the aspects of social, political, economic and cultural life. This is the condition for an authentic affirmation of democracy. Without this, the human being is reduced by the laws imposed on him or her to a mere provider of labour power, an impotent spectator confronted with decisions handed down by those in charge, a consumer propelled toward the worst waste. The affirmation, in law and in deed, of the absolute equality of sexes is an integral part of authentic democracy. One of the conditions of this democracy is the eradication of all forms of the patriarchy, either admitted or hidden.

3. Construct a universal civilisation offering in all areas the full potential of creative development to all its diverse members: For neo-liberalism, the affirmation of the individual—not that of the politically active citizen—allows the spread of the best human qualities. The capitalist system's unbearable isolation, imposed on the individual, produces its own illusory antidote: imprisonment in the ghettos of alleged common identities, most often those of a para-ethnic and or para-religious type. We want to construct a universal civilisation that looks to the future without nostalgia; one in which the political di-

versity of citizens and cultural and political differences of nations and peoples become the means of reinforcing individual creative development.

4. Construct socialisation through democracy: Neo-liberal policies aim to impose as the sole method of socialisation the force of the market, whose destructive impact on the majority of human beings no longer needs to be demonstrated. The world we want conceives sociability as the principle product of a democratisation without boundaries. In this framework, in which the market has a place but not the predominant place, economy and finance should be put at the service of a societal program; they should not be subordinated to the imperatives of dominant capital that favour the private interests of a tiny majority. The radical democracy that we want to promote re-establishes the creative force of political innovation as a fundamental human attribute. It bases social life on the production and reproduction of an inexhaustible diversity, and not on a manipulated consensus that eliminates all meaningful discussions and leaves dissidents weakened and trapped in ghettoes.

5. Construct a world founded on the recognition of the non-market- driven law of nature and of the resources of the planet and of its agricultural soil: The capitalist neo-liberal model aims at submitting all aspects of social life, almost without exception, to the status of a commodity. The process of privatisation and marketisation to the ultimate degree brings with it devastating results on a scale without precedent in human history: the threat to the fundamental biogeochemical processes of the planet; destruction of biodiversity through the undermining of ecosystems, the waste of vital resources (oil and water in particular); the annihilation of peasant societies threatened by massive expulsion from their land. All these areas of society-nature metabolism must be managed as the common wealth and in accordance with the basic needs of all of humanity. In these areas, the decisions must be based not on the market but on the political powers of nations and peoples.

6. Construct a world founded on the recognition of the non-market-driven status of cultural products and scientific acquisitions, of education and of health care: Neo-liberal policies lead to turning cultural products into commodities and to the privatisation of the most important social services, notably those of health and education. This option is accompanied by the mass production of low quality para-cultural products, the submission of research to the exclusive

priority of short-term profits, the degradation of education and health care for the poorest sectors of the people, including even their exclusion. The reinstatement and expansion of these public services should reinforce the satisfaction of needs and rights essential to education, health care and providing food.

7. Promote policies that closely associate democracy without pre-assigned limits, with social progress and the affirmation of autonomy of nations and peoples: Neo-liberal policies deny the preconditions of social progress—that some claim are a spontaneous product of the market—preconditions such as the autonomy of nations and peoples, necessary to the correction of inequalities. Under the regime of market hegemony, democracy is emptied of all effective content, made vulnerable and compromised in the extreme. To affirm an authentic democracy demands giving to social progress its determining place in the management of all aspects of social, political, economic and cultural life. The diversity of nations and of peoples produced by history, in all its positive aspects along with the inequalities that accompany them, demands the affirmation of autonomy of peoples and nations. There does not exist a unique universal recipe in the political or economic spheres that would permit any bypassing of this autonomy. The task of building equality necessarily requires a diversity of means to carry it out.

8. Affirm the solidarity of the people of the north and the south in the construction of an internationalism on an anti-imperialist basis: The solidarity of all the peoples—of the North and of the South—in the construction of a universal civilisation cannot be founded on the illusory notion that it is possible simply to ignore the conflicts of interest that separate different classes and nations that make up the real world. Such genuine solidarity must necessarily transcend the antagonisms inherent to capitalism and imperialism. The regional organisations behind the alternative globalisation movement must seek to strengthen the autonomy and the solidarity of nations and of peoples on the five continents. This perspective is in contradiction to that of the present dominant model of regionalisation, conceived as consisting of mere building blocks of neo-liberal globalisation. Fifty years after Bandung, the Bamako Appeal calls for a Bandung of the peoples of the South, victims of really existing capitalism, and the rebuilding of a peoples' front of the South able to hold in check both the imperialism of the dominant economic powers and U.S. military hegemony. Such an anti-imperialist front would not oppose the peoples of

the South to those of the North. On the contrary, it would constitute the basis of a global internationalism associating them all together in the building of a common civilisation in its diversity.

III. Long-Term Objectives and Proposals for Immediate Action

In order to progress from a collective conscience to the building of collective, popular, plural and multipolar actors, it has always been necessary to identify precise themes to formulate strategies and concrete proposals. The themes of the Bamako Appeal deal with the following 10 fields, including both long-term goals and proposals for immediate action: The political organisation of globalisation; the economic organisation of the world system; the future of peasant societies; the building of a workers' united front; regionalisation for the benefit of the peoples; the democratic management of the societies; gender equality; the sustainable management of the resources of the planet; the democratic management of the media and the cultural diversity; and the democratisation of international organisations.

The Bamako Appeal is an invitation to all the organisations of struggle representative of the vast majorities that comprise the working classes of the globe, to all those excluded from the neoliberal capitalist system, and to all people and political forces who support these principles—to work together in order to put into effect the new collective conscience, as an alternative to the present system of inequality and destruction.

Proposals of The Bamako Appeal

Only by building synergies and solidarity beyond geographical and regional borders is it possible to find methods of action that can lead to real alternatives in this globalised world. Working groups will continue during the year to inquire further into and concretise the topics addressed below, to prepare for the next meeting and to propose strategic priorities for action:[2]

1. For A Multipolar World System Founded On Peace, Law, And Negotiation
2. For An Economic Reorganisation Of The Global System
3. For Regionalisations In The Service Of The People And Which Reinforce The South In Global Negotiations
4. For The Democratic Management Of The Planet's Natural Resources
5. For A Better Future For Peasant Farmers

1) Proposals to assure food sovereignty:
   —At the national level
   —At the sub-regional level
   —At the international level
2) Short-term proposals to prevent the Doha Round and the Economic Partnership Agreement

6. To Build A Workers' United Front

7. For A Democratisation Of Societies As A Necessary Step To Full Human Development

8. For The Eradication Of All Forms Of Oppression, Exploitation, And Alienation Of Women

9. For The Democratic Management Of The Media And Cultural Diversity

1) For the right to education
2) For the right to information and the right to inform:
   —Initiatives towards the large media
   —To support the alternative media
   —Don't allow the television networks of the North a monopoly of the images broadcast to the world
3) For the right to express oneself in one's language

10. For The Democratisation Of International Organisations And The Institutionalisation Of A Multipolar International Order.

Note

1. Editors' Note: The Bamako Appeal was sponsored by the World Forum for Alternatives, the Third World Forum, Forum for Another Mali, and ENDA, Senegal. Samir Amin and François Houtart, both of the World Forum on Alternatives, were the key people behind the Bamako Appeal initiative, which was launched at a meeting in Bamako, Mali, on January 18-19 2007, the day before the start of the polycentric World Social Forum held at Bamako. The Appeal was then circulated on the NIGD listserve on 7 February 2006, after receipt from Samir Amin. The full text of the Appeal, including the signatories to the Appeal and other details as received from François Houtart, is available @ http://thirdworldforum.net/fren/index.htm and @ http://www.openspaceforum.net/twiki/tiki-read_article.php?articleId=66.

2 In this section, and because of space limitations, we give only the headlines/titles of the topics that, in the full Appeal, are followed by discussion and proposals. For the full text, see the link given in note 1 above.

CALL FROM THE CARACAS SOCIAL MOVEMENTS ASSEMBLY JANUARY 2006[1]

Call from the Social Movements Assembly held in the Teresa Carreño Theatre in the polycentric World Social Forum in Caracas, Venezuela, on the morning of January 29 2006.

In recent years, the popular struggles against neo-liberalism and imperialism in the Americas and in other parts of the World have generated a crisis of legitimacy for the neo-liberal system and its institutions. The most recent expressions of this are the defeat of the FTAA in Mar del Plata and the Agreement for a European Constitution in France and Holland.

We live in a time in which military intervention by the United States and European governments and their allies is the order of the day in order to control and pillage the riches of the planet, or to abort the processes of liberation and deny the peoples' sovereignty to control their own destiny; at times with the collusion of the local elite.

During this time in Latin America, we have seen an explosion of mobilisations against free trade, militarisation, and privatisation, and in defence of natural resources and food sovereignty. In some countries, these mobilisations have translated into alternative politics rising to government, emerging from the groundswell of popular struggles.

The most recent example of this process is the victory of Evo Morales in Bolivia. Its origin lies in the struggle against the privatisation of water and the grassroots, peasants, workers, and indigenous struggles which have been developing in this country since 2000.

Therefore, in the face of announcements by transnational corporations such as Repsol (and others) to withdraw their planned investments as a means to place conditions on the new government's policies, especially in terms of the recuperation of natural resources, this Assembly calls upon the workers' unions of these companies, and the social movements in the countries where they are located, to stop this blackmail from happening and to diligently monitor these companies in order to guarantee the sovereignty of the people and of the Bolivian government to freely make their own political choices.

In the face of the access to government by alternative politics related to popular struggle, we, social movements, must maintain our political and programmatic autonomy, driving social mobilisation to achieve our goals and apply pressure to prevent any adaptation by these governments of the neo-liberal model.

Finally, the social movements gathered during this World Social Forum in Caracas, in our commitment to confront the neo-liberal model, imperialism, and war, will advance in four central campaigns throughout the year 2006:

1. International Day of Mobilisation Against the Occupation of Iraq, March 18
Against the war and occupations: No more wars, peace is the only solution!

We demand the immediate and unconditional withdrawal of foreign troops from Iraq and an end to the privatisation of energy resources.

We oppose all occupations by foreign troops and, as such, we call for an end to the Israeli occupation of Palestine and for the creation of an independent Palestinian State.

We oppose the threats of occupation of Syria, Iran, and of Latin America countries through the Plan Colombia, military bases, and other means, as well as the use of economic embargos as a weapon of war, such as the US embargo against Cuba.

We demand the disarmament and elimination of nuclear weapons and weapons of mass destruction.

We demand respect for human rights, civil liberties, and an end to tortures, kidnappings, and illegal detentions, including secret prisons.

We call upon all to mobilise on March 18, 2006 for a global day of protest against the occupation of Iraq, as part of the global campaign that will continue until the foreign troops in Iraq are withdrawn.

We also call for participation in the conference in Cairo (Egypt) against US hegemony and the occupation of Iraq, which will be held on March 24-27, 2006.

2. Against the Conclusion of the WTO Doha Round
After the ministerial meeting of the WTO in Hong Kong, which in spite of great efforts, popular movements were unable to stop, the ministerial declaration of the WTO now opens the way for finalising free trade negotiations within the

Doha Round. The agreement on this declaration was the fruit of European Union and United States intimidation tactics, as well as the decisive role played by the governments of Brazil and India in their choice to obtain a place in the power structure of the WTO.

Despite this, all is not lost. In the next three months, the WTO has to conduct complex negotiations and the social movements must carry out campaigns and common actions that put pressure on the governments to reverse the outcomes of Hong Kong, in order to derail the WTO in the next meeting of the General Council, in May 2006.

3. Against the G-8 Summit, July 2006, in Saint Petersburg, Russia
Following on the convening of social movements and organisations of Russia, we call on the people of that country, and on all social movements and organisations that share the principles of peace, democracy, and social justice, to resist and to support our initiatives by participating in the People's Counter Summit, in opposition to the G8 Summit in Saint Petersburg to be held in July. Contact: alternativy@tochka.ru

4. Against the World Bank and IMF Annual Summit, September 2006
The Social Movements Assembly adopts the call from the Peoples of the South Assembly for an international day of direct action confronting the headquarters of the IMF and the WB in several countries, coinciding with the annual meetings of these institutions in September 2006.

It will be a mobilisation day to denounce the illegitimacy of the financial debt imposed on the countries of the South, and to defend their repudiation and non-payment, together with a recognition of the peoples of the South as creditors of an immense historical, social, and ecological debt, whose restitution and reparation we demand.

Beyond these four central campaigns, the VI World Social Forum in Caracas has been a convening point for movements to promote several networks and campaigns, whose resolutions are listed below:

Against the FTAA
The Continental Social Alliance calls for maintaining a continental alert against any possible attempt to revive FTAA negotiations in any of its forms, and to forward the struggle against bilateral or regional free trade agreements in Central America, the Andean region, the Caribbean, and the new generation of agreements promoted by the United States, as expressed in the North Amer-

ican Security and Prosperity agreement, which furthers subordinate integration to the United States, including the area of "security."

We also call for the construction of a bi-continental network for the Latin American-European Union Summit to be held in Vienna in May 2006, and especially for action against transnational abuse. In the face of new Latin American political scenarios, we also call for the increasing development and concretisation of development and integration alternatives, arising from the social movements as the new priority in this period.

And finally, with the necessity to orchestrate a whole new strategy, plan of action and new forms of convergence and organising, the Continental Social Alliance is convening a large Hemispheric Gathering of Social Movements in the continent, which will be held at the end of April in Havana, Cuba.

For Indigenous Peoples' Rights

We, indigenous peoples and movements, seek to deepen our presence in the WSF framework, maintaining our identity and our own spaces of action, and we ratify our rejections of the Free Trade Agreements in defence of our lands and water, calling for joint actions to build another world.

We stand in solidarity with all countries and peoples who struggle for sovereignty, such as Venezuela, Cuba, and Bolivia, and we call for participation in the III Continental Summit of Indigenous Peoples which will take place in Guatemala City in October 2006, and which was called for from the II Continental Summit in Quito.

For Food Sovereignty and Holistic Agrarian Reform

Land, water, genetic resources, and biodiversity belong to the people; we will not allow their privatisation nor their commercialisation; we defend and promote small farmer and peasant agriculture.

We demand the recuperation and protection of native seeds, and at that same time we categorically reject the sale and use of seeds produced with Terminator technology, because it is immoral and is an attack on the foods of humanity and denies seeds to 1,400 million small farmers and peasants around the world.

We call on the small farmer and peasant peoples, both organised and non-organised, to globally rise up against these policies on April 17—the International Day of Peasant Struggle—and on October 16—the World Food Sovereignty Day—and we extend this call to all networks and social sectors because this is a threat to all humanity and the planet. The drive for holistic agrarian reform and land protection will be the basis of our daily struggle.

For the Rights of the Palestinian People

We support the struggle of the Palestinian people for justice, self-determination, and the return of refugees, and the creation of an independent and sovereign state with its capital in Jerusalem.

Inspired by the South African struggle against Apartheid, we support the Palestinian civil society campaigns of boycotts, divestments, and sanctions against the Zionist colonising efforts driven by the State of Israel.

We demand:

- The end of occupation and colonisation of all Arab lands and the destruction of the wall.
- The full enjoyment of social, political, and economic rights by the Palestinian people.
- The application of the right of return for Palestinian refugees to their homes and properties. (Res. 194 of the UN).

We support:

- The call by representatives of the Palestinian civil society for a global day of struggle on May 15 (the 59th anniversary of the Nakba catastrophe), and invite all social movements to send civil missions to Palestine on this day.

The IVth Week of National and International Action Against the Apartheid Wall will be held November 9-16 2006.

Against the Commercialisation and Exploitation of and Violence Against Women (World March of Women)

We call for a permanent fight against racist, machista, and homophobic violence in all its forms, taking on the feminist struggle for equality as a common challenge in the building of our efforts and alternatives to the politics of commercialisation and war. The World March of Women and the Campaign of Women Say No to the War will organise on March 8 2006, days of feminist action against the tyranny of the market and war.

For the Right to Sexual Diversity (Di·logo Sur/Sur LGBT)

We affirm our respect for sexual diversity and the autonomy of individuals. We respect each person's right to freely make decisions about their body and sexuality. We reject any form of discrimination related to personal choice and we call for support of the mobilisation on June 28 for the full recognition of sexual diversity.

Health is Not for Sale (World Health Forum)

We highlight the Right to Health as a central axis of the WSF in Africa in January 2007, bearing in mind the dramatic health situation in Sub-Saharan Africa.

We call for mobilisation and participation in the regional and national health-related preparatory events for the WSF in Africa, culminating in participation in the II World Social Forum of Health to be held within the WSF framework in Nairobi.

We support the international mobilisation of April 3–7, 2006, as well as the Humanitarian Camp to be held in Bogotá, Colombia, April 4–7. On the 7th will be a continental / global day for the Right to Health.

We will organise an International People's Tribunal for the Right to Health, asserting the concept of genocide arising from the inequalities generated by neo-liberal policies.

In this year of 2006, we add ourselves to the Global Campaign for the Right to Health and to the focus on health promoted by a coalition led by the Peoples Health Movement—PHM—in conjunction with the World Social Forum on Health.

Week in Defence of Public Education for All, November 2006

Education is an inalienable public right that must be guaranteed and financed by the State. Education is not a commodity nor can it be included in any free trade agreement. We will keep fighting to keep education as a right of the people.

We confirm that the next World Education Forum will take place within the framework of the World Social Forum and we will convene a week of mobilisation in defence of public school for all, in the third week of November 2006.

Youth and Student Campaign Against the Privatisation of Education

The V International Student Gathering calls for mobilisation against the inclusion of education in free trade agreements, the privatisation process, and in defence of free public education. We will mobilise on November 17, International Students Day, against the commercialisation of education and the war.

Right to Housing (Frente Continental de Organizaciones Comunitarias, FCOC)

The organisations that fight for the rights of the city and urban reform understand that fighting against the eviction of millions of men, women, and children ensures the social function of private and public property, fighting for the universalisation of the right to water and environmental sanitation, as well as all social rights.

We call for all to join the Zero Eviction Campaign and to participate in the X Gathering of the FCOC and the People's March that will be held May 4-6 simultaneously in Brazil, Argentina, Uruguay, Mexico, the Dominican Republic, as well as other countries.

For the Right to Communication

Understanding Communication as a right and not a commodity, we see the fight for the democratisation of communication as a key component in the fight against neo-liberalism and imperialism, and for the construction of a new society. This means that the articulation and development of our own solidarity involves building citizenship, promoting policies that guarantee diversity and pluralism of media and preserve information and knowledge as public goods, reclaiming their access and resisting their privatisation.

Campaign Against the Privatisation of Water

We declare water to be a common good and access to it to be a fundamental and inalienable Human Right. Water is not a commodity! Therefore we reject all forms of its privatisation, including those carried out through public-private associations. We demand that water be excluded from the market laws imposed by the WTO, NAFTA, and the rest of the free trade and investment agreements. We commit ourselves to creating committees that will fulfil these objectives through education, organising, and mobilisation (at local, national, regional, and global levels). We also commit ourselves to the "citizen days" in March in Mexico City.

Triple Border: Gathering of Peoples in Defence of Life and Natural Resources

We put forth a call for the Gathering of Peoples in Defence of Life and Natural Resources, especially for the Guaraní Aquifer. We demand the withdrawal of US troops from Paraguay and the end of World Bank and IDB intervention in the country.

We will convene the II Social Forum of the Triple Border, June 21–23, 2006 in Ciudad del Este, Paraguay.

Campaign Against Climactic Change, November 11 2006

We recognise the threat of "global warming," climactic change, for all humanity. We must put pressure on businesses and government to reduce CO2 emissions.

We call for global mobilisations next November 11 2006, the date in which the United Nations will hold discussions on the climate.

Energy is Not a Commodity

Energy resources cannot be treated as commodities, but rather as strategic goods that belong to the people and not to transnational companies. We will work to have our countries regulate frameworks that guarantee access to energy for future generations.

We reaffirm the deliberations from the I Forum of Latin American and Caribbean Energy Workers (Caracas, March 2005) and we support the convening of its 2nd edition in Mexico City. These proposals should orient the actions of the social movement in energy issues during the upcoming period.

Energy and IIRSA

In terms of the integrations of energy and physical infrastructures, the model can not be based on purely economic logic that only looks at profits and ignores indigenous communities, peasant farmers and their families, and quilombos, among others. For us, the model has to be based on a social logic of inclusion, with respect for diversity, the environment, and workers' rights.

IIRSA—Initiative for the Integration of Regional Infrastructure in South America—will have to attend to the interests of the people and not generate more inequality. We denounce this initiative for being conducted with a lack of transparency and dialogue with the parliamentarians and civil societies of the countries involved. The current IIRSA proposal creates an infrastructural integration that perpetuates the role of our countries as exporters of non-valued-add raw materials and products, aggravating the problem of natural resources year after year.

From the point of view of alternative energies, the processes have to be both renewable and sustainable, and also not reinforce the logic of agribusiness, monoculture, and latifundio estates.

Campaign for the Demilitarisation of the Americas (CADA)

The Campaign for the Demilitarisation of the Americas demands the withdrawal of North American troops from Paraguay and the withdrawal of foreign troops from Haiti.

Campaign Against North American Military Bases

We condemn the action of the CIA, the M16, and the European secret police who carry out illegal detentions, kidnap civilians and carry them in secret flights to US military bases in Europe that are the "European Guantánamos" of today.

We express our solidarity with the 28 Pakistanis who were illegally detained and kidnapped in Greece. We will not sacrifice our civil liberties in the name of the "war on terror" of Bush, Blair, and their allies.

[We are preparing an international gathering of the movements that make up the campaign, to be held in Ecuador in March 2006.]

For the Freedom of the Five Cuban Prisoners Held in the United States

The United States government, with its double-standard morals in the fight against terrorism, refuses to extradite or try in its territory Luís Pozada Carriles (responsible for the explosion of a Cuban civilian plane that cost the lives of 73 passengers), while at the same time, it continues to hold five courageous Cuban fighters against terrorism. We demand their immediate release as well as the trial of Pozada Carriles.

Solidarity Days with Haiti, February 15 and 29 2006

We demand the withdrawal of foreign troops from Haiti and the annulment and reparation of the financial debt that the international financial institutions and other supposed creditors hold against the people. We call for carrying out actions on February 15 for troop withdrawal and the annulment of Haiti's debt. At the same time, we call for March 29 (Haitian Constitution Day) to be a World Day of Solidarity with Haiti.

Campaign for Self-Determination for the Last Colonies on the American Continent

We strongly condemn the presence on the continent of French, US, Dutch, and British colonies, and we denounce the pretence of the French colonial power in presenting this colonisation as a positive act.

We declare our solidarity with the struggle for self-determination of the peoples of Puerto Rico, Martinique, Guadalupe, French Guyana, Surinam, and Saint Martin.

We insist that these countries be included in the UN list of countries yet to be decolonised.

Campaign Stop Coca-Cola Assassin

The Assembly of Social Movements adopts the campaign "Stop Coca-Cola Assassin" being carried out by the US Students Against Sweatshops in defence of workers' rights and of people who have been victims of violence imposed by this transnational.

European Union/Latin America and Caribbean Counter-Summit, Vienna (Austria), May 2006

Marking the fourth presidential summit between the EU and Latin America / the Caribbean, social movement networks and NGOs of both continents will organise a large parallel event in Vienna (Austria), May 10–13, under the name Linking Alternatives 2. The event will include the People's Tribunal Against European Transnationals, bi-regional forums on alternatives to neo-liberalism and militarisation, meetings and public demonstrations, etc.

(This summit will organise a mobilisation from the European Social Forum in the preceding days, which will take place in Athens, Greece, on May 7, 2006)

Statement of the WSF on Childhood (WSFC), held in Caracas, January 24-29 2006

In the framework of the WSF on Childhood, held January 24-29 2006 in Caracas in the Andrés Bello school, the children, adolescent, and adult participants declare:

1. That another world is only possible with the pro-active participation of children and adolescents and the full, direct implementation of all their rights.

2. We suggest to all organisers of the Forum that they consider having Childhood be a crosscutting axis for the next Forum, and that they guarantee spaces for the direct participation of children and adolescents in that axis.

3. We request that the WSF Hemispheric Council include organisations made up of children and adolescents.

4. That the agreements, proposals, and conclusions coming out of the various tables of the WSF on Childhood be promoted and disseminated through the various mechanisms available through the WSF, with the aim of inviting the organisations, children, adolescents, and adult participants of this forum to share and discuss the suggestions and proposals coming out of the Forum.

5. We commit ourselves to building a network to promote the implementation and follow-up of the agreements, conclusions, and recommendations from the FSMI tables, and principally the pro-active participation of children and adolescents in future world social forums.

Sourced from <http://www.alternatives.ca/article2395.html>mk 27.09.09

AFRICAN STRUGGLES, GLOBAL STRUGGLES[1]

We, social movements from across Africa and across the world, have come together here in Nairobi at the 2007 World Social Forum to highlight and celebrate Africa and her social movements; Africa and her unbroken history of struggle against foreign domination, colonialism, and neo-colonialism; Africa and her contributions to humanity; Africa and her role in the quest for another world.

We are here to celebrate and reaffirm the spirit of the World Social Forum as a space of struggle and solidarity which is open to all people and social movements regardless of their ability to pay.

We denounce tendencies towards commercialisation, privatisation, and militarisation of the WSF space. Hundreds of our sisters and brothers who welcomed us to Nairobi have been excluded because of high costs of participation.

We are also deeply concerned about the presence of organisations working against the rights of women, marginalised people, and against sexual rights and diversity, in contradiction to the WSF Charter of Principles.

The social movements assembly has created a platform for Kenyans and other Africans from different backgrounds and communities to present their struggles, alternatives, cultures, talents, and skills. It is also a space for civil society organisations and social movements to interact and share the issues and problems affecting them.

Since the first assembly in 2001, we have contributed to building and strengthening successful international networks of civil societies and social movements and reinforced our spirit of solidarity and our struggles against all forms of oppression and domination.

We recognise that the diversity of movements and popular initiatives against neo-liberalism, world hegemony of capitalism and imperial wars, is an expression of a world resistance.

We have now to move towards a phase of effective alternatives. Many local initiatives are already existing and should be expanded: what is happening in Latin America and other parts of the world—thanks to the joint action of social movements—shows the way to establish concrete alternatives to world capitalist domination.

As social movements from all five continents gathering in Nairobi, we express our solidarity with the social movements in Latin America whose persistent and continuing struggle has led to electoral victories for the Left in several countries.

Actions

We are calling for a broad international mobilisation against the G8 in Rostock and Heiligendamm (Germany), 2-8 June 2007.

We will mobilise in our communities and movements for an International Day of Action in 2008.

Note

1. Statement of the Social Movements Assembly at the World Social Forum, Nairobi, 24 January 2007. Sourced from Focus on Global South @ http://www.focusweb.org/social-movements-assembly-in-nairobi.html?Itemid=94 accessed mk on 27.09.07.

Part 4

Looking Beyond: Possible Futures, Possible Worlds

The World Social Forum: Where To Now?[1]

Michael Albert

The worldwide Social Forum phenomenon is thriving. In contrast, the WSF once-a-year international event has run up against internal limits and needs renovation. Forums worldwide include relatively local events for small towns, cities, counties, whole states, and even regions. Examples are Forums for Ithaca, New York, USA, Brisbane Australia, South Africa, and Asia. There are many instances at each level, including, for example, about a hundred in towns throughout Italy. These Forums worldwide have two universal aims, and beyond that, much variation. One, to promote respectful communications and solidarity and two, to prioritise vision and strategy as well as analysis.

Moreover by all evidence, the Forums worldwide cause even activists who disagree to congregate, to hear one another, to develop new ties, and to take seriously, economic, political, gender, race, culture, ecology, globalisation, and international goals and strategies. Some local Forums excellently generate shared programme and actions among sub-sets of participants. But even short of that, by at least enhancing solidarity and enlarging vision, all the local Forums powerfully aid movements.

Another attribute of the Forums worldwide, more in evidence the more local they are, is accountability and transparency. Local Forum organisers are generally well known to the people participating and attending. Even for Forums lacking a fully democratic process, the decision-makers are at least known enough to the attendees to be accountable. Decisions are subject to challenge, refinement, and renovation.

Similarly, local Forums have a manageable scale. Arrangements, fees, setting up panels and getting people to them, all occur relatively smoothly. Local agendas tend to include many interactive sessions so that everyone involved participates more or less equally. People can access one another. Presenters and audience aren't sharply divided. A few people don't enjoy elite status. Others aren't marginalised.

Without exaggerating the virtues of the Forums worldwide, they are having positive effects and moving in participatory, transparent, and democratic directions.

The WSF—the *world* meeting of the WSF process—is, however, different.

The World Social Forum

The bottom-up Forums worldwide were spurred into existence by a very top-down WSF. The former has yet to reform the latter. So in contrast to the Forums worldwide, the WSF is not yet transparent or accountable, much less democratic. It has become unmanageable. And while it has profoundly valuable participation, there are often sharp and even destructive differences between the WSF's layers of participants. While some of these difficulties certainly derive from doing a massive event with unreliable and insufficient resources, there are other avenues of improvement as well.

The WSF's Decision-Making

The originators of the WSF took a great idea, made a courageous leap, and inspired effective work. In time, however, they became a leadership in a tighter, more determinative, and less exemplary manner. They began and remained unaccountable, save perhaps tangentially to their own organisations. This was caused likely in part by the difficulties of operating on such an unprecedented scale, partly by the structure and philosophies of some of the NGOs and other organisations involved such as the French ATTAC, and probably due to more singular factors as well.

After WSF 2, I was enlisted to help with a variety of Forum-related projects and, as a means to facilitate my doing so, I was asked to join the WSF's International Council. I missed a spring and a summer meeting, one in Thailand, the other in Barcelona. However, I did attend a meeting in Italy in the fall. My experience was that the Council wasn't a serious seat of power, and that the IC was barely a rubber stamp.

It wasn't that the people sitting around the table in Florence weren't an impressive group. They were worldly and wise, and many of them came from movements and constituencies of great importance around the world. And it wasn't that the people at the table didn't want a more democratic and participatory approach. This desire was raised repeatedly. But after a short time at that meeting, it became obvious that despite the members' stature and desires, the people on the Council and at the table were not the real locus of WSF power. The powers that be had some functionaries present, chairing the meeting. And it was clear that the powers that be had decided what the agenda was, what would be made known regarding the overall WSF situation to the people in the room, and what the International Council could be permitted to discuss —and that those attending had only very limited influence.

I circled around the room asking many of those present, "Who are the real decision-makers in the WSF? Who is it that allots limited choices to this group, saving important matters for their own eyes? Who is it that makes the bigger decisions that never come before this group?"

While a few folks could hesitantly name a leader or two based on knowing the history of the WSF, no one I talked to was confident about even that, much less a whole *list* of leaders. I felt I had been dragged onto a Central Committee that had a still higher body that dictated *key* results. But when I asked my fellow committee members who those higher authorities were, no one knew.

The *real* WSF leadership, I think, makes many key decisions. Will the event have Lula present, and in what capacity? What about Castro, or Chavez? Will there be exclusions and if so on what grounds? What about the Zapatistas? Will being in a party, advocating violent tactics, or even just being from some group that the inner circle finds too radical or otherwise dislikes (such as the Disobedienti from Italy, or the international People's Global Action) preclude prominent participation? What content will be part of the core of the events (more on this below), and what content will be left as periphery? Who will have their way paid and who will not? Will there be a march, and who will be the key speakers? Will there be a collective statement, with what content? What efforts will or won't be made to achieve gender balance, race balance, geographic balance? How will class differences be addressed, if at all, within the process and more broadly? How will press be handled, both mainstream and alternative? Will the WSF start to discuss facilitating an international movement of movements, or will it persist only as a Forum? What will be the accommodation between advocating reform of capitalism and advocating a new system entirely?

The decision-making of the WSF is not transparent though transparency could be easily attained: just post the relevant names and make known significant decisions. The decision-making is not accountable. This would be far harder to attain, but could at least be better approached, even for so complicated an entity. There is no widespread democratic input from regions around the world. While this could be difficult, it ought to be on the agenda, and implies some obvious organisational changes.

The WSF's Operational Viability

At WSF 3, most people probably perceived great success in terms of the actual details of speaking, listening, eating, sleeping, and marching. This is because what happened, happened well. People going to events largely enjoyed them

—be they marches or rallies, big panels or meetings, or the youth camps. People perceived and will report that what they attended was carried off adequately and even smoothly, as indeed, most of the events were, as they were perceived. This in itself is quite amazing and immensely praiseworthy.

But what about the 400 or so panels that were cancelled very near the time of the WSF, and long after people *planned* to participate in them? No one attended or presented at those panels, because they didn't take place at all. No one saw that they weren't there, other than those who suffered the cancellations. What about the events that weren't on any printed schedule, and that attendees couldn't find and that therefore attracted a fraction of the participation they deserved? Only very few people attended those events, all others being ignorant of their existence. Though the few who did attend were quite distraught, the full loss was again unrecorded, since it was a loss of the benefits that might have been had, if people who didn't know of sessions, had been able to go to them under better conditions. And what about the events whose rooms kept being changed, again disrupting or even obliterating their attendance? In some cases even presenters couldn't find panels. Again, few knew about this.

Maybe all these problems could have been avoided by stricter limits on the numbers of events and panels, by earlier scheduling, and so on. Or maybe, while there might have been less chaotic disruption with better preparations, most of the chaos wasn't ultimately the fault of those doing the work—but was a nearly inevitable by-product of the WSF's having grown too large and embodying too many unpredictable factors for the resources available.

In short, the WSF at its current size seems to a considerable extent unmanageable. It isn't that leftists can't handle large scale, per se. It is that having so few resources, no one could effectively manage so many unpredictable variables.

WSF Hierarchies

Each year, the WSF anoints a sub-set of events as its own. These events are prominent in the official schedules, have appropriate-sized rooms and resources, and their presenters are afforded considerable comforts, including paid hotel rooms and sometimes travel allowances. Moreover, the housing was at hotels that were better, the more prominent the person, not the more needy. I would guess this group to be roughly 100 people. I am quite sure that among them were some people who needed the financial aid, but also a great many who did not, relatively speaking.

On the other hand, there were the rest of the presenters who numbered maybe a few thousand or so. The events that these participants planned in many cases did not even appear in the official schedules and were subject to last minute termination or, short of that, to room changes. These second-tier presenters were afforded few comforts and little financial support though they included overwhelmingly less well off people than the 100 or so at the hotels. Gender still seems to play a horrible and destructive role in people's roles and visibility, as well. Beyond presenters, moreover, there were the youth who were housed in a camp with barely sufficient water and barely acceptable sewage. That the roughly 30,000 people in the youth camps made it a vibrant community in which there were no hierarchies is immensely admirable. But the many virtues of those who endure harsh conditions joyfully don't excuse the fact that they were treated as a separate entity with little visible effort to incorporate them.

Is there no alternative to having some participants living in camps, others in bearable environs, and a few in luxurious hotels? Couldn't there be sliding scales of fees and accommodations more in accord with need than with notoriety and with those better able tithed to help those less able? Younger folks can bear worse conditions better. Older folks need better conditions to manage such a strenuous undertaking. Some variation of accommodations is certainly warranted on this account, but being prominent shouldn't be the criterion.

Without attention, layering of participants' material circumstances abets even less warranted differences—due to gender, race, class, place of origin, and fame—in how people are regarded in general, in the media attention they are accorded, and in the visibility and promotion they receive. Often, attention afforded rises in nearly inverse proportion to the activism people do, to the extent they are anti-hierarchical in their own lives, and to the lessons and insights they have to offer and to share with other people at the WSF events. It isn't surprising that in the youth camps there is sharing and equity, dwarfing what prevails in the hotels. So while it would probably be impossible to do without the hotels, it is the logic and culture at the hotels that needs examination.

Of course, we need presentations, sometimes even to very large audiences, but it ought to be possible to reduce or even eliminate relative passivity and subordination of those who come to the WSF mainly to listen, and of those who present but have less known names.

There is another odd, if very much unintended layering effect at the WSF. The WSF is called a World Forum. We all say, "The WSF had 100,000 participants." And when I say and hear phrases like that, to me it sounds like a claim that 100,000 people from all over the world gathered. While WSF 3 attracted roughly 100,000 people, perhaps as many as 70,000 were from Brazil and perhaps another 15,000 were from neighbouring countries in South America. So one might reasonably say that this was a major *South American* Forum that invited 10–15,000 people from around the world to attend as presenters or guests, as well as say it was a World Forum. Shouldn't a *World* Forum be worldly representative, with some degree of proportion among its delegates to movements and activism around the world?

Where to Now?

The WSF has been a remarkable phenomenon three times so far. It has propelled Forums worldwide. It has educated, inspired, and engendered ties and connections. Its structure and processes were a miracle the first year, amazing the second year, but have begun to fall short the third year. The WSF, with all its virtues, is in diverse ways reaching the limits of its current incarnation.

The issues raised above and many more that other participants no doubt have on their minds, must be explored and debated. New ideas need to be put forth, evaluated, refined, and implemented. Here are eleven thoughts that may have some merit—but whether they do or not, certainly changes must be made:

- Emphasise local Forums as the *foundation* of the worldwide Forum process.
- Have each new level of Forums, from towns, to cities, to countries, to continents, to the world—be built largely on those below.
- Have the decision-making leadership of local events locally determined.
- Have the decision-making leadership at each higher level chosen, at least in considerable part, by the local Forums that are within the higher entity. The smaller local Forums in Italy choose Italy's national Forum leadership. The European Forum's leadership is chosen by the national Forums within Europe, and similarly elsewhere.
- Mandate that the decision-making leadership at every level should be at least 50 per cent women.
- Have the Forums from wealthier parts of the world charge delegates and organisations and attendees a tax on their fees to apply to helping finance the Forums in poorer parts of the world.
- Make the once-a-year international WSF a delegate event. Cities and states in Brazil should have a Forum. So should Brazil as a whole. So should other countries in South America, and so should South America as a whole. And,

likewise for India and South Asia, for South Africa and Africa, and so on. But the world event should be different. It should be representative.

- Keep the WSF attendance at 5,000–10,000 people delegated to it from the major regional Forums around the world. Have the WSF leadership selected by regional Forums. Mandate the WSF to share and compare and propose, based on all that is emerging worldwide—not to listen again to the same famous speakers whom everyone hears worldwide all the time anyhow —and have the WSF's results, like those of all other Forums, published and public, and of course reported by delegates back to the regions.

- Feature grassroots activists from movements around the world much more prominently in major events and throughout all Forums to strengthen the WSF and local Forums as vehicles for their activity and counter tendencies toward elitism.

- Ensure that the WSF as a whole, and the Forums worldwide do not make the mistake of trying to become an international, a movement of movements, or even just a voice of the world's movements. To be a Forum, the WSF and the smaller component Forums need to be as broad and diverse as possible. But being that broad and that diverse is simply being too broad and too diverse to be an organisation. The Forums can and should be venues for meeting. They can and should facilitate networking among mutually congenial participants that lead to shared actions. But to be an organisation that takes decisions about anything other than its component Forums would transcend the Forum project's degree of unity.

- Mandate Forums at every level, including the WSF, to welcome people from diverse constituencies—using the Forums and their processes to make contacts and develop ties that can in turn yield national, regional, or even international networks or movements of movements which do share sufficiently their political aspirations to work closely together, but which exist alongside rather than *instead* of the Forum phenomenon.

Note

1. Edited version of 'The WSF's Future,' on *ZNet*, 2 February 2003; renamed 'WSF: Where to Now?' on 3 February 2003. <Http://www.zmag.org/content/owarticle.cfm?SectionID=41&ItemID=2956>

The Twilight Of Vanguardism[1]

David Graeber

For most of a century now, revolutionary thinkers have been saying that the age of vanguardism is over. Outside of a handful of tiny sectarian groups, it is almost impossible to find radical intellectuals who seriously believe that their role should be to determine the correct historical analysis of the world situation, so as to lead the masses along in the one true revolutionary direction. But (rather like the idea of progress, to which it is obviously connected), it seems much easier to renounce the principle than to shake the accompanying habits of thought. Vanguardist, even sectarian, attitudes have become so ingrained in academic radicalism it is hard to say what it would mean to think outside them.

The depth of the problem first really struck me when I became acquainted with the consensus modes of decision-making employed in North American anarchist and anarchist-inspired political movements. This, I realised, bore a lot of similarities to the style of political decision-making current where I had done my anthropological fieldwork in rural Madagascar. There is enormous variation among different styles and forms of consensus but one thing almost all the North American variants have in common is that they are organised in conscious opposition to the style of organisation and debate typical of classical sectarian Marxist groups. These groups invariably organise around some master theoretician, who offers a comprehensive analysis of the world situation and, often, of human history as a whole, but very little theoretical reflection on more immediate questions of organisation and practice. Anarchist-inspired groups, by contrast, tend to operate on the assumption that no one could, or probably should, ever convert another person completely to ones own point of view, that decision-making structures are ways of managing diversity, and therefore, that one should concentrate instead on maintaining egalitarian processes and considering immediate questions of action in the present.

One of the fundamental principles of anarchist political debate, for instance, is that one is obliged to give other participants the benefit of the doubt for honesty and good intentions, whatever else one might think of their arguments. In part, this emerges from the style of debate encouraged by consensus decision-making: whereas voting encourages one to reduce opponents' positions to a hostile caricature, or whatever it takes to defeat them, a consensus process is built on a principle of compromise and creativity duromg which one is constantly mdifying proposals until one can come up with something *everyone* can at least live with; therefore, the incentive is always to put the best possible construction on others' arguments.

Why so Few Anarchists in the Academy?

As I have learned from experience, established academic practices are largely the opposite of these anarchist practices. And while I still believe that the growing prevalence of these new, and to my mind far healthier, modes of discourse among activists will have its effects on the academy, it is hard to deny that so far the change has been very slow in coming. Why so few anarchists in the academy?

One might argue this is because anarchism itself has made such small inroads into the academy. As a political philosophy, anarchism is going through a veritable explosion in recent years. Anarchist or anarchist-inspired movements are growing everywhere; anarchist principles—autonomy, voluntary association, self-organisation, mutual aid, direct democracy—have become the basis for organising within the globalisation movement and beyond, taking the place Marxism had in the social movements of the sixties. As the core revolutionary ideology, it is the source of ideas and inspiration; even those who do not consider themselves anarchists feel they have to define themselves in relation to it. Yet this has found almost no reflection in academic discourse. Most academics seem to have only the vaguest idea what anarchism is even about; or dismiss it with the crudest stereotypes ("anarchist *organisation*! But is that not a contradiction in terms?") In the U.S. —and I do not think it is all that different elsewhere—there are thousands of academic Marxists of one sort or another, but hardly anyone who is willing to openly call herself an anarchist.

I do not think this is just because the academy is behind times. Marxism has always had an affinity with the academy that anarchism never will. Anarchism was never really invented by anyone. True, historians usually treat it as if it were, constructing the history of anarchism as if it is basically a creature identical to Marxism: it was created by specific 19th century thinkers, perhaps Godwin or Stirner, but definitely Proudhon, Bakunin, Kropotkin; it inspired working-class organisations, and became enmeshed in political struggles. But, in fact, the analogy is rather strained. First of all, the 19th century thinkers generally credited with inventing anarchism did not think of themselves as having invented anything particularly new. The basic principles of anarchism—self-organisation, voluntary association, mutual aid—are as old as humanity. Similarly, the rejection of the State and of all forms of structural violence, inequality, or domination (anarchism literally means 'without rulers'), even the assumption that all these forms are somehow related and reinforce each other, was hardly some startlingly new 19th century doctrine; one can find evidence of people making similar arguments throughout history. We are talking less about a body of theory than about an *attitude*, or perhaps even a faith: a rejection of certain types of social relation, a confidence that certain others are much better ones on which to build a decent or humane society, a faith that it would be possible to do so.

One need only compare the historical schools of Marxism and anarchism, then, to see we are dealing with a fundamentally different sort of thing. Marxist schools have authors. Just as Marxism sprang from the mind of Marx, so we have Leninists, Maoists, Trotskyites, Gramscians, Althusserians. Note how the list starts with heads of state and grades almost seamlessly into French professors. Pierre Bourdieu once noted that, if the academic field is a game in which scholars strive for dominance, then you know you have won when other scholars start wondering how to make an adjective out of your name. It is, presumably, to preserve the possibility of winning the academic game that intellectuals insist on continuing to employ Great Man theories. Yet, for instance, Foucault's ideas, like Trotsky's, are never treated as primarily the products of a certain intellectual milieu, as something that emerged from endless conversations and arguments in cafes, classrooms, bedrooms, barber shops, involving thousands of people inside and outside the academy (or Party), but always as if they arose from a single man's genius. It is not quite that Marxist politics organised itself like an academic discipline or became a model for how radical intellectuals treated one another; rather, the two developed somewhat in tandem.

Schools of anarchism, in contrast, emerged from some kind of organisational principle or form of practice: Anarcho-Syndicalists and Anarcho-Communists, Insurrectionists and Platformists, Co-operativists, Individualists, and so on. (Significantly, those few Marxist tendencies that are not named after individuals, like Autonomism or Council Communism, are the closest to anarchism). Anarchists are distinguished by what they do, and how they organise themselves to go about doing it. And indeed, this has always been what anarchists have spent most of their time thinking and arguing about. They have never been much interested in the kinds of broad strategic or philosophical questions that preoccupy Marxists, such as: are the peasants a potentially revolutionary class? (which anarchists consider something for the peasants to decide); or, what is the nature of the commodity form? Rather, anarchists tend to argue about what is the truly democratic way to go about a meeting, or at what point organisation stops empowering people and starts squelching individual freedom. Is 'leadership' necessarily a bad thing? Or, alternately, about the ethics of opposing power: what is direct action? Should one condemn someone who assassinates a head of state? When is it okay to break a window?

One might sum it up like this: 1) Marxism has tended to be a theoretical or analytical discourse about revolutionary strategy; 2) Anarchism has tended to be an ethical discourse about revolutionary practice.

Now, this does imply that there are a lot of potential complementarities between the two, and indeed there have been. One could easily imagine a systematic division of labour in which Marxists critique the political economy, but stay out of organising, and anarchists handle the day-to-day organising, but defer to Marxists on questions of abstract theory; ie., in which Marxists explain why the economic crash in Argentina occurred and the anarchists deal with what to do about it. (I also should point out that I am aware I am being a bit hypocritical here by indulging in some of the same sort of sectarian reasoning I am otherwise critiquing: there are schools of Marxism which are very open-minded and tolerant, and democratically organised, as there are anarchist groups which are insanely sectarian.) This also makes it easier to understand why there are so few anarchists in the academy. Anarchism is primarily an ethics of practice; and it insists, before anything else, that ones means must be consonant with ones ends; one cannot create freedom through authoritarian means; that as much as possible, one must embody the society one wishes to create. This does not square very well with operating within universities that still have an essentially medieval social structure, presenting papers at conferences in expensive hotels, and doing intellectual battle in language no one who has not spent at least two or three years in grad school would ever hope to be able to understand.

All this does not, of course, mean that anarchist theory is impossible —though it does suggest that a *single* Anarchist High Theory in the style of university radicalism might be a contradiction in terms. One could imagine a body of theory that presumes and indeed values a diversity of sometimes incommensurable perspectives in much the same way that anarchist decision-making process does, but which nonetheless organises them around a presumption of shared commitments. But clearly, it would also have to self-consciously reject any trace of vanguardism; which leads to the question: if the role of revolutionary intellectuals is not to form an elite that can arrive at the correct strategic analyses and then lead the masses, what precisely is it? This is an area where I think anthropology is particularly well positioned to help. And not only because most actual, self-governing communities, non-market economies, and other radical alternatives have been mainly studied by anthropologists; but also, because the practice of ethnography provides at least something of a model, an incipient model, of how non-vanguardist revolutionary intellectual practice might work. Ethnography is about teasing out the hidden symbolic, moral, or pragmatic logics that underlie certain types of social action; the way people's habits and actions makes sense in ways that they are not themselves completely aware of. One obvious role for a radical intellectual is precisely to look at those who are creating viable collective alternatives, and try to figure out what might be the larger implications of what they are (already) doing.

History of the Idea of Vanguardism

Untwining social theory from vanguardist habits might seem a difficult task because modern social theory and the idea of the vanguard were born more or less together. On the other hand, so was the idea of an artistic avant garde, and the relationship among the three might itself suggest unexpected possibilities.

Henri de Saint-Simon coined the term 'avant-garde' in a series of essays he wrote at the very end of his life. Like his onetime secretary and disciple (and later, bitter rival, Auguste Comte), Saint-Simon was writing in the wake of the French revolution and was essentially asking what had gone wrong: why the transition from a medieval, feudal Catholic society to a modern, industrial democratic one seemed to create such enormous violence and social dislocation. The problem, he concluded, was that modern society lacked any force of ideological cohesion that could play the same role as the medieval church, which gave everyone the sense of having a meaningful place in the overall social order. Towards the end of their lives, Saint-Simon and Comte ended up creating their own religion: Saint-Simon called his the 'New Christianity,' Comte, the 'New Catholicism.' In the first, artists were to play the role of the ultimate spiritual leaders; in an imaginary dialogue with a scientist, Saint-Simon has an artist explaining that in their role of imagining possible futures and inspiring the public, they can play the role of an avant garde, a "truly priestly function," as he put it. In his ideal future, artists would hatch the ideas that they would then pass on to scientists and industrialists to put into effect. Saint-Simon was perhaps the first to conceive the notion of the withering away of the State: once it had become clear that the authorities were operating for the good of the public, one would no more need force to compel the public to heed their advice than one needed it to compel patients to take the advice of their doctors. Government would pass away into, at most, some minor police function.

Comte, of course, is most famous as the founder of sociology; he invented the term to describe what he saw as the 'master-discipline,' which could both understand and direct society. He ended up taking a far more authoritarian approach, ultimately proposing the regulation and control of almost all aspects of human life according to scientific principles, with the role of high priests in his New Catholicism being played by sociologists themselves.

It is a particularly fascinating opposition because in the early 20th century, the positions were effectively reversed. Instead of the left-wing Saint-Simonians looking to artists for leadership, while the right-wing Comtians fancied themselves scientists, we had fascist leaders like Hitler and Mussolini who imagined themselves as great artists inspiring the masses, sculpting society according to their grandiose imaginings, and the Marxist vanguard which claimed the role of scientists.

At any rate, the Saint Simonians actively sought to recruit artists for their various ventures, salons, and utopian communities, though they quickly ran into difficulties because so many within avant garde artistic circles preferred the more anarchistic Fourierists, and later, one or another branch of outright anarchists. Actually, the number of 19th century artists with anarchist sympathies is staggering, ranging from Pissaro to Tolstoy or Oscar Wilde, not to mention most early 20th century artists who later became Communists, from Malevich to Picasso. Rather than a political vanguard leading the way to a future society, radical artists almost invariably saw themselves as exploring new and less alienated modes of life. The really significant development in the 19th century was less the idea of a vanguard than that of Bohemia (a term first coined by Balzac in 1838): marginal communities living in more or less voluntary poverty, seeing themselves as dedicated to the pursuit of creative, un-alienated forms of experience, united by a profound hatred of bourgeois life and everything it stood for. Ideologically, they were equally likely to be proponents of 'art for art's sake' or social revolutionaries.

The idea of the political vanguard was used very widely and very loosely in the 19th century for anyone seen as exploring the path to a future free society. Radical newspapers for example, often called themselves 'avant garde.' It was Marx though, who began to significantly change the idea by introducing the notion that the proletariat were the true revolutionary class—he didn't actually use the term 'vanguard' in his own writing—because they were the most oppressed, or as he put it 'negated' by capitalism, and therefore had the least to lose by its abolition. In doing so, he ruled out the possibilities that less alienated enclaves, whether of artists or the sort of artisans and independent producers who tended to form the backbone of anarchism, had anything significant to offer. The results we all know. The idea of a vanguard party dedicated to both organising and providing an intellectual project for that most-oppressed class chosen as the agent of history, but also, actually sparking the revolution through their willingness to employ violence, was first outlined by Lenin in 1902 in 'What Is to Be Done?' and has been echoed endlessly ever since. All this had a curious effect on the artistic avant garde who increasingly started to organise themselves like vanguard parties, beginning with the Dadaists and Futurists, publishing their own manifestos, communiqués, purging one another, and otherwise making themselves (sometimes quite intentional) parodies of revolutionary sects. The ultimate fusion came with the Surrealists and then finally the Situationist International, which on the one hand was the most systematic group in trying to develop a theory of revolutionary action according to the spirit of Bohemia, thinking about what it might actually mean to destroy the boundaries between art and life; on the other hand however, in its own internal organisation, it displayed a kind of insane sectarianism full of so many splits, purges, and bitter denunciations that Guy Debord finally remarked that the only logical conclusion was for the International to be finally reduced to two members, one of whom would purge the other and then commit suicide. (Which is actually not too far from what actually ended up happening.)

Non-Alienated Production

Why is it that artists have so often been so drawn to revolutionary politics? It seems to me the answer must have something to do with alienation. There would appear to be a direct link between the experience of first imagining things and then bringing them into being, on the one hand—(that is, the experience of certain forms of un-alienated production)—and the ability to imagine social alternatives, on the other, particularly the possibility of a society premised on less alienated forms of creativity. This might allow us to perceive in a new light the historical shift between seeing the vanguard as the relatively un-alienated artists (or perhaps intellectuals) and seeing them as the representatives of the 'most oppressed.' In fact, I would suggest, revolutionary coalitions always tend to consist of an alliance between a society's least alienated and its most oppressed. This is less elitist a formulation than it might sound because it seems that actual revolutions tend to occur when these two categories overlap. That would at any rate explain why it almost always seems to be peasants and craftspeople—or alternately, newly proletarianised former peasants and craftspeople—who actually rise up and overthrow capitalist regimes, and not those inured by generations of wage labour. Finally, I suspect this would also help explain the extraordinary importance of indigenous people's struggles in that planetary uprising usually referred to as the 'anti-globalisation' movement: such people tend to be simultaneously the very least alienated and most oppressed people on earth, and once it is technologically possible to include them in revolutionary coalitions, it is almost inevitable that they should take a leading role.

The role of indigenous peoples, in turn, leads us back to the role of ethnography as a possible model for the would-be non-vanguardist revolutionary intellectual—as well as some of its potential pitfalls. Obviously what I am proposing would only work if it were, ultimately, a form of auto-ethnography, combined, perhaps, with a certain utopian extrapolation: a matter of teasing out the tacit logic or principles underlying certain forms of radical practice, and then, not only offering the analysis back to those communities, but using them to formulate new visions ("if one applied the same principles as you are applying to political organisation to economics, might it not look something like this?") Here too, there are suggestive parallels in the history of radical artistic movements, which became movements precisely as they became their own critics; there are also intellectuals already trying to do precisely this sort of auto-ethnographic work. But I say all this not so much to provide models as to open up a field for discussion, first of all, by emphasising that even the notion of vanguardism itself is far richer in its history, and full of alternative possibilities than most of us would ever be given to expect.

Note

1. Edited form of essay published by the San Francisco Bay Area Independent Media Center at <http://sf.indymedia.org/news/2003/06/1615559.php> Keynote address during the 'History Matters: Social Movements Past, Present, and Future'Conference, New School for Social Research, New York City. (<http://www.newschool.edu/gf/ historymatters>, for more information).

The World Social Forum And The Future: The Future Of The World Social Forum[1]

Boaventura de Sousa Santos

From Realistic Utopias to Alternatives

The WSF symbolises a critical and democratic utopia. This utopia manifests itself as an imbalance between negative expectations (what is rejected) and positive expectations (what is proposed as alternative). The success of the first WSF and the increasing counter-hegemonic globalisation up until 11 September, convinced movements and NGOs in charge of the organisation of the WSF, that the movement of movements might be entering a new phase, a politically more consistent one, which would require a higher level of concretisation of alternatives. Once the idea of an *alternative globalisation* to hegemonic globalisation was consolidated, the political strength of the movement of movements would depend on its capacity to formulate credible proposals for the political agendas of nations and multilateral organisations alike.

By the middle of 2001, the WSF's organising committee (OC) was spreading to the movements, organisations and the co-ordinators of the four major themes, the recommendation that interventions and debates were to focus on formulating concrete proposals. The *mot d'ordre* was, "We must advance more proposals." Besides formulating more proposals, some participants also engaged in the formulation of general objectives or principles that identified the need for alternatives and justified them ethically. Vandana Shiva, for example, argued for what she termed "the living democracy movement" as an alternative to globalisation in and of itself. For Shiva, by keeping the commitment to democracy alive at all levels of everyday life, we will both create and sustain an alternative world.

Theses were also formulated that had a higher level of concretisation, but which lacked the format as well as the substantive and procedural concreteness that might push them on to a political agenda. I myself presented fifteen theses for deepening democracy, and François Houtart proposed thinking of alternatives on three levels: 1) in terms of "re-building utopias," not in the sense of impossible things but rather in the sense of mobilising objectives; 2) defining medium-term alternatives, e.g. those goals that will take time to achieve because they involve lengthy struggles with the purpose of resisting the capitalist system itself; and 3) defining short-term alternatives, or those goals that are feasible in the foreseeable future and can serve as mobilisers, even though the objectives are partial.

Hundreds of more focussed proposals have been submitted and discussed in the workshops put together at the initiative of the movements and organisations present at the 2002 WSF. Among those focussing on economic and institutional changes were, for instance, the following: a) a proposal by Focus on the Global South for a 'Pluralistic System of Global Economic Governance' that would reduce the power of TNC-driven multilateral institutions, while strengthening some others or creating new ones intended to devolve control of the economy to national or local levels; b) a proposal by ATTAC (Association for the Taxation of Financial Transactions for the Aid of Citizens) for restoring control of financial capital to nation-states through national and international fiscal measures, such as the Tobin Tax; c) a proposal by CorpWatch for greater corporate responsibility and accountability; d) a proposal by the Committee for Cancellation of Third World Debt as an alternative to neoliberal adjustment programmes in the South, including endogenous development models and different trading practices; e) a proposal by the Institute for Research and Application of Methods of Development (IRAM) for agrarian reform and land policy based on a new social definition of land rights in terms of use, not ownership, and a new structure of programmes and incentives; f) A series of proposals concerning water, food sovereignty, knowledge and patents, and health under Thematic Area II—'Access to Wealth and Sustainability,' for instance, against the privatisation of water and for mechanisms of control based on coalitions of civil society, sustainable water management through territorial control of water sources, international water agreements and so forth; and g) The fight against dams, which contemplates a moratorium on new dams until all economic, social, cultural and environmental impacts they have caused are resolved, the promotion of new energy models, and so forth. Besides proposals of global scope, others of regional scope have also been presented. One of the more consensual ones among Latin American social movements is to subject Free Trade Zone of the Americas (ALCA) to a referendum in each one of the Latin American countries.

The great majority of the proposals have their origins in the articulations among movements concerned with the same thematic area. In this way, contrary to what the corporate media reports, the WSF has been 'a machine of proposals.' The design, complexity, and technical detail of many of them are of higher quality than many of those presented by the institutions of neoliberal globalisation. This entails a long-range challenge because, for these proposals to become part of political agendas, national and transnational political institutions must be changed. And many such institutional changes will occur only on the basis of non-institutional struggles. They will require rebellion, non-violent, but often illegal, direct action.

Self-Democracy and the Theory of Translation

In the WSF, the new and the old face each other. As utopia and epistemology, the WSF is something new. As a political phenomenon, its novelty co-exists with the traditions of thought on the Left or, more generally, counter-hegemonic thought, both in its western, southern and eastern versions. The newness of the WSF is consensually attributed to its absence of leaders and hierarchical organisation, its emphasis on cyberspace networks, its ideal of participatory democracy, and its flexibility and readiness to engage in experimentation.

The WSF is unquestionably the first large international progressive movement after the neoliberal backlash at the beginning of the eighties. Its future is the *future of hope* in an alternative to *la pensée unique* (single thinking). This future is completely unknown, and can only be speculated about. It depends both on the movements and organisations that comprise the WSF and the metamorphoses of neoliberal globalisation. For instance, the fact that the latter has been acquiring a bellicose component fixated on security will no doubt affect the evolution of the WSF. In light of this, the future of the WSF depends in part on the evaluation of its trajectory up till now and the conclusions drawn from it, with a view to enlarge and deepen its counter-hegemonic efficaciousness.

The evaluation of the WSF is one of the exercises that best discloses the confrontation between the new and the old. From the point of view of the old, the WSF cannot but be assessed negatively. It appears as a vast 'talk-show' that hovers over the concrete problems of exclusion and discrimination without tackling them; a cultural movement without deep social roots, therefore tolerated and easily co-opted by the dominant classes; it has no definite agents or agency, because, after all, it doesn't have any definite enemies either; its inclusiveness is the other side of its inefficaciousness; its efficaciousness, besides having an effect on the rhetoric of hegemonic discourse, has been minimal, since it has achieved no changes as far as concrete policies go, nor contributed to ameliorate the ills of exclusion and discrimination. In this evaluation, the WSF is assessed according to criteria that prevailed in progressive struggles up until the eighties. Such criteria do not concern strategies and tactics alone; they also concern the time frames and geopolitical units that are the reference of their applicability. The time frame is linear time, a time that gives meaning and direction to history; the temporality or duration is that of the State's action, even if the action aims to reform or revolutionise the State. The geopolitical unit is the national society, the boundary within which the most decisive progressive struggles of the last 200 years have occurred.

It seems obvious that the positivist epistemology underlying this evaluation is completely different from the one I ascribed to the WSF above.[2] In order to be minimally adequate, the evaluation of the WSF must be carried out according to the epistemology of the WSF itself. Otherwise, the assessment will be always negative. In other words, the evaluation must be carried out on the basis of the sociology of absences and sociology of emergences. In this case, the geopolitical unit is trans-scale: it combines the local, the national, and the global. Its time is not linear. From the standpoint of linear time, many of the counter-hegemonic experiences will always be absent or impossible. The temporalities of these experiences are indeed multiple, from the instant time of mass protests to the long-durée time of utopia.

In this light, the evaluation of the WSF cannot but be positive. By affirming and rendering credible the existence of a counter-hegemonic globalisation, the WSF has contributed significantly towards enlarging social experience. It has turned absent struggles and practices into present struggles and practices, and shown that alternative futures, declared impossible by hegemonic globalisation, were after all giving signs of emergence. By enlarging the available and possible social experience, the WSF created a global consciousness for different movements and NGOs, regardless of the scope of their action. Such a global consciousness was crucial to create certain symmetry of scale between hegemonic globalisation and the movements and NGOs that fought against it. Before the WSF, the movements and NGOs fought against hegemonic globalisation without being aware of their own globality. This consciousness of globality was decisive to make credible among the movements and the NGOs themselves the trans-scale nature of the geopolitical unit wherein they acted. By encompassing all those movements and NGOs, however, the WSF incorporated that same trans-scale nature, and that is why its efficaciousness cannot be assessed exclusively in terms of global changes. It has to be assessed as well in terms of local and national changes.

The WSF is today a more realistic utopia than when it first appeared. Increased realism, however, poses considerable challenges to utopia itself. The challenges consist in deepening its political existence without losing its utopian and epistemological integrity. I identify two main challenges, one short-range, the other long-range.

Self-Democracy

The first, short-range challenge I designate as self-democracy. The WSF's utopia concerns emancipatory democracy. In its broadest sense, emancipatory democracy is the whole process of changing power relations into relations of shared authority. Since the power relations against which the WSF resists are multiple, the processes of radical democratisation in which the WSF is involved are likewise multiple. In brief, the WSF is a large collective process for deepening democracy. Since this is the WSF's utopian distinction, it is no wonder that the issue of internal democracy has become more and more pressing.

The WSF's initial phase corresponds, as I said, to the three main Forums held in Porto Alegre, together with all the others—local, national, regional, and thematic—also held under the aegis of the WSF. It was a phase of beginnings and consolidation. The organising structure was based on the International Council (IC) and OC. For this phase, the organising structures were, to my mind, the most appropriate. Admittedly, the criteria of representation and participation could have been better tuned up to the diversity of the movements and NGOs. But it should be stressed that the successive editions of the WSF tried to respond to the criticisms advanced. If the response was not always satisfactory, I believe the reason has more to do with administrative incapacity than politically motivated design.

The challenge consists in changing the organising structure according to the demands of the new phase, with a view to deepening the internal democracy of such a structure. Two paths to reach this goal may be identified. One of them consists in transferring the WSF's core from the global event to the national, regional, and thematic Forums. The point here is that at these more circumscribed levels, the issues of representation and participatory democracy are easier to solve. The WSF, as a global event, will continue to affirm the globality of counter-hegemonic globalisation, but it will lose some of its centrality. The OC will continue to have a decisive role, but a role that will tend to be increasingly more executive while the IC will continue to be charged with defining broad thematic options and the organising structure. The democratising effort must therefore focus on the IC, urging it to go on reflecting on the multiple diversity that congregates in the WSF. This path, which seems to be close to what some members of the IC have been proposing, assumes its continuity with the previous phase.

This path does not claim to solve the issue of participatory democracy. That is to say, however representative and democratic the leading and organising structures of the Forums may be, the issue of the participation of the rank-and-file will be always there. Information and communication technologies today offer new possibilities to resort to voting and carrying out referendums during the Forums. If it is true in general that cyberdemocracy has an individualistic bias in reducing the citizen's political capacity to handling the terminal, it is no less true that such a bias is neutralised by the meetings of the Forum where inter-communication is so intense, precisely among the rank-and-file.

The second, far more structured path, aims to increase the WSF's internal democracy constructing it from bottom up. On the basis of the smaller Forums or Forums of narrower scope such as local or city Forums, representative structures are created at different levels in such a way that the structures at higher ranks are elected by the immediately lower ranks. The result envisaged is a pyramidal organisation having at the tip, the WSF turned into a Forum of delegates. The most recent and complete version of this path is the one proposed by Michael Albert, of ZNet (in this volume). Besides recommending the pyramidal construction of the WSF's democracy, Albert's proposal includes measures to correct structural deficiencies of representation, derived for example, from gender and North/South inequality and difference.

This proposal poses a radical break with the organisational model adopted up until now. Although there is a widespread feeling that the present model is exhausted, one suspects that such a radical break may stir up the fear that one might be throwing away the baby with the bath water. Needless to say, any proposal, especially one so radical, must be debated and ultimately voted. But by whom? By the current IC, certainly not representative of the whole WSF, let alone democratically elected by its members? By the participants of the Forums? Which Forums? These questions show that there is no machinery of democratic engineering capable of solving the problem of internal democracy at a single blow. To my mind, such a problem will end up being taken care of through successive partial solutions. Its cumulative effect will be the result of a learning process, which, on each democratisation landing, consolidates its force and gathers energy to venture on to an upper landing.

The Theory of Translation

The second challenge is long-range. The challenge of internal democracy concerns the processes of decision-making, rather than the content of the decisions, let alone the practices of struggle that may evolve thereof. In the long run, the evaluation of the WSF will depend on its capacity to transform the immense energy that is congregated in itself into new forms of counter-hegemonic agency—more efficacious forms that combine the strength of different social movements and NGOs.

The political theory of modernity, whether in its liberal or Marxist version, constructed the unity of action from the agent's unity. According to it, the coherence and meaning of social change was always based on the capacity of the privileged agent of change, be it the bourgeoisie or the working classes, to represent the totality from which the coherence and meaning derived. From such capacity of representation derived both the need and operationality of a general theory of social change.

The utopia and epistemology underlying the WSF place it in the antipodes of such a theory. The extraordinary energy of attraction and aggregation revealed by the WSF resides precisely in refusing the idea of a general theory. The diversity that finds a haven in it is free from the fear of being cannibalised by false universalisms or false single strategies propounded by any general theory. The time we live in, whose recent past was dominated by the idea of a general theory, is perhaps a time of transition that may be defined in the following way: we have no need of a general theory, but still need a general theory on the impossibility of a general theory.

We need, at any rate, a negative universalism that may give rise to the ecologies made possible by the sociology of absences. I cannot pursue this point here. I shall concentrate rather on what derives from it: what is the alternative to the general theory? To my mind, the alternative to a general theory is the work of translation. Translation is the procedure that allows for mutual intelligibility among the experiences of the world, both available and possible, as revealed by the sociology of absences and the sociology of emergences.

The WSF is witness to the wide multiplicity and variety of social practices of counter-hegemony that occur all over the world. Its strength derives from having corresponded or given expression to the aspiration of aggregation and articulation of different social movements and NGOs, an aspiration that had been only latent up until then. The movements and the NGOs constitute themselves around a number of more or less confined goals, create their own forms and styles of resistance, and specialise in certain kinds of practice and discourse that distinguish them from the others. Thus is constituted the identity that separates each movement from all the others. The feminist movement distinguishes itself from the labour movement, both distinguish themselves from the indigenous movement or the ecological movement, and so forth. All these distinctions have actually translated themselves into very practical differences, if not even into contradictions that contribute to bringing the movements apart and create rivalries and factionalisms. Hence derives the fragmentation and atomisation that are the dark side of diversity and multiplicity.

Movements and NGOs have only lately acknowledged this dark side. The truth is, however, that none of them individually has had the capacity or credibility to confront it. Hence the extraordinary step taken by the WSF. It must be admitted however that the aggregation and articulation made possible by the WSF is low intensity. The goals are limited and circumscribe themselves to recognising differences and wishing for exchange in order to make the differences more explicit and better known. Under these circumstances, joint action cannot but be limited. A good example was the European Social Forum. The differences, rivalries, and factionalisms that divide the various movements and NGOs that organised it are well known and have a history that is impossible to erase. This is why, in their positive response to the WSF's request to organise the ESF, the movements and NGOs that took up the task felt the need to assert that the differences among them were as sharp as ever and that they were coming together only with a very limited objective in mind: to organise the Forum and a Peace March.

The challenge that counter-hegemonic globalisation faces now may be formulated in the following way—the aggregation and articulation made possible by the WSF were enough to achieve the goals of the phase that has now reached its end. However, deepening the WSF's goals requires forms of aggregation and articulation of higher intensity. Such a process includes articulating struggles and resistances, as well as promoting ever more comprehensive and consistent alternatives. Such articulations presuppose combinations among the different social movements and NGOs that are bound to question their very identity and autonomy as they have been conceived of so far. If the idea is to promote counter-hegemonic practices and knowledges that have the collaboration of ecological, pacifist, indigenous, feminist, workers' and other movements, and if the idea is to go about this horizontally and with respect for the identity of every movement, an enormous effort of mutual recognition, dialogue, and debate will be required to carry out the task.

This is the only way to identify more rigorously what divides and unites the movements, so as to base the articulations of practices and knowledge on what unites them, rather than on what divides them. Such a task entails a wide exercise in translation to enlarge reciprocal intelligibility without destroying the identity of what is translated. The point is to create, in every movement or NGO, in every practice or strategy, in every discourse or knowledge, a contact zone that may render it porous and hence permeable to other NGOs, practices, strategies, discourses, and bodies of knowledge. The exercise of translation aims to identify and make manifest what is common in the diversity of counter-hegemonic drive. Cancelling what separates is out of the question. The goal is to have host-difference replace fortress-difference. Through translation work, diversity is celebrated not as a factor of fragmentation and isolationism but rather as a factor of sharing and solidarity.

To describe fully the procedures of the translation work is beyond the limits of this paper. Elsewhere I have proposed translations between the concept of human rights and the Hindu and Islamic concepts of human dignity[3]; between western strategies of development and Gandhi's *swadeshi*; between western philosophy and African oral sagesse; between 'modern' democracy and traditional authorities; between the indigenous movement and the ecological movement; between the workers' movement and the feminist movement.[4] To be successful, the work of translation depends on demanding conditions. Nonetheless, the effort must be taken up. On it depends the future of counter-hegemonic globalisation.

Notes

1. Edited version of a two-part paper presented at the XXIV International Congress of the Latin American Studies Association, Dallas, USA, March 27–29 2003.
2. See Part I in this volume, the chapter on "The World Social Forum: Toward a Counter-Hegemonic Globalisation."
3. Santos 1995, p. 337–346.
4. Santos 1995, 2002a, 2002b.

Women's Global Charter For Humanity

World March Of Women

Adopted on 10 December 2004 in Kigali, Rwanda, the Charter describes the world women want to build. This world based on five values: equality, freedom, solidarity, justice and peace.

Preamble

We women have been marching a long time to denounce and demand an end to the oppression of women and end the domination, exploitation, egotism, and unbridled quest for profit breeding injustice, war, conquest, and violence.

Our feminist struggles and those of our foremothers on every continent have forged new freedoms for us, our daughters and sons, and all the young girls and boys who will walk the earth after us. We are building a world where diversity is considered an asset and individuality a source of richness; where dialogue flourishes and where writing, song, and dreams can flower. In this world, human beings are considered one of the most precious sources of wealth. Equality, freedom, solidarity, justice, and peace are its driving force. We have the power to create this world. We represent over half of humanity. We give life, we work, love, create, struggle, and have fun. We currently accomplish most of the work essential to life and the continued survival of humankind. Yet our place in society continues to be undervalued.

The World March of Women, of which we are a part, views patriarchy as the system oppressing women and capitalism as the system that enables a minority to exploit the vast majority of women and men. These systems reinforce one another. They are rooted in, and work hand in hand with, racism, sexism, misogyny, xenophobia, homophobia, colonialism, imperialism, slavery, and forced labour. They breed manifold forms of fundamentalism that prevent women and men from being free. They generate poverty and exclusion, violate the rights of human beings, particularly women's rights, and imperil humanity and the planet.

We Reject This World!

We propose to build another world where exploitation, oppression, intolerance and exclusion no longer exist, and where integrity, diversity, and the rights and freedoms of all are respected. This Charter is based on the values of equality, freedom, solidarity, justice and peace.

EQUALITY

• *Affirmation 1:* All human beings and peoples are equal in all domains and all societies. They have equal access to wealth, to land, decent employment, means of production, adequate housing, a quality education, occupational training, justice, a healthy, nutritious and sufficient diet, physical and mental health services, old age security, a healthy environment, property, political and decision-making functions, energy, drinking water, clean air, means of transportation, technical knowledge and skills, information, means of communication, recreation, culture, rest, technology, and the fruit of scientific progress.

• *Affirmation 2:* No human condition or condition of life justifies discrimination.

• *Affirmation 3:* No custom, tradition, religion, ideology, economic system or policy justifies the inferiorisation of any person or authorises actions that undermine human dignity, and physical and psychological integrity.

• *Affirmation 4:* Women are full-fledged human beings and citizens before being spouses, companions, wives, mothers, and workers.

• *Affirmation 5:* All unpaid, so-called feminine tasks related to supporting life and social maintenance (household labour, education, caring of children and intimates) are economic activities that create wealth and that should be valued and shared.

• *Affirmation 6:* Trade among countries is equitable and does not harm peoples' development.

• *Affirmation 7:* Every person has access to a job with fair remuneration, in safe and sanitary conditions, and in which their dignity is respected.

FREEDOM

• *Affirmation 1:* All human beings live free of all forms of violence. No human being is the property of another. No person may be held in slavery, forced to marry, subjected to forced labour, trafficked, sexually exploited.

• *Affirmation 2:* All individuals enjoy collective and individual freedoms that guarantee their dignity, in particular: freedom of thought, conscience, belief and religion; freedom of expression and opinion; to express one's sexuality in a free and responsible manner and choose the person with whom to share one's life; freedom to vote, be elected and participate in political life; freedom to associate, meet, unionise and demonstrate; freedom to choose one's residence and civil status; freedom to choose one's courses of study and choose one's profession and exercise it; freedom to move and to be in charge of one's person and goods; and the freedom to choose one's language of communication while respecting minority languages and a society's choices concerning the language spoken at home and in the workplace, and to be informed, learn, discuss, and gain access to information technologies.

• *Affirmation 3:* Freedoms are exercised with tolerance and mutual respect and within a democratic and participatory framework, democratically determined by the society. They involve responsibilities and obligations towards the community.

• *Affirmation 4:* Women are free to make decisions about their body, fertility, and sexuality. They have the choice about whether they will have children.

• *Affirmation 5:* Democracy is rooted in freedom and equality.

SOLIDARITY

• *Affirmation 1:* International solidarity among individuals and peoples is promoted free of any form of manipulation or influence.

• *Affirmation 2:* All human beings are interdependent. They share the responsibility and the intention to live together and build a society that is generous, just, and egalitarian, based on human rights; a society free of oppression, exclusion, discrimination, intolerance, and violence.

• *Affirmation 3:* Natural resources and the goods and services necessary for all persons to live are quality public goods and services to which every individual has equal and fair access.

• *Affirmation 4:* Natural resources are administrated by the peoples living in the area, in a manner that is respectful of the environment and promotes its preservation and sustainability.

• *Affirmation 5:* A society's economy serves the women and men composing that society. It is based on the production and exchange of socially useful wealth distributed among all people, the priority of satisfying the collective needs, eliminating poverty and ensuring the balance of collective and individual interests. It ensures food sovereignty. It opposes the exclusive quest for profit to the detriment of social usefulness, and the private accumulation of the means of production, wealth, capital, land, and decision-making power by a few groups and individuals.

• *Affirmation 6:* The contribution of every person to society is acknowledged and paves the way to social rights, regardless of the function held by that person.

• *Affirmation 7:* Genetic modification is controlled. There are no patents on life or the human genome. Human cloning is prohibited.

JUSTICE

• *Affirmation 1:* All human beings regardless of their countries of origin, nationality and places of residence are considered to be full-fledged citizens, with fair and equal entitlement to human rights (social, economic, political, civil, cultural rights, sexual, reproductive, and environmental rights), within an egalitarian, fair, and genuinely democratic framework.

• *Affirmation 2:* Social justice is based on the equitable redistribution of wealth to eliminate poverty, limit wealth acquisition, and satisfy essential needs to improve the well being of all people.

• *Affirmation 3:* The physical and moral integrity of every person is protected. Torture and humiliating and degrading treatment are forbidden. Sexual violence, rape, female genital mutilation, violence against women, sex trafficking, and trafficking of human beings in general are considered crimes against the person and crimes against humanity.

• *Affirmation 4:* An accessible, egalitarian, effective, and independent judiciary is put in place.

• *Affirmation 5:* Every individual benefits from social protection guaranteeing her or him access to care, decent housing, education, information, and security in old age. Every individual has sufficient income to live in dignity.

• *Affirmation 6:* Health and social services are public, accessible, quality and free of charge; this includes all treatments, and services for all pandemic diseases, particularly HIV.

PEACE

• *Affirmation 1:* All human beings live in a peaceful world. Peace is achieved principally as a result of: equality between women and men, social, economic, political, legal and cultural equality, rights protection, and eradication of poverty, ensuring that all people live in dignity and free of violence, and that everyone has employment, enough resources to feed, house, clothe and educate themselves, is protected in old age, and has access to health care.

• *Affirmation 2:* Tolerance, dialogue and respect for diversity are foundations of peace.

• *Affirmation 3:* All forms of domination, exploitation and exclusion, of one person over another, one group over another, of a minority over a majority, of a majority over a minority, or of one nation over another, are excluded.

• *Affirmation 4:* All human beings have the right to live in a world free of war and armed conflict, foreign occupation and military bases. No one has the right to decide on the life or death of individuals and peoples.

• *Affirmation 5:* No custom, tradition, ideology, religion, political, or economic system justifies the use of violence.

• *Affirmation 6:* Armed and unarmed conflicts between countries, communities and peoples are resolved through negotiations, which bring about peaceful, just and fair solutions at the national, regional and international levels.

OUR CALL

This *Women's Global Charter for Humanity* calls on women and men and all oppressed peoples and groups of the planet to proclaim, individually and collectively, their power to transform the world and radically change social structures with a view to developing relationships based on equality, peace, freedom, solidarity and justice.

It calls on all social movements and all forces in society to take action so that the values promoted in this Charter can be effectively implemented and political decision-makers adopt the measures necessary for their implementation.

It is a call to action to change the world. The need is urgent!

No aspect of this Charter may be interpreted or utilised to express opinions or conduct activities that contravene the Charter's spirit. The values defended in it form a whole. They are of equal importance, interdependent, and indivisible, and the order they appear in the Charter is interchangeable.

What Is The World March Of Women?

The World March of Women is a movement composed of women's groups of diverse ethnic, cultural, religious, political, and class backgrounds, and different ages and sexual orientation. Far from dividing us, this diversity unites us in greater, more far-reaching solidarity.

In 2000, as part of the World March of Women, we wrote a political platform containing 17 practical demands for the elimination of poverty throughout the world, wealth sharing, the eradication of violence against women and the respect of women's physical and moral integrity. We transmitted these demands to the leaders of the International Monetary Fund, World Bank and United Nations. We received not even one concrete response. We also transmitted these demands to elected officials and leaders in our countries.

Ever since, we have ceaselessly continued to defend our demands. We are proposing alternatives to build another world. We are active in the world's social movements and in our societies. We are furthering the thinking about women's place in the world and the place we should be occupying.

With this 'Women's Global Charter for Humanity,' and our upcoming actions, we reaffirm that another world is possible, a world filled with hope and life that is truly a fine place to live. We proclaim our love of the world, its diversity and its beauty.

Note

1. This version of the charter was sourced on 9 September 2006 from <http://www.marchemondiale.org/qui_nous_sommes/charte/en>.

Other Worlds Are (Already) Possible: Self-Organisation, Complexity, And Post-Capitalist Cultures[1]

Arturo Escobar

This paper is a call for greater awareness of the theoretical frameworks that we use to understand the world and what to do about it. It stems from the realisation that there is always a tight connection between social reality, the theoretical framework we use to interpret it, and the sense of politics and hope that emerges from such an understanding. This connection is often overlooked. Our hopes and politics are largely the result of a given framework. It is particularly important that we reflect on this fact in times of profound transformations, such as today. Here, my intention is not so much to critique established frameworks (say, Marxism and liberalism), as to present the elements of another way of looking at social reality that can at least provisionally explain some of the social dynamics we are witnessing today—and in a novel way. The implications for politics should be apparent.

This new way of seeing is emerging from unsuspected quarters, chiefly, a set of alternative (but increasingly visible) theories that find their source in mathematics and the natural and physical sciences, which usually go under the label of 'complexity theory.' One of the most interesting and controversial claims of this theory is that the same dynamics and processes might be at play in many domains of material, biological, and social life. Categories such as self-organisation, non-linearity, strange attractors, and non-hierarchy are used to spell out these processes. In addition, for many, complexity in natural and social life unveils an underlying and until now largely uncharted, principle networks. This principle is clearly revealed in the domain of cyberspace, and is increasingly visible in the domain of global movements.[2]

The Argument for a New Way of Looking at Reality

Over the past few hundred years, economic and social life has tended to be largely organised on logic of order, centralisation and hierarchy building. Pushed by capitalism and its drive to accumulation, this logic has resulted in systems in which the few benefit at the expense of many. What has remained largely hidden, however, is that this logic is present not only in those social structures that are evidently exploitative but that similar logics have animated allegedly alternative systems, including socialism and most organisations on the Left. A different logic of social organisation (which was always at play, albeit marginalised) has become increasingly visible in the most recent decades. This logic seems most clearly manifested in two domains: digital technologies (cyberspace, as the universe of digital networks, interactions and interfaces); and the sciences of complexity, particularly in biology and other aspects of natural life. I would like to describe what I believe is the appeal of complexity and its potential for explaining and providing clues for social movements opposed to neoliberal globalisation. As a prelude, however, I would like to introduce briefly the argument for looking at cyberspace.

Cyberspace: Towards Subaltern Intelligent Communities?

The concept of cyberspace is based on a model that is very different from that of modern media. In the conventional model, information flows one way from a world of active emitters to that of passive receivers; there is tight ideological control so that the media reflect the world as seen by those who rule it. In other words, modern media operate on the basis of a top-down, action-reaction model of information. The model fostered by information, computer and communications technologies (ICTs) contrasts sharply with this dominant model. First, it is based on 'interactivity,' which refers to an altogether new framework of interaction—a profoundly relational model in which negotiated views of reality may be built, where all receivers are also potential emitters, a space of truly dialogical interaction, as in the best examples of net art. Second, at least in principle, cyberspace can be seen as a de-centralised archipelago of relatively autonomous zones in which communities create their own media and process their own information.

Third, ICTs and cyberspace tend to promote the creation of networked cultures without the homogenised identities assumed by the mass media; they foster routes for the circulation of ideas that are not so subject to centralised controls and the irruption of subcultures that are aware of the need to re-invent social and political orders. As a space for inter-cultural exchange and for the construction of shared artistic and political strategies, cyberspace affords unprecedented opportunities to build shared visions with peoples from all over the world (in this sense, the WSF can be seen partly as a result of this dynamics). At play is a micro-politics for the production of local knowledge made possible by the 'fluid architecture' of cyberspace, emphasising the 'molecular' (as opposed to molar, or characterised by large, homogeneous conglomerates) nature of cyberspace. This micro-politics consists of practices of mixing, re-using, and re-combining of knowledge and information.

In other words, cyberspace may be seen as embodying a new model of life and world-making. Variously called a knowledge space, a space of collective intelligence, and a 'noosphere' (sphere of collective thought), cyberspace, in these views, constitutes a signifying space of subject-subject interaction (individually and collectively) for the negotiation of visions and meanings. The resulting systems of networked intelligence could be of great cultural, social, and political potential. They could make up an inter-networked society of *intelligent communities*, centred on the democratic production of culture and subjectivity. Rather than at the service of capital, this new economy of knowledge would be at the service of an emerging humanity of co-operation, pluralism (singularity), and collective learning. It would be receptive to a multiplicity of life forms and cultures rather than contributing to the flattening of identities affected by capital's steam-rolling media. For cyberspace visionaries, this realisation could enable a re-signification of social and biological life and of freedom, a platform for the self-production of social and natural worlds.[3]

Networks, Complexity, and the Principle of Self-Organisation

In its utopian conception, cyberspace can thus be seen as enacting a de-centralised, non-hierarchical logic of self-organisation. Self-organisation is also at the heart of complexity in biological and social life. Ants, swarming moulds, cities, and certain markets are among the entities that show what scientists call 'complex adaptive behaviour.'[4] These examples evince the existence of bottom-up processes in which simple beginnings lead to complex entities, without there being any master plan or central intelligence planning it. In these cases, agents working at one (local) scale produce behaviour and forms at higher scales (e.g., the great anti-globalisation demonstrations of the last few years); simple rules at one level give rise to sophistication and complexity at another level. Scientists have a new word for this discovery, *emergence*, when the actions of multiple agents interacting dynamically and following local rules rather than top-down commands result in some kind of visible macro-behaviour or structure. There is more: these systems are (sometimes, not always) 'adaptive'—they learn over time, responding more effectively to the changing environment.

Emergent behaviour—such as, in the examples mentioned above—usually shows a mix of order and anarchy, self-organising networks and hierarchies (e.g., myriad encounters on sidewalks vs. rule-governed behaviour, to mention the example of cities). The important issue is to recognise the self-organising potential of diverse agents or multiplicities. It is important to respect and build on this logic (some new software and interfaces attempt to do just this, by learning to recognise complexity). This entails building on the logic of distributed (neither centralised nor de-centralised, but mesh-like), bottom-up intelligence as opposed to unified, top-down forms.

Complexity theory points at a pervasive logic underlying many domains of biological, social and economic life, and of networks and interconnection. Networks constitute the basic architecture of complexity. Networks are 'in' at present in the explanation of many types of processes; from nature to computers, from business to movements, anywhere one looks there seems to appear a web-like universe. Physical and natural scientists are currently busy mapping networks of all kinds, and trying to ascertain network structures, topologies, and mechanisms of operation. Social scientists are beginning to get onto the bandwagon of complex network research. As a pioneer and advocate of this research said in a comprehensive introduction to the subject, "networks will dominate the new century to a much greater degree than most people are yet ready to acknowledge...Network thinking is poised to invade all domains of human activity and most fields of human inquiry."[5] Be that as it may, the fact is that network thinking is here to stay, at least for a while, and it has interesting lessons for re-thinking many aspects of Left (and perhaps all kinds of) politics, from organisational structures to movement dynamics.

Often, networks assemble themselves by following the logic of self-organisation. The scientists' most striking claim, however, is that there are some basic laws governing all networks. For instance, networks are highly inter-connected, so that huge networks constitute 'small worlds' in the sense that all elements in the network are only a few links away from all others, particularly due to the presence of clusters, hubs and connectors. And of course not everything goes in networks, since some sites and hubs are much more connected than others are, so that there are hierarchies of inter-connection. Often, an entire network topology is determined by a few large hubs, as in the case of the World Wide Web, where links such as Google, Yahoo or Amazon have a much greater weight in defining the web's architecture than millions of much smaller nodes. These hubs determine preferential attachments; in the emerging global economy, large corporations have a profound role in shaping the networked economy. Something similar happens in global movement networks, in which Zapatista and a few other key nodes (including the WSF) are crucial to the structuring of the overall network. In sum, even if self-organised, networks of this type follow certain rules, which scientists refer to as 'power laws.'[6]

The Mexican theorist, Manuel de Landa, has introduced a useful distinction between two general network types: *Hierarchies*, and flexible, non-hierarchical, de-centralised and self-organising *meshworks*.[7] This is a key distinction that underlies two alternative philosophies of life. Hierarchies entail a degree of centralised control, ranks, overt planning, homogenisation, and particular goals and rules of behaviour; they operate under the tyranny of linear time and tree-like structures. The military, capitalist enterprises and most bureaucratic organisations have largely operated on this basis. Meshworks, on the contrary, are based on de-centralised decision making (such as the 'swarming effect' described above), self-organisation, and heterogeneity and diversity. Since they are non-hierarchical, they have no overt single goal. They develop through their encounter with their environments, although conserving their basic structure. Other metaphors used to describe these phenomena are tree-like structures or 'strata' (for hierarchies) and 'rhizomes' or 'self-consistent aggregates' for meshworks (by philosophers Deleuze and Guattari).[8] The metaphor of rhizomes suggests networks of heterogeneous elements that grow in unplanned directions, following the real-life situations they encounter. Hierarchies shun heterogeneity and diversity, meshworks welcome it. In short, they represent two very different life philosophies. An open question is whether rhizomatic meshworks escape the power laws that characterise most ('scalefree') regular networks.

These two principles are found mixed in most real-life examples. They could also give rise to one another (as when social movement meshworks develop hierarchies and centralisation). The internet is a case in point: having grown mostly on the model of self-organisation, it became increasingly colonised by hierarchical forms (from the military to e-business), which have attempted to turn it into another space of mass consumption of commodities and information. Today, the internet can be said to be a hybrid of meshwork and hierarchy components, with a tendency for the elements of command and control to increase. The reverse could be said about the global economy. Twentieth century corporate economy was based on a tree-like hierarchical model; today, corporations are seeking to evolve towards a networked form with flexible command structures. This contradicts the trend towards large conglomerates, so that capitalist economy continues to be a mixture of de-centralised networks and hierarchies. As de Landa put it, "the new view of markets stresses their de-centralisation (hence corporations do not belong there), and this can hardly justify globalisation which is mostly the result of corporations."[9] Global movements could get ahead of the game by opting decidedly for the meshwork logic.

To sum up, I am suggesting that in cyberspace and complexity we find a viable and at least potentially meaningful model of social life (in terms of, say, less hierarchical and more meshwork-like possibilities). This model is based on self-organisation, non-hierarchy, and complex adaptive behaviour on the part of agents, a model that contrasts sharply with the dominant model of capitalism and modernity, particularly in their incarnation as neoliberal globalisation. It is closer in spirit to philosophical and political anarchism and anarcho-socialism and may provide cues for internationalist networking. The model of self-organisation finally constitutes an *entirely different form* for the creation of biological, social, and economic life. Without proposing it as the only model and for all efforts worldwide, I suggest that leftist and progressive people in many parts of the world should consider this model seriously in their organising, resistance, and creative practices. In the long run, this may amount to re-inventing the dynamics of social emancipation itself. The Left is thus confronted with a novel sociology and politics of emergence from this perspective.[10]

Some Questions of Strategy

The transformation in question may already be happening as anti-globalisation social movements indicate. These movements may be seen as fostering a sort of 'emergence' in their attempt to counter the deadening, hierarchy-laden systems of neoliberal globalisation. None of the movements making up the anti-globalisation movement can by itself tackle the entire 'system' or the global situation, yet they have shown that they can work together in some fashion. They do not take their cues from any central committee, but act largely in response to local/national concerns, albeit having in mind some global issues.[11] In short, with anti-globalisation movements we have a case where local collective action results in global behaviour at least sometimes.[12] In other words, no single movement can 'see the whole' (e.g. for an Italian movement it is hard to see the complexity of a local movement in a Colombian rainforest, and for both, hard to see the complexity that their combined action might create, let alone when linked to a greater number of more diverse movements). But the fact that there are forms of globally emergent behaviour affects what particular movements think and do. In other words, place-based and other local movements contribute to emergent behaviour, that is, to forms of macro-intelligence and adaptability, even if the 'overall state of the system,' or the character of 'the enemy' might be difficult to assess. Such assessments are in fact always a perilous reduction; even if having some strategic sense of the whole might be important. In these cases, global forms of knowledge and strategy, making cannot be reduced to the individual movements making it up. The 'global movement' may indeed develop its life and adapt over a much longer time span than any individual movement that contributes to it.

In other words, anti-globalisation movements can be thought about in terms of self-organising networks (a meshwork) of movements that produce behaviour that goes beyond each individual movement. There have to be means for enabling suitable interactions (through face to face encounters, cyberspace, flexible and innovative organisational structures). These interfaces would have to foster complex learning that does not happen just locally. And it is important to think about two dynamics: the day-to-day lives of individual movements, and the historical scale of collective movement over the years. To this we might add the macro-scale of human society over long periods. Movements (and persons) are not very good at keeping these various levels in mind and at responding to changing patterns over time, for good reasons. It is important to recognise the role of self-organising behaviour so as to foster it, to the extent that is possible or desirable.[13]

Of course, not every interface or collection of agents is likely to produce adaptive, emergent behaviour. Many environments suppress such behaviour, hence the need to nourish it. There has to be both connection and organisation that promote higher-level learning. Self-organisation needs to be steered in specific ways to produce the kinds of collective intelligence that are needed. The greater the inter-connectedness, the greater the likelihood of positive feedback. Negative feedback is also important in attempting to steer a system into particular goals, making it into a complex adaptive system. From a theoretical perspective at least, a combination of ever-widening positive feedback and some negative feedback is needed—again, self-organisation with some measure of leadership, structure, and regulation. Theoretically again, the need for a measure of self-regulation and de-centralised control arises when the community/system cannot reach a constructive balance on its own. Movements would need to learn to 'read the signs' and adapt, but also learn to capitalise on the swarming behaviour and positive feedback of self-organisation. To foster interactivity conducive to these ends it is necessary to think about the rules of interaction. In the jargon of ICTs, the system needs to be wired accordingly.[14]

This double dynamic seems already present in principle in the proposal for a Social Movements World Network. Taking advantage of the virtual and real spaces created by the WSF, this proposal aims at creating a minimal basis for a world network of social movements. The proposal stems from the recognition of the need for "new structures, decision-making processes and new formations to articulate and drive a radical democratic, feminist, internationalist and anti-imperialist agenda."[15] The network "would help us develop the conditions so that the diverse social movements of the world can exchange analyses, opinions and information on the present conjuncture and establish some shared priorities and necessary tasks."

The objective is to go beyond episodic encounters among the movements, to construct a deeper political debate, to establish horizontal structures that facilitate exchange and common actions, and to extend the reach of the movements in all the continents. At this level, the proposal resonates with the logic of complexity and self-organisation, combined with some elements of structure and regulation just described.

As Adamovsky has rightly warned, however, the danger could start if and when those facilitating the process—themselves working within hierarchical organisations—attempt to create a structure that claims to represent 'the totality' of the social movements, or impose agendas instead of letting each node enter and exit network coalitions in terms of their own interests and needs.[16]

To get back to movements, anti-globalisation movements could be thought about as building de-centralised intelligence partly with the help of and following the non-colonised logic of ICTs, particularly cyberspace. Adaptive self-organisation is the best alternative available. This 'politics of emergence' shows that there can be collective intelligence and 'real results' (in terms of power) in self-organising behaviour. If it is true that global capitalism and information society are attempting a re-structuring towards the network form, movements could be better off by building on this logic and getting ahead of the game. Movements have the advantage since, unable to really pursue a strategy of collective intelligence, capitalism will progressively lose out to an anti-globalisation movement which, when all is said and done, will have learned to "think like a swarm."[17] Movements will develop a degree of self-awareness that only distributed intelligence can muster, of contributing with every action and political act to long term processes of alternative world-making.[18]

In conclusion, can anti-globalisation movements create a sort of collective intelligence that opposes the sociology of absences of neoliberal globalisation? If so, social movements would exhibit complex adaptive and emergent behaviour of their own, and would promote it for society as a whole out of their own local work. The 'behavioural ecology' of anti-globalisation movements shows that they have indeed developed adaptive behaviour to the changing environment of cyberspace. Leftist visions of the future could then build on the relational, radically self-organising principle of networking as the one most appropriate to the social movements of today. Perhaps it is on this basis that an internationalist challenge and alternative to neoliberal globalisation can be most effectively advanced.

A final caveat is in order. What does all this have to do with power? Is there a sense of power in complexity? For the vision presented above to have a chance it has to be accompanied by an ineluctable obligation: "To the local/locale; to the marginalised; to the public sphere; to a constant critical self-examination."[19] This is not easy to accomplish since the very same ICTs foster a disregard for locality, body and place, plus tremendous forms of inequality; they produce a degree of global de-localisation and erasure of place perhaps greater than ever before. Some feminists and environmentalists are very much aware of this fact:

> Who are most marginalised and disempowered by these trends? Often women, ethnic minorities, and the poor. We need to pay special attention to the political economy of ICTs and to the capitalist, patriarchal, and ethnocentric tendencies and structures that regulate ICTs and net practices today.[20]

This analysis should also give us clues about which agents should be—and at times actually are—at the forefront of struggles over ICTs.[21]

There is a political ecology of cyberculture that suggests that the 'cultures' developed out of ICTs-supported networking need to be conscious of the double character of the struggle: over the very nature of cyberspace and ICTs, and over the real re-structuring of the world effected by ICTs-led transnational capitalism. This means that if the aim is to create subaltern intelligent communities, these need to be ecological and ethical in the broad sense of these terms. There is thus a cultural politics of cyberspace that resists, transforms, and presents alternatives to the dominant real and virtual worlds. Consequently, this cybercultural politics can be most effective if it fulfils two conditions: awareness of the dominant worlds that are being created by the same technologies on which the progressive networks rely; and an ongoing tacking back and forth between cyberpolitics and place-based politics, or political activism in the physical locations where networkers or netweavers sit and live. This is precisely the politics that some of today's movements are attempting to develop in creatively combining local and global strategies for action, local and global goals, local and global interaction.[22]

Notes

1. Revised and edited version of January 2003 paper, "Other Worlds Are (Already) Possible: Cyber-Internationalism and Post-Capitalist Cultures." Draft Notes for the Cyberspace Panel, 'Life after Capitalism Programme,' World Social Forum, Porto Alegre, 23–28 January 2003. Available on www.zmag.org/lac.htm. I have preserved the general spirit of the 'Life after Capitalism' panels organised by Peter Waterman, that is, focus on the vision ('What do we want?') and strategy ('How do we get it?') Hence the generally utopian and tentative character of the piece, which is here offered as food for thought more than an accomplished proposal.
2. Calls for a new way of looking at reality came initially in the mid-eighties, from scientists advocating for a transition from the rationalistic, linear, and predictability assumptions of classical science to positions highlighting irreversibility, unpredictability, non-linearity, becoming, and the like. The most well known statement in this regard was Prigonine and Stengers's book, *Order out of Chaos* (1984). At about the same time, Boaventura de Sousa Santos was calling for a similar paradigmatic transition in the social sciences (1992).
3. Pierre Lévy (e.g., 1997) has most powerfully articulated this thesis in recent years. The liberation theologian Leonardo Boff's recent work on *religación* (2000)—a "reconnecting" of humans with nature, each other, the earth, the cosmos, God—could also be interpreted in this light (he appeals explicitly to complexity). Discussions of the impact of ICTs on daily life abound, including those examining "cybercultures" (e.g., Harcourt, ed. 1999; Bell and Kennedy, eds. 2000; Burbano and Barragán, eds. 2002). Kari-Hans Kommonen and the ARKI Research Group at the Media Lab at the Helsinki University of Art and Design are developing a framework to study the impact of growing digitalisation on everyday life. For these researchers, the internet is a first step in the development of a far more complex

Mediaspace that is emerging as a result of pervasive digitalisation. This Mediaspace will be central to crafting and negotiating ideas, structures and practices, hence the need to develop an explicit approach to designing this space as a means to social, cultural and political innovation. See < http://arki.uiah.fi>

4. Common examples include: thousands of invisible single-celled mould units which occasionally coalesce into a swarm and create a visible large mould; ant colonies that develop over a long time span with no central pacemaker; local markets which, in the past, efficiently linked myriad producers and consumers, allowing prices to set themselves in a way that was understood locally, without great hierarchies or central control; and the way in which cities developed without much central planning on the basis of interfaces between pedestrians, vehicles, goods and services. See the fine introduction on emergence in complex systems by Johnson (2001). A more technical work that attempts to re-think social structure from the perspective of complexity is Kontopoulos (1993); it pays attention to issues of emergence, stability, scale, and heterarchical forms of organisation in ways that could be useful for thinking about emergent structures and possibility spaces in AGMs. Above all, I have relied on Manuel de Landa's sustained effort at pushing complexity forward by focussing on social systems.
5. Barabási 2002, pp. 7, 222.
6. Barabási 2002.
7. de Landa 1997 and 2003.
8. Deleuze and Guattari 1987.
9. de Landa 2003, p. 5.
10. Santos, this volume.
11. A somewhat similar argument has been made by Osterweil (2002) for Italian movements, Peltonen (2003) for the Finnish environmental movement, and my own studies of the social movement of black communities of the Pacific (2000). Peltonen (2002), Chesters (2003), and Escobar (2002) are among the few applications of complexity to social movements to date.
12. Or is there a global effect *always going on*, besides and beyond the visible global events? Is there a stifling "Seattle effect" that does not let us see the always on-going swarming that goes on at the local/regional levels, that in some way is also "global?"
13. From the perspective of complexity, the theoretical utopia would be a phase transition as a result of AGM activity, that is, a radical change in state and organisation at a critical juncture, perhaps promoted by some sort of non-linear dynamics in the mechanisms of the world economy, ecology, ideology.
14. Some of the concerns with the WSF expressed by critics in this volume can be interpreted in this light. What kinds of interfaces and correctives would be needed to foster the movement networks adumbrated by Adamovsky and George, for instance, or for lessening the invisibilities unveiled by Osterweil?
15. CUT, World March of Women, ATTAC, and Focus on the Global South, this volume.

16. Adamovsky 2003.

17. Johnson 2002.

18. Electronic art, net art and software design are also fields where great innovation is taking place in the direction of self-organisation, multiplicity, and non-hierarchy. See the original version of this article for some references. See also *Critical Art Ensemble* (1996); Burbano and Barragán, eds. (2002) for recent Latin American experiments. Application of network theory to movements and global issues include Waterman (1992), King (2000), and the dissertations on Zapatista networks by Solano-Leyva (2001) and Olesen (2002). A study of networks from a dominant perspective is Arquilla and Ronfeldt (2001).

19. Waterman 2003.

20. Harcourt, ed 1999; Escobar 1999; Virilio 1999.

21. See, for instance, Maria Suárez's work with the FIRE radio and internet network in Costa Rica 2003, and in this volume.

22. See, for instance, the 'Women and the Politics of Place' project, organised by the Society for International Development, SID (www.sidint.org).

Glossary

ABONG	*Associação Brasileira de Organizações Não Governamentais* [Brazilian Association of Non-Governmental Organisations]
ACP	African, Caribbean, and Pacific Group of States
ADB	Asian Development Bank
Adivasi	Tribal person; literally meaning original inhabitant (India)
AFL-CIO	American Federation of Labor-Congress of Industrial Organisations (USA)
AGMs	Anti-Globalisation Social Movements
AIDWA	All India Women's Democratic Association
ALW	Alliance for Workers' Liberty
ANC	African National Congress (South Africa)
APA	Asian Peace Alliance
AGOA	African Growth and Opportunities Act
ASF	Asian Social Forum
ATTAC	*Association pour la Taxation des Transactions pour l'Aide aux Citoyens* [Association for the Taxation of Financial Transactions for the Aid of Citizens] (started in France, now in many countries)
AWID	Association of Women in Development
BOC	Brazilian Organising Committee
BJP	*Bharatiya Janata Party* [Indian People's Party] (India)
CADA	Campaign for the Demilitarization of the Americas
CBJP	*Comissão Brasileira Justiça e Paz* [Brazilian Justice and Peace Commission, of the National Council of Bishops (CNBB)]
CEDAW	Convention on the Elimination of All Forms of Discrimination Against Women
CIA	Central Intelligence Agency (USA)
CIVES	*Associação Brasileira de Empresários pela Cidadania* [Brazilian Business Association for Citizenship]
CJG	Centre for Global Justice
CJTF-HOA	Combined Joint Task Force-Horn of Africa
CLACSO	Latin American Council of Social Sciences, Buenos Aires (one of Latin America's premier research institutes)
COSATU	Congress of South African Trade Unions (South Africa)
CPI	Communist Party of India

CPI(M) Communist Party of India (Marxist)
CPI(ML) Communist Party of India (Marxist-Leninist)
Crore Ten million, in the Indian numerical system
CSN *Confédération des syndicats nationaux* [Confederation of National Labour Unions] (Canada)
CUT *Central Única dos Trabalhadores* (Central Trade Union Confederation) [Brazil]
DSF Durban Social Forum
EPAs Economic Partnership Agreements
ETUC European Trade Union Confederation
EU European Union
EZLN *Ejercito Zapatista de Liberacion Nacional* [Zapatista National Liberation Army] (Mexico)
FBI Federal Bureau of Investigation (USA)
FFQ *Fédération des Femmes du Québec* [Quebec Women's Federation]
FSQ *Forum Social Quebecois* [Quebec Social Forum]
FTAA Free Trade Area of the Americas
FWCW Fourth World Conference on Women, People's Republic of China, 1995
GGJ Grassroots Global Justice
Giovani Comunisti The youth organisation of the *Rifondazione Comunista*
GJ&SM Global Justice and Solidarity Movement
GJM Global Justice Movement
Global Fire The official newspaper of the WSSD civil society process
GUF Global Union Federation; formerly 'International Trade Union Secretariat'
Has Hemispheric Social Alliance
IBASE *Instituto Brasileiro de Análises Sociais e Econômicas* [Brazilian Institute for Social and Economic Studies]
IC International Council of the World Social Forum
ICFTU International Confederation of Free Trade Unions
ICPD International Conference on Population and Development, Egypt, 1994
ICTs Information and Communication Technologies
IDWIP International Decade of the World's Indigenous Peoples
IIRSA Initiative for the Integration of Regional Infrastructure in South America
ILC International Liaison Committee for a Workers' International
ILO International Labour Organisation
IMC Indymedia Centre

IMF International Monetary Fund
IUCN International Union for the Conservation of Nature
JwJ Jobs with Justice
Lakh Hundred thousand, in the Indian numerical system
LCR *Ligue Communiste Revolutionaire* [Revolutionary Communist League] (France)
LGBT Lesbian, Gay, Bisexual, and Transgender people
LPM Landless People's Movement
MAI Multilateral Agreement on Investment
MCC Millennium Challenge Corporation (USA)
MERCOSUL *Mercado Comum do Sul* [Southern Common Market, in Portuguese]
MERCOSUR *Mercado Común del Sur* [Southern Common Market, in Spanish]
MR Mumbai Resistance (an event in Mumbai, January 2004)
MST *Movimento dos Trabalhadores Rurais Sem Terra* [Movement of Landless Rural Workers] (Brazil)
MTD *Movimiento de Trabajadores Desocupados* [Movement of Disemployed Workers]
NAFTA North American Free Trade Agreement
NAM Non-Aligned Movement
NATO North Atlantic Treaty Organisation
NEPAD New Partnership for Africa's Development
NGOs Non-Governmental Organisations
NIEO New International Economic Order
NLG Neo-Liberal Globalisation
NPC National Planning Committee (for the U.S. Social Forum, June 2007)
NSM New Social Movements
NWICO New World Information and Communication Order
NWSF Northwest Social Forum (USA)
ODA Overseas Development Assistance
ORIT *Organisation Regional Interamericana de Trabajadores* [Inter American Regional Organisation of Workers] (Latin America)
OSAL *Observatorio Social de América Latina* [Latin American Social Observatory]
PAN Planetary Anarchist Network (also: Pesticides Action Network)
PGA People's Global Action
POWER People Organized to Win Employment Rights, San Francisco, USA
PQ *Parti Québécois* [Quebec Party]
PRC *Partito Della Rifondazione Comunista* [Reformed Communist Party] (Italy)

PSOE *Partido Socialista Obrero Español* [Spanish Socialist Party]
PT *Partido dos Trabalhadores* [Workers' Party] (Brazil)
PUC Pontificia Universidade Católica [Catholic University] (Porto Alegre, Brazil—the main location of the WSF in 2001 and 2002)
QS *Québec Solidaire* [Solidary Quebec]
Red Pepper The UK-based monthly magazine of the independent left
Rede Social de Justiça e Direitos Humanos [Social Justice and Human Right Network]
REDOIL Resisting Environmental Destruction on Indigenous Land, Alaska
Rifondazione Comunista Short version of *Partito Della Rifondazione Comunista* [Party of the Reformed Communists] (Italy)
RWA Revolutionary Writers' Association (Andhra Pradesh, India)
SAPs Structural Adjustment Policies
SDP Social Democratic Party (Germany)
SDS Students for a Democratic Society (USA)
SESF Southeast Social Forum (USA)
The Big G Globalisation
TINA There is No Alternative
TIUI Traditional International Union Institutions
TRC Truth and Reconciliation Commission (South Africa)
UNCTAD UN Centre for Trade and Development
UNDP UN Fund for Development
UNICEF UN Children's Fund
UNIFEM UN Fund for Women
USAID United States Agency for International Development
WB World Bank
WCAR World Conference Against Racism, South Africa, 2002
WEF World Economic Forum
WLUML Women Living Under Muslim Law
WMW World March of Women
WSF World Social Forum
WSFC WSF on Childhood (Caracas, Venezuela, January 24-29, 2006)
WSIS World Summit on the Information Society (2003, 2005)
WSSD World Summit on Sustainable Development (South Africa, 2002)
WSSD World Summit on Social Development (Copenhagen, Denmark, March 1995)
WTO World Trade Organisation
WWF World Wildlife Fund
ZANU Zimbabwe African National Union

References

This is a combined list of all the references given in the essays appearing in this book—making this a rich resource list by itself. It contains references both to documents and to websites. To make finding the latter easier, we have listed them separately, at the end.

The bibliographic system used in this list for documents is a little different from standard formats. It is a product of an ongoing separate effort to make bibliographic presentation more reader-friendly and counter-hegemonic. This includes providing translations (into the language of this book) of all titles in other languages. For those interested, there is a Note at the end of this list that explains the layout system used.

An additional feature of this list is that we have double-checked all the web links that were given in the first edition of this book and list, and given or made corrections wherever necessary; and we have also noted where the links given no longer work but we have found no substitute.

ABONG, ATTAC, CBJP, CIVES, CUT, IBASE, CJG, and MST, April 2001, 'World Social Forum Charter of Principles,' first edition, dt April 9 2001, 2 pp. Document earlier available at http://www.forumsocialmundial.org.br/main.php?id_menu=4&cd_language=2. Published in Jai Sen, Anita Anand, Arturo Escobar, and Peter Waterman, eds, 2004, *World Social Forum: Challenging Empires*. New Delhi: Viveka, pp 67-69. Available @ http://www.choike.org/nuevo_eng/informes/1557.html and @ http://www.openspaceforum.net/twiki/tiki-index.php?page=WSFChallengingEmpires2004

Abramsky, Kolya, ed, 2001, *Restructuring and Resistance, Diverse Voices of Struggle in Western Europe*, 565 pp. Available at reseryev@yahoo.com

Adamovsky, Ezequiel, 2003, 'The World Social Forum's New Project: 'The Network of the World's Social Movements'.' Unpublished manuscript

Adamovsky, Ezequiel and Susan George, 2003, 'What is the Point of Porto Alegre?,' first published in *openDemocracy*, @ http://www.opendemocracy.net/debates/article.jsp?id=6&debateId=91&articleId=906. Republished in Jai Sen, Anita Anand, Arturo Escobar, Peter Waterman, eds, 2004, *World Social Forum: Challenging Empires*, New Delhi: Viveka, pp 130-135. Available @ http://

www.choike.org/nuevo_eng/informes/1557.html and @ http://www. open spaceforum.net/twiki/tiki-index.php?page=WSFChallengingEmpires2004

Adams, J, February 2002, 'WSF2002: Hopes for a True International,' in *Z Magazine*, @ http://www.zmag.org/content/VisionStrategy/AdamsWSF.cfm

Africa All Party Parliamentary Group, March 2006, *The Other Side of the Coin: The UK and Corruption in Africa*, available @ www.africaappg.org.uk

African Social Forum, January 2003, Addis Ababa Consensus: Another Africa Is Possible!, in Jai Sen, Anita Anand, Arturo Escobar, and Peter Waterman, eds, 2004, *World Social Forum: Challenging Empires*. New Delhi: Viveka, pp 312-314. Available @ http://www.openspaceforum.net/twiki/tiki-index.php?page=WSFChallengingEmpires2004

Agrawal, A and K Sivaramkrishnan, 2000, 'Introduction: Agrarian Environments,' in Agrawal, A and K Sivaramkrishnan, eds, 2000, *Agrarian Environments: Resources Representation and Rule in India*, Durham: Duke University Press

Aguiton, Christophe, 2001, *Le Monde nous appartient* [*The World Belongs to Us*, in French], Paris: Plon

Aguiton, Christophe, nd, 'An Activist's Guide to the G8,' Translated by Barbara and David Forbes, 10 pp

Albert, Michael, 2002, *Trajectory of Change*, Boston

Albert, Michael, February 2003, 'WSF: Where to Now?' Available from http://www.zmag.org/content/showarticle.cfm?ItemID=2956 . Republished in edited form as 'The World Social Forum: Where To Now?' in Jai Sen, Anita Anand, Arturo Escobar, and Peter Waterman, eds, 2004, *World Social Forum: Challenging Empires*, New Delhi: Viveka, pp 323-328. Available @ http://www.choike.org/nuevo_eng/informes/1557.html and @ http://www. openspaceforum.net/twiki/tiki-index.php?page=WSFChallengingEmpires2004

Albert, Michael, nd, *Anarchism?!*. Available at http://zmag.org/anarchism.htm

Ali, Tariq and Susan Watkins, 1998, *1968: Marching in the Streets*, New York: Free Press

Alternatives Sud, April 2005, *'Le miracle chinois vu de l'intérieur: Points de vue d'auteurs chinois'* ['The Chinese miracle seen from the inside: The points of view of Chinese authors,' in French], volume 12, April 2005

Alvarez, Sonia E, Autumn 2000, 'Translating the Global: Effects of Transnational Organising on Local Feminist Discourses and Practices in Latin America,' in *Meridians: A Journal of Feminism, Race, Transnationalism*, vol 1, no 1, p 16

Alvarez, Sonia E, 2000a, *'A 'Globalização' dos Feminismos Latino-americanos: Tendências dos Anos 90 e Desafios para o Novo Milênio'* ['The Globalisation of Latin American Feminism: Trends of the 90s and Challenges for the New Millenium,' in Portuguese], in Sonia E Alvarez, Evelina Dagnino, and Arturo

Escobar, eds, 2000, *Cultura e Política nos Movimentos Sociais Latino-americanos: Novas Leituras* [title of English edition: 'Cultures of Politics/ Politics of Culture: Revisioning Latin American Social Movements'], pp 383-426. Belo Horizonte: Universidade Federal de Minas Gerais

Alvarez, Sonia E, 2000b, 'Translating the Global: Effects of Transnational Organizing on Latin American Feminist Discourses and Practices,' in *Meridians: A Journal of Feminisms, Race, Transnationalism*, vol 1, no 1, pp 29-67

Alvarez, Sonia and others, 2002, 'Encountering Latin American and Caribbean Feminisms,' in *Signs*, Volume 28, Number 2, pp 539-579

Alvarez, Sonia E, Evelina Dagnino, and Arturo Escobar, eds, 1998, *Cultures of Politics, Politics of Cultures, Re-Visioning Latin American Social Movements*, Boulder, Colorado: Westview Press

Alvarez, Sonia E, Nalu Faria and Miriam Nobre, eds, 2003, *'Dossiê: Fórum Social Mundial e Feminismos'* ['Introduction: World Social Forum and Feminisms,' in Spanish], special issue of *Revista Estudos Feministas* [*Journal of Feminist Studies*] (Brazil), Vol 11, No 2, 2003. Available online at www.portalfeminista.org.br and @ http://www.scielo.br/scielo.php?script=sci_serial&pid=0104-026X&lng=en&nrm=iso

Amin, S, G Arrighi, A G Frank, and others, 1990, *Transforming the Revolution: Social Movement and the World System*, New York: Monthly Review Press

Amin, Samir, interviewed by V Sridhar, January 2003, 'For struggles, global and national,' in *Frontline*, volume 20 issue 2, http://www.flonnet.com/fl2002/stories/20030131008201200.htm. Republished in Jai Sen, Anita Anand, Arturo Escobar, and Peter Waterman, eds, 2004, *World Social Forum: Challenging Empires*. New Delhi: Viveka pp 5-11

Amin, Samir, January 2007, *'Forum Social Mundial, Quel Altermondialisme?'* ['The World Social Forum—What Kind of Alterglobalisation?' in French], in *Le Monde Diplomatique*, January 2007, p. 28; @http://www.monde-diplomatique.fr/2007/01/AMIN/14356

Amin, Samir and François Houtart, eds, 2002, *Mondialisation de resistances: L'etat des lutes 2002*, ['The Globalisation of Resistance: The State of the Struggles 2002,' in French], Paris: L'Harmattan/Forum Mondial des Alternatives

Anand, Anita, Arturo Escobar, Jai Sen, und Peter Waterman (Hrsg), 2004, *Eine Andere Welt: Das Weltsozialforum* ['Another World: The World Social Forum,' in German]. Translated from the original English edition (*World Social Forum: Challenging Empires*, New Delhi: Viveka, 2004) by Carla Krüger and Wolfram Adolphi of the Rosa Luxemburg Foundation, Berlin: Karl Dietz Verlag

Anand, Nikhil, 2004, 'Bound to Mobility? Identity and Purpose at the World Social Forum,' in Jai Sen, Anita Anand, Arturo Escobar, and Peter Waterman, eds,

2004, *World Social Forum: Challenging Empires*, New Delhi: Viveka, pp 140-147. Revised version of paper for Seminar on 'Environment and Development: Dilemmas of Power and Place,' Yale University, May 2003. Available @ http://www.choike.org/nuevo_eng/informes/1557.html and @ http://www.openspaceforum.net/twiki/tiki-index.php?page=WSFChallengingEmpires2004

ANC discussion document, August 2002, 'The Balance of Forces,' cited in *Mail and Guardian*, dt 16 August 2002

Anderson, Benedict, 1983, *Imagined Communities: Reflections on the Origin and Spread of Nationalism*, London: Verso

Anheier, Helmut, Marlies Glasius, and Mary Kaldor, eds, 2001, *Global Civil Society Yearbook*, 360 pp, Oxford: Oxford University Press

Anon, nd, c. December 2001, 'Report on World Social Forum Meeting, Fireflies Ashram, Bangalore, December 15th and 16th, 2001.' 4 pp

Andhra Pradesh Vyavasaya Vruthidarula Union, National Alliance of People's Movements, National Agricultural Worker's Forum–India, and others, January 2003, 'People's Movements–Evolving Our World: End Imperialist Globalisation, Fundamentalism and War.' Statement of the People's Movements Encounters at the Asian Social Forum, Hyderabad, India, January 2-7 2003. 4 pp. Issued by P Chenniah, Coordinator, Andhra Pradesh Vyavasaya Vruthidarula Union and National Alliance of People's Movements, at Chenniah@nettlinx.com; available at the WSF India website http://www.wsfindia.org/. Published in Jai Sen, Anita Anand, Arturo Escobar, and Peter Waterman, eds, 2004, *World Social Forum: Challenging Empires*, New Delhi: Viveka, pp 275-278. Available @ http://www.openspaceforum.net/twiki/tiki-index.php?page=WSFChallengingEmpires2004

Anon, 2003, 'Statement of the Arab Social Movements participating in the World Social Forum, January 2003,' in Jai Sen, Anita Anand, Arturo Escobar, and Peter Waterman, eds, 2004, *World Social Forum: Challenging Empires*, New Delhi: Viveka, pp 365-367. Available @ http://www.openspaceforum.net/twiki/tiki-index.php?page=WSFChallengingEmpires2004

Anon, nd, c. December 2001, 'Report on World Social Forum Meeting, Fireflies Ashram, Bangalore, December 15th and 16th, 2001,' 4 pp

Appadurai, Arjun, 2002, 'Deep Democracy: Urban Governmentality and the Horizon of Politics,' in *Public Culture*, Volume 14, pp 21-47 Available @ http://www.ucl.ac.uk/dpu-projects/drivers_urb_change/urb_governance/pdf_democ_empower/IIED_appadurai_demo.pdf. [The text available on this link is without references.]

Arquilla, John and David Ronfeldt, 2001, *Networks and Netwars*, Santa Monica, CA: Rand Corporation

Arrighi, G, T K Hopkins, and I Wallerstein, 1989, *Antisystemic Movements*, London: Verso

Ashman, Sam, 2003, 'The Anti-Capitalist Movement and the War,' in *International Socialism*, number 98

Asian Peace Alliance, October 2001, 'Founding Declaration,' Available @ http://www.yonip.com/main/APA/pr.html

Asian Social Mass and Peoples' Movements & Organisations, January 2003, 'Statement of the Asian Social Mass & Peoples' Movements & Organisations, Hyderabad,' in Jai Sen, Anita Anand, Arturo Escobar, and Peter Waterman, eds, 2004, *World Social Forum: Challenging Empires*. New Delhi: Viveka, pp 272-274. Available @ http://www.openspaceforum.net/twiki/tiki-index.php?page=WSFChallengingEmpires2004

Aufheben, *Autumn 2001, issue no 10*

Bakunin, Michael, 1970, *'La Commune de Paris et la notion de l'état'* ['The Paris Commune and the notion of the state,' in French], reprinted in Guérin, *Ni Dieu, ni Maître* (Not God, Not Master), New York

Bandarage, Asoka, 1998, *Women, Population, and Global Crisis*, London: Zed Books

Barabasi, Albert László, 2002, *Linked: The New Science of Networks*, Cambridge: Perseus Publishing

Barber, Benjamin R, 1995, *Jihad vs McWorld, Terrorism's Challenge to Democracy*. New York: Ballantine Books, www.ballantinebooks.com

Barbiero, Alan and Yves Chaloult, 2003, *Poder e déficit democràtico do MERCOSUL. Estado, Centrais Sindicais e Sociedade Civil* ['Power and the democratic deficit in MERCOSUR: State, Trade Union Federations, and Civil Society,' in Spanish], Porto Alegre, EDIPUCRS

Barlow, Maude and Tony Clarke, 2002, *Global Showdown*, Toronto: Stoddart

Basu, Amrita, Autumn 2000, 'Globalisation of the Local/Localisation of the Global: Mapping Transnational Women's Movements,' in *Meridians: A Journal of Feminism, Race, Transnationalism*, vol 1, no 1, pp 68-84

Bayes, Jane H, and Rita Mae Kelly, 2001, 'Political Spaces, Gender, and NAFTA,' in Rita Mae Kelly et al, 2001, *Gender, Globalization and Democratization*, pp 160-161. Lanham, MD: Rowman & Littlefield

Bell, B, 2002, *Social Movements and Economic Integration in the Americas*, New York: Centre for Economic Justice

Bell, David, and Barbara Kennedy, eds, 2000, *The Cyber Cultures Reader*, London: Routledge

Bello, Walden F, 2001, *The Future in the Balance, Essays on Globalization and Resistance*, Oakland, CA: Food First Books

Bello, Walden, January 2002, 'Porto Alegre Social Summit Sets Stage for Counter-offensive against Globalization,' on *Z Magazine*, @ http://www.zmag.org/Sustainers/content/2002-01/31bello.cfm

Bello, Walden, May 2007, 'World Social Forum at the Crossroads,' in *Foreign Policy in Focus*, May 4 2007. Source: Transnational Institute @ http://www.tni.org/detail_page.phtml?act_id=16771

Benasayag, Miguel and Dardo Scavino, 1997, *Pour une nouvelle radicalité* ['For a new radicality,' in French], Paris: La Découverte/Poche

Benasayag, Miguel and Diego Sztulwark, 2002, *Du contre-pouvoir* ['On counter power,' in French], Paris: La Découverte/Poche

Bhushan, Prashant, March 2003, 'Bush Must Be Stopped Now Before It Is Too Late.' Note circulated over email, dt 15 March 2003

Biccum, April, 2005, 'The World Social Forum: Exploiting the Ambivalence of Open Spaces,' in *Ephemera*, volume 5(2), pp 116-133, www.ephemeraweb.org, @ http://www.ephemeraweb.org/journal/5-2/5-2biccum.pdf

Bloch, Ernst, 1995, *The Principle of Hope*, Cambridge, Mass: MIT Press

Boff, Leonardo, 2000, *El Cuidado Esencial*['The Essential Care,' in Spanish], Madrid: Editorial Trotta

Bond, P, 2002, *Unsustainable South Africa: Environment, Development, and Social Protest*, Pietermaritzburg: University of Natal Press

Bond, P, February 2003, 'Battle of the Trevors,' in *The Sowetan* (South Africa)

Bond, Patrick, 2003, *Against Global Apartheid*, London: Zed, and University of Cape Town Press

Boyd, Andrew, 2003, 'The Web Rewires the Movement,' in *The Nation*, dt 4 August 2003. Available at http://www.thenation.com/doc.mhtml?i=20030804&s=boyd

Bradford, Sue, and Bernardo Kucinski, eds, 2003, *Politics Transformed: Lula and the Workers Party in Brazil*, London: Latin America Bureau

Brand, Ulrich, January 2007, '*Die Netzwerke für eine andere Welt werden dichter*' ['The networks for another world become poets,' in German], *Frankfurter Rundschau*, 27 January 2007

Brenner, Johanna, 2000, 'Women and the Politics of Class,' in *Monthly Review*

Brosius, J P, 1999, 'Green Dots, Pink Hearts: Displacing Politics from the Malaysian Rain Forest,' in *American Anthropologist* 101(1), pp 36-57

Brunelle, Dorval, April 1999, 'Free trade illusions in Quebec,' in *Le Monde Diplomatique*

Buckley, Coady, Spring/Summer 2003, 'Introduction: Neoliberal Governance and Social Resistance: A Chronology of Events,' *The Commoner*, No 7 @

http://www.thecommoner.org. Also available as 'Neoliberal Governance and Social Resistance,' @ http://www.ainfos.ca and http://ainfos.ca/index24.html

Burbano, Andrés, and Hernando Barragán, eds, 2002, *hipercubo/ok/. arte, ciencia y tecnología en contextos próximos* ['hibercube/ok/. art, science and technology in proximal contexts,' in Spanish]. Bogotá: Universidad de Los Andes, Goethe Institute

Buzgalin, Aleksandr, October 2003, 'The Specter of "Alter-Globalization",' in *Russian Politics & Law*, Vol 41 No 5, September-October 2003; special issue on 'Russian Views of Globalization and Its Opponents,' pp 62-76. Available @ http://www.mamacoca.org/FSMT_sept_2003/en/lat/Buzgalin_spectre_of_alterglobalization.htm Callinicos, Alex, 2003, *An Anti-Capitalist Manifesto*, Cambridge: Polity

Cardon, Dominique, and Fabien Granjon, 2003, 'The Alter-Globalisation Movement and the Internet,' in *Sand in the Wheels*, ATTAC Weekly Newsletter, dt 19 February 2003, translated by Jane Holister. Available @ http://archive.attac.org/attacinfoen/attacnews163.pdf

Carr, Barry, 1998, 'The Many Meanings of [Mexico] 1968,' in *Enfoque*, pp 1-2, 6. Centre for U.S.-Mexican Studies, University of California, San Diego

Caruso, Giuseppe, December 2004, 'Conflict management and hegemonic practices in the World Social Forum 2004,' in *International Social Science Journal*, Issue no 182, pp 577-590. Available @ http://www.blackwell-synergy.com/servlet/useragent?func=showIssues&code=issj&open=2004#C2004/

Caruso, Giuseppe, October 2006, 'Difference and Conflicts in the World Social Forum India: Towards an "open" cosmopolitanism?' Mss for inclusion in Jai Sen and Peter Waterman, eds, forthcoming, 2008, *World Social Forum: Challenging Empires Globally* [title under finalisation], Volume 3 in the *Challenging Empires* series, New Delhi: OpenWord Books

Caruso, Giuseppe, April 2007, 'Open Spaces and Hegemonic Practices in Global Civil Society: The World Social Forum 2004.' A thesis submitted to the University of London in partial fulfilment of the requirements for the degree of PhD in Development Studies. Department of Development Studies, School of Oriental and African Studies, University of London

Cassen, Bernard, 2002, *'Comment est né le Forum Social Mondial'* [How the Forum was born,' in French]. Unpublished manuscript

Castells, M, 1996, *The Rise of the Network Society*, London: Blackwells

Castells, M, 1997, *The Power of Identity*, London: Blackwells

Celiberti, Lilian, April-June 2001, *'El Foro Social Mundial: nueva cultura política'* ['The World Social Forum: New Political Culture,' in Spanish], in *Cotidiano Mujer*['Everyday Woman,' in Spanish], no 34, pp 2-3

Celiberti, Lilian, 2002, *Metaforo, Documento de la Articulación Feminista Marcosur* ['Metaphor,' Document of the Marcosur Feminist Articulation; in Spanish], Montevideo: Articulación Feminista Marcosur

Chattopadhyay, Kunal, November 2003, 'The World Social Forum: What it could mean for the Indian left,' in *Labor Standard*, Information Education Discussion, 10 November 2003. Available @ http://www.laborstandard.org/WSF/Kunal.htm

Chen, Martha Alter, 1996, 'Engendering World Conferences: The International Women's Movement and the UN,' in Thomas G Weiss and Leon Gordenker, eds. *NGOs, the UN and Global Governance*, pp 139-158. Boulder, Colorado: Lynne Rienner

Chenoy, Kamal, S P Shukla, K S Subramanian, and Achin Vanaik, April 2002, *Gujarat Carnage 2002: A Report to the Nation*. Available @ http://www.sacw.net/Gujarat2002/GujCarnage.html

Chomsky, Noam, October-December 1992, '2 papers,' *Z Papers Special Issue*, @ http://www.zmag.org/ScienceWars/index.htm

Christian Aid, July 2006, 'UK profits from sub-Saharan Africa despite aid and debt pledges,' 5 July 2006

Clark, Ann Marie, Elisabeth J Friedman, and Kathryn Hochstetler, 1998, 'The Sovereign Limits of Global Civil Society: A Comparison of NGO Participation in UN World Conferences on the Environment, Human Rights, and Women,' in *World Politics* vol 51, no 1, pp 135

Clark, J, 2001, 'Ethical Globalisation: The Dilemma and Challenges of Internationalising Civil Society,' in Edwards and Gaventa, eds, *Global Citizen Action*, pp 17-28. Boulder: Lynn Reiner

Cleaver, Harry, 1998, 'The Zapatista Effect: The Internet and the Rise of an Alternative Political Fabric,' in *Journal of International Affairs*, Vol 51, No 2, pp 621-640. Available @ http://www.uff.br/mestcii/cleaver.htm, http://auto_sol.tao.ca/node/view/1764

Cock, J, July 2001, 'Butterfly Wings and Green Shoots: The Impact of Peace Organisations in Southern Africa,' in *Track Two*, Volume 10, Number 1, pp 4-33. Available @ http://ccrweb.ccr.uct.ac.za/archive/two/10_1/p04_butterfly_ wings. html

Cock, Jacklyn, February 2003, 'A Better or Worse World? The Third World Social Forum, Porto Alegre 2003.' Centre for Civil Society, Durban, South Africa, Research Report 5. http://www.nu.ac.za/ccs. Edited excerpt published in Jai Sen, Anita Anand, Arturo Escobar, and Peter Waterman, eds, 2004, *World Social Forum: Challenging Empires*. New Delhi: Viveka, pp 191-198. Available @ http://www.choike.org/nuevo_eng/informes/1557.html and @ http://www.openspaceforum.net/twiki/tiki-index.php?page=WSFChallengingEmpires2004

Cock, J and E Koch, 1991, *Going Green: People, Politics and the Environment*, Cape Town: Oxford University Press

Cock, J and D Fig, 2001, 'The Impact of Globalisation on Environmental Politics in South Africa 1990-2002,' Paper presented to the ISA Environmental Sociology Conference, Kyoto, Japan. Published in African Sociological Review, 5, (2), 2001. Available @ http://www.codesria.org/Links/Publications/asr5_2 full/Cock_Fig.pdf

Cockburn, Alexander, April 2000, ''New' and 'Left' Are Not Oxymoronic,' in *The Los Angeles Times*, 20 April 2000, Available @ http://www.common dreams.org/views/042000-103.htm

Cohen, Jean, ed, 1985, 'Social Movements,' in *Social Research*, Vol 52, No 4

Conference of the European Anti-capitalist Left, June 2002, 'Declaration,' available @ http://www.internationalviewpoint.org/spip.php?article384

Coomaraswamy, Radhika, 2002, 'Are Women's Rights Universal? Re-Engaging the Local,' in *Meridians: Journal of Feminism, Race, Transnationalism*, vol 3, no 1, pp 1-18

Corcoran-Nantes, Yvonne, 2000, 'Female Consciousness or Feminist Consciousness? Women's Consciousness Raising in Community-based Struggle in Brazil,' in Smith, Bonnie G, ed, 2000, *Global Feminism Since 1945*

Corey, Charles W, nd, *'Le Conseil d'administration de la MCC approuve un accord avec le Mali'* ['The Council of Administration of the MCC approves an agreement with Mali,' in French]. Available @ http://usinfo.state.gov/xarchives/display.html?p=washfile-french&y=2006&m=October&x=20061027164406WCyeroC4.128665e-02

Correio do Povo, January 2001, *'Grupo afro lamenta pouco espaço'* ['Afro group laments restricted space,' in Portuguese], 30.1.2001, p 11

Cotidiano Mujer/CFMEA, 2003.*Tu boca fundamental contra los fundamentalismos* ['Your Mouth is Fundamental against Fundamentalisms,' in Portuguese]. Flash Programme, Articulación Feminista Marcosur, @ www.cotidian omujer.org.uy

Critical Art Ensemble, 1996. *Electronic Civil Disobedience*. Brooklyn: Autonomedia

Crossley, Nick, 2002, 'Global Anti-Corporate Struggle, A Preliminary Analysis,' in *British Journal of Sociology*, Volume 53, Number 4, pp 667-91

Custers, Raf, April 2006, *'L'Union Européenne veut et obtient une force militaire au Congo'* ['The European Union wants and gets a military force to Congo,' in French]. April 8 2006, available @ http://www.indymedia.be/en/node/2014

Custers, Raf, May 2006, *'Patrons allemands partisans d'une guerre des matières premières'* ['German employers favour war around primary resources,' in French] May 7 2006, available @ http://www.indymedia.be/nl/node/2375/

CUT, World March of Women, ATTAC, and Focus on the Global South, November 2002, 'Building a Social Movements World Network,' in Jai Sen, Anita Anand, Arturo Escobar, and Peter Waterman, eds, 2004, *World Social Forum: Challenging Empires*. New Delhi: Viveka, pp 315-318. Available @ http://www.openspaceforum.net/twiki/tiki-index.php?page=WSFChallengingEmpires2004

Cyberspace after Capitalism, 2003, 'Cyberspace,' Life after Capitalism, ZNet, @ http://www.zmag.org/lac/dohertycyber.htm

Dakhli, Leyla, 2003, 'Gaps and tensions between social movements, political parties and political institutions: How to face these questions for achieving a participative democracy?' Roundtable debate at the World Social Forum, Porto Alegre, Brazil, on January 26 2003

Daulatzai, Anila, December 2004, 'A leap of faith: Thoughts on secularistic practices and progressive politics,' in *International Social Science Journal*, Issue no 182, pp 565-576. Available at http://www.blackwell-synergy.com/servlet/useragent?func=showIssues&code=issj&open=2004#C2004

Daulatzai, Anila, November 2006, 'Opium for the Masses: Notes on the Place of Religion in Progressive Politics.' Mss for inclusion in Jai Sen and Peter Waterman, eds, forthcoming, 2008, *World Social Forum: Challenging Empires Globally* [title under finalisation], Volume 3 in the *Challenging Empires* series, New Delhi: OpenWord Books

De Angelis, Massimo, 2002, 'Reflections on Alternatives, Commons and Communities, or: Building a New World from the Bottom up.' Draft submitted in Occasion of the European Social Form Workshop on Commons and Communities, Florence, November 7-10 2002, 16 pp. m.deangelis@btinternet.com. Edited version published in *The Commoner*, Winter 2003, available @ http://www.commoner.org.uk/deangelis06.pdf

De Angelis, Massimo, May 2004, "There Are Many Alternatives!' versus 'There is No Alternative!' A World Social Forum Book and the WSF Process.' Review of *World Social Forum: Challenging Empires* (New Delhi: The Viveka Foundation), edited by Sen, Anand, Escobar, and Waterman. Available @ http://www.choike.org/nuevo_eng/informes/1884.html@ http://www.openspaceforum.net/twiki/tiki-index.php?page=WSFChallengingEmpires2004

e la Grange, Bernard, and Maite Rico, 1998. *Marcos, La Genial Impostura*['Marcos, the Brilliant Impersonator,' in Spanish]. Mexico DF: Nuevo Siglo/Aguilar

De Landa, Manuel, 1997, *A Thousand Years of Nonlinear History*, New York: Zone Books

De Landa, Manuel, 2003, '1000 Years of War,' CTHEORY Interview with Manuel De Landa. Available @ http://www.ctheory.net/articles.aspx?id=383

De Landa, Manuel, nd, 'Meshworks, Hierarchies and Interfaces.' Available @ http://t0.or.at/delanda/meshwork.htm

Deblock, Christian and Dorval Brunelle, 2000, 'Globalization and New Normative Frameworks: the Multilateral Agreement on Investment,' in Guy Lachapelle and John Trent, eds, 2000, *Globalization, Governance and Identity: the Emergence of New Partnerships*, Montréal, Presses de l'Université de Montréal, pp 83-126. A 1998 version available @ http://www.er.uqam.ca/nobel/ieim/IMG /pdf/gric-98-6.pdf

della Porta, Donatella and ors, 2006, *Globalization from Below: Transnational Activists and Protest Networks*, Minneapolis: University of Minnesota Press

Deleuze, Gilles and Felix Guattari, 1987, *A Thousand Plateaus*, Minneapolis: University of Minnesota Press

Desai, Arvind, 2000, *We are the Poors*, New York: Monthly Review Press

Desh Bachao Desh Banao Abhiyan ['Save the Nation, Build the Nation Campaign,' in Hindi],2003, 'Ayodhya Declaration-National People's Agenda,' [URL given http://www.andolan.org/ server not found]

Dietrich, Gabriele and Nalini Nayak, 2001, 'Exploring Possibilities of Counter-Hegemonic Globalisation of Fishworkers Movement in India and Its Global Interactions.' Contribution to the Project on Reinventing Social Emancipation. Available from Centre of Social Studies, University of Coímbra, Portugal

Diniz, Simone Grilo et al, 1998, 'Not Like Our Mothers: Reproductive Choice and the Emergence of Citizenship Among Brazilian Rural Workers, Domestic Workers and Housewives,' in Petchesky and Judd, eds, 1998, *Negotiating Reproductive Rights*, pp 61-62

Drainville, André, 2004, *Contesting Globalisation: Space and Place in The World Economy*, New York: Routledge/RIPE Studies in Global Political Economy

Edwards, M, 1999, *Future Positive International Cooperation in the 21st Century*, London: Earthscan Publications

Edwards, Michael and John Gaventa, eds, 2001, *Global Citizen Action*, Boulder, Colorado: Lynne Rienner. www.rienner.com

ENDA, Water and Urban Poverty

Enzensberger, Hans Magnus, 1976 [1970], 'Constituents of a Theory of the Media,' in *Raids and Reconstructions, Essays in Politics, Crime and Culture*, pp 20-53, London: Pluto. Available @ http://www.religion-online.org/showarticle.asp? title=1567, http://www.arras.net/circulars/archives/000606.html

Erickson, Christian, 2002, 'Shock Wave: Conclusion. Transnational Revolt in the Space of the University.' Published by Education Department, UC Davis, California, USA. Original URL, http://trc.ucdavis.edu/erickson/mru/conclu.htm, but link not working. Abstract available @ http://faculty.ucr.edu/~rhead/earlymod/abstracts.html#erickson (accessed on 07.10.07)

Eschle, Catherine, 2002, 'Engendering Global Democracy,' in *International Feminist Journal of Politics*, Volume 4, Number 3, pp 315-41. Available @ http://www.niad.susx.ac.uk/Units/SPT/journal/archive/pdf/issue3-3.pdf.

Escobar, Arturo, November 2000, 'Notes on Networks and Anti-Globalisation Social Movements.' Presented at AAA Annual Meeting, San Francisco, November 15–19 2000. Available @ www.unc.edu/~aescobar/

Escobar, Arturo, 2000, 'Gender, Place and Networks, A Political Ecology of Cyberculture,' in Wendy Harcourt, ed, 2000, *Women@Internet, Creating New Cultures in Cyberspace*, London: Zed Books

Escobar, Arturo, January 2003, 'Other Worlds Are (Already) Possible: Cyber-Internationalism and Post-Capitalist Cultures. Draft Notes for the Cyberspace Panel, Life after Capitalism Programme, World Social Forum, Porto Alegre, January 23-28.' Available @ www.zmag.org/lac.htm. Revised version published as 'Other Worlds Are (Already) Possible: Self- Organisation, Complexity, and Post-Capitalist Cultures' in Jai Sen, Anita Anand, Arturo Escobar, and Peter Waterman, eds, 2004, *World Social Forum: Challenging Empires*, New Delhi: Viveka, pp 349-358. Available @ http://www.choike.org/nuevo_eng/informes/1557.html and @ http://www.openspace forum.net/twiki/tiki-index.php?page=WSFChallengingEmpires2004

Escobar, Arturo, 2003, 'Actors, Networks, and New Knowledge Producers: Social Movements and the Paradigmatic Transition in the Sciences,' in *Conhecimento Prudente para uma Vida decente: 'Um Discurso sobre as Ciências' Revisitad* ['Prudent Knowledge for a Decent Life: 'A Discourse on the Sciences' Revisited,' in Portuguese], edited by Boaventura de Sousa Santos, pp 605-630. Porto: Afrontamento

Escobar, Arturo, 2004, 'Other Worlds Are (Already) Possible: Self-Organisation, Complexity, and Post-Capitalist Cultures' in Jai Sen, Anita Anand, Arturo Escobar, and Peter Waterman, eds, 2004, *World Social Forum: Challenging Empires*, New Delhi: Viveka, pp 349-358. Available @ http://www.choike.org/nuevo_eng/informes/1557.html and @ http://www.openspaceforum.net/twiki/tiki-index.php?page=WSFChallengingEmpires2004

ETUC, 2002a, *'Foro Social Mundial 2002 Porto Alegre 31 Enero. 5 Febrero 2002,' Informe de la Delegacion de la CES'* ['World Social Forum 2002 Porto Alegre January 31-February 5: Report of the ETUC Delegation,' in French]. 9 pp. Brussels: European Trade Union Confederation

European Commission, nd, 'EU Development Cooperation in Africa, Caribbean and Pacific countries,' @ http://www.deleri.ec.europa.eu/acp_eu_cooperation/eu_acp.htm

European Social Movement Assembly, November 2002, 'Call of the European Social Movements,' in Jai Sen, Anita Anand, Arturo Escobar, and Peter Waterman, eds, 2004, *World Social Forum: Challenging Empires*. New Delhi: Viveka, pp 359-359. Available @ http://www.openspaceforum.net/twiki/tiki-index.php?page=WSFChallengingEmpires2004

EZLN, 1997, 'Summons to the Second International Encounter For Humanity and against Neoliberalism (26th July to 3rd Aug. 1997).' Available @ http://216.239.39.104/custom?q=cache:QWpaVO0UpRkJ: www.pangea.org/encuentro/convocatoria_in.htm+zapatistas+world+include+other+worlds&hl=en&ie=UTF-8. 07.10.07: Server not found, article not found

Featherstone, David, 2001, 'Friend-Enemy Relations and the Construction of Maps of Grievance: The Political Geographies of the Inter-Continental Caravan.' Available from author at Department of Geography, Faculty of Social Sciences, Open University, Milton Keynes, UK; D.J.Featherstone @open.ac.uk

Featherstone, David, forthcoming, 'Towards the Relational Construction of Militant Particularisms: Or Why the Geographies of Past Struggles Matter for Resistance to Neo-Liberal Globalisation.' Available from Department of Geography, Open University, Milton Keynes, UK

Feldman, Shelley, Summer 2001, 'Exploring Theories of Patriarchy: A Perspective from Contemporary Bangladesh,' *Signs: Journal of Women in Culture and Society*, vol 25, no. 4, p 1108

Fisher, William F and Thomas Ponniah, eds, 2003, *Another World Is Possible, Popular Alternatives to Globalization at the World Social Forum*, London/New York/Nova Scotia/Capetown: Zed/Fernwood/Sird/David Philip

Florini, Ann, 2001, 'Transnational Civil Society,' in Edwards, Michael and John Gaventa, eds, 2001, *Global Citizen Action*, Boulder: Lynn Reiner

Florini, A M, ed, 2000, *The Third Force, The Rise of Transnational Civil Society*, Washington: Carnegie

Fortun, Kim, 2001, *Advocacy After Bhopal: Environmentalism, Disaster, New Global Orders*, Chicago: University of Chicago Press

Forum for Another Mali, World Forum for Alternatives (France), Third World Forum Forum (Senegal), ENDA (Senegal), and ors, January 2006, 'The Bamako Appeal,' January 18 2006. Text as circulated by Samir Amin, President of the World Forum for Alternatives. Available for signing @ http://thirdworld forum.net/fren/index.htm, and otherwise @ http://www.openspaceforum.net/twiki/tiki-read_article.php?articleId=66, http://www.monthlyreview.org/mrzine/bamako.html, http://deletetheborder.org/node/698

Foster, John, 2005, 'The Trinational Alliance against NAFTA: Sinews of Solidarity,' in Bandy, Joe and Jackie Smith, 2005, *Coalitions Across Borders. Transnational Protest and the Neoliberal Order*, Lanham: Rowman & Littlefield Publishers, Inc, pp 209-230

Foucault, M, 1995, *Discipline and Punish: The Birth of the Prison*, 2nd edition, New York: Vintage Books

Friedman, Elisabeth J, 1999, 'The Effects of 'Transnationalism Reversed,' in 'Venezuela: Assessing the Impact of UN Global Conferences on the Women's Movement,' in *International Feminist Journal of Politics* vol 1, no 3, pp 357-381. Available @ http://www2.ucsc.edu/globalinterns/cpapers/Friedman.pdf

Friedman, Elisabeth Jay, 2003, 'Gendering the Agenda: The Impact of the Transnational Women's Rights Movement at the UN Conferences of the 1990s,' in *Women's Studies International Forum* vol 26, no 4, pp 313-331

Garavito, Rodriguez, A A César, P S Barrett, and D Chavez, eds, 2007, *La nueva izquierda en América Latina. Sus origines y trayectoria futura* ['The New Left in Latin America: Its Origins and Future Trajectory,' in Spanish], Bogotá, Vitral

Gasa, N, November 2002, 'It's a New Model of Masculinity,' in *The Star*

Gentle, L, October 2002, 'Social Movements in South Africa,' in *South African Labour Bulletin*, Volume 26, Number 5, pp 16-19

George, Susan, Summer 1997, 'How to Win the War of Ideas: Lessons from the Gramscian Right,' *Dissen*t (New York) Volume 44, Issue 3. Available @ http://www.global-labour.org/Dissent%20Summer%201997%20-%20George.pdf

George, Susan, 2002, 'The Global Citizens Movement,' in *New Agenda*, Second Quarter. Available @ http://www.tni.org/detail_page.phtml?act_id=1431&username=guest@tni.org&password=9999&publish=Y

Gera, Prema, Jude Howell, and Jai Sen, June 2002, 'Civil Advocacy for Rights-Based Inclusive Development.' A Scoping Report for DFID India on SARBID (Supporting Action for Rights-Based Inclusive Development)

Gerassi, John, ed, 1971, *The Coming of the New International*, New York: World Publishing Company

Gibson-Graham, J K, 1996, *The End of Capitalism (As We Know It): A Feminist Critique of Political Economy*, Oxford: Blackwell Publishers

Gitlin, Todd, 1980, *The Whole World is Watching, Mass Media in the Making and Unmaking of the New Left*, Berkeley: University of California Press

Glasius, Marlies, Mary Kaldor, and Helmut Anheier, eds, 2002, *Global Civil Society*, Oxford: Oxford University Press

Global Fire, August 2002, *The Official Newspaper of the WSSD Civil Society Process*, dt 22 August 2002

Godbout, Jacques 2000, *Le Don, la Dette et l'Identité: Homo donator vs homo oeconomicus* ['The Gift, the Debt, and Identity: Man the Donor vs Economic Man,' in French], Paris: La Découverte/MAUSS

Gordon, Linda, and Allen Hunter, 1998, 'Not All Male Dominance is Patriarchal,' in *Radical History Review*, no 71

Graeme, Chesters, 2003, 'Shape Shifting: Civil Society, Complexity and Social Movements.' Available from Centre for Local Policy Studies, Edge Hill University College, Lancashire, UK. Available @ http://www.shiftingground.freeuk.com/shapeshifting.htm

Gray, J, 1998, 'False Dawn,' in *The Delusions of Global Capitalism*, London: Granta

Greenberg, Bruce, October 2006, '*Des africanistes discutent des enjeux sécuritaires de la Somalie*' [Africanists discuss the security issues of Somalia,' in French], *Washington File*, 10 October 2006

Grubacic, Andrej, February 2003, 'Life after Social Forums: The New Radicalism and the Forum Process,' 10 February 2003

Grubacic, Andrej, 2003, 'Life After Social Forums: New Radicalism and the Question of Attitudes Towards the Social Forums.' Available @ http://zmag.org./content/print_article.cfm?itemID=3010§ionID=4

Grzybowski, Cândido, 1998, '*Lógica econômica vs. lógica democrática*' ['Economic logic vs Democratic logic,' in Portuguese], in Grzybowski et al, 1998, *Neoliberalismo: Alternativas?* ['Neoliberalism: Alternatives?'], pp 6-34, Rio de Janeiro: Publicações Novamerica

Grzybowski, Cândido, 2002, 'The democratic reinvention of globalization,' Chapter 5 in Rikkilä, Leena and Katarina Sehm Patomäki, eds, 2002, *From a Global Market Place to Political Spaces*, the North South Dialogue continues; pp 57-86. NIGD Working Paper 1/2002, published by NIGD-Network Institute for Global Democratisation, info@nigd.unet.com Rikkilä and Sehm Patomäki document available in full at http://www.nigd.org/nigd/nigd-publications/working-papers-nigd-publications

Grzybowski, Cândido, January 2003, '*Fórum Social Mundial: a construção de uma utopia*' ['World Social Forum: Construction of An Utopia,' in Portuguese], in *Terraviva*, January 24 2003, p 5

Gupta, A, 1998, *Postcolonial Developments: Agriculture in the Making of Modern India*, Durham: Duke University Press

Harcourt, Wendy ed, 2000, *Women@Internet, Creating New Cultures in Cyberspace*, London: Zed Books

Hardt, Michael, March 2002, 'Today's Bandung,' in *New Left Review*, Vol 14, pp 112-118. Circulated in July 2002 as 'Porto Alegre: Today's Bandung?' by *Worker* a-infosen@ainfos.ca dt 30 July 2002 11:23:57-0400 (EDT). Available in the World Social Forum WSF2002 Assessments, @ http://www.forumsocialmundial.org.br/eng/ and @ http://www.newleftreview.org/A2381

Hartmann, Betsy 2002, 'The Changing Faces of Population Control,' in Silliman, Jael and Anannya Bhattacharjee, eds, 2002, *Policing the National Body: Race, Gender and Criminalization*, pp 259-284

Heinrich Böll Foundation, 2002, *Fairness in a Fragile World: The Johannesburg Memorandum for the World Summit on Sustainable Development*, Berlin: Heinrich Böll Foundation. Available @ http://www.worldsummit2002.org/publications/memo_en_with.pdf

Hellman, Judith, 1999, 'Real and Virtual Chiapas: Magic Realism and the Left,' in Panitch, Leo and Colin Leys, eds, in *Socialist Register 2000*, special issue on 'Necessary and Unnecessary Utopias,' London: Merlin Press, and New York: Monthly Review Press. Available @ http://socialistregister.com/socialistregister.com/files/SR_2000_Hellmann.pdf

Hinkelammert, Franz, 2002, *Critica De La Razon Utópica* ['Critique of Utopian Reason,' in Spanish], Bilbau: Desclee de Brouwer

Hodkinson, Stuart, February 2003, 'Another European Social Forum is Necessary,' in *Red Pepper*, http://www.redpepper.org.uk/

Holloway, John, 1998b, *Zapatista Encuentro*['Zapatista Encounter,' in Spanish], Documents from the 1996 Encounter For Humanity and Against Neoliberalism, New York: Seven Stories Press

Holloway, John, and Elvoina Peláez, eds, 1998, *Zapatista! Reinventing Revolution in Mexico*, London: Pluto

Howard, Judith A and Carolyn Allen, eds, 2000, *Feminisms at a Millennium*, Chicago: University of Chicago Press

Hu Jin Tao, November 2006, *'Discours d'ouverture du Sommet Sino-africain'* ['Speech at the inauguration of the Chinese-African Summit,' in French], Beijing, November 3 2006

Hussain, Samir and Pranjal Tiwari, April 2003, 'Unimaginable Futures,' on *ZNet*, 28 April 2003. Available @ http://www.zmag.org/content/showarticle.cfm?ItemID=3532

Ichiyo, Muto, Summer 2003, 'Asian Peace Movements and Empire,' in *Multitude* no 13 (in French); forthcoming in English in *Inter-Asia Cultural Studies*, Vol 4, No 3 (Routledge). Reprinted in edited form in Jai Sen, Anita Anand, Arturo Escobar, and Peter Waterman, eds, 2004, *World Social Forum: Challenging Empires*, pp 44-50. New Delhi: Viveka. Available @ http://www.choike.org/nuevo_eng/informes/1557.html and @ http://www.openspaceforum.net/twiki/tiki-index.php?page=WSFChallengingEmpires2004

International Forum on Globalisation, 2002, *Alternatives to Economic Globalisation*, San Francisco: Berrett Koehler Publishers

INCITE! Women of Color Against Violence, eds, April 2007, *The Revolution Will Not Be Funded: Beyond The Non-Profit Industrial Complex!*, Boston: South End Press

International League for Peoples' Struggles (ILPS), World Peoples' Resistance Movement (WPRM), South Asia, Anti-Imperialist Camp (Austria), Bayan (Philippines), Confederation of Turkish Workers in Europe (ATIK), and others, September 2003, 'Introducing MR2004: Mumbai Resistance-2004. Against Imperialist Globalisation & War.' 5 September 2003. Available @ http://www.ilps-news.com/cenral-info-bureau/events/mumbai-resistance-2004/introducing-mr2004/

ISIS, 2003. 'The "Alternative WSIS" Rationale And Other Summit Critiques.' Available from http://www.isiswomen.org/onsite/wsis/alt-wsis.html [link not found, 07.10.07]

ITF (International Transportworkers Federation), 2002. 'Globalising Solidarity: The Popular Movement to Reform the Globalisation Process, Draft Resolution No. 5, ITF Congress, Vancouver.' Available from http://www.itfglobal.org/about-us/40thcongress-res.cfm

Iyer, P, 2001. *The Global Soul.* New York: Vintage

Jain, Devaki, January 2003, 'The Empire Strikes Back,' A report on the Asian Social Forum, in *Economic and Political Weekly,* 11 January, pp 99-100. Available from http://www.epw.org. Edited version published as 'Striking Back at The Empire' in Jai Sen, Anita Anand, Arturo Escobar, and Peter Waterman, eds, 2004, *World Social Forum: Challenging Empires*, New Delhi: Viveka, pp 289-292. Available @ http://www.choike.org/nuevo_eng/informes/1557.html and @ http://www.openspaceforum.net/twiki/tiki-index.php?page=WSFChallengingEmpires2004

James, P J, January 2003, 'World Social Forum's "Many Alternatives" to Globalisation,' in *Red Star*, Platform for Communist Revolutionaries, January 2003, pp 5-7. Edited version published in Jai Sen, Anita Anand, Arturo Escobar, and Peter Waterman, eds, 2004, *World Social Forum: Challenging Empires*, New Delhi: Viveka, pp 246-250. Available @ http://www.choike.org/nuevo_eng/informes/1557.html and @ http://www.openspaceforum.net/twiki/tiki-index.php?page=WSFChallengingEmpires2004

Juris, Jeff and Rodrigo Nunes, June 2005, 'Encounters in/Explorations of Open Space, I and II, A Report and Some Reflections.' Report on EIOS1 and EIOS2, workshops and meetings held at Integría, Picada Café, near Porto Alegre, and at the World Social Forum in Porto Alegre, Brazil, on January 21-24 and January 27-28 2005. Available @ OpenSpaceForum @ http://www.openspace forum.net/twiki/tiki-index.php?page=EIOS%201%20and%202%20Evaluation%20Report

Johnson, Steven, 2001, *Emergence*, New York: Scribner

Kandioyti, Denis, September 1988, 'Bargaining with Patriarchy,' *Gender & Society*, vol 2, no. 3, pp 274-290

Karat, Prakash, September 1988, *Foreign Funding & the Philosophy of Voluntary Organisations, A Factor in Imperialist Strategy*, New Delhi: National Book Centre. Expanded version of article in *The Marxist*, 1984, Earlier version available @ http://www.cpim.org/marxist/198402_marxist_vol_org_prakash.htm

Kagarlitsky, Boris, November 2002, 'Autumn Reflections,' *ZNet Daily Commentaries*, 21 November 2002. Http://www.zmag.org/sustainers/content/2002-11/21kagarlitsky.cfm

Kasse Tidiane, Mouhamadou, nd, c.2007, '*FSM 2007: L'heure de sortir des sentiers battus pour les Africains*' ['WSF 2007: Time to leave the way open to the Africans,' in French], available @ http://www.europe-solidaire.org/spip.php?article2190

Keck, Margaret E and Kathryn Sikkink, 1998, *Activists Beyond Borders*, Advocacy Networks in International Politics, Ithaca, NY: Cornell University Press

Kelly, Rita Mae and ors, eds, 2001, *Gender, Globalization and Democratization*, Lanham, MD: Rowman & Littlefield

Keraghel, Chloé, and Jai Sen, Editorial Advisers, December 2004, 'Explorations in Open Space: The World Social Forum and Cultures of Politics,' Issue no 182 of the *International Social Science Journal*. Contents of issue available at http://www.blackwell-synergy.com/servlet/useragent?func=showIssues&code=issj&open=2004#C2004

King, Mary, November 2000, 'Of Unknown Quantity: NGO Network Organizing and Global Environmental Politics,' Presented at the Session on Actors, Network, Networks, Meanings: Environmental Social Movements and Anthropology. AAA Annual Meeting San Francisco, November 15-19 2000

Kingsnorth, Paul, 2003, *One No, Many Yesses: A Journey to the Heart of the Global Resistance Movement*, London: Free Press

Kirkwood, Julieta, 1986, *Ser Política en Chile, Las Feministas y los Partidos* ['To Be Political in Chile: Feminists and Political Parties,' in Spanish], Santiago de Chile: FLACSO

Klein, Naomi, July 2000b, 'The Vision Thing: Were the DC and Seattle Protests Unfocused, or are Critics Missing The Point?,' in *The Nation*, dt 10 July 2000. Available @ http://www.commondreams.org/views/062300-103.htm and @ http://www.naomiklein.org/articles/2001/07/were-dc-and-seattle-protests-unfocused.

Klein, Naomi, March 2001, 'A Fete for the End of the End of History,' in *The Nation*, dt 19 March 2001. Available from http://www.thenation.com/doc /20010319/klein

Klein, Naomi, May 2001, 'Reclaiming the Commons,' in *New Left Review,* Number 9, pp 81-89. Available @ http://newleftreview.org/A2323

Klein, Naomi, 2001, 'Farewell to "End of History": Organisation and Vision in Anti-Corporate Movements,' in Panitch, Leo and Colin Leys, eds, 2001, *Socialist Register 2002: A World of Contradictions,* pp 1-14, London: The Merlin Press. Available @ http://socialistregister.com/socialistregister.com/files/SR_2002_Klein.pdf,

Klein, Naomi, 2002, *Fences and Windows, Dispatches from the Front Lines of the Globalization Debate,* London: Flamingo. Re-published by New Delhi: Left Word Books

Klein, Naomi, January 2003, 'What Happened to the New Left? The Hijacking of the WSF.' dt 30 January 2003. Available at http://www.nadir.org/nadir/initiativ/agp/free/wsf/naomiklein.htm

Koning, Hans, 1988, *1968: A Personal Report,* London: Unwin Hyman

Kontopoulos, Kyryakos, 1993, *The Logics of Social Structure,* Cambridge: Cambridge University Press

Kromm, Chris and Sue Sturgis, August-September 2007, 'Blueprint for Gulf Renewal: The Katrina Crisis and a Community Agenda for Action,' in *Southern Exposure,* August-September 2007. Available @ http://www.southernstudies.org/gulfblueprint.pdf

Lambert, R and E Webster, 2001, 'Southern Unionism and the New Labour Internationalism,' in Waterman, Peter and J Wills, eds, 2001, *Place, Space, and the New Labour Internationalism,* London: Blackwell

Lamy, Pascal, at http://www.tabd.org/media/2001/lamy060502.html. (Link not found, 06.10.07)

Archived @ http://web.archive.org/web/20021002052119/http://tabd.org/media/2001/lamy060502.html

León, Irene, ed, 2002, *Retos Feministas en un mundo globalizado: Foro Social Mundial, Porto Alegre, 2002* ['Feminist Challenges in a Globalised World: The World Social Fourm, Porto Alegre, 2002,' in Spanish], Quito, Ecuador: ALAI-Agencia Latinoamericana de Información [Latin American Information Agency]

Leon, Osvaldo, Sally Burch, Tamayo, and Eduardo, 2001, *Movimientos Sociales En La Red* ['Social Movements on the Web,' in Spanish], Quito: ALAI-Agencia Latinoamericana de Informacion

Levy, Pierre, 1997, *Collective Intelligence: Mankind's Emerging World in Cyberspace,* New York: Plenum Trade

Leyva Solano, Xochitll, 2002, 'Neo-*Zapatismo*: Networks of Power and War.' PhD dissertation, Department of Anthropology, University of Manchester, UK

Longhi, V, December 2002, in *Red Pepper*

Löwy, Michael, March 2003, 'Towards a New International?,' in *International Viewpoint*, No 348. Originally written for the Mexican magazine *Revista Rebeldia*; available @ http://www.internationalviewpoint.org/spip.php? article245. Edited version published as 'Towards a New International?' in Jai Sen, Anita Anand, Arturo Escobar, and Peter Waterman, eds, 2004, *World Social Forum: Challenging Empires*. New Delhi: Viveka. Available @ http://www.choike.org/nuevo_eng/informes/1557.html and @ http://www. openspaceforum.net/twiki/tiki-index.php?page=WSFChallengingEmpires2004

Ludden, D, 2000, 'Agrarian Histories and Grassroots Development in South Asia,' in Agrawal, A and K Sivaramkrishnan, eds, 2000, *Agrarian Environments: Resources Representation and Rule in India*, Durham: Duke University Press, pp 251-276

Mandel, R, 2001, 'The Privatisation of Security,' in *Armed Forces and Security*, Volume 28, pp 129-151. Available@ http://www.ciaonet.org/isa/mar01/

Marcosur Feminist Network, 2002, *Tu Boca Fundamental Contra Los Fundamentalismos* ['Your Mouth is Fundamental against Fundamentalisms']. Montevideo: Articulación Feminista Marcosur

Mariátegui, Jose Carlos, 1973 [1923], *'Internacionalismo y Nacionalismo'* ['Internationalism and Nationalism,' in Spanish], in *Historia de la crisis mundial. Conferencias años 1923 y 1924* ['History of the World Crisis. Conferences of 1923 and 1924']. Lima: Amauta

Marin, Gustavo, 2003, 'After Porto Alegre..., Alliance Presence at the World Social Forum,' contained in: Anon (Philippe Amouroux?), nd c.September 2003, 'Alliance coordination in the World Social Forum, Mumbai January 2004,' prepared for the preparatory meeting, Bangkok October 26-28 2003, pp 26-27

Martinez, Elizabeth (Betita), January 2000, 'Where Was The Color in Seattle? Looking for reasons why the Great Battle was so white.' Extended version of article appearing in *ColorLines*, February 2000, @ http://www.nadir.org/nadir/initiativ/agp/free/seattle/color.htm

Martinez, Elizabeth (Betita), July 2000, 'Where was the color in Seattle? Looking for reasons why the great battle was so white,' in *Monthly Review*

Massey, Doreen, June 1991, 'A global sense of place,' in *Marxism Today*, pp 24-29. Available @ http://www.unc.edu/courses/2006spring/geog/021/001/massey. pdf

Matte, Diane and Lorraine Guay, 2001, *'La marcha mundial de mujeres: por un mundo solidario y igualitario'* ['The world march of women: For a solidarious and equitable world,' in Spanish] in José Seoane and Emilio Taddei, *Resistencias mundiales: De Seattle a Porto Alegre* ['Global resistance: From Seattle to Porto Alegre,' in Spanish], Buenos Aires, CLACSO, pp 169-178

McDonald, D and J Pape, 2002, *Cost Recovery and the Crisis of Service Delivery*, Pretoria: HSRC Publishers

McDonald, K, 2002, 'From Solidarity to Fluidarity: Social movements beyond 'collective identity'- the case of globalization conflicts,' in *Social Movement Studies*, vol 1, pp 109-128

McGregor, Richard, November 2006. 'China's poorest worse off after boom,' in *Financial Times*, November 21 2006. Available @ http://www.ft.com/cms/s/0/e28495ce-7988-11db-b257-0000779e2340.html

McLeish, Phil nd, c.2003, 'The promise of the European Social Forum,' on *Navigation Multitudes* web, @ http://multitudes.samizdat.net/article.php3?id_article=1231

Mekata, M, 2000, 'Building Partnerships Toward a Common Goal, Experiences of the International Campaign to Ban Landmines,' in A M Florini, ed, *The Third Force, The Rise of Transnational Civil Society*. Washington: Carnegie

Melucci, Alberto, 1989, *Nomads of the Present: Social Movements and Individual Needs in Contemporary Society*, Philadelphia: Temple University Press

Mendez, Jennifer Bickham, 2002, 'Creating Alternatives from a Gender Perspective: Transnational Organising for Maquila Workers' Rights in Central America,' in Naples and Desai, eds, 2002, *Women's Activism and Globalisation*, pp 121-141

Meridians: feminism, race, transnationalism, Autumn 2002, vol. 3, no 1

Meyer, Mary K, and Elisabeth Prugl, eds, 1999, *Gender Politics in Global Governance*, New York: Rowman & Littlefield

Mindry, Deborah, Summer 2001, 'Nongovernmental Organisations, "Grassroots," and the Politics of Virtue,' in *Signs: Journal of Women in Culture and Society*, vol 26, no 4, pp 1187-1212

Mittelman, J, 2000, *The Globalization Syndrome: Transformation and Resistance*, Princeton: Princeton University Press

Mouffe, C, 1992, *Dimensions of Radical Democracy*, London: Verso

Munck, Ronaldo, 2002, 'Debating "Globalization and its Discontents",' 18 pp. Liverpool: Department of Sociology

Munnik, V and J Wilson, 2003, *The World Comes to One Country, An Insider History of the World Summit on Sustainable Development*, Johannesburg: Heinrich Boll Foundation. Available @ http://www.boell.de/downloads/rio+10/Summit2002_History.pdf

Muralidharan, Sukumar, 2003, 'Globalising Resistance,' in *Frontline*, Volume 20, Issue 2, January 18-31 2003; @ http://www.frontlineonnet.com/fl2002/stories/20030131009100400.htm. Edited version published in Jai Sen, Anita

Anand, Arturo Escobar, and Peter Waterman, eds, 2004, *World Social Forum: Challenging Empires*. New Delhi: Viveka, pp 279-283. Now available @ http://www.choike.org/nuevo_eng/informes/1557.html and @ http://www.openspaceforum.net/twiki/tiki-index.php?page=WSFChallengingEmpires 2004

Muricken, Ajit, 1999, 'Tyranny of Economic Globalism: Emerging Trends and Impact,' Paper to Conference of the Committee to Cancel Third World Debt (CADTM/COCAD). Available from http://users.skynet.be/cadtm/pages/english/angajit.html

Muto Ichiyo, May 2003, 'Asian Peace Movements and Empire: American War and Its Impacts,' in *Multitude* no 13 (in French) and in English in *Inter-Asia Cultural Studies*, Vol 4, No 3 (Routledge). Reprinted in edited form in Jai Sen, Anita Anand, Arturo Escobar, and Peter Waterman, eds, 2004, World Social Forum: Challenging Empires, New Delhi: Viveka, pp 44-50

Naples, Nancy A, and Manisha Desai, eds, 2002, *Women's Activism and Globalization, Linking Local Struggles and Transnational Politics*, New York: Routledge

NCDHR (National Campaign for Dalit Human Rights), nd, c.2003, 'NCDHR Dalit Swadhikar Rally-National Rally of Dalits for Assertion of Rights.' Issued by NCDHR, WSF Desk, Hyderabad, India, at desk4forum@hotmail.com

Nanga, Jean, October 2004, *'Darfour: les enjeux du conflit meurtrier'* ['Darfur: The issues of the deadly conflict,' in French], *Solidarities*, October 19 2004

Ndao, Babacar (*Réseau des Organisations Paysannes et des Producteurs Agricoles d'Afrique de l'Ouest* (ROPPA-Network of Peasant Organisations and Agricultural Producers of West Africa), November 2006. *'Libéralisation des produits agricoles et injustice sociale'* [Liberalisation of agricultural products and social injustice,' in French], 21 November 2006. Available on: http://www.pambazuka.org/fr/category/comment/38423

NextGENDERation, 2003, 'The NextGENDERation Network,' NextGENDERation (Utrecht, Netherlands), 4 pp. Available at http://www. nextgenderation.let.uu.nl/

The New Internationalist, September 2002

Ngwane, Trevor, 2003, 'Sparks in the Township,' in *New Left Review*, No 22 (new series). Available from http://www.newleftreview.net/NLR25603.shtml

Nzimande, Blade, 2003, 'New Possibilities for a Progressive Global Politics,' in *Umsebenzi Online*, Vol 2, No 4. Available @

http://www.sacp.org.za/main.php?include=pubs/umsebenzi/2003/uol009.htm

Obono, Danielle, March 2006. 'Unions lead popular resistance,' in *International Viewpoint* 376, March 2006, Available @ http://www.internationalviewpoint.org/spip.php?article989=

O'Brien, Robert, Anne Marie Goetz, Jan Aart Scholte, and Marc Williams, 2000. *Contesting Global Governance, Multilateral Economic Institutions and Global Social Movements*. New York: Cambridge University Press

Olea Mauleón, Cecilia, ed, 1998, *Encuentros, (Des)Encuentros y Búsquedas, El Movimiento Feminista en América Latina* ['Encounters, (Mis)Encounters, and Searches: The Feminist Movement in Latin America,' in Spanish], Lima: Ediciones Flora Tristán

Olesen, Thomas, 2002, 'Long Distance Zapatismo, Globalisation, and the Construction of Solidarity.' Available from Department of Political Science, University of Aarhus, Denmark

Olesen, Thomas, forthcoming, *International Zapatismo: The Construction of Solidarity in the Age of Globalisation*, London: Zed

Oloo, Onyango, 2007, '*Équilibre du genre au sein du Forum Social Mondial–Nairobi*' ['Gender balance within the World Social Forum, Nairobi,' in French], available @ http://www.pambazuka.org,/fr/category/comment/37892

Omvedt, Gail, 1993a, *Reinventing Revolution, New Social Movements and the Socialist Tradition in India*, New York: East Gate, and Armonk (NY): M E Sharpe

Ortega, Adriana Ortiz, Ana Amuchastegui and Marta Rivas, 1998, ' "Because They were Born From Me": Negotiating Women's Rights in Mexico,' in Petchesky, Rosalind P and Karen Judd, eds, 1998, *Negotiating Reproductive Rights*, pp 145-147

Osterweil, Michal, November 2002, 'Re-Thinking Politics and Resistance,' presented at the session on 'Ethnography and the Italian 'New Global' Movements' at the 2002 AAA Annual Meeting, New Orleans, November 20-24 2002

Osterweil, Michal, 2004, 'Decentering the Forum: Is Another Critique of the Forum Possible?,' in Jai Sen, Anita Anand, Arturo Escobar, and Peter Waterman, eds, 2004, *World Social Forum: Challenging Empires*, New Delhi: Viveka, pp 183-190. Available @ http://www.choike.org/nuevo_eng/informes/1557.html and @ http://www.openspaceforum.net/twiki/tiki-index.php?page=WSF ChallengingEmpires2004

OSAL/CLACSO, 2002, *América Latina en Movimiento* ['Latin America in Movement,' in Spanish], Video in Spanish. 14 mins. PAL N. Buenos Aires: Observatorio Social de América Latina. http://osal.clacso.org

Pailey, Robtel Neejai, February 2002, 'Modern-day slavery in Liberia,' February 2 2006. Available on: http://www.pambazuka.org/en/category/comment/31756

Pelda, Kurt, August 2006, '*Wie Kongo-Kinshasa seine Bodenschätze verschleudert. Undurchsichtige Verfahren bei der Erteilung von Bergbaukonzessionen*' ['How Congo-Kinshasa dissipates its ground treasures. Opaque procedures in the bestowing of mining concessions,' in German], in *Neue Zürcher Zeitung*, August 19-20 2006, p 29 (translation M J)

Peltonen, Lasse, 2003, 'Fluids Without a Cause? Tracing the Emergence of a Local Green Movement,' in Haila, Yrjö and Chuck Dyke, eds, 2003. *How Does Nature Speak? The Dynamics of the Human Ecological Condition* (Unpublished book manuscript, University of Helsinki)

Petchesky, Rosalind P and Karen Judd, eds, 1998, *Negotiating Reproductive Rights, Women's Perspectives Across Countries and Cultures*, London: Zed Books

Phillips, Carol, 2003, 'New and Old Social Movements: Current Confluence, Spaces, And Tension between Multiple Local and Global Actors.' Presentation at Panel at World Social Forum, Porto Alegre, Brazil, on January 24 2003

Pianta, Mario, 2001, 'Parallel Summits of Global Civil Society,' in Helmul-Anneier, Marlies Glasius and Mary Kaldor, eds, 2001, *Global Civil Society Yearbook 2001*, Oxford: Oxford University Press

Pillay, D, 1996, 'Social Movements, Development, and Democracy in Post Apartheid South Africa,' in J Coetzee and J Graaf, eds, 1996, *Reconstruction, Development and People*, pp 324 352, Cape Town: Oxford University Press

Polanyi, Karl, 1957, *The Great Transformation*, Boston: Beacon Press

Ponniah, Thomas, July 2007, 'The Contribution of the U.S. Social Forum: A reply to Whitaker and Bello's debate on the Open Space,' on the World Social Forum website @ http://www.forumsocialmundial.org.br/noticias_textos.php?cd_news=40

Ponniah, Thomas and William Fisher, interviewed by Solana Larsen, February 2003, 'Under a Tree in Porto Alegre: Democracy in its Most Radical Sense,' first published in *openDemocracy* @ http://www.opendemocracy.net/globalization-world/article_954.jsp. Republished in Jai Sen, Anita Anand, Arturo Escobar, and Peter Waterman, eds, *World Social Forum: Challenging Empires* (New Delhi: Viveka), pp 178-182. Available @ http://www.choike.org/nuevo_eng/informes/1557.html and @ http://www.openspaceforum.net/twiki/tiki-index.php?page=WSFChallengingEmpires2004

Poster, Winifred and Zakia Salime, 2002, 'The Limits of Microcredit: Transnational Feminism and USAID Activities in the United States and Morocco,' in Nancy A Naples and Manisha Desai, eds, 2002, *Women's Activism and Globalisation*, pp 189-219

Pratap, Vijay, January 2002, Letter of invitation to WSF Consultation in India on January 9-10 2002, dt January 1 2002

Pratap, Vijay and Jai Sen, on behalf of the India WSF Working Group, January 2002, Letter to Members of the WSF Brazil Organising Committee and the WSF International Council, through Sergio Haddad, Gustavo Marin, and Chico Whitaker. Dated 11 January 2002, 4 pp

Prestes, Paulo, 1999, *13 Leituras Petistas (Porto Alegre)* ['Thirteen PT Letters (Porto Alegre),' in Portuguese], pp 72-76

Prigogine, Ilya and Isabel Stengers, 1984, *Order Out of Chaos*, New York: Bantam Books

Putting People First, 2003, 'Putting People First in the Information Society, A Statement on WSIS Content and Themes, Endorsed by 22 NGOs and Civil Society Entities.' Available @ http://www.itu.int/wsis/docs/pc1/statements_content/cs_group.doc

Quijano, A, 2000, *'Colonialidad Del Poder y Clasificación Social'* ['Coloniality of Power and Social Classification,' in Spanish], in *Journal of World Systems Research*, Volume 6, Issue 2, pp 342-386

Raj, Rita et al, 1998, 'Between Modernization and Patriarchal Revivalism: Reproductive Negotiations Among Women in Peninsular Malaysia,' in Petchesky, Rosalind P and Karen Judd, eds, *Negotiating Reproductive Rights: Women's Perspectives Across Countries and Cultures*

Rebick, Judy, July 2007, 'Another U.S. is Possible,' in *Rabble News*, July 2 2007, http://www.openspaceforum.net/twiki/tiki-read_article.php?articleId=455

Rein, Marcy, July 2007, 'National Alliance of Domestic Workers Formed at Social Forum,' AFL-CIO Blog, @ http://blog.aflcio.org/2007/07/09/national-alliance-of-domestic-workers-formed-at-social-forum/

Revolutionary Writers' Association, Andhra Pradesh, December 2002, 'Struggle Against Imperialism is neither Fun nor Picnic! It is a Life and Death Practice!,' leaflet dt 31 December 2002. Published in Jai Sen, Anita Anand, Arturo Escobar, and Peter Waterman, eds, 2004, *World Social Forum: Challenging Empires*, New Delhi: Viveka, pp 284-288. Available @ http://www.choike.org/documentos/wsf_s407_writers.pdf and @ http://www.openspaceforum.net/twiki/tiki-index.php?page=WSFChallengingEmpires2004.

Richie, Beth E, 2000, 'A Black Feminist Reflection on the Anti-violence Movement,' in Howard, Judith A and Carolyn Allen, eds, 2000, *Feminisms at a Millennium*, Chicago: University of Chicago Press

Rikkilä, Leena and Katarina Sehm Patomäki, eds, 2002, *From a Global Market Place to Political Spaces–The North South Dialogue continues*. NIGD Working Paper 1/2002, Published by NIGD. Network Institute for Global Democratisation. Rikkilä and Sehm Patomäki document available in full at http://www.nigd.org/Working%20Papers.html

Riles, A, 2000.*The Network Inside Out*. Anne Arbor: University of Michigan

Rosenberg, Marta, 2002, *'Qué otro mundo es posible?'* ['What other world is possible?,' in Spanish], in *El Rodaballo*, vol 8, no 14 (Winter), pp 66-70

Rosenberg, Martha, 2002. 'Struggling for Sexual and Reproductive Rights: The Case of the 2nd World Social Forum, Porto Alegre 2002,' *Transnational Alternativ@s.* Available at http://www.tni.org/tat/. (Link not found, 06.10.07. For details, contact; tni@tni.org)

Roy, Arundhati, January 2003, 'Confronting Empire.' Text of speech given at the World Social Forum, Porto Alegre, Brazil, on January 27 2003. On *ZNet*, 28 January 2003. Available at http://www.zmag.org/content/showarticle.cfm?SectionID=51&ItemID=2919 (accessed 21.09.07). Republished in edited form as 'The World Social Forum: Where To Now?,' in Jai Sen, Anita Anand, Arturo Escobar, and Peter Waterman, eds, 2004, *World Social Forum: Challenging Empires*, New Delhi: Viveka, pp 51-54. Available @ http://www.choike.org/nuevo_eng/informes/1557.html and @ http://www.openspaceforum.net/twiki/tiki-index.php?page=WSFChallengingEmpires2004

RUPE (Research Unit for Political Economy), September 2003. The Economics and Politics of the World Social Forum, Lessons for the Struggle against 'Globalisation.' *Aspects of India's Economy* series, no 35. Published by Rajani X Desai for Research Unit for Political Economy, Sidhwa Estate, Ground Floor, N A Sawant Marg, Colaba, Mumbai 400 005, India. Available @ www.rupe-india.org

Santiago, Irene, 204, 'A Fierce Struggle to Re-create the World.' Foreword to Jai Sen, Anita Anand, Arturo Escobar, and Peter Waterman, eds, 2004, *World Social Forum: Challenging Empires*, New Delhi: Viveka, pp xiv-xvi. Available @ http://www.choike.org/nuevo_eng/informes/1557.html and @ http://www.openspaceforum.net/twiki/tiki-index.php?page=WSFChallengingEmpires2004

Santos, Boaventura de Sousa, 1992, 'A Discourse on the Sciences,' in *Review*, Volume XV, Issue 1, pp 9-47

Santos, Boaventura de Sousa, 1995, *Towards a New Common Sense: Law, Science and Politics in the Paradigmatic Transition*, New York: Routledge

Santos, Boaventura de Sousa, 1998, 'Oppositional Postmodernism and Globalisations,' in *Law and Social Inquiry*, Volume 23, Issue 1, pp 121-139

Santos, Boaventura de Sousa, April 2001, '*O principio do futuro*' ['The beginning of the future,' in Portuguese], at http://www.worldsocialforum.org (accessed 04.04.01)

Santos, Boaventura de Sousa, 2001, 'Nuestra America, Reinventing a Subaltern Paradigm of Recognition and Redistribution,' in *Theory Culture and Society*, Volume 18, Issue 2-3, pp 185-217

Santo, Boaventura de Sousa, October 2002, '*Para uma Sociología das ausencias e uma sociología das emergencias*' ['For a Sociology of Absences and a Sociology of Emergences,' in Spanish], in *Revista Critica de Ciencias Sociales* [*Critique of the Social Sciences*], no 63, pp 237-280

Santos, Boaventura de Sousa, 2002a, *Towards a New Legal Common Sense*, London: Butterworths

Santos, Boaventura de Sousa, 2002b, 'Towards a Multicultural Conception of Human Rights,' in *Moral Imperialism, A Critical Anthology*, pp 39-60. New York: New York University Press. Available @ http://www.ces.uc.pt/bss/documentos/toward_multicultural_conception_human_rights.pdf

Santos, Boaventura de Sousa, March 2003, 'The World Social Forum: Toward A Counter-Hegemonic Globalization.' First draft, March 2003. Presented at the XXIV International Congress of the Latin American Studies Association, Dallas, USA March 27-29 2003. 35 pp. Can be consulted at and cited from http://www.ces.fe.uc.pt/bss/fsm.php=A9 [link not found, 06.10.07]. Edited excerpts published in Jai Sen, Anita Anand, Arturo Escobar, and Peter Waterman, eds, 2004, *World Social Forum: Challenging Empires*, New Delhi: Viveka, pp 235-245 and pp 336-343. Available @ http://www.choike.org/ nuevo_eng/informes /1557.html and @ http://www.openspaceforum.net/ twiki/tiki-index.php?page=WSFChallengingEmpires2004

Santos, Boaventura de Sousa, 2003a, 'The Popular University of Social Movement: To Educate Activists and Leaders of Social Movements, as Social Scientists/Scholars Concerned with the Study of Social Change. Proposal for Discussion.' Email, 12 January. Available from: bsantos@sonata.fe.uc.pt , bsantos@facstaff.wisc.edu

Santos, Boaventura de Sousa, nd. 'A Critique of the Lazy Reason, Against the Waste of Experience,' in Immanuel Wallerstein, ed. *The Modern World System in the Long Durée*

Savio, Roberto 2002, 'First Draft for a Communication Plan to be Presented During the Fifth International Committee Meeting, Bangkok, August 12-14, 2002,' 6 pp

Savio, Roberto, January 2003a, 'Future of the WSF: Smaller Is Better,' on *Terra Viva Online*, 28 January 2003, @ http://www.ipsnews.net/fsm2003/28.01.2003/nota16.shtml

Savio, Roberto, January 2003b, *'Menor es mejor'* ['Smaller is Better,' in Portuguese], in *Terra Viva* 28.1.2003, p 6

Sehm Patomäki, Katarina and Marko Ulvila, August 2006, 'Democratic Politics Globally: Elements for a Dialogue on Global Political Party Formations.' NIGD Working Paper 1/2006, NIGD (Network Institute for Global Democratisation), Helsinki, Finland, @ http://www.nigd.org/globalparties

Sen, Jai, April 2001 (April 1975), *The Unintended City*, An Essay on the City of the Poor, in *Seminar* (New Delhi) 500, April 2001, pp 38-47. Originally published by Cathedral Relief Services, Calcutta, India. Reprinted in *The Hindustan Times*

(New Delhi), August 1975, in *Fulcrum* (Bombay), February 1976, and in *Seminar* (New Delhi), April 1976. Available @ http://www.india-seminar.com/2001/500/500%20jai%20sen.htm

Sen, Jai, January 2002a, 'The World Social Forum–Some Concerns and Considerations for a WSF Process in India,' dt January 5 2002. Available at http://www.choike.org/PDFs/concerns.pdf. Subsequently published in: Jai Sen with Madhuresh Kumar, compilers, August 2003. *Are Other Worlds Possible?, The Open Space Reader on the World Social Forum and its Engagement with Empire*, pp 198-206

Sen, Jai, March-April 2002. 'On Building Another World [Or: 'Are other globalisations possible?']: The World Social Forum as an instrument of global democratisation.' Published in abridged form as 'Are other globalizations possible? The World Social Forum as an instrument of global democratization,' Chapter 8 in Leena Rikkilä and Katarina Sehm Patomäki, eds, 2002, *From a Global Market Place to Political Spaces*, pp 167-205, NIGD Working Paper 1/2002, published by NIGD. Network Institute for Global Democratisation, em: info@nigd.u-net.com. Available @ http://www.nu.ac.za/ccs, http://www.forumsocialmundial.org.br/eng/tbib.asp, and http://www.choike.org/cgi-bin/choike/links/page.cgi?p=ver_informe&id=977

Sen, Jai, April 2002, 'Some thoughts on resource mobilisation, self-reliance, and internationalism.' Draft discussion note. Mss, 3 pp

Sen, Jai, July 2002, 'Towards the Formation of a 'Asian Solidarity Group' for the Asia Social Forum Being Organised by World Social Forum India in Hyderabad, India, during January 2-7 2003,' A Note for Discussion. Available from WSF India 14/187 Malviya Nagar–Lower Ground Floor, Shivalik Road (adjacent to Sunil Hospital), New Delhi 110017, India; wsfindia@vsn1.net, or from CACIM at cacim@cacim

Sen, Jai, August 2002, 'Report on Visit to Bangkok to attend the Asian Social Movements meeting and the meeting of the International Council of the World Social Forum, August 10-15 2002.' First draft, circulated for comments

Sen, Jai, November 2002d, 'Civilising Globalisation? Or Globalising Civilisation? Some reflections towards civil governance and a conscious, critical globalisation.' Paper for the 'Helsinki Conference 2002: Searching for Global Partnerships' held in Helsinki, Finland, December 2-4 2002, organised by the Crisis Management Initiative (Office of President Ahtisaari) on behalf of the Government of Finland

Sen, Jai, 2002, 'Are other globalisations possible? The World Social Forum as an instrument of global democratization.' Chapter 8 in Rikkilä and Sehm Patomäki, eds, 2002, *From a Global Market Place to Political Spaces*, pp 167-205. Abridged version of paper for the NIGD (Network Institute for Global Democratisation) Seminar at the World Social Forum, on 'Global Democracy? A North-South Dialogue' held on 4 February 2002, at Amarzen, Porto Alegre, Brazil. (Rikkilä and Sehm Patomäki document available in full at http://www.nigd.org/publications)

Sen, Jai, January 2003a, 'The Long March to Another World: Reflections on the World Social Forum process in India and internationally.' Available at http://www.choike.org/cgi-bin/choike/nuevo_eng/page.cgi?p=ver_informe&id=967

Sen, Jai, January 2003b, 'On The World Social Forum: Notes from Two Meetings in Hyderabad during the Asian Social Forum, January 5 and 7 2003,' dt 16 January 2003. Available at http://www.choike.org/PDFs/note.pdf

Sen, Jai, June 2003, 'Seeing Things Clearly: Towards Vision for the WSF World Meeting in India,' Some Urgent Comments on a WSF India Note. Published in Sen, Jai, with Madhuresh Kumar, compilers, August 2003. *Are Other Worlds Possible?*, The Open Space Reader on the World Social Forum and its Engagement with Empire, pp 239-252

Sen, Jai, August 2003, 'The WSF as logo, the WSF as commons: Take a moment to reflect on what is happening in the World Social Forum.' Available @ http://www.choike.org/cgi-bin/choike/links/page.cgi?p=ver_informe&id=1192

Sen, Jai, October 2003a, 'Are Other Worlds Possible?.' Comment, in *Seminar* (New Delhi) 530. Available @ http://www.india-seminar.com/2003/530/530%20comment.htm

Sen, Jai, October 2003b, *see entry for* Sen, Jai, 2004c.

Sen, Jai, December 2003c, 'Two Charters Compared.' Comparison of Original April 2001 WSF Charter of Principles with Revised Charter of Principles issued in June 2001, as found on the WSF website in October 2003. December 19 2003, 7 pp. Available @ http://www.choike.org/documentos/Two_charters_compared.pdf and @ http://www.openspaceforum.net/twiki/tiki-index.php?page=WSFChallengingEmpires2004

Sen, Jai, December 2003d, 'A Tale of Two Charters (Or: 'Another Charter Is (Im)Possible!'). Available at http://www.choike.org/documentos/Two_ Charters.pdf

Sen, Jai, December 2003f, 'How Open? The Challenge of Dogma: The Forum as Logo, the Forum as Religion: Scepticism of the Intellect, Optimism of the Will.' Available @ http://www.choike.org/nuevo_eng/informes/1192.html, http://www.choike.org/documentos/how_open.pdf, and http://www.openspaceforum.net/twiki/tiki-index.php?page=WSFChallengingEmpires2004

Sen, Jai, 2003, 'The Long March to Another World: Porto Alegre–Hyderabad–Porto Alegre. Reflections on the Past Year of the World Social Forum Process–in India and Internationally' (Summary), in 'Two, Three, Many New Social Forums?,' in *TransnationalAlternativ@s*, No 0. www.tni.org.

Sen, Jai, compiler, May 2004, 'Reactions to *World Social Forum: Challenging Empires* till April 2004,' revised February 2007. Available @ http://www.openspace forum.net/twiki/tiki-index.php?page=WSFChallengingEmpires2004

Sen, Jai, 2004, 'A Tale of Two Charters,' in Jai Sen, Anita Anand, Arturo Escobar, and Peter Waterman, eds, 2004, *World Social Forum: Challenging Empires*, New Delhi: Viveka, pp 72-75. Available @ http://www.choike.org/nuevo_eng /informes/1557.html and @ http://www.openspaceforum.net/twiki/tiki- index.php?page=WSFChallengingEmpires2004

Sen, Jai, 2004a, 'Challenging Empires: Reading the World Social Forum,' Proem to Sen, Anand, Escobar, and Waterman, eds, 2004, *World Social Forum: Challenging Empires* (New Delhi: Viveka), pp xxi-xxviii. Available at http://www.choike.org/documentos/wsf_proem_jai.pdf and @ http://www.openspaceforum.net/twiki/tiki-index.php?page=WSFChallengingEmpires2004

Sen, Jai, 2004c, 'The Long March to Another World: Reflections of a member of the WSF India Committee in 2002 on the first year of the World Social Forum process in India,' in Sen, Anand, Escobar, and Waterman, eds, 2004, *World Social Forum: Challenging Empires*, pp 293-311. Available @ http://www.choike.org/nuevo_eng/informes/1557.html and @ http://www.openspaceforum.net/twiki/tiki-index.php?page=WSFChallengingEmpires2004

Sen, Jai, January 2007 (February 2006), 'The World Social Forum as an emergent learning process,' in *Futures* vol 39 (2007), pp 505-522. Available through subscription @ http://dx.doi.org/10.1016/j.futures.2006.10.006. Unedited original available @ http://www.openspaceforum.net/twiki/tiki-download_file.php?fileId=34

Sen, Jai, May 2007, 'Opening open space: Notes on the grammar and vocabulary of the concept of open space.' Discussion draft 4 modified, May 17 2007. Available @ http://www.openspaceforum.net/twiki/tiki-read_article.php?ArticleId=42

Sen, Jai, compiler, May 2004, 'Reactions to *World Social Forum: Challenging Empires* till April 2004,' revised February 2007. Available @http://www.openspaceforum.net/twiki/tiki-index.php?page=WSFChallengingEmpires2004

Sen, Jai, Anita Anand, Arturo Escobar, and Peter Waterman, eds, 2004, *World Social Forum: Challenging Empires*, New Delhi: Viveka Foundation; available @ http://www.choike.org/nuevo_eng/informes/1557.html and @ http://www.openspaceforum.net/twiki/tiki-index.php?page=WSFChallengingEmpires2004

Sen, Jai, Anita Anand, Arturo Escobar, and Peter Waterman, eds, 2005, Japanese edition of *World Social Forum: Challenging Empires*, (New Delhi: Viveka, 2004). Tokyo: Sakuhin-Sha

Sen, Jai, Anita Anand, Arturo Escobar, y Peter Waterman (Editores), nd, c.2005, *El Foro Social Mundial: Desafiando Imperios* ['World Social Forum: Challenging Empires,' in Spanish]. Mataró (Barcelona): El Viejo Topo

Sen, Jai, Anita Anand, Arturo Escobar, and Peter Waterman, eds, 2006, *Nayi Subah Ki Or* ('Towards a New Dawn,' in Hindi), New Delhi: Prakashan Sansthan and CACIM. Associate editors: Kishan Kaljayee and Madhuresh Kumar. (Hindi edition of Jai Sen, Anita Anand, Arturo Escobar, and Peter Waterman, eds, 2004, *World Social Forum: Challenging Empires* (New Delhi: Viveka))

Sen, Jai with Madhuresh Kumar, compilers, August 2003, *Are Other Worlds Possible?, The Open Space Reader on the World Social Forum and its Engagement with Empire*. Available from CACIM @ cacim@cacim.net. See also: http://www.Openspaceforum.net/twiki/tiki-index.php?page=Open+Space+Seminar+Series

Sen, Jai, and Madhuresh Kumar, compilers, with Patrick Bond and Peter Waterman, January 2007, *A Political Programme for the World Social Forum? Democracy, Substance, and Debate in the Bamako Appeal and the Global Justice Movements. A Reader*. Published by CACIM (Critical Action: Centre in Movement), New Delhi, India, and University of KwaZulu-Natal Centre for Civil Society (CCS), Durban, South Africa. Soft copy available @ www.cacim.net and www.nu.ac. za/ccs

Sen, Jai, and Usha Ramanathan, September 2002, 'Reflections on the World Social Forum: Issues from Informal Meeting in Delhi, 30 August 2002,' dt September 9 2002

Sen, Jai, Teivo Teivainen, and Immanuel Wallerstein in debate, March 2006, 'Hard Questions on the WSF: Debate-the relationship between the WSF, political parties and governments.' Compiled by Ruby van der Wekken. Section II of *NIGD News and Notes*, Double Issue, 02-03/06: 'A Critical Utopia Moves to Africa,' @ http://www.nigd.org/docs/HardQuestionsIntro

Shephard, B and R Hayduk, 2002. *From ACT Up to the WTO*. London: Verso

Sherman, Stephen, July 2007a, *Monthly Review* web site MR Zine, @ http://www.monthlyreview.org/mrzine/sherman040707.html

Sherman, Steve, July 2007b, 'Achievements and Limits of the First United States Social Forum,' on MRZINE July 4 2007, @ http://www.openspaceforum.net/twiki/tiki-read_article.php?articleId=463. Source: http://canadiandimension.com/articles/2007/07/09/1206/

Silliman, Jael and Anannya Bhattacharjee, eds, 2002, *Policing the National Body*, Race, Gender and Criminalization, Cambridge, MA: South End

Simonson, Karin, March 2003, 'The Anti-War Movements–Waging Peace on the Brink of War.' Paper prepared for the Programme on NGOs and Civil Society of the Centre for Applied Studies in International Negotiation. Available @

http://se1.isn.ch/serviceengine/FileContent?serviceID=PublishingHouse&fileid=F420C2C8-7660-EA62-6A43-227575320489&lng=en

Slater, D, 1998, 'Rethinking the Spatialities of Social Movements: Questions of Borders, Culture and Politics in Global Times,' in Alvarez, S, E Dagnino, and A Escobar, eds,1998, *Cultures of Politics, Politics of Cultures*, Boulder, Colarado: Westview Press, pp 380-401

Smith, Bonnie G, ed, 2000, *Global Feminism Since 1945*, New York: Routledge

Smith, Jackie et al, 2008, *Global Democracy and the World Social Forums*, Boulder: Paradigm Press

Social Movement Assembly, Porto Alegre, January 2001, 'Porto Alegre Call for Mobilisation,' in Jai Sen, Anita Anand, Arturo Escobar, and Peter Waterman, eds, 2004, *World Social Forum: Challenging Empires*, New Delhi: Viveka, pp 95-101. Available @ http://www.openspaceforum.net/twiki/tiki-index.php?page=WSFChallengingEmpires2004

Social Movements World Network, São Paulo, January 2003, original url http://www.movsoc.org/htm/social_movements_meetings.htm, but no longer accessible there 06.10.07, but is archived at http://www.movsoc.org/htm/social_movements_meetings.htm,

Social Watch, 2003, 'The Citizens' Report on the Quality of Life in the World.' CD-Rom, multimedia. Montevideo: Social Watch, socwatch@social watch.org, www.socialwatch.org

Stanley Brehaut Ryerson, 1973, *Unequal union: Roots of crisis in the Canadas, 1815-1873*, Progress Books

Starr, Amory, 2000, *Naming The Enemy, Anti-Corporate Movements Confront Globalization*, New York: Zed Books

Starr, Amory and Jason Adams, 2003, 'Anti-Globalization, The Global Fight for Local Autonomy,' in *New Political Science*, Volume 25, Number 1

Stedile, J, 2002, 'Landless Battalions,' in *New Left Review*, Number 15, pp 77-104. Available @ http://newleftreview.org/A2390

Steinmeier, Frank-Walter, July 2006, '*Le monde entier peut y perdre*' ['The entire world there can lose,' in French], interview given to the magazine FOCUS, 9 July 2006

Suaraz, Maria, 2003, 'FIRE's Internet Radio Station, An Autochthonous Creation by Feminists in Cyberspace.' Available @ http://www.zmag.org/suarez cyber.htm

Sweeney, Anne Marie, 1997, 'Dancing in the Snow,' in *New Internationlist*, Number 296. Available @ http://www.newint.org/issue296/dancing.htm

Teivainen, Teivo, 2002, 'The World Social Forum and global democratisation: Learning from Porto Alegre,' in *Third World Quarterly*, vol 23, no 4. Originally circulated as a Note in May 2001, titled 'Democratizing the World: Reflections After Porto Alegre,' dt 31 May 2001. Available @ http://www.helsinki.fi/oik/globalgovernance/Mallisivusto/valinnat/Teivainen%20Third%20World%20Quarterly.pdf

Teivainen, Teivo, 2003a, 'Conference Synthesis of International Organisations and Architecture of World Power,' in Fisher, William F and Thomas Ponniah, 2003, *Another World is Possible: Popular Alternatives to Globalisation at the World Social Forum*, pp 290-295, London and New York, Zed Books. Also available at www.worldsocialforum.org (as of 03.02)

Teivainen, Teivo, 2003b, 'The World Social Forum: Arena or Actor?' Paper presented at the Latin American Studies Association (LASA) meeting, Dallas, Texas, USA, 28 March 2003. Revised and edited version published in Jai Sen, Anita Anand, Arturo Escobar, and Peter Waterman, eds, 2004, *World Social Forum: Challenging Empires*, New Delhi: Viveka, pp 122-129. Available @ http://www.choike.org/documentos/wsf_s303_teivainen.pdf

Thayer, Millie 2000, 'Traveling Feminisms: From Embodied Women to Gendered Citizenship,' in Michael Burawoy et al, eds, 2000, *Global Ethnography: Forces, Connections, and Imaginations in a Postmodern World*, Berkeley: University of California Press. Available @ http://sociology.berkeley.edu/mellon/mellon_pdf/ThayerTF.pdf

Tidiane Kasse, Mouhamadou, nd, c.2007, *'FSM 2007: L'heure de sortir des sentiers battus pour les Africains'* ['WSF 2007: Time to leave the way open to the Africans,' in French], available on http://www.europe-solidaire.org/spip.php?article2190

Toro, Maria Suarez, 2002, 'Draft Criteria for a Proposed Women's Summit about the State of the World,' in Jai Sen, Anita Anand, Arturo Escobar, and Peter Waterman, eds, 2004, *World Social Forum: Challenging Empires* (New Delhi: Viveka), pp 344-348. Available @ http://www.choike.org/nuevo_eng/informes/1557.html and @ http://www.openspaceforum.net/twiki/tiki-index.php?page=WSFChallengingEmpires2004

Townsend, Janet Gabriel et al, 1999, *Women and Power: Fighting Patriarchy and Poverty*, London: Zed Books

Transnational Alternatives, 2003, 'Two, Three, Many New Social Forums?,' Special Issue, *TransnationalAlternativ@s*, No. 0. Amsterdam: Transnational Institute, *web*: [original link www.tni.org.tat not working; for details, contact; tni@tni.org]

Transparency International, 2006, Summary of Report on Index of Corruption of Exporter Countries. http://www.transparency.org/

Treanor, Paul 2002, 'Who Controls the European Social Forum?' 9 pp. URL given as http://web.inter.nl.net/users/Paul.Treanor/esf.html, but article not found, 06.10.07. Available @ http://www.voiceoftheturtle.org/show_article.php?aid=301

Tsie, B, 2001, 'International Political Economy and Southern Africa,' in Oden, Bertil, Larry A Swatuk, and Peter Vale, eds, 2001, *Theory, Change and South Africa's Future*, London and New York: Palgrave, pp 110-147

Turok, B, 2002, 'Strange Silence From the Left,' in *New Agenda*, Issue 8, pp 6-12

U.S. Representative for Foreign Trade, October 2006, *'Entretiens entre Mme Schwab et quatre ministres africains du Commerce'* ['Agreement between Mme Schwab and four African Ministers of Commerce,' in French], Press release, October 27 2006

Uhlenbeck, Max, July 2007, 'A Light Within (the Heart of Empire): The 2007 U.S. Social Forum'; @ http://www.openspaceforum.net/twiki/tiki-read_article.php?articleId=439. Source: MR Zine @ http://mrzine.monthlyreview.org/uhlenbeck060607.html

Vague, Tom, 2000, 'The Boy Scout's Guide to the Situationist International: The Effect the SI Had on Paris '68 and All That, through the Angry Brigade and King Mob to the Sex Pistols.' Available from http://library.nothingness.org/articles/SI/en/display/240

Vanaik, Achin, May-June 2001, 'The New Indian Right,' in *New Left Review*, May-June 2001. Available @ http://www.sacw.net/2002/achin_NewIndianRight.html

Vargas, Gina, 2003, *'El Foro Social Mundial III y las tensiones en la construcción del pensamiento global alternativo' (Para Cuestion de Estado, Lima)* ['The World Social Forum III and the tensions in the construction of a global alternative (On the Question of the State, Lima),' in Spanish]. Available from http://www.mujeresdelsur.org.uy/fsm/fsm_doc03.htm. Translated and edited version published as 'WSF 3 and tensions in the construction of global alternative thinking,' in Jai Sen, Anita Anand, Arturo Escobar, and Peter Waterman, eds, 2004. *World Social Forum: Challenging Empires*. New Delhi: Viveka, pp 228-232

Vargas, Virginia (Articulación Feminista Marcosur), April 2007, 'A look at Nairobi's World Social Forum,' chapter in Jai Sen and Peter Waterman, eds, forthcoming, 2008, *World Social Forum: Challenging Empires Globally* [tentative title, under finalisation], Volume 3 in the *Challenging Empires* series, New Delhi: OpenWord Books

Vargas, Virginia, ed, 1998, *Roads to Beijing*, Fourth World Conference on Women in Latin America and the Caribbean, Lima; Santafé de Bogotá; Quito: Ediciones Flora Tristán; UNICEF; UNIFEM

Vera-Zavala, America, February 2003, 'An Extraordinary Coup at the WSF,' on *ZNet*,,Vision/Strategy, Part 1, 9 February 2003. Available @ http://www.zmag.org/content/Activism/zavala_wsfpt1.cfm

Virilio, Paul, 1999, *Politics of the Very Worst*, New York: Semitext

Vision Machine, 2002, 'The Globalisation Tapes.' Video. English. 71 mins. PAL. London: Vision Machine/International Union of Food and Agricultural Workers/Independent Plantation Workers' Union of Sumatra (Indonesia). visionmachine@unreal.at

Wahl, Asbjorn, June 2002, 'European Labour: Social Dialogue, Social Pacts, or a Social Europe?' in *Monthly Review* (New York), pp 23-33. Available @ http://findarticles.com/p/articles/mi_m1132/is_2_54/ai_87424636

Wainwright, Hilary, December 2002, Keynote speech at the European Social Forum, in *Red Pepper*. http://www.redpepper.org.uk

Wainwright, Hilary, 2003, 'Porto Alegre: Public Power beyond the State,' in Bradford, Sue and Bernardo Kucinski, eds, 2003, *Politics Transformed: Lula and the Workers Party in Brazil*, pp 103-133. London: Latin America Bureau

Wainwright, Hilary, 2004, 'The Forum as Jazz,' Foreword to Jai Sen, Anita Anand, Arturo Escobar, and Peter Waterman, eds, 2004, *World Social Forum: Challenging Empires*, pp xvii-xx, New Delhi: Viveka. Available at http://www.choike.org/nuevo_eng/informes/1557.html and @ http://www.openspaceforum.net/twiki/tiki-index.php?page=WSFChallengingEmpires2004

Walger, Eduardo, 2002. *El Pensamiento Critico a Comienzos del Siglo XXI: Un Documental de Eduardo Walger* ['Critical Thought at the Beginning of the XXI Century: A Documentary of Eduardo Walger,' in Spanish]. NTSC, Eng/Spa. Buenos Aires: Coop de Trab. Videola Ltda. [Link given in original citation as www.conlamismared.com.ar, but the site has moved/this one redirects on 06.10.07 to http://www.montacargas-y-racks.com/, on agricultural implements.]

Wallerstein, Immanuel, December 2002, 'New Revolts Against the System,' in *New Left Review*, 18, November-December 2002, special issue on 'A Movement of Movements?,' pp 29-39. Available @ http://www.newleftreview.org/A2420

Wallerstein, Immanuel, and Etienne Balibar, 1991, *Race, Nation, Class: Ambiguous Identities*, New York: Verso

Walsh, Shannon, February 2007, 'We won't pay to discuss our own poverty! Activist interventions into the 'open space' of the World Social Forum,' on Debate listserve, 4 February 2007, 4:06:20 PM GMT+05:30; available @ http://www.openspaceforum.net/twiki/tiki-read_article.php?articleId=497

Walton, John, David Seddon, eds, 1994, *Free Markets and Food Riots: The Politics of Global Adjustment*, Oxford: Blackwell

Waterman, Peter, 1982, 'Seeing the Straws, Riding the Whirlwind: Reflections of Unions and Popular Movements in India,' in *Journal of Contemporary Asia*, Vol. 12, No 4

Waterman, Peter, 1992, 'International Labour Communication by Computer, The Fifth International?,' Working Paper Series No 129. Available from Institute of Social Studies, The Hague

Waterman, Peter, 2001, *Globalization, Social Movements and the New Internationalisms*, London: Continuum

Waterman, Peter, 2001, *'Nueve Reflexiones Sobre Un Internationalismo De Communicacion En La Era Seattle'* ['Nine Reflections on a Communications Internationalism in the Era of Seattle'], in *Communicacion en elTercer Milenio* ['Communication in the Third Millenium,' in Spanish], edited by Ivan Rodrigo Mendizabal & Leonela Cururella, Quito: Universidad Andina Simon Bolivar

Waterman, Peter, 2001a, 'Globalisation, Networking, Solidarity, Internationalism,' Convenor's Discussion Paper, Workshop on 'Globalisation, Networking, Solidarity, Internationalism,' World Social Forum, Porto Alegre, Brazil, January 31-February 5 2002

Waterman, Peter, 2001b, 'Emancipating Labour Internationalism (From 20th Century Labour, Unions and Socialism).' Available at http://groups/yahoo.com/groups/GloSoDia

Waterman, Peter, 2001c,'16 Propositions on Internationalist Labour (and Other?) Networking,' Background paper for Panel at Conference of the Global Studies Association, Manchester, UK, July 2-4 2001, 22 pp. http://www.antenna.nl/~waterman/ELIlong%20281101.doc

Waterman, Peter, 2002a, '*Omnia Sint Communia*: A New/Old Slogan for International Labour and Labour Internationalism.' Contribution to a Workshop on 'The Commons and Communities: A Strategic Alternative to the State-Market Nexus,' European Social Forum, Florence, Italy, November 7-10 2002

Waterman, Peter, 2002b, 'What's Left Internationally? Reflections on the 2nd World Social Forum in Porto Alegre,' Institute of Social Studies, The Hague, Working Paper Series No 362, 38 pp. http://groups/yahoo.com/groups/GloSoDia

Waterman, Peter, 2002c, 'Learning to Talk across Difference in an Interconnected World of Labour,' in *Transnational Associations* (Brussels), no 2, pp 92-109

Waterman, Peter (guest editor), November 2002, 'Two, Three, Many New Social Forums...?,' Special Issue, *TransnationalAlternativ@s*, (Transnational Institute, Amsterdam), No 0. URL given as www.tni.org.tat or www.tni.org/alternativ/htm, but not working; for details, contact; tni@tni.org

Waterman, Peter, 2003a, 'Some Propositions on Cyberspace after Capitalism,' Presented at Cyberspace Panel, Life after Capitalism Programme, World Social Forum, Porto Alegre, January 23-28, 2003. Available at http://www.zmag.org/lacsite.htm

Waterman, Peter, 2003b, 'From "Comrades Agreements" to the Reinvention of Social Emancipation on a World Scale.' Available from http://www.voiceoftheturtle.org/show_article.php?aid=324

Waterman, Peter, 2003c, 'Second Thoughts on the Third World Social Forum: Place, Space and the Reinvention of Social Emancipation on a Global Scale'.' Available from http://groups.yahoo.com/group/GloSoDia/files%21%21%21%20FORUMS%20OF%20THE%20FUTURE%21%21%21/. Revised version published as 'The Secret of Fire' in Jai Sen, Anita Anand, Arturo Escobar, and Peter Waterman, eds, 2004, *World Social Forum: Challenging Empires*, New Delhi: Viveka, pp 148-160. Available @ http://www.choike.org/documentos/wsf_s307_waterman.pdf

Waterman, Peter. 2003d, 'Women, Workers, the World Social Forum and the World Wide Web in the Civilising of Global Society.' Review article, *International Feminist Review of Politics*, vol. 5, no. 2, pp. 301–9

Waterman, Peter (guest editor), November 2002, 'Two, Three, Many New Social Forums...?' Special Issue, *TransnationalAlternativ@s*, (Transnational Institute, Amsterdam), No.0. URL given as www.tni.org/alternative/htm, but not working; for details, contact; tri@tri.org

Waterman, Peter, 2004, 'Globalisation from the Middle? Reflections from a Margin,' in Jai Sen, Anita Anand, Arturo Escobar, and Peter Waterman, eds, 2004, *World Social Forum: Challenging Empires*, New Delhi: Viveka, pp 87-94. Available @ http://www.choike.org/nuevo_eng/informes/1557.html and @ http://www.openspaceforum.net/twiki/tiki-index.php?page=WSFChallengingEmpires2004

Waterman, Peter, forthcoming (b) 'Women, Workers, WSF and WWW in the Civilising of Global Society.' Review article, *International Feminist Review of Politics*. Available @ http://www.nu.ac.za/ccs/files/Global%20CS%20Review%202002.pdf

Webster, E, October 2002, 'On the March,' in *South African Labour Bulletin*, Volume 26, Issue 5, pp 33-34

Webster, E, 2002, 'Message From the Director,' Annual Report of the Sociology of Work Unit

Weekes, Anna, August 2002, 'Barometer of Resistance,' in *Khanya: A Journal for Activists*, No. 1, pp 29-36. Johannesburg: Khanya College. Available @ http://www.khanyacollege.org.za/Documents/journal12-pdfs/j12_15.pdf

West, Lois A, 1999, 'The United Nations Women's Conferences and Feminist Politics,' in *Gender Politics in Global Governance*, edited by Mary K. Meyer and Elisabeth Prugl, pp 177 93. New York: Rowman & Littlefield

Whitaker, Chico (Francisco), February 2002, *'Lições de Porto Alegre'* ['Lessons of Porto Alegre,' in Portuguese], dt 21 February 2002. Revised version of Note to the Comissão Episcopal de Pastoral of the CNBB, on 19 February 2002. Original in Portuguese; translated into English by Thomas Ponniah and Flávia Miranda Falcão. Published in Laura Nisula and Katarina Sehm Patomäki, eds, 2002, *We, the Peoples of the World Social Forum*. NIGD Working Paper 2/2002, Chapter 2, pp 13-16. Helsinki: NIGD. Network Institute for Global Democratisation

Whitaker, Francisco, April 2002, *'Fórum Social Mundial: origins e objetivos'* ['World Social Forum: Origins and Objectives,' in Portuguese], at http://www.forum socialmundial.org.br/por/qorigem.asp (13.4.2002)

Whitaker, Chico, March 2003, 'Notes about the World Social Forum,' dt 17 March 2003. Available from WSFitself@Yahoogrupos.com.br . Edited version published as 'The WSF as Open Space,' in in Jai Sen, Anita Anand, Arturo Escobar, and Peter Waterman, eds, 2004, *World Social Forum: Challenging Empires*. New Delhi: Viveka, pp 111-121

Whitaker, Chico, 2004, 'The WSF as Open Space,' in Jai Sen, Anita Anand, Arturo Escobar, and Peter Waterman, eds, 2004, *World Social Forum: Challenging Empires* (New Delhi: Viveka), pp 111-121. Available at http://www.choike.org/nuevo_eng/informes/1557.html, @ http://www.choike.org/documentos/wsf_s302_whitaker.pdf, and @ http://www.openspaceforum.net/twiki/tiki-index.php?page=WSFChallengingEmpires2004

Whitaker, Chico, May 2007, 'The crossroads do not always close roads (Reflections in continuity to that of Walden Bello,' translation of original article in Spanish, *'Las encrucijadas no siempre cierran caminos (Reflexión en continuidad a la de Walden Bello)'*; available @ http://www.openspaceforum.net/twiki/tiki-read_article.php?articleId=496

Wiesebron, M and P Vizentini (coords), 2003. *Free Trade for the Americas? The United States' Push for the FTAA Agreement*, London: Zed Books

Williams, Raymond. *Towards 2000*. Harmondsworth/London: Penguin/Chatto and Windus

Wolfwood, Theresa, 'Another World Is Possible', in Jai Sen, Anita Anand, Arturo Escobar, and Peter Waterman, eds, 2004, *World Social Forum: Challenging Empires*, New Delhi: Viveka

Workers' Liberty, 2000, 'Globalisation,' Special Issue of *Workers' Liberty* (London), no 63

World March of Women, 2003, '2003 World Social Forum: Perspective of Women of the World March of Women,' available @ http://www.ffq.qc.ca/marche2000/en/fsm2003.html. Republished in Jai Sen, Anita Anand, Arturo Escobar, and Peter Waterman, eds, 2004, *World Social Forum: Challenging Empires*. New Delhi: Viveka, pp 233-234. Now available @ http://www.openspaceforum.net/twiki/tiki-index.php?page=WSFChallengingEmpires2004

WSF Brazilian Organizing Committee, March 2002, 'Note from the Organising Committee on the Principles That Guide the WSF.' Available at www.forumsocialmundial.org.br/main.asp?id_menu=4 2&cd language=2

WSF Brazil Organising Committee, August 2002 [April 2002], 'IC-Nature, Responsibilities, Composition and Functioning.' Available at www.forumsocialmundial.org.br/main.asp?id_menu=4_2_2_1&cd_lanuage=2 and also at http://www.forumsocialmundial.org.br/eng/ qconselho_1.asp (11.4.2002). Reprinted in Jai Sen, Anita Anand, Arturo Escobar, and Peter Waterman, eds, 2004, *World Social Forum: Challenging Empires*. New Delhi: Viveka, pp 251-252

WSF India, April 2002, 'WSF India Process: The Bhopal Document.' As accepted in the WSF India National Consultation, Bhopal, April 19-21 2002,draft

WSF India, June 2002, 'Building another world-The WSF India Process: A note for discussion.' Available from WSF India Secretariat @ wsfindia@vsnl.net

WSF India, July 2002a, 'WSF India Policy Statement: Charter of Principles-World Social Forum India.' Earlier available at the WSF India website www.wsfindia.org. Reprinted in Jai Sen, Anita Anand, Arturo Escobar, and Peter Waterman, eds, 2004, *World Social Forum: Challenging Empires*, New Delhi: Viveka, pp 269-271. Now available @ http://www.choike.org/nuevo_eng/informes/1557.html and @ http://www.openspaceforum.net/twiki/tiki-index.php?page=WSFChallengingEmpires2004

WSF India, April 2003, 'WSF India General Council–Affiliation letter,' dt April 12 2003

WSF India, 2004. 'WSF 2004, Mumbai, India: The Global South Joins Hands,' in Jai Sen, Anita Anand, Arturo Escobar, and Peter Waterman, eds, 2004, *World Social Forum: Challenging Empires*, New Delhi: Viveka, pp 260-268. Edited version of WSF India, nd(a), 'WSF 2004, Mumbai, India: The Global South Joins Hands.' 10 pp. Available from WSF India Secretariat; wsfindia@vsnl.net or www.wsfindia.org. Now available @ http://www.choike.org/nuevo_eng/informes/1557.html and @ http://www.openspaceforum.net/twiki/tiki-index.php?page=WSFChallengingEmpires2004

WSF India, nd(a), 'Programme Note' for the Asian Social Forum, Hyderabad, India, January 2003

WSF India, nd(b), 'Affirmation Letter-India General Council.' Download form, 1 p, available in November 2003 at http://www.wsfindia.org/affirmation-letter-1.php; also as 'WSF 2004 Affirmation Forum' on p 9 in WSF India, nd(a), 'WSF 2004, Mumbai, India: The Global South Joins Hands'

WSF International Secretariat, January 2003, 'The Directions of the World Social Forum process,' in Jai Sen, Anita Anand, Arturo Escobar, and Peter Waterman, eds, 2004, *World Social Forum: Challenging Empires*, New Delhi: Viveka, pp 253-255. Available @ http://www.openspaceforum.net/twiki/tiki-index.php?page=WSFChallengingEmpires2004

WSF Organising Committee, June 2001, 'World Social Forum Charter of Principles.' Available at http://www.forumsocialmundial.org.br/main.asp?id_menu=4&cd_language=2 and @ http://www.openspaceforum.net/twiki/tiki-index.php?page=WSFChallengingEmpires2004

Wright, Colin, 2005, 'Opening Spaces: Power, Participation and Plural Democracy at the World Social Forum' in *ephemera, theory & politics in organization*, Vol 5, No 2, pp 409–422. Available @ http://www.ephemeraweb.org/journal/5-2/5-2wright.pdf, accessed 03.08.07

WSF Thematic Area 3, 2003. 'Media, Culture and Counter-hegemony.' Available from http://www.forumsocialmundial.org.br/dinamic.asp?pagina=paineis_eixo3_ing

Youmbi, Victor, 2003, 'Another Cameroon Is Possible!' first published in *openDemocracy*. Republished in Jai Sen, Anita Anand, Arturo Escobar, and Peter Waterman, eds, *World Social Forum: Challenging Empires*, New Delhi: Viveka, pp 207-209. Available @ http://www.choike.org/nuevo_eng/informes/1557.html and @ http://www.openspaceforum.net/twiki/tiki-index.php?page=WSFChallengingEmpires2004

Zibechi, Raúl, January 2003, '*Los Movimientos Sociales Latinoamericanos: Tendencias y Desafios*' ['Latin American Social Movements: Trends and Challenges,' in Spanish], in *Observatorio Social de America Latina* ['Social Observatory of Latin America'], Number 9, pp 185-88

Useful Web Links

ALAI: www.alainet.org

Alianza Continental Social: http://www.asc-hsa.org/

Alternatives International: http://alternatives-international.net/?lang=en

Anarchist Studies Network: http://www.anarchist-studies-network.org.uk/

Art-For-A-Change: http://www.art-for-a-change.com/Paris/paris.html

Articulación Feminista Marcosur: http://www.mujeresdelsur.org.uy/

CACIM–Critical Action Centre in Movement: www.cacim.net

CADTM: www.cadtm.org

Call of Social Movements: [original url http://www.movsoc.org/htm/social_movements_meetings.htm, but as of the time of writing (06.10.07), is redirected to a golf course website]

CCPA-Canadian Centre for Policy Alternatives: www.policyalternatives.ca Choike-A Portal on Southern Civil Societies: www.choike.org

Ciranda News Service: http://www.ciranda.net/

CLACSO: http://www.clacso.org/,

Counter Currents: www.countercurrents.org

Democracy Now: www.democracynow.org

Dissident Voice: www.dissidentvoice.org

Ecumenical Advocacy Alliance: http://www.e-alliance.ch/wsf.jsp

Focus on the Global South: focus-on-trade@yahoogroups.com

Foreign Policy In Focus: www.fpif.org

Global Civil Society Yearbook: http://www.lse.ac.uk/Depts/global/Yearbook/

Global Policy Forum: www.globalpolicy.org

Hub/Inventati List: http://www.inventati.org/mailman/listinfo/hub

Indymedia Centre NYC: http://nyc.indymedia.org/

International Viewpoint: www.internationalviewpoint.org

IPS: www.ipsnews.net

Journal of International Women's Studies: http://www.bridgew.edu/SoAS/jiws/index.htm

Life after Capitalism, Zmag/Znet: www.zmag.org/lac.htm

Migrant Diaries: www.migrantdiaries.com

MR ZINE: www.monthlyreview.org/mrzine/

NIGD-Network Institute for Global Democratization: www.nigd.org

North American Congress on Latin America: http://www.nacla.org/

Open Democracy: www.opendemocracy.org

Open Ed News: www.opednews.com

OpenSpaceforum: www.openspaceforum.net

OSAL: http://osal.clacso.org/

Pambazuka News: http://www.pambazuka.org/

Peace Journalism: www.peacejournalism.com

People's Global Action: http://www.nadir.org/nadir/initiativ/agp/en/

Political Affairs: www.politicalaffairs.net

Press Latina: www.plenglish.com Rabble News: www.rabble.ca

Radio Fire: www.fire.or.cr

Reclaim the Streets: http://rts.gn.apc.org/diary.htm

Reinventing Social Emancipation: http://www.ces.fe.uc.pt/emancipa/en/index.html

Social Movements World Network: http://www.movsoc.org/htm/social_movements_meetings.htm

Socialist Worker Online: www.socialistworker.co.uk

Spero News: www.speroforum.com

Spiegel Online International: www.spiegel.de

The Commoner: http://www.commoner.org.uk/

The Guardian: www.theguardian.co.uk

The Nation: www.thenation.com

TNI-Transnational Institute: www.tni.org

Voice of the Turtle: http://www.voiceoftheturtle.org/

Web Community of Social Movements/*Comunidad Web de Movimientos Sociales:* http://movimientos.org

World Social Forum: http://www.forumsocialmundial.org.br/home.asp

World Social Forum 2008: www.wsf2008.net

World Social Forum India: www.wsfindia.org

WSF 2007 Consultation Workspace: http://consultation.wsf2007.org/

WSF International Committee Consultation: http://www.delibera.info/fsm2003ci/GB/

WSF Library: wsflibrary.org

WSFitself: WSFitself@yahoogrupos.com.br

Yes Magazine: www.yesmagazine.org

Zapatista index: http://flag.blackened.net/revolt/zapatista.html

ZNet: www.zmag.org

Plus

For documents earlier available but now not so:

Internet Archive: http://www.archive.org/index.php (Internet Archive is a project to archive the whole internet under shareable licences.)

Explanatory Note Regarding Bibliographic Style Used In This Book:

The style used in this reference list has been developed to make it as understandable to non-specialists as possible, and yet provide full bibliographic data in a format comprehensible to specialists.

References may contain up to twelve items of information, in the following order: 1) Author(s) Name(s), 2) Author(s)' Role, 3) Date of Publication, 4) [Original date of publication, *in square brackets]*, 5) Document Title, 6) [Translated Title, and 7) Language of the document], 8) Compilation Title, 9) Volume Number, 10) Issue Number, 11) Page Number(s), and 12) Publication or Availability details.

Details

Author(s) role: No special indication if author; otherwise indicated by 'ed(s)' for editor(s), or by 'compilers.'

Date of Publication: Generally, indicated by publication year, but in cases of journals or newspaper items, or of multiple publications in the same year, the month is also given. In cases of multiple publications in the same year (or month), suffix (a), (b), added. 'nd' indicates 'not dated,' but if date can be reasonably estimated, indicated by 'c.[date].' ('c' = circa/about.)

Original Date of Publication: If the document is a reprint, then the original publication date is given after the (current) publication date, within square brackets.

Document Title: In case of freestanding documents, such as books or journals, the title is in italics; and in the case of non-freestanding documents, it is given within single quotation marks. Italics also indicate titles in languages other than English.

Translated Title, and Language of the document: Whenever the title is in a language other than English, then the translated title in English is provided next to the original title, followed by the language of the document; all in square brackets.

Compilation Title: In case of non-freestanding documents, the compilation title is mentioned after the Document title, and is in italics.

Publication details: In case of well-known publishers or institutions publishing, the format used is 'Place of Publication: Name of Publisher.' In case of publishers not well known, or where only the availability details are known, the format used is 'Published by' (or Available from') followed by the name and most current contact details for the publisher/source.

Example: Alvarez, Sonia E, 2000a, *'A 'Globalização' dos Feminismos Latino-americanos: Tendências dos Anos 90 e Desafios para o Novo Milênio'* ['The Globalisation of Latin American Feminism: Trends of the 90s and Challenges for the New Millenium,' in Portuguese], in Alvarez, Sonia E, Evelina Dagnino, and Arturo Escobar, eds, 2000. *Cultura e Política nos Movimentos Sociais Latino-americanos: Novas Leituras* [English title: 'Cultures of Politics/Politics of Culture: Revisioning Latin American Social Movements'], pp 383-426. Belo Horizonte: Universidade Federal de Minas Gerais

SCRAMBLE FOR AFRICA: Darfur—Intervention and the USA

Steven Fake and Kevin Funk

The Scramble for Africa analyzes the current humanitarian crisis in Darfur and the activist movements surrounding it, thereby taking on both the U.S. Government and the Save Darfur coalition alike. The authors present the basic information on the political and military aspects of the conflict, examine the options, and suggest ways forward, always with a concern for the broader international implications and for the hundreds of thousands of victims.

"This extremely well-documented work ... combines deep compassion with a keen critical analysis to show how we might best support the suffering people of Darfur." —Stephen R. Shalom, *Imperial Alibis: Rationalizing U.S. Intervention After the Cold War*

"One of the few works to tackle honestly the vexing question of what is to be done about Darfur." —Rahul Mahajan, *Full Spectrum Dominance: U.S. Power in Iraq and Beyond*

"Offers a fresh analysis of Darfur in its larger geopolitical context. It belongs on every Darfur activist's bookshelf." —David Morse, activist and journalist

"This excellent book is exactly what is needed and I hope it is very widely read. I will recommend it to everyone." —Justin Podur, writer and activist

STEVEN FAKE is an activist and political commentator. He is a graduate of the University of Pittsburgh, and a member of the Lucy Parson Center. KEVIN FUNK earned degrees in Journalism, Political Science, and Latin American Studies from the University of Pittsburgh. An activist himself, Funk writes frequently on U.S. foreign policy.

2008: 208 pages
Paperback ISBN: 978-1-55164-322-9 $19.99
Hardcover ISBN: 978-1-55164-323-6 $39.99